T0315041

The Modern
World-System IV

Underwood and Underwood, *Mrs. Pankhurst Arrested*. Mrs. Emmeline Pankhurst was a leader of the British suffragettes. Although much criticized at the time for her militant tactics, she is now credited with a major role in obtaining female suffrage in Great Britain. The photograph was taken on June 2, 1914, when Pankhurst was en route to presenting a petition to Parliament. It was published by the *New York World-Telegram & Sun*. (Courtesy of Prints and Photographs Division, U.S. Library of Congress)

The Modern World-System IV

Centrist Liberalism Triumphant, 1789–1914

Immanuel Wallerstein

UNIVERSITY OF CALIFORNIA PRESS

Berkeley   Los Angeles   London

The publisher gratefully acknowledges the generous support of the General
Endowment Fund of the University of California Press Foundation.

University of California Press, one of the most distinguished university
presses in the United States, enriches lives around the world by advancing
scholarship in the humanities, social sciences, and natural sciences. Its
activities are supported by the UC Press Foundation and by philanthropic
contributions from individuals and institutions. For more information,
visit www.ucpress.edu.

University of California Press
Berkeley and Los Angeles, California

University of California Press, Ltd.
London, England

Library of Congress Cataloging-in-Publication Data

Wallerstein, Immanuel Maurice, 1930–.
    Centrist liberalism triumphant, 1789/1914 / Immanuel Wallerstein.
        p.   cm.—(The modern world-system ; 4)
    Includes bibliographical references and index.
    ISBN 978-0-520-26760-2 (cloth : alk. paper)
    ISBN 978-0-520-26761-9 (pbk. : alk. paper)
    1. Liberalism.   2. Capitalism.   3. Ideology.   I. Title.
    HC51 .W28   1974 vol. 4
[JC574]
    320.5109′034—dc22   2010040366

20   19   18   17   16   15   14   13   12   11
10   9   8   7   6   5   4   3   2   1

In memory of and homage to Giovanni Arrighi

CONTENTS

List of Illustrations   ix
Preface: On Writing about the Modern World-System   xi

1. Centrist Liberalism as Ideology   1

2. Constructing the Liberal State, 1815–1830   21

3. The Liberal State and Class Conflict, 1830–1875   77

4. The Citizen in a Liberal State   143

5. Liberalism as Social Science   219

6. The Argument Restated   275

Bibliography   279
Index   359

ILLUSTRATIONS

Frontispiece: Underwood and Underwood, *Mrs. Pankhurst Arrested*   *ii*

Preface: David Wilkie/Abraham Raimbach, *Village Politicians*   *x*

Chapter 1: Victor Delaive, *Bourgeois et Ouvriers*   *xviii*

Chapter 2: Sir Thomas Lawrence, *Prince Metternich*   *20*

Chapter 3: Lechard (?), *Insurrection du Lyon, 9–14 avril 1834*   *76*

Chapter 4: Auguste Saint-Gaudens, *Robert Gould Shaw and 54th Regiment*   *142*

Chapter 5: André Dutertre, *Murad Bey.* In Napoleon's *Description de l'Egypte/Etat Moderne*   *218*

Chapter 6: Punch, *To the Temple of Fame*   *274*

David Wilkie/Abraham Raimbach, *Village Politicians*. This painting by the Scottish genre painter David Wilkie was the hit of the Royal Academy exhibit in 1806 in London and made his reputation. Wilkie later entered into collaboration with Raimbach to make engravings of his paintings to ensure wide distribution. The first such engraving was this one, done in 1813. The importance of the work was its illustration of how political debate had become a local activity of the populace and was no longer confined to the upper strata. (Courtesy of Prints and Photographs Division, U.S. Library of Congress)

This is the fourth volume in a series whose first volume was published in 1974. The overall work was conceived as a multivolume analysis of the historical and structural development of the modern world-system. Each volume was designed to stand by itself but was also intended simultaneously to be part of the singular larger work. This poses some problems both for the author and for the reader. I think it might be useful to the reader for me to spell out how I have approached these difficulties, not all of which were apparent to me when I started out. I do this in the hope that it makes my intentions and methods more clear to the reader.

Each volume, and each chapter within a volume, has a theme and tries therefore to establish a point. The whole book is simultaneously historical/diachronic and structural/analytic/theoretical. This is in accord with my epistemological premise that the much-vaunted distinction between idiographic and nomothetic epistemologies is outdated, spurious, and harmful to sound analysis. Social reality is always and necessarily both historical (in the sense that reality inevitably changes every nanosecond) and structural (in the sense that social action is governed by constraints deriving from the historical social system within which the described activity occurs).

If, however, one tries to describe reality over a large space and a long time (say, the modern world-system as a whole from its inception in the long sixteenth century [1450–1640] to today and tomorrow), one encounters the elementary difficulty that one cannot do everything at once. So I decided to take the story forward more or less chronologically, introducing structural aspects of the modern world-system when they first occurred or became evident in a significant way. There seemed to me no point in discussing, in a volume largely devoted to the long sixteenth century, structural issues that became salient only in the nineteenth century.

But equally, it did not seem to be useful to discuss, in a volume largely devoted to the nineteenth century, structural issues that had already been discussed in the first volume and whose characteristics had not significantly changed in the intervening centuries. Since, however, my views on when a phenomenon such as "industrialization" first occurred is somewhat different from the one argued by many other analysts, readers might not locate it in the volume in which they expect to see it discussed. I have tried to make clear, as I have proceeded, the logic of my choices.

So, let me first say how I decided to handle chronology. When I wrote volume 1, I said in my introduction that I would divide the overall work into four epochs, to which I gave specific dates in that introduction. Volume 1 sought to cover the long sixteenth century, defined as running from 1450 to 1640. However, when I came to write volume 2, I saw immediately that the story I wished to tell did not start in 1640 but rather, more or less, in 1600 and ran, more or less, to 1750. I put these years in the subtitle. I had now adopted, quite deliberately, the concept of overlapping long periods, a concept I continued in volumes 3 and 4. But this meant, of course, that I could not reach the present in merely four volumes, as I had thought in 1974.

The concept of overlapping time periods turned out to be crucial for my analyses. For time boundaries are of course fairly arbitrary and can be justified only in terms of the immediate issue that one is treating. The story of Dutch hegemony in the world-economy (chapter 2 of volume 2) may be thought to have started in 1600 (or even earlier) but definitely was not over in 1640 and is not really part of the story of the long sixteenth century. It belonged in volume 2, devoted to the consolidation of the European world-economy in the seventeenth century—again, more or less.

Furthermore, this raises the question of when one should seek to enter structural notions into the text. There was, at least in my opinion, no hegemonic power in the sixteenth century. It would have been out of place to introduce the concept, therefore, in volume 1. The Dutch were the first hegemonic power in the modern world-system. It is also true that they were not the last. But the concept of hegemony was not discussed within the context of Great Britain's assuming that role, nor will it be in the context of the assumption by the United States of that role. The concept, as such, once discussed, was taken for granted, and reference, when appropriate, was made to it without reviewing the logic of the concept. The theoretical debate had already taken place.

The chronology of each chapter follows its own internal logic as well, provided only that it stays somewhat within the parameters of the chronological limits of the volume. A good example of this is found in volume 3. Whereas the overall volume presumably ends in the 1840s, chapter 3, on incorporation, goes to 1850 (according to its title), and actually somewhat beyond. On the other hand, chapter 4, on the settler decolonization of the Americas, goes from 1763 to 1833.

Since I cannot presume that the reader of this volume will have read the three previous volumes, I believe it would be useful to resume the diachronic/theoretical story that I have heretofore told. Should readers of this volume feel that I have failed to discuss something that they think ought to have been included in it, perhaps they will discover that it is something I have extensively treated previously. For example, most books devoted to the nineteenth century will discuss—indeed, discuss at length—the so-called industrial revolution. I have treated this as chapter 1 of volume 3 and see no point in repeating this in volume 4, especially when I wish to tell a different kind of story about the nineteenth century.

So let me start by summarizing what I think is the overall argument of each of the successive volumes. Volume 1, defined as covering the long sixteenth century, is the story of the creation of the modern world-system and the creation of some of its basic economic and political institutions. Volume 2 is the story not of refeudalization but of the consolidation of the European world-economy in a period running from 1600 to 1750; it seeks to explain how capitalists in different zones of the world-economy responded to the phenomenon of overall slow growth. Volume 3, defined as running from 1730 to the 1840s, is the story of the renewed expansion—both economic and geographic—of the capitalist world-economy. Volume 4, which I think of as running from 1789 to 1873/1914, is devoted to the creation (and only at this late point) of a geoculture for the modern world-system, a geoculture largely fashioned around and dominated by what I am calling centrist liberalism.

I have said that the various chapters make successive theoretical points. In volume 1, I discussed in chapter 1 why and how the modern world-system emerged from the medieval prelude. I later considered this chapter inadequate to its theme, and elaborated the argument considerably in an essay first published in 1992.[1] The key chapter of volume 1 is chapter 2, in which I outlined the concept of an axial division of labor that leads to the construction of different zones in the world-economy—the core, the periphery, and the semiperiphery (this last being a concept I added to the core/periphery distinction that had been put forward by Raúl Prebisch). I also made the case that this was the construction of a capitalist world-economy, the form that was taken by the modern world-system, and that initially this capitalism was constructed in the agricultural arena, with different modes of labor control for different zones of the world-economy.

---

1. "The West, Capitalism, and the Modern World-System," *Review* 15, no. 4 (Fall 1992): 561–619; reprinted in *China and Historical Capitalism: Genealogies of Sinological Knowledge,* ed. Timothy Brook and Gregory Blue (Cambridge: Cambridge Univ. Press, 1999), 10–56.

Chapter 3 analyzed the creation of the states within the modern world-system and the role played therein by the absolute monarchies of the sixteenth century. Chapter 4 elaborated the distinction between a world-economy and a world-empire, and why the attempt by Charles V to create a world-empire was a failure. Chapter 5 looked at the core zones of the nascent world-economy and analyzed why strong state structures were established there, and the role that class played in this process. Chapter 6 looked at the peripheral zones and analyzed why their state structures were weak. It further elaborated the distinction between peripheral zones inside the world-economy and external arenas—that is, zones that remained outside the axial division of labor of the capitalist world-economy.

Volume 1 set the basic argument of the overall work in place, and concluded with a theoretical reprise that summarized and conceptualized the concrete empirical transformations described in the rest of the volume. During the long sixteenth century, and indeed for some time thereafter, the capitalist world-economy existed in only a part of the globe—essentially, western Europe and parts of the Americas. The rest of the globe was not yet part of this historical social system and therefore not subject to its rules and constraints.

If volume 1 went against the common argument that there was nothing we could call "modern" or "capitalist" before the late eighteenth century, it also argued with the position of those who said that there was a beginning of capitalism in the sixteenth century but that capitalism had a big setback in the seventeenth century. See the very extensive literature about the "crisis of the seventeenth century." I treated this literature in the introduction to and chapter 1 of volume 2. I wished to argue that the so-called crisis was not at all a setback but a normal B-phase (or downturn) of the world-economy, one that advanced rather than disrupted capitalist development.

Chapter 2 dealt, as we have already indicated, with Dutch hegemony and the general patterns that explain why and how one country becomes hegemonic—for a while. Chapter 3 explored what happens when a hegemonic power first begins to decline. Empirically it dealt with English and French aspirations to be the successor state. Chapter 3 discussed how peripheral zones cope with a B-phase and why "turning inward" is not anticapitalist but survivalist. Chapter 4 was the first serious discussion of the characteristics of a semiperiphery; the role that semiperipheries play in the life of the modern world-system; and the distinction between those that are "rising" and those that are "declining." Chapter 6 dealt with the continuing Franco-British rivalry in the period after there was no longer a significant political role for the Dutch. It described the lead that was taken by Great Britain and why this lead was the result not of more advanced economic structures (the usual argument) but of the fact that the British state, for various reasons, was *stronger* than the French state (contrary to the usual argument).

If the period of the late eighteenth and early nineteenth centuries is widely recognized as a period of economic and geographic expansion of the capitalist world-economy, credit is usually given to something called the "industrial revolution"—and often to something called the "first industrial revolution," which presumably occurred in England. Analytically, I thought this conception was weak on two grounds. One is that there were not, could not be, separate "industrial revolutions" in different countries. If there were any such thing, it had to be a phenomenon of the capitalist world-economy as a whole. And second, although what happened in that period did indeed reflect an upward blip in the mechanization and the value output of world production, it was no more significant than several previous and several subsequent blips. This is what chapter 1 sought to demonstrate.

Chapter 2 took up the story of the French Revolution. The voluminous literature on this "event" is currently divided between the adherents of the social (or classical) interpretation that had been so prominent for a long time and those of the liberal (or revisionist) interpretation that gained so much force in the last third of the twentieth century. My contention was that both interpretations are wrong, since they both focused attention on phenomena said to be internal to France and on the kinds of changes that occurred in the French state and economic structures. The argument of this chapter was that the French Revolution was a part of, a consequence of, the last phase in the British-French struggle for hegemonic succession—one that was won, of course, by Great Britain—and that the changes internal to France as a result of the Revolution were far less fundamental than is usually contended.

One of the outcomes of this Franco-British struggle was the second great geographic expansion of the capitalist world-economy, in which four large zones were incorporated into the axial division of labor: Russia, the Ottoman Empire, the Indian subcontinent, and West Africa. The key argument is about what happens to a zone, previously in the external arena, when it becomes incorporated as a peripheral zone of the capitalist world-economy. The transformations of both the political and economic structures in the four zones, starting from very different existing structures before incorporation, seem to have brought the four zones to all having more or less similar structures as a result of incorporation.

Finally, chapter 4 dealt, for the first time, with the concept of formal decolonization—why it occurs and why it is linked to the emergence of a new hegemonic power. But I argued also that the decolonization of the Americas was a "settler" decolonization and not a reassumption by the indigenous peoples of control of their own lives. The one exception was Haiti, and I tried to show here why and how Haiti was isolated and largely destroyed economically precisely because it was *not* a settler decolonization.

When I came to volume 4, which I had intended to be the story of the "long" nineteenth century, I faced two problems. As we move forward chronologically, the geography of the world-system widens, which expands the amount of material to be considered. But the amount of scholarly literature, even about a single country, has expanded at least arithmetically and probably geometrically. This poses a real problem of reading time and of difficulties of synthesis. This is my perhaps feeble excuse for having taken so long to produce volume 4. (The other part of the excuse is that, as time went on, I became more involved in many other intellectual activities that competed with the time available to me to write volume 4.)

The second problem was to decide what would be the central theme of this volume. Given my previous analyses, it could not be the industrial revolution—nor could it be the creation of a capitalist system, since I believed that this had occurred earlier. It was also not the great democratic revolution(s), of either the French or the American variety, since I thought that the role of both kinds of revolutions was quite different from that most often ascribed to them. I decided that the key happening was to be located in the cultural consequences to the modern world-system as a whole of the French Revolution. I conceived of this as the creation of a geoculture for the world-system—that is, a set of ideas, values, and norms that were widely accepted throughout the system and that constrained social action thereafter.

As the reader will see, I consider that the French Revolution had legitimated the concept of the normality of political change and the idea that sovereignty lay not with the sovereign but with the people. The consequences of this pair of beliefs were manifold. The first was the creation, as a reaction to these newly widespread concepts, of the three modern ideologies—conservatism, liberalism, and radicalism. The argument of the volume as a whole is that centrist liberalism was able to "tame" the other two ideologies and emerge triumphant in the course of the century. This then took the form of privileging the creation of liberal states, first of all in the two strongest states of the time—Great Britain and France. It took further form in stimulating the creation, and limiting the impact, of the major kinds of antisystemic movements (a new concept treated here). It is here that I treat the advances permitted by the concept of citizenship, and the illusions concerning the extent of these advantages. And finally, it took the form of encouraging and constraining the formation of the historical social sciences. The story as a whole runs from 1789 to 1914, or perhaps, one should better say, from 1789 to 1873/1914.

It took me a while to realize that this emphasis meant that three stories I intended to tell in this volume should be postponed to volume 5. They were the scramble for Africa and the rise of movements of national liberation; the U.S.-German economic and political rivalry for succession to Great Britain as the hegemonic power, and the ultimate triumph of the United States; and the incorporation of East Asia, its peripheralization, and its resurgence in the late twentieth century.

All three stories had their start somewhere in the middle of the nineteenth century. But one could not reasonably tell these stories as though they ended somehow in 1914. The nineteenth-century story was integrally linked to its continuation in the twentieth century. The year 1914 was not a turning point for any of the three stories per se. The essential part of each story was located in a sweeping curve of rise and decline, or decline and rise. In any case, I decided that each of these stories was a story of the "long" twentieth century, a story of America's century and not Britain's century. So I beg the reader's indulgence and patience.

If volume 5, as I project it now (but this may change in the writing), will go from 1873 to 1968/89, there will have to be, if I can last it out, a volume 6, whose theme will be the structural crisis of the capitalist world-economy and whose parameters would go from 1945/1968 to somewhere in the mid-twenty-first century—say, 2050. And then, I feel, we will be into a totally new situation. The modern world-system will have seen its definitive demise, ceding place to a successor or successors yet unknown, unknowable, and whose characteristics we cannot yet sketch.

Victor Delaive, *Bourgeois et Ouvriers*. This cartoon appeared in May 1848 in the midst of the social revolution in France. The worker tells the bourgeois that he confiscated two previous revolutions (1789 and 1830) and that this time "we workers demand our fair share. It's only just." (Courtesy of Bibliothèque National de France)

Centrist Liberalism as Ideology

The French Revolution . . . is the shadow under which the whole nineteenth century lived.

—GEORGE WATSON (1973, 45)

In 1815, the most important new political reality for Great Britain, France, and the world-system was the fact that, in the spirit of the times, political change had become normal. "With the French Revolution, parliamentary reform became a doctrine as distinct from an expedient" (White, 1973, 73). Furthermore, the locus of sovereignty had shifted in the minds of more and more persons from the monarch or even the legislature to something much more elusive, the "people" (Billington, 1980, 160–166; also 57–71). These were undoubtedly the principal geocultural legacies of the revolutionary-Napoleonic period. Consequently, the fundamental political problem that Great Britain, France, and the world-system had to face in 1815, and from then on, was how to reconcile the demands of those who would insist on implementing the concept of popular sovereignty exercising the normality of change with the desire of the notables, both within each state and in the world-system as a whole, to maintain themselves in power and to ensure their continuing ability to accumulate capital endlessly.

The name we give to these attempts at resolving what prima facie seems a deep and possibly unbridgeable gap of conflicting interests is *ideology*. Ideologies are not simply ways of viewing the world. They are more than mere prejudices and presuppositions. Ideologies are political metastrategies, and as such are required only in a world where political change is considered normal and not aberrant. It was precisely such a world that the capitalist world-economy had become under the cultural upheaval of the revolutionary-Napoleonic period. It was precisely this world that developed the ideologies that served during the nineteenth and twentieth centuries as both the handbooks of daily political activity and the credos justifying the mundane compromises of such activity.

Was the French Revolution inspired by liberal ideology, or was it rather the negation of liberal ideology? This was a central theme of the French (and world-wide) debate during the bicentennial of 1989. The question, however, is perhaps not very meaningful, because liberalism as an ideology is itself a consequence of the French Revolution, and not a description of its political culture.[1] The first ide-ological reaction to the French Revolution's transformation of the geoculture was in fact, however, not liberalism, but conservatism. Burke and de Maistre wrote about the Revolution immediately, in the heat of the events, in books that have remained founts of conservative ideology to this day. Of course, the concepts pre-ceded the terms. The term *conservative* apparently first appeared only in 1818,[2] and the noun *liberal* was probably first used in 1810.[3]

1. See Kaplan (1993) for the story of the French debate in all its gory detail. This book makes clear how inconclusive the debate was, largely because the question cannot be posed in these terms. Or rather, the reason the question was posed in these terms was in order to confront the political issues of the late twentieth century rather than to clarify the historical reality. Posing the question in this way makes it impossible to understand the rise and historical role of liberal ideology. In our previous vol-ume, we have discussed how to understand the French Revolution in terms of the historical evolution of the modern world-system (Wallerstein, 1989, chaps. 1, 2).

2. Bénéton (1988, 6) traces the term to Chateaubriand's journal, *Le Conservateur,* and its use in Great Britain as a party label to an article by J. W. Crocker written in 1830. *Reaction* or *reactionary* seem to have entered the vocabulary even later. Tudesq (1964, 2:1028) argues that these terms became common (*se vulgarisent*) only in 1848, but this doesn't really say anything about the issue of first usage.

3. As an adjective with political connotations, the term seems to have first been used during the years of the Directory in France. Cruz Seoane (1968, 157) attributes first use "probably" to Benjamin Constant in 1796 speaking of "liberal ideas." Brunot and Bruneau (1937, 2:660–61) locates the start of its career in Year VIII (1797–98) as a term opposed to *sectarian* and to *Jacobin*. But he also finds its use as a political verb (*se libéraliser*) in the *Ami des Patriotes* in 1791.

Everyone seems to agree that the adjective became a noun in Cádiz in 1810–11, when it was applied to a group of the Spanish Cortés. A member of the Cortés, the Conde de Toreno, writing some sixty years later, says that the public described the "friends of reform" as *los liberales* (cited by Marichal, 1955, 58). Billington (1980, 554, n. 33) says this led to the creation of a *partido liberal* in 1813 (see also Cruz Seoane, 1968, 158). Marichal finds it ironic that "Spain, the least 'bourgeois' country in western Europe, coined the theme word of the European bourgeoisie in the nineteenth century" (1955, 60). But it is not at all ironic: Spanish liberals in 1810 were in the midst of a tempestuous struggle, and ideological clarity served as a political rallying point for them.

Manning (1976, 9) claims that "the original implications of the term liberal, like the term imperial-ist, were for the most part derogatory." But this is not at all clear from the description of the Cortés. What he may be thinking of is Lord Castlereagh's speech in Parliament on February 15, 1816, in which he said that the Spanish party, though anti-French militarily, "were politically a French party of the very worst description. They had declared they would not admit Ferdinand's right to the throne, unless he put his seal to the principles which they laid down, and among the rest to that of the sovereignty be-ing in the people. The 'Liberals' were a perfectly Jacobinical party in principle" (*Parl. Deb.,* xxxvii, 602, cited in Halévy, 1949a, 82, n. 3). Ferdinand obviously agreed, since he banned the use of the term in the same year (see Marichal, 1955, 60). It comes into French and British political usage in 1819 (see Bertier de Sauvigny, 1970, 155; Halévy, 1949a, 81, n.3), but it would be another quarter century before the Whigs renamed themselves the Liberal Party.

Conservative ideology has been deeply tied to a vision of the French Revolution as the exemplar of the kind of deliberate political change that disrupts the slow-moving evolution of "natural" social forces. For conservatives, this disruptive process had a long and dubious heritage:

> The French Revolution was but the culmination of the historical process of atomization that reached back to the beginning of such doctrines as nominalism, religious dissent, scientific rationalism, and the destruction of those groups, institutions and intellectual certainties which had been basic in the Middle Ages. (Nisbet, 1952, 168–169)

Conservative ideology was thus "reactionary" in the simple sense that it was a reaction to the coming of what we think of as modernity, and set itself the objective either of reversing the situation entirely (the hard version) or of limiting the damage and holding back as long as possible the changes that were coming (the more sophisticated version). The conservatives believed that, by imposing their "rational," deductive schema on the political process, the partisans of revolution (or reform; it makes little difference in the conservative dogma) create turmoil, undo the wisdom of the ages, and thereby do social harm.

Like all ideologies, conservatism was first and foremost a political program. Conservatives knew full well that they had to hold on to or reconquer state power, that the institutions of the state were the key instrument needed to achieve their goals, When conservative forces returned to power in France in 1815, they baptized this event a "Restoration." But as we shall see, things did not really go back to the status quo ante. Louis XVIII had to concede a "Charter," and when Charles X tried to install a true reaction, he was ousted from power and in his place was put Louis-Philippe, who assumed the much more modern title "King of the French."[4]

The ideal solution for conservatives would have been the total disappearance of movements reflecting liberal impulses. Barring that—it did not happen in 1815 and came to be recognized as utopian after 1848—the next best solution was to persuade legislators of the need for utmost prudence in undertaking any political change of great significance. The continuing political strength of conservatism

---

4. The Charter conceded by Louis XVIII was politically crucial to his "restoration." In his declaration at St.-Ouen, the future king announced that he was determined to "adopt a liberal constitution," which he designated as a "charter." Bastid (1953, 163–164) observes that "the term Charter, whose meanings in former times had been multiple and varied, above all brought to mind the memory of communal liberties." He adds that, "for those of liberal bent, it evoked quite naturally the English Magna Carta of 1215." According to Bastid, "Louis XVIII would never have been able to win public acceptance had he not satisfied in some way the aspirations for liberty." When, in 1830, Louis-Philippe in turn also proclaimed a Charter, this time it had to be one that was "assented to" (*consentie*) rather than one that was "bestowed" (*octroyée*) by the king.

would be located in the popular wariness that multiple disillusions with reforms would repeatedly instill in the "sovereign people." On the other hand, conservatism's great weakness has always been that it was essentially a negative doctrine. "[Conservative doctrine] was born in reaction to the French Revolution. . . . [I]t was thus born counterrevolutionary."[5] And counterrevolution has been in general even less popular in the nineteenth and twentieth centuries than revolution; it is a label that has been an albatross for conservatives.

Conservatives felt, nonetheless, that they had an unassailable case. The greatest objection conservatives had to the French Revolution was the belief espoused by its partisans and theoreticians that all was possible and legitimate through politics. Conservatives argued, instead, for an organic conception of society, and the "radical inadequacy of the political as a final account of man."[6] Conservatives supported the state insofar as it incarnated authority, but suspected the central state insofar as it might legislate. The consequence was a penchant for localism, in part because notables had greater strength at local levels and partly because inherently less could be legislated at that level.[7] To be sure, this antipolitical bias was not

5. Bénéton (1988, 9), who continues: "[T]he essence of conservatism remains an antimodernist critique by fidelity to its traditionalist convictions, and its fate is impotence to prevent the progressive elimination of the traditional order. . . . Conservatives appeal to history but in a way history gives them the lie" (p. 10). Gash makes the same point: "[Conservatism] was born of reaction; part of the defensive mechanism traceable to the age of the French Revolution which began in 1789" (1977, 21). As a consequence, it would always be limited in its ability to construct any proactive proposals, and eventually would find itself constrained, as we shall see, to become a variant of reformist liberalism.

6. White (1950, 4). See also Quintin Hogg: "The Conservative does not believe that the power of politics to put things right in this world is unlimited" (*The Case for Conservatism*, 1947, in White, 1950, 31). Similarly, Crick defines conservatism as "above all, a renunciation of possibilities in favor of prescription which was born from the lesson or the fear of the French Revolution" (1955, 363). Finally, in the beginning of the twentieth century, Lord Cecil defined political conservatism as deriving from "natural conservatism," which involved the "distrust of the unknown" and the "preference of that to which we are accustomed because custom had actually assimilated our nature to it" (1912, 14).

White (1950, 1–2) shows how this attitude is profoundly antipolitical and, derivatively, anti-intellectual: "Conservatism is less a political doctrine than a mode of feeling, a way of living. . . . What holds this field full of folk together is obviously not so much a body of intellectually formulated principles as a number of instincts, and the governing instinct is the instinct of enjoyment. . . . The political importance of this instinct of enjoyment, this largely thoughtless devotion to the life of here and now in all its richness and variety, is that it puts politics in its place as something secondary or incidental."

7. Roberts (1958, 334) describes the attitude of the Tories in Great Britain: " 'Centralization' was an evil word. It evoked the deepest of Tory prejudices and touched the most sacred of Tory interests. . . . The Tories guarded their local privileges vigilantly and defended with equal regard the right of the clergy to educate the poor, the right of the borough to run its prisons, and the right of the parish to repair its roads. . . . The Conservative's attachment to local government arose from many sources: from traditionalism, from vested interests in local power and patronage, from a loyalty to the Church and from a fear of higher rates. The last motive was of no small magnitude."

universal among those who were "counterrevolutionary"; it was merely dominant. Henry Kissinger makes a very cogent distinction between Burkean conservatism (which is what I have been describing here as conservatism) and the conservatism of Metternich:

> To fight for conservatism in the name of historical forces, to reject the validity of the revolutionary question because of its denial of the temporal aspect of society and the social contract—this was the answer of Burke. To fight the revolution in the name of reason, to deny the validity of the question on epistemological grounds, as contrary to the structure of the universe—this was the answer of Metternich. The difference between these two positions is fundamental. . . .
>
> It was this rationalist conception of conservatism which imparted the rigidity to Metternich's policy. . . .
>
> It was thus that the Enlightenment retained deep into the nineteenth century its last champion, who judged actions by their "truth," not by their success.[8]

Success. This was the clarion call of the liberals. But success in what? This is the key question we must address. Liberalism as an ideology, as opposed to liberalism as a political philosophy—that is, liberalism as a metastrategy vis-à-vis the demands of popular sovereignty, as opposed to liberalism as a metaphysics of the good society—was not born adult out of the head of Zeus. It was molded by multiple, often contrary, interests. To this day, the term *liberalism* evokes quite varied resonances. There is the classic "confusion" between so-called economic and so-called political liberalism. There is also the liberalism of social behavior, sometimes called libertarianism. This mélange, this "confusion," has served liberal ideology well, enabling it to secure maximal support.

Liberalism started ideological life on the left of the political spectrum, or at least on the center-left. Liberalism defined itself as the opposite of conservatism, on the basis of what might be called a "consciousness of being modern" (Minogue, 1963, 3). Liberalism proclaimed itself universalist.[9] Sure of themselves and of the truth of this new world-view of modernity, liberals sought to propagate their views and intrude the logic of their views within all social institutions, thereby ridding

---

8. Kissinger (1973, 193, 194, 196). The political rigidity of the Metternich position would not, in the long run, serve well the interests of those who wished to conserve their privileges and power. It would in fact get them into deep trouble and into paradoxical forms of disruptive "radicalism," as we shall see happened to the Bonaldian conservatives during the Restoration in France. The Metternichian version of conservatism was revived only in the last decades of the twentieth century. Once again, it may not be serving well the interests of those who wish to conserve privileges and power.

9. "It is to mankind as a whole that liberals have, without major exception, addressed themselves" (Manning, 1976, 80).

the world of the "irrational" leftovers of the past, To do this, they had to fight conservative ideologues, whom they saw as obsessed with fear of "free men"[10]— men liberated from the false idols of tradition.

Liberals believed, however, that progress, even though it was inevitable, could not be achieved without some human effort, without a political program. Liberal ideology was thus the belief that, in order for history to follow its natural course, it was necessary to engage in conscious, continual, intelligent reformism, in full awareness that "time was the universal friend, which would inevitably bring greater happiness to ever greater numbers" (Schapiro, 1949, 13).

After 1815, liberal ideology presented itself as the opponent of the conservative thrust,[11] and as such was considered by conservatives to be "Jacobinical." But as liberalism gained momentum, support, and authority as an ideology, its left credentials weakened; in some respects it even gained right credentials. But its destiny was to assert that it was located in the center. It had already been conceptualized in this way by Constant[12] in the eighteenth century. It was institutionalized as the centrist position in the nineteenth century. And it was still being celebrated as the "vital center" by Schlesinger (1962) in the mid-twentieth century.

To be sure, the center is merely an abstraction, and a rhetorical device. One can always locate oneself in a central position simply by defining the extremes as one wishes. Liberals are those who decided to do this as their basic political strategy. Faced with the normality of change, liberals would claim a position between the conservatives—that is, the right, who wanted to slow down the pace of normal change as much as possible—and the "democrats" (or radicals or socialists or revolutionaries)—that is, the left, who wanted to speed it up as much as possible. In short, liberals were those who wished to control the pace of change so that it occurred at what they considered to be an optimal speed. But could one really know what is the optimal speed? Yes, said the liberals, and their metastrategy was precisely geared to achieving this end.

Two emblematic figures arose in the development of this metastrategy: Guizot and Bentham. Guizot was a historian, a man of letters, and of course a politician. Bentham was a philosopher and an advocate of concrete legislative action. In the

10. In Stendhal's *The Charterhouse of Parma*, the revolutionary Ferrante Palla always introduces himself as a "free man."

11. Rémond (1982, 16) dates the beginning of the ongoing gulf in France between the politics of conservatism and of liberalism not in 1789 but in 1815, "the moment when right and left became social realities and givens of the collective psyche."

12. "'Liberal' meant for Constant a 'moderate' and 'central' position between the two extremes of Jacobinism (or 'anarchy') and Monarchism ('the fanatics')" (Marichal, 1956, 293).

end, the eyes of both of them were focused on the state. Guizot himself defined *modernity* as "the substitution in government of intellectual means for material means, of ruse for force, Italian politics for feudal politics" (Guizot, 1846, 299). He said it began with Louis XI, and this may be so. But even if it were so, it became fully institutionalized only in the first half of the nineteenth century, precisely when Guizot was in the government of France.

Guizot sought a way to mute popular sovereignty without returning to the divine right of kings. He found it by claiming the existence of an "irresistible hand" of reason progressing through history. By arguing this more political version of the Smithian "invisible hand," Guizot could establish, as a prior condition for the exercise of the right to popular sovereignty, the possession of "capacity," defined as the "faculty of acting according to reason."[13] Only if suffrage were limited to those having this capacity would it then be possible to have a "scientific policy" and a "rational government." And only such a government would eliminate the triple menace of "the return of arbitrary government, the unloosing of popular passions, and social dissolution" (cited in Rosanvallon 1985, 255–256; see also 156–158). The reference to science is not casual, but fundamental. Manning (1976, 16, 21, 23) develops the links between liberal ideology and Newtonian science. He shows the derivation of what he argues are the three principles of liberal ideology from Newtonian thought: the principle of balance, the principle of spontaneous generation and circulation, and the principle of uniformity. First, the stability of the world "depend[s] upon its constituent parts remaining in balanced relationships." Second, "any attempt to transform the self-moving society into the directed society must necessarily destroy the harmony and balance of its rational order." Third, "we may expect democratic institutions to materialize in human societies whenever they reach the appropriate level of development, just as we may expect any physical phenomenon to materialize given the principle of its sufficient condition for its occurrence."

13. Rosanvallon (1985, 91, 95), who goes on to point out how this viewpoint distinguished Guizot and the other *doctrinaires* from Bonald on the one hand and Rousseau on the other: "[They] sought to introduce into political thought a sociological point of view which integrated as an irreversible and positive fact the achievement of civil equality and the full recognition of the modern individual. This overcame the antagonism between reactionary thought and liberal-democratic thought, consciously removing philosophy from what was considered to be the vicious circle of their confrontation. . . .

"Capacity being a faculty, and not a quality, it has both a personal and an impersonal dimension. It enables one to distinguish those who are endowed with it, the capable, from the rest of the population, without the latter being able to incorporate themselves in it or take total possession of it." The principle of capacity thus allows one to unite stability and social mobility, order and movement. "We must fix the things themselves," wrote Guizot, "and men will find their places around them" (p. 97).

In short, Guizot supported neither Louis XVI (or Charles X) nor Robespierre, for neither was a rational choice. And of the two, Guizot (and his epigones) probably worried about Robespierre and Rousseau more. "What is still generally called 'liberalism' in the beginning of the nineteenth century was an attempt to conceive of politics against Rousseau. Revolutionary terror was the child of political voluntarism (*artificialisme*); everyone agreed with that analysis" (Rosanvallon, 1985, 44).[14]

Guizot's reputation faded, sullied no doubt by his increasingly conservative role in the July Monarchy, and is only today being resuscitated by France's political neoliberals. But Bentham's reputation as Great Britain's quintessential liberal has never ceased to be asserted (and acclaimed).[15] Guizot's triple menace was equally there for the Benthamites, of course, but they were perhaps even more adept at countering it.[16] It was the great French Anglophile and liberal Elie Halévy (1900, iii–iv) who pointed out how Bentham took a starting point actually not too different from that of Rousseau but had it end up not with revolution but with classic liberalism:

> England, like France, had its century of liberalism: the century of the industrial revolution across the Channel was the equivalent of the century of the French Revolution; the utilitarian philosophy of the identity of interests that of the juridical and spiritualist philosophy of the rights of man. The interests of all individuals are identical. Each individual is the best judge of his own interests. Hence we ought to eliminate all artificial barriers which traditional institutions erected between individuals, all social constraints founded upon the presumed need to protect individuals against each other and against themselves. An emancipatory philosophy very different in its inspiration and in its principles but close in many of its practical applications to the sentimental philosophy of J.-J. Rousseau. The philosophy of the rights of man would culminate, on the Continent, in the Revolution of 1848; the philosophy of the identity of interests in England in the same period in the triumph of Manchesterian free trade concepts.

On the one hand, for Bentham, society was the "spontaneous product of the wills of its individual members [and therefore] a free growth in which the State

14. Rosanvallon adds in a footnote (p. 45, n.2): " 'Liberalism' must thus be distinguished radically from a democratic liberalism founded on the concept of human rights."

15. Eric Hobsbawm (1962, 228) calls the Benthamite philosophic radicals "the most self-consciously bourgeois school of British thinkers."

16. Roberts cautions about giving too much direct credit to Bentham. "What indeed was so remarkable about Bentham was not so much his influence over numerous men, but the foresight, the clarity, and the logic with which he expressed those truths which other forces, far stronger than his own ideas, would bring to pass" (1959, 207). But this is generally true of early ideological statements. They are cogent expressions of views that reflect the underlying metastrategy of political forces that are often incapable of articulating clearly, even to themselves, exactly what policy they are following. The early ideologists thus may not be the actual initiators of the metastrategy. It is only later that these ideological statements are utilized as a mode of socialization and of rationalization.

had no part." But at the very same time—and this is crucial for Bentham and liberalism—society was "a creation of the legislator, the offspring of positive law." State action was therefore perfectly legitimate, "provided the State were a democratic State and expressed the will of the greatest number."[17]

Bentham shared Guizot's penchant for scientific policy and rational government. The state was the perfect, neutral instrument of achieving the "greatest good of the greatest number." The state therefore had to be the instrument of reform, even of radical reform, precisely because of the triple menace:

> Bentham and the Benthamites . . . were never complacent about the condition of England. They were "Radical Reformers," and they worked hard at their reforms: by working out detailed blueprints for them; by propaganda, agitation, intrigue, conspiracy; and if truth be told, by encouragement to revolutionary movements up to—but not beyond—the point where resort to physical force would be the next step.[18]

We come here to the heart of the question. Liberalism was never a metastrategy of antistatism, or even of the so-called nightwatchman state. Far from being

17. Halévy (1950; 3:332). The proper use of the state, not too little but not too much, was an evident concern, but the Benthamites did not lack in self-confidence. "[N]one knew, or thought they knew, better that those second-generation *laissez-faire* philosophers, the Benthamite Utilitarians, how to regulate most efficiently and least wastefully" (Evans, 1983, 289).

18. Viner (1949, 361–362). Viner lists the many reforms with which the Benthamites, after the death of Bentham, were associated: fundamental law reform, prison reform, suffrage (including women's suffrage), free trade, reform in colonial government, legalization of trade unions, general education at the public expense, free speech and free press, secret ballot, appointment and promotion of the civil service on merit, reform of local government, repeal of the laws of usury, general registration of titles to property, safety code for merchant shipping, sanitary reform and preventive medicine at public expense, systematic collection of statistics, and free justice for the poor. Bentham also advocated birth control before Malthus. As we can see, this is a mixed list, including elements associated with implementing laissez-faire, protection of civic rights, intrusion of the government in the workplace, and the provision of social rights to individuals. What all of these had in common was the need to adopt legislation and, ultimately, the enforcement of these reforms by the state.

Perkin (1977, 107) emphasizes the importance of the element of enforcement in Benthamite reform: "the injection of the vital x-ingredient, the appointment of administrative officers who were the chief link in the recurring chain of feedback." See also Roberts (1959, 207): "[Bentham] saw more comprehensively than his contemporaries the necessity of an expanded administrative state."

It was Dicey (1914 [1898]) who portrayed Bentham as exclusively the great advocate of laissez-faire. Brebner (1948, 59–60) said this was a myth. Even those, however, like Parris (1960, 34–35), who think that Brebner overreacted merely argue that the "twin themes" of laissez-faire and state intervention were "equally characteristic of the middle years of the nineteenth century" and that "it is not necessary to assume that they were in contradiction to each other." The reason, for Parris, is obvious: "The main principle of Utilitarianism was what its supporters themselves believed and

contrary to laissez-faire, "the liberal state was itself a creation of the self-regulating market" (Polanyi, 1957, 3). Liberalism has always been in the end the ideology of the strong state in the sheep's clothing of individualism; or to be more precise, the ideology of the strong state as the only sure ultimate guarantor of individualism. Of course, if one defines individualism as egoism and reform as altruism, then the two thrusts are indeed incompatible. But if one defines individualism as maximizing the ability of individuals to achieve self-defined ends, and reform as creating the social conditions within which the strong can temper the discontent of the weak and simultaneously take advantage of the reality that the strong find it easier than the weak to realize their wills, then no inherent incompatibility exists. Quite the contrary!

Great Britain and France had been precisely the two states where relatively strong state machineries had already been created between the sixteenth and the eighteenth centuries. But these states did not have a deep popular legitimacy, and the French Revolution had undermined what legitimacy they had. Nineteenth-century liberalism set itself the task of creating (re-creating, significantly increasing) this legitimacy and thereby cementing the strength of these states, internally and within the world-system.

Socialism was the last of the three ideologies to be formulated. Before 1848, one could hardly yet think of it as constituting a distinctive ideology. The reason was primarily that those who began after 1789 to think of themselves to the left of the liberals saw themselves everywhere as the heirs and partisans of the French Revolution, which did not really distinguish them in the first half of the nineteenth century from those who had begun to call themselves "liberals."[19] Even in Great Britain, where the French Revolution was widely denounced and where "liberals" therefore laid claim to a different historical origin, the "radicals" (who were more or less the future "socialists") seemed at first to be merely somewhat more militant liberals.

In fact, what particularly distinguished socialism from liberalism as a political program and therefore as an ideology was the conviction that the achievement of

---

asserted—the principle of utility. The application of this principle led to considerable extension both of laissez-faire and of state intervention simultaneously." Ruggiero (1959, 99) says substantially the same thing: "Bentham's projects of reform, though demanding considerable activity on the part of the state, do not and are not meant to contradict the principles of individualism, but only give them a necessary complement."

19. Plamenatz points out that, although there were four factions in France among those opposed to the July Monarchy whom one might designate as being on the "left" and who later supported the Revolution of 1848, the term used to refer to them collectively at the time was not *socialists* but *republicans* (1952, 47, and passim).

progress needed not merely a helping hand but a *big* helping hand, without which achieving progress would be a very slow process. The heart of their program, in short, consisted in accelerating the course of history. That is why the word *revolution* appealed to them more than *reform,* which seemed to imply merely patient, if conscientious, political activity and was thought to incarnate primarily a wait-and-see attitude.

In sum, three postures toward modernity and the "normalization" of change had evolved: conservatism, or circumscribe the danger as much as possible; liberalism, or achieve in due time the happiness of mankind as rationally as possible; and socialism/radicalism, or accelerate the drive for progress by struggling hard against the forces that were strongly resisting it. It was in the period 1815–1848 that the terms *conservatism, liberalism,* and *socialism* began to be widely used to designate these three postures.

Each posture, it should be noted, located itself in opposition to something else. For conservatives, the target was the French Revolution. For liberals, it was conservatism (and the ancien régime, whose revival the conservatives were thought to seek). And for socialists, it was liberalism that they were rejecting. It is this fundamentally critical, negative tone in the very definition of the ideologies that explains why there are so many versions of each ideology. Affirmatively, as a positive credo, many varied, even contradictory, propositions were put forward within each camp, each affirming itself as the true meaning of the ideology. The unity of each ideological family lay only in what they were against. This is no minor detail, since it was this negativity that succeeded in holding together the three camps for 150 years or so (at least until 1968).

Since ideologies are in fact political programs to deal with modernity, each one needs a "subject," or a principal political actor. In the terminology of the modern world, this has been referred to as the question of sovereignty. The French Revolution asserted a crystal clear position on this matter: against the sovereignty of the absolute monarch, it had proclaimed the sovereignty of the "people."

This new language of the sovereignty of the people is one of the great achievements of modernity. Even if for a century thereafter there were lingering battles against it, no one has since been able to dethrone this new idol, the "people." But the victory has been hollow. There may have been universal agreement that the people constitute the sovereign, but from the outset there was no agreement about who were the "people." Furthermore, on this delicate question none of the three ideologies has had a clear position, which has not stopped their supporters from refusing to admit the murkiness of their respective stances.

The position that seemingly was least equivocal was that of the liberals. For them, the "people" was the sum of all the "individuals" who are each the ultimate holder of political, economic, and cultural rights. The individual is the historic "subject" of modernity par excellence. One can credit the liberals at least with having debated extensively this question of who this individual is in whom sovereignty is located.

Conservatives and socialists ought in principle to have been debating this issue as well, since each proposed a "subject" quite different from the individual, but their discussion was far less explicit. If the "subject" is not the individual, who, then, is it? It is a bit difficult to discern. See, for example, Edmund Burke's *Reflections on the Revolution in France* (in White, 1950, 28):

> The nature of man is intricate; the objects of society are of the greatest possible complexity; and therefore no simple disposition or direction of power can be suitable either to man's nature, or to the quality of his affairs.

If one didn't know that this was a text attacking French revolutionaries, one might have thought it was intended to denounce absolute monarchs. The matter becomes a bit clearer if we look at something Burke stated almost two decades earlier (1926 [1780], 357): "Individuals pass like shadows; but the commonwealth is fixed and stable."

Bonald's approach was quite different, because he insisted on the crucial role of the Church. His view shares, however, one element common to all the varieties of conservative ideology: the importance they confer on social groups such as the family, guilds (*corporations*), the Church, the traditional "orders"—which become for the conservatives the "subjects" that have the right to act politically. In other words, conservatives gave priority to all those groups that might be considered "traditional" (and thus incarnating continuity) but rejected identifying conservatism with any "totality" as a political actor. What has never in fact been clear in conservative thought is how one can decide which groups incarnate continuity. After all, there have always been arguments around contending royal lineages.

For Bonald (1988 [1802], 87), the great error of Rousseau and Montesquieu had been precisely to "imagine . . . a pure state of nature antecedent to society." Quite the contrary, "the true nature of society . . . is what society, public society, is at present."[20] But this definition was a trap for its author, because it so legitimated the present that it virtually forbade a "restoration." Precise logic, however, has never been the forte or main interest of conservative polemics. Rather, conservatives were concerned to issue warnings about the likely behavior of a majority constituted by adding up individual votes. Their historical subject was a far less active

---

20. As Tudesq notes (1964, 235): "The Legitimist opposition to the July Monarchy was an opposition of notables to established authority." Were the Legitimists not thus contradicting Bonald's dictum?

one than that of the liberals. In their eyes, good decisions are taken slowly and rarely, and such decisions have largely already been taken.

If conservatives refused to give priority to the individual as historical subject in favor of small, so-called traditional groups, socialists refused to do so in favor of that large group that is the whole of the people. Analyzing socialist thought in its early period, G. D. H. Cole (1953, 2) remarked:

> The "socialists" were those who, in opposition to the prevailing stress on the claims of the individual, emphasised the social element in human relations and sought to bring the social question to the front in the great debate about the rights of man let loose on the world by the French Revolution and by the accompanying revolution in the economic field.

But if it is difficult to know which individuals constitute the people, and even more difficult to know of what "groups" the people are constituted, the most difficult thing of all is to know how to define the general will of the whole people. How could one know what it is? And to begin with, whose views should we take into account, and how?

In short, what the three ideologies offered us was not a response to the question of who the appropriate historical subject is, but simply three starting points in the quest for who incarnates the sovereignty of the people: the so-called free individual, for the liberals; the so-called traditional groups, for the conservatives; and the entire membership of "society," for the socialists.

The people as "subject" has had as its primary "object" the state. It is within the state that the people exercises its will, that it is sovereign. Since the nineteenth century, however, we have also been told that the people form a "society." How might we reconcile state and society, which form the great intellectual antinomy of modernity?

The most astonishing thing is that when we look at the discourses of the three ideologies in this regard, they all seem to take the side of society against the state. Their arguments are familiar. For staunch liberals, it was crucial to keep the state out of economic life and to reduce its role in general to a minimum: "*Laissez-faire* is the nightwatchman doctrine of state" (Watson, 1973, 68). For conservatives the terrifying aspect of the French Revolution was not only its individualism but also and particularly its statism. The state becomes tyrannical when it questions the role of the intermediate groups that command the primary loyalty of people—the family, the Church, the guilds.[21] And we are familiar with

---

21. See the discussion of Bonald's views in Nisbet (1944, 318–319). Nisbet uses *corporation* in the sense of "associations based on occupation or profession."

the famous characterization by Marx and Engels in the *Communist Manifesto* (1976 [1848], 486):

> [T]he bourgeoisie has at last, since the establishment of Modern Industry and of the world market, conquered for itself, in the modern representative State, exclusive political sway. The executive of the modern State is but a committee for managing the common affairs of the whole bourgeoisie.

These negatives views of the state did not stop each of the three ideologies from complaining that this state, which was the object of their critique, was out of their control and said to be in the hands of their ideological opponents. In point of fact, each of the three ideologies turned out to be in great need of the services of the state to promote its own program. Let us not forget that an ideology is first and foremost a political strategy. Socialists have long been under attack for what has been said to be their incoherence in that most of them, despite their antistatist rhetoric, have always striven to increase state activity in the short run.

But were conservatives more seriously antistatist? Were they regularly opposed to achieving reforms by state action? Not at all, in reality. For we must take into account the question of the "decline of values," which conservatives have seen as one of the central consequences of modernity. To reverse the perceived current decadence of society, to restore society to the purer state in which it existed before, they have always needed the state. It has been said of one of the great English conservatives of the 1840s, Sir Robert Peel, that "he believed that a constitution issuing in a strong executive was essential to the anarchic age in which he lived" (Gash, 1951, 52). This comment in fact applies more generally to the practice of conservative politicians.

Note the way in which Halévy (1949, 42–43) explains the evolution of the conservative position vis-à-vis the state during the "Tory reaction" in England at the beginning of the nineteenth century:

> In 1688 and in the years following, the King regarded himself, and was regarded by public opinion, as the Sovereign. It was always to be feared that he would make his sovereignty absolute, and the independence of his authority enjoyed by all the powers of the State constituted a deliberate limitation of the prerogative, a system of constitutional guarantees against royal despotism. At the opening of the nineteenth century it was the people who in America, in France, in England even, had asserted, or were about to assert, the claim to be supreme; it was therefore against the people that the three powers now maintained their independence. It was no longer the Whigs, it was the Tories who supported institutions whose significance had changed, while their form remained the same. And now the King presided over the

league formed by the three powers for the defence of their autonomy against the new claimant for sovereignty.

The analysis is limpid. Conservatives were always ready to strengthen the state structure to the degree necessary to control popular forces pushing for change. This was in fact implicit in what was stated by Lord Cecil (1912, 192): "[A]s long as State action does not involve what is unjust or oppressive, it cannot be said that the principles of Conservatism are hostile to it."

Well then, did not at least the liberals—champions of individual freedom and of the free market—remain hostile to the state? Not at all! From the outset, liberals were caught in a fundamental contradiction. As defenders of the rights of the individual vis-à-vis the state, they were pushed in the direction of universal suffrage—the only guarantee of a democratic state. But thereupon the state became the principal agent of all reforms intended to liberate the individual from the social constraints inherited from the past. This in turn led liberals to the idea of putting positive law at the service of utilitarian objectives.

Once again, Halévy (1950: 99–100) clearly pointed out the consequences:

> The "utilitarian" philosophy was not solely, nor even perhaps fundamentally, a liberal system; it was at the same time a doctrine of authority which looked to the deliberate and in a sense scientific interference of Government to produce a harmony of interests. As his ideas developed, Bentham, who as a young man had been an advocate of "enlightened despotism," was converted to democracy. But he had reached that position by what we may call a long jump, which carried him at a bound over a number of political doctrines at which he might have been expected to halt—aristocracy, a mixed constitution, the balance of powers, and the doctrine that the statesman's aim should be to free the individual by weakening the authority of the Government and as far as possible dividing its powers. In Bentham's view, when the authority of the state had been reconciled by a universal or at least a very wide suffrage with the interests of the majority there was no further reason to hold it suspect. It became an unmixed blessing.

And thereupon, the conservatives became now the upholders of the genuine liberal tradition: the old system of aristocratic self-government, with its unpaid officials, against a new system of bureaucratic despotism administered by salaried officials.

Is it possible, then, to think that Benthamism was in fact a deviation from liberalism, whose optimal expression is to be found rather in the classical economists, the theoreticians of "laissez-faire"? No, because we shall see that, when the first Factory Acts were passed in Great Britain, all the leading classical economists of the time supported the legislation—a phenomenon spelled out (and approved) by none other than Alfred Marshall (1921, 763–764), the father of neoclassical

economics. Since that time, the great bureaucratic state has never stopped growing, and its expansion has been sponsored by successive liberal governments.
When Hobhouse wrote his book on liberalism as an answer to that of Lord Cecil
on conservatism, he justified this expansion in this way: "The function of State
coercion is to overcome individual coercion, and, of course, coercion exercised by
any association of individuals within the State" (1911, 146).

No doubt the justifications that each ideology invoked to explain its somewhat
embarrassing statism were different. For socialists, the state was implementing the
general will. For conservatives, the state was protecting traditional rights against
the general will. For liberals, the state was creating the conditions permitting
individual rights to flourish. But in each case, the bottom line was that the state
was being strengthened in relation to society, while the rhetoric called for doing
exactly the opposite.

All this muddle and intellectual confusion involved in the theme of the proper
relation of state and society permits us to understand why we have never been
entirely sure how many distinct ideologies came into existence in the nineteenth
century. Three? Two? Only one? I have just reviewed the traditional arguments
that there were three. Let us now look at how one can reduce the three to two.

It seems clear that in the period from the French Revolution to the revolutions of 1848, the "only clear cleavage" for contemporaries was between those who
accepted progress as inevitable and desirable, and thus "were globally favorable"
to the French Revolution, and those who favored the Counter-Revolution, which
took its stand against this disruption of values, considering it as profoundly wrong
(Agulhon, 1992, 7). Thus the political struggle was between liberals and conservatives; those who called themselves radicals or Jacobins or republicans or socialists
were regarded as simply a more militant variety of liberals. In *The Country Parson*
(*Le Curé de village*), Balzac (1897 [1839], 79) has a bishop exclaim:

> Miracles are called for here among an industrial population, where sedition has
> spread itself and taken root far and wide; where religious and monarchical doctrines
> are regarded with a critical spirit; where nothing is respected by a system of analysis
> derived from Protestantism by the so-called Liberalism of to-day, which is free to
> take another name tomorrow.

Tudesq reminds us (1964, 125–126) that in 1840 a Legitimist newspaper, *l'Orléanais*,
denounced another newspaper, *Le Journal de Loiret*, as a "liberal, Protestant,
Saint-Simonian, Lamennaisian paper." This was not completely wild, since, as
Simon notes (1956, 330): "[t]he Idea of Progress, in fact, constituted the core and
central inspiration of Saint-Simon's entire philosophy of thought" (cf. Manning,
1976, 83–84).

Furthermore, this liberal-socialist alliance has roots in liberal and egalitarian thought of the eighteenth century, in the struggle against absolute monarchy

(see Meyssonier, 1989, 137–156). It continued to be nourished in the nineteenth century by the ever-increasing interest of both ideologies in productivity, which each saw as the basic requirement for a social policy in the modern state. "Both Saint-Simonism and economic liberalism evolved in the direction of what we call today economic rationalisation" (Mason, 1931, 681). With the rise of utilitarianism, it might have seemed that the alliance could become a marriage. Brebner speaks with sympathy of the "collectivist" side of Bentham, concluding (1948, 66), "What were the Fabians but latter-day Benthamites?" And he adds that John Stuart Mill was already in 1830 "what might be called a liberal socialist."

On the other hand, after 1830 a clear distinction began to emerge between liberals and socialists, and after 1848 it became quite deep. At the same time, 1848 marked the beginning of a reconciliation between liberals and conservatives. Hobsbawm (1962, 117) thinks that the great consequence of 1830 was to make mass politics possible by allowing the political triumph in France, England, and especially Belgium (and even partially in Switzerland, Spain, and Portugal) of a "moderate" liberalism, which consequently "split moderates from radicals." Cantimori, analyzing the issue from an Italian perspective, thinks that the question of a divorce was open until 1848. Until then, he notes (1948, 288), "the liberal movement . . . had rejected no path: neither a call for insurrection nor reformist political action." It was only after 1848 that a divorce was consummated between these two tactics.

What is crucial to note is that after 1848 socialists stopped referring to Saint-Simon. The socialist movement began to organize itself around Marxist ideas. The plaint was no longer merely poverty, susceptible to repair by reform, but the dehumanization caused by capitalism, whose solution required overturning it completely (see Kolakowski, 1978, 222).

At this very time, conservatives began to be conscious of the utility of reformism for conservative objectives. Sir Robert Peel, immediately following the Reform Bill of 1832, issued an electoral manifesto, the Tamworth Manifesto, which became celebrated as a doctrinal statement. It was considered by contemporaries as "almost revolutionary," not merely because it announced the acceptance of the Reform Bill as "a final and irrevocable settlement of a great constitutional question," but because this position was announced to the people rather than to Parliament, which caused a great "sensation" at the time (Halévy, 1950, 178).[22]

---

22. Halévy quotes an article that appeared in the *Quarterly Review* of April 1835 (vol. 53, p. 265), entitled "Sir Robert Peel's Address": "When before did a Prime Minister think it expedient to announce to the *People*, not only his acceptance of office, but the principles and even the details of the measures which he intended to produce, and to solicit—not from parliament but from the people—that they would so far maintain the prerogative of the king as to give the ministers of his choice not, indeed, an implicit confidence, but a fair trial?" (1950, 178, n. 10).

In the process, conservatives noted their convergence with liberals on the importance of protecting property, even though what interested them about property was primarily the fact that it represented continuity and thus served as the foundation for family life, the Church, and other social solidarities (see Nisbet, 1966, 26). But beyond this practical convergence, there was the concrete menace of real revolution—a fear they shared, as Lord Cecil noted (1912, 64): "For it is an indispensable part of the effective resistance to Jacobinism that there should be moderate reform on conservative lines."

Finally, we should not entirely neglect the third possible reduction of three to two—conservatives and socialists joining hands in opposition to liberals—even if this seems the least likely theoretically. The "conservative" character of Saint-Simonian socialism, its roots in Bonaldian ideas, has often been noted (see Manuel, 1956, 320; Iggers, 1958a, 99). The two camps could come together around their anti-individualist reflex. Equally, a liberal like von Hayek denounced the "socialist" character of the conservative Carlyle's thought. This time, it was the "social" side of conservative thought that was in question. Lord Cecil (1912, 169) did not in fact hesitate to declare this affinity openly:

> It is often assumed that Conservatism and Socialism are directly opposed. But this is not completely true. Modern Conservatism inherits the traditions of Toryism which are favourable to the activities and the authority of the State. Indeed Mr. Herbert Spencer attacked Socialism as being in fact the revival of Toryism.

The consequence of liberal-socialist alliances was the emergence of a sort of socialist liberalism, ending up with two varieties of liberalism. The conservative-socialist alliances, more improbable, were originally merely passing tactics. But one might wonder whether one might not think of the various "totalitarianisms" of the twentieth century as a more lasting form of this alliance, in the sense that they instituted a form of traditionalism that was both populist and social. If so, these totalitarianisms were yet another way in which liberalism remained center stage, as the antithesis of a Manichean drama. Behind this facade of intense opposition to liberalism, one finds as a core component of the demands of all these regimes the same faith in progress via productivity that has been the gospel of the liberals. In this way we might conclude that even socialist conservatism (or conservative socialism) was, in a way, a variant of liberalism—its diabolical form. In which case, would it not be correct to conclude that since 1789 there had only been one true ideology—liberalism—which has displayed its colors in three major versions?

Of course such a statement has to be spelled out in historical terms. If during the period 1789–1848 there was a great ideological struggle between conservatism and liberalism, conservatism failed in the end to achieve a finished form, as we shall see. After 1848, liberalism would achieve cultural hegemony in the world-system and constitute the fundamental core of the geoculture. In the rest of the long nineteenth century, liberalism dominated the scene without serious opposition. It is true that Marxism tried to constitute a socialist ideology as an independent pole, but it was never entirely able to succeed. The story of the triumph of liberalism in the nineteenth century is the theme of this volume.

Sir Thomas Lawrence, *Prince Metternich*. This photomechanical print reproduces a portrait by the British painter of Klemens Wenzel, Prince von Metternich, the leading figure of the reactionary Holy Alliance during the period 1815–1848. (Courtesy of Prints and Photographs Division, U.S. Library of Congress)

2

Constructing the Liberal State,
1815–1830

[The French Revolution] overthrew or terrified the princes, disconcerted the philosophers, changed the form of problems.

—ELIE HALÉVY (1901A, 276)

During the half-century following the French Revolution from the fall of the Bastille to the final collapse of English Chartism, the danger of revolution was never entirely absent from any European country.

—FRANK O. DARVALL (1934, 304)

Great Britain and France fought a long battle for hegemony within the capitalist world-economy from 1651 to 1815.[1] It was only in 1815 that Great Britain at last won its definitive victory. At once, and with a celerity that is remarkable, the two countries entered into a tacit but very profound alliance in the effort to institutionalize a new political model for states located in the core zones (or aspiring to locate there). This model was that of the liberal state, which was a key element in the legitimation of the capitalist world-economy in the era of popular sovereignty.

The alliance between Great Britain and France was based not only on the fact that they faced somewhat comparable internal pressures but also on the fact that they needed each other in order to achieve this end. They needed each other for mutual support and learning in the construction of the model, to be sure. They needed each other also to maintain a geopolitical balance in their mutual interest.[2] But most of all, they needed to present a common standard to the rest of

---

1. This story was analyzed in vol. 2, chaps. 3 and 6, and in vol. 3, chap. 2.

2. "After 1815, the peace treaties effectively curbed French expansion. . . . Increasingly, Russia was perceived [by Great Britain] as the new menace. . . . British policy was generally directed to shoring up obstacles to Russian aggressiveness" (Evans, 1983, 196–197). Of course, in the second half of the nineteenth century the menace began to be Germany. However, as we know, the British-French alliance held firm throughout the nineteenth century and the next.

the world in order more effectively to sweep away alternative models and turn all eyes toward theirs. Thus began the complicit although quite often less than totally cordial entente. The crucial period for this process ran from 1815 to 1875, after which the model was firmly established and would remain so for at least a century, enabling the capitalist world-economy to maintain a certain structural stability amid the very stormy turmoil to which it would be subjected. Still, on the morrow of Waterloo there seemed to be very few advocates of the liberal state in places of power, even in Great Britain and France. Indeed, the very term did not yet exist.

Construction of the modern state, located within and constrained by an inter-state system, had been a constituent element of the modern world-system from its beginnings in the long sixteenth century. The concern of rulers had been to strengthen the state in two ways: to strengthen its authority—that is, its capac-ity to make efficacious decisions within its frontiers; and to strengthen its world power—that is, its capacity to impose its will on other states and diminish their possibility of doing the converse. There had long been much debate about the proper distribution of decision making within the state: how much of it should be concentrated in the head of state as sovereign, how much shared with legislative bodies. For three centuries, however, the debate remained one of distribution of power among branches of government. It is true that in 1776, the U.S. Declaration of Independence was proclaimed in the name of "we, the people", but it was not at all clear (even to the signers of this declaration) how seriously one was to take the idea of popular sovereignty, and what its implications were. For the world-system as a whole, it was "the French Revolution [that] let the genie out of the bottle. After 1789 it was impossible to keep political debate within a privileged circle of propertied interests" (Evans, 1983, 66). The French Revolution and its Napoleonic aftermath made the concept of popular sovereignty one with which every govern-ment in the modern world had to come to terms, and none more so than the gov-ernments of the two rivals for hegemonic power. The question in 1815 was whether 1789–1815 was merely a sort of revolutionary interlude, to be interred by a "Res-toration" and a "Tory reaction," or whether the concept of popular sovereignty would have an enduring political impact. To the surprise of the restorers of global order, it was an idea that had taken deeper root than they had realized. They could not inter it, whatever they wished. The specter that haunted the notables[3] was that of democracy. The distinction between the liberal state and democracy was, in Max Beloff's words, "the most important distinction in nineteenth-century poli-

---

3. I borrow the term from the July Monarchy, where it was used to designate the ruling stratum and lumped together "aristocrats, pseudo-nobles, and the grand bourgeoisie. . . . The notable is usually an heir" (Jardin and Tudesq, 1973, 1:157).

tics."[4] Democracy, in nineteenth-century usage, meant taking popular sovereignty seriously. The notables were not, and have never been, ready to do that. It was the realization of this new reality that would give birth to that extraordinary invention of the nineteenth century—the political ideology.

In 1789, no one really knew what transferring sovereignty from the monarch to the people really meant. They thought it had something to do with limiting the arbitrary power of the executive authority associated with the concept of an absolute monarch. And so it did, but that done, there was still the need to find a legitimation for the decisions of passing coalitions of sundry political leaders. Taking seriously the slogan of popular sovereignty has seemed ever since to all those with effective political power to be threatening, to suggest the unpleasant prospect of submission to the vagaries of uninformed capricious masses. The problem for the notables, therefore, was how to construct a structure that would seem to be popular and in fact was not, but would nonetheless retain the support of a significant proportion of the "people." That would not be easy. The liberal state was to be the historic solution.

In 1815, looking back on the long adventure from 1789 to 1815, in terms of internal social tensions in France and Great Britain, what did one see? Michel Vovelle (1993, 7) said of an essay of his about the French Revolution that it would be pretentious to entitle it "the birth of a nation" and that instead, "more modestly," he would call it "the discovery of politics."[5] But is this different? What else do we

4. He says this distinction "was sensed by Tocqueville and by a few others, but was brushed aside by the heirs of the Jacobins and by the Utilitarians. For these regarded the distinctions as an excuse for maintaining such indispensable class-privileges as the narrow propertied franchise of the July monarchy, which it was, but also as nothing more than an excuse, which it was not" (Beloff, 1974, 49). This nineteenth-century fear of democracy is similarly noted, and implicitly approved, by Rosanvallon (1985, 75, 76, 80):

> Mme. de Stael, Ballanche, Chateaubriand, Lamennais, Royer-Collard, Bonald, Saint-Simon, Benjamin Constant or Auguste Comte all spoke the same language, despite their [liberal-conservative] differences. . . .
>
> At the center of their common preoccupations was the desire to shy away from the model of popular sovereignty, considered to be responsible for all the excesses of the preceding [revolutionary-Napoleonic] period, the matrix of revolutionary disorder and the breeding-ground of Napoleonic despotism at the same time. . . .
>
> The recognition of the *ambivalence of democratic reality* in modern societies elaborated and completed this recognition of its fragility. An ambivalence that one can summarize succinctly in the following terms: democracy was at one and the same time for the *doctrinaires* the positive foundation of the new society and what threatened to subvert it; it represented both a just principle on which to build (civil equality) and a potential for destruction (the anarchic eruption of numbers in political decision-making).

5. See also Billington (1980, 57): "In the French Revolution, . . . the concept of a 'nation' was central even though no new country was created. The word *nation* soon predominated over the older and more paternalistic term *patrie*."

mean by a nation except that within which the pursuit of politics by its nationals is considered to be legitimate? In a profound sense, the sovereignty of the people is a concept that incarnates the legitimacy of politics. And therefore the debate about the implementation of this concept is a debate about the limits of the political—not only about who may be involved and how they may be involved, but also about what matters are subject to the collective decision of the nation. France, in this sense, had a rude beginning as a nation. But so did the rest of Europe. For, in effect, "the invader" Napoleon "with his ideas of emancipation and social liberation . . . spread the concept of the nation" (Ponteil, 1968, vii)[6] and spread with it France's rude beginnings. The question for France, as for all the other new nations, became what difference the politics of a nation would make for the lives of ordinary people, as opposed to their lives when politics did not exist and decisions were subject to the intrigues of a court. It was intended to make a profound difference. Still, there are those who would come to view the Revolution, as did Elton (1923, 7), as having been "primarily a movement for order; a movement against chaos." In that case, one could say of Napoleon (but not only of him) "indifferently that he 'organized the *ancien régime*' or that he consolidated the Revolution: for the two processes were identical" (Elton, 1923, 69).

In terms of the politics of the period following 1815, there were two main political legacies of the revolutionary-Napoleonic era. One was the image of the Terror, which informs French and world politics to this day—a Terror that is inextricably associated in the minds of many with democracy. For a long time, the Terror was in fact the chief argument the notables used against the extension of the suffrage. "In the name of this experience, men like Louis Guizot or Benjamin Constant refused the extension of political rights to the needy classes" (Donzelot, 1984, 21–22). The second legacy, which was intimately tied to the first, was the unceasing drive to seek to exclude the lower strata from the political arena of the nation entirely.

The story was not really very different in Great Britain. We often think of absolutism as having disappeared in Great Britain much earlier than in France. But in fact it is only at this very time that the king's power to make and unmake ministries—that is, to control the executive—was undone in practice. The French

6. See also Demangeon and Febvre (1935, 111): "[T]he Reformation [was] the first of repeated shocks which, over 300 years, would shake the old edifice of medieval Europe before Napoleon, with one brutal push of his shoulder, sent it crashing down." The post-1815 unavowed ideological alliance between France and Great Britain was, in a sense, already operative during the Napoleonic Wars. See Billington's analysis of the spread of radicalism in southern Europe: "British leadership in the anti-Napoleonic struggle encouraged the blending of Right and Left throughout southern Europe—from Greece through southern Italy to Spain and Portugal. The British *medium* for mobilizing elites politically was often the conservative Scottish orders of Masonry; but the main English *message* (constitutional limitation on royal power) was a revolutionary concept in these lands of absolutism" (1980, 119).

Revolution, it is true, drew a modest amount of support at first from the so-called English Jacobins, but they were relatively fainthearted, "eschew[ing] revolutionary means" (Thomis and Holt, 1979, 11).[7] Rather, as Evans says (1983, 23), "it may seem bizarre, and it is certainly too simple, to argue that [it was] Pitt the Younger [in office from 1783 to 1801] who destroyed the powers of the monarchy, but the observation contains a grain of truth."[8]

The period of the revolutionary-Napoleonic wars was a period of repression of the working class in Great Britain. There were the Anti-Combination Acts of 1799–1800. These were, of course, not totally new. There had been such laws as early as 1339, but they had been largely neglected. George argues that these were, too.[9] Indeed, she argues (1936, 177), the acts were "in practice a very negligible instrument of oppression." But if so, one must wonder why Pitt bothered, and the answer of course it that they were passed "principally against the background of Jacobin agitation" (Evans, 1983, 158), an agitation we have already noted to have been exaggerated by the government of the time.

It was less the immediacy of the threat to order than the fear that a serious threat might be in gestation. Clearly, there was an ideological message being conveyed to the urban workers, who were beginning to take too seriously the doctrine of popular sovereignty. The message became more concrete with the notorious Peterloo Massacre of 1818, but from the point of view of the authorities, the events

7. They continue: "[W]hen popularly voiced demands are ignored . . . , reform movements must disintegrate unless they are prepared to escalate their protests by more direct means." This was not the case here. See also Evans (1983, 69): "It is frequently remarked how easily authority triumphed over reform in 1794–95; it is less frequently appreciated how ill-prepared were the reformers in Britain for any struggle which spread beyond the comfortable limits of the printed pamphlet or the discussion group." The government suspended habeas corpus in 1794, prosecuted twelve leading London radicals in May 1794, and in 1794 passed the "Two Acts"—the Seditious Meetings Act (any meeting of more than fifty persons needed the permission of a magistrate) and the Treasonable Practices Act (which forbade even speaking or writing against the Constitution). "Radicalism after 1795 was driven underground." (p. 72).

Lest this repression be put to traditional anti-French sentiment in the England of the eighteenth century, it should be noted how sides changed with the Revolution of 1789. Before then, to be anti-French was the preserve of the "radicals," who saw it as a mode of being against the upper classes. With 1789, "the movement lost its claim to defend England and hence its claims to popularity; and instead it was again reduced . . . to the position of being a hated cult of supposed anti-English traitors, friends of France and of French ways" (Newman, 1987, 230).

8. At the same time, Evans continues (1983, 60), Pitt's post-Whig realignment of 1794 "was a true conservative coalition [which] drew ideological support from the arguments of Burke in *Reflections*, . . . [and] sought to resist the malign might of France." Destroying the power of the monarchy had clearly rather little to do with democracy.

9. "If the law was not enforced, the reason, of course, was that the masters did not choose to take legal proceedings either because the men's organization was too strong for them, or because they did not care to risk the expense and uncertainty of the law, or because they did not wish to provoke ill-feeling" (George, 1927, 227).

that led to Peterloo were in fact merely the culminating acts of a steady stream of civil disobedience going back to 1789, which had by 1818 given Manchester "a particular reputation for turbulence in the eyes of contemporaries" (Read, 1958, 93). Particularly perturbing to the notables was the fact that the character of the protest movements was changing. Local food riots, still the dominant mode of protest in the late eighteenth century, had ceased to be the preferred form. Rather, popular movements were becoming "national in scope and acquiring organization. . . . [They were] increasingly identified [after 1800] with the new industrial districts" (Thomis and Holt, 1977, 29). The Luddites, despite the fact that their slogans were seemingly backward-looking, because anti-industrial in tonality, alarmed the notables not because they seemed to be against progress or for the violence in itself but primarily because of their demonstration of the "remarkable capacity for organization within working-class ranks."[10] As a consequence, the Luddites united both Tory and Whig against "working-class Jacobinism" (Thomis, 1970, 174).

It is not accidental that this period of affirmation of popular sovereignty and therefore of nationalism led directly to the attempt to justify the exclusion of the working class from the right to participate, on the excuse that they were not yet prepared for it. The upper strata were willing to sacrifice even their own hedonism in order to validate this argument. The eighteenth-century aristocratic culture in England had been "expansive, bucolic, and roistering," permitting lavish entertainment, licentiousness, and alcoholism. The turn of the nineteenth century was the epoch of the rise of the Evangelicals, preaching "regularity, self-discipline and moderation in personal habits" (Evans, 1983, 46). The notables began to change their own behavior (institutionalized later as Victorianism), thereby allowing the Evangelicals to make working-class conversion implicitly become the gateway of resocialization, before whose conclusion there could be no thought of extending political rights or social acceptance.

The demand was paternalistic, to be sure. But we must see that it was merely the replacement of a more expensive form of paternalism by a less expensive form. The same period was the one in which the Elizabethan social security system (wage regulation, poor laws) was being repealed as "anachronistic and impractical":

> By the end of the French Wars paternalism sanctioned by legislation was dead; relations between masters and men were defended "objectively" by market forces. A decade before the frontal attack on tariffs, it was the first triumph of the new political economy and a talisman for the new age. (Evans, 1983, 44)

This demand of a prior resocialization, a transformation of the "moral order," as a way of postponing participation in the political rights that went with popular

---

10. "and a remarkable solidarity in the protection of law-breakers and their secrets" (Thomis and Holt, 1977, 33).

sovereignty was voiced not only in relation to Great Britain's working classes but also as a requirement for the unwashed, dangerous classes of what we would today call the Third World or the South. The same Methodists who led the evangelical thrust internally were the first Christian group to organize (in 1787) "a regular system of foreign missions" (Halévy, 1949a, 1:446).[11] This was also the moment of the rise of the abolitionist movement. There were of course many economic as well as humanitarian motives behind the pressure within Great Britain for the abolition of both slavery and the slave trade.[12] However, what we note here is the cultural message. Wilberforce's first bill had been introduced in 1789. At this time, the antislavery movement had a substantial "radical following" and was profiting from the general revolutionary upheaval. But the Jacobin phase of the Revolution "divided [British] abolitionist ranks" and provoked a "counter-revolutionary mobilisation," which set back the movement. Ten years later, the abolitionist movement was able to revive within a much more conservative climate, precisely because it was seen as "not so much the most urgent, as the least controversial reform that could be undertaken" (Blackburn, 1988, 147, 295). This conservatization of the message can best be understood within the context of the major change in British attitudes toward their "subject races" that was occurring at just this time. As Bayly (1989, 7) notes:

> Between 1780 and 1820, . . . Asians, Eurasians, Africans and even non-British and non-Protestant Europeans were widely excluded from positions of authority in government [in the colonies], while steps were taken to decontaminate the springs of British executive power from the influence of native corruption. Ironically, the growing and orchestrated contempt for Asian, African and even European subordinates was derived in part from the very same humanitarian drives which saw the abolition of the slave trade and the beginnings of the moves for the emancipation of the slaves. It was morally necessary to bring slaves back from social death into civil society. But if so, the hierarchy of civil society must be closely defined both through institutions and by an ideology which derived from the idea that cultures attained "civilisation" by stages of moral awakening and material endeavour. The "discovery" of the urban poor and the criminal classes in [Great] Britain were part of a very similar project and undertaken by the same civil and religious agencies.[13]

Great Britain and France had been precisely the two states where relatively strong state machineries had already been created between the sixteenth and

---

11. The only earlier European Protestant mission was that of the Moravian Brethren of Germany.

12. The economic interests were complex and multiple, which rendered British "slave-trade diplomacy" quite ambivalent in the years following the Act of 1807 abolishing the Atlantic slave trade. See Blackburn (1988, 316–326).

13. Bayly (1989, 12–13) is also very interesting on the degree to which Irish and Scottish nationalism of this period, whatever their other roots and aspirations, derived, at least in part, from "perceived exclusion from empire, not . . . inclusion within it." Once again, when the people are sovereign, the key question is, Who are the people?

eighteenth centuries. But these states did not have a deep popular legitimacy, and the French Revolution had undermined whatever legitimacy they had had. Nineteenth-century liberalism set itself the task of creating (re-creating, significantly increasing) this legitimacy and thereby cementing the strength of these states, internally and within the world-system.

Of course, Great Britain and France did not find themselves in quite the same economic situation in 1815. Indeed, in some ways their economic conditions had come to be sharply in contrast. By the end of the Napoleonic wars,

> Britain had been made safe from invasion and had developed productivity, technical skills, and financial strength. Instead of a debtor, it had become practically the sole creditor country in the world. In the course of a long and exhausting struggle, France, then the greatest power on the continent of Europe, and its reluctant allies, had been cut off from the expanding overseas world and impoverished. (Condliffe, 1951, 203)[14]

To be sure, the end of the Napoleonic wars ended Great Britain's "abnormal [wartime] development in agriculture, shipbuilding, and in the re-export trade," and these branches went into a "severe and chronic depression" (Rostow, 1942, 18).[15] But Great Britain simply placed a greater emphasis on domestic investment in the period 1815–1850, making what Rostow (1942, 22) terms an "incredibly easy" adjustment.[16]

14. In Condliffe's view, "the position of Britain at the end of the Napoleonic wars in many ways parallels the position in which the United States found itself at the close of the Second World War." The contrast can be seen to be particularly dramatic if one looks at the merchant marine. Before 1789 there were some two thousand French ships, but by 1799 "not a merchant ship on the high seas [was] flying the French flag" (Bruun, 1938, 86–87). On the other hand, Great Britain's fleet, even during active warfare, went from fifteen thousand to eighteen thousand in number.

Lévy-Leboyer (1964, 246) says that in the first half of the nineteenth century, the battle for control of the seas came to be exclusively between Great Britain and the United States, and that western European states were out of it, their combined merchant marine fleet of a million tons being half that of the United States and a third that of Great Britain. "Such a relative elimination (*effacement*) was hardly possible to envisage at the end of the eighteenth century, especially in the case of France." He puts the turning point at 1793.

15. See also the somewhat plaintive description by Buer (1921, 169) of the depression in Great Britain following the end of the Napoleonic wars: "It is not difficult to account for the long stagnation. The country was exhausted by a colossal struggle. The heavy burden of taxation could not be lightened; debt charges absorbed half the national revenue and the military and civil expenditures included a large proportion of fixed charges. National expenditures, therefore, diminished little with the falling prices, while the real burden on the taxpayer was increased. The ratepayers were in a similar plight. Poor relief, again, in spite of falling prices, continued a disastrous burden."

16. Rostow, therefore, does not believe that Great Britain's economy during the period 1815–1847 deserves its "bad name in economic history." True, the conditions of health and housing in the new

The gap in industrial production between Great Britain and its neighbors on the Continent grew bigger.[17] But then the gap with France (and Belgium, and perhaps some others) began to close, such that, somewhere between 1835 and 1850, it virtually disappeared.[18] Nonetheless, Great Britain would continue to be dominant in world trade (i.e., trade beyond northwestern Europe) for another quarter

---

industrial cities were bad, and there were periods of severe unemployment, bad harvest, and high food prices. True, the agricultural community was unhappy, and there was pressure on profit margins. But to compensate, there was the intensive domestic development: "interest rates fall; real wages rise; and the terms of trade shift favorably to Britain" (Rostow, 1948, 19).

17. "Between 1789 and 1848 Europe and America were flooded with British exports, steam engines, cotton machinery, and investments" (Hobsbawm, 1962, 51). See the explanation of Lévy-Leboyer (1964, 32, 41):

Everything leads us to think, in fact, that in taking the technological lead, a country or a city will come to be in a position of force to assemble and train a specialized labor force, build and rapidly amortize factories—in short, heavily influence the cost price (*prix de revient*), keep potential competitors out of the market, and become almost the sole beneficiary of the anticipated increase in demand. In any case the abundance of energy resources was a factor in favor of the industrialization of Great Britain. In 1817 she produced 16 million tons of coal compared with eight hundred thousand in France. This gave a very large freedom of maneuver to the English, allowing them to abandon early factory sites, dispersed along the rivers, concentrate the spinning mills near the coal fields, and possibly enlarge their scope of operations. . . .

Whatever the modalities of the concentration, one fact stands out: the Manchester group became stronger in the first third of the nineteenth century.

But France was not helpless in the face of the British juggernaut. See Johnson (1975, 143–144):

Lévy-Leboyer's "massive deceleration" thesis for the whole Revolutionary-Napoleonic era needs some modification. Still, in 1815, as in 1830, French industry was at a severe competitive disadvantage vis-à-vis the giant across the Channel.

France adapted to this situation in the first place by restrictive tariff policy. . . . Less appreciated until recently are the other adaptive strategies to which French businessmen resorted. The stock-in-trade of British industrial production were common, mass consumption goods, especially in textiles. Capital-intensive production was the mainspring of success in this realm. But in higher quality items, *articles de goût,* France had a historic reputation and, more importantly, a competitive chance. . . . [O]n a general level French industrial wages were approximately two-thirds of those paid in England. This meant that the higher the quality of goods produced, the greater the labor input and therefore the stronger the relative position of French industry. . . . All this meant that handwork, particularly in weaving, maintained its significance much longer in France than it did in England. Moreover, the better part of the first half of the nineteenth century witnessed a phenomenon that, at first glance, seems strange indeed for a country undergoing industrialization—the massive development of rural outworking in the textile industry. The reason, of course, was not hard to find. Rural labor was cheaper.

18. See the same Lévy-Leboyer (1964, 115, 326, 409): "In 1820, it might be asked whether [France] would ever overcome her lag behind England. In 1840, the task was virtually completed. . . .

"By 1835, whether we look at textiles or transport, the balance sheet of continental achievements seems positive: the lag accumulated at the beginning of the century was significantly reduced; it would

century at least,[19] a dominance Great Britain would maintain by its loans of capital abroad.[20] "[T]he contribution made by foreign trade and foreign investment to the consumption levels attained by British families" (O'Brien and Keyder, 1978, 63) essentially explains the higher standard of living that Great Britain was to main-

---

be eliminated totally when automatic looms and machines, railroads and steamships came to have their full effect upon the whole economy. . . .

"[W]hether we look at industrial production, which grew at an annual rate of 3 percent between 1815 and 1850, or at income from foreign investments, which had a slightly higher annual growth rate of 4 percent, the overall results compare quite favorably with the British statistics."

Markovitch (1966, 122) asserts that France's industrial growth was higher in the period 1815–1848 than at any other point in the nineteenth century. See also Sée (1927, 70), who considers the most characteristic feature of this period "the progress of machinism," manifested in the improvement of textile looms and the spread of the steam engine.

Similarly, Demoulin (1938, 298–299) argues that Belgian industry was transformed between 1800 and 1830 by the widespread introduction of machinery in the traditional industries and that its growth accelerated after 1830.

For a dissenting view on the gap between Great Britain and continental Europe, including France, see Crouzet (1978, 19), who believes that, in the first half of the nineteenth century, this gap "became scarcely smaller" in relative terms, and grew in absolute terms. He points out that in 1860, Great Britain represented 2 percent of the world's population and 10 percent of Europe's, but 40 to 45 percent of world production and 55 to 60 percent of Europe's. In a previous article, Crouzet (1972b, 115–116) explains this inability of western Europe to "catch up" with Great Britain in the period 1815–1850 by the narrowness of home markets and the difficulties of developing a strong export trade, given Great Britain's "almost complete monopoly" of trade to the United States and Latin America. He thereupon takes a position very close to that of Lévy-Leboyer concerning the coercive effect of economic hegemony: "It appears . . . that once a major 'modern' industrializing economy—[Great] Britain—had been established, the whole international trading context became unfavourable for other nations, and the mere presence of the new industrial giant restricted greatly the opportunities for them to base a major industrial impetus upon foreign markets."

Hobsbawm's statement on Great Britain's continuing industrial strength is similar but more restrained than that of Crouzet: "Britain [in 1850–1870] was the industrial country *par excellence* and . . . managed to maintain its relative position, though its productive steam power had begun to lag seriously" (1975, 40). And Cameron's characterization is also in between: on the one hand, he notes that "by 1850, France had 6,800 steam engines, more than all other Continental countries combined," but then he adds in a footnote: "On the other hand, [Great] Britain probably had a larger number than all Continental countries combined, including France" (1961, 66, and n. 9).

19. "[T]hrough British ports in the mid-century flow goods constituting nearly a quarter of the value of all international trade" (Imlah, 1950, 194). This had risen from a mere 3 percent in 1800 (p. 191, n. 24). "The British market was paramount." (p. 192, n. 24).

20. "[T]he volume of exports was significantly influenced by the direction of British lending. Capital exports were successfully transferred in the form of goods, and, possibly, to an overwhelming extent in the form of British goods. The swollen exports to the Continent during the war years, to South America in 1808–10 and 1820–5, to the United States in the thirties, to India and China in the forties, cannot be dissociated from the lending of those periods; nor, of course, can the subsequent decline be viewed apart from the cessation of these lending activities" (Gayer, Rostow, and Schwartz, 1953, 2:842).

In this process of world trade, continental Europe (and especially France) came to play a semiperipheral role in this period: "[B]y developing in tandem the sale of spun cotton in Europe and that of

5

tain over France throughout the nineteenth century, despite the rough parity of the two countries in per capita domestic commodity output.

Thus, the conventional view of early nineteenth-century Great Britain as the "workshop of the world"[21] is coming under a certain amount of sniper attack.

---

finished products in the new countries, England was able to share risks and prepare the future, for what was happening on the Continent was bound to reproduce itself overseas. The French profited indirectly from the industrialization of third countries by providing them with luxury items, the English directly by providing them with cloth, spun cotton—ever finer in quality—occasionally machinery, and always technicians" (Lévy-Leboyer, 1964, 181). By the mid-nineteenth century, nonetheless, it would be France, "the world's second industrial power," and not Great Britain that would play the "leading role" in the industrialization of continental Europe via the export of technology and capital (Cameron, 1953, 461).

Though Bairoch (1973, 592–593) considers that, throughout the nineteenth century, the trade of continental Europe with the Third World was "relatively marginal," this was not true of that of the United Kingdom. "As early as the mid-19th century, [the U.K.'s] exports to the Third World accounted for 40% of its total exports while exports to Europe only 35%." Similarly, Evans (1983, 340) notes that in 1815 Europe had taken more than half of Great Britain's exports and Asia a mere 6 percent, whereas in the mid-1850s, Europe was down to 32 percent, Asia up to 20 percent, and no less than 37 percent went to the Americas. See also Condliffe (1951, 207). Schlote (1952, 41) finds that the sharpest rise in overseas trade in relation to the size of the population occurs precisely between 1845 and 1855, which further emphasizes the importance of the extra-European trade.

Nonetheless, Imlah (1950, 176) agrees with Gayer, Rostow, and Schwartz: it was not exports that accounted for Great Britain's great advantage. Indeed, the net barter terms of trade (index numbers of export price series divided by import price series) was falling steadily until midcentury. No change in indexes "stands out more clearly. . . . It was caused by a more rapid fall in export prices than in new import prices, and much the greater part of the decline in net barter terms occurred by the year 1839." See also Checkland (1964, 62).

These import surpluses "preceded [the freer trade policies of the 1840s] by many decades" (Imlah, 1958, 6). "[T]he decline in raw-material prices [was] an effect of tariff reform" (Imlah, 1950, 189). McCloskey (1964, 313) inverses the order of the relationship of import surpluses to lower tariff rates: "A deliberate policy of free international trade . . . was responsible for only a part—a small part, indeed—of the reduction in tariff rates. The accident of a higher ratio of imports to the national income, itself only partly a consequence of British financial reform, accounts for much of the reduction, the triumph of free-trade ideology for very little of it." Whatever the order of the process, it followed that "Britain's new industrial system did not create export surpluses, and . . . her phenomenal accumulation of overseas credits in the nineteenth century cannot be explained by this time-honored assumption." Rather, it was the invisible credits (the merchant marine, commercial commissions, savings of personnel remitted, and income from investments abroad) that "made up the deficit of her visible trade and supplied whatever new capital was invested abroad" (Imlah, 1948, 149).

21. In the fourth edition (1907) of William Cunningham's principal work, he wrote the following:

During the period of Whig Ascendancy attention was concentrated on the promotion of industry of every kind, and no effort was spared to make England the workshop of the extensive spheres where her influence and her friendship availed to keep the markets open to our manufactures. (p. 494)

I am not certain if this was the origin of the now classic formula, England as "workshop of the world" (or whether this segment is to be found in earlier editions, the earliest of which was published in 1890), but it is quite possible that it was Cunningham who launched the concept.

Already in 1934, Darvall (1934, 12) had argued that "England in 1811 was still largely a rural and agricultural country."[22] This theme was renewed by Samuel (1977, 19) some forty years later:

> The most complete triumph of the machine was in the cotton trade of industrial Lancastershire. Elsewhere its progress was more halting, and there were major sectors of the economy . . . where down to the 1870s steam power made very little impression at all. . . . Even in textiles, the progress of mechanisation was uneven.[23]

If mechanization was less widespread and advanced than our conventional imagery has it, how then did Great Britain achieve its remarkable industrial growth? Recent scholarship is even questioning how remarkable it was, or at least whether the growth was quite as great as previous scholars (such as Walther Hoffmann, Phyllis Deane, and W. A. Cole) had led us to believe. By recalculations based on occupational data of the 1841 census, Harley (1982, 267; see also 285) concludes that this growth was "a third lower" than they had asserted for the period 1770–1815. And Bairoch (1962, 318, 323) asserts that the rate of growth in the nineteenth century of Great Britain (also of France and the United States) was less than 2 percent per annum. Bairoch calls our impression that it was higher "a great exaggeration" having its origin at a time when the 1930s theory of slow growth in mature economies was very influential, and which consequently led to backward overestimates.[24]

Still, it would be dangerous to go to the other extreme and lose sight of Britain's relative strength. The revisionist analyses enable us to see Britain's weaknesses despite her strength, and therefore the political dilemmas that the government faced even at this time of relative strength in the world-economy. The basic problem for the core countries in the period 1815–1873 was that growth led to a decline in prices,[25] and in particular a decline in industrial prices relative to prices of raw

22. See also Rousseaux: "Up to 1830, the English economy was still at the agricultural stage" (1938, 62). The phrase is almost identical to that of Henri Sée about France in the years 1815–1848. "In the period of the monarchy based on limited suffrage [*la monarchie censitaire*], France was essentially an agricultural country" (1927, 11). Darvall (1984, 12–13) continues: "Industry was still situated chiefly in the country. Even the newer industries, like the great and growing cotton manufactures of the north, were still situated more in the country than in the town. . . . The typical worker, in 1811, in the new, industrial north as well as in the older, more rural south and east, worked at home or in a small country workshop by hand on a single machine."

23. Samuel (1977, 47) attributes this "slow process of mechanization" to "the relative abundance of labor, both skilled and unskilled."

24. Compare, however, Bairoch's figure with that of Hoffman (1949, 165–66), who says that Great Britain had a growth rate of 2.8 percent from 1781 to 1913.

25. Gayer, Rostow, and Schwartz (1953, 1:486) speak of "a secular decline [in prices in Great Britain], the low point of which appears to be reached in 1850." See also Marczewski (1987, 34–36) on France. Recession was still inflationary, linked to the traditional problems of bad harvests reducing

materials (Markovitch, 1966, 228–229). From the middle of the eighteenth cen-tury to the middle of the nineteenth, cost control for producers focused on the large role of wages in the total price. A combination of repression and mechani-zation was used to reduce these costs, successfully. These techniques had in fact succeeded too well. For this had the negative consequences of both stimulating political turbulence and leading to the relative decline on the world market of industrial prices. It was only by means of the creation of the liberal state that this dilemma was overcome and capitalist producers in the core zones could benefit from a restored internal order and a return to favorable terms of trade. The key mechanism utilized by the liberal state was a shift in the central focus of cost con-trol from the domestic front to the periphery—a process incarnated in the colo-nial expansions of the last third of the nineteenth century.

But until that happened, Great Britain in particular, and western Europe in general, had to live with the dilemmas of deflation, particularly acute from 1815 to the late 1840s. Wage-workers were hurting, since wage levels went down both absolutely and relatively.[26] Agricultural producers were hurting, since there was a "steady fall in English wheat prices in the first three-quarters of the nineteenth century" (Fairlie, 1969, 105).[27]

Were even British industrialists doing all that well? We have already noted that their initial edge as of 1815 over western Europe, a quite significant one, seemed to fritter away by 1850, not to mention the emergence of Germany and the United States in the second half of the nineteenth century. The profitability of British industry risked being ephemeral. Alternatives needed to be secured, and were. If British hegemony in the world-system served to create any long-lasting economic advantage, it did so by making possible the remarkable growth in British foreign investments, "one of the most important facts of British economic development

---

GNP while driving up the price of daily consumption. This would change once improvements in world transport removed the capacity of local harvest difficulties to have such an impact, which is probably true after the 1870s and certainly in the twentieth century.

26. Rousseaux (1938, 229), who is referring to the period 1822–1848/50. See also Evens (1983, 141): "The worst years for laborers were those after 1815 when a market glutted by demobilized service-men coincided with depressed arable prices. In those years wages were beaten down and poor-rate expenditure reached its peak. . . . Most unkindly of all in the twenty years—1811–1831—when employ-ment opportunities were contracting most severely the population of the worst affected counties in the South and East increased by 31 percent."

27. See also Thompson (1963, 232). Fairlie (1969, 108) continues: "Once we grant a steadily increas-ing wave of scarcity in Europe as a whole until about 1870, the only way this can be reconciled with the apparent steady fall in English wheat prices is to maintain that the previous protected wheat prices had been so high—in relation to potential internal European sources of supply—that a shift to unre-stricted trade between [Great] Britain and Europe meant a net fall in England, even though the under-lying trend continued upwards." One can see why there was such strong resistance to Repeal of the Corn Laws.

in the nineteenth century and by no means a minor one in world affairs" (Imlah, 1952, 222).

France, of course, seemed, especially to the industrialists, to be in even more difficult straits. France did, to be sure, have a few advantages. Its technical education, thanks to the Revolution and Napoleon, flourished and was considered to be the best in the world in the first half of the nineteenth century. It could export its technical and commercial expertise (see Cameron, 1957a, 245–246; 1961). And its industrial base did steadily expand, as we have seen. Still, it has long been thought that France's industrialization, and hence its competitive edge in the world market, had been impeded by the slow growth of the population, and by the particularly large role of small as opposed to large industry.[28] This view has been challenged by Nye (1987, 650, 668), who has argued that small size was in fact a "rational response to prevailing economic conditions and in no way hampered the process of French industrialization," since "by any standard the returns to scale [were] rather low." And Gille (1959b, 163) has argued that there was more large industry than has been thought. Indeed, he locates the birth of large-scale capitalist industry in France in precisely the period 1815–1848.

Did not, however, Great Britain and France take opposite stances on the crucial question of free trade in the world-economy? The answer is less evident than we have been led to believe. In the first place,

> [i]n 1815, [Great] Britain was still a protectionist power and the state played an important role in directing foreign trade and overseas expansion. Tariff protection was extended not only to agriculture but also to [Great] Britain's growing manufacturing industries. Severe restrictions were placed upon the emigration of skilled labour and the export of machinery. (Evans, 1983, 12)

In the second place, quite aside from government protection, British industries were "riddled with price-rings or equivalent arrangements, often only on a regional basis but sometimes on a national basis" (Cain, 1980, 20). In the third place, British industrialists, including those in Manchester, were not at all unequivocally in favor of free trade. As late as the 1840s, free trade "was seen as a weapon in [the] commercial war [with other countries], and when it did not seem to answer [the needs of winning this war] it was not supported" (Evans, 1983, 20).[29]

---

28. This is a frequent theme of the literature (Markovitch, 1966, 316; Landes, 1949; Kindleberger, 1961a). Cameron (1957a, 441) explains it in part by relative scarcity on the supply side, with a consequently high cost of industrial raw materials. But since we have already seen that raw materials costs were high for Great Britain, too, this can be only a comparative statement: higher than for Great Britain.

29. Cain (1980, 24) reminds us that, among other reasons for hesitation, "free trade also meant the end of colonial privilege and made close control of colonies, when they had developed maturely, seem impossible to maintain." See also Musson (1972b, 18–19): "Historians have tended to emphasize too

And finally, Imlah (1949, 307–309) observes that British protectionism was at "its worst" in its last years:

> It was so much more severe in its effects after the Napoleonic Wars than in the preceding infant period of British industrialism that it constituted virtually a new system. . . .
>
> Tested by real [i.e., not "official"] values, British customs duties at the end of the eighteenth century were very moderate. . . . The compelling problem [which explained the considerable rise in customs duties in the early nineteenth century] was revenues.

Imlah argues that these duties were sufficiently severe that, by reducing imports significantly, they affected the purchasing power of potential customers. And since international trade was essential to Britain's economic health, her "fiscal system [was throwing] her international economy out of balance."[30]

Perhaps some of this protectionism was for show; it was surely not all strictly enforced.[31] But it tarnishes the image of the centrality of free trade in British policy, at least before 1850, especially when we put it in relation to the reality, and not the theory, of French protectionism. French tariff rates were in fact "substantially lower" than British rates for the whole period 1800–1840, despite the perception that the opposite was true. Nye (1991, 25; 26, table 1; 42) explains this misperception triply: by the attention the world has given Repeal of the Corn Laws; by the

generally Britain's competitive advantage, ignoring the fact that British manufacturers had developed behind a protective wall and that many of them still felt the need for its maintenance. . . . Manchester manufacturers—whilst demanding removal of duties on raw cotton imports and abolition of the Corn Laws—at the same time remained stubbornly protectionist in their opposition to removal of restrictions on the export of machinery, especially for manufacturing cotton goods, which would boost foreign competition."

30. The customs duties by 1830 were 38 percent of government revenue and 45 percent by 1840, which was almost twice the prewar proportion. Furthermore, "the toll taken on market values was substantially heavier and tending to grow" (p. 311).

31. See Jeremy (1977, 2): "In the early 1780s, no skilled artisan or manufacturer was legally free to leave [Great] Britain or Ireland and enter any foreign country outside the Crown's dominion for the purpose of carrying on his trade." But, of course, many did. Jeremy estimates that one hundred thousand persons emigrated from Ulster to the United States between 1783 and 1812. The restrictions on artisan emigration were lifted in 1824. In 1825, the outright ban on the export of machinery was also lifted and replaced with a licensing system. It was only in 1843, however, that Gladstone, as president of the Board of Trade, finally lifted all restrictions. Jeremy believes that these prohibitory laws, nonetheless, "failed signally to stem the flow of technological information spreading abroad, either via men or machines, in the early industrial period" (p. 34). See also Henderson (1954, 6), who asserts that the British authorities "let many labour recruiting agents and smugglers of machinery and blueprints slip through their fingers."

fact that analysts took into account only certain industries instead of the pattern of the economy as a whole; and by the fact that the British tended to talk free trade while the French tended to talk protectionism, even under Napoleon III. But, Nye says, in fact "the traditional stories of free trade counterpoising a liberal [Great] Britain against a protectionist France, reluctantly dragged into a world of more enlightened commercial policies, must now be seen as false." Indeed, Imlah, himself a great believer in the economic merits of free trade, explains (1958, 123) the *deficiencies* of Great Britain's economic performance during this period precisely by the relative absence of free trade:

> In many respects the first half of the nineteenth century should have been bonanza times for British trade. The technical efficiency of her increasingly mechanized industries, the possibilities of developing demand at home and abroad for her coal and for her machinery, both more freely exportable after 1825, the potentialities of her merchant marine and business services and the demand for her capital created an opportunity with few parallels in economic history. The opportunity was not finally realized under the high protectionism of the postwar years.[32]

This false contrast between Great Britain and France[33] is the background against which we should review another revisionist discussion—that concerning the presumed slowness of industrialization of France,[34] or the asserted "lateness" of "take-off" in France.[35] O'Brien and Keyder (1978), running a series of comparisons of Great Britain and France for the period 1781–1913, found the follow-

---

32. Furthermore, Imlah (1958, 23) blames protectionism for social unrest. He says that if one uses real (and again not the deceptive "official") values, the export trade stagnated. Comparing 1842 with 1816, both depression years, export trade was only 14 percent higher, whereas population had risen 40 percent and new imports 55 percent. "This suggests hardening of the arteries instead of sinews [as Bismarck had called it in praise of British protectionism in this period] and it more adequately accounts for the symptoms of rising social blood pressure which were evident at the time. Adoption of a free-trade policy [after 1842] may have been an escape from premature senescence." This analysis seems too simple, as we shall argue later on.

33. We have seen throughout this work how frequently our historiography has fed us these false contrasts. This historiographic perversion is part of the legacy of nineteenth-century social science in its function as liberal ideology.

34. The background to this particular subdebate has already been treated in vol. 3, chaps. 1 and 2 (Wallerstein, 1989).

35. The now almost forgotten fad for the concept of "take-off" was launched in 1960 by W. W. Rostow (1971), who situated that of France as occurring in 1830–1860, whereas that of Great Britain had occurred in "the two decades after 1783" (p. 9). The existence of a single period of "take-off" for France is contested by Marczewski, or rather he says that if there was one, it had occurred at the latest in the beginning of the nineteenth century (1961; 1963, 123); see also Bouvier (1965, 270), Markovitch (1966), and Lévy-Leboyer (1968b, 801).

ing: Per capita domestic commodity output was roughly equal. Wage levels were markedly lower in France, but since fewer persons were wage-workers, this tells us little about average level of earnings. British labor productivity was higher, which was offset by the allocation of a larger share of France's potential labor to agricultural and industrial production.[36] British agricultural productivity was higher, which the authors attribute not to greater efficiency but to better land endowment and greater allocation of land to animal-intensive agriculture.[37] In industry, French labor productivity was higher, the British not catching up until the 1890s, although there was less mass industry. In conclusion, O'Brien and Keyder (1978, 198) criticize any suggestion of a "relative backwardness" of France, seeing its economic choices as no doubt different but equally rational; indeed, they go further and say that they are "inclined to see a more humane and perhaps a no less efficient transition to industrial society in the experience of France."[38] The

36. Hence, France had a smaller service sector and fewer parasites, which leads O'Brien and Keyder (1978, 32) to comment that they now "see the force of Nietzsche's remark that 'the strength of a civilization' is to be measured by the number of parasites it can support."

37. "Agricultural 'backwardness' [lower output per worker] in France came from the maintenance of high labour densities in the countryside, which inevitably leads to the intensive cultivation of inferior soils and a crop mix dominated by basic foodstuffs. But in France the landless formed a far smaller proportion (in fact a minority) of the rural population and for decade after decade the majority displayed no desire to move from their 'inferior' land into the cities. . . . Critics of French economic performance sometimes forget that the agrarian institutions of France had been consolidated by the actions of militant peasants during the Revolution" (O'Brien and Keyder, 1978, 190, 195).

Hobsbawm also reminds us that French peasants, looking back in the middle of the nineteenth century on the period since 1789, and comparing themselves with rural workers in Great Britain, "could hardly doubt which of the two had made the better bargain" (1962, 201). Hobsbawm then reproduces the appreciation of a British author, H. Colman, in a book written in 1848 entitled *The Agricultural and Rural Economy of France, Belgium, Holland and Switzerland.* Colman writes (pp. 25–26): "Having been much among the peasantry and labouring class both at home and abroad, I must in truth say that a more civil, cleanly, industrious, frugal, sober, or better-dressed people than the French peasantry, for persons in their condition . . . I have never known. In these respects they furnish a striking contrast with a considerable portion of the Scotch agricultural labourers, who are dirty and squalid to an excess; with many of the English, who are servile, broken-spirited and severely straitened in their means of living; with the poor Irish, who are half-clad and in a savage condition" (cited on p. 201, n. a).

Finally, Hohenberg (1972, 238–239) argues that "throughout the nineteenth century, rural France underwent more change [in social structure, demographic behavior, and land-use institutions] than appears on the surface. Paradoxically, it was change that made it possible to preserve, indeed to strengthen, a basic equilibrium built on the family-run, family-owned farm."

38. See similar reevaluations of the rationality of French economic choices and the relatively good performance of French industry in the nineteenth century in Lévy-Leboyer (1968b), Roehl (1976), and Cameron and Freedeman (1983). But Lévy-Leboyer, who in 1968 praised the "flexible adaptation of the [French] economy and its vigorous industrial élan," which characterized its "relatively harmonious expansion" throughout the nineteenth century (p. 801), took a less happy view in the book he published with Bourguignon in 1985. They spoke (pp. 103–104) of "the French problem"—too large a

impact of this revisionism has been strong, such that even those who wish to insist on British "superiority," like Crouzet, are reduced to "nuancing" the views of the revisionists and to insisting that French economic achievements in the nineteenth century were "creditable, but not more."[39] Crafts (1984, 59, 67), who undertakes to demonstrate that "the revisionist interpretation [of French economic performance in the nineteenth century] exaggerates French achievements," nonetheless seems forced to conclude, after indicating his various reservations, that "even if all the above points are accepted, it is true that French economic performance looks substantially better than was once thought."[40]

Both Great Britain and France, then, as of 1815, sought to concentrate the worldwide accumulation of capital within their frontiers, and how well they did so was only in part a function of the strength of their respective industrial enterprises. It was also very much a function of their ability to restrain the costs of labor, to ensure the constancy of external supply, and to obtain adequate markets for their production. And this was more a political task than a matter of improving their respective economic efficiencies, which on a world scale were rather high for both. The operative role of the states was therefore crucial, but their use was a delicate matter, since the states could wreak damage as well as ensure advantage.

---

portion of consumption going to food, too small a diversified demand, too little industrial export, too little investment—and blamed the French peasantry:

> The fact that the technological initiative had thus escaped the country, something that had its origins in the 1790s, when political troubles, inflation, and wars had interrupted the first industrial revolution, is to be accounted for by two factors: (1) In the long term, the fact that the fringe of rural poverty, inherited from the preindustrial era, had been reduced only very slowly [a different image from that of Hobsbawm in the previous footnote]. This explains the deformations observed, in periods of accelerated growth, in the wage structure and consumption budgets. The entry into the labor market of a less qualified work force and the movement of rural migration changed the numbers in different social categories each time, . . . increasing the groups at the bottom (*les classes défavorisées*). The insufficient rise in the wage levels and in demand for industrial goods in the cycle is due to the change in the subgroups we have to include to calculate the means valid for the total population.

This amounts to saying that in the second half of the nineteenth century, France still had a large rural population that industrialists could draw on when necessary in order to reduce urban wage levels, a reserve army of labor that Great Britain had used up to a greater extent in the first half of the nineteenth century. (The second factor that the authors blame is the excessive role of state intervention in the 1870s and 1880s.)

39. The first quote is to be found in Crouzet (1970, 86) and the second in Crouzet (1972a, 278). In his 1985 book, supposedly on the "superiority" of England over France, Crouzet nonetheless comes up with a long list of joint "firsts" and concludes rather wanly: "[B]etween these two destinies there are so many resemblances and convergences" (1985, 454).

40. He also characterizes it as "responsible but not outstanding" (p. 67), which is a bit stronger than "creditable, but not more."

The states had to be tamed, manipulated, and directed rationally. The politics of the next sixty years was to center around this effort to "rationalize" the role of the state— that is to say, to fine-tune the structure of the state so as to maximize the possibilities of increasing the "wealth of the nation" and, especially, of those who accumulated capital within its frontiers.

This process began at the interstate level. From September 18, 1814, to June 9, 1815, Europe's monarchs and foreign ministers met in Vienna to decide the peace that was supposed to govern Europe—what would come to be called the Concert of Europe. In the middle of this long conclave, Napoleon returned from Elba for a "Hundred Days," but then was defeated, finally and definitively, at Waterloo on June 18, 1815. It is always harder to achieve consensus about peace than about war. Its objectives are more long-term, and more multifold; hence they divide the peacemakers. It was only Great Britain that had been unremittingly opposed to France (and from a time predating Napoleon). Austria, Russia, and Prussia had had a checkered history over the period of the wars. Great Britain was therefore the prime winner of the 23-year-long series of wars (which might better be considered a single war) as well as the 150-year-long struggle for hegemony in the world-system. She had every reason to be calm, balanced, and forceful. She wanted to be certain, of course, that France could never again rise to challenge her. But after the failure of the Hundred Days, this could not have seemed too big a problem. What was probably more on Lord Castlereagh's mind was how to prevent the other three great powers from expanding their power unduly, especially since they did not fully share Great Britain's political worldview—nor, of course, her economic interests.

On the one hand, now that French military power had been broken, Great Britain needed to worry only about Russian military strength and possible expansionist ambitions. In twentieth-century language, there were only "two superpowers," although in fact there was no real possibility of a military confrontation between them.[41] Castlereagh's real problem was that he had a rival in the construction of political order, Prince Metternich, who used his diplomatic skill and the fact that he represented the political sensibilities of the "eastern" trio—Austria, Prussia, and Russia—to counterbalance Great Britain's world strength. The assessment of

---

41. See Kraehe (1992, 693). Schroeder (1992a, 684) even talks of a "shared British and Russian hegemony," but this seems to me to be verbal inflation. See also Jervis (1992), Gruner (1992), and Schroeder (1992b). As for Austria and Prussia, they were "great powers by courtesy only" (Hobsbawm, 1962, 129).

Halévy (1949a, 95) captures well the British assessment of the military situation as of 1815: "There was certainly no reason of national security to prevent the English reducing their expenditures on the Army. England had now no enemies to fear. After a war extending over more than a century the power of France was at last broken. Carthage had conquered Rome."

Henry Kissinger (1973, 5) is that Castlereagh "negotiated the international settle-ment" but that it was Metternich who "legitimized it":

> Castlereagh, secure in the knowledge of England's insular safety, tended to oppose only *overt* aggression. But Metternich, the statesman of a power situated in the cen-ter of the Continent, sought above all to *forestall* upheavals.[42]

I'd say myself that Metternich tried to impose a certain form of legitimation, which was not really to the taste of Great Britain, and that Great Britain would in fact eventually prevail. In any case, it would soon become evident that Metternich could not forestall too much.[43]

It was, however, clearly in Great Britain's immediate interest (not to speak of her long-term strategy) to restore France to a position where she could serve as a potential ally in the politico-diplomatic struggles (even if France would occasion-ally resent the role of being a junior partner). Indeed, one could argue that France was the great victor of the Congress of Vienna, in that "the most striking feature of the post-Napoleonic peace settlement was, beyond doubt, the leniency showed toward the vanquished power" (Schenk, 1947, 45).[44] This is usually, and with some

---

42. On Metternich, see also Schroeder (1992a). On Great Britain, Webster (1925, 48–49) similarly emphasizes her sense of separateness from the continent of Europe and the continuing priority she tried to give to maritime and imperial problems.

> Sea power and maritime rights were still and truly regarded as the bulwark of power. . . . The "Maritime Rights" were not even admitted to discussion. The "Right of Search," and other prin-ciples of International Law, accepted by no other Great Power, were thus preserved in all their vigour. . . . [Yet] the "Maritime Rights" were never again [after 1815] exercised.

It is true that Castlereagh was more "isolationist" than his successors would be, but it would be a mistake to confuse Tory arrogance with long-run strategy. Momentarily, in 1815, between Castlereagh's insularity and Tsar Alexander's moment of romantic exuberance, we can observe what Weill (1930, 14) called the "curious fact that most of the constitutional projects had as their defender [in 1815] the Rus-sian aristocrat and as their adversary British diplomats: these proud Tories believed that their country alone was capable of operating a system of liberty which would leave power in the hands of the aristoc-racy." Bravo! Well said, in the best spirit of French acerbic commentary on the world of power.

In any case, Castlereagh obtained at Vienna what Great Britain thought crucial and immediately wanted: "She retained her command of the seas; she obtained general and local security; she acquired important possessions" (Nicolson, 1946, 211)—to wit, a series of strategic islands and ports on the world's sea lanes, acquired in the period 1783–1816. The list may be found in Wallerstein (1989, 122).

43. Metternich would in fact recognize this when, in 1830, he said of the July Revolution in France that it had "the effect of breaking the dike" (cited, without footnote, in Vidal, 1931, 34). Hobsbawm (1962, 132) agrees: "The revolutions of 1830 destroyed [the 1815 settlement] utterly." But, to be more exact, they destroyed the Metternich version, the better to ensconce the British version. Weill (1930, 4) calls the period 1815–1847 that of the "failure" of the Holy Alliance, which "could resist neither the progress of the national idea nor the passionate propaganda of the liberal parties."

44. Indeed, Clapham (1930, 317) considers them all too generous: "Continentals agreed with the islanders [in the years following 1815] that the islands carried a fearful burden of debt and a tax-system

justice, attributed to Talleyrand's ingenuity. One shouldn't, however, underestimate the role of Great Britain's understanding of what it would take to stabilize a non-Napoleonic regime in France. A secret report written (by M. Gallars) in April 1816 to the British ambassador in Paris (Sir Charles Stuart), and conveyed in turn to Lord Castlereagh, indicates exactly what the British feared:

> The general upheaval caused by the revolution still subsists in the spirits because authority, which had been so long placed in vile hands, has lost its majesty which had been the basis of confidence and respect; . . . [and] because religion has lost all its control over that class of men who, lacking a suitable education, do not know the laws of morality and cannot be intimidated by the fears of hell and of the scaffold. (Cited by Schenk, 1947, 49)

Because of these fears, the British, even ultra-Tories like Wellington, were on the side of the more moderate advisers around Louis XVIII, for fear that a full reactionary dose of medicine would be refused by the "patient," who might thereupon "relapse into his old left-wing revolutionary illusion" (Schenk, 1947, 130–131).[45] Nothing Great Britain could do could more enhance the authority of Louis XVIII than France's diplomatic rehabilitation.

In fact, France's rehabilitation served Great Britain's ability to exercise its hegemony. Castlereagh's somewhat simplistic formulas—Nicolson (1946, 155) speaks of his dream of an "ideal equilibrium, calculated almost mathematically in terms of population and power"—were eventually softened and improved by Talleyrand's "more realistic conception," which enabled Talleyrand (and thus the British as well) to confront the world with "lucidity, elasticity, and speed." So it was that France was admitted to the inner circle. The so-called Quadruple Alliance forged at Vienna in 1815 was replaced by the Quintuple Alliance (or Pentarchy of Great Powers) at Aix-la-Chapelle in 1818. As Dupuis (1909, 165) notes, this changed everything:

> The entry of France in the European Directory seemed to increase the latter's strength and authority; in reality, it weakened them. . . . The French peril faded away into the haze of the past; it would now become easier to express differences of opinion or pursue contradictory interests.[46]

---

radically bad. It was seldom noted that one reason for the burden of debt was the political and gentlemanlike refusal of Castlereagh and Wellington to consider extracting from France war indemnities of any consequence."

45. Schenk (1947, 132) further notes that "Wellington . . . foresaw with remarkable penetration that the fate of the Stuarts awaited the Bourbons."

46. Whereas Gross (1968, 45) says that the process of consultation and conferences on mutual interest instituted by the Concert of Europe "provided some sort of a self-appointed directing body for the maintenance and manipulation of that balance of power on which the European peace precariously reposed for about a hundred years," Dupuis (1909, 192) seems to me more accurate in suggesting that this didn't really last very long at all: "The Congress of Verona [1822] ended the trial period of a common government of Europe, by means of frequent deliberations among great powers on matters

Metternich had of course a quite different vision from that of Great Britain. In September 1815, the three monarchs of the "east"[47] signed the document that became known as the Holy Alliance—the pledge to work together to maintain the status quo in Europe, if necessary by intervention in countries threatened by revolution.[48] Great Britain did not join the signatories. The Prince Regent excused himself on the grounds that, constitutionally, he needed a minister to cosign. He contented himself with endorsing the "sacred maxims." Castlereagh declined to pass the document on to his government on the grounds that it was "a piece of sublime mysticism and nonsense" (Weigall, 1987, 111; see also Ruggiero, 1959, 93). But Metternich was anything but a mystic. He was merely a true believer in the ancien régime, as can be seen clearly from his *Memoirs,* when he discusses the movements for change in France, Germany, Italy, and Spain:

> In all four countries the agitated classes are primarily composed of wealthy men— real cosmopolitans securing their personal advantage at the expense of any order of things whatever—paid State officials, men of letters, lawyers and the individuals charged with public education. . . . This evil may be described in one word: presumption. (Cited from 3:465, 467, in Boyle, 1966, 832–833)

Great Britain was strong enough to ignore presumption. "When Castlereagh opposed revolution, it was not, as with Metternich, because it was 'unnatural' but because it was unsettling" (Kissinger, 1973, 32, 35). He continues: "Revolutions, although undesirable, are not [for him] an actual danger." There seemed to remain for Great Britain no obstacle for "the only major expansionist interest" it had— that of trade and investment (Hobsbawm, 1962, 134). Gash (1979, 282) calls Great Britain "a satiated power." It therefore sought, and could well afford merely to seek,

---

of general concern." The Concert of Europe had become at the very most an "intermittent syndicate of interests" (p. 503).

Renouvin (1954, 57) marks the end of concerted action even earlier, with the British Cabinet's State Paper of May 5, 1820, concerning the proposed intervention in Spain. The paper asserted that the Alliance was "never intended as a union for the government of the world or for the superintendence of the affairs of other States. . . . [Great Britain] cannot and will not act upon abstract and speculative principles of precaution" (cited in Crawley, 1969, 674–675).

47. Lest I be accused of using a post-1945 concept, see the discussion by Temperley (1925a, 23) of the Circular of Troppau (8 December 1820) issued by Austria, Prussia, and Russia at a conference at which Great Britain and France insisted on remaining merely observers: "The doctrine thus proclaimed was that revolutionary insurrection, even if purely an affair of internal change, could never be recognised by the three military despots of East Europe."

48. On the Holy Alliance as a pillar of the post-1815 settlement, see Seton-Watson (1937, 47–49). Schenk (1947, 41) reminds us that the invitation to join the Holy Alliance went to all European states *except* the Ottoman Empire. "[T]he Christian character of the pact offered a justification."

"influence without entanglement" (Evans, 1983, 196–203).[49] With "pragmatic pacifism" (Polanyi, 1957, 5), Great Britain "knew how to get the most out of her preponderance" (Renouvin, 1954, 131).

One way to do this was to concentrate not merely on world commerce but
on becoming the supplier of public loans to other states. Such loans were largely
a Rothschild monopoly for a generation, and tended to be "loans in support of
revolution rather than legitimacy"—that is, loans to Latin America, Greece, Spain,
and Portugal. The offerings on the stock exchange thus "appealed to that blend of
political idealism and commercial strategy which was the dominant tone of British public opinion." In turn, the securities on these loans (reaching some 750,000
between 1815 and 1830) represented an "accumulation of assets readily negotiable
abroad," proving to be a currency available for "financing the corn trade" (Jenks,
1927, 44–45, 61–62).[50]

A structure of hegemony in the world-system could not be stable unless the
home front was secure, and as of 1815 Great Britain was in trouble. The combination of a growing population, expanding urban and industrial zones, and the
severe postwar slump represented "an aggregate of social evils which took half a
century to bring under control" (Gash, 1979, 2). The essential choice in budgetary
terms for the government was whether it would emphasize reduction of expenditures, including social expenditures, and opening the economy maximally, or the
more cautious and protectionist policies advocated by the majority of the supporters of the Tories in power. "In fact, [the government] oscillated between the rival
policies" (Halévy, 1949b, 46).[51]

Although this was the moment of the so-called Tory Reaction, the British variant of conservative ideology was relatively "enlightened" from the beginning,
albeit sometimes grudgingly. To be sure, Toryism emphasized the "sense of harmony of the society" (Brock, 1941, 35).[52] The question is how much this meant in

49. See also Condliffe (1951, 203–209). Imlah (1958, 2) typically puts the best gloss on this: "[W]hat
became distinctive in the *Pax Britannica* [more than military power] . . . was the influence she exerted
on the attitudes of other peoples, and therefore on the policies of other governments, by her own liberty and highly rewarding policies."

50. Jenks (p. 63) also notes that in the case of Latin America, these loans were "vicious," since
they were used primarily to buy armaments. "The violence, the corruption, the instability, the financial recklessness which characterized most of the South American republics during a large part of the
century are in no small way attributable to the early laxity of the London money market." Are we sure
it was laxity?

51. Halévy goes on to say that "the former was plainly triumphant when, in 1819, by the restoration of specie payment, the school of Ricardo won a signal victory, and, moreover, at the very moment
when Ricardo purchased himself a seat in the Commons."

52. Brock continues: "Neither King, Lords, Commons, nor people should govern, but each had its
allotted sphere, and each could disturb the balance by moving beyond that sphere."

practical terms. For Halévy (1949a, 199), the Tory Reaction amounted, when all is said, to very little. The political passions exploited by the Tory leaders, the catchwords so frequently on their lips, differed in no essential point from the mass of sentiments and commonplaces that had composed the Whiggery of sixty years earlier.[53] And Brock (1941, 35, 76) dates the marginalization of the old, or High, Tories, "who resisted reform wherever it appeared," from the ministry of Lord Liverpool (1812–1827, but especially in its reorganized version after 1822). He calls this ministry "the first of those nineteenth-century governments which, without being called 'reforming,' may certainly be called 'improving.' "[54] It was less that the conservatives thought that improvement should be slow than that they thought it should not be consciously planned or intellectually constructed; it should simply emerge as the quiet consensus of wise men.[55]

The immediate problem with such a tactic was that, in a time of economic distress, the patience of the working classes sometimes proved to be limited. It is rather difficult to implement improvement as quiet consensus amid social disorder. Before Great Britain could launch the improvements, the governments felt, therefore, that they needed to bring the disorder under control, and the route they chose was repression. The war years had already not been without repression of social unrest, from that of the English Jacobins in the 1790s (see Thompson, 1997) to that of the Luddites in 1811–1812. In 1815, peace brought the provocative adoption of the Corn Laws (precisely those that were to be repealed with such commotion in 1846). These laws produced "a petitioning movement of unprecedented scale" (Stevenson, 1979, 190).[56] In 1817, the so-called Pentrich Rising of hand-loom weav-

53. Halévy lists (1949a, 200) as points of consonance of policy: the government as the party of war and of strong defense of freedoms in Europe; social support of the government; no intrusion of the military in government; reform of the public services; a mixed constitution with a blurred allocation of powers.

54. Asa Briggs (1959) describes the period between the 1780s and 1867 in Great Britain as the "age of improvement."

55. Indeed, in the twentieth century, conservative academics would argue that this is what actually happened. Hart (1965, 39) analyzes what she calls the "Tory interpretation of history" (referring to historians such as David Roberts, Oliver MacDonagh, and G. Kitson Clark), in counterpoise to the Whig interpretation, which emphasized men and ideas: "In explaining progress in nineteenth-century England, they belittle the role of men and ideas, especially the role of the Benthamites; they consider that opinion, often moved by a Christian conscience, was generally humanitarian; that social evils were therefore attacked and dealt with when people felt them to be intolerable; that many changes were not premeditated or in some sense planned, but were the result of 'historical' process or of 'blind forces.' The implication is that social progress will, in the future as in the past, take place without human effort; all will turn out for the best if we just drift in an Oakeshottian boat."

56. In London, it "created scenes which once again evoked memories of the Gordon Riots" of 1780. On the adoption of the Corn Law of 1815, see Holland (1913, chap. 10). The government had

ers (not quite a revolution, but so it seemed to some at the time) led to the suspension of habeas corpus and the hanging of the leaders.[57] A mass meeting of some sixty thousand people in Manchester in August 1819 in St. Peter's Field, Manchester (following similar meetings in Birmingham, Leeds, and London), triggered a panic reaction, which has come to be called the Peterloo Massacre. (This sardonic play on Waterloo has become irrevocably engraved in the manuals of history.) The state responded to its own panic by creating "Eleven Martyrs" and passing "Six Acts," and increasing the size of the military establishment (ten thousand troops and two thousand marines) (see Read, 1958, 186–189).[58] Finally, in February 1820, the Cato Street Conspiracy to blow up the entire Cabinet was exposed by its agent provocateur, and five persons were hanged. How are we to appreciate this period of disorder? Brock (1941, 1) claims that it "remains the one period during

---

implemented the Corn Laws ostensibly to secure food supply. Hilton (1977, 303) offers this justification: "When the 1814–15 price fall threatened heavy losses on wartime agricultural investment, massive decultivation, and a flight of capital from the land, ministers stepped in to prevent an inappropriate [*sic!*] diversion of sums to industry, and also to exclude foreign surpluses that were large enough to have ruined farmers, but too slight to feed consumers." The argument seems self-serving.

The arguments against the Corn Laws were scarcely more altruistic. Read (1958, 11–12) outlines the motives of the industrialists: "The Manchester opponents of the Corn Laws in 1815 did not think in the terms of social justice later used by the Anti–Corn Law League. Their arguments were undisguised cheap labour ones. High food prices, they argued, would force masters to pay high wages, and in consequence their products would become unimportant in world markets."

See the assessment by Coleman (1988, 35, 39) of the whole period that led up to and culminated in Peterloo: "The 'habit of authority' which has been attributed to the ruling classes of nineteenth-century Britain turned to authoritarianism when challenged at the beginning of the century. Some of the means of repression were informal—like social pressure and harassment, the diversion of custom by the wealthy, the encouragement of or connivance at the violence of loyalist movements—while others were formal and legalistic, like the tightening of statutory prohibitions and controls, campaigns of prosecutions, the increase of military establishments to overawe or put down the disaffected. . . . [The] government found itself strengthened. Whatever posterity was to make of Peterloo, that was the real lesson of 1819."

57. See Briggs (1967, 43); Evans (1983, 181–186). White (1973, 175) observed of the hangings that "Lord Colchester expressed his gratification that the event had served to remove the mischievous delusion that 'High Treason was an offense for which low persons were not punishable.' Another privilege of the aristocracy had been extended to the oncoming democracy." On the central role of weavers in the radicalism of this period, see Clapham (1930, 1:178–180); Prothero (1979); and Read (1958).

58. The Six Acts, passed on November 23, 1819, were the Training Prevention Bill (no training in the use of arms); the Seizure of Arms Bill (the right to search for arms, and to arrest); the Misdemeanors Bill (to reduce delays in the judicial process); the Seditious Meetings Bill (to prevent meetings of more than fifty persons, who could meet only in the parish in which they were normally domiciled, and even then could be ordered to disperse; and in any case could not bear arms, display flags, use drums or play music, or present themselves in military array); the Blasphemy and Seditious Libels Bill (restricting the role of the radical press); and the Newspaper Stamp Duties Bill (extending stamp duties to publications appearing more than once in twenty-six days and costing *less than* sixpence without tax). See also Prothero (1979, 75).

the nineteenth century in which a revolution could have taken place."[59] This seems a bit of unfriendly hyperbole. By contrast, Thomis and Holt (1979, 124) draw the conclusion about the "revolutionary threat" that "the most abiding impression" it leaves is that of the "weaknesses" of "a purely working-class movement with no middle-class involvement."[60] Perhaps so, but in any case, one can agree with White (1973, 192) that, as a result, "with Peterloo, and the departure of Regency England, parliamentary reform had come of age." The quiet consensus of wise men would be that the combination of repression followed by reform (but not the one without the other) was the best guarantee of long-term political stability.

This is all the more clear when one remembers that upheaval was not limited to Great Britain. It was Europe-wide in 1819–1820. Metternich reacted by promoting intervention in Naples and Spain at the Congress of Troppau in 1820. As we have already seen, the British Cabinet formally rejected this idea, despite the "increasing sympathy" that Tory supporters felt for Metternich, in the light of their own sense of insecurity "in their control over the masses of the people" (Webster, 1925, 176–177). Cooler heads saw that the day was already won and that it was now time to move on from repression to reform, or at least to improvement.

France in many ways initially suffered less popular discontent from the post-war slump than did Great Britain. Perhaps it was the fact that the French were so involved in the reconstruction of the government apparatus. Perhaps it was the legacy of revolutionary structures despite the fact that France was supposed to be living a Restoration. Perhaps it was the greater need to restrain a group of "Ultras" that quickened the pace of the liberal center. Perhaps, most of all, it was the excessive presumption of the "Ultras," which may have distracted attention from social issues.

Napoleon might even be said to have been the one who launched the restructuring. In his Hundred Days, he was "converted to liberalism." Faced with a Louis XVIII who had proclaimed a liberal constitution in the Charter, he told the Chamber of Peers two weeks before Waterloo: "I have come to inaugurate the constitutional monarchy" (Suel, 1953, 180). What his "messianic reappearance" from Elba did in fact accomplish was to cloud over the image of Napoleon as tyrant and reestablish his image as revolutionary. He thereby ensured a legacy. "The three nations

59. In a tut-tut mood, Brock (pp. 35–36) argues that "the radical disturbances of 1816 to 1819 retarded rather than advanced the cause of Parliamentary Reform. The Tories were more convinced than ever of the wickedness of the reformers, and the Whigs became lukewarm in a cause which they saw so supported."

60. Thomis and Holt further deprecate (p. 127) the fear of imminent revolution: "In view of such evidence of weakness on the revolutionary side, the explanation of the non-occurrence of revolution in late eighteenth or the early nineteenth century does not require to be sought in the strength of the government's position and the forces at its command."

which dominated the revolutionary tradition of the early nineteenth century—France, Italy and Poland—were precisely those in which the cult of Napoleon was most developed" (Billington, 1980, 129).

The king in 1814, not yet certain of his throne, sought support in the center. Not wishing to concede in principle the concept of popular control, he instead *edicted* a Charter that guaranteed a large number of the "popular" gains of the Revolution: equality before the law, in taxes, and in military service; freedom of expression and religion (although Catholicism would once again be the state religion); maintenance of Napoleon's Civil Code; continuity of titles and ranks accorded in the previous regime; security of the properties that had been confiscated and sold under the revolutionary procedures; and above all, continuity of the centralized state. Of course, one element in this compromise was the fact that, politically, the first restoration was effectuated with the connivance of many of Napoleon's leading supporters, who had bargained for their own continuity in posts (see Zeldin, 1959, 41). But it is important to note that, although some of these same persons compromised themselves with the king during the Hundred Days and were thereafter purged—in some cases, hanged—in the White Terror of the second Restoration, the Charter remained. It obviously reflected more than a circumstantial arrangement; it was a political choice.

To the dismay of the king, the first parliamentary elections brought in an ultraroyalist assembly—the disciples of de Maistre, Bonald, and Chateaubriand. Within a year, the "moderates" loyal to the preferences of the king found themselves in a parliamentary minority. And France entered into the ironic situation in which ultraroyalists, those who stood for "tradition made into a system and put forward as policy,"[61] a tradition of which the monarchy was a pillar, stood at cross-purposes with the incarnation of this pillar of tradition. The king dissolved this assembly and managed to get one that was somewhat better for him, but the struggle would go on until 1824, when the ultraroyalists got a major boost with the succession of Louis XVIII's brother as Charles X. However, this definitive rightward turn would of course lead directly into the July Revolution of 1830.

The crucial, definitive battle over the creation of the liberal state was fought not in Great Britain—where, as we have seen, it had won out even within the Tory party by the 1820s—but in France, where the Legitimists fought hard and unremittingly during the Restoration to achieve what they thought the ouster of Napoleon ought to have signaled: the restoration of a privileged aristocracy and a privileged Church—that is, in their view, "the destruction of equality!" (Elton, 1923, 103). So, when they found themselves under the authority of a king who wished to

---

61. This is the definition Rémond (1982, 22) gives of the "Ultras" as one of the three "rights" of France, the other two being the Orléanists (conservative-liberal) and the nationalist-Bonapartists.

govern rationally and moderately—that is, in the center—because he was aware that the real problem was how to channel popular sentiment that could no longer simply be ignored as unworthy of notice, the Legitimists turned against the king, and therefore tradition. Already in 1817, Bonald (cited in Mellon, 1958, 102–103) observed clearly what was happening:

> We who call ourselves Royalists want royalty to be affirmed by legitimacy; if then, we begin to act somewhere like Leaguers, we must be excused—even praised—since it is because we think that royalty is being opposed to legitimacy, and that we are right to serve [royalty] against itself.[62]

The Legitimists self-destructed. On the one hand, they came to be in favor of an authoritarian state, which is not the same as being in favor of an absolutist one, since it implies a populist, or at least antielitist, tonality.[63] At the same time, "their attachment to absolute monarchy and divine right [their effort to serve royalty against itself] led them to oppose the constitutional monarchy and become partisans of parliament" (Ruggiero, 1959, 174).[64] Worse yet, they turned to an extension of the suffrage, thinking that a middle-class suffrage could be diluted by a "traditionalist" peasant suffrage. And in so doing, they further emphasized the role of parliament. Louis Blanc, writing in 1841 (1:73), was lucid:

> What does it matter to history what the Chamber of 1815 intended? Their legacy is what they did. It is they who proclaimed the dogma of the absolute sovereignty of the legislature, and thus it is they who unknowingly laid the foundations of the syllogism out of which, after fifteen years of struggle, 1830 represents the conclusion drawn. . . . [The result of Louis XVIII dissolving the Chamber was that] those who

---

62. *Archives*, I, 1817, 10 (cited in Mellon, 1958, 102–103).

63. Lecuyer (1988, ii) points out in his editor's preface to a 1980s republication of Bonald that when Bonald's *Théorie du pouvoir politique* . . . was published in 1796, it was banned by the French government (the Directory) and thus had few readers in France. But Bonald did have "one notable reader: Bonaparte heard about it at the time and seems to have been particularly taken by it." That Bonald would himself be ferociously anti-Napoleon in the years to come, precisely on the grounds that he was a tyrant (see Koyré, 1946, 57, n. 6), is irrelevant, since the logic of his position pushed him into a modern authoritarian direction, as Béneton (1988, 43) appreciates: "[S]ince true reason is entirely social, all innovation must be *a priori* considered pernicious and dangerous. . . . [W]hat is most dangerous is a new *idea*. . . . Censorship of books is therefore necessary. . . . The primacy of the social justifies the appeal to the secular authorities. The radical traditionalism of Bonald thus culminates in an authoritarian formula."

64. This permits Ruggiero (1959, 85), a quintessential liberal, to attack the Legitimists as revolutionary: "[T]here is nothing [in the thought of Maistre, Bonald, etc.] to which the word 'restoration' in its proper sense can be applied. It is rather a continuation of the same revolution, showing a new side of itself. . . . The monarchs of the modern period really arose from a break-up of the universalism of the Middle Ages. . . . The religious universalism of the Holy Alliance is therefore wholly unconnected with tradition; it is aimed against the *Declaration of the Rights of Man,* and is itself no less revolutionary in character."

called themselves *ultra-royalists* were dismayed, and those who called themselves *liberals* applauded. It should have been the other way around.

It is therefore no surprise that it was these same Legitimists who by 1840 were forming the first organized political party in France.

The Legitimists gave the opening to the liberals, allowing them to appropriate the Revolution (and even Napoleon) for true tradition, dissociating themselves in the process from the Revolution's overly democratic overtones.[65] The Revolution had been virtuous, but had gone wrong by deviating from its original liberal intent, said Guizot[66] and other liberal historians (a theme Furet would revive in the late twentieth century), but "with the Charter, it became possible to complete the catechism—the Revolution is over and has triumphed." In that way, "the Liberals become the true royalists, the Ultras the true revolutionaries" (Mellon, 1958, 47).[67] Mellon calls this reading of the history of the French Revolution "a milestone in the development of European Liberalism." Thereby, the liberals were deradicalized, and were distinguished in their own minds, and more and more in the minds of others, from "democrats." *Liberalism* became a term linked with a moderate status quo.[68] It lost its "partisan meaning by being semantically dissolved into a general qualifier of various French 'achievements' after 1789" (Marichal, 1956, 293). And with that, it could shift from representing opposition to Napoleonic despotism to continuing the Napoleonic experience:

> Liberalism as the practice of government derived from the same matrix as Napoleonic administration, with the single and practically restricted exception of elected representation as a check on arbitrary rule. Like the Napoleonic functionaries, liber-

65. See Mellon (1958, 3, 7): "The first political task faced by the Liberals . . . was to sell the French Revolution. Their very existence during this period depended upon their ability to justify the Revolution, to acquit it of crimes, to explain away its criminals. . . . Instead of glorying in the 'newness' of the Revolution, its revulsion from centuries of darkness and tyranny, the Liberals of the Restoration would seize upon its connections with this past; they would counter the Conservative effort to read the Revolution out of French history with a version that would suggest its debt to the past, its continuity."

66. "[T]he revolution, the outcome of the divine necessity of a society in progress, founded on moral principles, undertaken on behalf of the public good, was the *terrible but legitimate* struggle of law against privilege, or liberty against the arbitrary, and . . . it alone is able, by regulating itself, by purging itself, by founding the constitutional monarchy, to consummate the good it began and repair the wrongs that it did" (Guizot, 1820b, 28). Thus, as Rosanvallon (1985, 199) puts it: "Understood from this perspective, the Charter of 1814, far from being a bastard, circumstantial compromise, seems on the contrary the endpoint of a long history."

67. This analysis by Mellon in 1958 of the historiography of the French Revolution during the Restoration should be read in conjunction with the analysis by Kaplan in 1993 of the historiography written during the bicentennial of the French Revolution. *Plus ça change. . . .*

68. As indeed Ruggiero (1959, 89) asserts in his defense of liberalism: "[T]he true Restoration is not contained in the territorial Treaty of Vienna, nor yet in the policy of the Holy Alliance, but comes about by degrees in the history of the European nations in which tradition and revolution, reactionaries and Jacobins, collaborated in opposite ways in a common work of restoring equilibrium and effecting a fusion of the old and the new."

als were convinced that they embodied social and economic progress, were favorable to science and technology, and proclaimed rational, utilitarian principles as the basis for a superior and neutral administration. The continuity between the Napoleonic experience and liberalism was accentuated by the strong defense of the former imperial administrators against the legitimist claims of some Restoration monarchies, as well as by their leading role in statistical propositions to resolve social problems. (Woolf, 1991, 242)

Once liberalism had thus cast off its radical associations, both in Great Britain and France, it was launched on its technocratic, reformist path. For the British government at the time, the most urgent problem to solve was that of money. Actually, W. Cooke Taylor said in 1851 that Great Britain had three urgent problems to solve after 1815—"cash, corn, and Catholics"—but note that he put cash first. In 1797, because of economic difficulties resulting from wartime expenditures and a weak military position, Pitt suspended "cash payments" on the notes of the Bank of England "temporarily," thus preserving its bullion reserves[69] but also "precipitating a controversy that continued for over three-quarters of a century" (Fetter, 1965, 1). To be more exact, there were two controversies. The resumption marked the culmination of the so-called bullionist controversy, and this in turn led to a second controversy, that between the so-called Banking School and the Currency School.[70] The bullionists took fright in 1809–1810 at inflationary pressures, which they attributed to excessive issue of notes; they preached the remedy of convertibility. The antibullionists argued that the problem could not be solved by a change of monetary policy, since it was the result of the extraordinary pressures of wartime and would pass. The compromise was to put off resumption until peacetime. At that point, however, acute deflation set in, and considerable opposition emerged to any tightening of credit, which resumption amounted to doing.[71] It was in large part at this point a controversy between those (such as the leaders of the cotton industry) who emphasized Great Britain's foreign-exchange position,

69. On the drain on the Treasury from 1793 to 1797, see Clapham (1944, 1:259–272). Clapham (p. 172) speaks of the "critical importance of [the] bullion" of the Bank of England "just before suspension of the cash payments in 1797" (1:172). Bank of England notes were not legal tender at this time, and "as long as the public would accept the Bank's notes without benefit of legal tender, the Government and the Bank preferred it that way." One element in avoiding the term *legal tender* was that it "was associated in the public mind with the *assignats* of the French Revolution" (Fetter, 1965, 59). The collapse of the *assignats* in 1795 had in fact led to an increase in the use of metallic currency in France, which in turn had been one of the factors that caused such a drain on the British Treasury (see Fetter, 1965, 11–21).

70. For a summary of the intricacies of these two controversies. see Laidler (1987) on the bullionist controversy and Schwartz (1987) on the banking versus currency schools. On both controversies, see also Fetter (1965, 28, 187–192).

71. On the political implications of the debate about resumption, see Jenks (1927, 25–31) and Fetter (1965, 95–103).

which a gold standard would enhance, and those who worried about maintaining the prices of agricultural products,[72] who were not only the large landowners but the "little man" as well.[73]

How much place there should be for the "little man," once Peterloo had shown the stiff backbone of the government, was a question that absorbed more and more public concern in Great Britain. The underlying cause of popular discontent, it was evident, was "distress," and the existing institutions of relief were clearly insufficient to keep the working classes from "resorting to disturbances" (Darvall, 1934, 199).[74] Despite the fact that Peterloo had been an effort to intimidate the working classes, and did intimidate them up to a point, the governing classes were fearful of their increased social power.

The debate between liberals and conservatives (better language than Whigs and Tories, or even radicals and Tories) was not over whether there existed a "problem" to be resolved. It was, rather, over how it could best be resolved. The liberals looked to legislation empowering experts, whereas the conservatives looked to a vague entity called "interests."[75] The timid beginnings of the legislative approach were made nonetheless under a Tory government in 1817 with the Poor Employ-

72. "The agricultural discontents were aggravated by the resumption of cash payments. Contracts had been made, money had been borrowed, and taxes assessed under the paper regime; with the return to the gold standard the value of money would rise, prices would fall, and debts contracted would have to be paid in currency of an enhanced value" (Brock, 1941, 186).

"At this point in the movement of protest, the corn and currency questions clearly overlapped—indeed, for a time, they became one and the same question. . . . [A] heavy burden was placed upon debtors. . . . One of the most important groups of debtors was the farming group. . . . The technical details of currency manipulation were . . . of great importance to corn growers however little they understood them. And it was easy for critics to forget the details and attack political economists, with their 'false speculation' and 'abominable theories,' and 'change-alley people' who seemed to be in charge of high policy. 'Faith! they are now becoming *everything*. Baring assists in the Congress of Sovereigns, and Ricardo [who introduced the resumption legislation] regulates things at home'" (Briggs, 1959, 204–205).

73. "It was all very well for the rich, who could raise all the credit they needed, to clamp rigid deflation and monetary orthodoxy on the economy after the Napoleonic Wars: it was the little man who suffered, and who, in all countries at all times in the nineteenth century, demanded easy credit and financial unorthodoxy" (Hobsbawm, 1962, 58). "The return to the Gold Standard after 1819 was regarded as a reinstatement of the monopolistic power of the rich class who controlled the supply of money" (Cole, 1953, 1:110). The middle-class Radicals were on the side of resumption because they thought that it would let the country "return to normal peacetime rates of taxation" (Read, 1958, 64).

74. This was of course equally true in the rural districts, where there were "two separate classes whose interests were totally distinct and discordant. . . . When the capitalists grew wealthy, the labourers suffered. [By 1815] there had grown up in the country districts of England and Scotland a proletariat ripe for revolt" (Halévy, 1949a, 249).

75. "Dominating the attitude of the Tory party towards the laboring classes was the idea of 'vested interests.' That which resisted most persistently the efforts of the Liberal Reformers to mould public administration on intelligible rational lines was the old eighteenth-century prejudice in favor of 'interests' rather than the state as the unit of government" (Hill, 1929, 92).

ment Act, which provided work on canals, roads, and bridges. The act represented "a significant new departure" in that it "implicitly acknowledged" an obligation to help the "little man" in a time of depression (Flinn, 1961, 92).[76] To the timid legislative effort we must add the pacifying elements of Methodism, emigration, and empire. The role of the Protestant sects in ensuring the political stability of Great Britain has long been argued.[77] Wilmot Horton's proposals to encourage emigration as a solution to poverty has been termed a policy of "shoveling out paupers."[78] And emigration was in turn linked to empire.

The keynote of British policy in the period immediately following 1815 seems to have been caution. They were cautious about lifting protectionist structures. They were cautious about resuming cash payments. The same caution could be seen vis-à-vis the colonies and the mercantile system. The liberal political economists were anti-imperial in principle,[79] but there was opposition to any "sudden overthrow of

76. Flinn (pp. 84–85) notes that four times between 1793 and 1811, Parliament voted Exchequer Bills offering relief to merchants, manufacturers, and colonial planters in difficulty. The fourth such act did mention "the consequent threat to employment." But before 1817, the acts merely assisted in increasing liquidity of the entrepreneurs and promoting specific public works. The 1817 Act involved as well "the desire to raise the level of employment." In fact, government social legislation predated the 1817 Act. There had been the Health and Morals Apprentices Act of 1802, which limited the work of pauper apprentices in cotton mills to twelve hours a day. Although this was perhaps really more an offshoot of the Elizabethan Poor Laws than a response to the new social strength of the working classes (see Heywood, 1988, 218), a second bill along these lines was introduced by Peel in 1815 at the prompting of Robert Owen (see Ward, 1973, 56). It is hard to draw a line, if one exists, between Tory social charity (noblesse oblige) and Tory prudent accommodation to the need to limit social upheaval. In any case, "Peelite Conservatism was not unanimous on labor questions. The attention of the official party under Wellington and Peel was engaged elsewhere" (Hill, 1929, 181).

77. "They offered an outlet by which the despair of the proletariat in times of hunger and misery could find relief, opposed a peaceful barrier to the spread of revolutionary ideas, and supplied the want of legal control by the sway of a despotic public opinion" (Halévy, 1949b, vi). "With their passion for liberty, [the Nonconformists] united a devotion to order, and in the last resort the latter predominated" (Halévy, 1949a, 424).

78. Johnston (1972, 64) defends Horton against this denigration by saying that he had a true "belief in the value of colonial possessions." Perhaps so, but the emigration was significant in size (ca. eleven thousand persons, or one out of nineteen emigrants) and did reduce the problem. And the government did push it, as Johnston (pp. 1–2) himself makes clear: "Between 1815 and 1826, the government of Lord Liverpool conducted six separate experiments in state-aided emigration. . . . Emigration like parliamentary reform and the repeal of the Corn Laws was a question which found roots in the distress of the lower classes."

Another worry was that the Irish and Highland Scots would migrate into "the economically developed areas of the United Kingdom" (Clapham, 1930, 63). Obviously they would, and obviously up to a point this was very useful for the entrepreneurs. But after a point, it added to the problem of urban social distress, whereas emigration of these same people outside the United Kingdom did not have this disadvantage. The *Emigration Inquiry of 1826-7* talked of the "infinite increase of would-be Irish migrants, and . . . the threat to the British standard of life" (cited in Clapham, 1930, 64).

79. "As sworn foes of mercantilism and all its works, the economists [Ricardo, Malthus, Mill, McCulloch] were of course opposed to the colonial system, and at a time when empire without

the existing system." Here, as everywhere else, the liberals hedged their bets. Yes, a free market, but not at the expense of the accumulation of capital. The modifications eventually came, although "it seemed to free-traders that the old system, like Charles II, was an unconscionable time a-dying" (Schuyler, 1945, 103).

The liberals were prudent even in their teaching about colonies. The liberal economists were in general very worried about the decline of profits. Wakefield drew the conclusion that colonies were a partial answer to the shortage of profitable investment opportunities. James Mill (cited in Winch, 1963, 398), though he accepted the strictures of Ricardo in general, did concede: "If colonization was an economic necessity for Britain, then it would require government support."[80] Wakefield developed a "new, liberal conception of empire," with a properly Benthamite justification for efficient and self-financing colonies.[81] The colonies in the Regency empire were thus indeed different from the earlier colonies, as Harlow (1953) has argued. They became "an extension of social change overseas, an example of social imperialism" (Bayly, 1989, 252–253).[82]

---

commercial restrictions seemed an anomaly, their teaching was naturally anti-imperialist in tone" (Schuyler, 1945, 70). One of the strongest statements ever made was by Huskisson (1825, 24) on the occasion of a parliamentary debate about ending the navigation monopoly: "In point of fact, . . . the [colonial] monopoly is either useless or pernicious: It is useless when the mother country can furnish the colony with commodities at the same or a lower rate than others; and when she cannot do this, the monopoly, by forcing a portion of her capital into employments for which she has no particular aptitude, is plainly and certainly pernicious." He points to the example of continued vigorous trade with the United States after its independence as verification of these truths. As for keeping out foreign competition, he says (p.285): "All the tyrannical regulations and *guarda costas* of Old Spain did not prevent her colonies from being deluged with the prohibited commodities of England, France, and Germany."

80. Huskisson (1825, 287), however, had a quite different view: "The truth is that the RATE of profit is not in the slightest degree dependent on the magnitude of the field for employment of capital, but that it is determined entirely by the productiveness of industry at the time."

81. "Wakefield stressed the 'scientific' nature of this proposal. . . . A parallel can be drawn between Wakefield's Central Land and Emigration Board and another Benthamite creation, the Central Board of the revised Poor Law system. Both were centralized bureaucracies of a type which was uncommon and uncongenial to the existing British mentality. Both required a body of full-time experts, fully versed in the principles underlying the system, to administer economically and efficiently, with a clear chain of command and responsibility reaching down to their subordinates. . . . Colonies were no longer to be merely military outposts, or convict dumping grounds; nor were they to be maintained for the sinecures they provided for the aristocracy or for the trading advantage of special interest groups. New communities were to be built, free from the political and religious restraints of English life, but possessing some of the attributes of an old civilization" (Winch, 1965, 149–150).

82. Bayly continues: "Of course, there was no crude sense in the mind of statesmen that picking up a Caribbean island here or an Indian province there would help discipline the working class and provide a field for the emigration of pauper Highlanders or disaffected Irish peasants. It was more that the sense of national mission, forged out of conflict and unease in Britain, and spread particularly by a newly militarised gentry, spilled overseas and regenerated the sleepy ambitions of complaisant governors in colonial outposts."

Social change overseas for the British in practice meant colonization by the British when it was an economic necessity for them, and decolonization of other countries' colonies when it was economically useful for the British. For an insular people, without Napoleonic universalist pretensions, the world had suddenly become their oyster. "Ever since 1815 England had been sending out her swarms over the entire Globe"—as tourists, as emigrants, as colonizers, and as romantic revolutionary supporters (Halévy, 1949b, 126–127).[83] Great Britain, after a long period filled with both hesitations about and encouragement of the settler independence movements of Latin America, finally came down decisively in 1823 in opposition to any European country other than Spain sending troops there to quash these movements; this was recognized as the definitive moment in the struggle.[84] For Great Britain was ready to fight here, as it had not been ready to fight in opposition to French intervention in Spain itself in 1820.[85] This is of course what one expects of a hegemonic power, and how such a power asserts itself—by making implicit threats that it expects will not be called, but also by knowing when it is not

83. Halévy continues: "Noblemen and members of the middle class had betaken themselves to Paris or Italy to enjoy cheaper living, lighter taxation [note this, all who think Great Britain was the super nightwatchman state], a better climate, and more abundant pleasures. Unemployed labourers left England to find work on the virgin soil of North America, South Africa, and Oceania; and the revolutions which were breaking out well nigh throughout the entire world afforded to all who were goaded by the spirit of adventure and found a life of peace insipid an opportunity to come forward as the sworn champions of liberty. In Paris Sir Robert Wilson aided La Vallette to escape; at Ravenna Byron came into conflict with the Austrian police. But South America offered these knights-errant the most glorious adventures. Lord Cochrane was in command of the Chilean fleet, Commodore Browne commanded the fleet of the Republic of La Plata stationed before Buenos Aires. In Venezuela, General MacGregor passed from battle to battle, and General English was at the head of an Anglo-German corps of three hundred men. It was estimated that more than 10,000 men sailed from Irish ports in 1819 'to fight against the cause of despotism in South America,' and that one brigade alone contained over fifteen hundred who had fought at Waterloo."

84. "How Canning met the problem [of the threatened European intervention] is well-known. He gave a timely warning that the British navy would be used to prevent the departure of French and other non-Spanish troops from Europe. . . . Continental governments were given sobering bases for calculating the risks before they committed themselves" (Imlah, 1958, 9).

85. The Monroe Doctrine was also issued in 1823, but its efficacy should not be overstated. Perkins (1927, 256–58) speaks of its "temporary, rather than enduring, interest to most Europeans," adding that "the notion that it struck fear into the hearts of the diplomats of the Old World is legend, and nothing more." The different reaction to Great Britain is clear, as Seton-Watson (1937, 88) notes: "[I]t is hardly too much to assert that Canning's attitude rather than the Monroe Doctrine was the decisive factor in the 'creation of the New World': for the United States were admittedly not ready to go to the length of war, whereas Canning quite definitely was, and Europe, realising it, was clearly impressed." In the case of the proposed intervention in Spain itself, Castlereagh and his then Foreign Minister Canning declined to participate. To be sure, they made clear that they disapproved of French intervention, but they did so "completely passively, so long as France kept clear of Portugal and Spanish America" (Seton-Watson, 1937, 84).

quite strong enough to issue ultimatums.[86] Having thus successfully maneuvered the European states into a do-nothing position, "Canning eventually obtained the chief credit among South Americans" (Temperley, 1925b, 53), and thus Great Britain secured her status as the standard-bearer of liberty despite the obvious economic self-interest that was at play.

This readiness of Great Britain to play the role of limited supporter of independence movements was extended to the Balkans/Ottoman Empire as well, most particularly in the case of Greece. Public opinion in Great Britain was torn between a disdain for autocracy, seen as somehow not quite civilized, and a prudent desire not to become too entangled. "Influence without entanglement" is how Evans (1983, chap. 21) describes British foreign-policy aims in Europe at this time. Another way to describe these aims, however, is to say that their primary objective was the slow eating away of the Holy Alliance by embarrassing it where its principles were most shaky. The case of Greece offered a golden opportunity. The Greek revolution started in the wake of, and at the same time as, others in Europe in 1820–1822. In the case of the others, Great Britain, as we have seen, disapproved "passively" of intervention. The Greek uprising, however, had the special characteristic of being an uprising of Christians against a Moslem empire, and in particular an uprising of Orthodox Christians. Metternich might remain unmoved, but it was harder for the Tsar of All the Russias. Even then, Alexander hesitated, but Nicholas, who acceded to the throne in 1825, was ready to join Great Britain, and then France, in forcing the issue,[87] which was ultimately fully to be resolved only in 1830.

In Great Britain and elsewhere, on the one hand, the Greek uprising was the cause of the radicals:

> Greece . . . became the inspirer of international liberalism and "philhellenism," which included organized support for the Greeks and the departure of numerous volunteer fighters, played a part in rallying the European left wing in the 1820s

86. See the analysis by Temperley (1925b, 37) as to the clear authority of Great Britain in this matter: "Castlereagh got Alexander at Aix-la-Chapelle (1818) to abandon any design of forcible intervention in Latin America. . . . But the fact that the Neo–Holy Alliance submitted to Castlereagh in 1818 was no reason why it should do so [in 1823] if France were prepared to risk something to achieve this purpose." But was France? France seemed to suggest it was. Louis XVIII had already tried to rehabilitate the Family Compact in 1815, and therefore offered support to Spain. Subsequently, France hoped to encourage the creation of Bourbon monarchies in Latin America. But by the end of 1823 France became convinced that "Spain could not reconquer her former colonies" (Robertson, 1939, 319) and that therefore it was not worth taking on Great Britain, despite the fact that the Ultra party (including Monsieur, soon to be Charles X) strongly supported intervention.

87. Schenk (1947, 41) reminds us that when the Ottoman government had been excluded in 1815 from Holy Alliance, it "felt disposed to look for ulterior motives behind this exclusion. After all, it could not easily be forgotten that so recently as 1808 Russia had laid claims to Constantinople."

analogous to that which support for the Spanish Republic was to play in the later 1930s (Hobsbawm, 1962, 145).[88]

But, on the other hand, Greek nationalism served as a wedge that the British government could use to undermine what remained of the Holy Alliance. If from "monstrous portent" still in 1822 the Holy Alliance had become a "thing of contempt" by 1827 (Temperley, 1925a, 474), it was primarily because of the Greek revolution. "[T]he prime artisan of this ruin [of the Holy Alliance] was George Canning" (Weill, 1931, 68).[89]

The ambiguous role of the Greek revolution—both archetype of nationalist revolution for the later "springtime of the nations," and crucial pawn in the British struggle to strengthen its hegemonic hold on the world-economy; ergo both myth of the radicals and excuse for clever maneuver by the Tories—precisely reflects the ambiguities of romanticism. For Greece became the prime inspirer of European romanticism, even as the good classicists of Europe celebrated the rationality of the ancient Greeks. Romanticism "comes of age between 1780 and 1830." It was naturally associated with the French Revolution, since romanticism had to do with "creating a new society different from its immediate forerunner" (Barzun, 1943, 52). Thus it was individualist, voluntarist, and poetic. It stood for a liberation of the imagination. But precisely because it wanted a liberation of the imagination, and rejected the limitations of the present. But at the same time it was "also the love of the past, the attachment to old traditions, the curiosity for epochs when the peoples, suffused [bercés] with legends, created naive poetry, a bit childish, but sincere and spontaneous" (Weill, 1930, 215).

> Thus, although romanticism involved spontaneity and hence could sanction revolution, it was strongly opposed to any universalistic tone in revolution, particularly as this had been incarnated in the Napoleonic imposition of the universalist project on

88. See also Billington (1980, 135): "[The Greek Revolution of 1821] raised the prestige of constitutional revolution throughout Europe at the very time when that cause seemed most humiliated. It gave an imaginative boost to the cause of national—as distinct from social—revolution, and it mobilized politically the influential romantic writers." The fact is that nationalism needed this boost. It was a very young doctrine, born to some extent in the Napoleonic years, but still confused with resistance to an occupying force. It is only after 1815 that it becomes a conscious doctrine that argues that state and nation should coincide. As Renouvin (1954, 12) says, "[N]owhere in 1815 . . . had this doctrine yet fully emerged."

89. Weill (p. 95) argues: "[T]he dissolution of the Holy Alliance, begun with regard to Spain and Spanish America, was completed in the Orient. . . . It is the decomposition of this European group that made possible the victory of liberalism in 1830." See Temperley (1925a, 474–475), who similarly credits Canning: "The work thus done was permanent. The security which England enjoyed amid the storms of 1848 is due more to Canning than to any other man. . . . The revolutions of 1830 and 1848 proved that the world could be 'made safe for constitutional monarchy.' And it was Canning who had foreseen its moderating influence in the twenties."

unwilling peoples.[90] For that reason, a radical, rationalist revolutionary like Blanqui considered romantics to be the enemy. When Blanqui, the great practical revolutionary of the nineteenth century, had finished fighting in the revolution of 1830, he burst into the editorial room of the paper on which he had worked. Standing in the doorway, he flung down his rifle and shouted with young enthusiasm [surely a romantic quality!] to the elderly journalists sitting there: "*Enfoncez, les romantiques!*"— "That finishes the Romantics." For him, the Revolution for which he had just risked his life was not primarily the victory of republican workers over their oppressors; what first occurred to him was that the ornate romantic style of Chateaubriand, the idealisation of the Middle Ages, fake Gothic and the aping of feudalism, would all now disappear in favour of a purer classical style, which would model itself, in writing, drama, and architecture, on the noble tradition of Republican Rome. (Postgate, 1974, 97)

Nonetheless, says Barzun (1961, xxi), "romanticism is populist . . . even when the Romanticist, like Scott or Carlyle, preaches a feudal order." Perhaps Hobsbawm (1962, 306) best catches the overall tone:

[T]hough it is by no means clear what romanticism stood for, it is quite evident what it was against: the middle. Whatever its content, it was an extremist creed. Romantic artists or thinkers . . . are found on the extreme left . . . , on the extreme right . . . , leaping from left to right . . . , but hardly ever among the moderates, or whig-liberals, in the rationalist centre, which indeed was the stronghold of "classicism."[91]

Where, then, does Greece fit in terms of this all too malleable concept? Here, Bernal's [1987, 1991] important work on the conceptualization of the ancestry of Europe comes in. He points out that Renaissance thinkers had seen Egypt, not Greece, as "the original and creative source," and that both Egypt and China had maintained "a high reputation for [their] philosophy and science, but above all for [their] political system" (Bernal, 1987, 16) until precisely the time of the French Revolution, at which point, led by Romantic thinkers, the focus shifted to Greece:

By the end of the eighteenth century, "progress" had become a dominant paradigm, dynamism and change were valued more than stability, and the world began to be viewed through time rather than across space. Nevertheless, space remained

90. "To [the romantics] the idea of imposing any nation's ways, sphere, or art upon another was repellent. For this was precisely the rationalist mistake that the French Revolution had attempted to carry out and that they were combatting" (Barzun, 1943, 129). Weill (1930, 216) asserts that "[t]he alliance between antirevolutionary politics and the new literature seemed evident to many contemporaries."

91. Hobsbawm continues: "It would be too much to call it an anti-bourgeois creed, for the revolutionary and conquistador element in young classes still about to storm heaven fascinates the romantics also. . . . The demonic element in capital accumulation . . . haunted them. . . . And yet the romantic elements remained subordinate, even in the phase of bourgeois revolution." Hobsbawm (p. 310) reminds us, too, that "the most lasting results of these romantic critiques were the concept of human 'alienation,' which was to play a crucial part in Marx, and the intimation of the perfect society of the future."

important for the Romantics, because of their concern for a local formation of peoples or "races." . . . Real communication was no longer perceived as taking place through reason, which could reach any rational man. It was now seen as flowing through feeling, which could touch only those tied to each other by kinship or "blood" and sharing a common "heritage." (Bernal, 1987, 28)

And this is exactly why Egypt had to be cut out of the line of anteriority for Europe. For eighteenth- and nineteenth-century Romantics and racists it was simply intolerable that "Greece—which was seen not merely as the epitome of Europe but also as its pure childhood—could be the result of the mixture of native Europeans and colonizing Africans and Semites" (Bernal, 1987, 28). Greece represented, was made to symbolize, the line between Europe and the outer world, the Orient, the lands of barbarism. Nationalism was acceptable, even desirable, within the zone of "Europe" (especially if protesting against a non-Christian imperial entity)— hence, both White settlers in Latin America and Greeks could have British support against "autocracy"—but this had nothing to do with what was appropriate in distant cultural climes like India.

The existence of more conservative and more revolutionary forms of romanticism correlates with a split in both time and place. In time, the romanticism that was nurtured against the universalism of the revolutionary-Napoleonic period was dominant in the earlier years, and in the core countries. Circa 1830, it gave way in Italy, Germany, and Poland, following in the footsteps of Greece, to a "romanticism of progress," which became "an important factor in the movements of national liberation" (Renouvin, 1954, 19). But in the core, and especially in Great Britain, it remained identified "with tradition and with the maintenance of authority in church and state," as opposed to the "revolutionary or semi-revolutionary character" it had on the Continent (Seton-Watson, 1937, 40).

Romanticism served British hegemony well. It undermined the Holy Alliance, which, as we have already noted, was quite rationalist and universalizing. It undermined the vestiges of the revolutionary-Napoleonic tradition. It encouraged a reorganization of the geopolitical space in Europe (and the Americas), which served Great Britain's immediate economic interests and its ability to maintain and reinforce its hegemonic order. And it drew a clear line between Europe and the outer world, creating a basic justification for imperialism and racism—both so crucial to the geopolitics and geoculture of the post-1789 world. Of course, it was a loose cannon and could not always be controlled. So romanticism would also eventually become part of the undoing of the British hegemonic order, but not until this order was undermined by the economic and political transformations of the last third of the nineteenth century.

It was of great help to the British that France's internal evolution went in tandem with this grand schema. As in Great Britain, so in France, the period after 1815 had "brought neither prosperity nor abundance for the working classes," but rather unemployment, worsened by internal migration toward the large urban centers (Ponteil, 1968, 285).[92] Socially, the gulf between the workers and the urban bourgeoisie was enormous.[93] The rights of the workers to organize were strictly limited to mutual aid societies under police surveillance.[94] There was worker unrest in Lyon in 1817, in which the workers raised the tricolor cockard, an event that the prefect of the Rhône attributed to contagion from the news about uprisings in England (as well as the rebellion of the Americas and the plot in Lisbon).[95] Still, a liberal like Guizot could say in 1820: "I do not despair of obtaining the support of the masses (*saisir les masses*), especially with regard to the political institutions."[96]

The mid-1820s, however, created a serious inflammation in the political process. At the very moment that Liberal Toryism was taking hold in Great Britain, Charles X, by the accident of the king's premature death, came to power in France in 1824 and began to implement his particularly reactionary views. This led to strains with the British, strains with large segments even of the *pays légal* at home, and strains with the working classes. In addition, the accession of Charles X coincided with an economic downturn that began in 1825 and greatly intensified in 1829. The combination of political sclerosis and economic troubles tends to be explosive, and led directly into the revolutionary atmosphere of 1830 (see Bourgin, 1947, 203; and Gonnet, 1955, 250–280).

Instead of seeking to moderate his policies and appease some of the malcontents, Charles X asserted his authority all the more arbitrarily.[97] When 221 deputies found the courage to send him a public address, asking him to respect the rights of the legislature, he saw this, not incorrectly, as the defense of the essential

92. See also Bruhat (1952, 186–87): "Conditions for the workers got considerably worse from 1815 to 1830. Wages went down as the number of hours of work and the cost of living went up. . . . Gas lighting, which had begun to spread, served primarily to make it possible to lengthen the work day during the winter season."

93. "It was, for a worker, an act of 'courage' to assert himself as an equal of a bourgeois" (Daumard, 1963, 517).

94. Bruhat (1952, 206–07), who however notes: "Nonetheless, even though their activities were restricted to mutual aid, these associations contributed to giving a sense of organization to the workers, if only by the regular collection of dues, the holding of meetings, and the designation of collectors" (p. 208).

95. See Rudé (1969, 61–62) on the report by the Prefect, the Comte de Chabrol, on June 24, 1817. Rudé also mentions a pamphlet, "Lyon en 1817," issued by a Col. Fabvier, which similarly implicates contagion from the movements in Lisbon and the revolution in Pernambuco, Brazil.

96. Letter to Fauriel, cited in Rosanvallon (1985, 39).

97. Labrousse (1949a, 19) argues that this was one of the common characteristics of the French revolutions of 1789, 1830, and 1848. They were all spontaneous; the causes were endogenous; in each case they had a social character; they were all preceded by economic difficulties. "In order that these two linked phenomena, economic and political tension, cause an explosion, they have to encounter resistance. . . . In England, policy of flexibility: timely concessions, and nothing explodes. In France, resistance—and everything explodes."

principles of the French Revolution, as upheld in the Charter of Louis XVIII, and he ignored the plea. This was in a sense Charles X's last chance. "If there was a revolution in 1830, it was a revolution that had been provoked." Charles X issued a repressive press decree on July 26. The deputies temporized; a crowd of workers acted. This crowd was composed neither of the "desperate and dispossessed" nor of the "substantial middle class" but "largely of men from skilled crafts, reasonably mature in years" (Suel, 1953, 188).

Was this then the revolution that Buonarroti, Europe's "first professional revolutionary," was hoping for when, "on the eve of the Revolution of 1830, he actually prayed for the triumph of reaction" (Eisenstein, 1959, 49)?[98] Not really. It was a three-day popular revolution—July 27–29, *les Trois Glorieuses*—which was quickly captured by Restoration liberalism and resulted in the July Monarchy, with Louis-Philippe, who was prepared to call himself not King of France but King of the French. Thiers said: "Without the Duke of Orléans . . . we could never have contained this rabble" (cited by Dolléans, 1947, 42). Against the Ultras, who had still hoped to truly restore some version of the ancien régime, the July Monarchy legitimated a liberal version of the French Revolution. "By the Revolution of 1830, the assault upon the Revolution of 1789 was finally defeated" (Elton (1923, 88).[99]

The workers would rapidly realize that, "in terms of the economy and the social structure, the Revolution [of 1830] had brought about no change whatsoever" (Bourgin, 1947, 205).[100] If the workers were disillusioned, the Ultras were nonetheless dismayed. On August 7, 1830, Chateaubriand (cited in Béneton, 1988, 56–57, n. 3) made a speech in the House of Peers refusing to support Louis-Philippe: "A useless Cassandra, I have wearied the throne and the fatherland with my disdained warnings; all that remains to me is to sit down on the debris of a wreckage that I have so often predicted." And big businessmen were unsure whether they should

---

98. What Buonarroti feared most was not the Holy Alliance but the "subtler enemy represented by the England of Canning and the Age of Reform. " (Eisenstein, 1959, 139).

99. This is celebrated to this day by the fact that the monument to the *Trois Glorieuses* stands in Paris on the Place de la Bastille. But the French Revolution that was celebrated was the one that was incarnated primarily in Louis XVIII's Charter of 1814. The opposition of the Parisian bourgeoisie to the Ultras "was not progressive; the Charter, in the minds of the notables, was an end point, not a starting point. Struggling against those whose reactionary views they denounced, the leaders of the Parisian bourgeoisie remained themselves just as much turned toward the past. Their conservative attitude manifested itself at the social level as well as in the domain of politics" (Daumard, 1963, 575).

100. Dolléans (1947, 44) concurs: "Nothing changed for the working class. . . . The ministers [of Louis Philippe] were more hostile to the people than the men of the Restoration." So does Daumard (1963, 576, 583): "It is a generally accepted thesis that, after the July Days, the bourgeoisie confiscated for its benefit a revolution made by the people. . . . At the end of 1831, bourgeois society was organized. The reforms were limited, but they represented what were then the wishes of the middle classes, whose representatives had, without exception, the impression of having obtained their proper place within the state."

applaud or not, fearing simultaneously "reaction, . . . the Legitimists, [and] social revolution by the masses" (Price, 1975b, 6).[101]

Finally, the British were also hesitant to applaud at first. In fact, in the weeks immediately following the revolution, the "menace of war hung heavily over France" (Pinkney, 1972, 303). The tricolor, the Marseillaise, the reorganization of the national guard all made the Holy Alliance states shudder; they even began to fear renewed French aggression. But the British government, under none other than Wellington, the spokesperson of the more conservative Tories, hastened to recognize the new government. And by October, so had everyone.

Why did the British move so rapidly? No doubt it helped that Louis-Philippe was both a "sincere admirer" of Great Britain's parliamentary institutions and a partisan of an alliance with Great Britain (see Guyot, 1901, 579). No doubt it was a clever move by Louis-Philippe to recruit the well-known exponent of these two views, Talleyrand, as ambassador to Great Britain, symbolizing that Great Britain was the country whose support "it was most important for [Louis-Philippe] to win" (Guichen, 1917, 186).[102] And no doubt the British had many reasons to be annoyed with the foreign policy that Polignac had conducted for Charles X. In particular, they were most unhappy about the implications of France's invasion of Algeria early in 1830, especially when they realized that Charles X saw in it virtually a revival of the Crusades.[103] At a moment when Great Britain had succeeded

---

See also Newman (1974, 58–59): "[The Revolution of 1830 was] the product of an alliance between constitutional liberals and the common people that had been building for several years. . . . [The two classes] could see themselves as part of a single political unit—the people—which was united against a common enemy, the priest-ridden aristocratic party led by Charles X. . . . [Only later would the common people] with the help of socialists like Louis Blanc [see that] liberty was not enough and that the liberal middle class did not and could not represent their interests."

The "later" was in fact almost immediately. By mid-August, there were many strikes in Paris. By October, there were "disturbances." "The working class found that the revolution, far from bringing them an amelioration of their lot, as they expected, had only worsened it" (Pinkney, 1972, 313). By October 7, 1831, the prefect of the Rhône would be noting the discontent of the working class "immediately following the revolution which, as [they] must feel, had been made on their behalf" (cited in Tarlé, 1929, 151).

101. For one thing, big business was already doing quite well, even under Charles X. Though the Revolution "did bring new men into public office"—indeed, it brought a "thorough . . . purge of the higher offices of the state" (Pinkney, 1972, 276–77)—it had "introduced no *new* regime of the *grande bourgeoisie*" (Pinkney, 1964b, 71). Indeed, they were wary of the economic impact of upheaval. The spring of 1830 had, in their opinion, represented "somewhat of an upswing after difficult times." Business conditions had "worsened in the months that followed the revolution." And, following the Revolution, there was "popular upheaval" (Johnson, 1975, 150–151, 153).

102. Although Talleyrand's appointment was controversial in both France and Great Britain, it was received very well by the British populace. See Masure (1893, 108–113).

103. "This far-off expedition against the Regency of Algiers, the repair of Berber pirates . . . pleased the King of France, Charles X, because his religious spirit conceived of it as, in the times of the Middle

in constraining the Holy Alliance, Charles X seemed to be upsetting the apple-cart.[104] Great Britain had been restrained from acting directly against him because of the strong support France was receiving from the other European powers, and from Russia in particular.[105] Now, however, it could hope for better from Louis-Philippe, as indeed would turn out to be the case.[106]

But with all the hesitations, the fact is that the July Revolution succeeded. That is, the liberal state was installed—in its primitive form, at least. One hundred years later, Benedetto Croce (1934, 101–102) could look back at what he called the "July sun" and exult:

> With [the July Days] all European absolutism was morally defeated and, on the con-
> trary, European liberalism, which was struggling and bridling in depression, became
> an example of how to face the enemy in extreme cases; a proof that in this way vic-
> tory is certain; an aid in the fact itself that a great power had reached the plenitude of
> liberty; and ground for confidence in revolutions soon to come.

As Croce indicates, the Revolution of 1830 was to be contagious, spreading most immediately to neighboring Belgium and Italy, but then also to Poland. "The peoples of Europe emerged from a long apathy. The Holy Alliance was shaken" (Rudé, 1940, 413).[107] Of the three revolutions, that of Belgium was the only successful one, and for good reason. It was the only one that fit into the project to create and consolidate the liberal state in the core countries of the world-economy. The Italian uprising of the Carbonari was supported by the more radical elements in France and various parts of the *Parti du mouvement* under the leadership of Lafayette. They organized the *Volontaires du Rhône* to come to the aid of

---

Ages, the kings had conceived of the Crusades" (Coulet, 1931, 2). This must have seemed dangerously provocative to the British.

104. Louis XVIII had been restrained in his colonial policy in order to appease the British. Charles X felt less restrained. True, he was at first involved in Greece, alongside Great Britain and Russia. But the Treaty of Adrianople in 1829 guaranteeing Greek independence, which for the British served to seal their hegemonic order, liberated French troops to engage in other and different overseas expeditions (see Schefer, 1928, 32–33).

105. See Guichen (1917, 65): "Public opinion in Europe considered the Algiers campaign as an expedient, intended to distract attention from the parliamentary situation, strengthen the political position of the government and of the throne itself, by a success that would impress all Europe." As a result, "the almost unanimous approval of the powers strongly constrained Aberdeen and Wellington" (p. 67). While "England ceaselessly protested, . . . the entente between Petersburg and Paris was becoming ever more cordial" (Schefer, 1907, 446).

106. Somewhat better, at least. Although Talleyrand proposed to Louis-Philippe that he give up Algiers as a gesture to the British, Louis-Philippe declined (see Guichen, 1917, 187). Nonetheless, the British could deal with Louis-Philippe as someone who shared their vision of Europe, as they could not have dealt with Charles X.

107. But for Masure (1892, 696), it had already been "shaken" before 1830: "By the beginning of the year 1830, the Holy Alliance was no more than a name."

Piedmont (and incidentally annex Savoy). They were. however. in part foiled by the French authorities themselves.[108] For the new French government wanted merely to contain Austria; and Charles-Albert, king of Piedmont, wanted the Austrians out but the liberals held in check. So in the end it was the liberals who lost out (see Renouvin, 1954, 73–75). As for Poland, the revolution there was suppressed without too much difficulty. The link between it and the revolution in France was spiritual but not more.[109] The French were very far away and neither able nor prepared to do anything.

Belgium was another story entirely. Belgium had never been an independent state, but in the long period between the Revolt of the Netherlands and the French Revolution, it had been a somewhat autonomous administrative unit first under Spanish, then Austrian rule. During this period, agriculture had flourished,[110] but industry thrived there as well, particularly following the "thirty-two years of prosperity" [1748–1780] under Prince Charles. The prince's deputy, the Count of Coblenz [1753–70], known as "the Colbert of the Low Countries," instituted a protectionist policy (Briavoinne, 1839, 7, 86–90), which resulted in "dazzling" growth between 1765 and 1775,[111] growth that continued steadily from that point on.[112] One of the advantages the Austrian Netherlands had over the United Provinces at that time was its combination of high population growth, low wages, and a skilled

108. See Rudé (1940, 433), who points out how, consequently, "the cadres of the *Volontaires du Rhône* survived in a certain number of workers' groups in Lyon secretly organized. . . . On November 21–22, 1831, it was the *Volontaires du Rhône* . . . who led the workers in battle in Lyon." Lafayette was a particular object of scorn and fear for the Holy Alliance. Pozzo del Borgo, the Russian ambassador in Paris, called him "the protector and obvious provocateur of this crusade of universal unrest." And Apponyi, secretary of the Austrian embassy in Paris, said he was the "idol of the people and the mannequin of the revolution" (cited in Guichen, 1917, 180).

109. See Leslie (1952, 121): "There is very little evidence to show that the leading conspirators [in Poland] rose in revolt in order to prevent the army from being used to quell the French Revolution of 1830. This is a justification after the event in order to lay claim to French sympathy, much as it has been argued that the Second and Third Partitions saved the French Revolution of 1789. The truth is that [Russian Grand Duke] Constantine [commander-in-chief of the army] had discovered the existence of Wysocki's conspiracy and for this reason it became necessary for the plotters to come to a quick decision."

110. Slicher van Bath (1963, 243) says that the "greatest development was in the period 1650–1750 because "the intensive type of Flemish agriculture was based less on cereals than on industrial and fodder crops." But this continued after 1750. Abel (1973, 286) notes: "Circa 1800 European travelers were unanimous in attributing once again [to Flanders] top rank in [the agricultural production] of Europe."

111. Hasquin (1971, 299), who is referring to Charleroi in particular. See also Garden (1978b, 21), who says that "even though they are incomplete and imprecise, the statistics for 1764 give the impression of a welter of industries in the greater part of the Austrian Netherlands."

112. Referring to the period 1770–1840, Lebrun (1961, 654) speaks of the "extremely rapid and compact character of the Belgian industrial revolution."

labor force.[113] One result was that Belgium was introducing industrial machinery almost as fast as England.[114]

France annexed Belgium in 1795. The main centers of industrial production—cotton in Ghent, wool in Verviers and Eupen, and heavy industry in Liège and Hainault—all underwent a further "remarkable expansion" in the French period (Mokyr, 1974, 366).[115] There seem to be two main reasons: "integration with a huge protected and unified area of 30 million customers" (Crouzet, 1964, 209), and transformation of the social structure—the removal of internal barriers to trade (customs, tolls), the abolition of guilds, civil equality, reform of codes and tribunals, and the abolition of feudal rights (see Wright, 1955, 90).[116] The two together seem to have worked splendidly, as everyone seems to agree: "brusk acceleration," the moment of a Rostovian "take-off," "total transformation, . . . [and] the moment of decisive expansion" are the phrases used (Lebrun, 1961, 555; Devleeshouwer, 1970, 618; Dhondt, 1969, 42, 44).[117] This was already the view of the Belgian analyst of the time, Natalis Briavoinne (1839, 113):

> The political events [of the French period], a unified civil legislation and, more relevant, the complete reorganization of the tribunals, [and] improved commercial

113. Mokyr (1974, 381) attributes the high population growth to the potato plus rural domestic industry and says that "the extraordinarily low wages paid in the protoindustry impressed contemporaries of the time as well as historians." He concludes that "lower wages may have been important in determining rapid industrialization in Belgium and higher wages in determining Dutch stagnation" (p. 385).

Milward and Saul (1973, 452–453) offer this explanation for Belgium's lower wages: "The structure of farming contributed . . . to breaking down the rigidities which handicapped France. So small were the farms that the same labor force was frequently shared between agricultural and industrial employment. The factory worker returned to his small holding after his day's work at a considerable distance. This was no transient stage in the development of a proletariat but a permanent feature of the Belgian economy. It seems to have developed from a long tradition of labor migration within Belgium and it was one reason for the relatively lower industrial wages in Belgium than France, for the entrepreneur did not need to entice his labor force permanently away from the land."

On skilled workers, see Ruwet (1967, 23): "That, from the beginning of the [eighteenth] century, the Elector of the Palatinate, the republic of Venice, the Elector of Bavaria, the [Holy Roman] Emperor, the king of Prussia, and later the Tsarina of Russia sought periodically to attract to their countries workers from Verviers abundantly testifies to the reputation of Verviers and its technicians."

114. Lebrun (1948, 24) speaks of "the smallness of the lag."

115. Crouzet (1964, 583) adds silk in Krefeld. Mokyr (1974, 368–369) notes a "considerable strain" in the Dutch period and then a loss of "some momentum" after 1830. Craeybeckx (1968, 123–24) adds a note of caution. He says that the Continental Blockade "stimulat[ed] certain industries" but also "held back . . . technical progress" in other sectors, notably metallurgy. He does note, however, that in the latter part of the French period, the impact of the removal of "the last hindrances left over from the ancien régime" was "particularly important."

116. Demangeon and Febvre (1935, 128) point out that Emperor Joseph II of Austria had tried to impose many of these reforms and failed, whereas Napoleon succeeded. "Napoleon thus assumed in Belgium the role of executor of the will of Joseph II."

117. Milward and Saul (1973, 292) essentially agree but put it more soberly. They say that the effects of French rule in Belgium were "complex but on balance beneficial." Dhondt and Bruwier (1973, 352)

institutions all underlie a remarkable momentum in Belgium as in France; but Belgium is the country which reaped the earliest and greatest benefits.

After Waterloo, Belgium was integrated into the Kingdom of the Netherlands. Local opinion was not consulted. This reunion (after 250 years of separation) was greeted with hostility in Belgium by both main groups of the population: by the democrats, strong in Wallonia, who wanted a parliamentary system; and by the Catholics, strong in Flanders, who were wary of being under a Protestant monarch without a prior pact to defend their religious rights (see Ponteil, 1968, 17). The immediate economic effect was negative, in part because of the general world economic downturn, and in part because of the contraction of the market for their goods.[118] In terms of policy, the central debate was about tariffs, between Dutch merchants who survived on open *entrepôts* and were much more concerned about Hamburg than about Manchester,[119] and Belgian industrialists. who were seeking protection against British competition.[120]

King William was primarily concerned about holding his enlarged kingdom together and servicing the enormous state debt.[121] In fact, the tariff quarrel subsided. The Belgians did better than the Dutch and became less protectionist. This became in turn part of the problem, because the Europe-wide downturn after

call this period the "peak" of the Belgian industrial revolution. Lebrun (1961, 574–76) points, however, to some "lost opportunities" caused by permitting too large urban agglomerations and insufficient attention to education.

118. Dhondt and Bruwier (1973, 349) note that the political restructuring plus the free flow of British products "led to the collapse of the Ghent cotton industry. The stagnation lasted until 1823." But then the industry found new outlets in the Dutch East Indies. Lis and Soly (1977, 480) record that living standards in Antwerp "declined drastically, both quantitatively and qualitatively," as measured by food consumption.

119. See Wright (1955, 28, 77): "At the end of the eighteenth century, much Dutch trade rested on custom rather than on clear economic advantage. Wartime conditions had forced foreign merchants to seek new connexions." The question is, Would the trade ever return? This was further complicated after 1815 by the opening of the Scheldt, which had been closed since 1585, and the reduction in the complications of German frontiers. "In 1816, most Dutch merchants met the challenge of the new age in the spirit of fifteenth-century Venice rather than of nineteenth-century Hamburg; they desired a *porto franco* which was limited by all possible restrictions in favor of Dutch commercial profits and traditions."

120. See Demoulin (1938, 124): "After the loss of the French market, Belgian industry was in disarray. . . . The demands of the Belgians were nonetheless exaggerated: they wanted prohibitions across the board. . . . [To be sure,] all of Europe was being protectionist at this time." Wright (1955, 100) notes that "most Belgian liberals were protectionists."

121. The debt of the Netherlands had been accumulating since the sixteenth century and required at this time an annual service charge of over 14 million florins. Belgium had had virtually no debt (less than three hundred thousand florins' service charge). To be sure, during the Napoleonic era the Belgians had paid 75–80 million florins annually, but the Belgians were comparing the Dutch with the Austrian periods in terms of fiscal regime. They complained in particular that the fiscal reforms

1825 created a pool of unemployed proletarians precisely in Belgium, who became "ready to receive revolutionary ferment" (Demoulin, 1938, 369).

Thus, the July Revolution in Paris had an immediate resonance in Belgium. It revived the always latent thought of possible reunion with France that animated some of the Walloon bourgeoisie. It revived the discomforts of the Catholics with Dutch Protestant overrule. But it needed a spark. Even if, as some argue, the August 25 uprising was inspired by "agitators arriving from Paris," they needed "troops," and the troops were to be found only among the unemployed workers (Harsin, 1936, 277). This was a "popular revolt," preceded by a social malaise, marked by Luddism and some violence.[122] But here, too, as in the case of the July Revolution, the uprising was quickly recuperated by middle-class forces and was transformed into a national, liberal revolution (see Demoulin, 1950, 152).[123]

Unlike the situation in France, there was no strong Ultra party in Belgium, precisely because Catholics were not in power. This made Belgian Catholics more open to the version of Catholic liberalism that Lamennais had pioneered in France, but which he could not really manage to turn there into a primary social force.[124] To be sure, the Vatican itself was very legitimist, and therefore very reserved about Belgian liberal nationalism, but "the policy of Rome was one thing and the

---

of 1821–1822 "sacrificed the agricultural and industrial zones of Belgium to the interest of the commercial cities of Holland" (Terlinden, 1922, 16). In face of Belgian protests, the king backtracked and accorded some further protection. As amended, "the system of 1821 proved broadly satisfactory to the Belgians. Their iron, coal, and cotton and woolen goods continued to enjoy valuable protection in the Dutch market, and acquired it in the Dutch colonies too" (Wright, 1955, 208). Furthermore, the Belgian bankers were drawing great profit from the persistence of the two sets of metallic coins—Dutch florins and Belgian francs—in a situation where the exchange rate favored francs, causing northern capital to move south (see Chlepner, 1926, 28–30).

122. Demoulin (1950, 17–21), who scoffs at the Dutch police argument that the agitators of popular revolt were the Brussels bourgeoisie: "That seems to us an *a posteriori* explanation; for the bourgeoisie were really afraid of the people and were too sensible to play the role of sorcerer's apprentices" (p. 17). For the case against interpreting the revolution as "proletarian" in origin, see van Kalken (1930).

123. The revolution was national not only in that it spoke for Belgium versus the Netherlands, but in that it included Liège in Belgium. Liège had not been part of the Austrian Netherlands. The French had annexed it along with Belgium and launched a process of assimilating the two. But as of 1815, the two were still considered separate. However, "in 1830, it had become everywhere a question of only [a single] Belgium" (Stengers, 1951, 105, n.1).

124. King William had offended even conservative Catholics when, in 1825, he sought to require that all Catholic seminarians attend his Collège Philosophique to learn common law and ecclesiastical history (claiming these subjects were not part of theology). By 1829, it had become for the Catholic church "the time of Lamennais and the liberals" (Simon, 1946, 8). Liberals and Catholics had been united by their "common enemy" (p. 10). Jacquemyns (1934, 433) suggests a role as well for romanticism in stimulating both religiosity and nationalism at the same time, and thus lending itself to a

behavior of the Belgian clergy another" (Demoulin, 1950, 143).[125] Walloon anti-clerical liberals were willing to make concessions to the (largely Flemish) Catholics to win their support on the national question.[126]

The issue quickly became not the status quo versus a change, but simply the form of the change. There were three possibilities: separation of the Netherlands and Belgium, but under a king coming from the House of Orange; reunion with France; or independence, with a king selected from elsewhere. The chances of the Prince of Orange, King William's son, were wrecked by the king's bombardment of Antwerp on October 27, which the Belgians saw as a way of aiding Dutch merchants against them. On the other hand, reunionist sentiment was never all that strong, and in any case had very powerful opposition outside Belgium. And both Orangism and reunionism had a very powerful enemy within—the Church, which saw the House of Orange as Protestant, and France as too anticlerical.[127]

But the internal social compromise would have been insufficient to carry the day had not Belgian independence served the larger needs of both Great Britain and France. The Holy Alliance had hoped that Great Britain would not rush to recognize the new regime as it had done with Louis-Philippe. They hoped that

---

Lamennaisian social reformism—which confirms some of the ambiguous consequences of the romantic movement that we previously discussed.

The role of Lamennais in France is a fascinating story. He started life as the most Ultra of the Ultras. He was so Ultramontane in his logic that he ended up seeing the monarchy, linked to Gallicanism, as the real enemy. He thereupon sought common cause with "the enemy of despotism, liberty. Once he ha[d] suggested this startling alliance, it quickly captivate[d] him," and he began to argue a historical congruence between the two, seeing both the sixteenth-century Catholic League in France and the Vendée uprising during the French Revolution as examples of such a congruence. It was in fact the Belgian situation that allowed him to develop his own ideas and foreshadowed his own further "drift to the left" (Mellon, 1958, 189). By 1832, when Pope Gregory XVI, in *Mirari Vos,* condemned liberalism, the separation of Church and state, and the link of religion to liberty, Lamennais was ready to "sacrifice the Church to democracy" (Ponteil, 1968, 308).

125. Although this was true before and during the Belgian revolution, the situation then began to change. As Lamennais and the Lamennaisians drifted leftward, the Church applied some brakes, and the Catholics began to play a moderating role in the nationalist revolution (see Guichen, 1917, 255).

Upon the publication of *Mirari Vos,* the Church succeeded in ending the alliance with the liberals. The Church in Belgium began to argue that there was a difference between the Catholic liberalism of Lamennais and the liberal Catholicism for which they stood. That is, they were not primarily liberals, but primarily Catholics, and if they accepted a separation of Church and state, it could only be as a *pis aller.* This is known as the teaching of the School of Malines (see Simon, 1959, 416). But though this was crucial for the future internal politics of Belgium as an independent state, the fact is that this pullback from liberalism was too late. Belgium had been created as a liberal state, divided between anticlerical liberals and Catholic liberals. And so it remained throughout the nineteenth century.

126. This process of compromise, primarily on the school issue, had already started in 1828 (see Renouvin, 1954, 62).

127. For a detailed account of this choice between the three options, see Stengers (1951).

British commercial links with Holland might induce them to take a hard line. They assumed as well that Great Britain would fear renewed French expansionism (see Guichen, 1917, 172 and passim).[128] They failed to understand the dynamism of the emerging British-French model, and how an independent Belgium, industrialized and liberal, would in fact consolidate it. "The idea of the 'liberal alliance' [was] from the 1830s on a constant theme of liberal journalism in London and Paris" (Lichtheim, 1969, 42).The French proclaimed the principle of "nonintervention" to dissuade the Prussian troops from intervening at the end of August, and got the British to concur.[129] "The confident relations of Great Britain and France in the first days of October 1830 were of paramount importance in keeping the peace" (Demoulin, 1950, 127)[130] and permitted thereby the declaration of independence by the National Congress on November 18. On November 24, the congress excluded all consideration of a king from the House of Orange. But at the very moment that Russia was mobilizing to send troops, the Polish insurrection broke out on November 29. The tsar was in effect restrained twice from intervention. Earlier, the opposition of Grand Duke Constantine and Foreign Minster Count Nesslerode had delayed action. They had counseled prudence, the grand duke fearing the decimation of the Polish army, his "private domain." And now the Polish uprising definitively "saved Belgium from intervention and perhaps Europe from war" (Guyot, 1926, 64). Indeed, the very mobilization by the tsar was itself an element in the Polish uprising, the Polish officers fearing decimation (see Morley, 1952, 412–414).[131] On January 15, 1831, Lafayette said: "Gentlemen, the war has been prepared against us. Poland was to form the advance-guard; the advance-guard has turned against the main army" (cited in Morley, 1952, 415).

128. It was not entirely absurd. The French attitude toward an independent Belgium was highly ambiguous. They supported it at the time, but Jean-Baptiste Nothomb believed that, except for Louis-Philippe and Guizot, most considered its "existence transitive" (Stengers, 1981, 29, n. 1). Michelet called Belgium "an English invention" (cited on p. 7). And as late as 1859, the French minister in Belgium called Belgium a "nationality by agreement [nationalité de convention]" (p. 8).

129. Talleyrand, in presenting his credentials to the king of England, took up the theme of nonintervention that Canning had once used as an expedient. "And thus from a momentary political expedient Canning had borrowed from Monroe [relating to the independences in Latin America] . . . , Talleyrand pretended to make a general and permanent law of interstate relations" (Guyot, 1901, 585).

130. See also Betley (1960, 245): "The views originating in London and Paris supplied the basis for the existence of the Belgian State, in spite of any differences on this account between the two governments."

131. Indeed, the Polish uprising then had repercussions within Russia itself. The Poles encouraged the Cadet conspiracy. They tendered the slogan "For your freedom and ours" as a gesture to the Cadets. "On the day that the Sejm voted the dethronement of Nicholas as King of Poland (January 25, 1831) the Cadet League organized an elaborate funeral demonstration to honor the memory of the five Russian Decembrists who had perished on the gallows. Banners inscribed with the words 'For your freedom and ours' were carried in the procession" (p. 415).

The Polish uprising thus marked the end of all possibility of Russian intervention against Belgium. To be sure, it did Poland itself little good. When Great Britain's prime minister, Lord Grey, received the Polish envoy, Prince Leon Sapieha, at the beginning of 1831, the latter reminded him of a pamphlet he had written on behalf of Poland. "Grey said he had not changed in principle; but in view of the existing danger that the French would be driven by public opinion to annex Belgium, Britain must have an ally capable of counteracting such a move. This could only be Russia" (Betley, 1960, 89).

The cynicism was de rigueur. It does, however, confirm the crucial difference between Belgium and Poland—the role that Belgium, but not Poland, could potentially play in consolidating the British-French model. Buonarroti at least was clear as to what had happened: Belgium, under the king finally chosen, Leopold I, had joined Great Britain and France to constitute the "bulwarks of that constitutional monarchy based on a parliamentary system and the broad consent of the middle classes," which he denounced as the "Order of Egoism" (Eisenstein, 1959, 86). Metternich was equally clear. In a letter to Count Nesselrode, he wrote: "My most secret thought is that old Europe is at the beginning of the end. . . . New Europe, on the other hand, is not yet at its beginning. Between the end and the beginning there will be chaos" (cited by Silva, 1917, 44).

Evans (1983, 200) calls this the "natural watershed in the history of European diplomacy"—autocracies in the East, liberal constitutionalism in the West.[132] It served as the material basis for that new cultural concept, the "West," which was developed precisely in the period between 1815 and 1848, in part by Auguste Comte, in part by various Russian theorists who looked longingly and in frustration at this "specific form of civilization" (Weill, 1930, 547). The concept of a West that was militarily strong and economically dominant, and which laid claim to the banner of individual freedom against an economically backward, "unfree East," would become the pattern for the rest of the nineteenth and twentieth centuries.

What Belgium had over Poland was its geographical location in northwestern Europe, combined with an already developed industrial base. It could therefore be included in the expanded core; indeed, it was needed as part of the enlarged locus of high-technology production required by a growing world-economy.[133] Belgium would recover quickly from its transitory economic difficulties caused by the tur-

---

132. See also Seton-Watson (1937, 151): "[T]he result [of the unrest in Europe in the 1830s] has been to divide Europe quite definitely into two camps—the Eastern Powers, as exponents of autocracy, . . . and the Liberal West, resting on constitutional progress at home and eager . . . to promote it in Spain and Portugal against the ferocious reaction of the Carlists and Dom Miguel."

133. Pollard (1973, 640) sees Belgium as still playing a semiperipheral role. Discussing Belgium's role in the period 1815–1865, he says that "some firms, the best and toughest, survived [in the face of British industrialization]. Their world lay between the more advanced British on one side and the more

bulence of a political revolution,[134] to be sagely governed by a king who would set himself the objective of "working at the Franco-British entente" (Ponteil, 1968, 327).

With France and Belgium in secure hands, Great Britain could make its own political adjustments with some ease. The story of reform started in fact not in 1830 during the Whig government of Lord Grey but in 1829 when the Duke of Wellington was presiding over a Tory government that was the nearest thing Great Britain had to an Ultra regime. The issue was not the enfranchisement of the urban middle classes but the "emancipation" of the Catholics. The question of Catholic emancipation had been under parliamentary discussion since 1778, when the penal laws were abrogated.[135] It was originally a question of extending civil rights to a minority—one element in the gradual liberalization of the political system. The Act of Union in 1800, however, complicated the issue. Once Ireland was juridically incorporated into the United Kingdom, extending Catholic rights could be seen as "the necessary completion" of the act. But it could also be seen as a way station to its reversal, one element in a possible decolonization of the British Empire.

At the same time, two other elements entered the picture. The first was the Protestant revival of the eighteenth century, which, although it was itself placing pressures on the Anglican Establishment, added a strong voice, which was "on the whole opposed to [Catholic] emancipation" (Hexter, 1936, 313). The second, which went in the other direction, was the French Revolution. Opposition to the Revolution led to a change in how Catholics were viewed in Great Britain: "Catholicism, no longer a soul-devouring ogre, was a virtuous Atlas, propping the tottering world against the onslaughts of a godless sansculottism" (Hexter, 1936, 301).[136]

---

backward Europe on the other. Belgium was the territory which became keyed first and most successfully into such an intermediate role, and Belgian industrial history can be fully understood only within this dual relationship." I think Pollard understates Belgian economic strength, especially after 1834.

134. Henderson (1954, 125) notes that "Belgium secured her political independence at the cost of a serious dislocation of her economy." Chlepner (1926, 57) also says that "the Revolution of 1830 provoked . . . a profound economic crisis." But by 1834, Belgium was beginning a great industrial expansion based on the construction of railroads. And the revival of Antwerp enabled her to become a locus for growing British-German trade. Furthermore, Belgium could then profit from being the latecomer. "Where French and German iron masters had good reasons for persevering with the older techniques, in Belgium there was every reason to convert to the new iron technology as soon as possible. Iron rail was the basic product for most of the big new Belgian forges after 1834" (Milward and Saul, 1977, 443).

135. The need to obtain Irish recruits and Quebec support in the war with the Thirteen Colonies in North America no doubt played a role (see Hexter, 1936, 297–298). The 1778 act was the immediate cause of the Gordon Riots by Protestants (see Stevenson, 1979, 76–90).

136. One immediate result was the Catholic Dissenters Relief Bill of 1791.

Still, it was undoubtedly the Irish lower classes who forced the issue, and their actions reflected not an urge for integration into the British political system but the beginnings of a popular Irish nationalism:

> It was rather that in Catholic emancipation [the Irish lower classes] foresaw vaguely the satisfaction of many desires, the expropriation of the Protestant landlords, and the division of land among themselves—in a word, the restitution to Catholics of the soil that had belonged to their ancestors. (Halévy, 1949a, 191)

By 1829 the nationalism had taken hold sufficiently that Ireland seemed poised to rebel. "At least so it seemed to the Duke of Wellington" (Reynolds, 1954, 30).[137] Required, he thought, to choose between emancipation and revolution, the Duke of Wellington—the Iron Duke, ferociously opposed to emancipation—"decided upon one of his strategic retreats. He wrung from the king permission"(Reynolds, 1954, 30)[138] to put forward a measure for unqualified emancipation.

Emancipation was to change the life of the Irish lower classes far less than they had hoped.[139] No matter! Wellington's retreat had the consequence that "it made reform respectable" (Moore, 1961, 17), and at the same time it had the final twist of turning the British Ultras themselves into partisans of electoral reform. This was the same reaction that the French Ultras in the Restoration had had in the face of what they considered Louis XVIII's insufficiently autocratic stance. Wellington and Peel were seen by the British Ultras to have turned out to be unreliable. Since they had been supported by the representatives of the rotten boroughs, these Ultras now argued, "paradoxically, but not irrationally," that only "a rational and widely-based electorate could be relied upon to rally round the 'No Popery'

137. Wellington had some clear indications of Irish Catholic political sentiments. The leader of the Catholic Association, Daniel O'Connell, was elected to Parliament from County Clare in 1828 against the newly appointed president of the Board of Trade, Vesey Fitzgerald, by a vote of 2,057 to 982. "Emancipation was inevitable. But its enactment in 1829 rather than five or ten years later is attributable directly to the Irish situation and in particular to the [Catholic] association" (p. 164).

138. He took counsel from his lieutenant, Robert Peel, who would emerge later as the architect of the repeal of the Corn Laws. Of course, they also had to persuade Parliament. Thomis and Holt (1977, 82) call this "a triumph for the new style of political campaigning and organization." Compare these ("enlightened") Tories with the Whig leadership. Halévy (1950, 255–56) observes that in the 1830s, "all over the world, in Ireland, Belgium, Poland, Canada, and Newfoundland, the malcontents, the clients of the advanced Liberals, were Catholics." Yet by 1838, these Whigs "had betrayed Poland, placed Lower Canada under martial law, and returned the Catholics of Luxemburg and Limburg to a Calvinist power [the Netherlands]." Similarly, Holland (1913, 77) acknowledges: "During [the Whigs'] decade of power [1830–1841; this was in fact interrupted from November 1834 to April 1835], Whig governments did not substantially change the national system of Corn Laws, Colonial Preference, Navigation Acts, and high protection duties upon manufactures." The Whigs almost never had the courage of their supposed liberalism. This is not really surprising, since "Whiggery always bore the stamp of aristocracy. . . . A 'Whig democrat' was a sport, not a genus" (Southgate, 1965, xv–xvi).

139. See Reynolds (1954, 168): "In Ireland itself the immediate effects of the measure seemed scarcely proportional to the energy and enthusiasm that had gone into six years of turmoil."

flag" (Evans, 1983, 206).[140] Wellington's timely retreat on Catholic emancipation ensured that there would be nothing like a July Days scenario, but the outcome turned out to be substantially the same, for it was equally the culmination of what were essentially parallel processes in both countries.

Catholic emancipation may have calmed things down in Ireland, but the failure of the harvest in England that same year revived the sense of turbulence. In the winter of 1830, unemployment in rural areas had become "widespread" and was followed by the failure of country banks, leading to agricultural riots (see Gash, 1935, 91). It was at this point, with new elections pending, that the July Revolution (the July Days) broke out. The reaction, as we have already noted, was mixed. The radicals were "triumphant." They saw July 1830 as "the renewal of 1789." The liberal center (the Whig aristocrats, the urban middle class notables) were hoping that the July Revolution would turn out to be "at once liberal and conservative, would in fact revive not 1789 or 1792 but 1688 and thus be a French tribute to the political wisdom of England" (Halévy, 1950, 5–6).

In any case, Wellington lost the election, which Halévy (1935, 53) sees as the "natural outcome of the fall of the last of the Kings of France."[141] Though July may or may not have hurt Wellington, we have already seen that Wellington was not in fact hostile to Louis-Philippe. As Louis Blanc (1842, 2:4) remarked at the time, if the Whigs embraced July as the "triumph of French liberalism," the Tories did so because they were seeking to maintain the "supremacy . . . in Europe" of Great Britain:

> The English aristocracy, like all aristocracies, is quite clairvoyant and coherent in seeking to accomplish its aims. It knew that, under Charles X, there was a serious

140. The first "thoroughgoing reform bill" was introduced by one of these Ultras, the Marquis of Blandford, in 1830. It called for "the transference of rotten borough seats to the counties, the disqualification of non-resident voters, the expulsion of Crown office-holders from Parliament, the payment of MP's and a general ratepayer franchise." Of course, there is more than one way of looking at the fact that a Parliament filled with representatives of rotten boroughs voted reforms. Halévy (1949a, 145, 147) puts a sympathetic gloss upon it: "Thus the very corruption of the electorate corrected to some extent the vices of the system and afforded a means by which the new classes of society could obtain seats in Parliament and the representation of their interests in the House. . . . [Voting reform bills twice in succession] proves that, unlike the House of Lords, the unreformed House of Commons already represented to a large extent the opinion of the country"—or at least that of "the bankers, merchants, and business men of all kinds," of whose membership in the House of Commons Halévy is speaking.

141. Gash (1956) contests Halévy's argument of a direct influence of the July Revolution on the British elections. He says that by the time news reached Great Britain on August 3, 60 of 120 members had already been returned. He admits that the remaining 60 included the quarter of the seats that were most contested but says that reform had become a significant issue before July, and that attributing a direct impact of the July Days on British opinion was primarily a retrospective claim of radical spokesmen. This assumes, however, that the impact of the July Revolution operated by affecting who was elected rather than by affecting the positions of those who were in fact elected.

possibility that France would take over the left bank of the Rhine and deliver Constantinople to the Russians. It knew that the Duke of Orleans was English in his tastes and inclinations.

The contagion of 1830 was clearly spreading. Still, reform might never have come, any more in Great Britain than in France or Belgium, had there not been a popular push. The new Whig government of Lord Grey reacted to the continuing agrarian disturbances by enforcing laws "with the utmost severity," bringing the riots and the arson successfully to an end (Halévy, 1950, 15). Once the riots were under control, Lord Grey moved his reform bill. When it carried only most narrowly, Parliament was dissolved, and a stronger reform majority was returned. But when the House of Lords voted down the readopted reform bill in October 1831, urban disturbances began. The middle-class reform leaders, like Francis Place, struggled to remain in the lead. Place launched the famous slogan "To stop the Duke [of Wellington], go for gold." This meant withdrawing private funds from the banks. The suggestion of armed resistance to a new Tory ministry was bruited, although "a revolution led by Francis Place would have been an incongruous phenomenon" (Evans, 1983, 211). Nonetheless, the threat worked. Wellington abandoned his opposition, the king promising Grey that, if need be, he would create new peers. "The test never came" (Thomis and Holt, 1977, 91, 98).[142]

Both supporters and opponents of reform agreed that at that moment Great Britain had been "standing on the edge of a precipice of disorder" (Fraser, 1969, 38). Rudé asserts there was no English revolution in 1830 because there was no "self-conscious working-class movement" and because the occasional angers of the laborers "lacked solid middle-class support" (Rudé, 1967, 102). But is this the way to analyze what happened? In response to the boast that the 1832 reforms were accomplished "without an insurrection," John Stuart Mill, writing in 1849 (p. 12), asks: "But was it without the *fear* of an insurrection? If there had been no chance of an uprising, would the House of Lords have waived their opposition, or the Duke of Wellington have thrown up the game in despair?"[143] The answer is almost surely not.

142. "And so the modern parliamentary reformers had their way, and the precedent they had established by extorting concessions under the threat of armed resistance was to be an acute embarrassment to them when the Chartists began to demand further measures of parliamentary reform and to employ similar tactics for their achievement" (Thomis and Holt, 1977, 99).

143. Ward's analysis (1973, 56) is quite different: "One does not have to search for Methodism or other restraints on revolution. A revolutionary situation did not exist. Reform succeeded because its supporters were largely elected at the last unreformed election, because Wellington was unable to form a ministry, because the peerage did not care to be swamped by new creations and because careful Whig manipulation of the Bill's clauses ensured a preponderantly bourgeois electorate." All true, but mostly intervening variables. It doesn't gainsay the factor adduced by Mill: fear of insurrection.

This does not mean, however, that the putative insurrectionaries accomplished their goals. For once again the process was taken in hand by the centrist liberals. The "primary purpose" of the Reform Bill was to "rally middle-class support round the aristocratic system" (Gash, 1979, 147).[144] The Whigs "made sure—to use their own language—that the 'age of improvement' would not be suddenly transformed into an 'age of disruption.'" For this, they needed a bill, any bill, that seemed to include the middle classes in the polity.[145] Even John Bright, who wanted much more, would say: "If the bill was not a good bill, . . . it was a great bill when it passed" (Briggs, 1959, 259–260).

The reforms had some unanticipated consequences for British politics. "[E]nfranchised Scotland and Catholic Ireland became powerful reinforcements for the Whig-liberal parliamentary strength" (Gash, 1979, 154). The Celtic fringe would be the bulwark first of Gladstone and Lloyd George, and then later of Labor. At the same time, the Conservatives could shift from being merely the "party of the Crown and the Peerage" to being the "party of England" (Halévy, 1950, 182). Still, it could be argued that it was as much by integrating the Celtic fringe as by integrating the middle classes that the reforms of 1829–1832 established the national liberal state in Great Britain.

In addition, by eliminating rotten boroughs, the bill weakened the power of the ministries vis-à-vis the individual members, who now needed to be responsive to their constituencies. This would be undone fifty years later by the development of centralized parties, which brought the members and their constituencies back under control. In the meantime, this weakening of an autocratic, if ministe-

---

As Southgate (1965, 21–22) puts it very well: "The only argument for extensive Reform, perhaps the only argument for *any* Reform, which all Grey's ministers could consciously utter in unison was that it was necessary for the safety, influence and reputation of the governing class. Convinced that their task was essentially conservative, a rescue operation on behalf of rank and property, the authors of the Bill were able to play the role which Whig hagiography ascribed to heroes of old. . . . They were endeavouring to detach from the ranks of those opposed to the constitution the middle classes, a large inchoate body of people distinguished from 'mere mechanics' and labourers by wealth, property, education, by 'respectability,' and therefore qualified to enter the *pays légal*. To the masses the Reform Bill offered nothing. It was an undemocratic, and anti-democratic, measure."

144. And of course, it worked: "The validity of the Whig claim to have detached the middle classes from lower-class radicalism was never more clearly demonstrated than in the years 1831–6. . . . The achievement of parliamentary reform was followed by a collapse in the membership and finances of the London National Political Union" (Gash, 1979, 191).

145. Once again, we shouldn't exaggerate. The Reform Bill doubled the electorate from a half a million to a million (see Halévy, 1950, 27). But, as Clark (1962, 7) argues, "the middle class, however defined, [did not] dominate the country after 1832. Certainly they were deemed to be politically important at the time of that Reform Bill, and that Bill was proposed and passed largely as a recognition of their importance; but after the Bill the final control in politics still lay without question in the hands of the old governing classes, the nobility and the gentry."

rial, center actually caused "dismay" to many radicals, liberals, and even Whigs, because they found new reform legislation often harder, not easier, to obtain. It was no longer sufficient to persuade a few men at the very top to make timely, essential changes. The interests of a much larger, but still quite narrow-minded, group had to be taken into account:

> The fondness of the Benthamites for Wellington and Peel in 1829 and 1830 may, indeed, be extremely significant. If history followed a logical progression (which it never does), it might be argued that the first Reform Act did more to delay such measures as the Repeal of the Corn Laws than it did to accelerate them. (Moore, 1961, 34)

If the middle classes got less than they might have wanted, they did get honor, and they would be turbulent no more. However, all the working classes got, in Great Britain as in France, was "disillusionment" (Briggs, 1956, 70) and a weakened position for the next round of battle.[146]

By 1830/1832, a liberal state governed by a liberal center had been fabricated in Great Britain, France, and Belgium—the three most industrialized states of the epoch. Collectively, the three formed the economic and cultural core of the world-system. The model of the liberal state was intended for their use and for the use of those others who were aspiring to achieve comparable prosperity and stability. The Holy Alliance and the Ultras in the core had been checked; indeed, they had been routed. The conservatives and the radicals had begun their de facto transformation into mere variants of centrist liberalism. If the Ultras were effectively neutralized, the insurrectionary revolutionaries had scarcely been able to achieve any political presence whatsoever, especially in the three model liberal states.

The machinery of the liberal state now needed to be developed. The process of electoral reform was still timid. But it had been launched, and it would roll on inexorably until it reached its peak as universal suffrage within a century. Suffrage was accompanied by the extension of civil rights to all citizens—even subjects, even residents. What had not yet quite begun was the second great pillar of the liberal state in its taming of the dangerous classes—state protection of the economically and socially weak. This process would be launched in the next period—that of the consolidation of the liberal states between 1830 and 1875.

---

146. See Southgate (1965, 24): "The social 'grand strategy' of the Reform Bill received its vindication in the Chartist fiasco of 1848, when Britain with her reformed constitution rode the storm unleashed by a new revolution in France."

Lechard (?), *Insurrection du Lyon, 9–14 avril 1834*. The strike of the *canuts* in Lyon deterio-
rated into an armed confrontation between the workers and the forces of order, resulting in a
massacre of the workers. The flag the workers are flying reads: "Live working or die fighting."
(Courtesy of Bibliothèque National de France)

3

The Liberal State and Class Conflict, 1830–1875

British state intervention was growing like a rolling snowball throughout the [nineteenth] century which most historians were inclined to characterize as one during which Government kept its hands off business.
—J. BARTLETT BREBNER (1948, 108)

[R]evolutions merely happen, they neither fail nor succeed.
—JOHN PLAMENATZ (1952, XII)

The struggle of the Orders suffuses or rather creates all this history. . . . Facts don't just disappear because ministries and parties want them to or find it useful that they do so.
—FRANÇOIS GUIZOT (1820, 6)

During the first half of the nineteenth century, socialism as a concept was still not separate from "bourgeois democracy" as a concept or, as Labrousse (1949b, 7) says, "Jacobinism and socialism remained muddled in political life." In some sense, it probably remained for at least a century thereafter that a full distinction of the two concepts did not exist. Nonetheless, liberalism (which seems to me a better locution than "bourgeois democracy") and socialism began to have diverging trajectories as political options after 1830. Indeed, as Hobsbawm (1962, 284) argues:

> Practical liberals . . . shied away from political democracy. . . . The social discontents, revolutionary movements, and the socialist ideologues of the post-Napoleonic era intensified this dilemma [of relying upon the majority to carry out the dictates of reason] and the 1830 Revolution made it acute. Liberalism and democracy appeared to be adversaries rather than allies.[1]

The concept of class and class conflict was not a contribution of socialist ideologues, much less of Karl Marx. It is a Saint-Simonian idea, developed and

---

1. Hobsbawm continues (p. 285): "While the liberal ideology thus lost its original confident swoop, . . . a new ideology, socialism, reformulated the old eighteenth-century verities. Reason, science, and

pursued by Guizot as part of the liberal project.[2] Saint-Simon's view of the class structure in the modern industrial world was that there were *three* classes: the property owners, the propertyless, and the savants. He saw the class conflict between the "industrials" (those who work) and the idlers as a transitional phase, to be superseded by a harmonious society of productive industrial classes under the aegis of the savants, a meritocratic vision in which the old aristocracy of birth would be replaced by an aristocracy of talent (Manuel, 1956; Iggers, 1958b).[3] For Guizot, the concept of class was an essential element in his efforts to "legitimate the political aspirations of the bourgeoisie" (Fossaert, 1955, 60).[4]

---

progress were its firm foundation." The year 1830 marks "a breakpoint" for Coornaert as well (1950, 13), and "a point of departure" in the history of the proletariat. He, too, notes (p. 26) the adoption of eighteenth-century philosophy: "faith in reason, in science, a simplistic faith in the endless progress of humanity."

2. This is spelled out quite clearly and quite early from the Marxist perspective by Plechanow (1902–1903). Nor is this all: the classical Marxist definition of socialism in the *Critique of the Gotha Program*—"from each according to his ability, to each according to his works"—is in fact taken directly from the *Doctrine de Saint-Simon* (1830, 70): "*A chacun selon sa capacité; à chaque capacité selon ses œuvres*" (cited in Manuel, 1956, 227). To be sure, Marx specifies that this is an interim formula. In the subsequent period of "communism," it will be "to each according to his needs."

3. Iggers originally taxed Saint-Simon with being "totalitarian" (1958a, 3) but recanted in a later book, in which he preferred to talk of the conservative bases of Saint-Simonian thought: "Like de Maistre, whom [the Saint-Simonians] deeply admired and unlike other advocates of the theory of progress, they were convinced that man possessed '*penchants vicieux*' and that these propensities made necessary the existence of a state which restricted and regulated the liberty of the individual" (1970, 689). Stark (1943, 55) calls him a "prophet of the bourgeoisie." See also Brunet, who emphasizes Saint-Simon's clarity about what he was against and his vagueness about what he was for, characterizing him (1925, 9) as "Oedipus before the sphinx," looking at the nineteenth century before him, trying to divine the future. See also Hayek (1952, 156–188), who traces his influence in three directions— on the young Hegelians and post-1848 socialism, on "continental capitalism," and on Comte and positivist sociology. And G. D. H. Cole (1953, 1:43) is severe: "There was, in all this, no element of democracy."

4. Fossaert continues the exposition of Guizot's thought: "The bourgeoisie which asserts itself and aspires to dominate the State does not fear to turn to revolutionary methods; 1830 is proof of that. Nor does it fear scientific theories. It is conscious of being a class in struggle and accepts that it be defined in this way." As late as 1847, when Guizot was pursuing a much more politically conservative line, he was being vilified by his opponents for this espousal of the doctrine of class. In the Chamber of Deputies, one Garnier-Pagès declared: "There are no classes in this country. . . . And you, M. Guizot, this is one of the most detestable theories you espouse, that there are different classes, that there is the bourgeoisie and the poor, the bourgeoisie and the people. . . . You wanted to divide us, but you will not succeed; . . . in France there are only French citizens." Daumard (1963, xi), who cites this peroration, notes that Garnier-Pagès, almost immediately, continues his address to the Chamber thus: "I see here many bourgeois." At least, the Chamber laughed.

But in 1830, Guizot and his friends succeeded, as they were simultaneously succeeding in Great Britain,[5] in establishing a form of middle-class rule "as a permanent *juste milieu* or golden mean between the extremes of revolution and reaction" (Starzinger, 1965, viii).[6] The Chamber of Deputies on August 7, 1830, suppressed the Preamble to the Charter of 1814 "as wounding the national dignity by appearing to *grant* to Frenchmen rights which belong to them essentially" (Collins, 1970, 90). The liberals politically and the *grande bourgeoisie* socially had at last won their *droit de cité*.[7]

Since, in addition, this coincided with a period of accelerating economic and social change, the most urgent problems facing France and Great Britain had now become the "social problems" of industrialism, and especially those of the "new proletariat, the horrors of uncontrolled break-neck urbanization" (Hobsbawm, 1962, 207). Class conflict would therefore come to mean something different from what Saint-Simon and Guizot had had in mind. The Revolution of 1830 itself came at a moment of particular economic difficulty for the workers (high unemployment, unusually high wheat prices).[8] It provided evidence of the utility of political

5. Gash (1977, 39) notes that Lord Liverpool's Cabinet of peers was in fact made up of sons and grandsons of the middle class. In 1835, Sir Robert Peel, giving a speech in the City, referred to the fact that his father had been a cotton manufacturer. "Did I feel that by any means a reflection on me?. . . . No, but does it not make one, or ought it not to make you, gentlemen, do all you can to reserve to other sons of other cotton-spinners the same opportunities, by the same system of laws under which this country has so long flourished, of arriving by the same honourable means at the like destination?" (cited on p. 71).

6. Guizot "neither rejected nor accepted the Revolution en bloc. . . . The society of 'reason' and 'justice' was the basic philosophic concept with which the Doctrinaires rejected the exclusive claims of either the Revolution or the Ancien Regime" (Starzinger, 1965, 20–21).

7. Both Lhomme (1960, 36) and Pouthas (1962, 258) speak of the substitution of one class for the other as the dominant force. Tudesq (1964, I, 335) cautions us, however, on how we should interpret this phenomenon: "There is no question of denying the supremacy of the *grande bourgeoisie* in the July Monarchy; but it less evicted the old aristocracy than it assimilated it." The social consequences of this shift were nonetheless real, as is attested by the letter the prefect of Paris addressed to the mayors of the various *arrondissements* shortly after the Revolution of 1830, in which he discussed necessary preparations for possible festivities at the palace: "You will no doubt find it appropriate . . . to draw up in advance a list of persons in each *arrondissement* who might be included in the honor of receiving invitations from the King. Eminent merit, wealth honorably acquired, a justly famous name, great industry, such . . . are the conditions which, in addition to an honorable life, should guide you in the choices you make. Please therefore list the Magistrates, the large property-owners, the bankers, the *agents de change,* the notaries, the attorneys, the manufacturers, the military officers, the artists, the men of letters residing in your district, five or six of the most notable persons in their profession." This letter is cited by Daumard (1963, 305), who comments: "It is no longer a question of ancestry, except in passing and in order not to exclude anyone with 'a justly famous name,' and even then this is not necessarily one that is traditional."

8. "In creating discontent among the population, in habituating it to riots, the crisis created the revolutionary ambiance" (Gonnet, 1955, 291).

uprising and served to stimulate workers' consciousness, a sense of having common interest "solely as proletarians," a sense of the "dignity of the worker" (Festy, 1908, 330).[9] The liberals perceived this change immediately. Thiers said in a statement to the Chamber of Deputies: "The day after the Revolution of July, we saw our duty to moderate it. In effect it was no longer liberty, but order which was in danger" (cited in Bezucha, 1974, 137).[10]

The next few years were to see worker unrest of a new intensity and quality in both France and Great Britain. It has been increasingly noted in the literature on strikes and workers' unrest how much of this activity was that of "artisans" as opposed to "workers." Although the line is not always as clear as some seem to think, in general those referred to as "artisans" had more technical skills, higher real income, and more workplace autonomy than other kinds of workers. Many of these "artisans" were members of organizations that had been in existence long before the nineteenth century, and which functioned to advance the welfare of their members through social support and mutual help. The organizations were hierarchical and built around rituals.

These organizations were the only ones permitted at all in the periods when trade-union organization had been strictly forbidden,[11] and then only under the careful surveillance of the authorities. In the changing political situation after 1830, however, even mutual aid societies began to take on new roles, as Sée (1951, 2:199) pointed out: "Many of these societies served . . . to hide veritable *resistance organizations*, hostile to the employers; by creating *auxiliary monetary reserves* (*bourses auxiliaires*), they created funds to support the unemployed and strikers."[12] Thus it could be, as Stearns (1965, 371–372) has argued, that such "artisans" were

9. See also Moss (1975a, 204): "The *Trois Glorieuses* inspired both a revival of the egalitarian ideals of the First Republic and an unprecedented wave of working-class protest."

10. One month after the Revolution of 1830, the *Journal des Débats* warned the middle classes about the rise of proletarians in modern society, comparing them to the barbarians in the Roman Empire (see Daumard, 1963, 515). And one hundred years later, that other liberal, Benedetto Croce (1934, 150), analyzed the Revolution of 1830 in a similar way: "The terms had changed. It was no longer a struggle between liberalism and absolutism, but one between liberalism and democracy, from its moderate to its extreme and socialist form. This struggle, which was the truly present and progressive struggle of the nineteenth century, was developed . . . in the countries that enjoyed liberty."

11. See Wallerstein (1989, 107, 120–121) on the *Loi Le Chapelier* in France and the Anti-Combination Acts in Great Britain.

12. Rudé (1969, 22) argues that the militancy of these associations was visible prior to 1830: "In fact, the events of October–November 1831 cannot be considered to have been a surprise. For the members of the association of heads of silk workshops in Lyon called the *Mutuellisme*, it was not in 1831 that 'the signal of the emancipation of workers was given,' but rather three or four years previously, when their organization was founded [1828]. . . . And throughout the Restoration, the worker's movement, which expressed itself as 'coalitions' and conspiracies, never stopped exhibiting astonishing vitality."

more likely to engage in strike action at this time than the "factory workers," who, being in an even weaker position, were "almost totally quiescent."[13]

The distinction made by many scholars between artisans and factory workers seems to be asserted primarily on the basis of differing workplace organization. But in fact the artisans were usually in "workshops," which were not all that different in structure and even social organization from the rather small "factories" that existed in this era. I suspect the real difference was in the social origins of the two groups of workers. The "artisans" were males, and males who came for the most part from the immediate area. The "factory workers" were largely either women and children (Bezucha, 1974, 35) or "migrants," which included both those who came from rural communities and workers speaking another language.[14]

The most dramatic expression of protest by the "artisans" was that of the *canuts*[15] of Lyon, first in 1831 and then in 1834. The struggles began right after the July Revolution, and included machine destruction and eviction of "foreign" workers.[16] The background to this was an eighteenth-century militancy of journeymen, which had erupted in 1786 in the so-called tuppenny riot (*émeute de deux sous*), in which the journeymen sought to obtain a fixed minimum rate for finished cloth.

13. Tilly on the one hand says that 1830 "made little difference" to workers' politics in the north of France. He talks of the "near-absence of strikes." But on the other hand he tells us that "the increased tempo of industrial conflict during the 1830s and 1840s normalized the strike, at least to some degree" (1986, 262, 263, 265).

14. See Bezucha (1974, 23), who has 1833 statistics for a workers' district in Lyon, showing that, of 3,257 journeymen, only 547 were born in Lyon. The rest were foreigners or from rural communities. "[I]mmigration was the principal factor in Lyon's growth during this period" (p. 158). Aguet (1954, 4) recounts a report in *Constitutionnel* of August 16, 1830, of a march on the Prefecture of Police in Paris, in which the local workers demanded that "foreign" workers ("foreign" included French workers of rural origin) be asked to leave Paris. The prefect refused on the grounds that the presence of the "foreign" workers represented "a competition which undergirds emulation, favors the spirit of improvement, and has contributed considerably to strengthening French industry." Aguet (p. 9) reports similar occurrences in Lyon and Grenoble.

Then, as now, the "foreign" workers were paid less than local workers but were attracted by wages higher than those available to them in their zones of origin. Sée (1924, 494, 498) cites an 1840 study by Villermé with data on Paris workers, which allows him to conclude both that the peasants were attracted by the relatively "high wage levels offered by manufacturing industry" and that, nonetheless, "the existence of the worker seemed quite precarious."

15. *Canut* apparently derives from the word *canette*, meaning "spool," and was the name that had been used in marionette shows since the sixteenth century in Lyon to caricature silk workers in Lyon. Levasseur (1904, 2:7) insists it was "not a term of scorn."

16. "If more jobs were to be made available to Frenchmen, this meant that foreigners in France would have to be expelled by their employers and the state. . . . This issue of expelling foreign workers was one of the principal points of disagreement between the workers and the government during the first months after the July Revolution" (Newman, 1975, 23). See also Bruhat (1952, 1:223), who complains that "the workers did not directly attack either the regime (capitalism) or the men (the capitalists) who were the cause of their suffering."

The ongoing turmoil continued up to the French Revolution and the enactment of the *Loi Le Chapelier*. Bezucha (1974, 11) concludes that "the French Revolution, in fact, broke the momentum created prior to 1789 and may have retarded the development of a workers' movement in Lyon." In the years between 1789 and 1830, however, the relatively stable system of the *compagnon* had been replaced by a more "fluid one of piece-work laborers" (Bezucha, 1974, 46).

Levasseur (1904, 2:6) asks the questions, Why Lyon? Why 1831? His answer is that Lyon was living off a luxury industry, silk, which made it more "sensitive . . . to economic crises and political turmoil." The immediate issue, as in 1786, was a minimum wage, which had been agreed to by the prefect but subsequently revoked by the central government. The first strike was relatively nonpolitical. But discontent continued. There was a strike in Paris in 1832. The atmosphere was more and more politicized, partly by the dissatisfaction of the working classes with the politics of the July Monarchy, partly (at least in Lyon) by the agitation of the Italian nationalist forces. Mazzini's aide-de-camp, General Romorino, was often in Lyon recruiting persons for their attempts to liberate Savoy and Piedmont (Bezucha, 1974, 122). On February 14, 1834, a general strike was called. It did not succeed. The local Republican party was divided in its attitude.[17] A repressive law caused a further reaction by the workers in April, an uprising in which some three hundred were killed. This attempt came to be viewed as a "landmark in the history of the European working class" (Bezucha, 1974, 124). This time the repression by the authorities was definitive. There was a "monster trial" in 1835, which the government used "to get rid of the republicans."[18] Faced with the beginnings of a serious class struggle by the urban working class, the liberal state initially reacted as repressively as did its predecessors.

The story was not very different in Great Britain. The moral equivalent of the July Revolution was the Reform Bill of 1832. Great Britain did not know "three glorious days" of "revolution." Instead, there was a parliamentary battle in which the revolution was "voted" in, on the crucial second reading in 1831, by a single vote.

---

17. How much support the workers got from the Republicans is a matter of controversy. Bezucha (1974, 171) plays it down: "In the last analysis, Republican participation in the Lyon uprising of 1834 was a result of the weakness, not the strength, of the local party." It was a workers' revolt, says Bezucha, not a political one as the government asserted. Bruhat also wishes to emphasize the primacy of workers' class consciousness (1952, I, 262). Levasseur (1904, 2:819) argues the opposite: the Republicans "were taking their revenge" for the deception of 1830 by supporting the 1834 uprising, whereas that of 1831 had in fact been nonpolitical. Dolléans (1947, 1:97) reverses the issue, saying that it was the workers who insisted on keeping their struggle limited to their immediate concerns: "They feared compromising their demands by working together with the republicans. They wanted to be prudent."

18. Plamenatz (1952, 55), who adds: "or, to come nearer to the truth, drove them underground." What followed, he says, were "the years of silence." See also Dolléans (1947, 1:107) on how the government used the strike as a pretext to suppress the republicans.

THE LIBERAL STATE AND CLASS CONFLICT

When, despite this, the bill was defeated in committee, Parliament was dissolved, and a pro-reform Parliament elected. At the time there was great awareness of events in France, and the possibilities of "worse" happening. Macaulay's speech on March 2, 1831, in favor of reform makes clear the reasoning of those who advocated it:

> Turn where we may, within, around, the voice of great events is proclaiming to us, Reform, that you may preserve. . . . Renew the youth of the State. Save property divided against itself. Save the multitude, endangered by its own ungovernable passions. Save the aristocracy, endangered by its own unpopular power. Save the greatest, and fairest, and most highly civilised country that ever existed, from calamities that may in a few days sweep away all the rich heritage of so many ages of wisdom and glory. The danger is terrible. The time is short. If this bill should be rejected, I pray to God that none of those who concur in rejecting it ever remember their votes with unavailing remorse, amidst the wreck of laws, the confusion of ranks, the spoliation of property, and the dissolution of social orders.[19]

Macaulay's argument was heard. And, exactly as in France, once the middle strata had won their *droit de cité,* attention turned immediately to containing the claims of the working classes. Chartism, "much the most important movement of working men" (Evans, 1983, 215)[20] and a continuation of the old radical reform movement, was contemporaneous with and strongest during the great industrial depression from 1837 to 1843. It gained considerable notoriety and seemed a real menace to the authorities for several years. A large part of Chartist ranks were drawn from members of trade societies.[21] But it also had support from middle-class radicals (Rowe, 1967, 85). The Chartist movement existed simultaneously with, and was in direct rivalry with, the free-trade movement of the Anti–Corn Law League. Halévy (1947, 9) raises the specter of a potential for "civil war." Briggs (1959, 312) speaks of the two movements as representing "a contrast between two segments of a divided society." Gash (1965, 2) says of the "Movement" ("a phrase borrowed from Continental politics") that it "had an undeniable air of class war."[22]

19. *Miscellaneous Writings and Speeches* (popular ed., p. 492), cited in Fay (1920, 33–34).

20. Ward (1973, 7) calls Chartism the "first working-class political party."

21. See Prothero (1971, 203, 209): "For what successes London Chartism achieved were due to its winning the adhesion of sections of the most important trades in the metropolis, such as carpenters, stonemasons, tailors, and shoemakers." Nonetheless, Prothero argues that Chartism received stronger and more consistent support from "the less strong, though organized, trades." The so-called aristocratic trades tended to join in only when their own interests were directly threatened by legislation such as the Masters and Servants Bill in 1844 (see Prothero, 1969, 84).

22. For Jones (1983, 57), this was the consequence of the disillusionment following 1832: "The Reform Bill was regarded as the great betrayal of what had been thought of as a common struggle [of middle-class radicals and workers]. The measures of the Whig government which followed it—the Irish Coercion Bill, the rejection of the Ten Hours' Bill, the Municipalities Acts and the New Poor

However, Chartism, after flaring up, fizzled. As of 1843 it was on the decline. Partly, there wasn't enough social support in Great Britain for a movement that was primarily and overtly a workers' movement. Partly, the movement also could not agree on the degree to which violence was a legitimate weapon. And partly, there was the "Irish factor": the working class in England was no longer just English, but English and Irish, and issues of Irish nationalism became intertwined with class issues. When Feargus O'Connor took the leadership of the Chartists, the confusion became too great, and the movement was "compromised."[23] Perhaps most important of all, times got a bit better, and Sir Robert Peel's program of economic reform removed some of the discontent.[24] In the end, class warfare did not do much better at this time in Great Britain than it had in France.

The internal problems of Great Britain and France never became large enough that those powers could not concentrate attention on the geopolitics of the world-system. The July Revolution, repeated and confirmed by the independence of Belgium and the Reform Act of 1832, was to have an immediate effect on Europe. Whereas the relations of Great Britain and France between 1815 and 1830 had been correct, and those countries often found themselves on similar sides of world issues, the heritage of the two-century struggle for hegemony continued to ensure enough mutual suspicion to preserve a degree of distance. The July Revolution overcame that, affecting even the Tory government of Wellington before the Reform Bill was enacted. Europe now entered the era of the entente cordiale, a marriage perhaps not of love but certainly of reason, one that would survive all subsequent quarrels until at least 1945. The term itself was probably coined by Palmerston in 1831, although it did not come into official use until 1842 (Guyot, 1926, 220; Halévy, 1950, 3:73, n. 1). The geopolitical basis of the alliance was clear. "As a Liberal power, France was [after the July Revolution] in the nature of things the ally of Liberal England" (Halévy, 1950, 3:73).[25] Great Britain could now pursue

---

Law—were seen as confirmation of the treachery of the middle class. The practical consequence to be drawn was that the working class must fight for its own emancipation."

23. See Halévy (1947, 208, 211): "The public imagination, it would seem, confused the Irish with the French. 'A Frenchman,' a journalist wrote, 'is a civilized Celt, an Irishman is a Gallic barbarian. What is Communism in France is brigandage in Ireland.' It was clear that the nation would have nothing to do with a movement led by Irishmen to launch in England a revolution after the French pattern."

24. The Chartist militants were perhaps not fooled. Halévy (1947, 149) says that "so far as the Chartists were concerned, the enactment of the Ten Hours' Bill was but a victory of a rearguard over one wing of the enemy." The point is less the views of the militants than that of their potential supporters.

25. The Duc de Broglie, in his preface to the *Mémoires de Talleyrand*, called the entente cordiale "the alliance of two liberal monarchies, founded on both sides on their national interests" (cited in Weil, 1919, 4).

with greater ease its containment of absolutism in Europe and expand the circle of liberal states (Guyot, 1926, 88, 117).[26]

But there were further motives. Great Britain and France faced the same internal problems, and even if France was not yet ready to embrace the free-trade nostrums of Great Britain, the entente cordiale seemed "in the eyes of democrats and socialists" as an "alliance of capitals" that was a "*fait accompli*" (Guyot, 1926, 302). Was this so wrong? Indeed, the two effects were not separate. In pressuring other powers to follow their example, Great Britain and France, with the entente cordiale, "discouraged the international revolutionary propaganda which counted on the divisions among the powers" (Guichen, 1917, 424–425).

Furthermore, 1830 launched a pattern that would discourage such propaganda even further. For France at least, 1830 served to restore France to a sense of world centrality and nationalist pride. It was not Guizot but the French socialist Louis Blanc (1844, 4:143–144) who would write:

> The July Revolution . . . was more than the *dénouement* of a struggle against the Church and royalty; it was the expression of national sentiment that had been excessively repressed by the treaties of 1815. We were determined to shake off the yoke of these treaties and restore the European equilibrium.[27]

One of the curious facts to note about the July Revolution was what happened in Algeria. Charles X's launching of the imperial venture had made Great Britain most unhappy, and Louis XVIII was ready to sacrifice it to appease the British. When, however, the French restrained themselves from direct intervention in Belgium, they felt they had done their share of pleasing the British, and simply continued the occupation, this time without British protest.[28] One reason

26. Jardin and Tudesq (1973, 1:179–180) argue that conditions for the alliance were "ripe": they had just collaborated in imposing an armistice on the Netherlands; the Treaty of Unkian-Skelessi that the Ottomans had signed threatened both their positions; they were both sympathetic to the liberals in the Germanies and the Italies in 1832.

27. In 1830, it was asserted in a workers' journal, *Étrennes d'un prolétaire,* that "we overthrew the government of the Bourbons, not because it made us unhappy, for the people were never happier than between 1816 and 1829, but because it had been imposed on us by the so-called victors, by foreign forces and by traitors within" (cited by Levasseur, 1903, 1:667).

28. Schefer (1928, 50–51), who says: "The Belgians . . . conquered Algiers for us a second time." Why the July Monarchy had continued the Algerian policy, which its supporters had criticized so vocally just before they came to power, is explained by Renouvin (1954, 109): "It's not at all surprising. The liberals who had fought Polignac had been hostile to the enterprise because it might consolidate a political regime they detested. Once this regime had disappeared, these same men believed that abandoning the acquisitions would be dangerous for the prestige of the Orleanist monarchy." He argues that the British went along in part because of their lack of clarity about the intentions of the July Monarchy and in part because "they had an interest in handling France carefully, since they needed France's collaboration in European affairs. It was good counsel to pursue a policy of holding fire" (p. 111).

clearly was its effect on worker unrest within France. The "floating" population of Paris, the potential revolutionaries, were being encouraged to settle in Algeria. Indeed, in 1838 Léon Blondel, a high civil servant in Algeria, could say with some confidence: "Africa is an element of order in France" (cited in Tudesq, 1964, 2:815).[29]

The liberal states thus combined legitimating the political role of the middle classes (and thereby receiving from them legitimation in turn) and internal repression of working-class discontent with an entente cordiale between themselves to ensure their dominance in the geopolitical arena. This seemed to work at first. But it was fragile, as the European revolution of 1848 was to demonstrate. More would have to be done to secure a stable political framework for the capitalist world-economy in the post-1789 situation.

The fragility lay in the fact that the liberal concessions to the working classes were extremely limited, and this made it difficult for liberal governments, if they were not ready to go further, to surmount the disarray caused by periodic severe economic downturns. This was the case most notably in France, where the July Monarchy, and its liberal epigone, Guizot, had become more and more conservative as the years went by, in face of the festering social discontent. The economic crisis of 1847–1848, one of the "most violent" crises that had thitherto been known, hit France hard. Profits fell severely. At the height of the crisis, 75 percent of Paris industrial workers were laid off (Markovitch, 1965, 256; Sée, 1951, 2:143; Labrousse, 1976b, 3:983–984).

The government did not prove itself flexible. Furthermore, it had failed to notice that its major political mechanism, the *vote censitaire,* was backfiring by alienating the very group of small merchants whose support they had acquired in 1830 by lowering the *cens.* The problem was that, as taxes were lowered by the government, this very fact pulled these voters off the rolls, undermining not merely the political rights of this group but also their social standing,[30] and thus making them receptive to the agitation for suffrage reform. Meanwhile, among the working classes the very moderate Icarians of Étienne Cabet, who had been in the

29. Nor were the socialists opposed to the Algerian policy. Louis Blanc affected enthusiasm for the struggle against Abd-el-Kader (1844, vol. 5, chap. 9), arguing both the civilizational and geopolitical legitimacy of imperialism: "It ensues from France's true genius . . . that she has the duty to expand. By temperament, even more than by geographical situation, France is a sea power. . . . The English alliance condemns us . . . to be nothing more than a continental nation, and if we assent even slightly to this role, competition will stifle us" (pp. 504–505).

30. Daumard (1963, 57), who notes that "the role of elector and of one eligible to be elected had a psychological value, almost one of worldly achievement; it was specifically listed for example after one's name in the *Almanach des 25 000 adresses.*"

1840s the major socialist voice—Christian, pacifist, legalist, nationalist, emphasizing class reconciliation—would now be squeezed out in the economic crisis and thereby yield place to more radical groups.[31]

The conservatization of the French regime contrasted with what was happening in the other liberal states. A liberal pope, Pius IX, had been elected in 1846, to the dismay of Metternich (Bury, 1948, 425). If Belgium remained "calm" in 1848, "it was because it had made its revolution, peacefully, in 1847" (Dhondt, 1949, 124). Similarly, the liberals and radicals had won their internal struggle against the Sonderbund in Switzerland in 1847, with the diplomatic support of the British but amid French hesitation (Halpérin, 1948, 1:157).[32] Indeed, this was a moment of temporary breakdown of the entente cordiale.[33] At home, the British had handled well the Chartist challenge at the same time that Sir Robert Peel was steering through the Repeal of the Corn Laws,[34] such that the "specter of Communism"[35]

31. "Cabet the *endormeur* bade the people rest when the situation demanded a revolutionary readiness, a militant vigilance on the part of the working class" (Johnson, 1974, 286). At this point, Cabet himself gave up and emigrated to Texas.

32. Halévy (1947, 193–194) notes: "Lucerne in 1847 [which fell to the cantons revolting against the Sonderbund] avenged the fate of Cracow in 1846. It was a serious defeat for Metternich and, consequently, for Guizot, who had openly made cause with him [but not for Louis-Philippe, whose 'caution had ... held [Guizot] back,'] and, therefore, an important victory for Palmerston and at the same time for Western Liberalism." Guizot's alienation from the British project of a liberal world order had been growing for some time previously. On March 16, 1844, he wrote a letter to the Comte de Flahaut, the ambassador of France to Austria, in which he said: "There is today no matter which deeply divides the great powers, no serious conflict of interests, no true struggle of influence. . . . There is but one concern in Europe, the same for everyone, to repress the anarchic spirit and to maintain peace towards this end." Prince Metternich in turn, having seen Guizot's letter, wrote a letter to the Comte Apponyi, his secretary of embassy in Paris, in which he cited this passage and said of it: "Such is also my conviction." The letters are cited in Weill (1921, 6, 8, 13).

33. The breakdown of the entente cordiale had begun in 1846 with the return of Palmerston to the Foreign Office. Greer attributes this to a long-standing hostility of Palmerston to the House of Orleans, dating back to the fact that he had been minister of war from 1809 to 1815; but this seems far-fetched, especially given the fact that it was Palmerston who had coined the very term. In any case, "this Anglo-French hostility was perhaps the most striking diplomatic fact of the beginning of the year 1848" (1925, 163)—and, one might add, one of the most consequential.

34. "Materially the repeal of the Corn Laws would protect the poorer classes in time of scarcity against any disastrous rise in food prices. Morally, it gave them assurances that, unenfranchised though most of them were, their welfare was an object of concern to an aristocratic Government and Parliament" (Gash, 1977, 97). Roberts (1958, 336) says of Peel that he "was the architect of the new conservatism ready to make its peace with the nineteenth century, attempting, as Burke preached, to blend cautious reforms with old traditions."

35. "When Marx in 1848 spoke of the 'spectre of Communism' which haunted Europe, he enunciated . . . a verifiable fact, at least for France and Germany. There existed, in mid-century, genuine sentiments of fear or hope of the rising of the masses" (Hammen, 1958, 199).

passed them by as well. The crisis of 1847 "provoked no revolutionary disturbance" (Halévy, 1947, 181),[36] although the Irish had to pay the price for this.[37]

Nonetheless, the weakening of the liberal project in France, one of the two pillar states, provided enough tinder for the revolutionary flame to be ignited throughout the nonliberal parts of Europe. To be sure, Metternich and the Austrians blamed the British, accused of being too liberal, for the uprisings,[38] but the blame

36. Indeed, it worked the other way. The debacle of April 10, a "fiasco," not only "marked the end" of Chartism as a political force but created the space for the British government, frightened by the example of revolutions in Paris, Berlin, and Vienna, to "beat it to death" (Bury, 1948, 1:415). Jenks, however, adds a cautionary note: "How closely financial England steered to the cataract in 1847 and 1848, her economists and public men never fully realized" (1927, 158). Jenks attributes Britain's salvation neither to her political wisdom nor to her "fetish" and "abracadabra" about free trade, but to the timely discovery of gold in California (1848) and Victoria (1851), which led to the "worldwide rise of prices and . . . consequent stimulus of enterprise in which the railway and free trade became for Great Britain leading assets instead of liabilities" (p. 162).

37. The Irish potato famine occurred just at the time of the debate on the Corn Laws. "With Cobden and Bright preparing for a decisive struggle at the next general election, due in 1847, and much of British middle- and lower-class opinion outside the purely agricultural areas converted to their views, it seemed clear to Peel and [Sir James] Graham [the Home Secretary] that to ask Parliament for a million or more of taxpayers' money to feed Ireland, while still retaining the Corn Laws in operation, would provide a storm of controversy" (Gash, 1977, 95). That the Irish famine became a ploy in the intra-Conservative political game is clear from Clark's account (1951b, 3) of repeal: "The traditional remedy for famine was to suspend the Corn Laws and open the ports. But Peel told his Cabinet that if he did this [in the case of Ireland at this time] he could not promise to reimpose them, and a majority in the Cabinet felt they could not support him in this policy on these terms. He therefore retired, but the Whigs could not, or would not, form a government. Peel therefore returned to office at the Queen's request [and] repealed the Corn Laws himself." See also Schuyler (1945, 145), who says: "The disastrous failure of the Irish potato crop in 1845 greatly strengthened . . . the movement for the repeal of the corn laws" but notes that repeal did not solve the food problem for Ireland, 1846 and 1847 remaining famine years (p. 186). The million pounds was never requested.

38. Metternich spoke of "the infernal role" of Palmerston, which was largely responsible for the revolutions, whereas Palmerston "firmly believed that a constitutional reform was the most efficacious barrier to revolution" (Bury, 1948, 1:420, 429). The Austrian ambassador to Belgium had written on November 16, 1847: "The Belgian liberals are blind; communism will devour them all." This is cited by Bartier (1948, 1:358), who remarks: "We know that the future gave the lie to these somber predictions. It was Louis-Philippe [of France] and not Leopold I [of Belgium] who lost his throne, and Metternich who took refuge in Brussels and not Charles Rogier [leader of the Belgian radicals] who took refuge in Vienna."

Metternich's views were shared one hundred years later by Fejtö in a book celebrating 1848, or celebrating it at least in part: "[T]he very fact of [England's] existence, the evolved state of its social structure, its inherent struggles, was a stimulant for ideas of reform. England can therefore be considered, from this point of view, one of the principal agents of the revolution. But, in the other direction, we can also observe that the very existence of England, its power against which France dared not pit itself, prevented the extension of the revolutionary wave" (1948c, 2:456). Whoever was to blame, what

is more legitimately placed at the feet of the French, who got cold feet and were not liberal enough. John Stuart Mill (1849, 7) was very severe on Louis-Philippe in assessing the causes of the February 1848 uprising in Paris, which was the beginning of the 1848 European revolution:

> No government can now expect to be permanent unless it guarantees progress as well as order; nor can it continue really to secure order, unless it promotes progress. It can go on as yet, with only a little of the spirit of improvement; while reformers have even a remote hope of effecting their objects through the existing system, they are generally willing to bear with it. But when there is no hope at all; when the institutions themselves seem to oppose an unyielding barrier to the program of improvement, the advance of tide heaps itself up behind them till it bears them down.[39]

The tide—that is, the European revolution of 1848—as all such great happenings, was made up of a mixture of movements and objectives. In France, it consisted essentially of the joining together of Europe's "first great proletarian insurrection" (Tilly, 1972, 228)[40] with the acute discontent of the left liberals who shared John Stuart Mill's view of the conservatization of the July Monarchy. Elsewhere in Europe, in states that were not as yet committed to liberalism, there were no proletarian insurrections; rather, there were liberal uprisings combined with nationalist uprisings. Two situations, with two solutions: Louis Napoleon handled the first; Palmerston, the rest.

The uprising of February 1848 illuminated the hopes of a "social republic," a vague socialist utopia that would provide jobs to the unemployed and liberation to all those who suffered indignities and inequalities. Everyone put forward their claims: the "artisans," who sought to restore their privileges and their mode of production;[41] the peasants, who sought to reestablish traditional rights of collective usage;[42] the women, who sought the extension of "universal" suffrage to include

---

distinguished 1789 from 1848 was precisely the "internationalism of the Revolution" (Beloff, 1974, 44; see also Hobsbawm, 1975, 10).

39. Another fault—even "more fatal"—of the government of Louis-Philippe was the "*culte des intérêts matériels*" and "the worship of the cash-box and the ledger," which made it, therefore, "a demoralising government" (Mill, 1849, 7–8).

40. "[I]t deserves the label," since for the first time, workers "*as such*" appeared in the "collective violence" (Tilly, 1972, 245).

41. Ellis (1974a, 41) says, somewhat harshly, that "the 1848 revolution . . . represented the dying fling of the decaying artisanal class."

42. This was an "effort by agricultural communities engaged primarily but not exclusively in subsistence farming to protect some of the diverse ways in which they made a living from encroachment by wealthier individuals who sought to improve farming techniques by means of enclosure and the abandonment of collective practices, agents of the government who sought to protect forests from degradation, or private forest owners who sought similarly to protect trees which constituted their capital" (Price, 1975b, 16).

them;[43] the slaves, who sought abolition.[44] The pendulum was beginning to swing too far, and in June the forces of order under General Cavaignac reined in the unruly dangerous classes.[45] "Pitiful provisional government!" cried Labrousse (1948, 2). "It feared the social revolution as much as it did the counter-revolution."[46]

43. Universal male suffrage was voted on March 6. On March 22, a delegation of women made this request to Armand Marrast, member of the provisional government and mayor of Paris. He replied that, since women had never before had political rights, it was not for the provisional government to take such a major decision but rather for the National Assembly when elected. See Thomas (1948, 36–37). Of course, there had never been universal male suffrage before, either.

44. Victor Schoelcher, who presided over the *Commission instituée pour préparer l'acte d'abolition immédiate de l'esclavage,* argued that abolition of slavery was the only way to save the colonies. As with the vote for women, Marrast wished to delay the issue, but this time he did not get his way, and on April 27, 1848, the government decreed immediate abolition. Just in time, says Césaire (1948, 1): "What would have come of the idea of abolition if, as Marrast, Mestro [Director of Colonies], and so many others had wanted, one would have waited for the elections and handed over the issue to the Constituent Assembly to resolve?" See also Schoelcher (1948, 175–184). The colonies in addition got the vote as of the day of abolition, including the ex-slaves, and the right "to determine the mode of their elections such that their representatives could participate with those of the metropole in the constitution of the republic" (Césaire, 1948, 23).

45. "[T]he middle classes were not in the least prepared to accede to workers' demands for either a reversion to the artisanal mode of production or for substantial reforms of the emerging industrial mode. Not only did they baulk [*sic!*] at socialistic plans for cooperative ownership, but they were equally loath to grant even modest wage increases. The conflict between the two groups is particularly well-indexed in the attitude of the bourgeoisie to their newly-won power. In every city affected by the insurrections of 1848 some sort of civilian militia was set up to protect the victors and their property. And in almost every case, once the first flush of euphoric enthusiasm had passed, the militia was used as a weapon against the lower classes" (Ellis, 1974a, 39–40). See the similar assessment of Bourgin (1948, I, 214–215): "At the beginning of the reign of Louis-Philippe a French general could say after the repression of the Polish insurrection: 'Order reigns in Warsaw.' After the June days [of 1848], order reigned in Paris, and Tsar Nicholas thought it appropriate to congratulate Cavaignac on his victory.... The social republic as dreamed by the proletarians and socialists of 1848 died during the June days, as Lamennais saw so clearly."

46. Labrousse (p. 3) contrasts the timidity of the provisional government with the boldness of the *Constituante,* who "did not fear to exceed by far their mandate." Labrousse's explanation of this timidity? "The men of 1848 lacked the 'will'? Let us not be too hard on them. Had they wished to, they probably could not have done more, did not 'know' how to.... France in 1848 was more like the old rural France of Louis XV than the France of the end of the Second Empire.... And the deep drama of the 1848 revolution was perhaps that it posed the great problems of the twentieth century in a society that had eighteenth-century structures."

Hobsbawm (1975, 20) offers a harsher judgment: "In 1848–49 moderate liberals made two important discoveries in western Europe: that revolution was dangerous and that some of their substantial demands (especially in economic matters) could be met without it. The bourgeoisie had ceased to be a revolutionary force."

Furthermore, as Bouillon (1956, 71) points out, although contemporaries spoke of the "Mountain" and of the "red list," "there was not in fact ... a Mountain 'party': this label hid a complex reality." It was

Cavaignac could repress; he could not relegitimize the state. Nor could the monarchs return; they had exhausted their credit. Into this void stepped Louis Napoleon, who sought to re-create a liberal, orderly, modern state and who, as Zeldin (1958, 6) puts it so well, "was not elected because he was [the] candidate [of the Party of Order], but . . . was their candidate because they saw he was bound to win."[47] But what did Louis Napoleon represent? He represented, first of all, the Napoleonic tradition, which combined the legacy of the French Revolution, a commitment to scientific and industrial progress, and nationalism. During the 1840s, Louis Napoleon had been a sharp critic of the July Monarchy because he felt that, by distancing itself from progressive liberalism, it was "building on sand and would surely tumble." And, unlike Guizot, he was aware that "with proper safeguards a democratic regime could be established without threatening the stability of the country."[48]

The liberals acted in 1848 just as they had in 1830. Dismayed by a regime that had become too rigid, too illiberal, they rose up and quickly won the day. Then, dismayed by the possibility that the lower strata would be able to take advantage of the situation and push things too far, they renewed their links with the political groups they had just ousted from power, because "the enemy, at present, is on the left" (Palmade, 1961, 255).[49] When Louis Napoleon made his coup d'état on December 2, 1851, the primary objective was to repress the left.[50] The secondary

---

at most a left-leaning coalition of diverse groups, and even then, when they presented themselves under the leadership of Ledru-Rollin at the elections of May 13, 1849, they won only a third of the votes.

47. Zeldin points out that they would have preferred Thiers. And of course they would get him— but they had to wait a bit more than twenty years.

48. These quotes are not Louis Napoleon's own words, but a summary of his ideas by Campbell (1978, 3–4). Campbell further reminds us that in the 1840s, "Bonapartism became part of the current of social romanticism [and] Louis Napoleon established a reputation as something of a socialist" (p. 5). The plan for class harmony through state action outlined in his book *Extinction du paupérisme* was similar to the ideas being propagated by the Saint-Simonians, a fit prologue to the role that ex-Saint-Simonians were to play in the Second Empire.

49. "What facilitated the rapprochement—which was, in fact, an integration of aristocratic elements with the business bourgeoisie—was that the social struggle, after the shock of 1848, had changed fronts."

50. "The repression after the *coup d'état* was worse than anything done by a French government since the Terror. Over 26,000 persons, nearly all of them republicans, were arrested and brought to trial before special commissions. . . . Their business was not to dispense justice but to make a political purge" (Plamenatz, 1952, 105–106). The exiles would not be allowed to return until 1859. See also Merriman (1976, 210): "The *coup d'état* of Louis-Napoleon Bonaparte on 2 December 1851 was . . . the culmination of a large series of blows struck against the radical Republican Party." Wright (1975, 2) makes essentially the same point. "[T]he repression was more far-reaching and appalling than official figures

objective was, however, to constrain the ability of conservative forces to act other than through him.[51] One can, if one wants, emphasize the Caesarist—the so-called Bonapartist—element in the regime.[52] If one does, however, one risks missing the degree to which the outcome of the repression, which was both real and effective,[53] was that of a centrist regime, oriented to capitalist expansion, constructing a liberal compromise[54]—one led not by a classical liberal but by an enlightened conservative.

---

might suggest," since, he says, we must add in the unrecorded, unofficial repression. However, he adds this caution: "[T]he repression, however terrible, could have been far worse" (p. 303). Bourgin (1948, 1:246–247) concludes that the accession of Louis Napoleon was a great defeat for the revolutionaries of 1848: "a triple fiasco—a social fiasco, with the elimination of the right to work; a political fiasco, with the reduction of electoral rights and the changes consequent to the coup d'état; an international fiasco, with the expedition of Rome."

51. At the same time that Louis Napoleon arrested the Republicans, he arrested conservative parliamentarians as well. Price (1975b, 56) sees this as primarily tactical: "Some potential opposition of the left was disarmed by proclaiming the restoration of universal suffrage, and even by the dissolution of the conservative, monarchist-dominated Assembly, for most of whose members neither the poor, nor the democrats, could be expected to have much sympathy. But rather than an anti-royalist coup, most of the measures taken signified a preventive assault against democratic organizations. More than anything else this was the culminating act in a long period of repression." But was this tactic not part of Louis Napoleon's underlying strategy? In any case, Price (p. 63) notes that, if conservatives "generally ... welcomed the *coup*," it was only "with misgivings."

52. See the view of a German historian in a paper given in a Franco-German colloquium on Bonapartism: "The year 1848/49 was that of the first all-European revolution. Thereafter, the psychological ground for Caesarism was laid, not only in France but on this side of the Rhine. The wreckage of liberalism on the national question, its indifference to the social question, the emergence of a political mass market in the wake of universal suffrage, the appeal to the masses and the establishment of a new legitimacy on the basis of an accord between a charismatic leader and his followers—all this belongs since 1848 to the alphabet in which, both in German and in French, the name of Caesar is spelled. The break with legitimacy would be sanctified by the support and jubilation of the masses. What would happen, however, if this support were once to be refused?" (Stürmer, 1977, 110). Schapiro (1949, 330) has a similarly bleak view of Louis Napoleon: "[A] new political method of fighting social revolution had been devised, to turn the revolutionary stream of working-class discontent into the new channel of a popular and socialized dictatorship."

53. Louis Napoleon's tactic was to make liberal forms serve repressive ends, the better to achieve safely liberal, but not democratic, objectives. The secret ballot is a good instance. Liberals were pleased with the decision to maintain the secret ballot instituted in 1848, seeing it as a guarantee of a free vote. Plamenatz (1952, 107–108) points out that Louis Napoleon's reasoning and that of his advisers was quite different: "What they wanted was to let fear operate untrammelled by shame." People assumed that the authorities would know how they voted. "The secrecy of the ballot would not, if they voted against the President, protect them from his police, but it might spare them the reproaches and abuse of their friends. The ballot was therefore made secret so that the timid might indulge their weakness without fear of the bold. . . . Terror combined with the secret ballot . . . first proved effective on Dec. 31st, 1851."

54. See a French historian's view at this same Franco-German colloquium: "Did it bring new ideas? Scarcely. Bonapartism came out of the French Revolution. . . . It is a democratic, tricolor ideology. But

If the liberal center was once more secure in France, it had required a Bonapartist form, given the strength of working-class rebelliousness combined with the rigidity of conservative forces—a consequence of France's narrower margin of maneuver in the face of economic recession, as compared at this time with that of Great Britain. Elsewhere in Europe, however, the problem was not resecuring the liberal center but allowing it to emerge. It was the role of the hegemonic power, Great Britain, to keep this process, which of course it favored, from upsetting the geopolitical calm too much.

Outside France, the specter of Communism did not have a comparable social base. Nonetheless, it seemed real for the ruling elites, who found it difficult to distinguish between liberals and socialists. A French author, writing about

---

for the Bonapartist, the revolution was not a bloc. One must sift its offerings. . . . [Bonapartism put forth the doctrine] of the perfect balance [*juste milieu*], of centrism" (Girard, 1977, 23). Girard cites Louis Napoleon in 1850: "We must take from the Revolution the good instincts and combat strongly the bad ones. . . . For me, order is the maintenance of everything that has been freely chosen and consented to by the people; it is the national will triumphing over factions." Duverger (1967, 191) similarly speaks of Bonapartism as "brilliant centrism." The initial brilliance was in coming to power at all: "In this unhappy republic without republicans, it soon became a race between those who favored the restoration of a dynasty (either a Bourbon or an Orléans) and the Bonapartists. By basing himself on the support of the center and by using force, Louis-Napoleon won it. He thus kept the power from falling into the hands of the true right" (p. 141).

See also Zeldin (1958, 44–45): "The elections of 1852 show what the second empire meant. It . . . sought to combine aristocracy with democracy. . . . The driving force within it was ambition and worldly honour open to all was its reward. It enabled peasants to vote for the left—for the revolutionary who had defied the constitution and against the old gangs and the nobles—but at the same time to vote for the right, for order, for property, for the family and for religion." Morazé (1957, 2) says essentially the same thing, but more acerbically: "For several months, the bourgeoisie was afraid of losing everything: 1848, the people of Paris tried to make themselves the masters of progress. But no, the hour of socialism has not yet sounded. It was an arrogant capitalism that Napoleon III and Bismarck put in power, seeking to catch up to and overtake England, fighting with each other to get there first, turning the competition between entrepreneurs into a competition between nations."

Blanchard (1956, 211–212) puts his emphasis on the liberal outcome: "If one believes that universal suffrage is the necessary instrument of national sovereignty, we can see that, despite the system of official candidates, the [Second] Empire represented at one and the same time an apprenticeship for universal suffrage and a decisive moment in the democratic evolution of the French peasant, most especially in the political formation of the French peasantry." Campbell (1978, 24) is equally positive: "Napoleon's authoritarian guarantee of order promised to provide what had escaped the 48ers. By preventing disorder, the government preserved the principle of universal suffrage. . . . By the 1860s universal suffrage had become an integral part of French political life." Campbell reminds us of Saint-Beuve's bon mot—that Napoleon III's great contribution was to rid France of previous regimes. "It was more correct than he realized" (p. 26). Hobsbawm (1975, 26) agrees but gives this a different twist: "Louis Napoleon's election signified that even the democracy of universal suffrage, that institution identified with revolution, was compatible with the maintenance of social order."

Spain in the *Revue des Deux Mondes* in January 1848, just before the revolutions began, said:

> I do not believe, I say again, that a revolution is possible, unless our government makes errors of which I think it incapable. But let us at least have no illusions. Let me be heard by those so imprudent as to excite the wrath of the people and so ambitious as to speculate on their fury! A revolution will not take place to the profit of a viewpoint, but to the profit of communism.[55]

Similarly, Cantimori (1948, 1:279) argues that in northern and central Italy, "the fear of social revolution . . . was but a reflection of the fear of the 'red specter,' of *jacqueries,* and of Communism, which all of European reaction felt." The revolutions broke out everywhere, taking different local colors according to the history: in the Austrian empire ("nowhere . . . more virulent" [Vermeil, 1948b, 2:46; cf. Endres, 1948]), in Germany and in Poland, in northern Europe and in southern Europe.[56] And everywhere the liberal/nationalist "blues" and the much weaker "reds" soon parted company (Fejtö, 1948c, 2:441).[57] The radical elements were easily contained, but in the process, the gains of the centrist nationalists and liberals were limited.[58] Nationalism could of course be used both to promote liberalism and to contain it, depending on the circumstances.[59]

55. Cited in Quero (1948, 1:323). The phrase "a viewpoint" reflects the cultural ambiance of the times. Tudesq (1964, 1:368), discussing the "party" system under Louis-Philippe, observes: "The press of the July Monarchy used excessively the term 'party' to designate tendencies of opinion. Only extreme political options, hostile to the very principle of the July regime, had an organization (not very structured) and a program (sometimes rather ambiguous) that could be said to have united their followers."

56. In Bohemia, the national question went well together with the social question: "The great majority of Czechs supported the revolutionary movement, in which the nationalist element soon became dominant. But since most Czechs were ordinary people, social demands were linked indissolubly with nationalist demands. The German bourgeoisie of Bohemia soon had the feeling that the Czechs wanted to ally themselves with the workers against the Germans" (Klima, 1948, 2:218).

57. Tissot (1948, 1:390) speaks of the "triumph of nationalist conceptions over ideas of reform."

58. See Luzzatto (1948, 86) on the fears of Mazzini liberals of communists and of their influence with urban workers: "For [the liberals] just as for the [Austrian police], the terror of communism was real, leading at the least to holding the lower classes at a great distance, fearing their participation in the political and social struggles. The result was precisely what [the liberals] said they wanted to avoid: the weakening of the forces that might have continued to struggle for liberty and independence, depriving the struggle of the fighting enthusiasm of popular forces."

59. On the one hand, in Greece, which already had a quite liberal constitution, the government fended off the democratic movement by brandishing "the flag of the Great Idea"—that is, of Hellenism, which "turned popular attention away from internal problems" (Sakellariou, 1948, 2:337). But in Sweden, long an independent state and therefore having no "national problem" per se, nationalism took the form of Scandinavism. This implied both shifting from a pro-Russian to a pro-"Western" (that is, a pro-British) foreign policy, and asserting Scandinavian "liberalism" against "germanism, particularly its authoritarian and feudal dimension" (Tissot, 1948, 1:394–395). And in Germany, the opposition at this time to unifying tendencies "also represented a reaction against liberalism" (Vermeil, 1948b, 2:30).

Great Britain entered the picture, here to support the liberals, there to make sure they didn't go too far, everywhere to maintain a balance, and consequently its sway over the interstate system. In Spain, where the government prior to 1848 had been closely tied to that of Louis-Philippe, Great Britain supported attempts by the liberals in March 1848 to change the government of General Narvaez. Palmerston actually sent a formal letter on March 16 to the government, in which he permitted himself to say: "[T]he Queen of Spain would be acting wisely, in the critical state of affairs, if she restructured the government by enlarging the bases on which her administration rests, and appealing for the counsel of some of those who have the confidence of the liberal party" (cited in Quero, 1948, 1:328).[60]

British intervention, if not directly successful, may have limited the repression. The British did better in Sicily, where they supported the insurgents against the Kingdom of Naples. Naples decided that her friend, Austria, was far off and otherwise occupied, and granted a constitution as demanded; in one fell stroke, "Italy [or at least Naples] found itself on the side of France, England, and Switzerland" (Cantimori, 1948, 1:265). Palmerston also asked the Austrians in 1849 to treat Hungary "with generosity," to which request the Austrian ambassador in London replied that Austria would be "the sole judge" of how it would deal with the rebels (Fejtö, 1948b, 2:202). On the other hand, Palmerston declined to intervene with the tsar concerning Poland, fearing the encouragement it might give to the Irish movement (Goriély, 1948a, 2:277). In short, Palmerston's policy was very simple: "[H]is foreign policy . . . had no other goal than to turn to England's advantage the situation created by the revolutionary events" (Fejtö, 1948a, 1:35). In general, the policy was efficacious, even when the diplomatic intrusions were rejected.[61]

60. Palmerston was speaking of the so-called Progressives, who were to the left of the Moderates in the government but who were still pro-monarchy and less radical than the Radicals. Nonetheless, this British attitude emboldened Spanish liberals, "encourag[ing] them to overthrow the government of General Narvaez by force" (Quero, 1948, 1:329). The uprising was abortive, and the government suppressed civil liberties and dissolved the Cortes, whereupon the British minister to Spain, Lord Bulwer, wrote to the government calling for the reopening of the Cortes, reminding them of the promise of Queen Isabel to preserve liberty, and concluding that "today the firmest guarantee of a sovereign's throne is to be found in national liberty and in an enlightened justice dispensed under its authority" (cited on p. 332). The press learned of the letter and published it. The Spanish foreign minister gave the letter a *fin de non recevoir*, asserting offense against an independent nation, and raising the question of Ireland. A break in diplomatic relations followed, lasting until 1850.

61. In any case, the British were self-congratulatory, as befits a hegemonic power. In 1851, Queen Victoria said: "When the revolutionary movement swept the Continent [in 1848], and shook up almost all the governments of Europe, England alone showed those qualities of order, of vigor, and of prosperity which were the due of a stable, free, and good government" (cited in and retranslated from Bury, 1948, 1:403). A less admiring attitude was assumed by Ledru-Rollin, leader of the Republicans in France, in his book *Décadence de l'Angleterre* (1850, 1:99): "Studying its laws and its customs, England reveals to us all the iniquities of privilege and all the corruptions of intelligence. The history of its conquests and its wars will make us know the perfidies of its policies, and give us the number and the

The European revolution of 1848 began as a threat to the world liberal regime that the hegemonic power, Great Britain—with the crucial aid of France—was establishing, but then became the crucible in which the dominance of liberalism in the geoculture was ensured. When Polanyi outlines in *The Great Transformation* (1957, 3) the four pillars of nineteenth-century civilization—the balance-of-power system, the international gold standard, the self-regulating market, and the liberal state—he says that "the fount and matrix of the system was the self-regulating market." If there was any moment in which this self-regulating market seemed to be functioning as close to its theoretical model as possible, it was in the years 1850–1873. And the crucial prelude to this moment of optimal operation of this principle was the Repeal of the Corn Laws in Great Britain in 1846. The story is worth reviewing in some detail.

The so-called Hungry Forties, coming in the wake of "the very real distress of the 1820s and 1830s," permitted a coming together of interests between the working classes, who were concerned with the price of basic commodities, and the liberals, who were preaching the virtues of the market. They both could find a target in those monopolists whose practices ensured a high cost of living: the West Indian coffee and sugar interests; the East India Company, which controlled the tea trade; and above all the English landowners, whose grain production was price protected by the Corn Laws (Mellor, 1951, 14).[62]

The political balance had begun to shift against continuing protection of grain. There had been a post-1815 grain glut in Europe because of the prior expansion of production due to military demands and the effects of the blockade, and this glut had served to justify the Corn Laws.[63] But by the late 1830s the glut had ceased to exist. Industrial expansion had increased urban populations, and land was being converted to industrial crops as well as to animal husbandry (a normal shift in a period of Kondratieff downturn). "[N]orthwestern Europe became collectively

---

measure of its crimes." But it was Ledru-Rollin who was to lose most, both symbolically and personally, by the Napoleonic solution in France—a solution that fit Great Britain's policy well.

62. See McCord (1958, 16): "[The Anti–Corn Law League was] essentially an offshoot of the Radical party, and its success was in great measure due to the fact that an attack on the Corn Laws was found an acceptable form for Radical energies at a time when the Radicals were sadly in need of such a rallying-point." After 1835 and the Tamworth Manifesto, the Conservatives had become "the enemy with which radicals had to contend, and from several points of view the Corn Laws were a better grounds for attack than the ballot. . . . It was obvious that a repeal of the Corn Laws under Radical pressure would be a blow not only to the economic, but also to the social and political, pre-eminence of the landed interest" (pp. 20–21). Attacking the Corn Laws was a way for Radicals to be in the center of political struggle without being *too* radical, especially since "the prevailing tendency of economic thought was against protectionism" (p. 21).

63. "One of the arguments put forward for the enactment of the British Corn Laws in 1815 was the fear that Polish wheat, produced by slave labour, might undercut home-grown wheat" (Leslie, 1956, 51).

deficient in bread grains" (Fairlie, 1965, 568).[64] The battle for repeal waxed strong, and its defenders were reduced to arguing a conservative position for its own sake. It is nonetheless interesting to note, since we have come to take the Repeal as a great defeat for the landed aristocracy, that opposition to repeal was far stronger among small tenant farmers than among large landowners.[65]

Why then all the fuss, since fuss there was indeed? The answer is that, for both sides, "the Corn Laws were a symbol"—for those who favored repeal, of the new and progressive against the old and privileged; for those who were opposed, of the defense of the landed gentry, "without which there can be no steady mean between democracy and despotism."[66] Into this symbolic battle, Sir Robert Peel devoted himself to the only objective worth achieving—not the triumph of the middle classes, but the triumph of the liberal state with the "perpetuation of the status of the landed classes in new technological conditions" (Moore, 1965, 651).[67] When Peel, on May 15, 1846, won the day for Repeal on its third reading, he had two-thirds of the Conservative Party against him. It was a rare parliamentary alliance that carried the day.[68]

64. There was even an increase of production in Great Britain at this time to compensate for the decline in imports from the traditional sources abroad, which were the German and Polish littoral and to a lesser extent the Atlantic coasts of Denmark, the Netherlands, and France (Fairlie, 1965, 562). This considerably reduced the case for protectionism, especially since even the increased British production was insufficient. "A situation in which the Corn Laws protected the British farmer against continental post-war glut was giving way to one in which their retention threatened Britain with famine" (pp. 571–572).

65. "[T]he leader of the Anti-League [Robert Baker] ... was not a member of the aristocracy, and not even a member of the landed gentry. Indeed, Mr. Baker was not even a landowner, ... merely a tenant farmer. ... It was the tenant farmers who led the Anti-League, and it was the landlords who were its reluctant and timorous followers" (Mosse, 1947, 134). For one thing, as Mosse points out, all this public agitation was too "democratic" for the taste of the large landowners, who demonstrated a "conservative disinclination to descend into the arena of everyday politics." (p. 139).

This political hesitation was combined with a lesser economic interest. As Clark (1951b, 10) points out, the case for repeal might seem reasonable enough to great nobles "whose rent rolls were comfortably supplemented by revenue from mines, or docks, or urban property" or whose large holdings in land provided a surplus large enough to tide them over while they installed new technology of deep drainage. "They did not console farmers who thought they might be ruined by one year's drop in prices, who had perhaps little capital and no science." See also Moore (1965, 544): "[By the 1840s] the economic value of the Corn Laws to the landed interest was no longer so clear."

66. This was the view expressed by John Wilson Croker, a prominent Tory, in a letter to Lord Brougham, written on February 19, 1843 (Jennings, 1884, 3:13).

67. See also Kitson Clark (1967, 27): "[Peel] did not repeal the Corn Laws until he had assured himself, after very careful enquiries, that agriculture did not need the protection of the Corn Laws, and would be better off without it."

68. Aydelotte's analysis (1972, 326) of parliamentary voting patterns is clear on this point: "The evidence of votes shows that substantial disagreements on important issues existed between the Peelites [those Conservatives who voted for Repeal] and the Whigs or Liberals, and that Peel sided with the

Peel pushed Repeal through Parliament on two conditions or two considerations. The first was that the stick of repeal to force the extension of high farming
techniques on British agriculture was accompanied by carrots that would ease the
transition financially: a reduction of tariffs on grass and clover seeds; laws making
it more difficult to return the urban poor to rural birth areas, thereby reducing the
needed local levies; and "most important of all . . . the drainage loan," which was
designed to popularize high farming among tenant farmers by giving loans to the
"settled estates," thereby enabling the tenants for life to charge the estates with the
costs of improvement (Moore, 1965, 554).[69] The second consideration was purely
political. Peel wanted to make sure that Repeal was seen as a decision of Parliament in its wisdom, and not one in reaction to popular pressure. Peel refused to
make repeal an issue in the general elections of December 1845. (It might in any
case have deeply split his own party.) By forcing it through Parliament, and in a
vote that crossed party lines, he made it "a victory over democratic agitation and
the [Anti–Corn Law] League, and a proof that parliament put the general welfare
above sectional interests" (Kemp, 1962, 204).[70]

What did Repeal of the Corn Laws actually achieve? Two things, really. On
the one hand, it ensured the reorganization of the axial division of labor in the
world-economy, such that wheat production once again became a peripheral
activity. The years following would see the rise of the United States and Canada
in North America and of Russia and Romania in eastern Europe as great wheat
exporters to western Europe, permitting an intensification of the industrial concentration in the western European zone.[71] But this shift was done in such a way

rest of his party, and against the Liberals, on most subjects of specific interest to Cobden with the single
exception of free trade."

69. This was done by requiring landlords "to compensate [the tenant farmer] for his improvements at such time as he quitted [the estate]" (Moore, 1965, 558).

70. McCord (1958, 203) captures this intent by underlining the consequence: "[N]othing shows
more clearly the fundamental impotence of the [Anti–Corn Laws] League . . . in the political conditions of the 1840s than its position during the final crisis. The League for eight years had headed the
agitation against the Corn Laws, but now that they were being repealed the Leaguers were without any
control over the procedure or the exact terms utilized." Nonetheless, after Repeal, "the growth of the
legend of the League" began (p. 208). Evans (1983, 263) argues similarly: "[W]hen Peel carried Corn
Law repeal, the League's influence was at a low ebb. It will not do to characterize the repeal of the Corn
Laws as the pre-ordained outcome of that middle-class pressure which the crisis of 1830–32 had taught
the aristocracy it was powerless to resist. It is at least arguable that the Corn Laws would have been
repealed even had the Anti–Corn Law League not existed." Furthermore, Evans (p. 267) says: "Peel . . .
denied the League its ultimate test by passing Corn Law repeal in advance of a General Election. . . .
[T]his may not have been coincidental."

71. The mechanism by which this shift occurred was very simple: "Under the Corn Laws,
merchants who could be reasonably sure of making a profit on imports from ports and depots in

that large British landowners could make the financial transition to new sources of wealth.[72]

On the other hand, it ensured the restructuring of British politics divided between a right-of-center Conservative Party and a left-of-center Liberal Party (eventually to be supplanted by a left-of-center Labor Party), both basically accepting the logic of centrist liberal politics. One may think of this as a victory for the middle classes, or just as easily as a concession by the aristocracy, "a timely retreat . . . from a forward position that had proved to be dangerous" (Kitson Clark, 1951b, 12).[73] The concept of Whigs and Tories, both coalitions of the eighteenth century, ceased to exist.

The initial advantage went to the Liberal Party because of the great split in Conservative ranks over Repeal.[74] But there now arose a new kind of conservatism, attuned to the normality of change, one that would regain power by "bas[ing] itself . . . squarely on the support and votes of the people" (Mosse, 1947, 142). Meanwhile, those Liberal Party members (radicals) who had wanted to associate their party with the working classes had lost out in favor of those who were

northwestern Europe when conditions warranted it hesitated to engage in the Black Sea and America even when famine conditions at home might have made this a great duty. In the first place, the journeys home were so long that the chances of the corn arriving after prices had fallen and duties had been reimposed were too large for comfort. In the second place, British ships . . . were scarce at the best of times in the Black Sea and other grain ports, and their freights soared wildly on the slightest expectation of grain price rises. Repeal of the Sliding Scale [1846] made distant grain trades 'respectable' and repeal of the Navigation Acts [1849] enabled merchants to use whatever shipping was currently available in grain-trade ports" (Fairlie, 1965, 571).

72. "For very many landowners a great new age of agricultural improvement was launched in the half-dozen years after Repeal" (Thompson, 1963, 247). This included improved field drainage, mass production of clay drainpipes, adding green crops (rutabagas, marigolds) to rotation, and increased stocking of cattle and sheep. "Essentially landowners thought of this whole complex of improvements as a rescue operation" (p. 248). The returns were "meagre" (p. 253) compared with those of the age of enclosure. Yet although "agricultural landownership did become an increasingly expensive luxury, [the shift in the mode of operation ensured a] long twilight of great honour, prestige, and personal wealth, [even] though their ascendancy was over" (p. 291). Thompson even calls the years 1880–1914 an "Indian summer" (title of chap. 11) before the final "eclipse" (title of chap. 12) of 1914–1939.

73. "After the battle the power remained in the same kind of hands as those in which it had rested before." The next reform bill would not be until 1867, proposed by none other than Disraeli, who had led the successful attempt within the Conservative Party to punish Peel for putting through Repeal. Thus did the intelligent conservatives continue down the path of sagely implementing a liberal program.

74. McCord (1958, 212) states somewhat overdramatically that the Conservative Party was "condemned to impotence for nearly thirty years." He does note, nonetheless, that Repeal also "impaired the unity of the Liberals," with a drift of the "moderate Whigs" to the Conservative Party.

more concerned with consolidating the state structure. As Briggs (1956, 72) said, "[W]hat the Reform Bill had decreed, the Corn Bill had realized."

You will note that I did not list as one of the great results of the Repeal of the Corn Laws the enshrinement of the doctrine of laissez-faire. That is because there is more myth than reality in the doctrine of laissez-faire. As a result, it cannot be taken as the defining characteristic of liberalism, surely not the fundamental message of liberalism as the geoculture of the world-system. To be sure, the public posture was that, as John Stuart Mill put it so tersely, "every departure from laissez-faire, unless required by some greater good, is a certain evil."[75] But the subordinate clause turned out to be a mighty big loophole. For example, in the very year of Repeal, 1846, in the debate on the Ten Hours Bill, Macaulay asserted that, although there was no *economic* justification for restricting hours, Parliament was required to take into consideration the *social* needs of women and children "who were incapable of entering into a proper contractual relationship with their employers" (Taylor, 1972, 44).[76] The simultaneity of the successful campaign to repeal the Corn Laws—opposition to the high symbol of state interference in the economy—with the beginning of serious social legislation in Great Britain (and on the Continent) is strong evidence for Brebner's dictum (1948, 107) that what was really happening was not a shift to laissez-faire but a shift "from intervention by the state in commerce to intervention by the state in industry." The classical economists and liberals were in fact aware of this and always took a nuanced position on laissez-faire, from Adam Smith to Bentham to Nassau Senior[77], as did

75. *Principles of Political Economy* (1921 ed., p. 950), cited in Taylor (1972, 13).

76. Macaulay's speech was given on May 22, 1846. Tory paternalism was of course a phenomenon that predated 1846. Such men as Richard Oastler, Michael Thomas Sadler, and George Bull had been campaigning in this fashion for decades. "They were skeptical of the benefits presumed to flow from unfettered competition and they saw the State as the natural agency whereby the most brutish aspects of industrial capitalism could be curbed" (Evans, 1983, 228). When "the greatest of Tory social reformers, Lord Ashley [Seventh Earl of Shaftesbury]" tried to get a Ten Hours Bill passed in 1833, it was already clear that the cause of industrial regulation drew support from many traditions: "Tory Evangelicals gave it impetus, the Utilitarians defined its form [the principle of inspection], and the Whigs, masters at compromise, passed [a milder bill] through Parliament" (Roberts, 1958, 325–326). Similarly, when the new Poor Law was passed in 1834, an "exaggerated fear of pauperism" led Parliament to accept the system recommended by the Royal Commission, "despite the fact that this contained a far greater degree of bureaucratic centralisation than would have been acceptable under normal circumstances" (Rose, 1974, 9). During approximately the same period in France, 1827–1841, there was considerable campaigning for a child-labor law, which, when finally adopted, became "the first example of social legislation in France: never before had the State intervened in the relationship between employer and employee" (Heywood, 1988, 231).

77. "Adam Smith was not a doctrinaire advocate of laissez-faire. . . . He did not believe that laissez-faire was always good, or always bad. It depended on circumstances" (Viner, 1927, 271–272). Furthermore, "Smith had himself undermined what is ordinarily regarded as his principal argument for

even the great neoclassical economist Alfred Marshall.[78] The distinction between recognizing the "value" of laissez-faire and preaching it as an "absolute dogma" was fundamental to all the classical economists (Rogers, 1963, 535).[79] They were all aware that "one man's *laissez-faire* was another man's intervention" (Taylor, 1972, 12).[80]

---

laissez-faire, by demonstrating that the natural order, when left to take its own course, in many respects works against, instead of for, the general welfare" (p. 218). "The classical economists as a whole were always prepared to assign a significant role to the state. . . . Moral and social improvement . . . was the characteristic aim of the classical economists rather than *laissez-faire* as an end in itself. . . . [I]n the writings of Bentham himself, there was no doubt of the importance attached to state action as a level for reform" (Gash, 1979, 45). Nassau Senior, generally considered one of those most resistant to social legislation, was also the one who called laissez-faire "the most fatal of all errors" (*Social Economy*, 2:302, cited in Sorenson, 1952, 262). Some analysts are a bit more reserved. Walker (1941, 173) says the classical economists "differed widely in their attitudes." And Ward, having read Brebner, Sorenson, and Walker, says (1962, 413) that "the conclusion to be drawn from the researches is generally a modification rather than a denial of the traditional view. The 'classical economists' might relent on children, but not on adults."

78. Alfred Marshall, in the autumn of his life, in the eighth edition of *Principles of Economics*, published in 1920, summed up his reflections on laissez-faire thus: "It has been left for our own generation to perceive all the evils which arose from the suddenness of this increase in economic freedom [during the industrial revolution]. . . . Thus gradually we may attain to an order of social life, in which the common good overrules individual caprice, even more than it did in the days before the sway of individualism had begun" (app. A, 750, 752, cited in Evans, 1978, 134).

79. Fay (1920, 44) argues: "[T]o the disciples of Bentham, *laissez-faire* did not mean . . . 'let things be, don't worry.' It was a war-cry, sounding the attack on every law or social convention which hindered freedom of development. It was a campaign for the overthrow of long-established abuses." Or, as Taylor (1972, 25) puts it: laissez-faire fell into "the prescriptive, not the analytical, area of economic thinking." And of course, the neoclassical economists believed that this campaign had had fruitful results. Marshall makes this quite clear: "The freedom to adopt whatever trade one would (*laissez faire* in its original sense), together with the freedom to send goods whithersoever one would, and fetch them whencesoever one would (*laissez aller*), made England the *entrepôt* of the world." Even so, Marshall (1921, 84–85) admits that this truth applied most strongly to Great Britain, and that this was not specified by the politicians on the grounds that they did not want to confuse the public. "But in the long run it might have been better both for England and for free trade, if [the politicians] had been compelled to make prominent these cumbrous qualifications which they omitted. For then other nations would have been warned beforehand that the removal of Protective duties could not be expected to confer the same unmixed benefits on their best industries as it had on those of England." Indeed, Marshall goes even further: "There is no general economic principle which supports the notion that industry will flourish best, or that life will be happiest and healthiest, when each man is allowed to manage his own concerns as he thinks best" (p. 736).

There are some, of course, who are skeptical that laissez-faire mattered even to Great Britain: "[I]f we compare English international commerce with that of other nations, and notably British exports with those of western Europe [in the nineteenth century], we are struck by the similarity of the two movements: in protectionist France, for example, as in free-trade England. . . . What credit then shall we give to the reforms of Huskisson and Peel?" (Labrousse, 1954, 1:45).

80. This contradiction was inbuilt in liberalism, as Halévy saw with such precision. Discussing John Stuart Mill as a centrist, torn between what Halévy called the philosophy of Westminster and the philosophy of Manchester, Halévy (1904, 387) ends by noting that Mill, when "faced with authoritarian

Still, Europe's liberals felt that the Repeal of the Corn Laws was a great event, which guaranteed economic progress.[81] And, as is true of many such beliefs, the years immediately following seemed to provide the evidence. For the world-economy was now entering into another Kondratieff A-phase, the "golden age of prosperity" of the 1850s and 1860s, and "many contemporaries came to attribute this to the repeal of the Corn Laws"—a "reconciling myth," according to Kemp (1962, 195). The years were particularly beneficent to the two key countries of the world-system at this time: Great Britain and France.

In Great Britain, this period has been labeled the "Great Victorian Boom" or, slightly more dramatically, the "High Noon of Victorianism," one that "rested upon the balance between industry and agriculture" (Kitson Clark, 1962, 31, 57).[82] It was a period during which British capitalists were doing so well that they primarily sought "to paddle their own canoes" (Clapham, 1932, 2:145), in the slang of the times. To be sure, they were obliged to do so, since Great Britain had become "an open market for nearly everything which she produced." This posed no problem as yet, since at this point Great Britain's superiority in everything was clear: in commerce, in finance, and in industry—that is, in the making of "those things which were chiefly needed" (Clapham, 1932, 2:2, 12).[83]

The 1850s marked the high point of growth in British exports. The export of cotton piece goods "just about doubled" in the decade, actually increasing even the *rate* of growth, which, Hobsbawm argues (1975, 30–31), provided "invaluable [political] breathing-space." Cotton textiles were still central to British wealth, but this was the period in which metals and machinery moved to the fore as the lead-

---

democracy[,] made the objections of liberalism, but [when] faced with the philosophy of competition, he made the objections of socialism. The contradiction between these two fundamental principles of utilitarianism has become clear to everyone. Philosophical radicalism exhausted its activity, in the history of English thought and legislation."

81. "If the repeal of the Corn Laws was seen as a great victory for the 'Left' as a whole, the fact that it brought with it the widespread conviction that the cause of 'cheap food' needed thoroughgoing free trade, and that protectionism was synonymous with taxation of the necessities as of life, was Cobden's personal triumph" (Biagini, 1991, 137).

82. After 1874, "a series of devastating blows struck British agriculture" (Kitson Clark, 1962, 57). Thus, Peel had managed to accord the great landowners nearly thirty years of reconversion time.

83. Clapham's euphoric assessment (pp. 20–21) continues: "Over her chosen ground, the ground where her engines toiled, England's control was in fact almost complete. Engines toiled in America too; but not much on goods for export and hardly at all on goods for export to England. Belgian machinery was abundant and good; but Belgium was very small. French machinery was relatively scantier and worse, all things considered. Holland was hardly thought of as a manufacturing country. . . . German machinery . . . was, as a whole, inferior and imitative. . . . Of other countries Britain might utilise the products, value the markets, or respect the arts; she did not affect to place them in an economic category with herself."

ing industry, and with them the emergence of "bigger industrial units all along the line" (Clapham, 1932, 2:114). Great Britain was clearly on the road to becoming an industrial state. "The course was set" (Clapham, 1932, 2:22). For Great Britain, these were "buoyant years," in which her economic dominance of the world-economy went "virtually unchallenged" and in which the new world of industry "seemed less like a volcano and more like a cornucopia" (Coleman, 1973, 7–8).[84] Great Britain was comfortably hegemonic, but also complacently so, not always feeling she had to watch over every fluctuation of the world-economy.[85]

Yet, we should not exaggerate. The voyage was "not half over." Agriculture remained "by very far the greatest of [Great Britain's] industries" (Clapham, 1932,

---

84. She seemed that way to other countries as well. Fejtö (1948a, 1:60) reminds us that even "the protectionists of [the various European] countries admired England . . . quite as much as the partisans of free trade. Friedrich List . . . invited his compatriots to follow the example of England, just as did the students of Cobden." Of course, List may have been remembering England's protectionist policies, which enabled it to achieve its economic dominance, more than the free-trade policies, which enabled it to maintain it.

85. Fetter (1965, 255) points out that after the First World War, the view became popular that the problem of the international economy was that Great Britain was no longer in a position to exercise leadership and that the United States was not yet in a position to do so, and that furthermore the United States lacked the vision and the training. "This is a plausible hypothesis, but I fail to find any suggestion that the British Empire or the people of England felt any such responsibility in the thirty years after 1845." He argues that Great Britain not only did not "manage" the world-economy but also did not serve as a "lender of last resort." On the other hand, Fetter himself cites (p. 271) Bagehot's article "The Duty of the Bank of England in Times of Quietude," published in the *Economist* of September 14, 1861 (p. 1009), in which Bagehot argues: "They have a national function. *They keep the sole bullion reserve* in the country. . . . The ultimate interest of the proprietors of the Bank, we believe, will be best addressed by the most complete discharge of the Bank's duty to the nation." Fetter then interprets this article thus: "In the eyes of Bagehot banking statesmanship and the profit motive were to be happily married, and his great service to the next half-century of central banking was that he convinced his countrymen that this was an honourable union blessed by the laws of free trade." This sounds like "managing" the economy to me, at least the British economy, which in 1861 meant in large part managing the world-economy.

Fetter admits that although "there was no formal acceptance of Bagehot's views by the Bank, . . . [nonetheless] from the middle 1870s the principle was no longer in doubt" (274–275). At which point, the orthodoxy included both the gold standard and the Bank of England as a lender of last resort: "That the gold standard was inviolate was a decision of Government. The task of maintaining the gold standard was entrusted to the Bank of England, and as long as it was carried out the mission the Government left to it the operating details" (p. 282).

Furthermore, this world role for the Bank of England, as the guarantor of "a sound currency and an active international trade," was well prepared by Peel when he passed the Bank Charter Act of 1844, which consecrated the victory of the so-called Currency School. "Although effective central bank management and techniques took years to evolve, the Victorians could look back to Peel as the architect of a confident economic order" (Briggs, 1959, 339).

2:22).[86] Church (1975, 76) believes that calling this period the "mid-Victorian boom" must be "severely qualified." Yes, there was a price rise,[87] business expansion, and an improved standard of living, but the growth rate in production was not all that big, and 1858 saw the most profound downward business cycle of the century. Like all economic leaders, Great Britain was preparing its own fall. It was resistant to innovation. It was in1856 that Bessemer first read his paper on his use of air blasts to make quality steel more inexpensively, but his ideas would not be widely adopted until the Kondratieff B-phase.[88] The expansion of the world-economy was bringing in its wake further industrialization in the United States and various parts of Europe, making Great Britain's competitive position "steadily more difficult," particularly because these countries indicated, with the significant exception of France, that they had "no intention of following Britain's example" in

86. This fact underlines the importance of Peel's concerns for providing a transition for the great landowners. It also underlines the dislocation that continued to present the British government with a problem of a refractory working class. "It is not easy to exaggerate the importance of the textile manufacturers in the industrial life of the country. Although not even that of cotton was completely mechanised . . . they stood as the representative industry of the age of machinery and power. . . . Because they were so mechanised their output was prodigious. Because they were not completely mechanised they carried with them in their march, and often left to fall by the wayside, a host of those who had become handworking camp-followers. Not counting hosiery and lace, they found employment for—or should we say gave a trade name to?—nearly eleven hundred thousand people" (p. 28). This group of handworkers were one in nineteen then; they were reduced to one in thirty-seven by 1901 (see p. 29).

87. The degree to which a price rise is necessarily beneficial to a hegemonic power is open to some question. Imlah (1950, 191, n. 28) gives three main explanations for the price rise in this period: the Crimean, American, and Prussian wars; new and large supplies of gold; and the export of capital goods. Rostow (1948, 20–21) is skeptical about the pluses of each of these happenings. The wars were economically "unproductive." The mining of gold was a tax on resources and "no service to the world." And capital exports were "unproductive ventures, or . . . ventures which yielded their resources only over a long period of time." As for railway building, it would pay off only after 1873 (p. 23). One might think Rostow preferred Kondratieff B-phases, but it is of course different groups, and smaller ones, that profit during the B-phases.

88. As almost always, an invention became a major innovation only during times of economic downturn. "The gigantic lock-up of capital and human capital sunk in puddling, and the as yet [1858] undisputed dominance of Britain's iron industry in the world's markets, were all against rapid change. The loss of this semi-monopolistic position and the accompanying economies in production—partly enforced—during the decade 1870–80 were the deciding factors in the ultimate transition" (Clapham, 1932, 56–57). That Great Britain's economic dominance would not be eternal was already evident to the perspicacious *Economist* of March 8, 1851: "From the relative progress of [Great Britain and the United States] within the last sixty years, it may be inferred that the superiority of the United States to England is ultimately as certain as the next eclipse" (cited in Clapham, 1932, 10).

adopting free trade (Schlote, 1952, 43).[89] Indeed, Great Britain itself would eventually sour on free trade.[90]

In this midcentury British glow, France seemed initially at a disadvantage because of the turmoil of 1848. Once again, its revolutions seemed to be hurting its economic development. But this time only most briefly, because the political solution to the turmoil—the populist authoritarianism of the Second Empire—served to resolve some of the political tensions precisely because this regime had made itself, as none had done before,[91] the proponent and propellant of a leap forward of French economic structures, thereby consolidating the liberal core of the world-system.

89. In its relation to other industrial countries outside the British Empire, "British manufactures showed a considerable decline [from 1850 to 1914] as a proportion of total exports. But, as a proportion of imports, manufactures increased considerably" (p. 87). As for the Empire, its "share of Britain's overseas commerce changed little up to the outbreak of the first World War" (p. 88), but after that it, too, declined. British shipping also entered into "relative decline" after its peak in 1847–1849 (Clapham, 1932, 211).

90. In 1850, "no one supposed . . . that Great Britain was 'young and rising' [which had been John Stuart Mill's permissible exception for protection]. She was old, risen, yet still rising. The exception did not apply. . . . It was most natural that after the collapse of the early 'seventies, and during the continued puzzling commercial and industrial difficulties which followed, plain men should begin to put the question—is it 'fair' to keep open market for nations who are closing theirs?" (Clapham, 1932, 242, 249). The Fair Trade League was founded in 1881, and Friedrich List was first translated into English in 1885 (p. 251). As Coleman (1973, 10) says: "By the 1880s the mid-Victorian optimism had evaporated."

91. "The Second Empire is the first French regime to have so clearly given priority to objectives in the economic sphere" (Plessis, 1973, 85). And this worked. See Marczewski (1965, lx): "The Revolution and the Napoleonic wars had caused a disastrous fall in foreign trade. With the Restoration, the relation between exports and physical product began to grow, but it did not exceed the level of 1787–89 until 1855. The liberal policies, inaugurated by the Anglo-French Treaty of 1860 and the stimulus to world trade of the discovery of new gold deposits, were certainly factors in the leap forward of French exports in the decade running from 1855 to 1864."

On the other hand, we should not pretend that the Second Empire was a miracle that came out of nowhere. The Belgian analyst Natalis Briavoinne was already asking this question in 1839: "Why are the scientific and industrial revolutions taking place primarily in France and in England?" To which he added a footnote in which he noted that there was of course some industrial development also in Italy, Germany, and Sweden, but he asserted that nonetheless "there is a sort of universal consensus that France is the site of the revolution in the chemical arts, and England of the revolution in mechanics" (1:191–192). Sée (1951, 2:226) similarly reminds us that "on the whole, under the regime of Louis-Philippe, there was a significant economic expansion that was remarked upon by contemporaries."

A detailed analysis by Coussy (1961) throws a skeptical eye on the degree to which the Second Empire represented a discontinuity with previous and subsequent French economic policy, arguing in particular that the economic liberalism of the regime was "a very relative liberalism, which would be labeled today a moderate protectionism" (p. 2). On the other hand, "moderate protectionism" has tended to be the liberal extreme in the continuum of governmental policies in the capitalist world-economy. Rarely has any country more than briefly exceeded this level of openness.

The economic indicators were clear: Foreign trade tripled (Palmade, 1961, 193). The production of the means of production grew relative to the production of consumable goods (Markovitch, 1966, 322).[92] There was a boom not only in domestic investment but also in foreign investment, such that by 1867 net income from external investments exceeded net export of capital. For Cameron (1961, 79), this meant that France had become "a 'mature' creditor nation."[93] And French public finances had become, along with those of Great Britain, "solid." The public subscription to government loans "demonstrated the strength of savings and the abundance of capital which existed in the *two* countries" (Gille, 1967, 280).[94] In short, this was a time of economic glory for France as well as for Great Britain. This was "to the benefit, if not the credit, of the Second Empire," but, as Palmade (1961, 127, 129) insists, "the externally favorable situation fell to a government firmly committed to taking advantage of it."

Furthermore, it was a government that thought governmental action was essential to this economic expansion, one that did not consider, in the words of Napoleon III, that state action was a "necessary ulcer" but rather that it was "the benevolent motor of any social organism." The intention nonetheless was to promote private enterprise thereby. Although the "primary concern" of the government was to "create as many [economic] activities as possible," still the government wished to "avoid this grievous tendency of the state to engage in activities which private individuals can do as well as or better than it can."[95] Furthermore, the public-works program of the government was directed not merely to aid industry, but to shore up the agricultural sector.[96] And behind this practice—"a precursor of

92. Markovitch is citing Raymond Barre. Markovitch takes this as evidence of fundamental structural change (see p. 321).

93. Cameron calls this an "important turning point in the history of France's international economic relations." As part of this process, "the decade of the 1850s . . . is also notable for the emergence of French leadership in railway promotion" (p. 213). See also Sée (1951, 2:355): "In 1871, France had more than 12 billion [francs] in foreign securities, from which 2 billion must be subtracted to cover war debts. But this loss soon turned into profit: France could acquire cheap the securities that Germany, Italy, and even England were obliged to sell on the Bourse de Paris to get out of the crisis of central Europe that occurred in 1873."

94. Gille says that "people called [these public subscriptions] at the time the universal suffrage of capital" (p. 276).

95. All these quotations from Napoleon III are reproduced in Palmade (1961, 129).

96. Vigier (1977, 18, 19, 21), in his appreciation of Bonapartism, emphasizes how much further the Second Empire took a program, already existing under the July Monarchy, of using public works "to permit the peasantry to profit fully from the rise in agricultural prices." He then asks if Bonapartism also enabled the peasantry to democratize local political life as well and "emancipate themselves progressively from the tutelage of the local notables." Noting the division of historians on this latter question, he says his own view would be a "quite nuanced one." Pouthas (1983, 459, 462) is more positive: "Agriculture was the great beneficiary of the regime. . . . The peasants, reassured against the menaces of socialism and of reaction, became the strongest supporters of the regime, to the point that the

technocratic Gaullist modernization"—was the objective of combating "political instability and class conflict" (Magraw, 1985, 159),[97] crucial for a regime that had emerged in the crucible of the Revolution of 1848.

This is where the famous Saint-Simonian link comes in. Actually, we should talk of the post–Saint-Simonians, those who had emerged out of the pseudoreligious phase under Enfantin and who retained only the "radical" spirit of Saint-Simon— rigorously modernist, technocratic, reformist, ultimately neither "socialist" nor "conservative" (as some have claimed) but essentially "liberal" in spirit, as became most clear in the Second Empire.[98] It was liberal in spirit because it combined the two key features of liberalism: economic development linked to social ameliora-tion. For liberals, the two are obverse sides of the same coin. The Saint-Simonians affirmed "the primacy of the economic over the political sphere" (Blanchard, 1956, 60). But they also argued, in the 1831 formula of Isaac Péreire, that economic progress would bring about "an amelioration of the lot of the largest and poor-est strata" (cited in Plessis, 1973, 86). This is of course why Napoleon III and the Saint-Simonians were "made for each other" (Weill, 1913, 391–92).[99] To be sure, the

English and Karl Marx called the Empire the empire of the peasantry." But, in the end, how different was Louis Napoleon's caressing and coddling of the peasantry from Peel's enforced modernization of British agriculture? In both cases, it appeased a substantial political force that controlled the country's food supply while allowing a gentle transition to a long-term declining role and profitability for this sector, which became clear to everyone after 1873. See Verley (1987, 166): "[I]nternal agricultural pro-ductivity in the 1860s could not keep pace with the needs of global growth." Mokyr and Nye (1990, 173) describe governmental policy as "redirect[ing] the economy toward agriculture, in which France apparently had a comparative advantage." If so, it lost it soon thereafter. I see Bonapartist policy as more overtly political, aimed at holding in check peasant discontent.

97. In Magraw's view, "the balance sheet of Bonapartism's political economy was uneven" (p. 163).

98. See Carlisle (1968, 444–445): "Saint-Simonian radicalism consisted in its determination to modify, from within, the outlook, customs and practices of the Liberal bourgeois business world in post-Napoleonic France. Saint-Simonian radicalism further consisted in bringing to this business world, governed by a concept of rigid, inescapable economic law, a conviction of the possibility, and the inevitability, of escape from that law. . . . [T]he Saint-Simonians were the creators of an attitude of initiative, risktaking, flexibility, and expansionism among French businessmen." Cole (1953, 1:52, 56), speaking of their global vision and involvement in the building of the Suez and Panama canals, says: "They were in fact the precursors of President Truman's 'Point Four.' Nothing was too grand for them to project. . . . They were the first to see (and approve) what is now called the 'managerial revolution.'"

99. Weill continues: "The Saint-Simonians . . . gave top priority to increasing production. . . . Were not large public works the best way rapidly to aid the poor? . . . It was the role of the state to undertake these large works. . . . [B]ut if the state neglected its duty, the Saint-Simonians did not hesitate to appeal to private initiative. . . . The imperial government had the same program." This was in no way a demo-cratic socialist program. See Bourgin (1913, 406): "Saint-Simonian socialism, founded on inequality, had nothing in common with the new schools based on democracy. The friends of a strong govern-ment were a source of distrust for all the adversaries of Napoleon III."

Saint-Simonians were "about the only intellectual group available to [Napoleon]" (Boon, 1936, 85). But also vice versa: the modernist sector of the bourgeoisie, the true liberals, "needed [Napoleon] to liberate themselves from the timidities of the well-to-do" (Agulhon, 1973, 234),[100] who had dominated the Party of Order in the July Monarchy. This is why Guérard (1943, chap. 9) called Napoleon III "Saint-Simon on horseback."

It is in this period as well that banks came into their own as key agents of national economic development. In this, too, the credit must go to the post–Saint-Simonians (such as the brothers Péreire), who were "the first to realize the role of stimulus and coordinator that banks could play in economic life" (Chlepner, 1926, 15). But the story predates the brothers Péreire. From at least 1815 on, the biggest banks—notably the Rothschilds and the Barings—shifted their emphasis to long-term loans, first in negotiating and promoting loans to governments and second in sustaining large private enterprises. Since, as Landes (1956, 210–212) notes, were these banks to show "too voracious an appetite," they could be under-cut by competitors, they tended to form cartels. The Rothschilds in particular found their best profits in a tacit link with the Holy Alliance and were thus able to locate themselves in the principal money markets, which at that time were "more markets of demand than centers of money supply" (Gille, 1965, 98).[101] Further-more, the "favorite gambit" of the Rothschilds—the short-term emergency loan to a government in difficulty—was not necessarily an aid to national self-sufficiency. Cameron (1957b, 556) argues that such governments "rarely ever regained [their] independence" and compares the practice to a "habit-forming drug."[102]

---

100. Kemp (1971, 158–159) downplays the significance of the Saint-Simonians on the grounds that "it was ... very much in the objective position of the Second Empire that ... the state should adopt the role of stimulator of the economy. ... [The state] offered to all the owners of mobile wealth the prospect of increasing it. It was this implicit appeal to the cupidity of the middle class and better-off peasants which constituted the great strength of the regime; only, of course, because it did pay off. It was in the fifties and sixties that Guizot's 'Enrichissez-vous' came true for large numbers of Frenchmen." His conclusion, therefore, is that "in view of the favorable economic conjuncture of the third quarter of the nineteenth century, it seems likely that appreciable economic growth, necessarily involving qualitative changes in the financial and industrial structure, would have taken place under any form of govern-ment able to maintain civil peace" (p. 200). This is true, of course, but it was Napoleon III's government that was able to maintain civil peace, and it was the Saint-Simonians who were around and willing to undertake the necessary initiatives.

101. Gille continues: "They may have let themselves be thought of as the bankers of the Holy Alli-ance, although Metternich ... was certainly not taken in. Above all, they profited from an extremely favorable moment (conjoncture), when they were able to push aside some serious competitors. They now set themselves to consolidating this position, even to improving it."

102. He says they "returned again and again for new injections." But how much choice did these governments have? Gille (1965, 79–80) points out that most of them could find subscribers to loans only on an international market, and particularly in the London and Paris markets. For that, they

The need, of course, was for more locally controlled sources of credit. Chlepner (1926, 19) reminds us that, before the Crédit Mobilier of the brothers Péreire, there were "predecessors" in Belgium—most notably the Société Générale, founded by King William in 1822. It was, however, only after Belgium marked its independence in 1831 with the enthronement of Leopold I that the bank became a major actor in economic development, primarily in the construction of railways. If this bank and the rival Banque de Belgique, founded in 1835, both went into relative hibernation after the financial crisis of 1838, they were even harder hit by the Anglo-French economic crisis of 1846–1847. With this in the background, February 1848 led to fear of revolution, fear of the loss of independence, and a "veritable financial panic" (Chlepner, 1926, 238; see also 1931), which caused the state to come to the aid of the bank and end the period of agitation. Belgium thus was able to avoid the revolutionary upsurge and could then move to a more truly liberal system, eliminating the semiofficial character of the Société Générale in 1851.[103]

The banking controversies in Great Britain, previously discussed, created a situation in which the banks were unable to play a direct role in promoting economic growth. These controversies culminated in the Bank Act of 1844, whose objective, from Peel's point of view, was primarily to "make more solid the foundations of the gold standard" and secondarily to remove the use of gold as an internal political weapon (Fetter, 1965, 192).[104] Perhaps Great Britain could afford, better than other countries, not to have a banking policy that would promote economic growth. Cameron (1961, 58–59) calls this "inefficient" but notes

---

needed an organizer, and not just any organizer, but one who inspired confidence. "It was enough, that the name [of a reputable firm] be part of the financial operation [sponsoring the loan] that it drained all the available capital to it. And if [this firm] had, via commissions, and facilities to place money, a certain number of active correspondents, its supremacy was ensured."

103. The reason the financial situation of 1838 had been particularly acute in Belgium was political, not economic. It was the result of the final acceptance by William of the Netherlands of the Treaty of 1831, which recognized Belgium's separation from the kingdom. This had been a treaty unfavorable to Belgium, accepted under duress in 1831, and which no longer seemed reasonable to a stronger Belgium in 1838 (Chlepner, 1926, 154 and n.2).

104. Gold had been a notable element in the politics of the Reform Bill of 1832. When the Reform Bill was defeated in the House of Lords, and Wellington was trying, without success, to form a government, Francis Place (as we previously noted) had launched the famous slogan "To stop the Duke, go for gold." The run on gold did occur and did affect the political situation. But this in turn had the effect of "strengthening public opinion that bank notes should be legal tender" (135–136). Perhaps Peel in 1844 was anticipating that such a weapon might be used once again, this time against him, in the battle over Repeal of the Corn Laws. Fetter also notes (p. 174) the simultaneity of the growth of free trade sentiment in Great Britain in the 1840s with the "growing acceptance of the idea that note issue was not a business activity, but a function of government." But he does not comment on how paradoxical this is in terms of laissez-faire doctrine. Obviously, the freer the trade in goods, the less free the free traders in goods wanted the trade in money to be. Freedom is not worth too much if it puts profit at risk.

that "paradoxically, . . . the very obstacles placed in the way of a rational bank-ing and monetary system stimulated the private sector to introduce the financial innovations necessary for realization of the full benefits of technical innovations in industry."

What the British state had promoted by its failures—an adequate supply of credit for the midcentury economic expansion—the French state under Napoleon III would create deliberately. The decree of February 1852 authorizing the forma-tion of mortgage banks, the Crédit Foncier of Émile Péreire being one of the first, provided the financial underpinning for the reconstruction of Paris by Hauss-mann. "[F]rom a laggard, France became a leader and innovator in mortgage credit" (Cameron, 1961, 129).[105] The Rothschilds were not happy. James de Roth-schild argued that this change in structure would concentrate too much power in untried hands. It seems a case of the pot calling the kettle black.[106] In any case, the rise of the great corporate banks of the Second Empire took the monopoly away from what had been called the *haute banque,* a "powerful group of private (unincorporated) bankers" (Cameron, 1953, 462). But the *haute banque* had not provided sufficient credit to *French* business enterprises.[107]

Toward the end of the Second Empire, in 1867, the largest of the new banks, Crédit Mobilier, failed. The Rothschilds, however, were still there, and are still there today. Nonetheless the liberal state, by its intervention, had changed the worldwide credit structure of modern capitalism: "[T]he banking system of every nation in Continental Europe bore the imprint of French influence" (Cameron,

---

105. These activities became a source of great wealth in the Second Empire: "[T]he bonds of the railways and of the City of Paris or of Crédit Foncier, regularly issued and with a high interest rate, gave savings a sure and remunerative place to invest" (Girard, 1952, 399). No wonder that, as Cameron goes on, "[t]he *crédit foncier* idea spread rapidly in the 1860ss, and by 1875 all European countries and several outside Europe had similar institutions."

106. For a detailed discussion of James de Rothschild's views, see Gille (1970, 132–134) and also Pouthas (1983, 457).

107. "Throughout the *monarchie censitaire* [monarchy with legislatures elected on limited suf-frage], there had been complaints about the lack of organized credit, indeed of its nonexistence. In the last year of the reign of Louis-Philippe complaints on this score had grown greatly. After the 1848 Revolution, there was general recognition that the crises were due in part to the absence of a devel-oped credit system" (Gille, 1959a, 370). Lévy-Leboyer (1964, 699) finds the complaints to have "little foundation." He says that in the 1840s, when the railways were being built, "the financial market gave the impression of being the vital part of the economy" of western Europe. He does admit that this was true mainly of Paris and Brussels, and a few other centers, and that "grave lacunae existed" (p. 705). This may be the clue to what really happened. Plessis (1987, 207) points out that, in the July Monarchy, the Banque de France opened local branches in order to shut out other banks, whereas in the Second Empire they were closing the local branches, to the protest of local notables. What the local notables wanted was both the Banque de France and the new banks, because that gave them multiple and com-petitive sources of credit.

1961, 203).[108] The creation of larger numbers of banks oriented to the international market may have diminished the power of the *haute banque*. This was not necessarily a great virtue for the weaker state structures in tight financial situations. Jenks (1927, 273) discusses the perverse effect of greater competition in the field of loans to governments:

> [C]ompetition simply augmented the risks of marketing the loan in the face of efforts of the unsuccessful banker to cry it down. . . . What the competition did encourage, however, was the pressing of more money upon frequently "bewildered" borrowers. . . . In a word, the loan business was monopolescent.[109]

The collapse of Crédit Mobilier gives credence to this analysis. It formed part of a sequence that led to the drying up of loans to weak governments and hence the accentuation of what was to become the Great Depression after 1873.[110]

The liberals had achieved what they had hoped to achieve in midcentury. The long upswing of the world-economy and the actions of the governments of the core zone—in particular, of Great Britain and France—secured a steady process of worldwide relocations, until at least the end of the twentieth century. We may call this the "strong market," one of the three pillars of the liberal world order that was to be the great achievement of the capitalist world-economy in the nineteenth and twentieth centuries. But there were two further pillars for a liberal world order: the strong state, and the strong interstate system. It is to the process of securing them that we now turn.

The absolute monarchies had not been strong states. Absolutism was merely the scaffolding within which weak states sought to become stronger. It would only be in the post-1789 world-system's atmosphere of normal change and popular sovereignty that one could build truly strong states—that is, states with an ade-

---

108. Cameron (1953, 487) makes this judicious assessment: "In properly judging the contribution to economic development of the Crédit Mobilier and its contemporaries, one must take account of possible offsets on its record. Did the export of capital hinder the economic growth of France itself? Could the Crédit Mobilier have made a greater contribution by limiting its activities to its own country? No brief answers to such questions would be satisfactory, but the combined weight of both orthodox economic doctrine and the specific economic conditions in France at the time indicate that the course which it pursued was in the direction of greatest social utility."

109. Of course, it's never hard to lend money to poorer states. As Jenks observes (1927, 263): "Governments borrow money immediately because they are torn between zeal for progress and the desire to propitiate the taxpayer."

110. See the analysis of Newbold (1932, 429): "The more conservative houses that remained, after the British financial crisis of 1866 and the French political collapse of 1870, were not readily disposed to throw good money after bad and to find for the Turks, the Egyptians, and the 'Liberal' republics of Latin America the means out of the capital of new loans to pay the interest on the old loans. . . . It was, therefore, only a matter of time when the Sultan, the Khedive, and a half-dozen Presidents would announce their utter inability to meet their obligations." Newbold says that, if we add in the aftereffects of the American Civil War, we can easily understand the "orgy of speculation" of 1869–1873.

quate bureaucratic structure and a reasonable degree of popular acquiescence (which in wartime could be converted into passionate patriotism). And it was the liberals, and only the liberals, who could construct such states in the core zones of the world-system. Bureaucratic growth was the essential pendant of economic growth, at least of economic growth at the scale that capitalists now hoped for and that was now technologically possible.

Of course, the construction of a strong bureaucratic state was a long process that had begun in the late fifteenth century. Resistance to such construction is what we really mean when we refer to an ancien régime, which of course existed quite as much in Great Britain as in France, as indeed it did throughout Europe and most of the world. What we may call generically Colbertism was the attempt to overcome this resistance by taking real power from the local level and concentrating it in the hands of the monarch. It was at best partially successful. Jacobinism was nothing but Colbertism with a republican face. It died in its original form in 1815. After 1815, it would be liberalism that took up the battle to create a strong state. Whereas Colbertism and Jacobinism had been brutally frank about their intentions, the fact that liberals refused to acknowledge that building the strong state was their intention—in many ways, their priority—was perhaps precisely why they were able to succeed better than the Colbertists and the Jacobins. Indeed, they succeeded so well that the enlightened conservatives took up this same objective, largely effacing in the process any ideological distinction between themselves and the liberals.

Of course, there are many reasons why capitalists find strong states useful. One is to help them accumulate capital;[111] a second is to guarantee this capital.[112] But after 1848, capitalists fully realized, if they had not before, that only the strong state—that is, the reformist state—could buffer them against the winds of worker discontent. Péreire put his finger on it: "The 'strong' state became the welfare state of large-scale (*grand*) capitalism" (cited in Bouvier, 1967, 166). Of course, "welfare state" here has a double connotation—the welfare of the working classes to be sure, but the welfare of the capitalists as well.

111. Daumard (1976, 3:150) cites Burdeau: "The theorists [of capitalism] repeat the slogan of laissez-faire, but businessmen demand of legislators *pouvoir faire* [the means to be able to do]. It has never been enough [for capitalists] that liberty permits them to act; they want it to be active."

112. In the spring of 1914, the secretary of the French *Comité des Houillières*, Henry de Peyerimhoff, made a speech in which he talked of world economic competition: "In this struggle, . . . what can we count on? On our capital. . . . It is a force, but it is a fragile force when it is not supported by others. Riches that are undefended make the most tempting prey and the most desirable hostage. Venice played this role and then the United Provinces. The financial claims of the House of Hope in Amsterdam on all the sovereigns of Europe did not produce a very great impression, it seems, on the hussars of Pichegru, and I am afraid that the coffers of the Most Serene Republic, actually half empty, attracted Bonaparte more than they intimidated him. Our money works for our empire to the degree that our empire will be able to defend our money" (cited in Bouvier, 1965, 175).

We think of Victorian Great Britain as the locus of antistatism in its heyday, and it is quite true that "in general, [most Englishmen] were suspicious of the State and of centralization" at this time (Burn, 1964, 226).[113] But in the jostle of conflicting interests between those (largely the "liberals") who wanted the state to cease propping up the agricultural interests and those (largely the "conservatives") who were inclined to favor local and more traditional authority, combining it with a rhetoric of social concern for the poor,[114] it was easy for the latter to find compensation for every victory of free commerce by pushing forward some project of state intervention in industry. Brebner calls it the "mid-century dance . . . like a minuet": parliamentary reform in 1832, the first Factory Act in 1833; Peel's budget in 1841; the Mines Act in 1842; Repeal of the Corn Laws in 1846; the Ten Hours Bill in 1847. "The one common characteristic [of the political initiatives of 1825–1870] is the consistent readiness of interested groups to use the state for collectivist interests" (Brebner, 1948, 64, 70).[115]

Before 1848 much of the argument among the middle classes for state social reform had been based on "widespread philanthropic enthusiasm and the uneasy con-

---

113. He notes, however, that these same Englishmen, when they "had some particular interest[,] . . . were prepared to use the action of the State to forward it."

114. Speenhamland, of course, was a major ploy in this battle. It was instituted in 1795 and ended in 1834. Hobsbawm (1962, 200) calls it "a well-meaning but mistaken attempt to guarantee the laborer a minimum wage by subsidizing wages out of poor rates"—mistaken because it in fact lowered wages. Polanyi (1957, 81) points out that it had this effect only because, at the same time, the Anti-Combination Laws were passed in 1799–1800. Thus the Conservative thrust had prevented the creation of a free labor market as the industrialists had sought, but without any real benefit to the working classes. The economic liberals eventually solved the problem, as Hobsbawm continues, in their "usual brisk and ruthless manner by forcing [the laborer] to find work at a social wage or to migrate." Migration occurred in two forms: country to town (see Cairncross, 1949, 70–71), and overseas. The latter was abetted by lifting the restrictions on the emigration of skilled artisans (see Clapham, 1930, 1:489, for a breakdown of who went where). For previous discussion, see Wallerstein (1989, 120–121).

115. See Brebner's appendix (70–73) for a long list of interventionist legislation in the nineteenth century. On the *non*-opposition of the classical economists to social legislation like the Factory Acts, see none other than Alfred Marshall (1921, 763–764): "[N]either Ricardo, nor any other of the great coterie by which he was surrounded, seems to have been quoted as having opposed the early Factory Acts." He points out that Tooke, McCulloch, and Newmarch were all supporters, and that Nassau Senior, opposed at first, later supported them. This readiness of the very spokesmen of laissez-faire to approve of some government intervention in the social arena was theorized by another liberal economist, Stanley Jevons, in 1882 in the following way: "We must neither maximize the functions of government at the beck of quasi-military officials, nor minimize them according to the theories of the very best philosophers. We must learn to judge each case by its merits" (*The State in Relation to Labour*, p. 171, cited in Clapham, 1932, 2:389). Jevons's statement is actually a fine example of what Burn (1949, 221) calls the "liberal equipoise" in midcentury Great Britain: "The balance, the equipoise held; both between the several classes and interests and between the 'individual' and the State. It both made for

science . . . at the spectacle of the poverty in which the workers were condemned to live" (Halévy, 1947, 218). However, the revolutions of 1848, which Britons could not help but feel they had averted by the beginnings of social intervention, added to mere guilt a sense of the political importance of reformist legislation.[116] Thus it was that, at the very height of the classical age of English liberalism, "the growth of the *central* government was staggering" (Katznelson, 1985, 274).[117] These foundations of modern government may have been, as Evans (1983, 285) said, "laid in the teeth of a gale."[118] But Gladstonian liberalism was "a restless, reforming creed" (Southgate, 1965, 324), albeit without the least semblance of any commitment to economic equality.

The origins of Gladstonian reformism were in Benthamism, as we have seen.[119] The result was the so-called administrative revolution, which transformed the

---

and was assisted by a notable change in the temper of the age. That change may be described, and was described by a contemporary, as the suppression of principle by expediency."

116. This was reinforced in Great Britain by the curious hangover of religious prejudice, as pointed out by Halévy (1947, 326): "We must go back in imagination to the year 1850 when the "Papal Aggression" caused such a stir in England. Throughout Latin Europe, in Austria and in Belgium, Catholicism had defeated Liberalism, atheism, and Socialism. Before the close of 1851 Louis Napoleon surrounded with the blessing of the entire Episcopate would overthrow the Constitution in France. Papal Aggression was but the prolongation beyond the Channel of this Catholic reaction against the hostile forces which, ever since 1789 and with renewed strength since 1830, threatened it everywhere. It was not, therefore, surprising that British public opinion took alarm. On the Continent the defeat of the revolution of 1848 had been the victory of Catholicism. But England had escaped that revolution; and, when the Catholic reaction reached England, it encountered an obstacle which had no existence on the Continent, the victory of the revolution of 1846, the victory of Liberalism."

Cahill (1957, 75–76) draws the opposite conclusion from the same description: "The year 1848, often claimed as the year of triumph for British Liberalism, actually witnessed the bankruptcy of that ideology, in the face of threats from abroad and at home. The year of revolution saw the victory of British nationalism, bolstered and reinforced by anti-French and anti-Catholic feeling. . . . British success of 1848 was the achievement of a patriotic press which, by associating Irish Repeal, French Radicalism, a Liberal Pope, Irish Popery and Democratic Chartism, eased the tensions of social unrest at home."

117. The central bureaucracy increased fifteen times between 1797 and 1869. "The unitary . . . English state concentrated distributive public policies at the center as a result of the passage of the Poor Law of 1834; the Public Health Acts of 1848, 1866, 1872, and 1875; the Police Acts of 1839 and 1856; the Food and Drug Acts of 1860 and 1872."

118. Evans (p. 289) finds this a "supreme irony," but in our analysis, there is no irony whatsoever. As he himself says, "[N]one knew better, or thought they knew better, than those second-generation *laissez-faire* philosophers, the Benthamite Utilitarians, how to regulate most efficiently and least wastefully." And henceforth, the Benthamite Utilitarians, and their successors in many guises, would have a permanent role, for with the growth in the power of the state went "the growth in the power of the expert" (Kitson Clark, 1967, 167).

119. See Coates (1950, 358): "[I]t was by the unrestricted use of the legislative power of the state that Bentham sought to effect his reforms." See also Checkland (1964, 411): "Benthamism meant identifying

functions of the state in the direction of a "new and more or less conscious Fabianism" (MacDonagh, 1958, 60).[120] Bit by bit, "the disciples of Smith and Ricardo [came to promote a series of] social reforms which brought a strong paternalistic state" (Roberts, 1958, 335). And then, in the last twist, English liberalism redefined in this fashion "found a complementary expression in the Conservative Party which . . . actually realized certain Liberal principles which the other . . . was in danger of obscuring" (Ruggiero, 1959, 135).

The situation in France was remarkably similar. There, too, laissez-faire had become "the dominant watchword." But there, too, "practice was rather different from theory." And there, too, "those in power were conscious of the industrial factor in the world struggle for preponderance, peaceful but then tending to become warlike" (Léon, 1960, 182).[121] And there, too, the nineteenth century was the century in which the strong state was constructed. To be sure, this creation had been and would continue to be a continuous process—from Richelieu to Colbert to the Jacobins to Napoleon to the *monarchies censitaires* to the Second Empire to the Third Republic to the Fifth.[122] But in many ways the Second Empire marked

---

the urgent tasks of society and prescribing the means for their discharge: it meant specific legislation, with inspectors in the field and administrators in centralized offices. It meant Members of Parliament who thought, as Bentham did, in terms of 'agenda.'" Between 1852 and 1867, this agenda included the police force, prisons, endowed schools, doctors, and veterinary medicine—all regulated and promoted by the state. See Burn (1964, 167–226).

John Maynard Keynes, in his book *The End of Laissez-Faire* (1926, 45–46), was quite lucid on Benthamism and the state: "Nineteenth-century State Socialism sprung from Bentham, free competition, etc., and is in some respects a clearer, in some respects a more muddled version of just the same philosophy as nineteenth-century individualism. Both equally laid their stress on freedom, the one negatively to avoid limitations on existing freedom, the other positively to destroy natural or acquired monopolies. They are different reactions to the same intellectual atmosphere."

120. This change was quite pragmatic: "The great body of such changes were natural answers to concrete day-to-day problems, pressed eventually to the surface by the sheer exigencies of the case" (p. 65). Aydelotte (1967, 226) makes the same case: "It is now generally appreciated that the mid-nineteenth century was not a period of administrative nihilism [in Great Britain] but, on the contrary, one of rapid and significant development of government regulation of social conditions." See also Watson (1973, 70): [I]t cannot be seriously doubted that the level of government activity rose, and rose largely, during the reign of Victoria." For critiques of this view, see Hart (1965) and Parris (1960).

It is important to remember that this was a change in the practice, not in the doctrine. The doctrine of free trade was predominant throughout much of Europe at this time. Indeed, Kindleberger (1975, 51) attributes the widespread turning to free trade between 1820 and 1875 as evidence that Europe was "a single entity which moved to free trade for ideological or perhaps better doctrinal reasons." But then, pragmatically, Europe would move away from free trade in the wake of the Great Depression. Reality kept overcoming doctrine.

121. The major difference between France and Great Britain in midcentury is that, given their relative strengths in the world-economy at that time, the French state, unlike the British, never renounced intervening in the commercial arena.

122. "The rationalization of the Administration began long before the Revolution [of 1789] and has not stopped since" (Théret, 1991, 141–142). See also Fontvieille (1976, 2011) on the steady expansion

a crucial step forward. Or perhaps the way to put it is that the Second Empire marked the locking in of the structure by laying the basis for popular acquiescence. Louis Napoleon was able to do this because, as Guizot (cited in Pouthas, 1983, 144) said, with what sounds like grudging admiration, he incarnated at one and the same time "national glory, a revolutionary guarantee, and the principle of order."[123]

What Napoleon III instituted was a welfare-state principle from the top down. The Second Republic had brought the "social question" to the fore of the agenda, arguing that the sovereignty of all the people contrasted with, was belied by, the "tragic inferiority in the conditions of some of the people." From this observation, two conclusions seemed possible: a definition of popular sovereignty that would lead to "unlimited political power," or an "absolute rejection of political authorities (*pouvoir*)" that risked making society "ungovernable" (Donzelot, 1984, 67, 70). Bonapartism represented the former definition, without ever forgetting that it had to use the power to provide a response to the "social question."

In his first decade in power, Napoleon III repressively reestablished order, used the state to build public works and modernize the banking system, and concluded the 1860 free-trade treaty with Great Britain. In this period, Napoleon III was primarily concerned with creating an "environment favourable to industrial capitalists," and therefore one in which the working class was "held in check" (Kemp, 1971, 181).[124] Once this was assured, he would then turn to integrating the working classes into the political process. He became quite popular with the workers in the years after 1858. They were years of great prosperity, years of political reform, years in which France was supporting oppressed nationalities in Italy and elsewhere. A pro-Bonapartist workers' group came into existence (Kulstein, 1962, 373–375; also 1964). In this atmosphere, there was a growing competition

---

since 1815: "[S]tatistically the expansion of the state is explained [*déterminée*] by its growing intervention in the economic structure."

123. Werner (1977, xi–xii) amplifies the bon mot of Guizot: "Bonapartism, despite some undeniably conservative, even reactionary, traits, demanded of its adherents commitment to the ideas of the Nation and the Revolution of 1789, in the version sanctioned by Napoleon I. . . . [T]he people, politically organized and voting in elections, were no longer subjects of a prince but the true sovereign which even the plebiscited president, even the emperor, had to serve. . . . Universal suffrage, the ideals of liberty, equality, and fraternity, the concept of the citizen all represented surviving achievements of the Revolution, which did not mean, in the mind of the proponents, that a strong and centralized power was not needed to prevent future revolutions."

124. Bourgin (1913, 224) also notes that "the working class felt its hands tied . . . , the authoritarian Emperor . . . clearly taking sides, in wage conflicts, against the working class. Still one cannot deny . . . the philanthropic preoccupations that were perhaps an exclusive mark of the Empire."

among republicans, royalists, and Prince Napoleon for the favor of the workers. They were all encouraging cooperatives on the grounds that such organizations were not "incompatible with the free economy in which they all believed" (Plamenatz, 1952, 126).[125]

In various ways, Napoleon III sought to "become closer to the new social left" (Duverger, 1967, 156).[126] In 1864, he legalized trade unions and strikes, which constituted, in the words of Henri Sée (1951, 2:342), "an act of major importance in the social history of France."[127] Indeed, the regime used its attempt to "ameliorate the conditions of the workers and the needy" as a central theme of its propaganda, boasting of its "cradle to the grave" assistance to the needy (Kulstein, 1969, 95, 99).[128] What Napoleon III, as the first among the "democratic Bonapartists," sought was a program that would "render the masses conservative . . . by giving them something to conserve" (Zeldin, 1958, 50). In this way, he made it possible to complete the project of transforming France into a liberal state—a project that would be consecrated in the constitution of 1875.[129] Furthermore, France was not only a liberal state but a national state, and it was France that had sealed the identification of the two in nineteenth-century Europe.[130]

The third pillar of the British/liberal world order was a strong interstate system. Metternich's Holy Alliance had not been considered a step in that direction, since

125. Prince Napoleon even arranged for a delegation of workers to attend the World Exposition in London in 1862. Once there, however, they joined in the formation of the International Working Mens' Association, and broke their relations with the prince upon their return.

126. Still, as Bourgin insists (1913, 232), "the government was hesitant in relation to the workers." And, he adds, they were right to be hesitant: "Insofar as the Empire made concessions which were ruining its authoritarian base, the workers began to feel their strength growing and came to see that the government that had successively bullied them and caressed them was falling apart."

127. Sée notes the various constraints that remained but says that nonetheless, the law represented "a serious step forward, all the more so since, up to the very moment of its adoption, striking workers were still being indicted by the judicial authorities."

128. Théret, very down-to-earth, observes (1989, 1160), however, that "the 'social' image of the Second Empire does not fare well . . . once one takes a close look at the statistics on governmental expenditures."

129. Daumard (1976, 138) defines the project thus: "[P]rogressively the French moved from being subjects to being citizens."

130. See Woolf (1992, 101): "It could be argued that the model of France, perhaps even more than that of Britain, was central in this construction of the political concept of modern Europe precisely because, in the hands of the liberals, national identity was combined with the leading role attributed to the state. For one of the most remarkable features of this legacy of the Napoleonic years was the growing association of liberalism and standardizing administrative reforms as the method to forge a unified state identity. . . . As new nation-states achieved independence in the nineteenth century their governments insisted on the same methods against what they saw as the dangers of anti-national regional or ethnic identities."

the oppressive interference had tended to stir the nationalist pots while trying to keep the kettle tops pinned in place—a sure remedy for further revolutions, as 1848 would show. Or so both the British and the French thought. What the British wanted, as the hegemonic power and the strongest actor in the world-economy at this time, was as much free trade as possible, which meant as much as was politically possible, with the least need for military expenditures. The British wanted to have their way without having constantly to use too much force to impose their way. In short, they wanted stability and openness to the degree that it served their economic interests. Of course, in some sense this objective was not new. But in midcentury the British were in a position to be more honest about it and for a short time to profit highly from the fruits of such a policy. To be sure, as Cunningham (1908, 869) noted:

> It may be pointed out with some truth that the system of unfettered intercourse was opportune for England, because she had reached a particular phase of development as an industrial nation, but that it was not equally advantageous to countries in which the economic system was less advanced.

And this was because, as Musson (1972b, 19) has argued, free trade is in fact simply one more protectionist doctrine—in this case, protectionist of the advantages of those who at a given time are enjoying greater economic efficiencies.[131]

Nor should we forget that, to the extent that one may argue that free trade prevailed in the capitalist world-economy in the nineteenth century, or at least among European powers, it was at most a story of the midcentury Kondratieff A-period, 1850–1873. "The nineteenth century began and ended in Europe . . . with restrictions of international trade" (Bairoch, 1976a, 11),[132] quite severe restrictions—the Continental Blockade at the one end and the multiplicity of protectionist tariffs at the other.

---

131. "[Free trade] was as protectionist as the old Mercantilist policies: it aimed at preventing or delaying the growth of foreign, industrial competition—foreign countries, it was hoped, would exchange their foodstuffs and raw materials for British manufactures which, by their cheapness, would swamp foreign industries."

Noting that British colonial preference was fully abolished only in 1860 (to be reinstated, of course, in the last third of the century), Schuyler (1945, 246) says: "There was no longer any need for the British to post themselves all over the globe in order to make way for their commerce; trade had become its own protection." And Evans (1983, 31), in discussing Great Britain's earlier "rage for commercial treaties" in the 1780s, which he attributes to the attempt to overcome being "starkly isolated in Europe" after the end of the American War, observes that only one treaty was ever concluded—the Eden treaty with France, in 1786. But that treaty, he says, "gave the first hint of that concealed monopoly which Britain was to enjoy as she became the world's first industrial nation. The liberalization of trade was bound to favour the most efficient producers." (On the Eden treaty, see Wallerstein, 1989, 87–93.)

132. Bairoch (1973, 561–562) lists the years 1860–1880/1890 as "Europe's free trade experience," during which there was "a more rapid increase in intra-European trade." In a later article (1989, 36), he gives the years 1860–1879. Polanyi (1957, 19) specifies the years 1846–1879 as "the free trade episode." Great Britain had formally adopted the principle of free trade in 1846.

It was only slowly that Great Britain itself had been won over to the merits of free trade. The political economists in the Board of Trade believed that the adoption of the Corn Laws in 1815 had been the stimulus to the *Zollverein,* which worried them doubly. It furthered the development of competitive manufacturing in the German states, and it also tended to cut the British off from using these states as the "excellent smuggling bases" into Prussia, Bavaria, Austria, and Russia that they had previously been (Clapham, 1930, 1:480–481; Kindleberger, 1975, 33–34).[133] In the 1830s, the worries about competitive manufacturing grew.[134] These worries, plus the internal considerations previously discussed, account for Peel's actions in the 1840s. Peel, let us remember, was not a free-trade ideologue; he was no Cobden. He was, in Schuyler's apt image (1945, 134), "a reformer on the installment plan, disinclined to push theories to their logical limit."[135]

The strongest theme of free trade in Great Britain—or, let us say, the theme that assembled the widest band of public opinion behind it—was what might be called the theme of "liberal interventionism." Free trade for the British was a doctrine that was intended to prevent other governments from doing anything that might hurt British enterprise. In this sense, one might regard the antislavery (and antislave-trade) movement as the first great success of liberal interventionism. We have previously discussed the degree to which the British abolitionist movement was predicated on economic considerations (Wallerstein, 1989, 143–146).[136] What

133. Kindleberger concludes: "On this showing, the repeal of the Corn Laws was motivated by 'free trade imperialism,' the desire to gain a monopoly of trade with the world in manufactured goods. *Zollverein* in the 1830s merely indicated the need for haste."

134. See Cain (1980, 19): "The attempts made in the 1830s to induce European countries to make concessions on the basis of reciprocity were often founded on the notion that there ought to be a 'natural' division of labour between industrial Britain and agricultural Europe. These negotiations failed largely because countries like France were determined to avoid dependence on Britain for their manufactured commodities."

135. It is precisely this centrist compromise that has allowed later observers to make such opposite assessments of his actions. On the one hand, Jenks (1927, 126) said Repeal of the Corn Laws (plus the railway mania) "brought about a revolution as complete [as the changes in production of preceding generations] in the conditions of the foreign trade of Great Britain." At about the same time, Walker-Smith (1933, 17, 27–28), himself a Conservative protectionist, argued: "Peel's revision of the Tariff was in the direction not of Free Trade, but of scientific and graded protectionism.... The protectionist house was set in order. To some at the time it may have appeared that the new Tariff and the revised sliding-scale were only the thin end of a Free Trade edge.... [But] Peel, as strongly as the party which he led, stood firm by the Protectionist system, as strengthened and amended by themselves."

136. Drescher (1981, 18) is a forceful spokesman against the idea that antislavery was "a means of universalizing a single middle-class perspective of the world" or a diversion from domestic reform, seeing it rather as "providing a strand of humanity against which the opposing capitalist exploitation could be devastatingly measured in quite specific terms." Blackburn, who is inclined to give economic factors a far larger role, concludes (1988, 520) nonetheless that "slavery was not overthrown for economic reasons but where it was politically untenable," meaning essentially the degree to which there

we wish to note here is the degree to which the antislavery movement provided a model of liberal reformism—a point underlined by Blackburn (1988, 439–440):

> In acutely troubled times anti-slavery helped middle-class reformers to highlight their socio-economic ideals. . . . [Anti-slavery] furnished a model of legislation dictated by general policy rather than particular interests. It justified state intervention in regulating the working class contract, while sanctifying the contract itself. The advocates of emancipation presented it as furnishing an economic stimulus via market expansion. The free worker was also a consumer.[137]

The same liberal belief in the legitimacy of state-led reformism was applied to free trade. The forced transformation of India, from being an exporter of cotton textiles to being an exporter of raw cotton, permitted British cotton manufacturers to embrace free trade unreservedly, once the British state had "secured Lancashire against any threat of Indian competition in the markets of Europe" (Farnie, 1979, 100).[138] Palmerston told Auckland on January 22, 1841: "It is the business of Government to open and secure the roads for the merchant" (cited in Platt, 1968b, 85).[139] Applying this logic even to European states, a Whig M.P. in the parliamentary debate of 1846 could describe free trade as a beneficent principle whereby "foreign nations would become valuable Colonies to us, without imposing on us the responsibility of governing them."[140] This sense of imposing beneficence could

---

was slave resistance and the degree of social mobilization of partisans of abolition. But this seems to me an artificial separation of the economic and political arenas.

137. Blackburn (p. 430) also notes that "the affinity between reform and abolitionism was by no means simply a product of parliamentary calculation. Both movements questioned what they saw as aberrant types of property. . . . Anti-slavery helped to mobilize the middle classes, and a popular following, without the danger that they would capsize into revolution."

138. The process of deindustrialization, not only of India but of other areas newly incorporated into the world-economy, is discussed in Wallerstein (1989, 149–152).

139. Platt comments: "All Victorians were agreed, politicians, traders, and officials, that the opening of the world to trade was an objective that the Government might be expected to pursue. They may well have differed about the means, but they shared a belief in the ends; material and even moral progress, they felt, might be expected automatically from the expansion of trade. Richard Cobden, for example, fiercely opposed as he was to the Anglo-Chinese Wars, welcomed their outcome—the opening of China to world trade. It was morally wrong, he argued, to open markets at the point of a bayonet, but access to those markets was in practice of mutual benefit and would, in the end, bring that expansion of trade which was the best guarantee of world peace. Most London-based officials shared the Cobdenite view."

140. *Parliamentary Debates*, 3d ser., LXXXIII, 23 February 1846, 1399–1400, cited in Semmel (1970, 8). Of course, some persons were aware of the fragility of the free-trade advantage, or rather its temporariness, and drew from it the conclusion that it shouldn't be tried at all. Disraeli was one. In 1838, he argued against Corn Law repeal on the grounds that it was a "delusion" to suppose that European countries "would suffer England to be the workshop of the world." And of course he was right in the long run. In a speech in 1840 he reminded Parliament that the Dutch, too, had once regarded all

lead to (was based upon?) the "quasi-religious" belief that cotton manufacturing was more vital to the "social regeneration" of civilization than the fine arts dear to John Ruskin, as one R. H. Hutton argued in 1870: "If we must choose between a Titian and a Lancashire cotton-mill, then, in the name of manhood and morality, give us the cotton-mill" (Farnie, 1979, 87–88).[141]

Free trade was free-trade imperialism, in the phrase made famous by Gallagher and Robinson (1953, 2–3, 11, 13), but their crucial qualification should always be borne in mind: "British policy followed the principle of control informally if possible, and formally if necessary." It was apparently necessary even in the mid-century free-trade years (that preceded the acknowledged colonial scramble of the last third of the nineteenth century) to occupy or annex a long series of colonies, to the point that, far from being an era of "indifference," this period might be thought of as the "decisive stage" in British overseas expansion, permitting a combination of commercial penetration and colonial rule such that Great Britain could "command those economies which could be made to fit best into her own."[142] Although intervention was considered somewhat distasteful, it rapidly became legitimate whenever there seemed to be a danger to the routes to India, or "an alarming threat" to the British position in the world-economy that was thought to be caused by "unfair" activities of rival trading powers (Platt, 1968b, 32).

Despite the entente cordiale, and despite the de facto collaboration of Great Britain and France in imposing a liberal world order, France was quite reluctant to abandon an overt protectionism. France had done so briefly in 1786, with unhappy

---

of Europe as "their farm" (*Parliamentary Debates*, 3d ser., XLI, 13 March 1838, 940; LIII, 1 June 1840, 383–384; cited in Semmel, 1970, 155).

In the great parliamentary debate in 1846 on Repeal of the Corn Laws, Disraeli called for a via media between prohibitive protection and unrestricted competition. He cited Spain and Turkey as examples of each, saying of the Ottoman Empire: "[T]here has been a complete application for a long time of the system of unmitigated competition, not indeed from any philosophical conviction of its policy, but rather from the haughty indifference with which a race of conquerors is apt to consider commerce. There has been free trade in Turkey, and what has it produced? It has destroyed some of the finest manufactures in the world" (cited in Holland, 1913, 265). Of course, this argument is somewhat specious, because it neglects to mention the role the free-trade Anglo-Turkish Commercial Convention of 1838 played in this destruction (see Wallerstein, 1989, 176–177).

141. Hutton wrote this in an article entitled "Mr. Ruskin's Philosophy of Art," *Spectator*, 6 August 1870, p. 953.

142. The list of new colonies acquired during those years includes New Zealand, the Gold Coast, Labuan, Natal, Punjab, Sind, Hong Kong, Berar, Oudh, Lower Burma, Kowloon, Lagos, the neighborhood of Sierra Leone, Basutoland, Griqualand, Transvaal, and further expansion in Queensland and British Columbia. Semmel (1970, 203) agrees that "the reputed mid-Victorian policy of 'anti-imperialism' is a myth." Platt (1973, 90) notes pertinently: "Over the period . . . 1830 to 1860, the incentives and opportunities for rapid [British] economic expansion into those regions of 'informal empire' where the trade was even remotely significant, into Latin America, the Levant, and the Far East, simply did not exist."

results (Wallerstein, 1989, 87–93). In the post-1815 period, Great Britain remained protectionist, as did France, albeit a little more intensively so.[143] When Great Britain moved toward free-trade protectionism, the French stood firm, for reasons that seemed quite cogent to them, as this 1845 speech by a French industrialist to his peers makes clear:

> Gentlemen, pay no attention to the theories that cry out, freedom for trade. This theory was proclaimed by England as the true law of the commercial world only when, following a long practice of the most absolute prohibitions, she had brought her industry to so great a level of development that there was no market within which any other large-scale industry was able to compete with hers.[144]

Indeed, in the early 1840s France was trying, albeit unsuccessfully, to create a customs union with neighboring states in order to strengthen its industrial position vis-à-vis Great Britain.[145]

It may therefore seem surprising that the greatest success in Europe of Great Britain's free-trade diplomacy of midcentury was the signing of the so-called Chevalier-Cobden treaty—the Anglo-French Treaty of Commerce of 1860, a treaty that "represented the most significant trade liberalization agreement of the nineteenth century" (O'Brien and Pigman, 1992, 98). What happened?

The treaty affected all the most important industries. France ended her prohibitions and limited the ad valorem duties, which were to be replaced within six months by specific duties. Great Britain agreed to let in nearly all French goods free, with the notable exception of wine. Coal would be exported duty-free from both countries. But since Great Britain was an exporter and France an importer, this was in reality a British concession—one that aroused much opposition in Great Britain. Furthermore, the treaty contained a most-favored-nation clause, which meant that, to the degree that France would enter into reciprocal tariff-cutting arrangements with other European countries, Great Britain would

143. Great Britain would abandon industrial protectionism only in the 1820s, holding on to agriculture until 1846 and shipping until 1849. France was less willing to relax restrictions. The Restoration monarchy, having behind it Napoleon's Continental Blockade, was required to make a conscious economic choice: "[T]he choice of 1814 was quite clear: French policy would link maximum economic liberty internally with maximum protectionism in the international market" (Démier, 1992, 97). Crouzet (1972b, 103) comments: "It is more reasonable, however, to recognize that protectionism was absolutely necessary [in the post-1815 period] for most Continental industry. The French mistake was to carry it to extreme lengths—to downright prohibition of most foreign manufactured goods."

144. Léon Talabot, *Conseil général des manufactures: Session de 1845* (1846, 4), cited in Lévy-Leboyer (1964, 15).

145. Such a union was almost reached with Belgium in 1842, and there was already talk of extending it to the Netherlands, Switzerland, and Piedmont, when "the combined opposition of French vested interests and the foreign offices of the other great powers, who feared a resurgence of French influence, effectively stifled it" (Cameron, 1961, 37).

automatically benefit. Each new treaty in turn containing the same clause, there cumulated rapidly a general reduction of tariffs such that "for a decade or so . . . Europe came as close as ever to complete free trade until after World War II" (Cameron, 1989, 277).[146]

British free-trade diplomacy had always centered on France. France was of course a major trading partner, but, even more important, France was the country with which Great Britain had the greatest and most persistent deficit in the balance of trade (Bairoch, 1976a, 46).[147] Every previous attempt since 1815 by Great Britain to negotiate a treaty with France had failed. The negotiations had been in fact half-hearted on both sides because the terms discussed had always involved strict reciprocity, and no doubt above all because the French government had "lacked the power to control the protectionist Chambers" (Dunham, 1930, 101).[148] What had changed was the desire of Napoleon III to consolidate a liberal state. Just as, after repression of revolutionaries, he would move a decade later to the recognition of trade unions, so after a decade of state-led strengthening of the French economy, he would move forward to the Treaty of 1860. He could do this effectively precisely because he did it in secret, by virtue of his authoritarian powers. One day in a letter to his minister of state, Achille Fould, Napoleon III simply announced the treaty. It was immediately branded a "new coup d'état of Napoleon III" (Bairoch, 1970, 6).[149]

146. Thus, "the Treaty of 1860 served as the first link in an ever-lengthening chain of commercial agreements" (Dunham, 1930, 142). It is important to appreciate that the treaty represented "substantial concessions on both sides" (Condliffe, 1951, 222). One important consequence of this free-trade interlude, often overlooked, was its effect on the geography of world trade. Whereas in 1790 intra-European trade was 76 percent of total European international trade, the period 1800–1860 was one of growing geographic diversification, which then was reversed in the period 1860–1880/1890, to be resumed again thereafter. Still, this movement should not be exaggerated. Intra-European trade as a percentage of the total was never less than two-thirds throughout the century. See Bairoch (1974b, 561–563).

147. Great Britain was in the same situation vis-à-vis France as that in which the United States would later find itself vis-à-vis Japan as of the 1980s and China in the 1990s and the early twenty-first century.

148. Dunham continues: "But, even if in 1840 or 1852 a treaty had been signed, it would have accomplished little, for in each case there was no conception of anything greater than a restrictive bargain over a handful of commodities." Furthermore, in no previous attempt had there been any question of a most-favored-nation clause.

149. Fohlen (1956, 418) argues that, in the long run, Napoleon III paid a heavy political price for his action: "The only serious tariff reform required an authoritarian route to achieve it, against the will of the bourgeoisie, and Napoleon III thereby lost his throne. The Anglo-French Treaty of Commerce of January 23, 1860, was considered to be an 'industrial coup d'état' so contrary was it to economic tradition and bourgeois ideology, even though it was far from bringing about real free trade. . . . Napoleon III had betrayed the bourgeoisie, and they would remember this in 1870."

What mattered in Napoleon III's negotiation of this treaty was not the economic change it brought, but the cultural meaning. Signing the treaty represented the full commitment of France to the concept of the liberal state. In economic terms, it was "the culmination, not the start of the opening of the French economy" (Mokyr and Nye, 1990, 173). It was at most a move from an openly protectionist system to a "moderately protectionist regime" (Rist, 1956, 943; cf. Coussy, 1961, 3).[150] What were its consequences economically? Dunham (1930, 1–2) claims that it revived "moribund French industries . . . by the salutary pressure of foreign competition."[151] But Bairoch (1972, 221) is not persuaded that there were economic benefits to France. Rather, he says "the liberalization of trade substantially slowed down [French] economic growth."[152]

In general, free trade was supposed to serve Great Britain well, and both its supporters and its enemies have tended to agree that, from a British point of view, it was "a success from the very beginning [1846]" (Imlah, 1950, 156). But there have come to be skeptical voices about how well it worked even for Great Britain: skepticism about the economic advantages,[153] and skepticism both about the degree of real support it had within Great Britain and about how influential the "free-

150. Broder (1976, 335) makes the same point more sharply: "[W]e should have no illusions about [the Treaty of 1860]. The debate about the treaty is basically a false debate. Throughout the [nineteenth] century, France was resolutely protectionist. One might categorize the protectionism as successively general (1820–1852), moderate (1852–1881), and selective (1882–)."

151. See also Rist (1956), who agrees that the consequences for France were generally favorable. As for Great Britain, Dunham argues, "it is doubtful that [it] influenced appreciably the general development of British industries." Thus it seems, according to this British singer of the praises of free trade, that the treaty was virtually a noble gift of the British (who scarcely profited from it) to the French (who needed to be cajoled into it for their own good). If so, one wonders why the British were so keen on it. Iliasu (1971) argues that the motivations of the treaty were more political than economic. After all, he says, concluding a treaty was "a breach of the principle" (p. 72) decided upon after 1846 not to enter into any commercial treaty. He attributes the treaty to the "unsettled diplomatic dispute" (p. 87) between the two countries over Italy. Napoleon annexed Nice in 1861, and the treaty was seen "rightly or wrongly . . . as a bribe to purchase Great Britain's assent to the annexation" (p. 96).

152. Not only was this so but, says Bairoch (1970, 7), "the reintroduction of protectionism [the Méline tariff of 1892] led to acceleration in the rate of growth." This period of freer trade, furthermore, lasted longer in France than in other continental countries. In a later work (1976a, 238) Bairoch concludes that "the inrush of agricultural products . . . was the most important explanatory factor in the failure of the French liberal experience."

153. Bairoch (1978a, 75) points out that, during the period 1860–1910, Great Britain's expansion of exports was slower than that of the rest of Europe; indeed protectionist countries did best. But in terms of global economic growth, "the liberal period was much less unfavorable to the more developed countries [such as Great Britain] than to the rest of Europe" (p. 163). McCloskey's conclusions (1980, 318) are harsher: "[F]ree trade caused the British terms of trade to deteriorate, reducing national income."

traders" were.[154] So, says Redford (1956, 11), the great events of 1860—the Anglo-French treaty and Mr. Gladstone's budget—may have had, probably did have, "less practical effect" than previously thought, but "they made a splendid coping-stone to the free trade edifice."

Still, quibbling over the degree of economic advantage to the one or the other party in the Anglo-French Treaty of Commerce may make us lose sight of the effort to construct an international order that would sanctify liberalism as the European ideology. We talk of the period 1815–1914 as the *Pax Britannica*. In fact, this is a deceptive way of describing it. It was actually a period of constant colonial wars, "some not so very 'small' as [some] are wont to call [them]" (Gough, 1990, 179–181).[155] For the creation of the liberal-national state was also and necessarily the creation of the liberal-imperial state.

To be sure, world conditions between 1815 and the 1870s favored "a more relaxed policy" of Great Britain toward the periphery. These were "halcyon days" for British trade. And the myth of "Little England" was a good way of denying the imposition of "informal empire" (Galbraith, 1961, 39–40).[156] Furthermore, Burn (1949, 222–223) argues that, as part of what he calls Great Britain's "liberal equipoise," it was crucial to direct the angers of the populace outward: "The instinct for violence was also being diverted abroad. . . . The English were by no means a pacific people, but they satisfied themselves by thinking of what ought to be done or what they would do to rebellious Sepoys, riotous negroes, Russians or Frenchmen or, in 1861, Americans." This diversion was not merely a matter of social psy-

154. See Farnie (1979, 39–41) on the degree to which the influence of free traders has been "exaggerated by its intellectual heirs." He thinks it remained no more than "a school of thought" with less impact on the Liberal Party than Whig grandees or the Nonconformist conscience. He sees the support of Manchester merchants coming from "motives of expediency rather than of principle." He notes all the antiliberal intellectual agitation coming after Repeal: Young Englandism in 1848, Christian Socialism in 1850, pre-Raphaelitism in 1851, and the widely read "bitter diatribes" of Carlyle. "Manchester became a standing rock of offence to poets, literati, and aesthetes." It may have had some long-run benefits, but in the short term, Repeal of the Corn Laws "ushered in a period of bitter debate which raged from 1846 to 1853 and ended only with the emasculation of the original gospel of free trade."

155. She adds: "In almost every circumstance, law, that underpinning of the Empire of the *Pax,* was ineffective in itself. It had to be backed by force. This was as true in the largest continental dominion—Canada—as it was in the smallest island colony or protectorate—Pitcairn."

156. Condliffe (1951, 254) is not willing even to accept the adjective *relaxed* vis-à-vis existing colonies: "Despite the views of the Little Englanders, after the loss of the American colonies, administration was not relaxed, but rather was tightened in the colonies that remained to Britain. . . . Manufacturers might protest against the costs of war and preparations for war, but the majority of Englishmen stubbornly maintained their faith in sea power and their pride of empire. There were, moreover, large vested interests at stake. The shipping interests fought against any relaxation of the Navigation Acts. The Army and Navy had a professional interest in maintaining such services and a personal interest in colonial patronage."

chology but of social mobility. Job opportunities in the colonies took "some of the sting" out of early nineteenth-century radicalism.[157]

In theory, liberal ideologists were opposed to colonialism on the grounds that it constituted an infringement on human freedom.[158] But this was very theoretical. In practice, British liberal (and socialist) economists and commentators had an evolving and increasingly favorable concept of British imperial rule over "barbarians" (which term did not include the White settler colonists), although there were a few moments (1780–1800, 1860–1880) when they were rather skeptical.[159] Even as strong a proponent of the self-determination of nations as John Stuart Mill intruded a criterion of "fitness."[160] India was of course the centerpiece of the British imperial project. It was not at first merely, even perhaps primarily, a matter of free-trade imperialism but of revenues, as Bayly (1989, 10) rightly insists.[161] And when the free-trade group successfully worked to eliminate the East India

157. Neale (1972, 97) says that this is true "for at least some of the aspiring professional and petty bourgeois members of the quasi-group from which a stronger middling class might have come." He adds, speaking of the situation in Australia between 1788 and 1856 (p. 108), that "the social profile of governors and executive councillors . . . suggests that they were mainly at least second-generation members of a middling set of people who lived either in the Home Counties or the Lowlands of Scotland and were members of the Anglican and Presbyterian churches."

158. For a classic statement of the official view, see this letter of Cobden to John Bright in 1847: "But you must not disguise for yourself that the evil has its roots in the pugnacious, energetic, self-sufficient, foreign-despising and pitying character of that noble insular character, John Bull. Read Washington Irving's description of him fumbling for his cudgel always the moment he hears of a row taking place anywhere on the face of the earth and bristling with anger at the very idea of any other people daring to have a quarrel without first asking his consent or inviting him to take a part in it" (cited in Condliffe, 1951, 255).

159. See Wagner (1932, 74), who traces the story from Adam Smith to G. D. H. Cole. As he says, "they objected to colonial policies, not to colonies or colonization." In any case, he goes on, "if economists were at times pessimistic [about the virtue of empire], they usually recovered their confidence and even helped to restore the credit of imperialism when it became dangerously low."

160. See Mill, writing amid the revolutions of 1848 (1849, 31): "Nationality is desirable, as a means to the attainment of liberty; and this is reason enough for sympathizing with the attitudes of Italians to re-construct an Italy, and in those of the people of Posen to become a Poland. So long, indeed, as a people are unfit for self-government, it is often better for them to be under despotism of foreigners than of natives, when those foreigners are more advanced in civilization and cultivation than themselves. But when their hour of freedom, to use M. de Lamartine's metaphor, has struck, without their having become merged and blended in the nationality of their conquerors, the re-conquest of their own is often an indispensable condition either to obtaining free institutions, or to the possibility, were they even obtained, of working them in the spirit of freedom."

161. "In the . . . case of India, the financial and military momentum of the East India Company's army was the mainspring of expansion with free traders no more than the fly on the wheel. India's territorial revenues, not its trade, remained the chief economic prize for the British in the East. Even after 1834 the Company retained many of its features of mercantile despotism. Anglo-Dutch rule in Java and British mercantilist despotism in Ceylon retained similar characteristics through to mid-century. The

Company entirely from the picture, they did so in a way that contributed to "the strength and the endurance of Britain's imperial connexion with India" (Moore, 1964, 145).

French liberalism was no less oriented to the imperial state. After all, for Saint-Simon, as for so many other believers in "the certainty of human progress," the "East" was thought to be still in the "childhood" of this progress (Cole, 1953, 1:41).[162] Louis de Bougainville had already made a tour of the Pacific, starting from St.-Malo on December 15, 1766. on a trip that had brought him to Tuamolu, Tahiti, Samoa, the New Hebrides, the Solomon Islands, and the Moluccas. It was, however, only after 1796 that missionaries and merchants began to show some interest in the Pacific. Beginning with Charles X's incursion into Algeria, and continuing under Louis-Philippe, France "constantly enlarged its overseas domain" (Schefer, 1928, 430).[163]

The July Monarchy evinced an economic concern to maintain order on whaling vessels in the Pacific. It was at this point that the entente cordiale almost disintegrated into warfare because of acute British–French rivalry in the so-called Pritchard affair of 1843. In 1838, the French had made a treaty with Tahiti. In 1840, the British had beat the French out by annexing New Zealand (Jore, 1959, 1: 186, 213). France "took her revenge" in 1842 by taking over the Marquesas and establishing a protectorate over Tahiti as well as sending missionaries to New Caledonia. It was just then that Great Britain, by the Treaty of Nanking, "opened" China (Faivre, 1954, 9, 338; Jore, 1959, 1:200–207, 213, 224; 2:81–106, 165–171, 181–353).

The climax of the rivalry occurred in Tahiti. Though the British "acquiesced" over the Marquesas, they were more unhappy about Tahiti. In 1842, the French arrested the British consul in Tahiti, one Pritchard. In 1843, C. V. Lord Paulet sought to place Hawaii, which the French also coveted, under a British protectorate. Passions rose on both sides. But then both sides pulled back. Guizot and Aberdeen agreed to calm the waters. The French voted an indemnity to Pritchard.

------

sale of British manufactures to India and other parts of the East was sluggish until the 1840s. Indeed, the expansion of British world trade between 1790 and 1830 can be considerably exaggerated."

And even when, later, trade came to the fore, revenues were by no means neglected. See Jenks (1927, 223–224): "The burdens that it was found convenient to charge to India seem preposterous. The costs of the Mutiny, the price of the transfer of the Company's rights to the Crown, the expenses of simultaneous wars in China and Abyssinia, every governmental item in London that was remotely related to India down to the fees of the charwomen in the India Office and the expenses of ships that sailed but did not participate in hostilities and the cost of Indian regiments for six months' training at home before they sailed—all were charged to the account of the unrepresented ryot."

162. On the active role of the Saint-Simonians in the colonial enterprise in Algeria, both in the July Monarchy and during the Second Empire, see Emerit (1941).

163. In addition to expanding their Algerian zone, there were conquests on the Guinea Coast, in the Indian Ocean, and in the Pacific islands.

Both Pritchard and the French consul in Tahiti, Moerenhout, were replaced. There would be no French protectorate over the Wallis Islands or New Caledonia, nor would there be a British protectorate over the Gambia (in West Africa). Both powers agreed to recognize Hawaii as an independent state (Faivre, 1954, 496–497; Jore, 1959, 2:385–387).

There were a number of reasons for this mutual withdrawal from the precipice. There was an upsurge of agitation in Ireland. And the United States was entering the picture. Great Britain and the United States were in active dispute over the Canadian Pacific border. The convention of the Democratic Party in the United States had proclaimed the slogan of "54°40′ or Fight." U.S. Secretary of State Webster had extended the Monroe Doctrine to Hawaii. Both the British and the French felt that the possible gains to be derived from their continued colonizing did not outweigh the damage to be done to their alliance—so essential to their mutual objectives. They were both determined not to let such an incident recur, as well as to maintain the status quo in the Pacific. They thus both decided to "*veiller au grain*" (or "look out for squalls," in the old mariner's expression) (Jore, 1959, 2:388).[164]

The importance for world order of this reassertion of the entente cordiale became clear in the 1850s with the Crimean War. Basically, the war was about Russia's long-standing attempt to expand its territory, power, and influence southward into the zone controlled by the Ottoman Empire. Since the British (and the French) were equally desirous of controlling the economic flows of this zone, and the British were in fact well into the process of turning the Ottoman Empire into being very dependent on them, the two powers decided to make it militarily clear that the Russians had to concede priority to the British. The war was thus, in Polanyi's words (1957, 5), "a more or less colonial event."[165] Since the British

164. In the view of Faivre (1954, 497), the British got the better part of the deal, for they now had, he says, "a stronger position [in the Pacific] than had had the Spaniards." Of course, in making this assessment, he lumps together Great Britain and the United States as "Anglo-Saxons."

165. Mutatis mutandis, Russia was playing the same role for British public opinion that the U.S.S.R. would later play for U.S. public opinion in the period 1945–1990. See Briggs (1959, 379–380): "The Crimean War . . . cannot be understood from a perusal of the motives of members of the British government. Throughout Britain there was a powerful current of popular Russophobia. . . . [Several English writers had] familiarized important sections of the reading public with the view that only enslaved peoples anxious for their own liberation could drive the semi-barbarous Russian despots back into the steppes of Asia. . . . [I]n the post-1848 world the critics of Russia stirred not limited sections of the reading public but large crowds of people. Ex-Chartists . . . warmed to a struggle against the universal enemy of the popular cause; David Urquhart . . . set up 'working men's foreign affairs committees' to study Russian 'crimes' as well as to condemn them. . . . When what [the very representative radical and co-operator G. J. Holyoake] felt was a premature peace was signed, he refused to illuminate his office in Fleet Street, preferring to display a large placard bearing Elizabeth Barrett Browning's verses on the continued plight of Poland, Italy, and Hungary."

were indeed the hegemonic power and commanded the support of the French (and of course the Ottomans), "Palmerston's war" could not but be a military success. Russia was forced into a "humiliating peace." But can it really be called that "rare example of a war that achieved what it set out to achieve" (Vincent, 1981, 37–38)?[166]

In retrospect, the Crimean War has been presented as a "minor" exception to the *Pax Britannica*, involving "localized theatres of operations and . . . limited objectives" (Imlah, 1958, 1). Hugh Seton-Watson (1937, 359) calls it "the most unnecessary war in the history of modern Europe."[167] It certainly did strengthen the British position in the Ottoman Empire.[168] But it had unexpected negative side effects for the British. The British government had to withdraw some troops from the colonies to use in the fighting. It even sought to recruit troops in the United States, which strained diplomatic relations.[169] But the use of these troops for the Crimean War backfired. For it proved that one could diminish the "burdens of Empire," thereby giving Conservatives further arguments for the "rise of a new imperialism" (Schuyler, 1945, 233).

Even more important, however, was that the war had to be fought at all. Hegemony depends in many ways on the fact that implicit strength is never challenged. Although Great Britain won, it did so only after "the much publicized defeats and disasters of the first Crimean winter." The resulting "paradox" was that Great Britain had now to spend much more on military preparedness and nonetheless witnessed "a decline of British influence in Europe" (Gash, 1979, 310–311). The defeat of Russia as a result was in fact only temporary. Russia found that she "only had to await patiently the moment when she would be able to shake off the restraints imposed on her in the Black Sea" (Seton-Watson, 1937, 359). And at home, the

166. He argues: "Its achievements were lasting. When Russia next attacked Turkey, she had to do it the hard way, by land, and not by means of naval supremacy in the Black Sea. Turkey has never again been in danger of becoming a Russian satellite."

167. "The chief gains of the war lay with Napoleon III, whose regime it stabilised, . . . and with the [Ottoman] Porte."

168. See Baster (1934, 82, 86): "The result of the War stirred up much English interest in the commercial and financial prospects of a regenerated Turkey, and increased the British bidding for the bank concession. . . . [T]he usefulness of such institutions as the Imperial Ottoman Bank as the weapon for the economic penetration of a backward country provided nineteenth-century diplomacy with a striking object lesson. The great capital-exporting nations of western Europe certainly were not slow to profit by it."

169. The British minister in Washington was dismissed by the U.S. government as a result (Schuyler, 1945, 221). This was because the United States had officially declared neutrality and viewed with a dim eye the setting up of a depot in Halifax for U.S. volunteers, who were in fact not that hard to recruit, given the depression (Brebner, 1930, 303–305, 320). During the U.S. Civil War, soon thereafter, the United States returned the favor by recruiting Canadians to serve in Union troops (pp. 326–327).

Crimean War persuaded previously recalcitrant British manufacturers of the importance of the liberal state being an actively imperial state.[170]

The 1860s should have marked the definitive installation of the British-dominated pacific world order, in crucial alliance with France. It was indeed the moment of its apogee, but it also marked the beginning of its decline. The very period when the "tendencies in Britain towards the disruption of the Empire reached their climax" (Schuyler, 1921, 538) was also the period of "the final demonstration of British powerlessness and pacifism over Schleswig-Holstein," and thus of the shattering of "the old confidence in the moral power of British influence" (Gash, 1979, 317–318).[171]

The same thing happened in France. In addition to Crimea (1854–1856) and the conquest of Cochin in 1862, Napoleon III sought to consolidate France's position as a world power by an adventure into Central America, seeking thereby to limit the power of the United States. In 1852, France and Great Britain proposed to the United States a tripower protectorate over Cuba. The "haughty refusal" by the United States increased the suspicions of U.S. intentions.[172] In 1859, in a situation

170. See Farnie (1979, 44): "The great debate inaugurated in 1846 was ended by the Crimean War which accelerated the transformation in the world outlook of the economic elite of Lancashire begun in 1850 by Palmerston's Don Pacifico speech. The first international conflict of the free-trade era generated economic prosperity rather than depression and dispelled the dream of perpetual peace cherished since 1851. The war infected all classes in Lancashire with the military spirit and encouraged Manchester's gravitation towards the Church of England. It rallied Mancunian opinion to the support of Palmerston and paved the way for the decisive rejection of the representatives of the Manchester School in the post-war general election of 1857 when the importance of state action in the extension of the China market and of the informal empire of Britain was clearly recognized by the electorate. As the economy of the market failed to achieve full independence from the State the ethic of free trade became an end in itself rather than a means to a higher end and was transformed from a sovereign method of social regeneration into a mere mechanical interchange of commodities."

171. By 1864, "Britain, the one supporter of the *status quo*, was isolated and impotent. . . . It was clear that in future Britain would either have to do more or say less. . . . The old antagonism between authority and liberalism was being resolved into a new and dangerous synthesis of the nationalism of 1848 and the militarism of the dynastic states." Seton-Watson (1937, 449, 465) reports the statement of Lord Russell, British foreign minister: "I remember Canning say, 'I am told we must have war sooner or later. If that be the case, I say later.' I say with Canning, 'later.'" The noninterventionists of the Manchester School were joined by the Conservatives, who preferred involvement in the colonial zones to involvement in continental affairs. The consequence was obvious to Moltke, who said in 1865: "England is as powerless on the Continent as she is presuming." Internally, it meant the return of the Conservative Party to power: "From the summer of 1870 onward, anti-imperialist sentiment waned rapidly. . . . Disraeli skillfully seized upon imperialism as a party issue, and probably no part of his political program appealed more powerfully to the British electorate than his pledge to maintain the integrity of the Empire. The Conservative victory in the general election of 1874 drove Little-Englandism completely from the field of practical politics" (Schuyler, 1921, 559–560).

172. Schefer (1939, 7–11): "Fear of the United States dominated in short British, Spanish, and French policies [in the Caribbean]."

of two competing governments in Mexico—that of Juárez in Veracruz and that of Zuloaga in Mexico City—President Buchanan spoke of U.S. ambitions in Cuba and Mexico, and threw his weight behind Juárez. Zuloaga turned to the French for military help. When the United States was then paralyzed by the outbreak of the Civil War in 1861, the French and the Mexican monarchists joined forces to support Archduke Maximilian of Austria as the king of Mexico. France had begun its American "Crimea."

When Juárez suspended debt payments, the French, British, and Spanish joined forces, demanding the installation of debt commissioners in Veracruz and Tampico. All three powers sent in troops in 1862, but only France was willing to support Maximilian. The other two powers and Maximilian himself pulled back, leaving France alone "forced into a real war." Napoleon III sent a whole expedition, which failed, and the Second Empire was "discredited," losing much of the "prestige on which [the Second Empire] was in large part based" (Schefer, 1939, 11, 241), and of course particularly in Europe.[173]

The British-French attempts to create a liberal world order that they would dominate was thus a great success, but it was also a great failure. On the one hand, they had stretched their economic and military power to the limit and would not be able to stop the steady ascent of Germany and the United States, whose joint increase in real power and whose mutual rivalry would begin to shape the increasingly conflictual world order after 1870. Both Great Britain and France would now be forced to change their pattern of colonial acquisition from one in which they alone set the pace to one in which everyone (or at least very many) were free to "scramble." But on the other hand, Great Britain and France had succeeded in imposing on the world-system the geoculture of liberalism, to which increasing homage had to be paid by everyone, at least until the outbreak of the First World War. Bismarck could not resume the language of the Holy Alliance, nor did he have the least interest in doing so. Rather, Bismarck and Disraeli would draw the positive lessons of the Second Empire and propound an enlightened conservatism, which was really a conservative variant of liberalism.

The turning point in the nineteenth-century world order would be the years 1866–1873—"a gigantic hinge on which the history of the later nineteenth century turns" (Clapham, 1944, 2:271). The United States had remained united, and in 1866 it seemed clear that Germany was about to become so. Thus, the two rising powers were in a position to increase their geopolitical role. At the same time, Great Britain was about to join France in the big leap to universal male suffrage.

---

173. See Girard (1977, 25): "It was foreign affairs that would be the downfall of the regime, after notable successes. France was no longer strong enough to open to continental Europe a middle road between the ancien regime and revolution. It was Bismarck rather who would impose this solution for several decades."

Parliamentary reform in Great Britain in 1867 is seen, quite correctly, as "the end of an epoch" (Burn, 1964, chap. 6). The British Reform Act of 1867 plus the paroxysm of 1870–1871 in France represent together the culmination of a process begun in 1815 of trying to tame the dangerous classes—in particular, the urban proletariat—by incorporating them into the system politically, but in such a way that they would not upset the basic economic, political, and cultural structures of the two countries.

In the prior fifty years, the extension of the suffrage had been in theory a proposition of liberals, resisted by conservatives. The classic evidence for this is the passage of the Reform Act of 1832. Is it not then strange that most of the other crucial advances were made under the aegis of, or at least the leadership of, conservative politicians: Catholic Emancipation in 1829, which preceded the Reform Bill of 1832; Repeal of the Corn Laws in 1846; and, most important, the Reform Act of 1867, which granted virtual universal manhood suffrage? Himmelfarb (1966, 117), in her analysis of 1867, says that liberals, believing that individuals mattered politically, were so cautious about putting political arrangements at the mercy of the mass of individuals that they considered universal suffrage both "serious and perilous." Conservatives, she says, with their "faith in eternal verities of human nature and society," worried less, which is why the Reform Act was "a Conservative measure, initiated and carried out by a Conservative Government."[174] This is no doubt a correct description, up to a point, of the reasoning process of members of these two political groups, but I am not sure that this is what really happened.

It seems to me that the Liberals never quite had the courage of their convictions, for the simple reason that they shared all the fears of Conservatives of the dangerous classes, with little of the political and social self-assurance of Conservative

174. Himmelfarb calls the act "one of the decisive events, perhaps *the* decisive event, in modern English history. It was this act that transformed England into a democracy and made democracy a respectable form of government (the United States was never quite respectable), but also, it was soon taken for granted, the only natural and proper form of government." This is quite correct, except for the word *democracy*. Universal suffrage is not democracy. Were that the case, no respectable Conservative, or for that matter no respectable Liberal, would ever have supported it. Universal suffrage is the granting of full citizenship to all adults (or at least all adult males), which is far short of their having an equal say in political decision making. However, it is the case that the definition of *democracy* as "universal male suffrage" did become commonplace in political discourse after the Reform Act of 1867. As for liberals and their caution, see Schapiro (1939, 131) on their moment of glory in 1832: "Despite their advocacy of universal suffrage, the Utilitarians accepted with equanimity the narrow suffrage restrictions of the Reform Bill of 1832. In truth manhood suffrage was to them more a logical conclusion from their premises of the 'greatest happiness' principle than a vital issue in practical politics. Logic compelled Bentham to advocate manhood suffrage but the spirit of compromise, which constantly hovered over the Utilitarians, inspired him to declare that he 'would gladly compound for householder suffrage.'"

aristocrats. Liberals were always afraid of being accused of being reckless. Con-servatives, on the other hand, were in no rush to reform, but when they saw that reform was essential, they were quite ready to move more decisively, free of the fear of being attacked for radical beliefs.[175] Besides, with a little cleverness they might turn the extension of the suffrage into votes for themselves rather than for the Liberals.[176] It thus might seem not totally coincidental that

> [t]he years 1869–70 seem clearly to mark a turning point in the attitude of public opinion in Britain towards the colonies. When confronted with what looked like

175. Not that Conservatives moved without being prodded. Hinton (1983, 12–13) reminds us that the 1867 decision was taken at a moment that had been preceded by a bad harvest, a hard winter, and a cholera epidemic—all of which "deepened discontent." The left had seized the initiative within the Reform League and was able to mount a demonstration in Hyde Park of 150,000 people waving the red flag. Disraeli's acceptance of a Radical amendment quadrupling the number that would be enfran-chised followed within two weeks. Nor was this yet universal suffrage. Not only were the urban poor not included (those who were not "registered" and "residential"), but, most important, neither were all *rural* workers, ensuring continued Conservative control of these ridings. Disraeli was primarily seek-ing to avert the threat of "more class-conscious definitions of politics."

Even with these caveats, it was a bold step, and Disraeli's supporters did know the twinge of fear. Briggs (1959, 513–514) reminds us that Lord Derby frankly admitted that he had made "a great experi-ment" and taken a "leap in the dark." And that Gathorne Hardy, one of those who helped Disraeli pass the bill, had said: "What an unknown world we are to enter. If the gentry will take their part they will be adopted as leaders. If we are left to demagogues, God help us!" But, as Briggs also says, we know that what actually happened after 1867 justified in retrospect the Tory gamble: "[T]here was no sud-den change in politics, . . . the 'age of improvement' did not suddenly end, . . . the working classes did not immediately come into their own, . . . the gentry still remained influential, . . . the middle classes continued to prosper."

To be sure, at the time there were Conservatives who thought that "Disraeli's audacity in 1867" (Goldman, 1986, 95) was sheer madness. In 1869, an anonymous article (probably written by Lord Cranborne, Third Marquess of Salisbury [see Southgate, 1977, 160]) complained that since the 1840s, British Conservative policy had "consisted in their constant efforts to defeat the moderate opponents by combination with their extreme opponents. There can be no doubt of the novelty of the idea." Our author applied his irony to an analysis of the Reform Act of 1867: "Two years ago it was a favourite subject of discussion whether household suffrage was a Conservative or Radical measure. . . . A vague idea that the poorer men are the more easily they are influenced by the rich; a notion that those whose vocation it was to bargain and battle with the middle class must on that account love the gentry; an im-pression—for it could be no more—that the ruder class of minds would be more sensitive to traditional emotions; and an indistinct application to English politics of Napoleon's (then) supposed success in taming revolution by universal suffrage;—all these arguments . . . went to make up the clear conviction of the mass of the Conservative party that in a Reform Bill more Radical than that of the Whigs they had discovered the secret of a sure and signal triumph" (Anon., 1869, 284–285).

176. For evidence on how this worked in the long run, see McKenzie and Silver (1968), who note that at the time, most analysts from Karl Marx to Walter Bagehot (with the notable exception of Disraeli) believed that this extension of the suffrage would doom the Conservative Party. Yet for a hun-dred years thereafter, the Conservative Party governed Great Britain three-quarters of the time, some-thing made possible by the "successful recruitment of considerable working class support" (p. 240).

an imminent dissolution of the Empire, the British people, it was evident, were not ready to follow the doctrinaire disciples of the Manchester School, whatever some of the political leaders might wish. (Schuyler, 1945, 276)

The political leaders who might have wished this were Liberals, not Conservatives. Having made the working class into citizens with something to defend, and having reassured the middle classes that they were not about to be dispossessed, the Conservatives could now lead Great Britain into being more avowedly a liberal-*imperial* state. In any case, Great Britain did not have much choice. Given the erosion of her dominant economic and political position in Europe, she sought solace and renewed strength in her imperial role.

Could the Second Empire have made the same smooth transition to the mature liberal-imperial state? France already had universal suffrage. What it lacked was a fully liberal parliamentary political regime. But Napoleon III saw that and was clearly trying in the 1860s to move in that direction. As Plamenatz says (1952, 162): "By making the Empire liberal, Napoleon III . . . really wished to placate . . . the republicans." True, his regime was being attacked for squandering money on prestige expenditures and for evading parliamentary controls through public borrow-

---

In terms of short-run considerations, see this analysis of Moore (1967, 54–55): "The real paradox of 1867—if such, indeed, it should be called—was not the franchise but the boundaries. . . . [O]n the borough franchise, there was little to choose between the Palmerston Bill of 1860 and the Derby-Disraeli Bill of 1867, as the latter was finally amended. . . . But there was much to choose between the two measures on the question of constituency boundaries. The paradox of 1867 lies in the fact that the Liberal majority in the Commons not only agreed to the appointment of boundary commissioners. They also agreed to instruct these commissioners to enlarge the boroughs 'so as to include within the limits of the borough all premises the occupants of which ought, due regard being had to situation or other local circumstances, to be included therein for Parliamentary purposes. . . . ' Apparently, they only realized what they had done when the commissioners took their instructions to heart, and when a Boundary bill was introduced based on their report by which every important borough was so enlarged as to absorb its suburban overspill. To the Conservatives, whose symbolic basis of power lay in the counties and who, perhaps, were more at home than many Liberals with a hierarchical society, such a measure was essential as a means of restoring the world they knew. To many Liberals, on the other hand, who appreciated its electoral consequences, it was a simple gerrymander." One sees here why merely extending the suffrage has little to do with instituting democracy.

The Reform Act of 1867, in addition to recruiting a segment of workers known as "Tory workers" and gerrymandering the districts, enabled the Conservatives to make inroads among formerly Liberal voters. See Smith (1967, 319): "Paradoxically, it was the Suffrage Reform Act of 1867, at first sight the coup by which Disraeli committed his party to the pursuit of 'Tory Democracy,' that in the long run did most to establish the conditions necessary for the assimilation of the bourgeoisie. While it gave the urban working men a substantial installment of political power, and made the consideration of working-class interests vital to politicians, it intensified the pressure and fears which tended to drive elements of the middle classes into the Conservative party, as the only reliable agency of resistance to the advocates of Radicalism and labour."

ing.[177] Still, the gradual liberalization of Napoleon III might well have succeeded were it not for the Franco-German War and the defeat of France.

Bismarck had correctly seen that the Second Empire was the weak link in the structure of British hegemony and that knocking down France would ensure a more rapid decline of Great Britain in the geopolitical structures of the world-system. What Bismarck did not anticipate was that knocking down Napoleon III also meant knocking down the political constraints that had been elaborately constructed on the French working classes and on French radical democrats in general. Hence the Commune of Paris. It was the siege of Paris and the armistice that aroused the workers of Paris:

> They had resisted the Prussians for over four months and were willing still to resist them. It was the provincials who had been defeated, and it was the provincials, dominated by the church and the bourgeoisie, who had supported the Second Empire. They were unpatriotic and reactionary. (Plamenatz, 1952, 137)

In the elections of February 5–8, Paris and other large towns voted republican, but the provinces voted royalist (and for peace). The Bonapartists were out of the picture. The republicans had become the war party. Nationalism and republicanism/socialism were deeply intertwined in the Commune, which was no doubt the most significant workers' insurrection in the history of western Europe, and furthermore the first that attracted significant support from *employés*—that is, from those whose work was "cleaner," better paid, and at the time more skilled:

> [I]t was the first time that those who were not yet "white-collar workers" [*cols-blancs*] but still merely "pen pushers" [*ronds de cuir*] joined in such large numbers the ranks of a workers' insurrection. In June 1848, the *employés* had been fighting on the side of order. (Rougerie, 1964, 128)[178]

What the middle classes feared vaguely in 1815 and more pertinently in 1848 was now occurring. The dangerous classes wanted democracy. They wanted to

---

177. For details of the criticisms, see Girard (1952, 400), who concludes: "A large part of the bourgeoisie refused to see in [the Second Empire] anything but an 'interim team' whereas it desired the application of the methods that had triumphed in England." What caused the disillusionment was exactly what had been the illusions: "The Empire and Saint-Simonian finance had always discounted the future. And the future of 1852 was the present of 1868. . . . Despite the creative audacity and so many public works accomplished at such a relatively modest cost, the ungrateful public, having obtained their houses, their railways, their steamboats, were astonished that they were costing so much. Napoleon III, the Péreires, the men of the political economy of December 2 had said too often that they would get this for nothing. So the public no longer wished to consider these magicians disappointed by credit anything but charlatans. It no longer wanted enchanters, but very solid currency following upon extensive public discussion" (p. 371).

178. The tables in Rougerie (1964, 127 and 129) contain breakdowns of participation in the Commune.

run their country, which they thought of both as their *country* and *their* country. The uprising was fiercely repressed by the troops of the provisional government at Versailles, which enjoyed the benign noninterference of German troops. The repression met equally fierce resistance by the workers, and after this resistance was overcome, there were widespread executions and sentences of exile.[179]

But once done, what were the consequences? I think Plamenatz (1952, 155–156) gets it just right:

> The Commune did for republicans in the 1870s what the June insurrection did in the middle of the century. It discredited the socialists and the revolutionaries. But this time it did not strengthen the conservatives. . . .
>
> The failure of the Commune did no harm to the republicans, but it did make the republicans more conservative than they would otherwise have been.[180]

For the republicans took up exactly where Napoleon III had left off, speaking the language of the liberal-imperial state, ready to repress the dangerous classes if they should ask too much, but also ready to give them citizenship, and citizenship in a liberal-imperial state.[181] Adolphe Thiers incarnated the transition. A man of many regimes, as were Talleyrand and Guizot before him, he had supported the workers in Lyon in 1834 but the Party of Order in 1848. He had not been compromised by participation in the Second Empire governments, was friendly with both royalists and republicans, and was a fierce enemy of revolutionaries. In 1870, he said that, though he had not wanted the Republic, it had one virtue (*titre*) in his eyes: "[I]t is, of all governments, the one that divides us least."

By 1875, it could be said that the liberal-imperial state was now securely in place in Great Britain and France and had shown its ability to contain the danger-

179. "The Versailles troops, especially their officers, behaved with the greatest brutality. . . . During the last bloody week, nearly 20,000 persons were killed in the streets of Paris. There is nothing uglier than the vengeance of the well-to-do and respectable classes when they have been frightened by the poor" (Plamenatz, 1952, 154). Similarly Rougerie (1964, 59) speaks of "the abject bourgeois terror, . . . the great fear of 1871, as demonstrated . . . by the ferocity of the repression. It took ten years before they were willing to give amnesty to the condemned insurgents."

180. Billington (1980, 346) has a slightly different appreciation of the political consequences of the Commune: "It triggered the triumph of the Right throughout Europe—and opened up new horizons for the revolutionary Left." Perhaps so, but until 1914 the liberal center was able to contain both right and left pressures with considerable ease.

181. See Elwitt (1975, 306–307): "[The radical rhetoric of the republicans] was both sweeping and circumscribed in its political nature, ruthlessly excluding any radical/socialist content that challenged the fundamentals of the existing order. . . . The republican bourgeoisie inherited universal suffrage, welcomed it, used it, and turned it to their political advantage. . . . As for the workers of France, their existence as a separate class was repeatedly denied. Republicans, when they spoke of 'reconciliation,' meant integration if possible, suppression when necessary." The Third Republic also, of course, continued the policy of the active state of the Second Empire. As Girard says (1952, 393), "the opportunist Republic would finally implement the promises made [by Napoleon III] in his letter of January 5, 1860."

ous classes. It had thus become a model for other states. What was most constant in the model was certainly not fidelity to the free market (a fidelity that varied with the shifting economic position of given countries in the world-economy and the impact of its cyclical rhythms). Nor was the liberal-imperial state marked by fidelity to the maximization of the rights of the individual (a fidelity that varied with the extent to which individuals used these rights to challenge the basic social order). What distinguished the liberal-imperial state was its commitment to intelligent reform by the state that would simultaneously advance economic growth (or rather the accumulation of capital) and tame the dangerous classes (by incorporating them into the citizenry and offering them a part, albeit a small part, of the imperial economic pie).

To this end, liberal-imperial states had to revolve around the political center and avoid regimes that smacked either of reaction or of revolution. Of course, to be able to do this, a state had to have no major unresolved nationalist problems vis-à-vis outsiders and no strong internal unhappy minorities. It had also to be strong enough in the world-economy that the prospects of collective prosperity were not unreal. And it had to have enough military power or strong enough allies that it was free from excessive outside interference. When all these conditions prevailed, the liberal-imperial state was free to reflect the collective conservatism of a majority that now had something to conserve.

Therefore, first of all the liberal-imperial state had to be a strong state, a strengthened state. To be sure, from the beginning, the extension of the state's powers was intended primarily to control the dangerous classes:

> [T]he centralization which Bentham and especially [Edwin] Chadwick meditated did no more than touch the dominant middle classes. Centralization, swept clear of theory, meant authorization of those services which affected the labouring classes. Centralization, it cannot be doubted, was never intended to curtail in the slightest degree the economic and social freedom of the more respectable classes. Nor did it. (Hill, 1929, 95–96)[182]

And second, the liberal-imperial state involved a commitment to the extension of the suffrage. But, as we have seen, this extension was managed prudently. "The

---

182. The success of this program is vaunted by Darvall (1934, 307): "As soon as the stream of modern legislation began, the incentive for, and the chance of success of, a revolution became rapidly less and less. On the one hand, the creation of a police force, of modern efficient units of local government, lessened the chances of the disorderly. Riots had far less opportunity to grow into revolution. On the other hand, the repeal of the Combination Acts, the passage of the Factory Acts, the movement towards Free Trade, the parliamentary reform programme, all had a moderating effect upon popular discontent, and removed the incentive for revolution. It became credible, as it had not been credible before, that a redress of grievances might be obtained, gradually but still effectually, by peaceful means." Darvall's analysis makes it clear why "the increase of State power implied by policing was one of the issues the Chartists most bitterly contested" (Evans, 1983, 257)

right to exercise freedom was only guaranteed to responsible adults by classical liberals" (Crouch, 1967, 209). The concept of responsibility, as applied to extension of the suffrage, involved both timing and an application of the Enlightenment faith in the educability of humanity. Therefore, the liberal advocacy of universal suffrage was "deeply ambiguous," as Rosanvallon (1985, 136–137) explains:

> In most cases, [such advocacy] was but a sort of bet on the future, expressing merely an anticipatory representation of the movement of civilization and of Enlightenment progress in the nation. . . . In the liberal and republican circles that were favorable to it, universal suffrage continued to be understood as a recognition of potential capacity, far more than as a consequence of the principle of equality, a symbolic translation of humans together in society. . . . Hence the great debate about the *prematureness* of introducing universal suffrage. It was often rejected because it was still too early. It was the suffrage of the ignorant and immature masses that was feared.[183]

That said, liberalism was identified with rationalism, with science, and with economic progress, and for that reason and in that sense, by midcentury "almost every statesman and civil servant . . . was a Liberal, irrespective of his ideological affiliation" (Hobsbawm, 1975, 105).[184]

The most interesting thing to notice about this period is the position of the Conservatives. If, in 1834, following the Reform Act, Sir Robert Peel "had rechristened his party 'Conservative,' it was to make it plain that it was not his intention to pursue in any respect a policy of reaction" (Halévy, 1947, 57).[185] At the very same

---

183. The link of education and order is explained well by Johnson (1970, 119): "[E]arly Victorian obsession with the education of the poor is best understood as a concern about authority, about power, about the assertion (or reassertion?) of control. This concern was expressed in an enormously ambitious attempt to determine, through the capture of educational means, the patterns of thought, sentiment and behaviour of the working class. Supervised by its trusty teacher, surrounded by its playground wall, the school was to raise a new race of working people—respectful, cheerful, hard-working, loyal, patriotic, and religious."

184. But it was also true, in this midcentury consecration of liberalism, that "the men who officially presided over the affairs of the victorious bourgeois order in its moment of triumph were a deeply reactionary country nobleman from Prussia, an imitation emperor in France and a succession of aristocratic landowners in Britain" (p. 3). Zeldin (1958, 46) sees no accident or paradox in this: "[Napoleon's] motley qualities were perhaps necessary for a man engaged in transforming a country in which the old and the new stood confronted and unreconciled. . . . Disraeli was in many ways his counterpart in England, pursuing a similar task, and bizarre and mystical like him. Their followers were equally divided in both countries, and they both had to deal with all extremes from the most progressive radicalism to the highest toryism."

185. Gash (1963, 163–164) elaborates the long-term effect of this shift:

> The essence of the internal conflict of the Conservative party in 1841–6 was precisely over what was principle and what was subject to the "flexible rules of politics." Peel could claim with justice that he never embarked on any policy that was not at bottom a conservative one. To encourage trade and industry, to dampen class and sectarian Chartism by prosperity and the

time in France, following the Revolution of 1830, conservatism was being elaborated in France as "the way one manages a post-revolutionary society," as a way of "concluding the revolution." As such, it is no longer in opposition to liberalism, as Rosanvallon (1985, 277–278) puts it so well: "Rather it conceived of itself as the completion of liberalism, as its eternity."

As a result, Conservatives, too, began to favor the strong state. For Conservatives, there were at least three considerations. The first was the inbuilt weakness of the appeal to tradition and continuity, which Burke had wanted to make the basis of conservative ideology.[186] For, as Bénéton (1988, 116) notes, this position leads to contradictions, once there are, as in France, durable interruptions that have led to creating other traditions. What can one do then? Political conservative thought began to oscillate "between fatalism and radical reformism, between the rule of a limited state and the appeal for a strong state." Hence, for many Conservatives the strong state became the road to the restoration, or at least the partial restoration, of tradition. Second, many Conservatives felt that conservatism was "an attitude that saw in law, order, and stable rule the first principle of government" and, like Peel, drew from this the conclusion that "the conservation and steady improvement of the institutions of the state [were] the necessary corollary in principle" (Gash, 1977, 59).

But the third reason was the most cogent, as perceived by the liberal ideologist Guido Ruggiero (1959, 136–137) in his discussion of how British Tories, influenced by German romanticists, transferred their defense of royal prerogatives to the state:

> It was the State whose importance and prestige were to be reasserted. The State was to be regarded not as a compromise between opposing self-interests but as what Burke had called it—a living communion of minds.
>
> For this reason the Conservatives recognized the need of broadening the basis of the State and building it not upon the tower of privilege but upon the humble yet solid platform of the feelings and interests of the whole people. The old Toryism had created an oligarchical government; but was not the Liberal government an oligarchy, less entitled to rule because based solely upon wealth detached from birth and the privileges of an ancient tradition?
>
> Why, asked the Conservatives, did Liberalism wish to weaken the State? The answer was easy. It wanted to allow free play to the strongest forces in competition

---

[Anti–Corn Law] League by timely concession, were in his view the surest means of preserving aristocratic leadership and the traditional structure of power.

186. Gash (1977, 27) resumes Burke's view thus: "Change was part of political life, as of all organisms; time itself was the greatest innovator. . . . But the continuity of the social fabric must be respected. Change should come in small gradations; by way of evolution not revolution; by adaptation not destruction. . . . For the doctrinaire reformer who acted as though human nature and existing society could be disregarded in the pursuit of abstract justice, he had nothing but scorn."

with the weakest, and full power to exploit the defenceless masses, which were the victims and not the protagonists of the struggle, by destroying all power superior to individuals and able to exercise upon them a moderating and equalizing function.[187]

When, in 1960, Lord Kilmuir (1960, 70–71) sought to explain how it was that the Conservatives in Great Britain always returned to power after great defeats by "social revolutionary movements" (he so terms 1832, 1846, 1906, and 1945), his answer is "the Shaftesbury tradition," which he defines as the association of Toryism with "state intervention to insure minimum standards in diverse forms, for example, factory acts, housing and public health acts, and acts on behalf of trade unions"—in short, because the Conservatives had used the state for their own version of social reformism.

This "mutually advantageous alliance between the [Conservative] party and the people" was the heart of Disraeli's so-called national Toryism. Despite the fact that Disraeli's original rise in the Tory party was the result of his fierce opposition to Peel's repeal of the Corn Laws, close observation of Disraeli's own later political practice shows it to be "largely 'Peelite' in spirit" (Smith, 1967, 4, 15).[188] What Disraeli essentially added to "Peelism" was imperialism. Liberal reformism was to be seen as "a means, a path, a discipline, in the service of a higher end, Empire" (Ruggiero, 1959, 140)—thereby tying the working classes more closely both to the nation and to some extent to the Conservative Party.

It could be said that, if the great political achievement of liberalism in the period 1830–1875 was the taming of the dangerous classes, the great ideological achievement was the taming of conservatism—transforming it into a variant of the rational state-oriented reformism that liberalism propounded. The common ground was nationalism and the strong state, which affected even the cultural outlook of conservatives. Barzun (1943, 143–144), in discussing the cultural shift from

187. The role of the monarchy as symbol was an interesting side effect of the political struggles, as Hill (1929, 100) notes: "[I]n fighting the centralizing tendencies of [liberal] Reformist legislation, Tories and Radicals were alike led in the direction of *étatisme* of another kind. Disraeli would check the overweening power of Parliament and the Cabinet by exalting the Sovereign. Richard Oastler would appeal to the good sense of the young Queen to limit by her prerogatives what he called the power of the Commissioners to inflict cruelty, and the cry was still heard when Oastler had sunk into old age. It was Kingsley and the Christian Socialists who would now exalt the Queen."

188. In the 1980s, when Margaret Thatcher was able for the first time since Wellington to make reformism illegitimate as Conservative doctrine and practice, there was an effort to redefine "the Disraelian legacy" by suggesting that in fact he had been "haunted" by the division of the party that Peel had brought about. See Coleman (1988, 157, 161–162): "[Disraeli's] main commitment was always to the interests of his party and its conservative purposes. . . . [I]t is the continuity and traditionalism of the Disraeli ministry that stands out, not any departure. . . . This conclusion will disappoint romantics who wish to find profound creativity in Disraeli's leadership. . . . [He] prevented [the party] from shifting to either a significantly more progressive or a more rigidly diehard position." Coleman also minimizes the radicalism of intent of the parliamentary reform of 1866–1867 (see pp. 131–138).

romanticism to realism in the period 1850–1885, calls it a "rebound from [the] disappointment" of 1848. He notes the rise of both Realpolitik and materialism, each bolstered by the "august authority of physical science." He argues:

> Liberals, conservatives, and radicals were united by their common desire for tangible, territorial nationhood; scientific hypotheses were tested by their suitability to mechanical representation or analogy . . . ; while force . . . was applied as the great resolver of social paradoxes and complexities."[189]

As liberalism and conservatism moved toward their "common policy of state intervention," some Conservatives (such as Chamberlain in the late nineteenth century) tried to insist on the distinction that for Conservatives it was an act of "patronage," whereas for the Liberals it was the belief that "all people should be assisted to govern themselves." But, as Ruggiero (1959, 151) says, "in practice, the difference was often very slight." Of course it was. In 1875, the socialists were still not totally tamed. That would be completed only in the period 1875–1914. Schapiro (1949, vii) would thus be able to conclude his book on liberalism: "When the nineteenth century ended historically in 1914, liberalism had been accepted as the way of political life in Europe."

189. The need to look for subtexts can be seen in the fact that just as realism was used to symbolize "tangible, territorial nationhood," so had romanticism in the earlier period. See Agulhon (1973, 13–14): "Everything pushed [in 1848] the intellectual elite to see in the people a reservoir of new and healthy forces. Taking up themes first put forward at the end of the previous century by German romanticism, the inspirers and leaders of nationalist movements in central and eastern Europe, in their struggle against the aristocracies and their cosmopolitan cultures, exalted the national virtues of folklore, of popular songs and tales, or the primordial health of the masses. France to be sure was not in the same situation, the national problem being considered there to have been solved. But the peoples and nationalities in revolt, from Greece to Ireland, from Poland to Italy, were cherished by our liberals and republicans, and thereupon the vaguely populist ideology that undergirded European struggles did not fail to influence their French friends."

Auguste Saint-Gaudens, *Robert Gould Shaw and 54th Regiment*. In the U.S. Civil War, the North somewhat reluctantly organized an African-American Volunteer Regiment, commanded by a White officer from a Massachusetts abolitionist family. The 54th Regiment became famous for its bravery in the attack on Fort Wagner. Some thirty years later, Saint-Gaudens was commissioned to erect a bronze monument in Boston. As one can see, the monument is largely about the White commander. It was not until 1982 that the names of sixty-four African-American soldiers who died in that battle were inscribed on the back of the monument. (Courtesy of Yale Collection of American Literature, Beinecke Rare Book and Manuscript Library, Yale Univeristy)

4

The Citizen in a Liberal State

That the principle of national sovereignty is at the very heart of the French Revolution is something on which we need scarcely insist. That this principle was created—and put into practice—by the transfer of absolute sovereignty from the king to the nation is a truism that is worth repeating. And worth examining.

—KEITH MICHAEL BAKER, "SOUVERAINETÉ" (1988)

I would say that the French revolutionary tradition . . . had a greater impact on the nineteenth century than on contemporaries.

—MERNEST LABROUSSE (1949B, 29)

Inequality is a fundamental reality of the modern world-system, as it has been of every known historical system. What is different, what is particular to historical capitalism, is that equality has been proclaimed as its objective (and indeed as its achievement)—equality in the marketplace, equality before the law, the fundamental social equality of all individuals endowed with equal rights. The great political question of the modern world, the great cultural question, has been how to reconcile the theoretical embrace of equality with the continuing and increasingly acute polarization of real-life opportunities and satisfactions that has been its outcome.

For a long time—for three centuries, from the sixteenth to the eighteenth—this question was scarcely mooted in the modern world-system. Inequality was still considered natural—indeed, ordained by God. But once the revolutionary upsurge of the late eighteenth century transformed the language of equality into a cultural icon, once challenges to authority everywhere became commonplace, the disparity of theory and practice could no longer be ignored. The need to contain the implications of this cultural claim, and thereby to tame the now "dangerous classes," became a priority of those who held power. The construction of the liberal state was the principal framework that was built to limit the claim. The elaboration of modern ideologies was in turn an essential mechanism in the construction of the liberal state.

THE FRENCH REVOLUTION AND THE CONCEPT
OF CITIZENSHIP

The great symbolic gesture of the French Revolution was the insistence that titles no longer be used, not even that of *Monsieur* and *Madame*. Everyone was to be called *Citoyen* (Citizen). This gesture was intended to demonstrate the repudiation of traditional hierarchies, the incrustation of social equality in the new society that was being constructed. The French Revolution came to an end. Titles were reinstituted. But the concept of "citizen" (if not its use as a title of address) survived. It did more than survive. It thrived. It became the rhetorical bedrock of the liberal state. And it was adopted juridically everywhere, to the point that by 1918 the world found it necessary to invent the concept of "stateless" persons to describe the relatively small portion of humanity who were unable to claim citizenship somewhere.

The concept of citizen was intended to be inclusive—to insist that all persons in a state, and not just some persons (a monarch, the aristocrats), had the right to be a part, an equal part, of the process of collective decision making in the political arena. It followed that everyone should have the right to receive the social benefits the state might distribute. By the second half of the twentieth century, the existence of rights that are guaranteed to citizens came to make up the minimal definition of what constitutes a modern "democratic" state, which virtually every state was now claiming to be.

But the other face of the inclusiveness of citizenship was exclusion. Those who did not fall into this new category of citizens of the state became by definition that other new concept: aliens. The aliens of one state might be the citizens perhaps of some other state, but not of this state. Still, for any given state, even the exclusion of aliens within its boundaries did not limit very much the number of persons theoretically included. In most cases, more than 90 percent of the residents of the country were citizens—*legally* citizens, that is, for citizenship had now become a matter of legal definition.

And this was precisely the problem faced by the states after the French Revolution. Too many persons were citizens. The results could be dangerous indeed.[1] The story of the nineteenth century (and indeed of the twentieth) was that some (those

---

1. "A specter haunted most political commentators [*publicistes*] at the beginning of the nineteenth century: that of social dissolution. . . . At the heart of these common preoccupations lay the wish to circumvent the model of popular sovereignty. . . . It was the numbers that were frightening" (Rosanvallon, 1985, 75–76).

with privilege and advantage) continually attempted to define citizenship narrowly and that all the others responded by seeking to validate a broader definition. It is around this struggle that the intellectual theorizing of the post-1789 centuries centered. It was around this struggle that the social movements were formed.

The *way* to define citizenship narrowly in practice, while retaining the principle in theory, is to create two categories of citizens. The effort started with Abbé Siéyès, just six days after the fall of the Bastille. In a report he read to the Constitutional Committee of the National Assembly on July 20–21, 1789, Siéyès proposed a distinction between passive and active rights, between passive and active citizens. Natural and civil rights, he said, are rights *"for* whose maintenance and development society is formed." These are passive rights. There also exist political rights, "those *by* which society is formed." These are active rights. And from this distinction, Siéyès drew the following conclusion:

> All inhabitants of a country should enjoy in it the rights of *passive* citizens; all have the right to the protection of their person, of their property, of their liberty, etc. But all do not have the right to play an active role in the formation of public authorities; all are not *active* citizens. Women (at least at the present time), children, foreigners, and those others who contribute nothing to sustaining the public establishment should not be allowed to influence public life actively. Everyone is entitled to enjoy the advantages of society, but only those who contribute to the public establishment are true stockholders (*actionnaires*) of the great social enterprise. They alone are truly active citizens, true members of the association." (Siéyès, 1789, 193–194)

Without blinking an eye, Siéyès then added that equality of political rights is a fundamental principle (but presumably only for active citizens), without which privilege would reassert itself. On October 29, 1789, the National Assembly translated this theoretical concept into a legal decree that defined active citizens as those who paid a minimum of three days' wages in direct taxation. Property became the prerequisite of active citizenship. As Rosanvallon (1985, 95) points out, "If reason is sovereign, men cannot invent laws. They must discover them. . . . The notion of capacity finds its logic in this framework."[2]

---

2. The theoretical justification was that a criterion of eligibility for the vote was "independence of judgment." It followed that "all those who were considered to be dependent on someone else in the exercise of their will, such as minors, women, or servants, were excluded from the suffrage" (Gueniffey, 1988, 616). This was the origin of what would later be called the *régime censitaire* (Théret, 1989, 519).

Competence of judgment continued to be the main justification for denying access to the suffrage. For example, in 1824, James Mill, a leading figure among English liberals of the time, argued against both female and working-class suffrage "on the grounds that their interests could be effectively represented by others who were better able to wield political power on their behalf: husbands and fathers in the case of women, and 'the most wise and virtuous part of the community, the middle rank' in the case of the working class" (Taylor, 1983, 16).

The attempt to circumscribe the meaning of citizenship took many forms, all of them necessarily involving the creation of antinomies that could justify the division into passive and active citizens. Binary distinctions (of rank, of class, of gender, of race/ethnicity, of education) are ancient realities. What was different in the nineteenth century were the attempts to erect a theoretical scaffolding that could legitimate the translation of such distinctions into legal categories, in order that such categories serve to limit the degree to which the proclaimed equality of all citizens was in fact realized.

The reason is simple. When inequality was the norm, there was no need to make any further distinction than that between those of different rank—generically, between noble and commoner. But when equality became the official norm, it was suddenly crucial to know who was in fact included in the "all" who have equal rights—that is, who are the "active" citizens. The more equality was proclaimed as a moral principle, the more obstacles—juridical, political, economic, and cultural—were instituted to prevent its realization. The concept of citizen forced the crystallization and rigidification—both intellectual and legal—of a long list of binary distinctions that then came to form the cultural underpinnings of the capitalist world-economy in the nineteenth and twentieth centuries: bourgeois and proletarian, man and woman, adult and minor, breadwinner and housewife, majority and minority, White and Black, European and non-European, educated and ignorant, skilled and unskilled, specialist and amateur, scientist and layman, high culture and low culture, heterosexual and homosexual, normal and abnormal, able-bodied and disabled, and of course the ur-category that all of these others imply—civilized and barbarian.

In states with citizens enjoying equal rights, the dominant groups were seeking to exclude, while the dominated groups were seeking to be included. The struggle was conducted both in the political and in the intellectual arena. All persons found themselves on one side or the other of each of the antinomies. Those who were on the dominant side tended to theorize the distinctions as in some way natural. The key problem of the dominant was to make sure that individually they were on the dominant end of each and every binary distinction. Facing them, those who were located on the dominated side began to organize, seeking to devalue, destroy, or redefine the distinctions in order to relocate themselves into the category of active citizens, into the category of the civilized.

The fact that there were multiple binary categories created a difficulty. It was possible to be on the dominating side in some categories and not in others. Those who did not have what might be called a perfect score had political decisions to make if they wished to be considered part of the group that comprised full-fledged citizens. They often, quite understandably, sought to give priority to those categories in which they were on the dominant side. The result could be some widening of the privileged group, but this merely increased the difficulties for those who remained excluded. It was this struggle about definitions of priorities of binary categories that was at the root of the continuing debates inside the social movements about the tactics of their struggles and the nature of potential and desirable alliances.

To be sure, the concept of citizenship was meant to be liberating, and it did indeed liberate us all from the dead weight of received hierarchies claiming divine or natural ordination. But the liberation was only a partial liberation from the disabilities, and the new inclusions made sharper and more apparent the continuing (and new) exclusions. Universal rights as a consequence turned out in actual practice to be somewhat of a linguistic mirage, an oxymoron. Creating a republic of virtuous equals turned out to require the rejection of others who were thereby deemed to be nonvirtuous.[3]

Liberalism, which would become the dominant ideology of the modern world, preached that virtue could be taught, and it therefore offered the managed progression of rights, the managed promotion of passive citizens to the status of active citizens—a road for the transformation of barbarians into the civilized. Since the legal process of promotion was thought to be irreversible, it had to be handled carefully, prudently, and above all gradually. On the other hand, those social movements that were being created to champion the interests of those whose rights were not fully recognized were always debating what might be done to end nonrecognition as rapidly as possible. There were those who insisted that the movements should be antisystemic—that is, that they should seek to destroy the existing historical system that made possible the travesties of equality. And there were those who were essentially integrationist—that is, who believed that the role of the movements was merely to speed up the already existing liberal program of the managed acquisition of rights.

The story, as we have already seen, began with the French Revolution itself. Siéyès, in that same memorandum, said: "All public authority, without distinction, is an emanation of the general will; all come from the people—that is, the Nation. These two terms should be considered synonyms" (1789, 195). The implementation of this view was simple and rapid. Everything that had been labeled royal was relabeled national.[4] "For the French revolutionaries, the nation was not a given; it

3. The distinction of Siéyès would be adopted everywhere in one form or another. "The Italian liberals, like their counterparts elsewhere in Europe, made a clear distinction between the citizenry (*i cittadini*) and the masses or populace (*il popolo*). In a liberal state the populace were entitled to civil rights, but only the citizenry, a minority fit for positions of responsibility by virtue of sex, property ownership, and formal education, could properly be entrusted with political rights. . . . [T]he liberal position . . . reflected the fear that political democracy might lead to unstable government and to 'mob rule'" (Lovett, 1982, 33).

4. Godechot (1971, 495) notes: "[D]uring the electoral campaign of 1789, nation suddenly took on a revolutionary resonance which made it very popular among the masses. In effect, the 'Nation

had to be created" (Cruz Seoane, 1968, 64). The concept of nation spread rapidly to other countries.[5] It was the French revolutionaries, too, who first used the concept of nation to justify the concept of the self-determination of nations. When the Assembly voted the annexation of Avignon and the Comtat Venaisson on September 13, 1791, it was done in the name of "the right of people to determine their own fate [disposer d'eux-mêmes]" (Godechot, 1965, 189).

However, once having noted that national sovereignty was constituted the moment sovereignty passed from the crown to the nation, Nora (1988, 893) asks pertinently, "But what nation?... And what society?" The enthusiasms of ordinary people during the heyday of the French Revolution may have given a momentary hyperegalitarian tonality to the concept of nation, but there existed as well a quite different Enlightenment tradition that had distinguished sharply between the "nation"—a concept used to denote the educated strata—and the "people," who were "not depraved but easily influenced, [and who therefore] required a moral, technical (and physical) education appropriate for their status, that would best equip them for a life of labour" (Woolf, 1989, 106). Linguistic games would continue to be played, with shifting emphases from fatherland (patrie) to nation to people.[6]

---

assembled,' and then just the *Nation,* would assume the position of the king in the hierarchy. Hence the motto adopted in September 1789: 'The Nation, the Law, the King.' The Nation which decides, which commands, the law; the king who only implements the law. Everything that had been 'royal' now became *national;* the National Assembly, national guard, national army, national education, national economy, national domains, national well-being, national debt, etc. Following the example of crimes of *lèse-majesté,* there were now crimes of *lèse-nation.*"

Nora (1988, 801) underlines the fact that the French Revolution brought together three senses of the term *nation:* "the social meaning: a body of citizens equal before the law; the juridical meaning: the constituent power in relation to the constituted power; the historical meaning: a group of men united by continuity, with a past and a future." Billington (1980, 57) emphasizes the social psychological importance of the concept: "[The nation is] a new fraternity in which lesser loyalties as well as petty enmities are swept aside by the exaltations of being born again as *enfants de la patrie:* children of a common fatherland." He calls it a "militant ideal."

5. The Cortes of Cádiz in 1810 made "national sovereignty" and "the sovereignty of the people" the new basic political principle, and here, too, everything that had been "royal" now became "national" (Cruz Seoane, 1968, 53, 64). Lyttleton (1993, 63) argues in the case of Italy: "The Italian question did not exist as a political reality before 1796. The Italian Jacobins were the first to pose the creation of a united Italy as a concrete political project, and their concept of the nation was derived from the French Revolution."

6. Godechot (1971, 495) argues that a reading of the *cahiers de doléance* reveals that it was the educated classes who tended to use the term *patrie,* and who seemed very aware of the historic controversy between Voltaire, who had defined *patrie* as "the country in which one feels comfortable" (*là où on est bien*), and Rousseau, who had insisted it was "the country in which one was born." The term *nation* was used by those who had more revolutionary tendencies. Robespierre seemed, however, to want

It would not be too long before the term *nation* had become too mild, and the term *people* had become so popular that even autocratic rulers sought to use it.

> By the 1830s, romantic revolutionaries were speaking almost routinely of *le peuple, das Volk, il popolo, narod,* or *lud* as a kind of regenerative life force in human history. The new monarchs who came to power after the Revolutions of 1830, Louis-Philippe and Léopold I, sought the sanction of the "people" as the king "of the French" and "of the Belgians," rather than of France or Belgium. Even the reactionary Tsar Nicholas I, three years after crushing the Polish uprising of 1830–31, proclaimed that his own authority was based on "nationality" (as well as autocracy and Orthodoxy)—and his word *narodnost,* also meaning "spirit of the people," was copied from the Polish *narodowość.* (Billington, 1980, 160)

But it was more than a game. It was part of the crucial debate about who was a true citizen. Nor was this merely an abstract debate. The National Assembly and then its successor structure, the Convention, were faced with three concrete issues about citizenship: women, Blacks, and workers. The record of the French Revolution was mixed, but in each case, they decided on exclusions that left bitterness.

In the case of women, the whole matter started out badly. The royal decree summoning the Estates-General specified that women who held seigniorial fiefs had to choose male proxies to represent them in the Electoral College—nobles for laywomen, clergy for nuns (Landes, 1988, 232, n. 5). Nonetheless, women (religious communities, societies of tradeswomen) did write *cahiers de doléance.* And some of their complaints foreshadowed later problems of alliances. Mme. B*** O***, Pays de Caux, wrote: "There is talk of liberating the Negro slaves; . . . could it be possible that [the nation] would be mute about us?"[7]

It is well known that women played a major role in various popular demonstrations during the French Revolution, most crucially in the so-called October days in 1789, when the Parisian market women (along with national guardsmen) marched on Versailles and forced the royal couple to come to the capital to reside. But this demonstration concerned the rights of poor people, not of women per se.[8] And two months after these riots, on December 22, 1789, the National Assembly formally excluded women from the right to vote. True, Condorcet did write

---

to rescue *patrie* for the revolutionary cause. He said: "In aristocratic states, the term *patrie* makes no sense, other than for patrician families who have confiscated sovereignty" (cited in Carrère d'Encausse, 1971, 222).

7. Duhet, 1989, 33. Shortly thereafter, in an appeal to the National Assembly, someone wrote: "Women are certainly as worthy as (*valent bien*) Jews and Coloreds" (cited in Rebérioux, 1989, x).

8. Hufton (1971, 95) argues: "[T]he most significant social division of the *ancien régime* . . . lay between those who could make the proud claim, 'there is always bread in our house,' and those who could not. . . . The woman of the bread riots owed her intensity to her appreciation of the need to stay

a famous pamphlet in 1790 calling for women to have *droit de cité,* but he didn't persuade those in power. The Constitution of 1791 renewed the exclusion, and this was reiterated in a vote of the Convention on July 24, 1793, specifying that women were excluded from all political rights, which actually was something that at least aristocratic women had had in the ancien régime.[9]

Some improvements in women's rights were instituted, it is true. Marriage and divorce became civil processes. Primogeniture was abolished, and the rights of illegitimate children and their mothers to financial support were promulgated. A law was passed permitting women to be witnesses in documents related to the *état civil,* although this matter continued to be controversial (Abray, 1975, 55). And in the heated atmosphere of the Jacobin period, women began to organize. They began to play a much larger role in the popular societies. They stood outside the doors of the Convention, trying to control who would enter. They packed the galleries and shouted their views (Landes, 1988, 139–140).

On May 5, 1793, the Society of Republican-Revolutionary Women was founded. They pushed vigorously the demands of women for bread. Their language had distinctly feminist overtones. They were allied to the *Enragés,*[10] who were critical of the Jacobins from the left. But above all, they were women, organized women, who insisted on being heard. When women in one Paris section petitioned for the right to bear arms, Fabre d'Eglantine sputtered in the Convention: "After the *bonnet rouge,* which the *Républicaines* wore during their meetings, comes the gun belt, then the gun" (cited in Abray 1975, 56). The Committee on Public Safety appointed a committee, headed by André Amar, to consider whether women should exercise

---

on the right side of the line between poverty and destitution. . . . [T]he destitute were not protesters, not rioters. . . . [T]hey gave up and expected nothing.

"The bread riots of the French Revolution then, whether the march to Versailles on 5–6 October 1789 or, to a lesser extent, the *journées* of Germinal and Prairial of Year III, were *par excellence* women's days. Where bread was concerned, this was their province; a bread riot without women is an inherent contradiction."

Applewhite and Levy (1984, 64) see the women's role somewhat differently: "Women of the popular classes in Paris made a major contribution to what is most significant, even unique, about the Revolution: its achievement of the most democratically-based popular sovereignty in the eighteenth-century western world. Feminist claims for civil and political rights growing out of Enlightenment liberalism never became central to the Revolutionary power struggles and were denied by the Napoleonic Code, but the political activities of non-elite women were at the heart of Revolutionary politics."

9. "When Philip the Fair solemnly convened the first Estates-General . . . in 1302, he received an assembly chosen by both men and women. For over five centuries, privileged women of all estates retained the vote, both local and national. Then in the 1790s, the revolution that proclaimed the rights of man abolished the political rights of women" (Hause, 1984, 3).

10. George (1976–1977, 420) says that the purpose of the *Républicaines* was "to organize the feminine half of the 'people' for zealous support of the program of the *Enragés.*"

political rights and whether they should be allowed to take part in political clubs. The answer to both would be no. The committee deemed that women did not have the "moral and physical qualities" to exercise political rights, and furthermore that it was the aristocracy that wanted women to have these rights "in order to put women at odds with men" (cited in George, 1976–1977, 434).

As for participating in political associations, Amar was quite explicit in explaining why women should not be allowed to be members:

> If we consider that the political education of men is at its beginning, . . . then how much more reasonable is it for women, whose moral education is almost nil, to be less enlightened concerning principles? Their presence in popular societies, therefore, would give an active role in government to people more exposed to error and seduction. Let us add that women are disposed by their organization to an overexcitation which would be deadly in public affairs and that interests of state would be sacrificed to everything which ardor in passions can generate in the way of error and disorder. (Cited in Landes, 1988, 144)

As Banks noted (1981, 28), advocating the "rights of man" did not necessarily lead to the "rights of women," since "it is quite possible to define women as having a different nature from that of men." To be sure, the exclusion of women was often put forward as a *temporary* provision. An earlier report by Lanjuinais in April 1793 called for the exclusion of women from political rights "for the time that it will take to remedy the vices of women's education." As Cerati (1966, 170) remarked acerbically: "[These vices] must have been terribly tenacious since it took a century and a half to overcome them."

Why it was the women's clubs that became the first victim of the Law of Suspects[11] has been a matter of considerable debate. George (1976–1977, 412) thinks that "Jacobin nerves were taut, and Jacobin patience snapping with apostles of participatory democracy," and that the women were an easy first target. Lytle (1955, 25) specifies that "the Revolutionary Women had become a danger to the Robespierrists [because the latter were] unable to satisfy the demands of Parisians for bread." Hufton (1971, 102) links the latter issue to that of the attitude of the *sans-culottes*:

> The *sans culotte*, Chaumette said when he dissolved women's clubs in October 1793, had a right to expect from his wife the running of the home while he attended political meetings. . . . Others have lingered on the pride of the *sans culottes* in his new-found importance in *société populaire*, [in] section[,] or as a professional revolutionary on commission. . . . While her husband was still talking she in some

---

11. Racz (1952, 171) notes the "irony" of this, since the *Républicaines* had been ardent supporters of this law.

areas had joined the food queues and the minute she did that her loyalty was potentially suspect.

Applewhite and Levy (1984, 76) see the outlawing of the women's clubs as "the
triumph of the bourgeois revolution over the popular revolution."[12] But of course
bourgeois feminists fared no better. Olympe de Gouges, author of the *Declaration of the Rights of Woman and Citizen*,[13] was sent to the guillotine on November
3, 1793. Whichever the explanation for the Jacobin attitude, the situation did not
change after the downfall of the Jacobins. In 1795, after the *journée* of 1er Prairial,
the Convention excluded women from its hall entirely, even as listeners, unless
accompanied by a man with a citizen's card (Abray, 1975, 58). And in 1796, the
Council of Five Hundred excluded women from senior teaching positions. In
1804, the Napoleonic Code regressed over even the ancien régime. Previously, at
least aristocratic women were allowed to handle property and legal matters. Now,
in the more egalitarian mood of the French Revolution, all women were treated
equally—all having no rights whatsoever (Levy et al., 1979, 310).

I have called this a mixed picture. One can emphasize the negative side. Abray
(1975, 62) says that it "stands as striking proof of the essential social conservatism [of the Revolution]." Knibiehler (1976, 824) insists that it marks a "relative
regression of the status of women," one that, for George (1976–1977, 415), was
"more clearly inferior than that of the Catholic, feudal past, because now defined,
cloaked and justified by the bourgeois deities of Reason and the laws of Nature."
Cerati (1966, 13) asserts that the claims of women for greater rights during the
French Revolution met with "a glacial reception from the [otherwise] enthusiastic
[masculine] partisans of equality." However, Landes (1988, 148) claims that part
of the problem was that the feminists themselves "bore the stamp of ambivalence
toward public women."

But one can also evaluate the experience more positively. Landes (1988, 170)
also points out that, after the French Revolution, "gender became a socially relevant category . . . in a way that it would not have mattered formerly." Kelly (1982,
79) compares the situation of the post-1789 feminists favorably with that of those
involved in the famous *querelle des femmes* launched by Christine de Pisan and
others in the fifteenth century. The earlier feminists, she says, lacked "the vision

---

12. So does Lacour (1900, 403): "Michelet was mistaken when he wrote: 'This great social question [the political rights of women] was strangled accidentally.' The Terror was logical in suppressing
women's clubs. What they strangled, or rather what they finished strangling, was the party that, in
the *Ami du peuple* of Leclerc and at the tribune of the *Républicaines révolutionnaires*, had demanded
urgently the implementation of the Constitution. It was the male and female party that wanted a social
revolution, . . . that which had taken seriously the socialist promises of Robespierre, and then the voting of the Constitution."

13. This declaration was not timid: "Women, wake up; the tocsin of reason is being heard throughout the whole universe; discover your rights" (reproduced in Levy et al., 1979, 92). See Scott (1981) for a
perceptive analysis of Olympe de Gouges's views and role.

of a social movement to change events," whereas after 1789 they "were animated by a notion of progress and of intentional social change." And Moses (1984, 14) insists that, whereas before 1789 feminism was an issue only for the upper classes, the French Revolution led to "the rise of a feminism more sweeping in its scope and more inclusive in its following." The negative evaluation lays emphasis on the changes actually achieved and the justifying ideas of the times. The positive evaluation lays stress on the development of the feminist movement and its mobilization. This tension would remain the principal cultural-political antinomy of the nineteenth (and twentieth) centuries: the dominant theorized; the dominated organized.

The story of Blacks was not too different. There were of course few Blacks in hexagonal France at the time of the Revolution. But there were plenty in the colonies, and above all in St.-Domingue. I have previously told the story of the successive rebellions there, the creation of the first Black state in the Americas, the wars, and finally the diplomatic isolation of the Republic of Haiti (Wallerstein, 1989, passim, esp. 240–244, 253–256). Here I wish to underline the debate that took place in Paris.

St.-Domingue had had a clear system of social stratification before the Revolution. There was a small White stratum, most of whom were planters. There was a stratum of free mulattos. But the largest group were the Blacks, and the Blacks were almost all slaves. This was an ordinal social ranking. But none of these groups had political rights. The French Revolution was thus received enthusiastically by all three strata, because they all hoped it would bring them political rights. However, the Whites did not wish social equality to be granted to the free mulattos, and neither the Whites nor the free mulattos wanted the enfranchisement of the slaves. Once again, the norm of equality raised the question of who is to be included. As Aimé Césaire (1981, 342) notes so acutely:

> Just as the royal authority could not oppress the Blacks without oppressing to various degrees all the classes, it became rapidly clear that the authority that emerged out of the French Revolution could not accede to the demand of one of the classes of colonial society for freedom without putting on the table the question of the very existence of colonial society. More specifically, the bourgeois power that emerged out of the French Revolution felt that liberty was indivisible, that one couldn't give political or economic liberty to White planters and keep mulattos under iron rule; and that one couldn't recognize the civil equality of free men of color and at the same time keep Blacks in the ergastulum. In short, to liberate one of the classes of colonial society, one had to liberate them all, one had to liberate St.-Domingue. And this seemed contrary to the interests of France.

It is not that there were not some in the National Assembly and the Convention who realized this. In the debate on the condition of the slaves, Abbé Grégoire declaimed: "There still exists one aristocracy, that of skin color" (cited in Césaire, 1981, 187). But, as Césaire suggested, beyond philanthropy and even antiracism lay anticolonialism, and even Grégoire and Robespierre were not prepared to go that far. Only Marat was. Marat noted the connection of this issue with the very principle of active citizens: "But how can we treat as free men persons with black skin, when we do not treat as citizens those who cannot pay one *écu* in direct taxes?" (cited in Césaire, 1981, 189–190).

The emancipation of the slaves in 1793 was not the fruit of the egalitarian impulses of the French revolutionaries. It was imposed by the power of Toussaint L'Ouverture, leader of the slave rebellion in St.-Domingue, and merely ratified by the Convention in a decree (Decree no. 2262 of February 4, 1794) that would be revoked by Napoleon in 1802 after Toussaint had been imprisoned (and one that would not be reenacted until 1848).

What is more revealing, however, is the prior debate on the rights to be accorded to free mulattos. Pushed by the Amis des Noirs and opposed by the Club Massiac, which represented the interests of the White planters, the Assembly decided "unanimously" on a curious compromise. After the adoption of the decree granting the vote to free men of color, Dupont de Nemours presented a "declaration" of the Whites explaining their assent on the grounds that the vote was being given only to "qualified mulattos of free parents" and was not being accorded, could not be accorded, "to unfree persons, or freedmen, since these were members of a 'foreign nation'" (cited in Blackburn, 1988, 187–188).[14] The *poor* Whites on St.-Domingue opposed any property qualification, since that would give the vote to some free mulattos while not to them. They applied the description of the White planters—"a species of foreigner with no entitlement to political rights"—to *all* free mulattos (Blackburn, 1988, 177). Even the free mulattos were by definition not part of the "nation"; they could not therefore be citizens.

As for French workers, we have already noted that the concept of active citizenship, by creating a property-based definition of political rights, resulted in excluding them, was intended to exclude them. In the heady revolutionary atmosphere, however, workers began to seek improvement of their situation by organizing. The Assembly had abolished the guilds. The employers and workers gave this opposite interpretations. For the former, the only law that now governed production was the law of supply and demand. The workers thought it meant they could not create organizations freely, as they wished (Soreau, 1931, 295).

The rapid rise of prices plus the collapse of the paper money, the *assignats*, fueled worker effervescence, peaking in the spring of 1791 just before the flight

14. In St.-Domingue the Whites would ignore this decree, and indeed, they executed the leader of the free men of color, Ogé, when he tried to secure its implementation. This led to a White–mulatto civil war, which was then rendered irrelevant by the rebellion of the Black slaves against both. Blackburn (1988, 176) calls the Amis des Noirs, the leading advocate of the rights of the mulattos, "ineffective" as a political group, noting that the slave interests had a "veto power not only in the Assembly but in the Revolutionary Clubs."

of the king and the enactment of the Constitution. Strikes and disorders seemed beyond the control of the Paris municipality, and led to calls for action by the Assembly. While maintaining the inegalitarian standards for voting, the Assembly sought to use the ideology of equality against the possibility of workers to organize by enacting an "anti-cabal" law. The notorious Loi Le Chapelier, adopted on June 14, 1791, outlawed any workers' combination, and on July 20 this proscription was extended to the *compagnonnages,* the long-existing mutual benefit societies (Wallerstein, 1989, 107 and n. 248).

Steven L. Kaplan (1979, 74–75) observes how, behind the facade of the new language of equality, the revolutionaries continued the very same practices that the royalist regime had followed:

> One would henceforth repress in the name of individual liberty what one had previously repressed in the name of collective and corporate public weal. . . . It is striking to notice that the two great means of social control of the world of labor utilized by the revolutionaries for the defense of liberty—the maximum, underpinned by a system of food supply obtained by constraint, and the anti-cabal law—had been the cornerstones of the prohibiting, paternalist *Ancien Régime.*

In his history of the French Revolution, Jean Jaurès (1968, 912) denounced this "terrible law" that, under the guise of symmetry between workers and employers, affected only the workers, and weighed upon them heavily for seventy-five years. He cites Marx, who called it a "bourgeois coup d'état," and finds it quite unsurprising that Robespierre should have tacitly supported enacting the law by his silence.[15]

The French Revolution appealed to nature, which was a universal phenomenon, belonging to everyone. But it also appealed to virtue, which was only a potential (but not necessarily the actual) characteristic of everyone. From these concepts, it derived the existence of human rights. Since there could be multiple "natures" and multiple capacities, the discourse had an "ambivalent quality" (Landes, 1981, 123). Scott (1981, 2) sums up "the persistent question of the relationship of specific, marked groups to the embodied universal" quite well: "[H]ow could the rights of the poor, of mulattos, blacks, or women be figured as the rights of Man? The general answer is: with difficulty."

---

15. Cobb (1970, 184) essentially agrees, although he refuses to call this class conflict: "The conflict between the Jacobin dictatorship and the popular movement, the parting of the ways between the *robespierristes* and the *sans-culottes,* was much more straightforward than has been suggested. Programme played little part in this divorce, nor can any 'inevitability' of conflict be discovered in terms of class. The two sides represented forms of government (un-government might be a better term to describe the communalism of the popular militants) that could not co-exist for more than a few months." On exactly how the *sans-culottes* might best be analyzed as a social category, see the discussions in Hobsbawm (1977, 88), Soboul (1962, 394), and Tønnesson (1978, xvii).

Still, the French Revolution had the consequence that "revolutionary action acquired a status whose promise, or menace, was at once qualitatively different from rebellious action and morally comparable to that with which, in other times and places, great religious changes had been (and sometimes still are) invested" (Sonenscher, 1989, vi). Of course, since revolutionary action was both promise and menace, it was polarizing, and this polarization "provided the subsoil for the politics of the next century and a half" (Roberts, 1978, 73).

The great socially unifying concept of the citizen thus led to the formalization of multiple cross-cutting binary categories and to the binary tension of political life—the split between right and left, the Party of Order and the Party of Movement—a split that centrist liberalism would devote all its efforts to rendering meaningless. The result was an intense zigzagging of public life, energized by the juggernaut of a belief in progress, and distorted by the continuous and increasing social and economic polarization of real life within the world-system.

In the nineteenth century, the so-called middle classes came to dominate the Western world, and Europe came to dominate the world. When one has achieved the top position, the problem is no longer how to get there but how to stay there. The middle classes nationally, and the Europeans globally, sought to maintain their advantage by appropriating the mantle of nature and virtue to justify privilege. They called it civilization, and this concept was a key ingredient of their effort. In the Western world, it was translated into education, and education became a way of controlling the masses.[16] And on the global scene, starting with Napoleon (but adopted subsequently by all the other European powers), "the concept of civilization as an ideology . . . became unashamedly a form of cultural imperialism" (Woolf, 1989, 119).

The French Revolution would come to a definitive political end in 1793/1799/1815 and become thereafter merely a political symbol and a cultural memory. It left, however, a monumental legacy to the whole world-system. Sovereignty now belonged to the people, the nation. And political debate and political change were the normal consequence of the sovereignty of the people. The privileged strata of the world-system had to come to terms with what was for them a poi-

---

16. See Thompson's summary (1997, 23): "Attitudes towards social class, popular culture, and education became 'set' in the aftermath of the French Revolution. For a century and more, most middle class educationalists could not distinguish the work of education from that of social control: and this entailed too often a repression of or a denial of the validity of the life experience of their pupils as expressed in uncouth dialect or in traditional cultural forms. Hence education and received experience were at odds with each other. And those working men who by their own efforts broke into the educated culture found themselves at once in the same place of tension, in which education brought with it the danger of the rejection of their fellows and self-distrust. The tension of course continues still."

sonous legacy. They would see whether they could incorporate it institutionally in ways that would contain its potential for the radical dislocation of existing hierarchies.

This process of containment took three forms. The first was the crystallization of what came to be called ideologies, which claimed to be philosophical constructs but were actually primarily political strategies. The second was the elaboration of conceptual categories as a new discourse with which to describe the world. This was initially and primarily, as we have said, the work of the dominant strata, who hoped thereby to frame the debate and justify the limiting of citizenship. Eventually, this work of creative conceptualization became transformed and institutionalized in the structures of knowledge known as the social sciences. And the third was the establishment of a network of organizations, initially primarily the work of the dominated strata, which were to serve as agents of furthering change but would act simultaneously as mechanisms of limiting change.

The period 1815–1848 was one in which all and sundry seemed to be moving uncertainly in this transformed political terrain. The reactionaries tried to turn the clock back, to undo the cultural earthquake that was the French Revolution. They discovered, as we have seen, that this wasn't really possible. The dominated (and repressed) strata, for their part, were in search of appropriate and effective modes of organizing. And the emergent liberal center was unsure of how it should, or could, construct the appropriate political base to get the turmoil under control. They concentrated, as we have seen, on constructing liberal states—first of all, and what was most important, in the most powerful countries: Great Britain and France.

THE WORLD-REVOLUTION OF 1848

It would be the world-revolution of 1848 and its immediate aftermath that would require resolving these uncertain searches and efforts in order to stabilize the world-system and restore a certain degree of political equilibrium. The revolution started once again in France, where the July Monarchy had exhausted its credibility and legitimacy. The rebellion of February 25, 1848, had widespread support, from both the middle and the working classes, from Bonapartists, even from the Church and the Legitimists, "who saw in the fall of Louis-Philippe revenge for 1830" (Pierrard, 1984, 145). And it had immediate resonance elsewhere in Europe—in Belgium, to be sure, but also in all those countries where nationalism was becoming a rallying point: Germany, Italy, Hungary. That is why 1848 came to be called by historians "the springtime of the nations." The one country where the revolution would not occur was England, something immediately explained in an editorial in the *Times* on February 26, 1848, as due to the fact that "the people feel that under the existing state of things they have a voice in the government of the country, and can utter that voice with effect."[17]

The *Times* may have been right about England, but the revolution took on a more social, more working-class and radical tone in France. Four months later, on June 25, came the second so-called social revolution.[18] The broad support evaporated almost immediately. By July 2, *Le Moniteur Industriel* was thundering: "[F]amily, property, nation—all were struck to the core; the very civilization of the nineteenth century was menaced by the blows of these new barbarians" (cited in Scott, 1988, 117). We know how this second revolution ended—in the overthrow of the social regime, and eventually the installation of Louis Napoleon and the Second Empire.

But the cat had been let out of the bag. The movement for socialism, which "had never been more than the tail, a lively tail, of the movement for bourgeois democracy" (cited in Droz, 1972a, 16),[19] would now separate itself clearly from centrist liberalism.[20] For Halévy (1947, 204), "Chartism had triumphed, but in

17. This editorial, published on February 26, 1848, is worth reading at length: "During the remarkable period [since 1830] the Sovereigns and Governments of England have been steadily improving and popularising all the institutions of the country. They have immensely expanded the basis of representation. They have evidently and deliberately increased the power of the Commons. They have opened the municipalities. They have qualified and destroyed the monopolies of companies and of classes. They have liberated manufactures and commerce. But why need we linger on details? In a word, they have thrown themselves into the arms of the people. *They have cut the very ground from under democracy* by satisfying, one by one all its just desires. Let any one, who has not yet attained to the midday of life, compare the popular agitations of the present kind and that preceding the last French revolution. England was then incessantly disturbed by clamour for organic change. The peerage, the church, the rights of property, law, monarchy, and order itself, were to disappear. Mark the change which has come upon that turbulent scene. Popular agitation is in these days of a purely rational, and, so to speak, legislative character. Thousands and tens of thousands meet to impress upon their representatives their opinion—and generally their wise opinion—on a pending question, not concerning the fundamentals of society or the reconstruction of the state, but some minor and debateable point. The discussion is lawful in its subject, and regular in its tone" (cited in Saville, 1990, 229).

18. "Of all the French revolutions, that of 1848 is clearly the most social, in the modern sense of the term, . . . in the sense of being 'working-class,' or 'proletarian'" (Labrousse, 1952, 183). This aspect was not unknown in other countries at the time. Droz (1972b, 462) cites the declaration of the *Arbeiterverein* of Frankfurt on May 14, 1848, that "the workers constitute the people itself." Conze and Groh (1971, 143) assert that during 1848/1849, "the basis of the democratic movement and the working-class movement was supported almost exclusively by a well-qualified minority, namely 'worker-journeymen,' whose social situation at that time can be described only as extremely precarious."

19. No doubt, it had stronger roots prior to 1848 in France than in any other country. Bruhat (1979a, 331) calls France "unquestionably the country of socialism" in this period.

20. The year 1848 was "the moment when an autonomous socialist labor movement had begun to emerge in Europe from the matrix of the democratic revolution" (Lichtheim, 1969, vii). See also Lehning (1970, 171). Bruhat (1972, 505) describes socialism as emerging in 1848 as a "doctrinal force." In Germany, "a clear separation between radical-democratic and socialist politics did not occur before 1848" (Kocka, 1986, 333).

France, not in England."[21] To be sure, this nascent movement "suffered a very great set-back after 1848" (Cole, 1953, 1:157). And an economist of the era, Louis Reybaud, a student since the 1840s of the socialist movement, would even proclaim in 1854: "Socialism is dead. To speak of socialism is to give a funeral oration" (cited in Droz, 1972a, 16). This would not be the last of such premature opining.

It would have been more audacious, even at the time, to suggest that nationalism was dead. Lovett (1982, 92) sees the revolution of 1848 as the transformation of local and regional Italian democratic movements into a "national democratic network," but one that would then have difficulty facing up to the "social" question.[22] The Hungarian nationalist movement discovered a different kind of problem. Whereas, for Kossuth, "nationalism coincided with liberalism" (Fejtö, 1948b, 133), for the Serbs, Romanians, and Croats who were located within the boundaries of Hungary, Hungarian nationalism seemed "a movement of the nobility, a family quarrel between Hungarian seigniors and the rulers in Vienna" (Fejtö, 1948b, 153).[23] Still, 1848 "put in motion the revolutionary wave in Europe" (Djordjevíc and Fisher-Galati, 1981, 106), and it would spread throughout the Balkans.

The revolutions of 1848 constituted the first world-revolution of the modern world-system. It is not that it occurred in all parts of the world-system; it did not. Nor is it that the revolutionaries achieved their objectives; by and large, the revolutions were defeated politically. It is that the revolutions centered around issues of exclusion—exclusion from the benefits of citizenship. It was in 1848 that we first see clearly that there would be two kinds of antisystemic movements, two separate ways of dealing with this exclusion: more rights within the nation (the social revolution), and separating one ethno-national group from another, dominant one (the national revolution).

And it was in 1848 that the question of long-term strategy first became clearly posed. From 1815 to 1848, the ideological struggle was considered to be one

21. The fact that Chartism did *not* triumph in England is, however, the important consideration for Lichtheim (1969, 5), since it permitted the "consolidation of Victorian society." Saville (1990, 227) sees it rather as "the closing of ranks among all those with a property stake in [Great Britain], however small that stake was."

22. "Most importantly, the revolutionary experience convinced many democratic activists that it was impossible to enlist the support of the masses for a cultural and political revolution without articulating the social goals of that revolution in more coherent and specific terms than Mazzini had done. . . . To reach a consensus, even a vague one, about the social goals of the Italian revolution proved much more difficult than to agree upon its cultural and political objective. Indeed, both before and after the unification the issue of social justice was the major cause of dissension in the democratic camp" (Lovett, 1982, 50–51).

23. Croat nationalists "were not liberals, but simply nationalists with plenty of resentment for all those who refused to accept that they formed a nation" (Fejtö, 1948b, 154–155).

between liberals and conservatives, between the heirs of the spirit (if not of all the tactics) of the French Revolution and those who fervently sought to restore the order derived from an older way of viewing the world. In this struggle, "democrats" and "radicals" had little place. Anathema to the conservatives, an embarrassment to the liberals, they played at most a gadfly role, pressuring the liberals to be more daring (without much success, be it noted). What the revolutions of 1848 did was to open up the possibility that these democrats/radicals, who now sometimes called themselves "socialists" but sometimes also "nationalist revolutionaries," would be more than gadflies, that they would organize mass action separate and distinct from the liberal center. This is what Chartism had foreshadowed, and this is what Halévy meant when he said that Chartism had triumphed not in England but in France.

This was a terrifying prospect not merely to the conservatives but also to the liberal center. And both reacted accordingly. Suppression of the radicals became the order of the day, not merely in the Russian and Austro-Hungarian empires, and among the various regimes in the Germanies and Italies, but in the liberal states of France and England as well. This is the "set-back" of which Cole spoke. Socialist and trade-union movements would now have a difficult ten to fifteen years. So would feminist movements. So would nationalist movements.

The suppression would be effective, but not long lasting, since all these movements would reemerge in a decade or two, and in far stronger forms. What was lasting were the lessons that the proponents of the three classical ideologies of the nineteenth century—conservatism, liberalism, and radicalism—would draw from the experience of 1848. The liberals drew two lessons. One was that they were in many ways closer to the conservatives than they had thought, and that alliances with radical elements often proved dangerous to their interests. But second, they determined that they had to elaborate better theoretical justifications for the distinctions that they continued to wish to make among the citizenry, between the active and passive citizens à la Siéyès, if they wished to sustain this distinction.

The conservatives drew a different lesson. The strategy of Metternich (really of de Maistre, Bonald, et al.) would not work. They were impressed that only Great Britain did not have an uprising, even though it had been the country where radical forces had been the strongest. They noticed that Great Britain had been the only country where conservatives had followed a more centrist path, ready to make some concessions, in order to absorb and co-opt at least middle-class forces into the arena of political decision making. And they noticed that this policy had succeeded, as the editorial in the *Times* suggested. The conservatives would now be ready to go down the path of pursuing some version of centrist liberalism, albeit a somewhat more conservative one—what historians have come to call "enlightened conservatism."

Radicals (erstwhile democrats) drew a still different conclusion. It was that spontaneity was not enough.[24] If one wanted to have a major political impact, systematic and long-term organization was a prerequisite. This would lead the "movements"—an ephemeral concept—down the path of bureaucratic organizations, with members and officers, with finance and newspapers, with programs, and eventually with parliamentary participation.

Sewell (1985, 82) says that the French Revolution changed the concept of revolution from "something that happened to the state . . . [to] something that people did to the state consciously and with forethought." What 1848 led the movements to see was that the "people" were unlikely to do something that mattered to the state without their prior uniting in organizational form.[25] This would inevitably make them focus on the state, the *national* political level. It would also eventually and inevitably call into question the degree to which these movements could continue to be truly antisystemic and not simply a variant of centrist liberalism, albeit a somewhat more impatient one.

The story of the rest of the nineteenth century, and indeed of a good part of the twentieth, was that the centrist liberals would theorize, the antisystemic movements (both of the socialist and of the national-liberation variety) would organize, and the enlightened conservatives would legislate. They would enact compro-

24. They already knew that conspiracy would not work. The utter failure of Blanqui's uprising in 1839 was telling. In 1846, Karl Schopper, on behalf of the London Communist Correspondence Committee, wrote in a letter: "[A] conspiracy has never been of benefit to anyone except our enemies. . . . We are certainly convinced that one cannot avoid a grand revolution, but to bring about such a revolution through conspiracies and silly proclamations . . . is ridiculous" (cited in Ellis 1974a, 42). But now the conclusion went beyond doubting the value of conspiracies to doubting the sufficiency of spontaneous rebellion.

25. Geary (1981, 26–28) seeks to distinguish three kinds of labor protest: preindustrial ("typically, the food riot"), early industrial (Luddism), and modern industrial, marked by the creation of formal organizations that have a "stable, continuous existence." Similarly, Tilly (1986, 389, 392) says that after 1848/1851, popular protest in France "shifted to national awareness." He describes previous protest as "parochial and patronized" and protest thereafter as "national and autonomous." Calhoun (1980, 115) also says: "On a sociological level, the critical shift in the transition to 'class' action came with the development of the formal organizations which could mobilize workers for national action." He says this begins in the 1820s. I think this is too early. I see at most weak beginnings of this in France, and at best partially class-based activity in England. Real national class organizations are a post-1848 phenomenon. I believe Hobsbawm (1975, 115) to be closer to the time mark than Calhoun: "[W]e can now see that two achievements of the 1860s were permanent. There were henceforth to be organized, independent, political, socialist mass labor movements. The influence of the pre-Marxian socialist left had been largely broken. And consequently the structure of politics was to be permanently changed."

mises, and in the process they seemed to compromise the antisystemic movements. It was the theorizing of the liberals about citizenship, however, that would make this possible. It is this story that we shall now tell.

LABOR AND SOCIAL MOVEMENTS

In the liberal states—western Europe and North America, and later central Europe—the strongest demand for inclusion in citizenship came from the urban working classes. It is their struggle, which they most frequently called the struggle for socialism by the proletariat against the bourgeoisie, which commanded most attention at the time and since. It is fitting to start with this part of the story. I shall organize it in the temporal division of socialism as idea and as movement, a division that was suggested by Labrousse (1949b, 5): 1815 to 1851—"powerful idea (*grandeur de l'idée*), weak movement"; 1851 to 1871—"movement on the rise, idea in decline"; 1871 to the end of the nineteenth century—"powerful idea, powerful movement."

We have previously noted the beginnings of labor movements in the 1830s and 1840s.[26] Jones (1983, 59) explains well their confused efforts: "The elements of working-class politics had to be forged together from the mixed inheritance of the Enlightenment, socialism, Dissent and traditional notions of moral economy, in a situation which had no precedent."[27] What they did feel was that they were somehow the heirs of the more radical elements of revolutionary traditions.[28]

26. This was a view expressed at the time. Bronterre O'Brien, who was a radical militant and trade unionist, wrote in 1833: "A spirit has grown up among the working classes, of which there has been no example in former times" (cited in Briggs, 1960, 68). Foster (1974, 47–72), however, insists that "extralegal unionism" existed in England earlier, in the period between the 1800s and the 1830s, and that its consequence was a "massive cultural reorganization of the working population" (p. 72). I suppose it depends on what you define as "trade unionism." Rule (1988, 10) finds evidence for its existence in eighteenth-century England in the references to conflicts that he finds in Adam Smith and in the passage of the Combination Acts in 1799, which, he claims, employers saw as "a strengthening of their arm against established trade unions." See also the discussion by Pelling (1976, 14) of pre-1825 trade unions in Great Britain, "almost invariably of skilled artisans rather than of laborers."

27. British workers "looked back to Locke as much as [they] looked forward to Marx. [Their theory] was not a theory of exploitation within production but a theory of unequal exchange. Capitalists were still primarily seen as middlemen or monopolists. . . . Profit was thus a deduction from the product of labor, enforced through ownership of the means of production. . . . The situation described . . . corresponded most closely to that of the depressed artisan or outworker" (pp. 57–58).

28. Rudé (1969, 52, 95, 112), speaking of the workers in Lyon—a key center politically and economically, where the majority of the workers had "reacted rather negatively to the Restoration," not to speak of their "far from enthusiastic" reception of the enthronement of Charles X—asserts that "Jacobin traditions had been conserved for a long time." Referring to the emergence of trade unions and workingmen's parties in the United States in the 1830s, Bridges (1986, 163–164) says: "This organizational life reveals the artisans of the Jacksonian era as the proud bearers of the ideology of [Tom] Paine and the American Revolution. . . . Their rhetoric opposed the freeman to the slave and aristocracy to

As we know, in 1830 there was a revolution in France but not one in England. Instead, England saw the enactment of the Reform Bill in 1832. This is largely because England had no equivalent of the regime of the Ultras under Charles X.[29] But "revolution" or not, the development of working-class consciousness began to take root in both France and England, not within the parties but outside them.[30] In order to do this, the nascent socialist movement had to carve out a place for corporate demands not previously admissible within the revolutionary rhetoric of the French revolution (and its generic citizen). They began to speak of "cooperation" and "association"—not of a single trade but of all "workers" as a class.[31] Even before

---

republicanism; . . . it based its claims squarely on equality and natural right." Mommsen (1979, 81) sees the workers' movements in Germany in the 1860s as "the heir of bourgeois radicalism."

Geary (1981, 49), however, cautions that the fact "that radical ideas found a more favorable reception among some sections of the British working class in the 1830s and 1840s than at a later date suggests that changing circumstances—affluence, a liberal state—rather than ideological activity itself determined the perceptions of labor."

29. Rudé (1969, 243) emphasizes the difference in the attitude toward the regime of the middle classes in England and France: "In short, there was no revolution [in England] in 1832 not so much because the Tories or the Lords surrendered to the threats of Whigs or Radicals, as because nobody of importance wanted one and because that combination of political and material factors that alone would have made one possible was conspicuously absent." Jones (1983, 57) sees the Reform Act of 1832 as a stimulus to working-class consciousness, insofar as it was regarded as a "the great betrayal" by the middle classes of "what had been thought of as a common struggle." This sense of betrayal was then deepened by the actions of the subsequent Whig government—Irish Coercion Bill, rejection of the Ten Hours Bill, attack on trade unions, Municipalities Act, and the new Poor Law—all of which were seen as "confirmation of the treachery of the middle class. The practical consequence to be drawn was that the working class must fight for its own emancipation."

30. "The great movement both in France and Great Britain between 1830 and 1836 did not need politicians. Quite the contrary, it was suspicious of them. The leaders of the parties were interested only in being in power and staying there" (Dolléans, 1947, 1:30).

31. Thus, Lichtheim (1969, 7) makes England and France the "twin birth-places" of the new movement of socialism and dates this to "about 1830." Sewell (1986, 61) concentrates on France and dates it as "during 1831, 1832, and 1833." He emphasizes that "the really massive development of socialism among the working class . . . was the consequence of an appropriation rather than an abandonment of the revolutionary political tradition" (p. 65). In Germany, in the 1830s and 1840s, "early radical associations like the 'Communist League' recruited their members largely from *Handwerksgeseller,* that is, journeymen or young artisans trained according to guild rules and working in dependent positions" (Kocka, 1984, 95).

Moss (1976, 38) views cooperative socialism as "the republican response to working class protest that appeared after the July revolution." To be sure, the radical republicans of the Société des Droits de l'Homme were middle class, but "the application of egalitarian principles to industrial society led them beyond their middle class interests toward an authentically socialist program." So, against Marx's view that this movement was "petty bourgeois socialism" and "middle class," Moss insists (p. 47) that its social base was "primarily working class" and "represented the aspirations of an authentic proletariat for trade socialism, the collective ownership of industrial capital by a federation of skilled trades." Plamenatz (1952, 177) also wishes to take issue with Marx but in the opposite direction. Socialism, far

1830, the need for collective action by workers came to be seen. The logic of their position derived directly from the consequences of the dissolution by the French Revolution of the guilds. The controller of production was no longer a master; he was now an employer. Whereas workers had thereby gained more freedom, they had lost all claims to the paternal solicitude of the master. To compensate, they adopted "a modified version of the corporate idiom of the Old Regime," creating workers' guilds with rituals and older organizational forms "to assert the continuing existence of a moral community of the trade, and to maintain vigilance over conditions of labor in the workplace" (Sewell, 1979, 55). It is these journeymen who became the strongest supporters of the early labor movements. Kocka (1986, 314–315) says they came largely from "urban crafts that had great continuity, stability, and cohesion, usually guild traditions, . . . and relatively good bargaining power."[32]

They began to use the weapon of strikes, even though strikes were illegal, through anonymous calls launched by informal social networks.[33] At the same time, the workers began to concern themselves with the "nationality" of their fellow work-

---

from being an ideology of the proletariat, "came to France before there was a demand for it by the class in whose interest it was invented. . . . It was the natural issue, born in bourgeois minds, of [bourgeois] ideology; and the workers took to it (or as much of it as they could understand) because they had first accepted the principles of 1789, because they had learnt that the 'rights of man' were meant as much for them as for other people."

32. "Artisans of this type lived outside the households of their employers. They were far advanced in the process of transformation from traditional journeyman to qualified wage worker, but they still retained much of what held the trade together traditionally and used this as a basis of protest and organization" (Kocka, 1986, 315). It is precisely this kind of "continuity, stability, and cohesion" that Calhoun (1980, 421) invokes as an explanation of the possibility of engaging in revolutionary action: "I suggest that social bonds which predate specific 'causes' are of critical importance in providing social strength for long-term, risky, and concerted collective action." Sewell (1986, 53) similarly explains the "artisans' proclivity for class-conscious action" compared with the "relative quiescence of factory workers" at this time by the way in which they "understood their labor." For artisans it was "largely a consequence of a social understanding . . . that derived from the corporate or guild system," whereas factory workers had "a less social, more individualized conception of the relations of production." See also Moss (1976, 22–23): "Skilled workers did not suffer the process of industrialization as passive victims but brought to it a set of values and orientations—autonomy, pride, and solidarity of the trade; organizational experience; and an egalitarian ethos nurtured through popular republicanism—that motivated an active transformative response. . . . The skilled worker combined a professional and a proletarian class consciousness."

33. "The notion that strikes during early industrialization were irrational outbursts of factory workers who had not yet learned to adjust to their new surroundings is contradicted by the high degree of rationality and organization exhibited by strikers and by the concentration of early strikes among artisans in handicraft industry, who were well integrated into traditional craft communities" (Aminzade, 1982, 63). Generally speaking, workers at this time had to be very careful about syndical action, since repression was quite rapid. In Spain, for example, a *Real Orden* authorized mutual benefit societies in 1839. But as soon as there were conflicts in Barcelona, the society involved was dissolved.

ers, the issue of non-"citizens" as competitors in the labor market. We have already discussed the ways in which the *canuts* of Lyon had made the employment of "foreign" workers one of their key complaints in 1831. Some of the artisanal guildlike structures would wither after 1830, especially because of the "ever growing migration to Paris in particular" (Judt, 1986, 57). The result would be a "new identification of the worker to the nation" (Derainne, 1993, 33). There would now come to be a debate about the bases of workers' unity. Flora Tristan, who was a very strong voice for workers' unity (as well as an important feminist figure), in her pamphlet on this topic written in 1843 (1983, 53), drew an inference that would become very controversial in the history of workers' movements—support for independence movements in colonial countries, the workers as a class blending into the "people" as a construct:

> If I constantly cite Ireland [the Catholic Association, headed by O'Connell] it is because Ireland is still the only country to realize that if the people want to leave their slavery, they must begin first by creating a huge, solid, and indissoluble union. For the union gives strength, and in order to demand one's rights and to bring the right of such a demand to public attention, one must above all be in a position to speak authoritatively enough to make oneself heard.

Perhaps Tristan could say this about Ireland because she was French. English workers were notably more reticent on the subject. Their only focus was England. It was Chartism that was central to English history of the 1830s and 1840s. The Charter adopted in 1838 famously made six demands, demands that had, however, long been demands of English radicals: annual Parliaments, universal suffrage, equality of electoral districts, the secret ballot, parliamentary immunity, and the removal of property requirements for eligibility for election. To the question of whether this was not at most merely a set of demands for parliamentary democracy, Dolléans (1947, 127) replies that this was merely an "appearance," that the Charter had a "clearly socialist character," and that, for the Chartists, "true democracy implied a social revolution." Whether this is the way to view Chartism has long been a matter of debate. On the one side there are those, like Evans (1983, 255, 257), who see Chartism as "much the most important political movement of working men organized during the nineteenth century" and claim that it was "a critical stage in the political education of the working people."[34] And there are those,

---

And after various kinds of unrest, all unions were suppressed in 1845 (Tuñon de Lara, 1972, 41–48). Speaking of England, Sykes (1988, 193) says that "there does seem to have been a particularly intensive and embittered spell of conflict at the onset of the 1830s. This whole experience . . . deeply influenced class attitudes and relationships."

34. Bédarida (1979, 319) agrees: "From a British point of view, Chartism represents the most powerful, the deepest, and the richest movement of popular emancipation that modern England has known. From a European perspective, it constitutes one of the two great revolutionary worker struggles of the nineteenth century, the other being the Commune of 1871."

like Gash (1979, 209), who see it rather as merely "a continuation under another name of the old radical reform movement." Jones (1983, 168, 171) provides a bridge between the two viewpoints by saying that "if Chartism became a movement of workers, it became so not out of choice but from necessity."[35]

Still, as we know, in the end, Chartism failed. Perhaps it was, as Royle (1986, 57–58) argues, that the Chartists had "no coherent or effective strategy to offer," torn as they were between "hopelessly naive" moral educationists and "physical force advocates, caught up in their own rhetoric." Nonetheless, as Royle (1986, 93) himself says, "the Chartists' greatest achievement was Chartism, a movement shot through not with despair but with hope." Chartism was an essential part of the process—crystallized by the world-revolution of 1848—of defining the great social antinomy of the nineteenth century and most of the twentieth: bourgeoisie versus proletariat.

Neither bourgeoisie nor proletariat are eternal essences. They were social creations, reflecting to be sure a certain social reality, which was then reified. And as with all such concepts, it was the dominant, not the dominated, stratum that began the process of reification, contrary to subsequent beliefs. We have already discussed Guizot's role, even before the July Monarchy, in elaborating the concept of class—a concept he had taken from Saint-Simon. He did this, of course, in order to justify the political role of the bourgeoisie as opposed to the aristocracy. But he also did this to situate the bourgeoisie (which he felt would in time assimilate the aristocracy) vis-à-vis the proletariat, and to distinguish between the two (Botrel and Le Bouil, 1973, 143). If he was seeking *droit de cité* for the bourgeoisie, and ultimately total political control, he was specifically opposed to the inclusion of the proletariat. The *droit de cité* was to be reserved for active—that is, propertied—citizens.[36]

35. "As a secular phenomenon, Chartism was the last, most prominent and most desperate—though not perhaps the most revolutionary—version of a radical critique of society. . . . The vision which lay behind this critique was of a more or less egalitarian society, populated exclusively by the industrious, and needing minimal government. . . .

"[R]adical and Chartist politics make no sense if they are interpreted as a response to the emergence of an industrial capitalism conceived as an objective, inevitable and irreversible economic process. The radical picture was of a far more arbitrary and artificial development whose source was to be found not in the real workings of the economy, but in the acceleration and accentuation of a process of financial plunder made possible by the political developments of the preceding fifty years." Of course, Chartism encompassed still other elements. On the role therein of a "radical Christian sensibility," see Yeo (1981, 110–112). On the so-called Tory-radical character of northern Chartism, by which is meant "traditional protectionism," see Ward (1973, 156 and passim).

36. In discussing the emergence of the concept in Spain, Ralle (1973, 124) cites the definition of *bourgeoisie* given by a Spanish socialist paper, *La Emancipación*, in 1871: "all those who, belonging to different classes and adhering to different parties, live in a regime of social injustice, and strive to a greater or lesser degree to enjoy the fruits of their advantages, and to contribute to maintaining the system."

As the bourgeoisie slowly evolved into that much vaguer and more inclusive category of the "middle class" or "classes,"[37] so eventually the proletariat evolved into that vaguer and more inclusive category of the "working class" or "classes." There would come to be a great deal of resistance to explicit class language by many politicians and social scientists, because the use of such language came to be identified with a particular political position—that of Marxism—and using it therefore came to signify for many people accepting Marxist analysis and politics. But the retreat to vaguer language did not eliminate the antinomy. If anything, it strengthened it—by making it easier for individuals to pass quietly over the line—while at the same time maintaining the line firmly. For those who passed, the important thing was that there be a line, one that might keep others from passing as well and thereby undermining the newly acquired privileged position of full citizenship of those who managed to pass.[38]

Since in the end the concept of the proletariat, even in its watered-down version of the working class, was intended to exclude, it is not surprising that the persons so designated often worked hard to redefine the terminology. For example, in Catalonia, retail-shop employees, whose working conditions were awful, refused to allow themselves to be called *obrers* or *proletaris*, insisting they were *treballadors*. This was because the latter term was less associated in the nineteenth century with unskilled manual labor than *obrers* (Lladonosa and Ferrer, 1977, 284). In Germany, the politics of naming was quite clear. From the 1830s on, the term *Arbeiter* began to widen from its original indication of unskilled laborer to include journeymen, and to be accepted by the latter in their politically radical phase. The self-employed craftsmen, however, resisted this category, and the workers' movements resisted including them (Kocka, 1986, 326–327).[39]

---

37. This would later allow social scientists to dispute, with true medieval clerical fury, the exact definition of the middle class. For one debate about definitions as they apply to France, see successively Cobban (1967), O'Boyle (1967), Stearns (1979a), O'Boyle (1979), and Stearns (1979b).

38. England has always been a notable exception to this queasiness about class language. Jones (1983, 2) notes the unusual "pervasiveness . . . of class vocabulary" in England, and offers the following explanation: "Unlike Germany, languages of class in England never faced serious rivalry from a pre-existing language of estates; unlike France and America, republican vocabulary and notions of citizenship never became more than a minor current . . . ; unlike the countries of southern Europe, vocabularies of class did not accompany, but long preceded, the arrival of social democratic parties and were never exclusively associated with them."

39. A discussion of the terminology concerning the working classes in England is to be found in Hobsbawm (1979, 59–63). Hobsbawm (1964, 116) also has a very useful discussion of the way we should conceive of cottage workers and outworkers: "The early industrial period was not one which *replaced* domestic workers by factory workers. . . . On the contrary, it multiplied them. . . . [T]he handloom weavers who were [later] starved out were not simply 'survivals from the middle ages,' but a class multiplied, and largely created, *as part of capitalist industrialization in its early phases* just as the factory workers were. . . . It is as unrealistic to leave the non-factory workers of the early industrial period out

Of course, this was a game that could be played by both sides. Scott (1988, 123–124) recounts the interesting story of a report by the Paris Chamber of Commerce in 1851 that attempted to recategorize the social structure in order to delegitimize the social revolution of 1848. The object was to reduce the number of workers by including in the category of heads of enterprises all self-employed persons; all persons making goods to order who employed others, even if these others were family members and not paid; all persons making goods for "bourgeois clientele" (this included washerwomen); and all those making goods to order for more than one manufacturer. By doing this, the report eradicated the class identification of these persons as workers or proletarians, which they had manifested in the February–June 1848 period. "Written in the wake of 1848, it was intended to dispute the revolution's most radical economic and political claims and to reassert a vision of economic organization [hierarchical and harmonious] that had been severely challenged, especially by socialist theorists." Thus it was that liberals theorized when radicals organized.

The period from the defeat of the revolutions of 1848 to the end of the 1860s was a very difficult one for workers' movements. The initial reaction of those in power was to repress anything that seemed to hark back to those revolutionary days. The defeat of Chartism and of the 1848 revolutions in turn created a sense of "disillusion" in the working classes. Jones (1983, 71) argues that "the permanence of industrial capitalism now seemed assured, and all except the most despairing of the outworkers were forced to adapt to this fact."[40] A closer look, however, seems to indicate that *adapt* may be the wrong word. It is perhaps more like *lie low* until better times come. Dolléans (1947, 1:225) seems to me to put it more aptly when he designates the period 1848–1862 as "the fire that is brewing."

What author after author emphasizes is the continuity between the patterns of the 1840s and those of the 1860s, as though the tactics of the workers were simply taken up again once the repression was slightly lifted. "Popular radicalism not only survived after 1848, but remained a major political force" (Biagini and Reed, 1991, 5).[41] And everywhere, we continue to see a primary role for the artisans, as

---

of the picture, as it would be to confine the discussion of the social effects of the introduction of the typewriter to the wages and grading of workers in the mass-production engineering factories which make them, and leave out the typists."

40. Kumar (1983, 16) gives a similar explanation of the "deradicalisation" of the English working class: "The demoralising defeats of Chartism, coupled with the fact that employers were, in several industries, at last succeeding in breaking craft control over the organisation and pattern of work, produced a largely apolitical factory work force which saw its best hopes for the future in industrial, trade-union terms."

41. Speaking of Great Britain, Musson (1976, 355) argues: "There was *not* a sustained, united, class-conscious 'mass movement' in the 1830s and 1840s, and a 'new labor aristocracy' was *not* suddenly created at mid-century. There was *not* a great 'discontinuity' around 1850, but a *continuity,* in the sense

opposed to the unskilled factory workers. Hinton (1983, 2) says of mid-Victorian England: "In the language of contemporary social commentary, 'skilled' and 'organized' were often used as synonymous."[42]

One can of course appreciate the warning that Kocka (1984, 112) makes "against exaggerating the continuity between *Handwerk* and working-class history."[43] And yet we find a certain "radicalization" in this period among the artisanal strata, says Sewell (1974, 88–89), especially among those who are "immigrants."[44] Hinton's comments (1983, 5) are helpful in unraveling this seeming paradox. He sees two kinds of skilled workers: those in craft industries, whose "trade-unionism was an outgrowth of the informal community of the trade"; and those in other sectors, where "skilled status was more commonly a product of trade-union organization" rather than preceding it. The first were sometimes quite radical, for they "experienced a greater relative deprivation" (Moss, 1975b, 7) than the factory worker, but they eventually were forced out of the picture, whereas the latter were going to be the mainstay of the future socialist and trade-union organizations.

---

of continuous, gradual change." Speaking of Germany, Conze and Groh (1971, 1:159) speak of "continuity—in terms of personnel, ideology, and to a lesser extent organization—of the working-class movement and thus of a major part of the democratic movement." And speaking of the United States, Hoagland says of the 1850s: "Stripped of universal and glowing ideals, without establishing a single labour paper to appeal to the country, the skilled trades settled down to the cold business of getting more pay for themselves by means of permanent and exclusive organizations."

42. On France, see Moss (1976, 8): "The French labor movement arose not among factory workers, . . . but among skilled craftsmen engaged as wage-earners in small-scale capitalist production." See also Sewell (1974, 81), in his study of Marseille: "[T]he artisanal trades nearly always had some form of labour organization, usually either *compagnonnages* or mutual aid societies until the late 1860s when *chambres syndicales* were legalized. . . . By contrast, I find no evidence of sustained labour organization in *any* of the proletarian trades." For Germany, see Geary (1976, 298): "[T]hose who made up the rank and file of the workers' clubs and associations in the 1860s were principally skilled workers in relatively small concerns and certainly not recruited from a concentrated and unskilled labour force." See also Kocka (1986, 314): "It is not surprising that journeymen were the main supporters of the early labor movement." Only for the United States do we get a slightly different tone: "By the 1850s there were more spokesmen for the unskilled parts of the working classes, and more who identified themselves as wage laborers" (Bridges, 1986, 177). But then, the United States suffered no particular repression of the free White working classes in the 1850s.

43. He reminds us (1984, 99) that, from the 1860s onward, "the rising social-democratic and socialist labour movement" in Germany "explicitly attacked craft and artisan traditions and loyalties among journeymen and (skilled) industrial workers because they correctly recognized that such traditions and loyalties were strictly craft-specific, particularistic and narrow, and that as such they stood in the path of the broad and comprehensive class solidarity which they were trying to promote."

44. His causal sequence (1974, 99–100) is as follows: repression of the workers' organizations during the Second Empire dismantled structures that had been exclusive clubs of nonimmigrant Marseillais, very Catholic and hence royalist, and led to the rise of a café culture, which in turn "opened the way for republican and socialist politics among the artisans." Thus, he argues, the rise of the "working class" was "a *cultural* as well as a political change" (p. 106).

During all this time, as indeed throughout the nineteenth and twentieth centuries, "fear of the masses, the concern with order, was the motif . . . always underlying the actions of the ruling class" (Moorhouse, 1973, 346). The question always remained for the dominant strata as for the working classes, Which tactics are optimal? From the point of view of the dominant strata, repression has its merits, but it also stokes the fire that is brewing, and eventually breeds revolt. So in the late 1860s, both Napoleon III and the British Conservative Party felt the need to loosen the constraints, to make it more possible for there to be workers' organizations and perhaps to expand a bit the de facto definition of citizenship. In a report written in 1860 for the Congress of the National Social Science Association, in Great Britain, "trade-unionism as an essay in self-government" was approved, and the authors declared that "leaders of a strike, where there is no regularly organized society, are likely to prove more unreasonable and violent than where there is" (cited in Pelling, 1976, 51). It seems an elementary bit of social science wisdom, one that signaled the beginning of an attempt to deal with the challenge to the definition of citizenship that organized working-class movements were now making. One hundred years later, another social scientist, looking back, opined that "in England lower-class protests appear to aim at establishing the citizenship of the workers" (Bendix, 1964, 67). Bendix saw this as distinguishing England from the Continent. He is probably doubly wrong. The objective was as true of labor movements in continental Europe as of those in England. And it is not true, even in England, that this was their only objective. This is, however, all they would achieve, and the liberal center in their theorizing and the enlightened conservatives in their practice endeavored to persuade them that it was all they needed or should want.

This period was the moment in which the so-called First International, the International Working Mens' Association (IWMA), was founded. It was a very small and weak organization, whose member organizations were equally weak and were pursuing objectives that were not entirely international.[45] But in terms of

45. See Kriegel (1979, 607): "In essence, the IWMA emerged as the product of a momentary convergence of different interests. . . . [It appeared] useful [to British trade unionists] to stop the importation of strikebreakers into England or of competing foreign workers working at lower wages. The French workers were looking for a model. They were unsure what route they should take: political struggle, in alliance with the republican bourgeoisie, against an Empire which oscillated between authoritarianism and an appeal for popular support? Or an economic struggle against employers aghast at new English competition and poorly adapted to the rapidity of the transformations through which the French economy was going? . . . The great utility of such a Franco-British dialogue furnished a concrete purpose to this new association." Van den Linden (1989) points to the inherent problems of the IWMA as an international *political* association, composed primarily of trade unions as members. He suggests, for example, that the essential reason the British unions quit the IWMA after 1867 was

the evolving strategy of the workers' movement, it served as the locus of the great debate of Karl Marx and Mikhail Bakunin (Forman, 1998, chap. 1). This debate had many aspects. But the heart of it was that the anarchists regarded the state as an implacable enemy, with which there could be no compromise, whereas the Marxists essentially had a two-stage theory of social transformation: somehow obtain state power, and then transform the world. How to obtain state power would of course come to divide the Marxists severely. But first they had to overcome the strength of the anarchist view.

The situation would evolve in the last third of the nineteenth century. Socialism became, in Labrousse's terms, a powerful movement as well as a powerful idea. So there seems to be a considerable "radicalization" of class conflict, starting with the Paris Commune and followed by the rise of socialist parties and trade unions, at least in all the more industrialized, wealthier parts of the world-system. "In 1880 [socialist parties] barely existed. . . . By 1906 they were . . . taken for granted" (Hobsbawm, 1987, 116–117).[46] But it is now also a truism that after 1890 there was a general deradicalization of these movements,[47] culminating in 1914 with the war votes of all the socialist parties (with the notable exception of the Bolsheviks).[48]

The picture that is offered us by most historical writing on the subject is one of a curve of militancy that went upward via popular mobilization and then downward via reformist sagacity (or betrayal, if one prefers that rhetoric). This is undoubtedly true in its crude outlines, although the upward part of the curve

---

that they no longer needed its assistance against the use in England of foreigners as strikebreakers and to give financial aid during strikes since they had become solidly implanted in Great Britain at the national level.

46. "[L]abour and socialist parties were almost everywhere growing at a rate which, depending on one's point of view, was extraordinarily alarming or marvelous. . . . The proletariat was joining its parties."

47. See Geary (1981, 109): "[T]he European working class did seem to abandon the barricade for the strike and insurrection for peaceful organization."

48. The ambiguous debates in the period immediately preceding the declarations of war are to found in Haupt (1965). The essential point is that virtually all the parties promised to refuse participation in the war, and virtually everyone voted the war credits. The shift in public position was a matter of days. Kriegel and Becker (1964, 123) explain the attitude of the French socialists in this way: "It appears that a certain socialism is nothing but a modern form of Jacobinism and, when the country is in danger, the voice of the 'great ancestors' prevails over socialist theories which are difficult to reconcile with the immediate situation." And Schorske (1955, 284) explains the vote of the German SPD for war credits as "but the logical end of a clear line of development, [in which] the command of crucial power positions in the party had passed to the reformist forces in the preceding decade." Actually, the Bolsheviks were not alone in condemning the war. During the war, in 1915, the Balkan socialist parties met in Bucharest and condemned both the war and the fact that most socialist parties were supporting it. They spoke of "the shame of the International" (Haupt, 1978, 78).

may never have been as great as some believe. As Michèle Perrot (1967, 702) says of so-called revisionism among the socialists of late nineteenth-century France, "In order that there be a 'revision,' there first has to be something to revise."[49]

The question is where the roots of this so-called radical political upsurge lie—an upsurge that, in the end (by 1914), no longer seemed to threaten any of the encrusted social structures of the modern world-system. It seems reasonable to interpret this as a clash about citizenship—that is, about who was to be included in the privileges and derived benefits of being designated the kind of citizen (active) who had these rights. It was a material issue, to be sure, but it was also a question of identity and identification. The narrowness of the prevailing definitions of real citizenship in the period 1815–1848 (justified by the premise that the workers were uneducated and propertyless, and therefore could have no reason to maintain social order) provoked a "world-revolution," which appalled the middle strata (since it threatened to go too far) and led to repression. When the pluses of repression were exhausted in twenty years,[50] there came to be more political space for popular maneuver. On the one hand, the liberal center urged the "education" of the working classes. And on the other hand, the working classes pushed for their own "education."

This is turn led to the creation of serious organizations that sought to force the pace of inclusion of at least the male, urban working classes. These organizations had to make their demands somewhat loudly in order to be taken seriously, both by the dominant classes and by those they were hoping to mobilize politically. Thus we heard a "radical" rhetoric. This rhetoric was effective, and the dominant strata reacted by various kinds of concessions—extension of the suffrage, the expansion of economic benefits (including the nascent welfare state), and inclusion in the "nation" via the exclusions resulting from racism and imperialism. Of course, this gave the results intended—the maintenance of the system in its major outlines, and the "moderation" of the workers' rhetoric. One does not need to intrude concepts of errors of judgment (false consciousness), self-interest of a leading, bureaucratic stratum (betrayal, the iron law of oligarchy), or the special interest of the better-paid workers (aristocracy of labor) to account for a process that seems more or less pandemic, more or less inevitable in retrospect, and which

49. Similarly, Geary (1976, 306), discussing the role of the official Marxism of the German Social-Democratic Party, says that "it is clear that the radicalism of the SPD in its early years has been exaggerated; and this raises problems for the usual theory of the embourgeoisement of the party."

50. And despite a second repression following the Commune. The International Working Mens' Association went out of existence after the Commune, partly because of such repression. The English members resigned in order to dissociate themselves from the publication of *The Civil War in France* by the General Council. And the French government pushed a campaign to accuse the IWMA of responsibility for the Commune, with whose origins and functioning it had virtually nothing to do. But any excuse will do (Forman, 1998, 61).

occurred in quite similar form throughout the world (the more industrialized, richer part of the world in the period 1870–1914) despite all the national variations in the details of their respective histories and immediate conditions—variations that proved ultimately to be of minor importance.

There is a sense in which the "radicalism" of the post-1870 period was actually a lot less radical in spirit than the "radicalism" of the pre-1848 period. As Jones (1983, 237–238) puts it:

> One of the most striking features of the social movements between 1790 and 1850 had been the clarity and concreteness of their conception of the state. . . . It had been seen as a flesh and blood machine of coercion, exploitation and corruption. . . . The triumph of the people would replace it by a popular democracy of a Leveller or Jacobin sort.

The concrete program, however, was "republicanism, secularism, popular self-education, co-operation, land reform, internationalism," and all these themes had by now become part of the litany of the liberal center, at least of its more progressive flank. The late nineteenth-century movements would shift their emphasis "from power to welfare," and with that, they were encased in a "defensive culture." In a sense, however radical the post-1870 movements were, they were less angry than the pre-1848 movements. The lure of the reward of citizenship was becoming too strong.

The period running from the 1870s to the First World War saw the first substantial organization of the working classes into political movements (primarily socialist and anarchist) and into trade unions. It therefore became the period of a major debate about strategy. The question that preoccupied all those who organized was how the working classes might achieve their goals, and in particular how they should relate to the existing states and parliaments. There was the debate between Marxists and anarchists. And there was the crosscutting debate between so-called revolutionaries and so-called reformists. At one level, these were real debates, and they absorbed a good deal of organizational energy and time. And on the other hand, they turned out often to be less consequential debates than people at the time and since have usually assumed.

It is important to note that the strongest and the most influential movements were located primarily in the countries that were strongest economically: Great Britain, France, Germany, the United States, Italy, Belgium, the Netherlands, and to a lesser extent elsewhere in Europe and Great Britain's White Dominions. And if one adds to this list Russia, then all the debates that subsequently formed the central historical memory of the world's social/labor movements and became the reference of discourse almost everywhere took place in these countries. What is striking, when one reviews the debates in these countries, is how amazingly similar they were, despite all the important and oft-noted historical specificities of each national situation, and despite the differences in rhetorical labels that are usually used to describe them.

Let us first remember that the post-1870 period was one in which male suffrage had become widely extended. Most notable had been the 1867 extensions in Great Britain instituted by Disraeli and in Germany by Bismarck. They matched those that had previously been instituted in the Second Empire and the United States, and would soon be matched elsewhere in Europe. Of course they were still less than universal.[51] Bendix (1964, 63) celebrates these extensions as channeling lower-class protest to "realizing full participation in the existing political community or establishing a national political community in which such participation would be possible." He is probably right.[52] The question is how much we should celebrate this.

In Great Britain, which served as one of the two principal loci of the pre-1870 movements, in the view of most observers, the so-called New Unionism of the late 1880s represented a new (or renewed) militancy. Of course, as Hobsbawm (1984c, 152–153) points out, we can have a "new" unionism in Great Britain because, unlike continental Europe, "we find an already established 'old unionism' . . . to combat, transform, and expand," a new unionism that would become the founding base of the Labour Party.[53] The new unions were intended to include more than the arti-

51. Hinton (1983, 77) estimates that, even after the further extensions in Great Britain in 1884, only two-thirds of adult males were qualified (because of registration residence requirements and the exclusion of paupers). Moorhouse (1973, 346) asserts that only half the male working class had the suffrage before 1918. Still, Hinton notes that, despite these figures, after 1884 "the extension of the franchise never became a central issue in working-class politics." Roth (1973, 35) insists that Bismarck saw the extension of the suffrage as providing "a conservative mass vote against the liberals, especially in the countryside." This was probably a consideration of Disraeli as well. Curiously, Groh (1973, 27) sees the 1867 extension in Germany as something to be explained by the exceptional "German constitutional system."

52. But see the arguments of Bridges (1986, 192) about the United States: "In emphasizing the importance of the suffrage some disclaimers should be made. I am not saying here, as Reinhard Bendix did, that workers in the United States were less angry about industrialization than voters elsewhere because they had the vote as 'compensation.' . . . I am arguing that when workers had political goals . . . , were entitled to vote, and were an urban minority, they were inevitably drawn into electoral politics and party politics—and these practices just as inevitably shaped their consciousness and their culture."

Shaping culture is also the concern of Langewiesche (1987, 517): "If one defines the society and culture of Imperial Germany as 'bourgeois,' then the socialist cultural labor movement was an instrument of *embourgeoisement*. The socialist workers who built up these cultural organizations and the socialist experts who contributed the lofty programs did not, however, view their efforts at cultural improvement in this way. On the contrary, they believed they were struggling not for a bourgeois culture but for a national culture—an inheritance which the class system of Imperial Germany *conspired to withhold from them*."

53. "[C]ontinental 'new unionism' of the late nineteenth century was new chiefly inasmuch as it established trade unions as a serious force, which they had not hitherto been outside some localities

sans or those with steady, continuous wage work. They were to be "general" unions for the highly mobile, unskilled workers who lacked scarce human resources and who had been unorganized because they couldn't use the tactics of craft unions. General unions were their hope as a weapon (Hobsbawm, 1949, 123–125).

The new unionism emphasized strategies and organizational forms, close links with the emerging socialist movements, and organizing the unorganized in order thereby to create a far stronger trade-union *movement*. Although the new unionism is often seen as a peculiarly British phenomenon. there were in fact analogous developments in various European countries (Hobsbawm, 1984d, 19; Pollard, 1984, 58). The new unionism led to a spectacular growth of trade unions at its outset in 1889–1891, but this sudden upsurge turned out to be quite short-lived. From 1891 to 1914, the numbers did continue to creep upward, but only at a very slow pace (Hinton, 1983, 45–53, 64).[54] Why was there such a "short heyday"? For Hyman (1984, 331), "various institutional correctives [checked and] considerably reduced the potential for disorder." For Hobsbawm (1964, 189), it was the fact that the ability of class-militant general unions to ride out slumps depended on their being "tolerated and accepted" by employers, and this in turn depended on "a more cautious and conciliatory policy." For Howell (1983, 111), similarly, given that the new unionism succeeded best when organizing workers (gas workers, metal trades) whose work had scarcity value, they found that they needed to abandon the "ecumenical hope of large-scale general unions," and it then followed that "prudence [was] a condition of survival." Burgess (1975, 309) lays emphasis on the development of a trade-union bureaucracy with a different "life style" from the average worker, which made the trade unions "reluctant" to be too militant insofar as disputes with employers might "endanger" union funds, the positions of the trade-union officials, and the friendly society benefits of the members.

---

and the occasional craft trade." On the other hand, G. D. H. Cole (1937, 21–22) is a voice to defend the "very considerable Trade Union militancy" of the older British trade unions. "That the Trade Union leaders of the 1860s and early 1870s were in no sense Socialists, I fully agree; but the same may be said of the leaders of Chartism. They were in no sense revolutionaries, I also agree; but it is one thing to abandon revolutionary attitudes and quite another to accept the philosophy of capitalism."

In any case, we should not forget that one of the things that facilitated the emergence of the new unionism were the two acts passed by Disraeli in 1875, which in effect legalized trade unions by excluding them from the law of conspiracy, allowing peaceful picketing, and abolishing imprisonment for breach of contract. These acts were notably more enabling than the previous 1871 legislation of a Liberal government (Hinton, 1983, 22; Pelling, 1976, 66, 69). Once again, it was conservative concessions that enacted liberal theories.

54. Hinton's explanation (1983, 50) for the briefness of the upsurge is that "the successes of New Unionism during 1889–90 rested on full employment, on the readiness of the police to tolerate vigorous picketing, and on the absence of concerted opposition from employers. None of these conditions lasted long."

The upshot was that British new unionism did accomplish a few things: It helped to wean the trade unions away from the Liberal Party to the Labour Party.[55] It organized new sectors of the labor force—those in which the organizers did not have to compete with already existing trade-union structures (Hobsbawm, 1984b, 166–167). And it contributed to the "narrowing of differentials" among the working classes (Hobsbawm, 1984b, 156). But in the long run, there would turn out to be "no essential difference in outlook" between the old unionism and the new (Duffy, 1961, 319).[56]

One of the central issues for the workers' movement in this period was the relationship of trade unions and socialist parties—a matter of much debate and some tension. In Great Britain, the trade unions were a major organizational base of the new Labour Party and received a greater institutionalized role within the party than would be the case in most other national situations. The new unionism in Great Britain was, however, perhaps the last instance in which the central locus of militancy of the workers' movement was to be found in trade-union action per se. As of the 1890s, the parties sought in general to control the trade unions rather than the other way around.

The Second International vigorously sought to make this relationship clear. Already in 1881, the Swiss trade unions "willingly" used the metaphor of man and woman to denote the relationship of party and trade union as one of subordination (Haupt, 1981, 31). Whereas the First International had often debated the relative merits of political and economic action, the Second International now went on to make an *organizational* distinction between them.[57] In 1891, its Congress passed a resolution calling on all socialist parties to establish a trade-union secretariat *within* the party structure (Hansen, 1977, 202). As the parties sought to control the unions more closely, the latter resisted, and the "idea of trade-union autonomy gained ground" (Haupt, 1981, 43). What had always been a "problematic" relationship of trade unions engaged in "the day-to-day processes with the existing social order" and the parties with a "project of social transformation" (Hinton, 1983, viii) led increasingly to "divergence" and "friction" (Hobsbawm, 1984b, 171) between them.

55. But, says Hinton (1983, 60), "[t]he growth of socialist politics in the 1890s represented not a political generalisation of industrial militancy, but a reaction to defeat in the industrial struggle, a search for political solutions where industrial ones had failed. Behind this lay the incompleteness and weakness of trade union organisation."

56. Or, as Hobsbawm (1949, 133) put it: "The 'new unionism' of 1889 thus became uncomfortably like the 'old unionism' it had once fought; and the politics of its leaders changed accordingly. The revolutionary marxists . . . were increasingly replaced by much milder socialists."

57. See Gaston Manacorda (1981, 185): "The moment of the separation was that of the birth of social-democracy in Germany." Marxist theorizing was ambiguous on this question. See Moses (1990) for the conflicting interpretations that were drawn from Marx's writings on the role of trade unions and their relationship to socialist parties.

Politically, the trade unions were pushed to the sidelines, and the strategic debates about degrees and forms of militancy would center henceforth within the parties. The "model party" in the world social/labor movement would be, up to the First World War, the German SPD.[58] It was the most powerful party in the Second International. It was the only party with a true mass base. It was the party of the most intense theoretical debates. When, in 1877, the SPD was able to get sixteen deputies elected to the German Reichstag, this resulted in increased repression (the antisocialist laws of 1878). It also resulted in the deflation of the anarchist case (Ragionieri, 1961, 57–62)[59] and the acceptance, at the Erfurt Congress in 1891, of Marxism as the official doctrine of the SPD.[60]

From this point forward, the SPD became the locus of the grand debate between Bernstein and Kautsky. Bernstein preached a "reformism" of a party that was no longer a "sect" and argued that, with universal suffrage, the party could achieve its objectives through the ballot. Kautsky represented "orthodox" Marxism, which was presumably the "revolutionary" option.

---

58. The phrase *model party* is the title of chap. 3 of Haupt (1986), in which he discusses the influence of the SPD on the various parties of southeastern Europe. Fay (1981, 187) says that "the dream" of all the Russian socialists, including even the Bolsheviks, was "to transpose onto Russia soil the German model, both in terms of organization and in terms of the relations of trade unions to the party."

59. Carlson (1972, 3) argues that there had been important anarchist groups in Germany, contrary to "misleading" assertions of other scholars. Unlike Ragioneri, he explains the decline of any serious anarchist movement in the 1880s in a sense to their own doings, notably the assassination attempts of 1878, which backfired (chap. 8). In addition, industrialization eliminated the stratum of "discontented handicraft workers" (p. 395), who had been the mainstay of the anarchist groups. Ragioneri's arguments can be combined with these.

60. Roth (1963, 165) interprets this occurrence as primarily "a response to the rigid power and class structure of the Empire and the isolation and powerlessness of the labour movement." Schorske (1955, 3) says that the German movement turned to Marxism in reaction to the "fury" that Bismarck had unleashed against them. "Marxism" as a doctrine was a product of the 1890s, "at the very moment when its exact nature began to be debated among the various tendencies and schools of Marxism" (Hobsbawm, 1974, 242).

The final split between anarchists and Marxists in the SPD occurred at this point. In 1880, a Social-Democratic deputy, Wilhelm Hasselman, who was a Blanquist, said, in speaking of Bismarck's antisocialist laws, that "the time of parliamentary chatter is over and the time of the deed has begun" (cited in Bock, 1976, 42). The anarchist faction formally quit the SPD in 1891 after the Erfurt Congress, because, it said, the SPD had fallen into the hands of the "petty bourgeoisie" who wanted "state socialism." But their new organization, the Verein der Unabhänginger Sozialisten, did not flourish, and it soon disintegrated (pp. 68–73).

In 1893 at Zurich, the Third Congress of the Second International excluded the anarchists by adopting, sixteen-to-two, a resolution admitting only organizations that "recognized the necessity of . . . political action," as it had been defined by Bebel at the congress. At the next congress, in London, in 1896, Liebknecht successfully moved a further specification. Member organizations had to recognize "legislative and parliamentary action as a necessary means to arrive at [socialism]" (Longuet, 1913, 27, 35).

How important was this theoretical debate? Geary (1976, 306) says it concerned "only a small group of intellectuals" and that trade unionists "often voted for party orthodoxy" because it didn't affect what they were really doing and they "disliked all theoreticians, both left and right." Even Liebknecht, who would later be a supporter of the Russian Revolution, argued (against a Dutch delegate to the International who objected in 1893 to electoral participation) that "tactics are essentially a question of practical politics" and that there are neither "revolutionary" nor "reformist" tactics (cited in Longuet, 1913, 29). There was an upsurge of revolutionary spirit after the 1905 Russian Revolution (Schorske, 1955, 28; Stern and Sauerzapf, 1954, xxxiv, xliii), but, like the 1905 revolution itself, it didn't last.

One can sum up this historical trajectory as "radical theory and moderate practice" (Roth, 1963, 163). And the basis of this contribution was "deterministic Marxism" in its two variants (Bernstein and Kautsky).[61] Roth (1963, 167) asserts that it was the "fitting ideology" for a Social-Democratic subculture, given the inability of the labor movement to "break out of its isolation." Nolan (1986, 389) states the same thing in more friendly terms, emphasizing that deterministic Marxism "provided the promise of a revolution in a nonrevolutionary situation, a theory of revolution in a country without an indigenous revolutionary tradition." Mathias (1971, 1:178) argues that making Marxism the official ideology of the SPD was a "precondition for the acceptance of the fatalistic interpretation of Marxism."

The key shift was not in the terminology but in the fact that, from the 1870s on, the socialists began to demand protective legislation. After 1871, the working classes "entered into a close relationship with the nation-states" (van der Linden, 1988, 333). Nolan (1986, 386) calls this a shift from "politics to social policy." In Germany, they were responding to "an agenda that Bismarck had set." This had to lead over time to "a general integration of the working-class into the state" (Mathias, 1971, 1:181).[62]

In the German case, Roth (1963, 8, 315) calls this "negative integration," which he defines as allowing "a hostile mass movement to exist legally, but prevent[ing]

---

61. See Bebel at Erfurt: "The bourgeois society is striving vigorously toward its own destruction; we need only wait for the moment to seize power as it slips from their hands!" (cited in Mathias, 1971, 1:178). Marxism, as Hobsbawm (1987, 134) reminds us, was not necessarily equated with "revolutionary" doctrine: "Between 1905 and 1914 the typical revolutionary in the west was likely to be some kind of revolutionary syndicalist who, paradoxically, rejected marxism as the ideology of parties which used it as an excuse for not trying to make revolution. This was a little unfair to the shades of Marx, for the striking thing about the western mass proletarian parties which ran up his banner on their flagpoles was how modest the role of Marx actually was in them. The basic beliefs of their leaders and militants were often indistinguishable from those of the non-Marxist working-class radical or jacobin left."

62. Mathias goes even further. He says that they "had finally accepted the Imperial State and the social order of capitalism as an unshakable reality." I do not agree that they "accepted" this consciously, certainly not in this era. But the de facto result may not be too different.

it from gaining access to the centers of power."[63] In any case, Kaiser Wilhelm I repealed the antisocialist legislation in 1890 and called for an international conference to promote international labor legislation (Ragionieri, 1961, 159) He gained the sobriquet of *Arbeiterkaiser* by making various small "reformist concessions," although he continued to vacillate by occasional "recourse to further repressive legislation" (Hall, 1974, 365). Roth wants to see this as quite different from what happened in Great Britain and the United States. I agree that the rhetoric was more strident in Germany, but were the ultimate results so different?

If we turn from the two "model" national cases—Great Britain and Germany— to the other major loci of growth of the socialist/labor movements, we find variation without significant difference. Everywhere the pattern is one of organizing with some difficulties in the light of state repression, rhetoric that is often radical with practice that is on the whole moderate, and a sort of "negative integration" into the national communities. In France, the heavy repression after the Commune eased up after 1875, the government recognizing the wisdom of a "social policy directed at the working class" (Schöttler, 1985, 58).

The Guesdists in France founded the Parti Ouvrier Français (POF) in 1882 and called themselves Marxists, but it was a limited version of Marxism, one still influenced by anarchism (Willard, 1965, 30). What Marxism seemed to mean most of all was the rejection of "associationism" based on class harmony and "a revolutionary strategy in the pursuit of trade socialism" (Moss, 1976, 157). What the POF seemed most to like in Marxism was the Saint-Simonian tradition of industrialism combined with a "vitriolic critique" of capitalism. They were "heralds of a transcendent future" (Stuart, 1992, 126).[64] The POF was never a mass party, unlike the later Section Française de l'Internationale Socialiste (SFIO) (Cottereau, 1986, 143). Stuart's epitaph (1992, 54) on the POF is that its story was that of "a prolonged and agonizing birth, an unpromising youth, a prosperous and hopeful maturity followed by apparent terminal crisis and final transfiguration [in 1905]." Metaphorically, might this not be said of all the socialist/labor movements—at varying paces, to be sure?

---

63. Groh (1973, 36) likes the concept and says it correlates with a "behavior pattern of revolutionary waiting [*Attentismus*]." The "reformist" tonality of the SPD was already observed by Ashley in 1904 (cited by Marks, 1939, 339), who attributed it to material improvement of conditions, a view Marks believes too simple, finding its sources in "the dependence of Social Democracy on its sympathizers (*Mitlänger*) in the labor bureaucracy, and in the organizational composition of the party membership" (p. 345). Maehl (1952, 40) finds that the end of persecution led the party to concentrate on "practical tasks" and the party was thereby led "far astray from the militant class struggle."

64. But at the same time, insistent as they were on the primacy of socioeconomic transformation, "Guesdists explicitly repudiated the insurrectionary conception of revolution. . . . In the Parti Ouvrier's political paradigm [the development and maturing of the new society within the very breast of the old], in themselves, constitute revolutionary social transformation" (p. 260).

French socialists were to take another path. It was Alexandre Millerand in 1896 who first coined the term *reformism* (Procacci, 1972, 164), and he would be the first socialist to enter a coalition government, one headed by Pierre Waldeck-Rousseau under the aegis of "republican concentration" (Willard, 1965, 422).[65] The subsequent failure of the general strike in 1906–1908 (as well as the second one in 1919–1920) "marked the death of a [last] dream: revolution via the strike of workers" (Perrot, 1974, 1:71).

In any case, all the parties seemed to follow the path of de facto reformism—that is, integration (even if negative) into the political structures of their respective countries. Heywood (1990, chap. 1) calls the Spanish socialists "decaffeinated Marxists." The Dutch party and trade unions "were clearly moving in a reformist direction" (Hansen, 1977, 199). The Italian party pursued an "edulcorated version" of the program of the German SPD (Andreucci, 1982, 221), and its great expansion in 1901–1902 occurred "under the aegis of reformism" (Procacci, 1972, 163).[66]

As for the United States (and Canada), which Lipset (1983, 14) insists are different because the absence of a feudal past "served to reduce the salience of class-conscious politics and proposals," one merely needs to change a bit of the rhetoric to see the similarities. Herberg (cited in Dubofsky, 1974, 275) showed the degree to which the relationship of the IWW ("with its stress on proletarian direct action") to the craft unionism of the AFL was parallel to the relationship of Kautsky's "orthodox Marxism" to Bernstein's "reformism." Laslett (1974, 115–116) makes the same point essentially about the American Socialist Party. Foner (1984, 74), responding to the literature on why there was "no socialism in the U.S.," says that the question should really be posed as "Why has there been no socialist transformation in any advanced capitalist society?" The most striking difference in the United States (and Canada) from the western European states was the ability of the Democratic Party in the United States (and the Liberal Party in Canada) to remain the prime

65. Guesde denounced this move but received no international support. The German SPD proclaimed its neutrality on the question. Guesde's position was quite consistent. He had always denounced the "Republican myth" and substituted for this chronicle of freedom a different "historical myth [based on] a chronicle of bourgeois repression which unrolled in bloody scroll from the Champ de Mars massacre in 1791 to the killings at Fourmies in 1891, a century-long working-class martyrdom which consecrated the socialist indictment of the Republican regime" (Stuart, 1992, 228).

66. Procacci (1972, 332–374) describes the inconclusive debate between Turati and Labriola over whether the Italian Socialist Party should participate in government and seeks to find virtue in Italian developments. "Late" in political development, he says, the "originality" of the Italian party was "its capacity to appropriate a large part of the patrimony of the democracy of the Risorgimento. . . . Its backwardness was its strength" (pp. 74–75). But Italy's "lateness" was not that striking, and the Italian movement was not the only one, as we have seen, to draw on earlier radical, nonsocialist traditions. The same was clearly true of England, which was not at all a "late" developer. I think Belloni (1979, 44) is nearer to the mark when he says that for the Partito Sozialista, "the revolution was a firm and unquestioned element in its own creed, projected into a future that was undefined but sufficiently far off not to have much effect in fact on political moves and strategy, in the short or middle term."

vehicle of working-class politics (Shefter, 1966, 270; Kealey, 1980, 273), something that might be explained more by the role of the city machines in incorporating immigrant workers than by anything else.[67]

What was crucial to all the social/labor movements in the end was their drive to participate in the nation. The unification of the Parti Ouvrier Belge occurred within the framework of the struggle for universal suffrage (Sztejnberg, 1963, 214). The demands of the socialists in France in the 1880s began to center around material needs that could be met only by "an appeal to the state, or rather, to the Republic" (Schöttler, 1985, 68). The U.S. trade-union movement became national in the 1860s to 1890s in order "to demand uniform wage scales" across the country— "that is, to impose some order on capitalism from below" (Montgomery, 1980, 90; see also Andrews, 1918, 2:43–44). And in discussing the Charte d'Amiens of the French trade-union federation, the CGT, in 1906, Bron (1970, 2:132) describes the "complementary battles" of the trade unions and the socialist party. The trade unions emphasized the productive role of the workers; the socialists, "the aspect of 'citizenship.' "

The workers regarded themselves as the working classes. The upper strata tended to think of them as the dangerous classes. A large part of the tactical struggle on the part of the workers revolved around how they could lose the label of "dangerous" and acquire that of citizens. In Germany, after 1871, the Social-Democrats had been accused on being "enemies of the nation" and "*Vaterlandlos*" (without a fatherland) (Groh, 1966, 17). They needed to overcome this label. Chevalier (1958, 461) expresses well the analytic issue, which in the end was a political issue:

> Distinguishing the working classes from the dangerous classes . . . is made all the more difficult by the fact that the borders between these categories are unclear, and that at the uncertain frontier between them there are found many intermediate groups, of whom it is difficult to say whether they belong more to the one or the other category. How can one finally distinguish them when they depend so greatly on economic, political, or biological circumstances that intermingle them, and make

---

67. See Commons (1918, 1:13), who describes the role of the Knights of Labor in the upheaval of the 1880s in the United States thus: "[N]ever before had organization reached out so widely or deeply. New areas of competition, new races and nationalities, new masses of the unskilled, new recruits from the skilled and semi-skilled, were lifted up temporarily into what appeared to be an organization, *but was more nearly a procession,* so rapidly did the membership change. With three-quarters of the million members on the books of the Knights of Labor at the height of its power, a million or more passed onto and soon out from its assemblies." Shefter (1986, 272) says of the city political machines that "they organized cleavages of ethnicity and community into politics, uniting under a common banner skilled workers who belonged to trade unions, unskilled workers for whom unions refused to accept responsibility, and members of the middle and upper classes. And these machines displayed a militancy in their campaigns . . . that was akin to that of contemporary trade unions, though the groups and issues on behalf of which they fought were rather different."

persons shift, according to the years or the season or the revolutions, crises, and epidemics, from one category to the other?

One key mechanism that was widely used was to distinguish workers by the category of ethnicity or of nationality. Racism internally and imperialism/colonialism externally served the function of displacing the label of dangerous to a subcategory of workers. To the extent that this was persuasive, some workers could become active citizens while others remained passive citizens or even noncitizens. Once again, inclusion was being achieved by exclusion.

The internal exclusions are most salient in the story of the United States—a zone of constant immigration during the nineteenth century—in which immigrants tended to settle in urban areas and start as relatively unskilled laborers, while native-born Americans formed a very large part of the artisanal strata and were more likely to be upwardly mobile, with their positions being filled in behind them by immigrant (and second-generation) workers. Already in the 1850s, the social distance between the native-born artisans and the predominantly immigrant wage workers took the political form of nativist parties (anti-immigrant, anti-Catholic) that "emphasized their artisan membership as well as their Protestantism" (Bridges, 1986, 176). In the Civil War, conscripted native labor was often replaced by foreign labor, and "race antagonism added intensity to the natural struggle between employer and employed" (Ely, 1890, 62). Immediately after the war, U.S. interest in and participation in the First International was spurred by the attempt of the newly formed National Trades' Union to regulate immigration by an arrangement with the IWMA (Andrews, 1918, 2:86)—an interest, as we have already noted, that was shared by British trade unions. The workers' organizations led the agitation for the Chinese Exclusion Act of 1882. Selig Perlman (1922, 62), in his famous history of the U.S. trade-union movement, goes so far as to say that this agitation "was doubtless the most important single factor in the history of American labor, for without it the entire country might have been overrun by Mongolian labor and the labor movement might have been a conflict of races instead of one of classes."

The Socialist Party disproportionately recruited immigrant workers. On the one hand, this was doubtless because the U.S. working class of the late nineteenth century, as was noted at the time, consisted "chiefly of men and women of foreign birth or foreign parentage" (Ely, 1890, 286). But this can also account for the decline of this party when immigration was cut off and the third generation shunned linkage with their immigrant past.

The employers took advantage of this ethnic split, of course, and often used "blacks, Orientals, and women" as strikebreakers (Shefter, 1986, 228). And it is certainly true that the top place of English-speaking White workers in the ethnic hierarchy was "implicitly accepted throughout [U.S.] history" (Soffer, 1960, 151) and that disorder was regularly blamed on the immigrants. But this is not enough to account for the continued centrality of ethnic/racial distinctions among American workers. Commons (1935, 2:xvii), it seems to me, captures well the essence of the issue—the relation of U.S. unions to "Americanism":

> [Anthracite mines had "open shop" agreements with the miners.] Consequently, with the weakness of the unions the companies in 1912 discovered that their mines were being invaded by syndicalists, the I.W.W. They reversed their attitude toward the union. It was discovered that the American labor movement, however aggressive it might be, was the first bulwark against revolution and the strongest defender of constitutional government. Upon the unions, indeed, falls the first burden of "Americanizing" the immigrants, and it has done so for more than fifty years. When President Wilson saw the need for unifying a heterogeneous nation for the World War he was the first president to attend and address the convention of the American Federation of Labor. When Samuel Gompers, at 74 years of age, and fifty years of leadership, returned from his alliance with the labor movement of Mexico, to which he had gone to prevent its capture by the communists, his last words on his dying bed at the Mexican border in 1924 were "God bless our American institutions."

The other arena in which inclusion/exclusion played a major role was outside the country—in other countries or in colonial possessions of a metropole. On the one hand, it was easy for workers in western Europe to keep within a certain radical/liberal tradition of favoring the struggles of far-off persons for their liberation. In 1844, 1,505 Parisian workers petitioned the deputies to abolish slavery in the colonies, noting that "the worker belongs to himself," that "whatever the vices of present-day organization of work in France, the worker is free, in a certain sense" (cited in Césaire, 1948, 11). British workers saw the Crimean War as pitting "free Englishmen against the Russian serf" (Foster, 1974, 242). And in the 1860s, the British working class supported Garibaldi, the North during the U.S. Civil War, and Polish insurrection (Collins, 1964, 29–30).[68]

But it is also true that the antislavery movement in early nineteenth-century England met with working-class hostility, because "black slaves were already better off than white slaves; freedom for the blacks would be bought by further oppressing the white slaves; and once freed, black slaves would become as badly off as white slaves" (Hollis, 1980, 309). And at the beginning of the twentieth century, British labor centered its critique of imperial policy in South Africa around the importation of Chinese labor to work in the Rand mines, which they saw as "further evidence of Government-sponsored blacklegging" (Hinton, 1983, 73).

---

68. Indeed, when Gladstone forced Garibaldi in April 1864 to cut short a visit to England, there was such an uproar that Gladstone "sought to redress the balance by calling publicly for an expansion of the working class franchise" (Collins, 1964, 24).

The Second International was deeply split on colonial questions (Haupt and Rebérioux, 1967a, 77–283). Those like Hyndman of the United Kingdom and Lenin, who denounced imperialism at every turn, were more than balanced by such as Henri van Kol of the Netherlands, who spoke of the "necessity of the colonial reality" and merely wished to limit its "crimes," and those like Bernstein, for whom "the colonial question [was] the question of the extension of civilization" (Rebérioux and Haupt, 1963, 13, 18). Even the Austrian socialists, so noted for their more nuanced understanding of the demands of the multiple nationalities in the Austro-Hungarian Empire, were vehement in their opposition to Hungarian "separatism."[69]

In the end, even for those who took an anticolonial position like the Guesdists, it was always a "minor combat" at best (Willard, 1965, 63). What dominated sentiments was the certainty expressed by the German SPD that, when the SPD prevailed, its "victory would sweep the peasantry along behind it and thus make the advent of socialism possible in economically backward countries" (Haupt, 1986, 57). This was argued as a question of priorities. But it rang a bell among the working class as a question of inclusion among the "civilized."[70] Socialists in colonial countries had to draw their own conclusions about priorities. When Connolly, who considered himself both a Marxist and an Irish nationalist, observed what he considered the betrayal by the European working class of proletarian internationalism in 1914, he hung a sign outside the Dublin headquarters of his party—"We serve neither King nor Kaiser, but Ireland" (Bédarida, 1965, 20)—and proceeded in 1916 to lead the Easter Rebellion.

WOMEN'S AND FEMINIST MOVEMENTS

The story of the feminist/women's movement in the nineteenth century is similar in very many ways to the story of the social/labor movement. But for the most

69. In 1905, "Karl Renner, for example, 'chastised the cowardice of the Austrian bourgeoisie who began to acquiesce in the separatistic plans of the Magyars [though] the Hungarian market is incomparably more significant for Austrian capital than [the] Moroccan is for the German.'" He opposed "the clamouring of [Hungarian] city sharks, swindlers, and political demagogues, against the very interests of Austrian industry, of the Austrian working-classes, and of the Hungarian agricultural population" (cited in Anderson, 1991, 107).

70. Jones (1983, 181–182) stresses the element of political apathy. In discussing the attitudes of the English working class in the last third of the nineteenth century, he says: "[I]f the working class did not actively promote jingoism, there can be no doubt it passively acquiesced to it. . . . The failure of radicals and socialists to make any deep impression on the London working class in the last Victorian and Edwardian period had deeper roots than subjective deficiency. . . . What Mafeking and other imperialist celebrations portended was not so much the predominance of the wrong politics among the mass of London workers, but rather their estrangement from political activity as such. There was general agreement that the politically active working man of the times was a radical or a socialist. Loyalism was a product of apathy." But apathy, of course, was a product of inclusion within the nation, and therefore at the very least a passive acceptance of the exclusion of others.

part, it is as though these two movement families were on widely separated and largely parallel tracks, almost never crossing each other and seldom collaborating. Indeed, in many ways the social/labor movement regarded the feminist/women's movement as a rival, a nuisance, a diversion, and even quite often as an enemy. This had everything to do with inclusion/exclusion.

There were of course a few voices who saw the two struggles as not merely compatible but intertwined. Flora Tristan in the pre-1848 period spent her life preaching this. Indeed, devoted as she was to the cause of the workers, she put into her book *The Workers' Union* (1983, 83), written in 1843, the message that "all working-class ills can be summed up in two words: poverty and ignorance. Now in order to get out of this maze, I see only one way: begin by educating women, because women are in charge of instructing boys and girls." She was, it must be said, a voice in the wilderness, as was Aline Vallette, disciple of Guesde, who wrote in *L'Harmonie sociale* on March 15, 1892, that "to renovate society, it is necessary that the two oppressed groups of society, women and proletarians, unite" (cited in Zylberberg-Hocquard, 1978, 89).

The issue seemed to the male worker in urban wage work quite straightforward. Women were paid less—indeed, before 1914, "considerably" less (Guilbert, 1966, 21)—and this posed a threat to the level of wages in general.[71] The asserted threat was raised in meeting after meeting (Guilbert, 1966, 188). Despite some mythology, the feminine component of the manufacturing work force was rather large. It is estimated at 40 percent for Paris in midcentury (DeGroat, 1997, 33). Women were relegated to the more "proletarian" positions (Judt, 1986, 44–46, 50–51), partly no doubt because they were barred by the skilled artisans from entering their trades (Hinton, 1983, 31), but partly because employers thought them more productive workers with more labor discipline (or docility) and more technical dexterity than men (Berg, 1993, 41).

Male workers reacted both at a personal level and at an organizational level. Alexander (1984, 144) sees their reaction primarily "as a desire to (legally) control and (morally) order sexuality." One should never underestimate sexual motivations, and no doubt this drive fitted in very well with the cultural mores of the time, particularly among middle-class women who favored "reducing women to unpaid work in marriage and family along with their total exclusion . . . from remunerated occupations" (Kleinau, 1987, 199). It is undoubtedly also the case that, among male urban wage-workers, "proletarian anti-feminism predominated" (Thönnessen, 1973, 19). The German male workers referred to women workers as *Fabrikmenschen* (a curious phrase, since it literally means "factory men" but had

71. But see Hartmann's comment (1976, 155): "That male workers viewed the employment of women as a threat to their jobs is not surprising, given an economic system where competition among workers was characteristic. That women were paid lower wages exacerbated the threat. But why their response was to attempt to exclude women rather than to organize them is explained, not by capitalism, but by patriarchal relations between men and women."

186   THE CITIZEN IN A LIBERAL STATE

the tonality of "factory girls") and tended to regard them as "morally depraved" (Quataert, 1979, 153). Hobsbawm (1978, 8) notes that workers' imagery evolved in the course of the century, so that by the last third of the nineteenth century the image of "inspiring women" (see Delacroix's painting *Les Trois Glorieuses*) with which the century had begun had been transformed into that of women who merely "suffer and endure," while the nude male torso now became the pictorial symbol of workers' energy and power.

The First International was divided on the question. At the first congress in Geneva in 1866, the representative of Lassalle's Allgemeine Deutsche Arbeitsverein proposed forbidding female employment on the grounds of "protection" of women (Hervé, 1983, 23). The final resolution compromised by saying that women's work was to be regarded positively, but criticizing its conditions under capitalist production (Frei, 1987, 39). The workers' organizations would now place their demands on three fronts: equality of wages, the family wage, and ending dangerous workplace conditions.

Equality of wages (for equal work) is a standard and obvious demand of trade unions. But it was frequently the secret hope that, if wages were made equal (for women, for minorities and immigrants, for workers in other countries), the hierarchically dominant worker (the male citizen worker of the ranking ethnic group) would then be employed in preference, if only for cultural-historical reasons. Notice, for example, the language of the resolution in the Ninth Congress of the French CGT in Rennes in 1898:

> That in all areas of life we seek to propagate the idea *that the man must nourish the woman;* that for the woman, widow or young girl, necessarily obliged to provide for herself, it shall be understood that the formula, for equal work equal pay, shall be applied to her; ...
>
> Keep men from taking jobs and work that belong to women, and reciprocally, keep women from taking work away from men that is their natural province. (Cited in Guilbert, 1966, 173)[72]

By and large, women did not join or were kept out of the trade unions. In the period 1900–1914, when trade unions had grown relatively strong, it is estimated that only 5 to 10 percent of women workers in France were members (Guilbert, 1966, 29, 34). There were some efforts to create special women's trade unions, and in England these grew relatively numerous in the same period, but they were less

---

72. The formula "the man must nourish the woman" in fact hides another. Yes, it was thought that the man must earn the money with which the woman would be physically nourished. But Hinton (1983, 32) reminds us that, for the male worker of the nineteenth century, the woman ought not to go out to work in order that she make possible "the construction of the home as an arena of physical comfort and emotional support"—for the man, of course, but also for the children.

bargaining structures than "benefit societies," from which they were "indistinguishable" (Olcott, 1976, 34, 39).

Of course, trade unions had a difficult time justifying the exclusion of women, as can be seen in the reluctant resolution of the Fédération Française des Travailleurs du Livre, notorious for having conducted the largest number of strikes aimed at excluding women from employment. Finally, the FFTL, admitting that for economic reasons even those workers opposed to the employment of women in their own trades regularly pushed their wives to work in other trades, offered the following compromise:

1. We shall support, morally and materially, those locals that . . . wish to react against the exploitation of women by obtaining for them the minimum trade-union rate of pay.
2. During a transitional period . . . women presently employed shall be admitted to the Federation on the same conditions as men. At the end of the transitional period only women employed at the trade-union rate will be admitted. (Cited in Guilbert, 1966, 62)

A second resolution simultaneously urged "workers who were heads of families to apply the principle of the woman at home and require their companions to refuse all work outside the home." If this seems somewhat inconsistent with the other resolution, it is because it is.

Social scientists lent their expertise to validate these positions. Dr. William Ogle explained to the Royal Statistical Society in 1890:

> There are men who work because work is a pleasure to them and there are others who toil because work is a duty; but the great majority of men are only stimulated to labour that in amount or character is distasteful to them, by the hope that they may be able, in the first place, to maintain themselves, and secondly to marry and maintain a family. . . . If therefore, the well-being of a state consists in the mature well-being of the people, a country is then most flourishing when the largest proportion of its population is able to satisfy these two natural desires. (*Journal of the Royal Statistical Society*, cited in Lewis, 1984, 45)

The "family wage" became a central demand of the trade-union structures. In part, this demand originated in a real problem. Whereas in the eighteenth century

---

Formulas are important. The idea that *young, unmarried* women might legitimately work was accepted everywhere. See, however, how it was justified in late nineteenth-century Japan: "More than any other group, young women in the textile mills were models of government and management attitudes toward women workers. They were not workers, but "daughters" or "students" spending a few years before marriage working for their families, the nation, and the mills. Lack of commitment and lack of skill justified both the low wages paid to this work force and its characterization as part-time or temporary" (Sievers, 1983, 58).

it had been considered normal that women and children work for remuneration as well as men, the shift of many productive activities outside the home meant the loss of income from the home work of women and children. This is probably a key element in the observed dip in real household income in the late eighteenth and early nineteenth centuries (Pinchbeck, 1930, 4; Wallerstein, 1989, 124).

The family wage was a simple idea. The minimum wage an adult male should receive for his waged work should be a sum sufficient to sustain him, his wife, and his nonadult children. This concept had wide appeal. It was strongly endorsed by the labor movement (Lewis, 1984, 49). It appealed to many employers, since it seemed to promise stability of the work force (May, 1982, 418). It fit in with the nineteenth-century value of the "responsibility" of men to care for their family (Evans, 1983, 281). It appealed therefore not only to the IWMA and other labor movements but to centrist politicians of all stripes. Only feminists objected to the concept (Offen, 1987a, 183).

The concept of special "protective" legislation for women workers was always a "thorny issue" (Rowbotham, 1974, 114). It seemed a virtuous idea, and it was long a preoccupation of the socialist movement (Guilbert, 1966, 413). Anarchists didn't like it, but only because it involved government intervention. Middle-class feminists opposed it in the name of equality. The women workers themselves often feared that it would result in reduced wages. The socialist movement was somewhat divided. Clara Zetkin, for example, argued that it was irrelevant since, following Marx and Engels, industrialization had destroyed age and sex as "distinctive" variables, but hers was a minority view in the German SPD (Quataert, 1979, 39). The Catholic Zentrum in Germany endorsed the family wage as part of its search for a more social capitalism. For most male workers, it served as an alibi for their unwillingness to see an equal role for women in the workplace, and hence in political society. The inclusion of male workers, they seemed to think, required that women be treated as a weaker, more vulnerable, and hence more passive part of the population.

The issue of women's rights got a somewhat more sympathetic audience in socialist parties than it received within the trade unions. The most famous and important locus of socialist debate about the relation of women and the party was in the German SPD, which Quataert described (1979) as "reluctant feminists." The important role of the Women's Conference and the Women's Bureau within the SPD was exceptional in socialist parties. It originated as the result of the restrictive laws of the German state. The Prussian *Vereingesetz* of 1851 forbade women not only to join political organizations, but even to attend meetings. There were similar laws in Bavaria and Saxony (Evans, 1976, 10–11). The SPD, in order to mobilize women, was obliged to set up separate structures that could claim legally to be apolitical. This turned out to be a double-edged sword. It enabled the SPD to organize women despite the government's laws. But it also enabled the women socialists to act as an organized faction within the party, "securing representation for women's special interests." In addition, it meant that the socialist women, precisely because they had their own organization, were extremely hostile to the middle-class feminist movements, with whom their split was "pronounced" (Honeycutt, 1979, 32–33).

The result was a curious in-between position on feminist issues. On the one hand, August Bebel wrote the most important and most cited book on women by any socialist leader, *Frau und Sozialismus,* one that was considered relatively "feminist."[73] And although the socialist women insisted there did not exist such a thing as a "women's question"—as did the Italian, French (Guesdist), and Russian movements—unlike the other movements, the German SPD did place emphasis on the political emancipation of women (Honeycutt, 1979, 37). Also, despite Rosa Luxemburg's views (she was never involved in the SPD women's movement), they did seek various reforms designed to "alleviate sex oppression under capitalism" (Quataert, 1979, 12). On the other hand, the SPD women's movement was in fact "largely a movement of married women"—housewives and not women workers (Evans, 1977, 165). And as soon as the German government passed a new *Vereingesetz* and ended its restrictions on women's political activities (1908), the SPD abolished the Women's Conference (1910) and then the Women's Bureau (1912). Honeycutt's assessment (1981, 43) is that the goal that Clara Zetkin, the leader of the socialist women, had set herself "of realizing feminist ideals through the socialist movement was utopian for the period in which she lived."

The French socialist women shared the hostility to bourgeois feminism of the German women. Louise Saumoneau, the organizer of the first Groupe des Femmes Socialistes in 1899, rejected completely any collaboration with bourgeois feminists (Hause and Kenney, 1981, 793). But, unlike the socialist women in Germany, who were nearly 20 percent of the SPD in 1900–1913, women made up only 2 to 3 percent of the party in France (Sowerwine, 1976, 4–5). On the other hand, socialism and feminism seemed less incompatible in France. First of all, there was the very strong image of women as leaders of the Commune (Rabaut, 1983, 6). Indeed, the popular image was so strong that even the bourgeois women's movements seemed tarnished by its subversive flavor.[74]

---

73. But see the caustic analysis of a Swiss socialist and radical feminist, Fritz Brupbacker, in 1935: "Bebel wrote a nice book. . . . But this kind of socialism was just a convenient decoration for Sundays, or if one had to give a speech on the great festival days of the party (*Märzfeier* [March 18, in celebration of the convocation of the Frankfurt Assembly in 1848] and May Day). On workdays one was very, very far from this kind of socialism. The workday paid no attention to Sunday socialism. There, one was for the bourgeois family" (cited in Frei, 1987, 56).

74. "Now just as the Third Republic's new breed of moderate politicians wished to obliterate the connotations of republicanism with the violence and disorder of the Commune, the June Days of Terror, so too the feminists were equally anxious to dispel the memories of previous links between

Second, there was the figure of Hubertine Auclert, to whom there was no equivalent in Germany. Auclert gave a famous speech to the Third French Workers' Socialist Congress of 1879, saying that she had come "not because I am a worker, but because I am a woman—that is, one who is exploited—a slave delegated by nine millions slaves." She appealed for an alliance between the workers and the women, ending with a peroration: "Oh, proletarians, if you wish to be free, cease being unjust. With modern science, with the awareness that science knows no prejudices, say: equality for all men, equality between men and women" (Auclert, 1879, 1–2, 16). And she did get from the congress a strong resolution in favor of "the absolute equality of the two sexes" and the right of women to work (emphasizing, to be sure, "equal work, equal pay"), albeit insisting at the same time that women had the obligation to nurse their children (Guilbert, 1966, 156–157).

But in France, too, the alliance, momentarily achieved, would ultimately fail (Rebérioux, 1978a, xvi; Sowerwine, 1978, 233–234). The split among the French socialists in 1882, generally considered to be that between a more reformist faction (the Brassists) and a more revolutionary one (the Guesdists), took as its immediate excuse a women's issue. Léonie Rouzade, a Brassist, had stood for election to the Paris Municipal Council in 1881, and the Guesdists were decidedly cool to her candidacy. This led to their expulsion from the party. The Guesdists then formed the Parti Ouvrier Français, alleging that Brousse advocated a "sex struggle" rather than a "class struggle." The Guesdists said that to advocate women's political rights was "reformist" since they could be achieved "legally" rather than by revolution, to which the Brassists replied that men had also achieved their "rights" legally. But then, nonetheless, the Guesdists incorporated women's rights into their own project (Sowerwine, 1982, 28–45).

In the end, both the feminists and the socialists in France gave up the idea of a coalition. What weighed on the socialists was the great fear that most women were too influenced by the Church and would use their suffrage against their party (Perrot, 1976, 113). When the SFIO created a feminine auxiliary, it was primarily to prevent the spread of feminism rather than to obtain full rights for women (Sowerwine, 1978, 1).

The unhappy relationship seemed at its fiercest in 1913 with the "Couriau affair." Emma Couriau, with the support of her husband, who had long been a militant trade unionist, sought admission to the typographers' union. She was refused, and her husband was expelled from the union for permitting her to work. A great fuss was created, and Couriau received support not only in feminist but also in some trade-union circles. The issue was then referred to the next national congress of

---

feminism and political radicalism. . . . Given the links between the two movements in the early days, it is hardly surprising that from the outset mainstream feminism in France opted for a course of prudence and moderation which might better be described as timidity" (McMillan, 1981b, 84).

the FFTL in 1915, which, however, never took place because of the war (Albis-tur and Armogathe, 1977, 361). Whereas many authors have emphasized that this incident demonstrates the depth of labor hostility to the right of women to work, Sowerwine (1983, 441) views it more positively: "If the Couriau affair is 'an indica-tion of attitudes toward women,' it indicates not the persistence of misogyny but a step in an evolution toward egalitarianism."

The Italian socialist movement also had a famous debate on women's suffrage, one between Filippo Turati, the party leader, and his life companion, Anna Kuli-scioff, in *Critica sociale*. In Italy, too, the male socialists wished to delay the strug-gle for women's suffrage in order to achieve more rapidly universal male suffrage. And in Italy, too, they used justifications of capacity—such as, for example, that women "were absent from politics." As Kuliscioff replied, if this is the argument, one has to ask "how many men participate effectively in politics?" And when the vote is offered to illiterate men, she said, how can one argue that the vote should not be given to women because they are illiterate? (Ravera, 1978, 77–79; see also Pieroni, 1963, 122–123; Pieroni, 1974, 9; Puccini, 1976, 30–31).

The ambivalence could be found everywhere. In England, the Labour Party was reluctant to put its support behind the move for women's suffrage, many of its supporters believing that "feminism was simply another name for increasing the privilege of propertied women" (Liddington and Norris, 1985, 28). The fear of a conservative women's vote made most Labour men "not enthusiastic" for women's suffrage (Fulford, 1957, 113). It was only in 1912 that Labour resolved not to support any further extension of the franchise that did not include women (Hinton, 1983, 79).

In the United States, there was a famous incident at the National Labor Con-gress in 1868, when the credentials of Elizabeth Cady Stanton were challenged on the grounds that she did not represent a labor organization. In finally accepting her credentials, the congress felt it necessary to assert that they did not agree with her "peculiar views" but that they accepted her simply because her organization was seeking the amelioration of the conditions of labor (Andrews, 1918, 2:128).

In Belgium and Austria (as well as Germany), socialist parties refused to sup-port women's suffrage in order not to jeopardize universal male suffrage (Evans, 1987, 86–88). On the other hand, in country after country, eventually (and to some extent painfully) the socialists came down on the side of women's suffrage (Evans, 1987, 76). And in postrevolutionary Russia, the Clara Zetkin brand of "proletarian women's movement" did get the endorsement of both Alexandra Kollontai and Nadezhda Krupskaya, Lenin's wife (Stites, 1957, 251).[75]

75. But *not more than* the Clara Zetkin version. Kollontai (1971, 59–60) is quite clear: "However apparently radical the demands of the feminists, one must not lose sight of the fact that the feminists cannot, on account of their class position, fight for the fundamental transformation of contemporary economic and social structure of society without which the liberation of women cannot be complete."

Still, Kennedy and Tilly (1985, 36) insist that feminists and socialists remained "at arm's length," at least from 1890 to 1920, and indeed "became bitter enemies." Klejman and Rochefort (1989, 231) say that "[f]rom 1889 to 1914, the relations between organized feminism and the Socialist Party never ceased being conflictual." For working-class women the basic choice seemed always to be: "Sisters or citizens?" (Sowerwine, 1982, 1). And in the end, working-class women who were politically active were not allowed to refuse the choice.

The feminist/women's movement must not, however, be seen primarily through the prism of the social/labor movement. It had its own dynamic, albeit one that was parallel in many ways. John Stuart Mill explained this dynamic well:

> The concessions of the privileged to the unprivileged are so seldom brought about by any better motive than the power of the unprivileged to extort them, that any arguments against the prerogatives of sex are likely to be little attended to by the generality, as long as they are able to say to themselves that women do not complain of it. (Cited in Rossi, 1970, 214)

Still, the story didn't really start with the women but with the men. As O'Neill (1971, 6) says of Victorian men (but was more generally true throughout the nineteenth-century European world), they "taught women to think of themselves as a special class. . . . [They] created The Woman, where before there had only been women."

In England, in the early years of the century, women organized primarily as part of the antislavery movement, and that would perhaps pay off well for feminist organizations later. As Banks (1981, 22) suggests, their active participation in this movement "gave them valuable experience in such fundamentals of routine political activities as fund-raising and collecting signatures for petitions." It was perhaps a little less than manning the barricades, but surely a little more than conversation in a parlor. Early Chartist politics was more radical in its tactics—it was a mass politics—and in those days women took their part. But the Chartists would be as ambiguous on women's rights (particularly suffrage) as the social/labor movement later on. While, at an early stage, the Charter's calls for universal suffrage "specifically included" women (Fulford, 1957, 38), in most later statements, "the matter was left vague" (Thompson, 1976. 132). The sentiment was that the main issue was "one of class."

Similarly in Italy, whereas Anna Monzoni insisted on the necessity to have alongside a socialist party an organization for woman's liberation, and if the socialists did not understand that, it was because the "working class was inheriting from the bourgeoisie a new form of antifeminism," Anna Kuliscioff (the same person who debated her companion, Filippe Turati, on the importance of woman's suffrage) argued against an "interclass" organization, which, she said, even for such a "clear objective as woman's emancipation," was unacceptable (Bortolotti, 1978, 105).

It was Owenite socialism that provided the friendliest environment for nascent feminism. Owenism had both a "theoretical and practical commitment to women's liberation" (Taylor, 1983, xiii).[76] But Owenism was to fade out with the collapse of Owenwood in 1845, just about the time Chartism was collapsing. Owen had seen women's liberation as part of the larger "social regeneration" he had been preaching. And with the disappearance of this movement "went the ideological tie between feminism and [English] working-class radicalism." After that, what had been seen as "twin struggles of a single strategy [became] separate struggles, organized from different—and sometimes opposing—perspectives" (Taylor, 1983, 264).

The last quarter of the eighteenth century and the first half of the nineteenth were marked by the contributions of a number of striking women intellectuals, from the feminist writings in England of Mary Wollstonecraft and Harriet Martineau to the cultural centrality of Mme. de Staël and Georges Sand in France to the Berlin salons of Rahel Varnhagen, Henriette Herz, and Dorothea von Courland (Hertz, 1988). But it was primarily in France that we would have the stirrings of feminist movements, albeit all inside the various, mostly small, socialist movements. Indeed, Abensour (1913, 222, 330) would explain the absence of significant success for French feminist demands between 1830 and 1848 (divorce, entry into the liberal professions, political rights) as the consequence of "their firm union with socialist doctrines."

Most notably, feminists were linked to the Saint-Simonians and to the Fourierists. The Saint-Simonians placed a great emphasis on regeneration by love, therefore by women, and at first gave women a major role in their organizational structure (Thibert, 1926, 78). They founded many women's journals: *La Femme Libre,* the work of a working-class Saint-Simonian woman, Désirée Veril[77]; the *Tribune des Femmes* in 1832, in which only articles by women were published (Moses, 1982, 251–257); *La Gazette des Femmes,* founded in 1836 by Jeanne Deroin, which sought to combine a Saint-Simonian spirit with democratic tendencies in general.[78]

---

76. "The only way to end property in women, they argued, was to end private property itself. It was certainly a more radical solution than Woolstonecraft had posed, yet there is a sense in which it was the logical outcome of the demands she and other feminists had raised."

77. Her founding editorial in issue number 1 was entitled "Apostolate of Women." It was an "appeal to women," which starts: "When all peoples have become restless for liberty and proletarians demand the vote, shall we women remain passive amidst this great movement of social emancipation that is taking place in front of our eyes? . . . Let us understand our rights; and our power. We have the power of our attractiveness, the power of our charms, an irresistible arm. Let us know how to use it" (Adler, 1979, 41). She changed her name to Jeanne-Désirée.

78. Bouglé (1918, 106) comments: "In the fire of 1848, this combination became a fusion." He also says that "in different forms this Saint-Simonian prophetic tone survives in the heart of our contemporary [1918] suffragists" (p. 110).

Thibert (1926, iii–iv) celebrates the "sentimental and idealistic" nature of Saint-Simonian feminism and speaks of "disinterested generosity." Moses (1982, 265) makes a perhaps more sober evaluation of what took place. She notes how, as the women came to assert themselves, the Saint-Simonian men moved to curtail their powers in the organization. But, says Moses, "ironically, the result was liberating," because in consequence "the Saint-Simonian women emancipated themselves from male tutelage" and created the first independent women's movement in history.

Fourier linked women's liberation to the "moral liberation" that was central to his socialism. But even more important, he argued that the moral and social freedom of women had as an "essential condition" women's economic independence, hence their "right to work" (Thibert, 1926, 99, 140). It is Fourier who is generally credited with having invented the term *feminism* (Perrot, 1988, 33),[79] but this is controversial.[80] In any case, it is better to be remembered as the inventor of the term than to be remembered, as is Proudhon (1846, 197, cited in McMillan, 1981b, 193), the leader of the other important early socialist movement (and one that would continue to be strong throughout the century), as the inventor of the formula "harlot or housewife" (*courtisane ou ménagère*), for which he was denounced immediately by Jeanne Deroin, and for which he has continued to be reproached ever since (Tixerant, 1908, 186).[81]

Flora Tristan, as we have already noted, made a valiant effort to insist that the struggle of women and that of the proletariat were a common cause, since both women and the proletariat occupied "an inferior station" in society (Puech, 1925, 337) and therefore the two struggles were "inseparable" (Albistur and Armogathe, 1977, 284). Indeed, she said, "the woman is the proletarian of the proletarian" (cited in Rebérioux, 1978a, xix; see also Dijkstra, 1992, 178; Portal, 1983, 95).

It seemed in the world-revolution of 1848 that such appeals might at last bear fruit. In 1848, feminism reasserted itself as part of the social revolution in France and elsewhere. In France, the demands were many. Pauline Roland tried to vote in the mayoralty election in Paris and was refused the right. Jeanne Deroin petitioned to stand for election to the National Assembly in 1849. The journal *Voix des Femmes* bore the subtitle *Socialist and Political Journal, Organ of the Interest of All Women*. Its editor, Eugénie Niboyet, even had the audacity to ask that the rooms of

79. Perrot notes, however, that the term was "institutionalized" only in 1892 with the creation of La Fédération Française des Sociétés Féministes.

80. Turgéon, in his book *Le féminisme français* (1907, 1:10; cited in Abray, 1975, 43), claims to have found it in Fourier's *Théorie des Quatre Vents* (1841), but Offen (1987b, 193, n. 4) says she couldn't find it there. Offen will agree only that its "obscure" origin predates 1972. Moses (1992, 80–81) could not find it anywhere in Fourier's writings and says its first important usage is in Auclert's journal, *La Citoyenne*, in 1885.

81. Proudhon said that feminism "smells of prostitution" and called feminism "pornocracy." He has in turn been called a "peasant attached to patriarchal mores" (Thibert, 1926, 171, 185, 190).

the Bibliothèque Nationale be open to women readers (Thibert, 1926, 313, 317–318, 327). But with the exception of a few tiny Communist groups, these demands were met by a "wave of puritanism" (Devance, 1976, 92). In 1850, Deroin, Roland, and others were imprisoned for having formed L'Association des Instituteurs, Institutrices et des Professeurs Socialistes, on the grounds that this was a "secret society with political goals" (Thibert, 1926, 332–334),

In the United States, the only expression of the world-revolution of 1848 was the Seneca Falls Convention, generally regarded as the founding moment of U.S. feminism. Its famous Declaration of Sentiments of July 19–20, 1848, echoing the Declaration of Independence, begins: "We hold these truths to be self-evident: that all men and women are created equal." Among the grievances listed on August 18 was the fact that women were deprived of "the first right of a citizen, elective franchise," a franchise that was given (this complaint foreshadowing future conflicts) to "ignorant and degraded men—both natives and foreigners" (Rossi, 1973, 416).

In Europe, the repression was severe. The June Days in France resulted in the "rejection of even limited acceptance of social change" (Thompson, 1996, 399), undoing the more liberal ambiance of the July Monarchy. The feminist press would be closed (Adler, 1979, 175). And on July 26, 1848, a decree assimilated the status of women to minors, forbidding them even to attend meetings of a political club (Tixerant, 1908, 63). In Italy, the initial sympathy for women's causes in the Provisional Government (February 25–May 4) was negated by the discriminatory measures of the Constituent Assembly (May 4–28), followed by a legislature in which there could no longer be any "illusion of improvements in the status of women" (Anteghini, 1988, 57). The German feminists, linked to the liberals, "fell victim to the repression that followed the 1848 revolution" (Hackett, 1972, 362).

The net result of 1848 was thus not merely a repression of the socialists but of the feminists as well. This did not, however, draw them together. Rather, the two "pariahs" would now, for the most part, go on their separate organizational ways. What had happened in the first half of the nineteenth century is summarized thus by O'Neill (1969, 17):

> The gap between women's narrowed sphere and men's expanding one appears to have reached its greatest extent at a time when liberal and libertarian ideas were in ascendance. In both England and America the exclusion became more obvious as the suffrage was broadened, and more difficult to defend.

Of course, this was equally true of continental Europe. It is this difficult-to-defend gap[82] that would be the focus of the feminist/women's movements from this point forward.

---

82. The response of Hubertine Auclert in 1879 to this wide gap was her famous proclamation: "Man makes the laws to his advantage and we are obliged to bow our heads in silence. Enough of resignation. Pariahs of society, stand up!" (cited in Bidelman, 1982, xiv).

The housewife had now become the dominant cultural image of the role the woman was supposed to play in the modern world. The woman had lost whatever element had existed in prior epochs of being an "appreciated collaborator in the economic sphere" (Ortega, 1988, 13). Of course, emphasis should be put upon the word *appreciated*, for most women did not cease to "collaborate" in the economic sphere. As Hall (1992c, 68) notes, "the bourgeoisie made their wives into ladies in a position of dependence economically and subordination ideologically and then used lower-middle-class and working-class women to service their households and produce their textiles."[83]

In the nineteenth century, the distinction between public and private spheres of life became central to the geoculture. It was being hailed as one of the great advances of modernity, and was the logical consequence of the demand for rationality, in which "good social organization" seemed to require "a stricter definition of spaces, roles and tasks" (Perrot, 1988, 35), which in turn "served as a justification for the assignment of personal characteristics and social roles to males and females" (Allen, 1991, 29).[84] This has been called the "gendering of the public sphere," and Landes (1988, 2) notes the difference between this nineteenth-century cultural definition and that of the ancien régime, in which, "because rights were not universal, women's exclusion from formal channels of power was not deemed to be particularly exceptional."[85] Precisely the point: rights were now supposed to be universal, as the feminists kept insisting. In 1876, Hedwig Dohn,

83. Hobsbawm (1984c, 93) says that it is "a paradox of nineteenth-century industrialization that it tended to increase and sharpen the sexual division of labour between (unpaid) household work and (paid) work outside." But why is this a paradox?

84. Rowbotham (1977, 47) argues the links between gendered spheres and economic structure: "The model of the free market and freely competing economic atoms required sentiment to give it cohesion, as long as this emotion was kept in a proper place. Otherwise bourgeois man was left in a Hobbesian world dissolved under its own rationality. The Victorian middle classes found their sentiment in their womenfolk encased in their crinolines." But of course, it was not only the Victorian middle classes. Perrot (1986, 99) notes that "masculine consciousness had its appearance as a dimension of class [in France] at the beginning of the twentieth century. . . . Syndicalism organized by taking over in its own behalf the bourgeois definition of public space as masculine space." I would say myself that this occurred much earlier than the beginning of the twentieth century.

85. Nye (1993, 47) asserts that this gendering of the public and private spheres became legally sanctioned in the period 1789–1815 and connects this with scientific theorizing: "[A] biomedical model of male and female was constructed by medical scientists in this era that made the sexes 'naturally' suited for their respective social and familial roles. The sexed bodies that emerged from this process were so constituted as to be both 'opposite' and 'complementary.' Because the public and private spheres of the bourgeois cosmos were delineated so sharply from one another, only two wholly different beings could occupy them."

a German feminist, proclaimed: "Human rights [*Menschenrechte*] have no sex" (cited in Clemens, 1988, 1).

However, feminist movements were from the beginning caught in the conceptual dilemma that had been created for them. On the one hand, they were heirs to the universalist, and individualist, tradition enshrined in the French Revolution. But when they asked for their full rights as active citizens, they found these refused on grounds of their difference from men in some important ways.[86] On the other hand, when they decided alternatively to seek "equality in difference," a concept adumbrated by Ernest Legouvé, a French mid-nineteenth-century feminist,[87] they were doubtlessly seeking "a way to expand liberalism and to negotiate the patriarchal political world which liberalism accepted" (Caine, 1992, 53). They were also fitting in with the "new scientific representation of the body" that saw male and female bodies "as a series of binary oppositions" that were incommensurable (Poovey, 1988, 6). But in doing this, they were inevitably acceding to their role as passive citizens, accepting, if you will, the role men had assigned themselves of "benevolent patriarchs" (Offen, 1983, 257).

Navigating the channel between Scylla and Charybdis has never been easy, and it has rarely been done successfully. Viewing this from a distance, one can come to some unusual conclusions. Yvonne Turin (1989, 359) suggests that perhaps we should think of nuns as the true women's liberation movement of the nineteenth century:

> They were the first students of medicine, of pharmacy, the first heads of enterprises, the first strikers, too. . . . Totally foreign to theorizing, whether feminist or not, they made their presence felt by their daily practice, by fulfilling what they called their vocation, which pushed them to assume responsibilities, but also to get their initiatives adopted by the Church and civil society. The Church was the only structure that offered them a sphere of liberty large enough for their activities. . . . Before acting, today's feminist asks herself if men also do what she is asked to do. If the answer is yes, she agrees. If no, she refuses. She knows how to copy, to repeat, to conform, and

---

86. "Individualism provided the ideological links between liberal movements . . . (anti-slavery organizations, nationalist societies, moral crusades, social reform associations, political parties and so on) and the emergence of organized feminism. These links operated in two ways. First, it seems likely . . . that many, if not most, early feminist activists came from families that were closely involved in liberal movements of this kind. . . . Secondly, these and other women usually played an active part in movements of liberal reform. . . . The common experience of women active in these movements was one of initial enthusiasm, followed by disillusionment with the restraints placed on their activities by the men who led them" (Evans, 1977, 33).

87. "Legouvé's slogan of 'equality in difference' became the leitmotif of the organized republican movement for women's rights, and the reform program he had outlined [in 1848,] their program during the early Third Republic" (Offen, 1986, 454).

kills female inventiveness. The nun of the nineteenth century, a woman to the tip of her toes, invented all over the place.

And in an orthogonal but strangely complementary argument, at the other end of the cultural divide, see how Rubin (1975, 185) analyzes (and criticizes) psychoanalysis:

> [Psychoanalysis] is a theory of sexuality in human society. Most importantly, psychoanalysis provides a description of the mechanisms by which the sexes are divided and deformed, of how bisexual androgynous infants are transformed into boys and girls. Psychoanalysis is a feminist theory *manqué*.

But neither Turin's sense of how to navigate the rapids nor Rubin's sense of how to understand how the rapids became so dangerous in the first place was central to the ways in which feminists thought about and organized themselves after 1848 and up to the late twentieth century. Feminism had to make its way in a world in which sexism was not merely legitimate but openly and aggressively argued and therefore had an impact on any and all potential allies. Rebérioux (1978b, 154) speaks of "the force of 'cultural' antifeminism common to all European societies in the nineteenth century and shared as well by the socialists: the [socialist] parties could function as the anti-State, but not as the anti-Society."

Neither the scholars nor the political commentators nor the political leaders were of much help. In England, Herbert Spencer's early support for feminism (derived from his individualist ideas) was transformed into antifeminism by his discovery of the principle of Darwinian selection (Paxton 1991). Michelet's *La Femme* (1981 [1859], 49) includes an incredibly sexist dialogue of two men about the limitations of women, who are "brought up to hate and disdain what all Frenchmen love and in which they believe"—that is, secular values, science, the Revolution of 1789. McMillan (1981a, 362–363) points out that Michelet, Proudhon, and Jules Simon—all staunch anticlericals—in fact shared the conventional views of the Church on the role of women in the home. As for the forces of the right, they made feminism into one more example of the degeneration of values, and connected their views to nationalist themes.[88] And in Italy in 1893, Lombroso and Ferrero published a book, *La donna delinquente, la prostituta, la donna nor-*

---

88. "The books and tracts produced by this [French] chauvinist school argued that France was invaded, indeed infected (these writers were inordinately fond of medical metaphors)[,] by morbid outside influences—Jews, Protestants, and Freemasons—all conspicuously present among the leaders of the French movement for women's' rights. The antifeminists argued that France was threatened to the core by 'Internationalism' and 'cosmopolitanism.' In shrill tones they denounced all forms of Anglo-Saxon cultural imperialism, of which feminism was the most reprehensible element" (Offen, 1984, 662).

male, that talked of the intellectual inferiority of women, their innate tendency to lie, and their genetic potential for deviance.[89]

Rendall (1985, 321) notes that "by 1860, the common language within which, in [the United States, France, and England], the question of women's political rights was discussed [. . .] was still the language of republicanism and citizenship"[90]—and of course not only in those three countries.[91] The search for political integration into the states became virtually the only political issue of a movement that had an "overwhelmingly middle-class composition" (Evans, 1977, 34). How does one demand to be an active citizen? The answer seemed simple enough: organize, ask that laws be changed, lobby for these changes. And that is what feminists did. And if one asked why it was important to become a citizen? The answer would be parallel to the two-stage theory of Marxism: first the vote, then everything else.[92]

The question was how to get the vote. It required organization—organization as women.[93] The French feminists gave names to the two possible alterna-

89. Casalini (1981, 17–18) argues that the position of the socialist leader Filippo Turati, who compared female prostitution to male delinquency, was not in the end all that different from that of Lombroso and Ferrero. Rather, it shows that there exists at best simply "gradations of positivism, from a rationalist positivism with Marxist influences to the more retrograde Darwinism."

90. The devotion of women's movements to republicanism was not necessarily reciprocated. Klejman and Rochefort (1989, 57) entitle one of their chapters on feminism in France "Feminism and Republicanism: A Dialogue of the Deaf." As a result, Hubertine Auclert wrote in 1889, on the occasion of the centenary of the French Revolution: "Women should not be celebrating a masculine 89 but creating a feminine 89" (Auclert, 1982, 126). She called her journal *La Citoyenne.* And see the very clear language of Louise-Otto Peters, one of the founders of the German bourgeois feminist movement: "We are fighting against the consequences of the capitalist societal order [*Gesellschaftsordnung*], not this societal order itself" (cited in Hervé, 1983, 19).

91. For example, it was not until 1905 that there emerged an organized feminist movement in Russia, but when it did emerge it was a women's suffrage movement (Stites, 1978, 191). On India, see Forbes (1982).

92. "Classical feminism . . . finally came to focus on the vote as the capstone of emancipation in the West. This does not mean that the vote was seen as the end of feminist aspirations. The evidence is clear enough that most feminists envisioned political equality as a means, a continuance of the emancipation process at a higher level: female voters would elect women; women would effect the desired reforms not only for their own sex (law, divorce, education, and the rest) but also (via an argument for female sensitivity that sometimes contradicted mainstream feminist rhetoric) contribute to national regeneration, and ensure the abolition of such evils as alcoholism, prostitution, and war" (Stites, 1978, xviii). Bidelman (1982, 190) sums up the viewpoint of French feminists thus: "[W]ithout a permanent liberal answer to the 'first stage' political question, there could be no answer to the 'second stage' woman question." See the defense by Dubois (1978, 17018) of this strategy: "[I]t is a mistake to conclude that the women's suffrage movement was a useless distraction in women's struggle for liberation because the vote did not solve the problem of women's oppression. . . . It was the first independent movement of women for their own liberation."

93. "Liberal feminism is not feminism merely added onto liberalism. . . . [F]eminism requires a recognition, however implicit and undefined, of the sexual-class identification of women as women. . . . [Woman] was excluded from citizen rights as a member of a sexual class. Her *ascribed* social status

tive tactics. They called them the "politics of the breach" (associated with Maria Desraines) and the "politics of the assault" (associated with Hubertine Auclert). The issue was whether priority should given to achieving civil emancipation or political emancipation (Bidelman, 1982, chaps. 3, 4). As a debate about tactics, this was not too different from the reformist-revolutionary debate among the German Social-Democrats. In general, the politics of the breach was dominant. "Almost everywhere, the radicals (i.e. above all those who demanded feminine suffrage) were a minority, often strongly opposed by the 'moderate' majority of feminists" (Evans, 1977, 37).

The usual explanation of the moderation of feminist movements is the fact that they were dominated by middle-class women with bourgeois values. "Bourgeois *mentalités* predisposed them to gradual, lawful solutions" (Hause and Kenney, 1981, 783).[94] But some feminists did move on to more radical tactics. Evans (1977, 189–190) credits the example of the socialist movements and the emergence of social-democratic women's movements for inspiring those who came to be called "militant" feminists by their "aggressive tactics and intensive propaganda methods. . . . Mass demonstrations in the streets, banners and placards, slogans and colours, and the hard-hitting aggressive approach to opponents were all tactics pioneered by the socialist movement."

The aggressive tactics took hold particularly in Great Britain and the United States. "The [British] suffragettes smashed the image of woman as a passive, dependent creature as effectively as they smashed the plate-glass windows of Regent Street" (Rover, 1967, 20). Chafetz and Dworkin (1986, 112) argue that it was precisely this militancy and "narrowing the issue to suffrage" that enabled the U.S. [and British] movements to achieve a "mass following." If this didn't happen in France, Moses (1984, 230) says, it was not because the French movement "burned itself out" but rather because "repressive governments repeatedly burned feminism."

---

prevented her from participating in individual *achievements* provided by liberal society" (Eisenstein, 1981, 6).

94. Although Hause and Kenney claim (p. 804) that this effect was especially strong in France, because feminism did not "receive the leavening of working-class experience that it did in Britain," Rover (1967, 61) describes the situation in Great Britain thus: "The early middle-class feminists who were to give organized support to women's suffrage from 1866 on [National Society for Women's Suffrage] were much more closely linked with the Anti–Corn Law League than with the early Reform Societies or Chartism, the support for which was mainly working class, and it is not entirely an accident that Manchester, the centre of anti–corn law agitation, was an important centre for women's suffrage activities." And Perrot (1988, 47) protests against Anglo-Saxon historiography that sees French feminism as significantly different from feminism in Great Britain or the United States. As for Germany, Evans (1976, 272) insists that the two major characteristics of feminism there were that "it was liberal and it was middle class."

The feminists who led the struggle for suffrage were faced with groups of organized women who placed other objectives ahead of suffrage, either as a goal or as a priority. The suffragists saw these other movements as essentially less militant, more socially conservative. But some invert the analysis:

> Far from radicalizing the women's movement, . . . the emergence of the Suffragist Movement led to a contraction of its aims and an emphasis on pragmatism and moderation which considerably narrowed the scope of the movement. . . . The dominating role of the suffragists led to an almost exclusive concern with an issue of direct importance only to some middle-class women, in place of the concern with the problems of all women evident in the Contagious Diseases Agitation and some of the earlier work in regard to marriage laws and employment. (Caine, 1982b, 549–550)[95]

The argument was not simply suffrage versus other priorities. The fundamental issue was whether, when women entered the public sphere, they were entering it in order to demand genderless individuality (equality before the law in all matters, equality in the market, equality in education and any other cultural arena) or in order to ensure the recognition of women's particular virtues and talents (and to insist that these should not be confined to a "private" sphere). This debate within the feminist/women's movement informed the nineteenth-century movements and has not ceased to this day.[96]

It is important to be aware that the social feminists were in fact as concerned with political questions (i.e., questions of the law) as were the political feminists who concentrated on suffrage. For the law impinged on women's rights and possibilities in countless ways. The illegalization (as opposed to the social disapproval) of abortion was an early nineteenth-century action (Rendall, 1985, 226). And its legalization has been a women's issue ever since (McLaren, 1978a; Evans, 1977. 108). So has birth control.[97] So was, especially in the United States, the issue of

95. The Contagious Diseases Act was a piece of legislation in Great Britain in the 1820s. On the issues at the time, and the "cross-class alliance between feminists and radical working men," see Walkowitz (1982, esp. 80–83).

96. Lewis (1984, 89) sees the latter group, those who "accepted the idea of women as the natural guardians of the moral order," as using the language of the evangelical tradition and science (which had previously contained women in the home) in order "to argue for an extension of maternal influence beyond the home."

97. "[V]ery few advocates of reproductive rights . . . adopted arguments based purely or even chiefly on the rights of women as individuals, without reference to the welfare of community, nation, or new generation. In this context, the German feminist movement—and not only the radical organizations—stands out for its relative advancement and daring, not for its conservatism" (Allen, 1991, 204). The question, however, is what is "conservative" in this regard. McLaren (1978b, 107) points out the ambiguities: "The early birth control ideology was a curious amalgam. Its 'progressive' dimensions were exemplified by its interest in women's rights and medical self-help; its conservatism, by its adherence to neo-Malthusian economics." And then the eugenicists entered the debate, and this "shifted

temperance, in which movement many suffragists participated.[98] And when German feminists argued for kindergarten education, it was in pursuit of their model of a liberal state, based on *Rechtsstaat*, "which required an active role for government not just in protecting individual freedoms but in positively encouraging a sense of community." Kindergartens were thought to promote this goal "by stimulating the child's early instinct for self-activity" (Allen, 1991, 65).

All these attempts of women to control the elements of their femaleness met one obstacle, newly important in the nineteenth century: the rise of the medical doctor as the governing expert, based on the new scientificity of medicine.[99] In general, these physicians "assumed that women and men were more different than alike and that the physiological differences between the sexes translated 'naturally' to different social roles" (Theriot, 1993, 19). The physician, in this more secular world, succeeded the clergyman as the "keeper of normalcy" in the sexual sphere (Mosse, 1985, 10).[100] In particular, the new concept of the "family physician" became a mode of "direct surveillance" within the home of approved behavior (Donzelot, 1977, 22, 46). It is no wonder that even conservative women sought to emerge into the public sphere, and thereby reacquire some personal autonomy.

Of course, in the shift from religious control to medical/scientific control of behavior, we shift from a concept of "natural" behavior, from which sinners may deviate but back to which repentant persons may return, to a concept of "physiologically essential behaviors" that can be dealt with by the scientist and to a degree "controlled" or "reformed" but not fundamentally changed. Foucault (1976, 59) shows how this works for sexuality: "The [seventeenth-century] sodomite was a relapsed person; the [nineteenth-century] homosexual is a species." It is the difference, he argues, between a forbidden act (sodomy) and a person (a character) with a past, an infancy, a mode of life (the homosexual). And of course, once one reifies these behaviors into persons/characters, one can link one kind of deviance to another, since they are all rooted in biology. And those who could do this best were not biologists (very few in number) but physicians:

> Medical men had enough training in basic science to be credible as scientific mediators between the mysteries of the clinic and the vexing problems of every-

---

attention from the rights of the mother to those of the state; from the quantity of the work force to its quality" (p. 154).

98. "Participation in the [Women's Temperance] Crusade by . . . suffragists was possible because an area of agreement existed between the two movements. Not only were both movements by and for women, but both also asserted women's right to be active in the public sphere" (Blocker, 1985, 471).

99. Before the Enlightenment, physicians and surgeons were not highly esteemed, by and large. "Molière testifies to this," say Kniehbiehler and Fouquet (1983, 4).

100. Of course, it was perhaps even worse when this did not occur, since at this time "the most persistent and intractable of [feminist] enemies [was] the Roman Catholic Church" (Evans, 1977, 124).

day life. Doctors were also well organized, thoroughly secular and political in their outlook, and fierce defenders of their professional and social prerogatives. (Nye, 1984, xi)[101]

Of course, the feminists were divided over what to emphasize in the public sphere. For some it was the "maternal metaphor" and the sense that "familial and maternal roles exert a positive influence on women's public and private behavior" (Allen, 1991, 1, 244). Some felt that the discourse on marriage and the family ended by confining women to a women's sphere, although very few advocated "free love." Either way they intended to strike "at the roots of . . . patriarchy" (Basch, 1986, 36) and create more space for women.

The last important public arena in which women sought to play a specifically feminine role was geopolitics. Women formed peace movements, often insisting that it was because women, unlike men, abjured military traits, and because they were "maternal," that they refused to see their sons die in pointless wars. Pacifism became a woman's specialty, with a special international organization, the Women's International League for Peace and Freedom (WILPF), which was formed in 1915 in the midst of the First World War to protest against the war.[102]

The state action that women had the least ability to affect, because it was not a matter of legislation, was census categories. In late nineteenth-century Australia, married women were all categorized as dependents, "a political act carried out in the interests of working-class men for the purpose of labor-market closure" (Deacon, 1985, 46). Such a classification had become widespread: "By 1900, the notion that married women without paying jobs outside the home were 'dependents' had acquired the status of a scientific fact" (Folbre, 1991, 482). When social science concepts are legislated, they have an effect and gain a degree of legitimacy that carries great weight in the day-to-day functioning of the social system.

---

101. Nye is discussing primarily France. There, he says, this biologization of social deviance was used to account for the defeat of 1870 and had "the thoroughly *cultural* aim of explaining to the French the origins of national decadence and the weakness of their population" (p. xiii). In chap. 10, on Great Britain and Germany, he does admit that "such concerns were not uncommon elsewhere" (p. 320).

102. But actual warfare could have the reverse effect. In Japan, the effect of the 1894–1895 conflict with China was to accelerate "conservative tendencies that were by definition anti-feminist" and encouraged the government to propagate "the roles that women could play as child bearers and supporters of government policy" (Siever, 1983, 103). During the First World War, Italian feminists "passed with relative ease from convinced pacifism to collaboration in the organization and propaganda of war" (Bigaran, 1982, 128). The same thing seemed to have happened in France (Klejman and Rochefort, 1989, 189). Vellacott (1987, 95) says that, in Great Britain, once the war was over, "the gilt was off on three 'isms'—feminism, pacifism, and socialism. . . . [T]he pacifists had indeed been proven right in their claim that a militaristic world was the death of women's vision."

ETHNIC AND RACIAL MOVEMENTS

We have seen that the social/labor movements had great difficulty in accepting the legitimacy of the feminist/women's movements in their demands for the rights of active citizenship. In a similar manner, the feminist/women's movements had great difficulties in accepting the legitimacy of the ethnic/racial movements in the latter's demands for the rights of active citizenship. It was as though there weren't enough room on the ship to accommodate everyone. Or perhaps the better metaphor is an unwillingness to accept the idea of a one-class ship—citizens all, citizens equal. In the nineteenth century, this second organizational conflict was to be found primarily in the United States, where the oppression of the Blacks played such a central role in political tensions and therefore gave rise to Black social movements. The struggle for Irish rights in Great Britain posed a parallel issue, except that it included a demand for political separation that was largely absent in the case of the Blacks in the United States.

From the point of view of the dominant strata, the issue of women's rights and that of rights for Blacks (and indeed for other ethnic "minorities") were not fundamentally different. Indeed, it often seemed that they fused the perceptions:

> Republican gender ideology eased the development of a racialized citizenship. Gender ideology opposed manhood to womanhood, fastening manhood to productivity and independence and womanhood to servility and dependence. . . . By assigning feminine traits to ethnic men, old-stock Americans not only neutered allegedly servile and dependent men but marked them as a peril to republican liberty as well. . . . The flip side of dependent womanhood was virtuous motherhood; the flip side of dependent manhood was the germ of tyranny. (Mink, 1990, 96)

In the early nineteenth century, women were quite active in the abolitionist movements, especially in Great Britain and the United States. It was a period in which women's rights were deteriorating everywhere—in the case of the United States, "dramatically" (Berg, 1978, 11). It should be remembered that the first *formal* exclusion of women from the vote was in the British Reform Bill of 1832, which was intended to enfranchise some who did not have the franchise before. But in doing this, the bill specified "male persons," a phrase that had never before been found in English legislation. This phrase "provided a focus of attack and a source of resentment," (Rover, 1967, 3) out of which British feminism would grow.[103]

Women turned quite pointedly to the concept of "natural rights," which was the legacy of the Enlightenment and the French Revolution, in order to lay claim

---

103. Fulford (1957, 33) says of this phrase: "There was no subtle intention to deprive women of their just rights because it never crossed the minds of these parliamentarians that such rights existed." This underlines the depth of women's subordinate position from which the feminist movement would be seeking to extract them.

to their freedom. Abolitionism was also based on the concept of "natural rights," and the abolitionist movement "served as a catalyst which transformed latent feminist sentiment into the beginnings of an organized movement" (Hersh, 1978, 1). Abolition, of course, involved the ending of slavery, and thus the entry into formal citizenship of those who had been slaves. But since, as we have seen, there were de facto two levels of citizens, the active and the passive, the immediate question was into which of the two categories the liberated slaves would be placed.

This was the kernel of the debate over the Thirteenth, Fourteenth and Fifteenth Amendments to the U.S. Constitution following the end of the Civil War. President Lincoln had emancipated the slaves on January 1, 1863 (actually not quite all the slaves, but most of them). The Thirteenth Amendment, passed in 1865, made slavery unconstitutional. The Fourteen Amendment, passed in 1868, declared that if the right to vote was denied in any states to citizens over twenty-one who were "male inhabitants" of that state, the basis of representation of that state would be reduced in Congress. And the Fifteenth Amendment, passed in 1870, declared that the right to vote shall not be abridged "on account of race, color, or previous condition of servitude."

The feminists saw the Fourteenth Amendment as a "political setback" because for the first time the world *male* was included and thus for the first time women were "explicitly excluded from politics" (Ryan, 1992, 20). This was precisely parallel to what had happened with the British Reform Act of 1832. The franchise was enlarged, and in the process women were consciously and specifically excluded. The women, of course, argued that extending the suffrage should be done for all that were excluded, and at the same time. Wendell Phillips, one of the leaders of the U.S. abolitionist movement, had said in May 1865 that the demands of women's suffrage should not be pressed at the moment, for "this is the Negro's Hour." This famous statement received a very strong and almost equally famous response from Elizabeth Cady Stanton in a letter to the editor of the *National Anti-Slavery Standard* on December 26, 1865:

> The representative women of the nation have done their uttermost for the last thirty years to secure freedom for the negro, and so long as he was lowest in the scale of being we were willing to press *his* claims; but now, as the celestial gate to civil rights is slowly moving on its hinges, it becomes a serious question whether we had better stand aside and see "Sambo" walk into the kingdom first. . . .

> It is all very well for the privileged order to look down complacently and tell us, "this is the negro's hour; do not clog his way; do not embarrass the Republican party with any new issue; be generous and magnanimous; the negro once safe, the woman comes next." Now, if our prayer involved a new set of measures, or a new train of thought, it would be cruel to tax "white male citizens" with even two simple questions at a time; but the disfranchised all make the same demand, and the same logic and justice that secures Suffrage to one class gives it to all.

The struggle of the last thirty years has not been on the black man as such, but on the broader ground of his humanity. (Gordon, 1997, 504–505)[104]

The women suffragists did not stand by mute. They managed to get the New York State Constitution in 1867 to eliminate the word *male* along with *white,* over the objections of Horace Greeley (O'Neill, 1971, 17). And in Kansas in 1867, Stanton and Susan B. Anthony supported the campaign of George Francis Train, a known racist, who, however, advocated women's suffrage.[105] In this struggle of the women with their long-time allies in the fight against slavery—the Republican majority in the U.S. Congress, the former slaves—"the women were defeated in every encounter" (Griffith, 1984, 118).

Not all women leaders took the Stanton–Anthony position. Lucy Stone argued that "if the women could not win their political freedom, it was well that the Negro men could win theirs" (Kraditor, 1967, 3). The outcome was a profound split in the feminist movement. In 1869, Anthony and Stanton founded the National Woman Suffrage Association, with more links henceforth to the Democratic Party. And Stone and Henry Ward Beecher formed the American Woman Suffrage Association, with more links to the Republican Party. The NWSA had the more social analysis, arguing that women's oppression was due to marriage and the sexual division of labor. The AWSA restricted itself to the central political issue of suffrage (Buechler, 1990, 50).[106]

104. Later, Stanton wrote an article on January 15, 1868, in *Revolution,* which she entitled "Who Are Our Friends?" In it, she said: "Charles Sumner, Horace Greeley, Gerrit Smith, and Wendell Phillips, with one consent, bid the women of the nation stand aside and behold the salvation of the negro. Wendell Phillips says, 'one idea for a generation,' to come up in order of their importance. First negro suffrage, then temperance, then the eight-hour movement, then women's suffrage. In 1958, three generations hence, thirty years to a generation, Phillips and Providence permitting, women's suffrage will be in order" (O'Neill, 1969, 117). Women's suffrage actually was enacted in the United States in 1919. But as Catt and Shuler (1923, 108) say: "Between the adoption of the Fifteenth Amendment (March 30, 1870), which completed the enfranchisement of the Negro, and 1910, lie forty years during which white women watched, prayed and worked together without ceasing for the woman's hour that never came." One could of course remark that, when White women in the United States got the vote in 1919, they really got it, whereas Black men (and women) didn't really get it until the Civil Rights Act of 1963, and even then many continue to be effectively deprived of it.

105. Frederick Douglass, the Black leader, denounced the association of Stanton and Anthony with Train (Dubois, 1978, 187). Hersh (1978, 70) says it was only a "brief association." But Dubois (1978, 95–96) argues that "by turning to Train [Anthony and Stanton] gave substance to the charges of anti-feminist Republicans that the women's suffrage movement was a tool that the Democratic party used against the freedmen." Douglass had long been a supporter of women's suffrage. He attended the Seneca Falls meeting in 1848, and he renewed his support in the 1870s. "But in the vital years of 1866–9 he withheld his support," believing that adding women's suffrage to the package would endanger obtaining the vote for the freedmen, and that the latter was more vital and urgent (Evans, 1977, 48).

106. The split would finally end in 1890, with their merger as the National American Woman Suffrage Association (NAWSA). The politics of the various women's leaders did not change, however,

As the women's movement became more conservative on all social/labor issues in the second half of the nineteenth century, so did it on all ethnic/racial issues within countries (as in the United States)[107] or colonial issues (as in Great Britain).[108] In the course of this conservative shift, many feminists abandoned the "natural rights" argument. In the United States, they began to argue that women be given the vote "to balance the impact of the foreign born" (Berg, 1978, 269). When the NAWSA in 1903 came out for an "educational requirement" for the vote (to the notable but lonely dissent of Charlotte Perkins Gilman), they had shifted from campaigning to extend the franchise to a proposal "to take the vote away from some Americans—Negroes in the South and naturalized citizens in the North" (Kraditor, 1965, 137; see Flexner, 1975, 316).[109]

To the antifeminist eugenicists, strong in both England and Germany, who argued against suffrage on the grounds that high fertility was essential for a superior race,

---

as can be seen by the stands they took thereafter on labor questions. Lucy Stone, showing her hostility to the labor movement in general, asked why the Homestead strikers, in their struggle with Carnegie Steel Company in 1892, did not "save their earnings to start their own businesses if they were dissatisfied with their jobs." Susan B. Anthony, on the other hand, called herself a "friend of Eugene V. Debs and of labor" but, true to her position on the vote for Blacks, said she would not support *any* cause until women had the vote (Kraditor, 1965, 158–159).

107. In the United States, the women's movement showed increasing resentment of the hostility of immigrant groups to women's suffrage. "In the process . . . votes for women, which had once been an expression of equal rights, became an issue of social privilege." The same thing occurred in terms of the relation with Blacks, following the conflict over the Amendments. "By the closing years of the century it was commonplace in the South for racist arguments to be used in support of women's suffrage" (Banks, 1981, 141). Cohen (1996, 708–709), speaking of the attitude of a later generation of feminists, remarks: "Feminists often have assumed that, by dividing women, white women's racism undermines their own interests and serves white men. Yet the leaders of the [U.S.] white women's suffrage movement were often quite explicit in their *opposition* to nonwhite (or foreign-born) women and men. Theirs was less an error in feminist analysis that a political strategy reflecting *and creating* real privilege."

108. "The birth of organized feminism in Britain took place against the background of anti-slavery enthusiasm but its development was consolidated during a period of popular imperialism" (Ware, 1992, 118). "[F]eminism, like imperialism, was structured around the idea of moral responsibility. In Victorian terms, *responsibility* was custodial, classist, ageist, and hierarchical. . . . [F]eminist argument, no less than imperialist apologia, was preoccupied with race preservation, racial purity, and racial motherhood. This was in part because it had to be. One of the most damaging attacks made against the case for female emancipation was that it would enervate the race" (Burton, 1990, 296, 299).

109. In a parallel way, the British feminist movement was divided on the issue of property qualifications for the vote (Banks, 1981, 133–134). In Russia, after the emancipation of the serfs in 1861, "women sensitive to their status were quick to contrast the liberation of fifty million illiterate serfs (and two years later of four million Negro slaves in the United States) to their own lack of liberation" (Stites, 1978, 43). Still, Stites adds that although the Russian suffragist movements between 1905 and 1917 "may have been indifferent to universal suffrage, . . . nowhere could be heard anything

some feminists felt it appropriate to respond that "unless women were granted their demands for a new social order their refusal to bear children would result in racial decline" (Rowbotham, 1974, 106).[110] The so-called Ruffin incident in 1900 illustrated the dominant tone. At the Milwaukee meeting of the National Federation of Women's Clubs, the Women's Era Club was admitted as a new member. When Josephine St. Pierre Ruffin showed up as its representative, the Executive Committee realized that this was a club of Black women and revoked the decision. Mrs. Ruffin was told she could enter the convention as a delegate of the Massachusetts State Federation, a "White club" of which she was a member, but not as a representative of a "colored club." The incident degenerated to the point of someone trying to snatch away her badge—unsuccessfully, since she resisted—but she then refused to attend (Moses, 1978, 107–108).[111]

At the height of this tension, some suffragists resorted to crude racism. For example, they issued a poster of a "brutish-looking Negro porter sitting next to a refined-looking White lady" with a caption that read, "*He* can vote; why can't I?" Of course, this received the obvious reply from antisuffragist men that the presumed infusion of intelligent votes by granting the vote to White women would be undone by the granting at the same time of votes to Black women. And in 1910, in the *Atlantic Monthly,* one antisuffragist wrote: "We have suffered many things at the hands of Patrick; the New World would add Bridget also. And—graver danger—to the vote of that silly, amiable uneducated Negro, she would add (if logical) the vote of his sillier, baser female" (Kraditor, 1965, 31). It did not help that Blacks like Mrs. Booker T. Washington would plead for consideration on the grounds of the moral superiority of Blacks to immigrants.[112]

---

equivalent to the strident hostility which Americans like Catt, Stone, and Stanton lavished upon labor, the Negro, and 'the steerage'" (p. 228). Nor was this style of feminist arguments restricted to Western countries. In the 1920s, a Filipino feminist of obviously upper-class status wrote: "My chauffeur, my cook and my man servant who are all under me can vote; why can't the government allow me and Filipino women in general the privilege of going to the polls?" (cited in Jayawardena, 1986, 155).

110. Worse yet, a leader of the presumably more radical wing of the German suffragists, Else Linders, came out against racially mixed marriages (Evans, 1976, 167).

111. Almost fifty years earlier, in June 1854, an almost parallel exclusion occurred, this time by (White) male antislavery militants against (White) women. The international antislavery conference being held in London spent its entire first day debating whether U.S. women could be seated as delegates. Finally, the assembly voted overwhelmingly that they could not. "For the remainder of the sessions they were obliged to sit behind a curtain—'similar to those used to screen the choir from the public gaze'" (Ware, 1992, 82).

112. In a letter to Edna D. Cheney, a White reformer, Mrs. Washington wrote on November 23, 1896: "I can not tell you how I felt since Miss Willard has taken up the Armenian question, not that she should not do this but it is so strange that these people who have no special claims upon this country should so take possession of the hearts of northern women, that the woman of color is entirely overlooked." And Booker T. Washington himself added in his Atlanta Exposition address: "To those of the

The First World War was in many ways a political turning point for feminist movements. In many countries, they had by then or at that time obtained the vote. And with that, the feminist/women's movements seemed to go into serious decline. One reason, of course, is that the process of mobilizing to obtain the vote had transformed the women's suffragist worldview from one that saw the suffrage "as a means of challenging traditions that were oppressive to a view that embraced many of those traditions and built on them to develop arguments for the vote" (Buechler, 1987, 78–79).[113] Evans (1977, 227) notes that in the United States, Prohibition and women's suffrage were voted in at virtually the same time, and largely supported by the same people:

> Both were associated with Populism and Progressivism. Both represented an attempt by middle class White Anglo-Saxon Protestants to control the blacks, the immigrants and the big cities. They were a response to what was felt as a growing threat to the supremacy of American values. They achieved victory in the war not least because with the conflict against Germany and—to an immensely greater extent— the Bolshevik Revolution of 1917 and the revolutions in Central Europe at the end of the war, the fear of the subversion of values by the Protestant middle classes reached panic proportions.

If citizenship—that is, active citizenship—was difficult to achieve for workers and women, it was even more difficult for persons of color (or other groups defined by some status-group characteristic and treated as somehow inferior). The intellectual justification for this had been building up since the beginning of the capitalist world-economy.[114] But it was only in the nineteenth century that the theme of superior and inferior "races" was constantly elaborated and considered to be by Whites virtually self-evident. Above all, the previous theories of race all allowed

---

white race who look to the incoming of those of foreign birth and strange tongue and habits for the prosperity of the South, were I permitted to repeat what I say to my own race: 'Cast down your bucket where you are.'" The editorial of the *Woman's Era,* a Black publication, went even further: "'The audacity of foreigners who flee their native land and seek refuge here, many of them criminals and traitors, who are here but a day before they join in the hue and cry against the native born citizens of this land is becoming intolerable" (Moses, 1978, 112–113).

113. Lindhohn (1991, 121) argues that the gains for women "came at considerable costs in terms of real structural change" and thus calls the campaign of Swedish feminism "the conservative revolution." O'Neill calls his book (1971, viii) "an inquiry into the failure of feminism" and says that suffrage proved to a "dead end" (p. 48). And Buhle argues (1981, 318), in her book on American feminism, that "feminism, once a dynamic force, became narrowly relegated to the individualistic aspirations of professional women."

114. "If one takes a closer look, one can see that European literature from the sixteenth to the eighteenth centuries was a gigantic laboratory of ideas, out of which emerged the central themes which served as the key arguments for the thesis of the inferiority of the peoples of color" (Poliakov et al., 1976, 52).

for some possibility of movement—for example, via "conversion."[115] "Beginning in the nineteenth century, . . . implicitly or explicitly, *there was a rupture in humanity; groups 'are'* and no longer have a mobile status" (Guillaumin, 1972, 25).

The racial divide was made almost inevitable from the beginning by the forms in which class ideology evolved.[116] When commoners asserted their rights to citizenship both in England and in France, one of the arguments they sometimes used was that the aristocrats were "strangers" and not of native origin. This was the theory of the Norman Yoke, put forward in England since the seventeenth century,[117] and the theory of the distinction between the "*race gauloise*" and the "*race franque*" in France, which had been bruited for some time but became prominent during the French Revolution.[118] A parallel argument emerged in Italy with Etruscomania (Poliakov, 1974, 65–66). But if the aristocrats were to be excluded from active citizenship on the grounds of their foreign origins, how much more obviously would persons of color be so excluded? *Jus sanguinis* as opposed to *jus soli* is by definition exclusionary and inevitably racist. Still, if there existed the theme of the racial superiority of commoners, there was of course an even stronger one of aristocratic "blue bloods" and their natural rights.[119]

115. "'[R]ace' as that term developed across several European languages was a highly unstable term in the early modern period. . . . At the beginnings of this era, *raza* in Spanish, *raça* in Portuguese, or 'race' in French or English variously designed notions of lineage or genealogy, as in the sense of noble (or biblical) 'race and stock,' even before its application in Spain to the Moors and Jews or its eventual extension to paradigms of physical and phenotypical difference that would become the basis of later discourse of racism and racial difference" (Hendricks and Parker, 1994, 1–2).

116. See the discussion in Balibar and Wallerstein, 1988, chaps. 10, 11.

117. The theory of the Norman Yoke is that the Norman conquest of 1066 deprived the Anglo-Saxon inhabitants of their heritage as "free and equal citizens" and that the struggle of the people was to reconquer ancient rights. On the Great Seal of the Commonwealth, created in 1651, was the inscription that freedom was "by God's will restored." As Hill (1958, 67) notes, this theory "also stirred far profounder feelings of English patriotism and English Protestantism. Herein lay its strength."

118. During the French Revolution, the "*race gauloise*" became identified with the bourgeoisie (and hence with the "people") and the "*race franque*" with the "aristocracy" (Poliakov et al., 1976, 69). They cite the earlier arguments of Boulainvilliers, Montesquieu, and the Comte de Montlosier. And Guizot later explicitly used this distinction as part of his effort to justify the French Revolution for the cause of his version of liberalism and the bourgeoisie. "If the July Revolution marked a political consummation, in that it established the bourgeoisie, once and for all, as the ruling class in France, it also marked the triumphant career of the Gallic view of France" (Poliakov, 1974, 32). Throughout the nineteenth century, this Gallic view was available to justify hostility to the Franks (the Germans), the Latins (the Italians), and the Semites (the Jews). Simon (1991) calls this a "Celtic culture."

119. "The dreams of racism actually have their origin in the ideology of *class*, rather than in those of nation: above all in claims to divinity among rulers and to 'blue' or 'white' blood and 'breeding'

If race became a theorized concept in the nineteenth century, and racism an institutionalized practice, it was the result primarily of the centrality of the concept of citizenship. For citizenship as a concept had two logical consequences: It led states to emphasize and to predicate and insist on homogeneity as the only sound basis on which to justify the theoretical equality of all citizens. And it led states to justify their political domination of other states on the grounds that their particular homogeneous quality incarnated a higher degree of civilization than that of the dominated state, equally homogeneous but inferior.

The organic quality of the nation is inherent in what we have come to call Jacobinism, the key concept of which is that there should exist no intermediary bodies between the state and the individual. All individuals being equal, they have no public (or state-relevant) qualities other than that of being a citizen. Groups, however formed, no matter what their basis, do not have legal or moral standing as such. Gilroy (2000, 63) calls the resulting nation "a violent, organic entity of a new type manifest above all in the working of the state." This organic entity represented progress. Bourguet (1976, 812) analyzes how this may be noted in the *Statistique des Préfets* of the year IX (1800):

> Progress was thus defined as the march toward a society ever more homogeneous, the triumph of man over nature, of the uniform over diversity. . . . The philosophy of the Enlightenment and of the French Revolution forged this ideal of a rational society, from which the abnormal, the pathological, the different were to be excluded.

It would not be difficult or even illogical to transform the concept of organic qualities into different ones for each nation and, more generally, for a difference between the civilized (European) nations taken together and all the others. The slide from a created homogeneity to a culturo-genetic organic reality, which could not be easily changed, was not difficult, either. A good example is that of Gustave Le Bon, who, in his 1886 work on race psychology, defined the greatest danger to the organic nation as that of assimilation—of criminals, of women, of ethnic groups, of colonials (Nye, 1975, 49–50).[120] Thus did we go from an organic whole that legitimated the equality of all citizens to an organic reality that justified a hierarchy among those citizens. Once again, from citizens all to an active/passive distinction. At which point, those excluded could demand inclusion. But

---

among aristocrats. No surprise then that the putative sire of modern racism should not be some petty-bourgeois but Joseph Arthur, comte de Gobineau" (Anderson, 1991, 149)

120. Like all thinkers of the extreme right in the modern world, Le Bon (1978 [1894], 9–10) seems to believe that the idea of the equality of individuals and races has in fact come to dominate the world. "Very appealing to the crowds, this idea ended by becoming solidly implanted in their psyches and soon bore its fruits. It has shaken the bases of old societies, engendered the most formidable revolutions, and thrown the Western world into a series of violent convulsions whose outcome is impossible to foresee."

they could also embrace the negatives, as angry riposte, rhetorical ploy, or organizer of identification.[121]

The nineteenth century was the apogee of Europe in the world. "[N]ever did white men of European descent dominate [the world] with less challenge" (Hobsbawm, 1975, 135).[122] This was based on their military power, no doubt, but it was secured by their ideological constructs. "Europe had been 'Europeanized' by the construction of a unifying grid of civilization, against which all other cultures could be measured and classified" (Woolf, 1992, 89).[123] As the states sought to create homogeneous nations of citizens, they simultaneously sought to create a White (European) race, in the "crusade against the backward areas of the world" advocated by Saint-Simon (Manuel, 1956, 195).[124] And the crusade involved colonization: "The identification of colour with less than human became . . . an essential part of the process by which the French defined their role as colonizers" (Boulle,

121. "[W]ords and notions such as 'proletariat,' 'dangerous classes,' haunted the discourse and imagination of the first half of the nineteenth century. These terrifying, negative, savage visions forced workers to situate themselves in relation to them, either to make them their own, or more commonly, to distinguish themselves from them. Workers sometimes emphasized negative traits, declaring themselves to be *lundistes* (Monday absenteeists), drunks, fighters, dirty talkers; in this regard, *ouvriérisme* is akin to *negritude*. Alternatively, . . . the image they wished to give of themselves contrasted reactively. . . . It was necessary to give a positive image of oneself against those who denied it; identity formed itself in this tension, in this relationship to the adversary" (Perrot, 1986, 95–96).

122. Hobsbawm specifies the moment as the third quarter of the nineteenth century. This view of an apogee was shared by one of the major racist books of the twentieth century, *The Rising Tide of Color against White World-Supremacy*, by Lothrop Stoddard, who said (1924, 153) that "1900 . . . was the high-water mark of the white tide which had been flooding for four hundred years. At that moment the white man stood on the pinnacle of his prestige and power. Pass four short years, and the flash of Japanese guns across the murky waters of Port Arthur revealed to a startled world the beginning of the ebb."

123. A student of John Stuart Mill reports: "He used to tell us that the Oxford theologians had done for England something like what Guizot, Villemain, Michelet, Cousin had done a little earlier for France—they had opened, broadened, deepened the issues and meanings of European history; they had reminded us that history is European; that it is quite unintelligible if treated as merely local" (Morley cited in Hammond and Foot, 1952, 25).

Delacampagne (1983, 200) wants to deny that European racism can be explained by imperial expansion or the class struggle or capitalism, but by "what characterizes Western culture from its beginnings, its total intolerance." And he sees this intolerance deriving from Europe's universalist pretensions. But this view simply turns essentialism against European perpetrators of essentialism and vitiates any historical understanding of the institutionalized racism of the nineteenth-century world.

124. Manuel (p. 176) cites Saint-Simon: "To people the globe with the European race, which is superior to all other races, to open the whole world to travel and to render it as habitable as Europe, that is the enterprise through which the European parliament should continually engage the activity of Europe and always keep up its momentum." Manuel adds that, by Europe, Saint-Simon meant western Europe and primarily England, France, and Germany. Manuel (p. 401, n. 11) sees Saint-Simon's call for a crusade against uncivilized disorder as parallel to Bonald's view that the virtue of modern states was that they had put an end to the conflict of feudal chieftains.

1988, 245–246).[125] Of course, this was equally true within countries. Jordan (1968, xiii) notes that, in post-Revolutionary America, what the intellectuals did "was, in effect, to claim America as a white man's country."

The concept of a racial hierarchy received the legitimation of science, itself the great cultural icon of the nineteenth century. Science did this by the "confusion of sociological reality and biological reality" (Guillaumin, 1972, 24),[126] egregious for avowed racists like Gobineau but evident in only milder form among centrist liberals.[127] In the mid-nineteenth century, "polygenism" enjoyed a vogue among anthropologists, despite the fact that it defied even biblical views. Or perhaps just the contrary: one of the reasons polygenism appealed was that it seemed more "scientific" than the book of Genesis.[128] Todorov (1989, 3) sees this "scientism" as

125. But, of course, so did the British. "[E]ven a cursory reading of [British] political speeches after 1890 . . . shows that in the interpretation of national as well as international problems an increasingly 'biological' vocabulary was used; one of the most prominent examples of which was certainly Salisbury's speech [1898] on the 'dying nations'" (Mock, 1981, 191).

126. She notes how this confusion was a new phenomenon of the nineteenth and twentieth centuries. In the eighteenth century, "evolution [was] a phenomenon internal to the social mechanism," and the origin of differences was "either geographical, or psychological, or pure social mechanism, but in all cases foreign to biology" (pp. 24–25). Similarly, Lewis (1978, 74–75) argues: "When all of its limitations have been noted it remains true that [the] reputation [of the eighteenth century] as the 'age of reason' was not an empty one. It was ready and eager to look at non-European peoples in a spirit of genuine curiosity. It no doubt tended to romanticize these peoples. . . . But it was willing to listen to black and brown voices, and to recognize that there were cultural and spiritual values in the non-European civilizations absent in Europe." What intervened was the universalism of the French Revolution and the dilemmas of citizenship.

Poliakov et al. (1976, 67) also date the moment of shift of emphasis as that of the French Revolution. The reverse side of the principles of liberty, equality, and fraternity—scarcely noticed at the time, they say—was "the new scientific mentality [which] tended to emphasize the determining character of biological elements. It substituted for ancient religious and cultural classifications new ones derived from observing physical characteristics (skin color, etc.). The latter were considered to be unchangeable, and affected, it was thought, the behavior of the individuals in question." To be sure, Poliakov (1982, 53) also says that racism "in its modern form, as a value-judgment bailed out by science, goes back to the eighteenth century." Jordan (1968, xiii) notes the same shift in the United States: "What seems particularly to make the debate on the Negro's nature different after the [American] Revolution than before was the rapid growth in Europe and America after 1775 of interest in anatomical investigation of human differences" and "the widespread interest in elucidating these differences with scalpels and calipers."

127. "The true extent of scientific racism can best be grasped through its appeal to what is not normally seen as its constituency, namely to the liberals among the scientists" (Barkan, 1992, 177). He cites specifically Julian Huxley and Herbert Spencer. Poliakov (1982, 55–56) speaks of the role of Voltaire, Kant, and Buffon in laying the groundwork for such ideas. Voltaire, the great symbol of civil liberties in the nineteenth and twentieth centuries, was explicitly anti-Black and anti-Jewish.

128. Cohen (1980, 233) says that "by the 1850s polygenism had swept France." Jordan (1968, 509) recounts that in the antebellum U.S. South, "a small but noisy 'American school' of anthropology

somehow a betrayal of the Enlightenment's "basic principle, the triumph of freedom over determinism," which he claims "refuses to subordinate what ought to be to what is." But Cohen (1980, 210), it seems to me, is more correct in asserting that the Enlightenment thinkers left "unresolved" the debate on whether differences between "peoples" were environmental or biological in origin. The question remained unresolved in public debate until 1945, and perhaps, albeit more sotto voce, to this day.[129]

One of the key scientific notions that contributed to this biological interpretation of social reality was the concept of the Aryan. It was originally and basically a linguistic concept—the discovery by nineteenth-century linguists of the links between a large series of languages: almost all of those that were spoken in Europe, in Persia, and some spoken in South Asia. Linguists call this family of languages Indo-European. In 1814, Ballanche suggested substituting the study of Sanskrit for the study of Latin. This was in fact to take the side of language as it was created by humans against language as revealed by God. Linguists like Schlegel and Grimm were discovering the incredible complexity of what had been thought of as "primitive" languages (Schwab, 1950, 190–191). During the nineteenth century, Aryan theory came to be "in the main current of scientific progress" (Poliakov, 1974, 327–328).

As the European powers moved into a more active imperial expansion in the late nineteenth century, the racist ideas that had previously supported slavery were "dressed up in a new pseudo-scientific garb and given a popular mass appeal" (Davis, 1993, 73). The concept of the Aryan now became the justification of European domination of the non-European world. The concept of the Aryan then met up with the concept of the Oriental.

Gilroy (2000, 72) suggests that all this scientific and pseudoscientific theorizing added up to what he calls "raciology," which he defines as the "variety of essen-

---

stridently denied the original unity of man while their clerical opponents grew increasingly rigid and dogmatic in defence of Genesis." For polygenism in Great Britain, see Stepan (1982, 3).

129. "[W]hen faced with apparently immutable racial difference, the best cosmopolitan intentions of an enlightened standpoint could be undermined. They were compromised by ambiguity and conflict over where the boundaries of humanity should fall and regularly defeated by the white supremacist thinking that rendered most enlightenment versions of reason actively complicit with the political project involved in classifying the world by means of 'race' and reading the motion of history through racialized categories. Allied with a weak sense of the unity of human life, this combination would be a dubious bequest to the Enlightenment's liberal and socialist successors. Indeed, we could say that it was only with the defeat of the Nazis and their allies in the mid-twentieth century that the utterly respectable raciology of the previous period was pushed briefly beyond the bounds of respectability. Prior to that, even voices of dissent from imperial misconduct and colonial expansionism had to engage with the same anthropological ideas of 'race,' nation, and culture that had applauded imperial power, directing them to more equitable ends against the very logic of their meshed interconnection" (Gilroy, 2000, 38).

tializing and reductionist ways of thinking [about race] that are both biological and cultural in character." It is important to stress that the essentializing is just as pernicious if it is cultural as when it is biological.

Racist theorizing bred antiracist movements. But it must be admitted that such movements were in fact quite weak in the nineteenth century, much weaker than the social/labor movements and the feminist/women's movements. And in the end, they got even less support from the liberal center than did the other kinds of movements. In part, this may reflect the even greater strength of racist ideology than of ideologies of bourgeois or of male dominance. In part, it reflected the numerical weakness of those as the bottom of the racial hierarchy in Western countries. This was not true of the United States, but then the United States was the country where precisely racist ideology was most deeply rooted, because it was the country first of slavery and later of Jim Crow.

The difficulty of the centrist liberals in confronting racism was their acceptance, fundamentally, of the active/passive distinction, which they framed as the difference between the inherent potential of all humans to be civilized (hence active citizens) and the current level of those who had not yet achieved their potential (hence passive citizens). They assumed that those with potential would take "generations—even centuries—to catch up, even given the most careful, paternalistic attention from benevolent Anglo-Saxons" (Bederman, 1995, 123).[130] This could be seen in the equivocation of Frances Willard, head of the U.S. temperance movement, on issues of racial equality within her own organization, and the strained public disputes she had with Ida B. Wells, Black woman leader, when both of them conducted speaking tours in Great Britain (Ware, 1992, 198–221). This could be seen in the choices made by workers' and nationalist movements regarding how boldly they would be willing to be antiracist.[131]

---

130. Lasch (1958, 321) points out that, in the debate about the acquisition of the Philippines by the United States, the difference between the imperialist and anti-imperialist camp did not revolve around different views on equality; rather, the difference was merely that the anti-imperialists "refused to believe that [Anglo-Saxon] destiny required such strenuous exertions of the American people, particularly when they saw in these exertions the menace of militarism and tyranny."

131. See the multiple ambiguities of Jaurès and the French socialists on the anti-Jewish angers of Algerian socialists. Nor were they ready to consider for Algerian Muslims anything other than "gradual assimilation"—a policy formulated casually and never pursued with any vigor "for lack of interest or because of doctrinal embarrassment" (Ageron, 1963, 6, 29). See also the remarkable account of the difficulties Daniel O'Connell encountered in the first half of the nineteenth century when, as leader of the Irish nationalist movement, he told Irish supporters in the United States that they must take an antislavery position. They refused, with some vigor, and in the end O'Connell softened his public stand. "Instead of the Irish love of liberty warming America, the wind of republican slavery blew back to Ireland. The Irish had faded from Green to white, bleached by, as O'Connell put it, something in the 'atmosphere' of America" (Ignatiev, 1995, 31).

It was extremely rare to hear the kind of statement that Eugene V. Debs (1903, 255, 259), the American socialist leader, made:

> The whole world is under obligation to the negro, and that the whole heel is upon the black neck is simply proof that the world is not yet civilized. The history of the negro in the United States is a history of crime without parallel. . . . We have simply to say: "The class struggle is colorless."

What is more pertinent is to remember that the nineteenth century was "an age of synthesis." And that if Marx synthesized economics and Darwin biology, it was Gobineau who synthesized racism, with at least as much effect (Cohen, 1980, 217).

The racist binary split that was theorized was intertwined with the binary splits of sexuality. As Bederman (1995, 50) says, " '[T]he white man' represented 'civilization' as a single human being defined equally by his whiteness and his manliness." It seemed always important to connect racial differences and ranking with differences in sexuality. This was logical insofar as one was making a biological case for hierarchy. Mosse (1985, 133–134) notes how, from the beginnings of a racist discourse, "the description of blacks included their supposed inability to control their sexual passions."[132] To regard the male racial inferior as someone who cannot control his sexual impulses served also to reinforce the man–woman binary distinction. Not only did it give a further excuse to the White male to act as the protector of the White female, but it also allowed the White male to treat the Black male as he would treat a female.[133] And should the White male somehow falter, he would then be taxed with "neurasthenia," which was seen as a "bodily weakness" that needed to be cured.[134]

Sexuality was in turn linked to nationalism. The prevailing nineteenth-century concept of bourgeois "respectability" spread to all classes via nationalism, which "hardly wavered in its advocacy of respectability." But at the same time, to be "abnormal" was to be not respectable. Enter the physician as "the keeper of normalcy" (Mosse, 1985, 9–10). The full circle of binary constraints thus englobed class, gender, race, and sexuality—all mechanisms of limiting the pervasiveness

132. He continues: "The stereotype of the so-called inferior race filled with lust was a staple of racism, part of the inversion of accepted values characteristic of the 'outsider,' who at one and the same time threatened society and by his very existence confirmed its standards of behavior."

133. MacDonagh (1981, 339) shows how this same relationship was forged in the colonial domination by the British of the Irish. He speaks of "the Irish nationalist conception of the brother island. One says 'brother' because, significantly, the sexual image was in constant use to express the dominator's concept of the relationship between the two islands—with the later Land Acts dimly perceived as a sort of counterpart to the Married Women's Property Acts, and the retention of the power of political decrees subconsciously validated by similar mixtures of assertion and insecurity."

134. "*All* healthy men, savage and civilized, were believed to have a strong and masculine sexual drive. . . . [But] primitive men [were] unable to wield civilized power because they lacked the racial capacity for sexual self-restraint" (Bederman, 1995, 84–85).

of citizenship. Nationalism required giving precedence to those who would, who could be active citizens.

Difference and inequalities of persons of different social origins—orders (*Stände*, Estates), class, gender, race, and education—were not invented in the nineteenth century. They had long existed and had been considered natural, inevitable, and indeed desirable. What was new in the nineteenth century was the rhetorical legitimacy of equality and the concept of citizenship as the basis of collective governance, as the centerpiece of centrist liberal ideology. This led, as we have seen, to the theorizing of the binary distinctions, the attempt to freeze them logically, to make de facto transiting across the boundaries not merely against the rules of society but against the rules of science. What was new as well were the social organizations created by all those excluded by these binary reifications in order to secure their liberation, or at least a partial liberation, from the legal con-straints. Each success of a particular group seemed to make easier by example and more difficult in practice the attempts of the next claimants of liberation. Citizen-ship always excluded as much as it included.

The nineteenth century saw the creation of our entire contemporary concep-tual apparatus of identities. Once rule was no longer an apparatus guaranteed by heritage—a system whose legitimacy, if not whose reality, the French Revolution had definitively undone—identities were required to delineate who had and who didn't have the right to power and wealth. The identities of the powerful were the most urgent. They were, however, relational—that is, they identified not only who they were but who they were not. In creating their own identities, the powerful thereby created the identities of the others.

The concept of the bourgeois preceded and provoked the concept of the pro-letarian/worker. The concept of the White preceded and provoked the concept of the Black/Oriental/non-White. The concept of the masculine male preceded and provoked the concept of the feminine female. The concept of the citizen preceded and provoked the concept of the alien/immigrant. The concept of the specialist preceded and provoked the concept of the masses. The concept of the West pre-ceded and provoked the concept of the "rest."

Concepts preceded and provoked organizations. But organizations institution-alized concepts. And it was organizations/institutions that guaranteed heritage for some and an oppositional role for others. Of course, all these categories were ancient, but they had not been previously defining concepts of one's identity in the modern world. Before the nineteenth century, identities were still a matter of "orders" (*Stände*), and persons were defined by their family, their community, their church, their station in life. The new categories were the mark of the new geoculture of the modern world-system, informed and dominated by the ideol-ogy of centrist liberalism, which came in the course of the nineteenth century to dominate mentalities and structures.

André Dutertre, *Murad Bey.* In Napoleon's *Description de l'Egypte/Etat Moderne* (Paris, 1809–1828). When Napoleon invaded Egypt at the end of the eighteenth century, he brought with him a large team of scholars, who produced an enormous work of reference entitled *Description de l'Egypte.* It would be one of the foundation stones of Orientalist knowledge. This is how one of the principal leaders of the military resistance is portrayed by an artist on the team. (Courtesy of Beinecke Rare Book and Manuscript Library, Yale University)

5

Liberalism as Social Science

The values liberals hold dear are absolute not relative values. . . . Where recognized, the liberal order of justice is eternal, immutable and universal.
—D. J. MANNING (1976, 79)

I do not know which makes a man more conservative—to know nothing but the present or nothing but the past.
—JOHN MAYNARD KEYNES (1926, 16)

[W]e tend to overstrain a new principle of explanation.
—FREDERICK A. VON HAYEK (1952, 209, N. 9)

The century stretching from the defeat of Napoleon to the outbreak of the First World War has been called the Age of Steam, the Age of Nationalism— and the Age of the Bourgeoisie. Defensible names all, but it might well be called, too, the Age of Advice.
—PETER GAY (1993, 491)

The French Revolution, as we have been arguing, had enormous consequences for the realities of the capitalist world-economy. It led to the construction of the three modern ideologies—conservatism, liberalism, and radicalism—and then to the triumph of centrist liberalism as the basis of the world-system's geoculture. It led to the construction of the liberal state in the core zones of the world-economy. It led to the emergence of the antisystemic movements and then to their containment. And it led to the creation of a whole new knowledge sector: the historical social sciences. Hayek sums up (1941, 14) the impact of the French Revolution on our knowledge systems thus:

> In the first place, the very collapse of the existing institutions called for immediate application of all knowledge which appeared to us as the concrete manifestation of that Reason which was the Goddess of the Revolution.

In this field, too, centrist liberalism would come to be triumphant. It is the story of this other pillar of the nineteenth-century world-system (one that lasted indeed for the first two-thirds of the twentieth century as well) that we wish to tell now in order to complete the picture of this triumph of liberalism in the nineteenth century.

The real social world changed remarkably during the nineteenth century. But the ways in which we perceived, analyzed, and categorized the world changed even more. To the extent that we do not take cognizance of the latter, we exaggerate the former. What had changed most in the real social world was the wide acceptance of the twin doctrines that were consecrated by the French Revolution—the normality of change, and the sovereignty of the people. For those who were immersed in the politics of the world-system, it now became urgent to understand what generated normal change in order to be able to limit the impact of popular preferences on the structures of the social system. This is the task for which the historical social sciences and its new conceptual language were invented.[1]

To be sure, social analysis and social theorizing were ancient activities, and eighteenth-century Europe in particular was the locus of important theoretical debates that we might find useful to read still today, were we to read them. However, this prior tradition of social analysis was not what we call today social science. The social science that was invented in the nineteenth century is the systematized, organized, and, yes, bureaucratized research on how our social systems operate, and in particular on how the modern world-system operates. This "social science" was conceived of as a knowledge activity that was to be distinguished from, and somehow situated between, "humanities" or "letters" on the one hand and "natural science" on the other (Lepenies, 1989).

THE INVENTION OF THE "TWO CULTURES"

The period between 1789 and 1848 was one of great confusion, in terms of both the content of the emerging ideologies and the content and structure of the emerging knowledge systems. Neither the terms to be used nor the boundary lines to be drawn, nor even the number of basic categories (the key question being whether there were two or three) had yet been clearly decided, and certainly these were not yet in any way institutionalized. At that time, these political and intellectual battles

---

1. See the discussion by Brunot and Bruneau (1937, 617) of the transformation of the term *revolution:* "The evening of the fall of the Bastille, Louis XVI, uneasy, enquired: 'Is this then a riot?'—'No, Sire, it's a revolution,' the Duke of Liancourt responded. This word was not new, even in the sense of a profound movement transforming an empire. Nonetheless, ... however old it was, it was beginning a new life."

took place for the most part in a geographically very restricted arena: primarily in Great Britain and France, and secondarily in the Germanies. the Italies, and the United States.

Social science did not emerge solely in the shadow of the political consequences for the world-system of the French Revolution. It also emerged in the context of a several-century-long transformation of the knowledge systems that had led, was leading, to a consecration of a concept that we would later call the "two cultures"—a term popularized much later by C. P. Snow's famous 1959 Rede lectures at Cambridge (1965).

Once upon a time, in Europe as elsewhere, there was only one knowledge culture—the search for the true, the good, and the beautiful. It was not divided into differing and opposed epistemologies. Rather, there was a continual struggle as to who would control this single knowledge culture. In medieval Europe, the Church laid claim to being the ultimate arbiter of knowledge. It claimed a privileged access to God's truth. In a sense, all knowledge in its view was theological. When Europe rediscovered, primarily via the Arabo-Muslim world, the knowledge of the ancient Greeks, the Church sought to absorb it as part of theological knowledge, as for example by St. Thomas Aquinas.

The creation of the modern world-system was accompanied by a long effort of nontheologians, who called themselves philosophers, to liberate themselves from the heavy hand of the Church. They argued in self-justification that human beings could acquire knowledge through the direct use of their intellects without passing through the straitjacket of revealed knowledge that had a special institutionalized guild of interpreters—the theologians. The philosophers argued that there were, as the Church had said, natural laws—of truth, goodness, and beauty. The philosophers insisted that they could perceive these natural laws as well as (if not better than) anyone else. Gradually, between the fifteenth and the eighteenth centuries, the philosophers were able to push the theologians aside and gain equality, even primacy, of place as the purveyors of knowledge.

Among the more practical persons involved in the economic and political institutions of the modern world-system, it was not clear that the philosophers offered much greater help than the theologians. Their work seemed too abstract, with too little immediate practical consequence. The universities, which had originally been the bailiwick of the theologians, were sorely weakened by the struggle of the philosophers and the theologians, and receded as a locus of the creation and dissemination of knowledge. Other institutions, like the Collège de France and the Royal Society in Great Britain, emerged as substitutes.

By 1750, there was great confusion and uncertainty about where and how knowledge could be constructed. There was even greater confusion about the names that could describe knowledge categories. There were a large number of terms that described phenomena we today call social science, and they were used indifferently and almost interchangeably.[2]

The natural scientists now began to assert that the search for truth could not depend on the proclamations of either theologians or philosophers but had to be located in the concrete world of empirical observations. Such observations, they argued, could lead to hypotheses that could be verified by other natural scientists and offered as tentative laws, which could then be applied to the solution of practical problems.[3] Although the natural scientists still suffered from lower prestige as of 1800,[4] their arguments nonetheless began to persuade more and more people. Turner (1974, 2:524) argues that, by 1820, *wissenschaftlich* had become "the supreme scholarly accolade" in Germany.[5]

2. "As for the social sciences, the terms physiology, psychology, analysis of ideas and sensations, anthropology, ideology, political economy, political arithmetic, the science of government, *art social,* morals, moral sciences, and science of man were employed indiscriminately, with no consensus as to their meaning" (Manuel, 1956, 130–131; see also n. 4 on p. 391). Baker (1964, 215) points out that Condorcet in 1792 used *science social* and *art social* as equivalent and that, when translated into English, these terms became "moral science" (p. 220).

3. This would then lead to distinguishing science from the nonscientific "arts," although this was not necessarily the only conclusion. Cunningham and Jardine (1990, 14) suggest another outcome, which was still a strong contender as of 1800:

"[The] classification of subjects [around 1800] would have put engineering among the arts, a useful rather than a fine art, while almost all other subjects now taught in universities, such as chemistry, history and theology, would have been sciences. The real division was between the realm of science, governed by reason, and that of practice, or rule of thumb, and apostles of science hoped to replace habit by reason in the affairs of life."

4. "In the early 1800s, science did not enjoy the cultural and institutional security that allowed [many] to see it as the dominant feature of the century. Its prestige was lower than rival forms of intellectual activity, such as theology and the classics, which, even if they did not attempt to explain the natural world, stood as powerful exemplars of culturally sanctioned bodies of knowledge. . . . The word 'science' had not entirely lost its earlier meaning of systematic knowledge, or *scientia*—for some people, logic, theology, and grammar were still 'sciences,' and the term was still used synonymously with 'philosophy'" (Yeo, 1993, 32–33).

5. Still, one should be prudent about how early the distinction between science and the humanities was consummated. Proctor argues (1991, 75): "The German scholar of the late eighteenth century and early nineteenth century was supposed to be a carrier of moral as well as intellectual culture. *Wissen* (science) was equally the study of theology, medicine, law, and philosophy. . . . *Scholarship* or *study* better reflects the meaning of *Wissen* than does the term *science*." Ross (1962, 69) asserts that the terms *philosophy* and *science* were still interchangeable in 1820 but were clearly distinct by 1850, philosophy having become the theological and metaphysical and science the experimental and physical branches of knowledge. And Schweber reminds us (1985, 2–3) that the early Victorian intellectual elite (ca. 1830–1850) still had the "cult of polymathy, [insisting] on mastering all that was known and could be known." He notes that Augustus de Morgan, the first professor of mathematics at the University of London, said that the "minimal standard for an educated man [was one] who knew something of everything and everything of something."

There was, to be sure, resistance to the rising prestige of science. Bonald had already in 1807 noted unhappily in *Des sciences, des lettres et des arts* that this was happening. As Lepenies (1989, 9) notes, he saw "in the widening divorce between science and literature a sign of modernity and thus a symptom of decadence."[6] Carlyle, on the other hand, writing in the *Edinburgh Review* in 1829, seemed far more sanguine about what was happening. He noted that

> metaphysics and moral sciences are falling into decay, while the physical are engrossing every day more respect and attention. . . . [W]hat cannot be investigated and understood mechanically cannot be investigated and understood at all. (Cited in Ross, 1962, 69–70)

In a certain sense, the organizational objective of the natural scientists (the word did not yet exist) was to secede from the combined blur of knowledge activity and create a haven for certain kinds of activity from which others were to be excluded. The natural sciences presented themselves as the sole guardian of the search for truth. They were to be distinguished from letters or philosophy, which was, in the view of the natural scientists, something quite different from the activity in which they were engaged. To succeed in this intellectual "divorce," the natural scientists needed a secure institutional base. They began to ensconce themselves in the universities and to create organizational niches in newly created faculties of natural science.

Once the natural scientists went down this path, the "humanists" felt impelled to respond defensively, by seeking to establish similar organizational niches (Lee and Wallerstein, 2004, esp. chaps. 1–3). In this way, the university began to revive as a locus both of the production and of the reproduction of knowledge systems. But it was a different kind of university than its putative ancestor, the medieval university. By the eighteenth century, the university had descended to being a site, perhaps primarily a site, of "brawling students" (Ziolkowski, 1990, 220–236). In the nineteenth century, it would be transformed into a professionalized university quite different from the medieval university. Scholars earned their basic income within it, and received full-time appointments in what were beginning to be the units of organization we would come to call departments and which presumably were based on distinctions between disciplines. In these departments, the students were now full-time as well and pursuing serious study.[7]

---

6. Bonald was the heir of the earlier, scornful views of Bossuet, who called social science "vain curiosities of knowledge" that could produce nothing useful. This is to be found in his *Traité de la concupiscence*, cited by Hauser (1903, 387), who says that Bossuet placed the doctors of social science "among the collectors of old medals and specimens of insects."

7. "The modern dualistic [teaching and research] professorate, and especially the use of predominantly disciplinary criteria in appointments, presupposes several conditions in the larger academic world. In particular, it presupposes the existence of well-defined academic communities, the

Such a structure took a while to construct. It would not be easy. Oxford adopted new statutes in 1800 and 1817, creating honors both in Literae Humaniores (classical studies, history, languages) and in science and mathematics (Engel, 1974, 1:307). The distinction between faculties of letters and of science dates from 1808 in France (Aulard, 1911). Nonetheless, as late as 1831, Sir William Hamilton still believed it necessary to write an article, "Universities of England—Oxford," in the *Edinburgh Review* (53, June, 384–427) in which he called upon the university to realize that "education had to be conducted by professionals who taught one subject they knew well, rather than by college tutors each of whom had to teach all subjects, though not qualified to teach any particular subject in depth" (cited in Engel, 1974, 313). The scholars were now beginning to find their appropriate and different places within the universities. The economic base for scholars now became double—university appointments and royalties from books, the latter more important for the humanists than for the natural scientists.[8]

The epistemological difference and quarrel between "science" and the "humanities" was being institutionalized. Science was being defined as an activity empirical in method, in search of general laws in objective, and consequently as quantitative as possible in description. The humanities were being defined as hermeneutic in method, considering general laws to be reductionist illusions, and consequently qualitative in description. Later, we would come to call this the difference between a nomothetic and an idiographic epistemology. Furthermore, it was more than a simple difference between epistemologies. Each side tended to consider the other side as engaged in activities that were intellectually dubious, if not useless and even harmful.[9]

---

reputation of whose participants can be at least roughly assessed by local administrators as a basis for their decisions about appointments" (Turner, 1974, 2:510).

"[T]he rise of *Wissen* in the German university, coupled with restrictions on and higher standards for admission to the university and the professions, had a pronounced . . . effect on students.

". . . [They] had to study more diligently because of the increased value placed on scholarship and increasingly rigorous professional examinations" (McClelland, 1980, 202).

8. "We should also note the importance of the *professionalization* of intellectuals [in the nineteenth century]. In the eighteenth century, philosophers were protected by, received stipends from, and were otherwise supported by powerful people. In the nineteenth century, they became financially more autonomous, for two reasons: importance of university appointments on the one hand, and the development of the sales of their books and hence of royalties on the other hand" (Rosanvallon, 1985, 169, n. 2)

9. By the mid-nineteenth century, Renan would predict that historical and critical studies would fall into a "deserved neglect" (cited by Super, 1977, 231). This was what made positivism a fundamental challenge to religious belief. It "questioned the ability of human beings to enter into any meaningful theological discussion at all, and nothing could be more fundamental than that" (Cashdollar, 1989, 6–7). Still, as Peter Gay observes (1993, 448): "Even devout Christians, though troubled by the drift away from religion, subscribed to the proposition [in the Victorian era] that theirs was the

In 1859, as president of the British Association for the Advancement of Science, Prince Albert asserted:

> The domain of the inductive sciences . . . is the domain of facts. . . . We thus gain a roadway, a ladder by which even a child may, almost without knowing it, ascend to the summit of truth. (Cited in Benson, 1985, 299)

To which John Henry Newman responded by saying that science simply "brings us phenomena. . . . We have to take its facts, and give them a meaning" (cited in Benson, 1985, 300). And Matthew Arnold further specified: "The humanist's task was to put what is 'only' knowledge into relation with our sense for conduct, our sense for beauty." (cited in Benson, 1985, 301).

Romanticism as a movement emerged in large part as a response to the increasing scorn by the natural sciences of all that was literary and metaphysical. As Dale argues (1989, 5):

> The essential intellectual history of the nineteenth century may fairly be described as a search [by the humanists] for an adequate replacement for the lost Christian totality, an effort to resurrect a saving belief, as Carlyle poignantly put it, on the ashes of the French Revolution. . . . [Romanticism remade] Christianity for the modern world, secularizing it as a metaphysical idea of social and individual wholeness.[10]

It is in this context that the need for a coherent understanding of social reality, the source of ordinary change, led to the construction of the social sciences—in effect, to new kinds of disciplines.[11] The natural scientists and the humanists both laid claim to controlling this emergent arena of knowledge. The scientists argued

---

scientific century. The conviction was so common, and so commonplace, that it requires virtually no documentation."

10. Yeo argues (1993, 65) that science and romanticism were less antithetical than related dialectically in a common search "to create an audience for their activities; in some cases they saw themselves as fighting over the same clientele." Knight adds to this the observation (1990, 8) that "the self-image of the new 'men of science' was to be largely constituted by Romantic themes—scientific discovery as the work of genius, the pursuit of knowledge as a disinterested and heroic quest, the scientist as actor in a dramatic history, the autonomy of a scientific elite."

One of the reasons the term *scientist,* which Whewell had invented in 1833, was not generally adopted in Great Britain until the close of the nineteenth century was that "some of the important men of science, such as Michael Faraday and T. H. Huxley, preferred to think of their work as part of broader philosophical, theological, and moral concerns" (Yeo, 1993, 5).

11. Henri Hauser wrote in 1903 (p. 5) that "the times following the French Revolution were eminently times of social dislocation, of class conflict, of open reflection and open criticism. No reason then to be astonished that it was following the French Revolution, and particularly in the second half of the nineteenth century, that the social sciences, for the first time, emerged fully into the sunlight."

Hauser also noted the impact of the Paris Commune on the institutions of knowledge: "After the terrible repression of May 1871, it seemed more necessary than ever to move social problems from the domain of the street to the domain of science. Furthermore, the Republic of September 4, like its earlier

that the rules of scientific method applied to human activity just as they applied to physical or biological activity, because the rules of scientific analysis were universal. The humanists argued, against this, that humans, unlike the subjects of the enquiries of natural scientists, were conscious actors affecting their own destiny and that therefore any analysis of their activities could not be subjected to the mechanical use of lawlike generalizations.

Which path would the social sciences take? The general answer is that the practitioners of what would be constructed as the social sciences were profoundly split over this question, and remain so to a considerable extent to this day. Some social scientists would opt for a scientistic path, others would opt for a humanistic path, while still others attempted to wiggle in between.[12] Whole disciplines made collective choices, but in addition there were individual choices being made within the organizational framework of each discipline. To appreciate this, we must look successively at (1) the degree to which social science was explicitly linked to social reformism and (2) the efforts to "professionalize" social science, which was linked to the debates about the nature of objectivity and the merits of value neutrality. Then we shall be better able to appreciate how and why what we have come to denote as the separate disciplines of the social sciences came into institutional existence.

SOCIAL SCIENCE AS SOCIAL MOVEMENT

In the wake of the French Revolution, its promises, and its perceived failings, science in general—and later, social science in particular—came to be seen as an

---

incarnation in 1848, needed civil servants. If one didn't want to recruit them among cadres of the imperial era, they had to be trained via a suitable education" (134–135).

12. The debate was intense: "The great revolution in thought brought about by the French Revolution was most notable in the handling of social problems. Ever since Descartes the notion of the unity of all knowledge had been generally prevalent. All phenomena . . . could ultimately be understood by the same method—the mathematical method of the social sciences. With the French Revolution, however, the idea arose that social phenomena constituted a special class, requiring special treatment and a special methodology. Eternally unchanging laws may be valid for the natural sciences, because nature is eternal and unchanging, but human society undergoes constant change (progress) from epoch to epoch. The particular task of the social sciences is therefore not to seek for eternal laws but to find the law of change itself" (Grossman, 1943, 386). But of course, if there were a law of change, then it would be an eternal law, in which case we have historicized nothing.

One could, however, draw the opposite conclusion about human society. One could say that that the traditional guides to social policy—philosophy, classics, and history—"had afforded guidance, if at all, in the form of precedent, precept, or disquisition on the ideal form of government. The new natural sciences seemed to offer the prospect of precise and relevant reasoning" (Checkland, 1951, 48). Checkland reminds us that already in 1783 Condorcet had called upon scholars "to introduce into the moral sciences the philosophy and method of the natural sciences."

alternative path to human betterment. Knight summarizes (1984, 3) this view succinctly:

> It was not political revolution but scientific development which would bring prosperity and reduce misery. This would happen both through science being applied to what were previously activities done by rule of thumb, traditional routines; and also by the general adoption of "scientific" ways of thinking. This was the programme of the Age of Science; an age of innocence and of faith.

It was in this context of innocence and faith that social science began its life in the nineteenth century—not as a set of university disciplines (nor even as a single one) but rather as a social movement, which in the words of L. L. and Jessie Bernard (1943, 33)

> was much more epochal than anything specific it may have accomplished. For it represented the transition from a theologically oriented society to a scientifically minded one. Social Science [in the first two-thirds of the nineteenth century] . . . was not a generic term for all the social sciences; it was the religion of a society in the throes of industrialization, just as theology had been the religion of the old feudal world.

And because it was a social movement, its initial expression was not within the universities but within structures that were called social science associations, the most important of which emerged first in Great Britain and the United States, and later in Germany. These associations were "the product of the urge to understand and correct the social evils of the times . . . , the child of the urge for social reform" (Bernard and Bernard, 1943, 25–26). When later the social sciences became institutionalized within the university structures, they would not lose this focus.[13]

In Great Britain, the earliest of these associations were statistical associations. Those who founded the Manchester Statistical Association were "united by common social ideology, [in particular] a commitment to social reform" (Elesh, 1972, 33). The two principal subjects on which they collected data were public health and education. It was "urbanization which dominated the minds of the statisticians" (Cullen, 1975, 135). Amid the political turmoil of 1832, William Jacob, then Comptroller of Corn Returns for the Board of Trade, called for the creation of a statistical department, giving as his argument that

> the best mode of allaying disquietude and of diffusing contentment on the subject of public affairs is an open and clear disclosure of their condition and management.

---

13. "There was . . . a close link between the new social sciences and a general societal concern about the formation of new political and cultural institutions to cope with the changing social conditions" (Wittrock, 1993, 303). However, see this somewhat different view of what happened: "It is not that a reformist social science 'frustrated' the development of an academic sociology; rather 'sociology' had its origins in the frustration of reform" (Goldman, 1987, 171).

> ... A more general diffusion of accurate knowledge regarding the state of public affairs would tend to check that excitement and party spirit which has often been created by misrepresentation or exaggeration, and has produced an annoyance to the government, and at least a temporary disaffection of the public mind. (Cited in Cullen, 1975, 20)

Jacob was not alone. Abrams suggests (1968, 38) that "in the 1830s the fear that poverty was the father of *sansculottism* was a powerful motive to social research."

In 1856 the National Association for the Promotion of Social Science—otherwise known as the Social Science Association (SSA)—was founded specifically to aid legislation.[14] Rodgers (1952) calls the combination of social reformers, social workers, lawyers, educationalists, economists, doctors, and businessmen who made up its members "an inchoate body" (p. 283), but one that "was pretty confident that everything could be accomplished by Acts of Parliament" (p. 289). Goldman sees the association as less incoherent than that: "[B]ehind its rhetoric of neutrality, its cultivation of a bi-partisan image, the Social Science Association was an essentially Liberal Forum" (1986, 101).[15]

There were parallel developments in the United States. As the Civil War ended in 1865, the American Social Science Association (ASSA) was founded,

---

14. The organization was founded as a result of a joint meeting of the Law Amendment Society and the National Reformatory Union, with the support of Lord Russell, former Liberal prime minister. It "was designed to provide expert guidance for a legislature lacking the commitment and specialised knowledge for social reform" (Goldman, 2002, 58). It went rapidly through two changes of names. First it was called the National Association for the Moral and Social Improvement of the People, then the National Association for Law Amendment, to settle on the permanent name of the National Association for the Promotion of Social Science. Since this name was still a bit long, it came to be referred to as the Social Science Association. Goldman gives the history of the organizational process on pp. 27–66.

These names reflect the "statist" orientation of the SSA: "Its liberalism was of the utilitarian variety, prizing rationality and systematization, largely unconcerned by the degree of control required to effect these aims, and relatively heedless of arguments premised on individual rights" (Goldman, 2002, 133). "In what circumstances did the Association turn reflexively towards state action? Three different types of intervention are evident and may be given the following names: 'emancipatory reforms'; 'protective legislation'; and, most significantly, 'administrative interventionism'" (Goldman, 2002, 266).

And in its belief that "social science would form the basis for enhanced social administration," it was vindicated by its success: "When the SSA disbanded in 1886, *The Times*, which had been its antagonist, was fulsome in its tribute: 'Not a single amendment in law, police, education and the art of national health has ever been carried into effect which had not been first inculcated in season and out of season by the Social Science Association'" (Goldman, 2002, 19, 21).

Goldman (2002, 14) makes the interesting observation that the SSA incarnated the features of Weber's ideal-type bureaucracy "in its reliance on expert and professional knowledge rather than charismatic authorities." It was a voluntary association that "was created, we might say, to fill the gap created in the absence of a competent and well-resourced bureaucracy of the ideal type in the mid-Victorian decades."

15. "[T]he overwhelmingly dominant motive [for empirical research in Great Britain] was the need to collect information that would be useful in bringing about social reform. . . . The self-image

"sponsored by genteel New England intellectuals [. . .] who wanted to understand and improve their rapidly changing society" (Haskell, 1977, vi). But at the same time, in addition to this reform sentiment, Haskell sees the ASSA as involved in

> a Tocquevillean impulse to defend authority, to erect institutional barriers against the corrosive consequences of unlimited competition in ideas and moral values in an interdependent mass society. (1977, 63)

He calls this a "movement of conservative reform"—what I have been calling *centrist liberalism.*

Indeed, Edwin Godkin, who in 1865 founded the quintessential left-liberal magazine in the United States, *The Nation,* was at the same time one of the principal creators of the ASSA in 1869. He wrote of the founding meeting that the ASSA would

> render society a great service if it simply helps to rouse the public into a perception of the fact that there is no subject of greater intricacy, and of greater importance, than the proper adjustment of the relations of men in society; and that with regard to it as with all other subjects, men who have made it a special study are better worth listening to than men who have not. (*Nation,* November 4, 1869, p. 381; cited in Goldman, 1998, 22)

While the social science reform movement was perhaps strongest in Great Britain and the United States, the Association Internationale pour le Progrès des Sciences Sociales was created at a meeting in Brussels in 1862, with delegates coming from Belgium, the Netherlands, Great Britain, France, Germany, Italy, Russia, Switzerland, and the United States (Villard, 1869), but it survived only until 1866 (Goldman, 1987).[16]

---

of the members of the Royal Statistical Society and the Social Science Association was that of social reformer. They thought of social research as a tool for bringing about social reform" (Cole, 1972, 99).

This sentiment was reinforced by the Crimean War, the extension of suffrage in 1867, and the need for conscription: "How could the confidence and support of the whole nation be secured when there was a canker of poverty at the heart of the Empire?" (McGregor, 1957, 156).

What Cole views as incoherence, Goldman (1998, 5) regards as the strength of the SSA: "Its annual congresses . . . helped to bring together provincial and metropolitan Liberal elites and cemented the complex and contradictory amalgam of social interests—religious non-conformists, businessmen, workers, university dons, social reformers, benevolent Whig aristocrats, and the provincial press—that together formed Gladstonian Liberalism, at once traditional and radical."

16. Still, Goldman insists (1998, 5): "It was a powerful example . . . of the resonance of 'social science' and of British liberalism, denoting free trade, free institutions, free expression and representative government, among similar political and professional constituencies on the continent." What Goldman calls "international liberalism" was "compounded of a common faith in scientific method and expertise; a common belief that social problems could be debated and resolved in national and international forums; a common interest in social consensus, measured reform and enlightened public administration; and a common adherence to political freedom, peace and free trade" (17–18).

It was only some time after the unification of Germany, in 1890, that a similar social science movement developed in Germany. It was called the Verein für Sozialpolitik. The Germans were more open about their objectives. Its name spoke not of social science but of social policy. Like the others, it brought together scholars and businessmen, civil servants, and free professionals (Lindenaub, 1967, 6). As Krüger (1987, 71) notes:

> The *Verein* was the manifest link between the dominant socio-scientific paradigm and socio-political conviction. Since the 1870s, the Historical School had emerged as the leading tendency in German political economy. . . . It was accompanied by the prevailing opinion among scholars and the cultured bourgeoisie that the outmoded institutional system should be amended in favour of an improvement in the situation of the working classes. Academic knowledge and socio-political convictions thereby legitimated and stimulated each other. . . . [T]he *Verein* was a "combat patrol of social reforms," that is, a platform for cultured bourgeois commitment to social reforms.[17]

The question was, What kind of reforms? On the one hand, "entrepreneurial circles sometimes put the *Verein für Sozialpolitik* and Social-Democracy in the same category, insofar as they were both accused of being too friendly to the working classes" (Plessen 1975, 59). Indeed, hostile critics accused the academics of the Verein of being *Katheder-Sozialisten,* or professorial socialists (Dorfman, 1955b, 18).

But that's just the point. They were *Katheder-Sozialisten,* not revolutionaries. Although the social reform movement began life in intellectual opposition to what was called the "Manchesterism" of the "Berlin economists" of the period 1820–1850, with their emphasis on the virtues of free trade (Lindenlaub, 1967, 2), the movement was also opposed to Marxist Social-Democracy.[18] Their essential analysis was very centrist:

> The founding generation of the *Verein für Sozialpolitik* believed that the reactionary social attitude of the economic liberal circles and the social-revolutionary commit-

---

17. "The one pervasive characteristic of German social research in the period 1848–1914 was its concern with working-class people and their problems. It was essentially motivated by the need for action and reform" (Oberschall, 1965, 137).

18. "[The mandarin reformers] wanted social reform without Marxism" (Ringer, 1969, 139). In 1897, Gustav von Schmoller, a commanding figure in the Verein and perhaps the leading *Katheder-Sozialist,* gave the opening address at the Cologne congress of the Verein, which was celebrating its twenty-fifth anniversary. He underlined the centrist political location of the Verein: "The Social-Democrats have always emphasized that it was their activity, not ours, which set the ball of social reform rolling. That is from a certain perspective true. Their activity is based on their politically organized power. Social-Democracy represents a powerful class interest. We are a small handful of scholars and humanist practitioners. We could not and did not seek to do what Social-Democracy could and wanted to accomplish. But does that mean that we did not accomplish other things?

ment of the Socialists aggravated social tensions and had to lead to the class struggle and revolution. They thought that only through social reforms could one stabilize the shaky social order. (Lindenlaub, 1967, 4)[19]

Plessen points to the congruence of the sociopolitical program of the Verein and Bismarck's program of social legislation. He goes further, arguing that "Bismarck's path breaking legislation would not have been possible were it not for the work of the Verein für Sozialpolitik" (1975, 127).

PROFESSIONALIZATION AND VALUE NEUTRALITY IN SOCIAL SCIENCE

Despite what might be considered to have been the manifest success of social science as a movement for social reform that was an incarnation of centrist liberalism, the academic half of the combination of academics and middle-class nonacademic reformers grew increasingly uncomfortable about the role that they were playing. The academics sought a more autonomous and a more distinctive role in the social order. This required breaking away from the social science associations and creating professional, exclusively academic structures.

"The entrepreneurs have always accused us of excessive friendliness to the working class. Worker-friendly we have been and wish to be, since we believe that the excessive gap of cultured behavior (*Gesittung*) and income represents the greatest danger for the future, to be remedied by raising up the standard of living of the lower classes of our society and our state. However, that does not mean that we are enemies of the entrepreneurs, whose merits as leaders and officers of the economic army we have always recognized" (Schmoller, 1920 [1897], 26).

Schmoller was very consistent. At the very first meeting of the Verein twenty-five years earlier, in 1872, he said that the founders were concerned about "the deep cleavage that cuts through our society, the conflict that pits entrepreneur against worker, the owning against the propertyless classes, the possible danger of a . . . social revolution" (cited in Rueschmayer and Van Rossen, 1996, 45). Brentano, another founder of the Verein and leading *Katheder-Sozialist,* expressed in a letter to Schmoller his opposition equally to "socialist or absolutist despotism" (cited in Gay, 1993, 469). See also Plessen (1975, 104), who called the Verein "a mediator between the classes."

The centrist position of the Verein was quite similar to that of the British SSA, which "was prepared to recognise the advance of trade unionism, but it sought leave, in recompense, to impose on the unions a series of expedients for industrial harmony calculated to limit their functions and audience. . . . The SSA thrived on such public displays of social solidarity—a manifestation of its self-appointed role in the reconciliation of classes" (Goldman, 2002, 201, 205).

19. Everywhere, centrist liberalism had two basic beliefs that seemed to be shared by social scientists. One was that "the citizen who was to be given full voting rights should be economically secure and educated. For most people, the liberal ideal of the citizen was not more than a model for the future, the achievement of which was the task of each individual" (Langewiesche, 1993, 49). This created the "vision" of a classless society, with a "continued attempt to promote such a development while also trying to guide and restrict it" (Langewiesche, 1993, 52). The second basic belief was the rejection of "violent forms of collective action" and a "commitment to the constitutional state" (Langewiesche, 1993, 41–42).

The academics would now reject the claim of the dilettante to pretend to scholarly knowledge, which had been so widely recognized in the seventeenth and eighteenth centuries (Torstendahl, 1993, 115) and was still being legitimated in the nineteenth century within the framework of the social science associations. Instead, the professionalization of academics was advocated as

> a means of establishing authority so securely that the truth and its proponents might win the deference even of a mass public, one that threatened to withhold deference from all men, all traditions, even the highest values. (Haskell, 1977, 65)

But authority to do what? Dale reminds us (1989, 14) that all the early social science positivists (such as Comte, Mill, and Spencer) felt that "social science theory was meant, in the end, to lead to the regeneration of social order. This, to be sure, is a political objective." One should not miss the antiegalitarian thrust that was the basis of this new tendency. Professionalization was directed against both the pretensions of popular culture and the narrow perspectives of profit-oriented businessmen.[20] This double objective could be accomplished by installing in authority what Haskell calls "the community of the competent."[21]

20. This was most explicit in the United States. "Outraged by the corruption and materialism that democracy had spawned, and rallying around the watchwords, 'civilization' and 'culture,' the 'better sort' of Americans . . . mounted a counteroffensive in the late nineteenth century to recoup some of the authority they had lost in preceding decades. Over and over again, one finds a common idealistic and elitist motive among the leading scholars of the later nineteenth century: a zeal to make 'a higher order of things' prevail over 'the base votaries of Mammon'. . . . Explicitly they were detaching themselves from the loosely structured, nontheoretical, community-based culture of Jacksonian America. Specialization, entrenched in newly created professional guilds, provided a means to these ends" (Higham, 1979, 9).

This was linked in the United States to the politics of the progressive movement, "with its emphasis on nonpartisanship, government efficiency, electoral reform, and the separation of politics and administration. . . . [It sought to shift] political decisions from elected officials to appointed officials; the latter were then to be provided with nonpartisan, expert advice. It was also a political movement in which the presumed excesses of popular democracy—and agitation by the working class—could be tempered by a recommitment to the principles of representational democracy. Social order and the public interest were to be preserved by returning government to the 'better element.' In these times, the 'better element' was not a moneyed aristocracy or landed gentry or clerical hierarchy; it was the well-educated professional class" (Prewitt, 2004, 782).

21. "The community of the competent is . . . a specialized kind of voluntary association, one which offers its members protection against the tyranny of public opinion, even as it compels their submission to professional opinion. When the individual joins such a community, he is elevated above the mass and made independent of it; but at the same time he is deliberately made more dependent on his peers and rendered less able to resist the consensus of the competent" (Haskell, 1977, 75, n. 29).

"[T]he community of the competent had to identify competence, cultivate it, and confer authority on those who possessed it in accordance with universalistic criteria—or, more realistically, criteria that were not in any obvious way personal, partisan, or particular" (Haskell, 1977, 89).

The authority of professional competence required a new "social organization of science" (Wittrock, 1993, 318). This was the research university, a structure that permitted the university to resume its central role in the production, and not merely the reproduction, of knowledge. The rise of the research university was "intimately linked to . . . the rise of the modern nation-state," as a result of which the universities were given "much greater resources than had previously been the case" (Wittrock, 1993, 305, 344).

This did not necessarily mean the abandonment of centrist social reform as an objective, but rather putting its implementation more solidly in the hands of experts.[22] This meant that direct advocacy was no longer safe, since the academics lacked the cover of prominent nonacademic figures. What was necessary was rather to cloak reform objectives in the garments of "objective" knowledge, knowledge that only the scientific experts were capable of establishing and offering to the public.[23]

The trick was to be political without appearing to be political. Furness notes that in the United States in the 1880s, both Herbert Baxter Adams and John Bates Clark believed that unregulated industrial capitalism caused injustices. They found that they could not directly denounce the injustices. Rather, "as they began to achieve scholarly recognition both also began equating moderateness of opin-

22. "Among nonacademics and academic social scientists alike, the tension between reform and knowledge provided an impulse to professionalization" (Furner, 1975, 3). Nonetheless, "[t]he social scientist served his society in the capacity of an expert. Expertise required research. . . . The believer in a useful higher education . . . valued research and performed a good deal of it; he did not sneer at it as humanists were often to do. But it remained for him a subordinate goal. It was always research for some ulterior (and serviceable) purpose, not primarily for the intrinsic rewards of discovery" (Veysey, 1965, 76).

23. "In the area of reformist social values, the social scientists were treading on particularly dangerous ground. The dependence of the universities on the support of the respectable public for funds and students made them anxious both to demonstrate the usefulness of their faculties and to avoid public criticism. College presidents [in the United States] urged their social science faculties to display their vital contribution to democracy. Yet identification with a controversial reform cause or service in the government under political appointment was frowned upon because they risked partisan identification. . . . Rather than risk their status as objective scientists, a status upon which their places in both university and profession rested, they limited their political advocacy to the liberal center, where their values were less conspicuous" (Ross, 1979, 122–123). Ross calls this a "centrist compromise."

Actually, the reformist social scientists were faced with a dilemma, as Hinsley indicates (1981, 286): "The role of the . . . social scientific elite . . . embraced two tendencies that coexisted uneasily. The scientist must spread scientific experience among the people as a means of spiritual uplift and social harmony—salvation would have to be known directly, not through hearsay. Concurrently, though, the drive to exclusiveness, which rested on the assumption that only the few were truly capable or inclined to devote their lives to science, demanded recognition of special status. The latter need impelled the drive against frauds and imposters and efforts to establish means of formal accreditation."

ion with objectivity, and objectivity with scholarly worth" (Furness, 1975, 91). Prewitt points out that searching

> for social theories to buttress politically derived goals . . . is difficult territory, full of traps for the unwary and not easily navigated even by those alert to the inherent contradictions. Can there be a social intelligence that is both useful and in fact used that stands outside partisan advocacy? Social science leaders schooled in pragmatic liberalism . . . have insisted that this can be so. (2004, 782)

The most famous debate about advocacy and value neutrality was the so-called *Werturteilstreit* (values controversy). In 1909, Max Weber and others withdrew from the Verein für Sozialpolitik to found the German Sociological Society, which was to be *wertfrei* (value free). This objective was not, however, as straightforward as it may seem; indeed, it has been plagued by ambiguity ever since. For the social scientists who claimed to be value free nonetheless believed that

> the progress of science would ensure prosperity for all time to come. . . . [S]cience, pursued for its own sake, would enable men to transcend their petty differences; science would triumph over war and social conflict as it had triumphed over ignorance and disease. Science was a harmonizing force, a unifying force. (Proctor, 1991, 96)

It was the particularly difficult political situation of German academics in the Wilhelmine period between 1871 and 1918 that created a very awkward squeeze on social scientists. On the one hand, they were being accused of being hidden socialists, while at the same time the socialists were pressing them to become their open allies. On the other hand, they were under pressure from German nationalists to identify openly with German military and imperial objectives.[24] Value freedom was the ideological expression of "science under siege."[25] Value neutrality involved moral and intellectual wiggling.

But did it work? Two later scholars, Ralf Dahrendorf and Raymond Aron, both deeply influenced by Weber, underlined the difficulties and the moral uncertainties of these arguments—what Dahrendorf calls their "explosive ambiguity." If

24. "Neutrality served to defend against the charge that *sociology* was just another name for *socialism*. But institutional autonomy was not the only social function served by the principle of neutrality. Neutrality was not just a shield, but a weapon: neutrality was used to thwart attempts on the part of feminists, social Darwinians, and (especially) socialists to politicize social theory. It was largely in reaction against these movements that [German] sociologists formulated the ideal of value-neutrality" (Proctor, 1991, 120).

25. Proctor (1991, 68), who continues: "Neutrality was a liberal response to pressures by governments for censorship, industries for practical results, and social movements for relevance. Neutrality was a political statement as well as an ontological position, part of a more general, liberal, vision of the relations between knowledge and power" (p. 70).

Weber's distinction between facts and values, between an ethics of conviction and an ethics of responsibility, is so clear, asked Dahrendorf,

> why did Weber himself find it all but unbearable to live with his distinctions? Could it be that the distinctions are, at the same time, intellectually compelling and impossible to sustain in practice? Are they a prescription for breakdown? (1987, 577–578)

Aron is less harsh in his analysis, but in the end is not very far from Dahrendorf's reservations:

> The originality and the grandeur of Weber derives first of all from the fact that he was and wanted to be both a political person and a scholar, or more precisely to the fact that he separated and united politics and science. Separated: science must be independent of our preferences, pure of any value-judgment. United: science is conceived in a way that it is indispensable to action. . . . Neither science nor reality impose any law; science, which is incapable of prophecy or total vision, leaves man entirely free; each of us must decide for ourselves. . . . [M]an must choose between the gods. . . . History is the story [of] the rivalry of the gods, the conflicts of faith and necessity. (1950, 97–98)

It is perhaps for these reasons that Novick said (1988, 7) that objectivity is like "nailing jelly to the wall." The debate has always centered around what one means by being "disinterested." As Rueschmayer and Van Rossen point out (1996, 150), the Verein claimed as evidence of their disinterestedness "their distance from capital and working class alike"—the fact that they were attacked by both "interested parties." But given the increased political and ideological conflicts *within* the community of scholars, Weber drew the "logical conclusion" (p. 147) that social science had to be insulated from morality and politics.[26]

The arena in which the objectivity of value-neutral social science most manifestly seemed to falter was eugenics. Eugenics was of course intimately linked to a basic characteristic of the modern world-system, its continuing racism—a phenomenon overtly in conflict with the theoretically egalitarian doctrines institutionalized in the geocultural structures spawned by the French Revolution.

When Linnaeus in the eighteenth century formulated a morphology with which biologists classified all biota, it became necessary to explain why, if homo

---

26. Gunnell (2006, 480–481) expresses this position quite clearly: "Weber's statement about the separation of fact and value was less a philosophical imperative than the recognition of the ineluctable difference, by the turn of the [twentieth] century, between the university and politics. . . . His point was not that it was logically incorrect or impossible for social scientists to engage in making value judgments but it was no longer a practicable role. In an increasingly ideologically and culturally pluralized society, the academy was in no position to perform this function. . . . An attempt by social scientists to persist in their moralizing attitudes would undermine their epistemic authority, which was the only kind of authority that they, in effect, now possessed and which was the only source of potential practical influence."

sapiens were in fact a unified genus/species, there seemed to be substantial visual differences between people in different parts of the world. Substantial visual differences are of course a matter of social definition. Few people create or utilize social categories according to the color of human eyes, but many do so according to the perceived color of human skin. By the late eighteenth century the term *race* was used primarily to classify groups differing in skin color.

In the eighteenth century, there were two basic theories about the origins of racial differences—monogenesis, which accorded with the traditional Christian concept of the unity of mankind (Heiniger, 1980, pt. 3); and polygenesis, which asserted clear lines of distinction between the races and thereby "provided a useful rationalization for the apparent historical subservience of non-whites to whites" (Lorimer, 1978, 132). By the second half of the nineteenth century, although polygenesis had been discredited, a sociobiological argument about significant differences between the races came to be articulated to which we have given the label "scientific racism." It presumed the existence of "impassable walls" (Guillaumin, 1992, 25) between biosocially unequal groups. And "significant efforts to popularize this authoritative scientific view were developed (Lorimer, 1990, 369).[27]

Eugenics was a social movement that derived from scientific racism. It called for state action to preserve the "purity" of the races and to favor in various ways the increase in numbers of the race that was considered superior, at the expense of the others. Despite what Hofstadter calls its "fundamental conservatism," it attracted strong support at first from liberal centrists:

> [T]he eugenics movement had about it the air of a "reform," for it emerged [in the United States] at a time when most Americans liked to think of themselves as reformers. Like the reform movements, eugenics accepted the principle of state

---

27. The biological argument did not have to be based on Mendelian principles of heredity. There were those who made the same case based on Lamarckian views. The last of the prominent British Lamarckian biologists, Ernest Macbride, believed that the lower classes were largely Irish who had, he thought, "permanently fixed [racial characteristics that] could not be improved by exposure to better conditions" (Bowler, 1984, 246). Macbride argued that evolutionary change could lessen but never eliminate these presumably racial differences.

Still, Mendelian arguments were dominant. "In the last years of the [nineteenth] century social hereditarianism had already undergone a complex evolution since its mid-century origins; the stage had been set for its tenaciously aggressive, nativistic, and formally eugenic metamorphosis. The vogue of Mendelism in the first decade of the twentieth century only crystallized and added impetus to well-established intellectual and emotional concerns. In the last quarter of the nineteenth century publicists, physicians, proto-social scientists, and social workers had already applied hereditarian explanations to the analysis of almost every social problem. Hereditarian explanations of human behavior had the virtue of seeming to embody the concepts and prestige of science, while at the same time being devoid of verifiable content." (Rosenberg, 1976, 49).

action toward a common end and spoke in terms of the collective destiny of the group rather than of individual success. (Hofstadter, 1992, 167)

"[T]he idea of race [was] linked to the development of nationalisms in Europe [and the pan-European world]; the two facts [were] at least contemporaneous" (Guillaumin, 1972, 37). What Parker (1981, 827, 846) terms "liberal racialism" was part of the search for national identity, one that "led all too easily to hostility to those beyond the pale."

Of course, as we know, eugenics was brought to its most horrendous, but logical, conclusion in Germany with the Nazi program of extermination of lesser breeds. The "reciprocal involvement of science and politics" took on a particularly strong form in Germany, where

> the small community of race hygienists (as eugenicists called themselves there), seeking status and recognition, formed a coalition with politicians of the conservative and radical right. (Weingart, 1989, 260)[28]

It was because eugenics led in Germany to the Nazi conclusion that the liberal center after 1945 so firmly rejected "scientific racism"—to be replaced in its turn by what might be called a scientific antiracism, which would also be put forth as value free.

THE CREATION OF SCIENTIFIC HISTORY

The professionalization of social science took the form, within the universities, of the establishment of distinctive disciplines and the creation of corresponding professional/academic national (and eventually international) organizations for the various disciplines.[29] It did so not as a single discipline, but "fragment[ed] into many sub-disciplines, new organisations, and specialisms" (Goldman, 2002, 356). As we shall see, a discipline, a profession, is "a vocabulary, an organisation, a journal and a conference" (Maloney 1985, 2).

The first discipline to assert its presence in the new university structures was the one with the longest presence as a university category—history. *History* is of course a very ancient term. And it is common today to speak of noteworthy ancient

---

28. Weingart (1989, 280) blames this trajectory of the racial hygienists in Germany on a more general phenomenon, "the institutional inertia of science," which he says "was not in the least disturbed by its political and moral corruption. Only a few scientists . . . saw the connection between the ideology of an apolitical science and its utility to and compatibility with immoral political goals."

29. "[E]ach of the specialized social sciences . . . formally declared its independence of all the others, and each . . . developed the familiar professional apparatus of journals and associations and more or less uniform training curricula at the university level. Intellectual authority now depended upon membership and rank within a readily identifiable community of peers, whose members shared a similar training experience and hence a substantially similar set of evaluative criteria" (Haskell, 1977, 24).

historians. There certainly were always writers who described the "past" and who eulogized important rulers. The major source for these historians had traditionally been the work of prior historians insofar as their written works survived.

What happened in the nineteenth century was the creation of a new concept of appropriate sources for the work of historians. It is sometimes called a "scientific revolution" in historiography, and is associated prominently with the work of Leopold von Ranke. It was Ranke who bequeathed to us the notable insistence that we write history *wie es eigentlich gewesen ist* (as it really happened).[30]

There are two things we should notice in this famous slogan: the belief that it is possible to achieve a true description of the past, and the assumption that not everything that had previously been done in the name of history adhered to this rule. Ranke was asserting the potential existence of an "objective" analysis of the past. For all those who shared this view, the questions ever since have been what renders an account objective, and what it is that historians are writing about. Nipperdey, who considers Ranke the "father" of the idea of scientific objectivity in history, insists (1988, 218) that the core of Ranke's ideas was the strict binding of the historian to both the "sources and their critique (*Quellenkritik*)," which he calls a "methodologically restricted objectivity." Herbst underlines (1965, 216) the contradictions of Ranke-ian historicism: "[A]s idealists they asserted the autonomy of their discipline and of all *Geisteswissenschaften*, while as empiricists they proposed to use the tools of natural science."

Sources are a very empirical concept. Originally (and for a very long time), they were thought to consist only in written documents. Later, the concept was extended to include material objects such as archaeological finds that were available for careful study. Archaeology was used primarily as a mode of studying zones and times for which written sources did not exist or were very rare—a sort of second-best.

But why were written sources the basis of objective knowledge? The principal argument was that they were not created for the eyes of later researchers but somehow reflected immediate reality as seen by the participants of the time. To be sure there was the possibility that such sources could be fakes that were

---

30. "The 'true' historians saw themselves as empiricists who—unlike the chronologists and literati of past generations—had brought the laboratory scientist's tools of observation and analysis to the investigation of past events" (Herbst, 1965, 101).

As is true of everything else about which we attribute origins, Ranke was not the first to come up with such a demand. Burke notes (1988, 190, n. 2) that, already in the sixteenth century, Sleiden had demanded that the historians "*prout quaeque res acta fuit*" and Popelinière had deemed it essential to "*réciter la chose comme elle est advenue.*" But few persons responded to these earlier demands, and consequently neither Sleiden nor Popelinière is today a household name, even among historiographers. Ranke's slogan made its mark because the time was ripe for it.

written later than the source seemed to indicate or were meant as modes of deceiving others at the time they were written. And it was for this reason that sources had to be subjected to *Quellenkritik*. Still, it was considered that there was no substitute for using such sources. Ranke "approached the past as virtually a revelation of God. . . . It was, as Ranke himself remarked, a sort of *Gottesdienst* [church service]" (McClelland, 1980, 173).

Historical research of this sort was "scientific" insofar as it was considered legitimate only if it was linked to empirical evidence. However, the historians were in other ways very unscientific. Most of them were antitheoretical, rejecting any search for lawlike statements that might be inferred from this empirical research.[31] They took this stance essentially because of their opposition to the Enlightenment radicals and their successors who wished to reform the world.[32] Novick believes (1988, 27) that Ranke's "abstention from moral judgment, rather than manifesting disinterested neutrality, [was], in its context, a profoundly conservative political judgment."[33]

And yet this "shrinking" of the analysis of politics to "events in the narrowest sense" (Burke, 1988, 197) served well the interests of the centrist liberals. For, when generalizations were shunned, historical writing became for the first time in the nineteenth century a "national religion" (Barrett-Kriegel, 1988, 264). The reason was very simple. If one was to construct liberal states, there had to be states within which people could create their identities as a "nation" to which they could offer their primary loyalties. The creation of the nation was essential as the basis of the liberal state. And to create a nation, one had to have a state.[34]

The historians were charged with the task of discovering/creating the memory of the historical past for a state. This was true for Great Britain and France, the

31. Ringer (1992, 262) discusses the degree to which Ranke's scientific history was idiographic: "Leopold von Ranke himself described his conception of history in the language of empathy and individuality. . . . Moreover, he was interested in the 'originality' of the 'particular,' not in the general. He believed that [states] represented cultural and moral energies, and that this gave a higher meaning to the struggles among them."

32. This antitheoretical bent could take different, almost opposite, forms. Novick notes (1988, 43) that in the early part of the nineteenth century, the Romanticist bent was to value "the warmth of the unique . . . over the coldness of abstract systems." But in the last decades of the century "it was the cold fact that was celebrated as an instrument of liberation from the suffocating temperature and humidity of overarching systems."

33. Bénéton has a similar view: "Because the Counter-Revolution took the opposing view to that of the Revolution, the tendency of conservatism is to devalue philosophy in favor of sociology and history" (1988, 49).

34. The importance of the existence of a state was reflected in Engels's notorious concept that there were "peoples without history." These included for him the Romanians and the Slavs (Czechs, Slovaks, Slovenes, Croats, Serbs, and Ukrainians/Ruthenians) on the grounds that these peoples had never created states. He exempted the Poles precisely because they had. See Rosdolsky (1964, 87–88).

original liberal states, but it was even more true for Germany and Italy, states to be created in the course of the nineteenth century, and then by extension for everywhere else.[35] The French revolution of 1830 had, as we know, an echo in Poland (under Russian rule).

And this in turn had an impact on German intellectuals, stimulating their concern with national unification. Ranke, for example, wrote a series of articles in 1832 around the theme previously argued by Berthold Niebuhr: "The historical development of a people is a function of its national genius." Ranke concluded that "we have a great German duty: create the true German state which will reflect the genius of the nation" (Renouvin, 1954, 75–76).[36] Younger historians at this time, "skeptical of Ranke's conservative leanings and looking to Prussian leadership in German unification, turned back to Humboldt, Fichte, and Hegel for inspiration." But the failure of the 1848 revolution convinced them, too, "of the primacy of state action and of the ethical rightness of political power." By 1871, conservatives, liberals, and even democrats (radicals) came to share in the "common religion of history" (Iggers, 1983, 11).[37]

The engagement of German historians in the construction of a German nation was matched by the engagement of British historians in what we have come to call the Whig interpretation of history. Great Britain being then the hegemonic power of the world-system, its historians took comfort in the belief that everything that had occurred to put Great Britain in this position was both inevitable and progressive. Manning (1976, 84) explains the logic of this position quite clearly:

> All events which helped to constitute the civil society liberals admire are necessarily progressive and all those which mark resistance to those changes are necessarily reactionary. By definition a civil society is more civilized than a feudal one. In the vocabulary of liberalism, part of the meaning of the word civil is something open

35. Late in the twentieth century, historians began to write about the "invention of tradition" (Hobsbawm and Ranger, 1992). They noticed this phenomenon first of all in the "new" postcolonial states that were being created at the time, but also in Europe in the thirty to forty years before the First World War (Hobsbawm, 1983, 263).

36. Revouvin further points out (1954, 164) that the writings in the 1840s of Savigny, the historian of legal systems, and Jacob Grimm, the historian of language, "had the same preoccupations as found in the writings of political history: to discover the antecedents that enabled one to show the close relationship of Germanic populations."

37. Iggers (1983, 42–43) sees the very concept of historicism developing. To Goethe's and Humboldt's concept of individuality, now applied to collective groups, and Herder's historical optimism ("a hidden meaning in the flow of history") there was added later "the concept of the primacy of the state in the nation and in society." The three concepts together "were to provide the foundations for the theoretical assumptions of much of German historiography in the nineteenth and twentieth centuries."

and progressive, and part of the meaning of the word feudal is something closed and reactionary.[38]

German historicism and the Whig interpretation of history (which was in fact a variant of historicism) concurred in placing the progress of the nation at the center of their analysis and their concerns.[39]

France, like Great Britain, began to make history central to the national state it was creating. Hauser (1903, 119) sees the July Revolution as the turning point:

> Precisely because it wasn't an "historic" royalty, the July monarchy could neither ignore history nor dispense with it. . . . Under the direct influence of political events, history turned towards questions of organizing society. The new state had every interest in having the Guizots, the Thierrys, using memories of medieval France and the lessons of English revolutions, create for it a new legitimacy founded on reason.

But whereas the July Monarchy legitimated history in order that historians legitimate it, it was the traumatic events of 1870–1871—defeat of France by Germany, the Paris Commune—that finally established history as central to integrating the state. The newly established Third Republic turned to the historians to help reinvigorate and reunify the nation by reforming the curriculum of the secondary school system. Logue (1983, 80) describes the thinking of leaders of the republic's education system this way:

> The hitherto ignorant and superstitious masses were seen in those early years [after 1875] as less formidable potential enemies of the republic than those middle- and upper-class youths who had received their education at the hands of priests, lay brothers, and—worst of all—Jesuits. It was disunity within the elite that most worried the liberals of the late nineteenth century, not disunity between the elite and the masses. . . . A truly republican and liberal elite would be the natural leaders of a democratic people.[40]

Hobsbawm (1983, 270), however, sees this emphasis on national history as motivated more by the fear of radical tendencies, arguing that the historians invented

38. "To liberalism, time was the universal friend, which would inevitably bring greater happiness to even greater numbers" (Schapiro, 1949, 13). Skinner (1965, 15) points out how this nineteenth-century view accorded with the economics of the Scottish Enlightenment: "[T]he exchange economy was seen to be the final product of a development which began with the primitive state. . . . [T]hey concluded that a higher degree of personal liberty was appropriate to the conditions that actually faced them."

39. Skinner (1965, 21) calls the Whig interpretation of history "a remarkable anticipation of Marx," at least about the "paternity of the new order" if not about its "funeral." But this is merely one more way in which Marxism and liberalism found common ground in the nineteenth, and indeed in the twentieth, centuries.

40. Gabriel Monod founded the *Revue historique* in 1875. Monod believed that there was a deficiency in the French historical tradition. "He was confident that the preconditions for such a

"imagery, the symbolism, and the traditions of the Republic" to control the working classes. The "men of the centre" (he is talking of the Radical Socialists) did this by "masquerading as men of the extreme left."

No doubt the centrist liberals were seeking to limit both the conservative forces, whom they identified with the Church, and the radical forces that had shown their face and vigor in the Paris Commune. They were able to make use of the new scientific history to establish in the public mind a past that could unify a nation, and render national identity the basis for a patriotism that would stabilize the state. It was not, to be sure, the only mechanism. Service in the armed forces for young men integrated and socialized them as much as the public school system. It was particularly effective for those who came from rural districts and from minority ethnicities. The construction of national monuments and the invention of public ceremonies (such as Bastille Day in France) were also part of the systematic campaign (Hobsbawm, 1983, 271).[41] But these, too, were the product of the work of the historians. The past was thus becoming secure. But what about the present?

THE CREATION OF THE NOMOTHETIC DISCIPLINES

Creating and reinforcing a national identity was only part of the liberal agenda, however important. A strong national identity served to legitimate the states and limit severely the justification of alternative and potentially oppositional loyalties—to class, religion, ethnicity, or language community. But the liberal states, in order to function smoothly and in particular to anticipate the antiliberal pressures

---

professional orientation existed in France, but he impatiently complained that the spirit of professionalism suffered from stunted growth." He sought a reform of the university to further this end. "Pending the creation of such an academic historical profession, he hoped that the *Revue historique* would serve . . . to encourage young men who intend to enter the career of history to adopt the methods of scientific scholarship" (Keylor, 1975, 52).

Such science was not without political implications for Monod. "Monod believed that German historians, and specifically the *Historische Zeitung*, had contributed greatly to German reunification. He hoped that the *Revue historique* would also contribute to a political objective: the revitalization of the French national spirit in the aftermath of 1870" (Stieg, 1986, 6).

Jules Ferry, the French minister of education, essentially had similar goals in mind. In a speech printed in the *Revue internationale de l'enseignement* in 1883, he called on professional historians to develop scientific ideas that could oppose "ideas of utopia and of error which, . . . when not regulated and enlightened by science, could become the spirit of disorder and of anarchy" (cited in Weisz, 1979, 83).

41. Trouillot (1995, 124) notes that this new emphasis on tradition went beyond France: "The second half of the nineteenth century saw an unprecedented attention to the systematic management of public discourse in countries that combined substantial working classes and wide electoral franchises. . . . [Nationalist celebrations] taught the new masses who they were, in part by telling them who they were not."

of the dangerous classes, needed to understand the ongoing reality of the present. This came to be the function of the three nomothetic social sciences: economics, sociology, and political science.

The first thing to notice about this trinity is that it is a trinity. When writing about the past (the role of history), the emerging university structures combined the so-called economic, political, and social domains into one single "discipline." But as soon as one engaged the present, the social scientists insisted that these were three separate domains, to be studied separately.

Wherefore this division? There is only one source—the insistence of liberal thinkers (but not of either conservative or radical ones) that the signal feature of "modernity" was the differentiation of the social structure into three compartments that were quite different from each other. They were so different that they had consequently to be isolated from each other in practice, and hence analyzed quite distinctly. These three domains were the market, the state, and the civil society. It was from the theoretical distinction of these three domains, which presumably had been differentiated as the outcome of modernizing, that the universities derived the three disciplines: economics for the study of the market, political science for the state, and sociology for the civil society.

Centrist liberalism has always devoted itself to the prudent and competent reform of institutions, and in the mid-nineteenth century this objective posed a fundamental question for the emerging social sciences studying the present, as we have seen. Were they to constitute themselves as social activists or merely as those who produced the analyses that the social reformers could use to implement their objectives? When thinkers like Mirabeau and Condorcet first used the term *social science,* they had made it synonymous with *social art,* which "carried practical and reformist connotations as a rational guide to public policy and social reconstruction" (Goldman, 1987, 141). The initial result had been the creation of the social science associations, as we have discussed. But in the late nineteenth century, the arena shifted to the universities and to the creation of disciplinary departments that would produce the needed specialized professionals.

1. Economics

The first of these nomothetic disciplines to be institutionalized was economics. The name *economics* was a late invention. Up until the late nineteenth century, the usual term in Great Britain and the United States had been *political economy.* In France, there was somewhat of a struggle between the terms *social economy* and *political economy.* A similar split existed in the Germanies, where the term *national economy* (*Nationalökonomie*) competed with *Volkswirtschaft,* with all the ambiguity of attaching the term *Volk* (literally "people," but with a strong ethnic overtone) to the term *Wirtschaft* (usually translated as "economy" with or without the prefix *Volks-*). Why did all these other terms come to be rejected eventually in favor of the shorter term *economics?*

The term *political economy* suggests that there is some relation between the political and economic spheres of life. But what kind of relation? One of the earliest expressions was the so-called Scottish historical school of the eighteenth century, which included such diverse figures as Adam Smith, Adam Ferguson, William Robertson, and John Millar. Diverse perhaps, but they shared some clear premises, both about history and about political economy. Their macrohistorical imagery was that of a world in which mankind had passed through a progressive succession of different stages. The most frequent list of stages at the time was that of hunting, pasturage, agriculture, and commerce. The basis of the list was a sort of "techno-economic determinism."[42]

If these men spoke of political economy, it was because they analyzed these successive forms of economic structuring, and particularly that of commerce, as occurring within a polity—that is, a state. They all therefore placed emphasis on the "mode of subsistence," a phrase invented by Robertson (Meek, 1967, 37). And they all believed that if one knew the state of property, one would know something about the political system, because there was a "causal connection between property relationships and the form of government."[43] For a later unremitting believer in the primacy of the market like Friedrich von Hayek, the eighteenth-century political economists would be seen as persons who could not decide whether they were scientists or moral and social philosophers (Hayek, 1952, 13). And neither they nor successive generations had particular training in the kinds of skills we would today associate with economics.[44]

Hayek was right, of course. Adam Smith in fact occupied the chair of moral philosophy at Glasgow University. And this concern both with moral philosophy and history explains the great difference between the political economy of what we now call the classical economists (from Smith to Marx) and the so-called neoclassical economists who came to define the field in the late nineteenth century.

> The classical economists hoped to unravel the skein of history, to find the great central forces which move (determine?) the course of nations and empires. . . . [T]hey were engaged in the delineation of the "magnificent dynamics." By contrast, the task set by [the neoclassicists] Walras and Marshall seems mean and petty, but it was

42. Meek says (1976, 242) that "we should look upon [this theory of stages] as the first great theoretical crystallization of a set of wider notions and attitudes—the law of unintended consequences, the idea of a social *science*, the comparative method, the notion of techno-economic determinism, and the principle of cultural evolution."

43. "Society, they argued, developed blindly" (Meek, 1967, 38). It was not "great men" who fashioned the state, but the underlying economic realities.

44. Fetter points out (1943, 60) that, as late as 1870, every so-called political economist in the United States was trained in something else—"theology, moral philosophy, literature, languages, law, practical politics, journalism, business, or some branch of the natural sciences. In political economy, they were all self-trained amateurs, who, as it were, happened to wander in this field."

their efforts to analyze the mechanics of markets that produced the problem-solving economics we now possess. (Gordon, 1973, 255)

The ambiguous relation of the market and politics had its parallel in France. Before the French Revolution, it was the Physiocrats who held center stage. The term *physiocracy* means the "rule of nature." And the nature that ruled for them was the land, the sole source of productive labor and therefore of net profit. Their emphasis on distinguishing who or what was productive from who or what was sterile became a constitutive element of political economy, even if there were differences of views as to which groups were indeed the productive groups. The Physiocrats, like the Scottish political economists, were materialist, not rationalist. Their economic determinist views were endorsed strongly by the words and deeds of the leaders of the French Revolution.[45]

But they were more than mere economic determinists. After Thermidor, their legacy was continued by a group called the *idéologues,* for whom, however,

> political economy was not an economism. It was one means among others to achieve the happiness of a society founded on the rights of man. The affluence which would result from understanding the laws of economics would render men "more virtuous," more able to govern freely. Political economy took its place alongside other moral and political sciences. The [French] Institute [which included an Academy of Moral and Political Sciences], created in 1795 [on the instigation of] the *idéologues,* was intended to promote [such good government]. (Le Van-Mesle, 1980, 272–273)

However, these views came to be considered dangerous, even subversive, first by Napoleon, and then even more so by Louis XVIII and the leaders of the Restoration. Political economy thus fell into disgrace. However, political economy soon returned to acceptability in France. It did so by revising its self-presentation. It shed its subversive image and emphasized rather the degree to which it was a "centrist" doctrine. As such, of course, it was attacked both on the left and on the right. It would nonetheless seek to establish its political utility by demonstrating the link between what it defined as the centrist principles of the French Revolution and economic liberalism. In 1845, the political economist Eugène Daire wrote:

> The glory of the French Revolution is to have inscribed in the law, on normal bases, the constitution of liberty, property, and family. . . . Today the task of men who accept these principles is simply to make them realized completely in reality, and to combat energetically any retrograde or so-called progressive doctrines which tend to

---

45. "Rationalism received a mortal blow. The [French] revolution and its aftermath demonstrated that moral and legal relationships did not depend on reason alone, that economic interests were a more important factor in determining the political position of each group in the population" (Grossman, 1943, 387).

undo the work of our fathers, and to deprive future generations of the rewards of the blood spilled on their behalf. (Cited in Lutfalla, 1972, 495)

It is because political economy became so centrist that some left Catholic thinkers sought to oppose "social economy" to "political economy." The 1835 catalogue of the Faculty of Social Sciences of the Catholic University criticized political economy for concerning itself only with how wealth was accumulated and failing to discuss the fact that the wealth was badly distributed.

> Thus the fortune of some was based on the misery of others. And society, awakened from its dreams by the clamors of the poor, discovered at last that it had lost in security what it had gained in opulence. (De Caux, 1835, 35)

Hence, it followed that there was need for a course in *social* economy.

The voice of these left Catholics was not heard by the political elite, and the clamors of the poor (De Caux was no doubt referring to the uprising of the *canuts* in Lyon) were not to find a significant political expression until the Revolution of 1848. One of the noteworthy decisions of the provisional government in 1848 was to abolish the chairs of political economy in the university, precisely because political economy was seen as linked to social conservatism, despite the vain protests of the Society of Political Economy. In turn, the Academy of Moral Sciences responded to the appeal of the government by asserting that it was "not sufficient to restore material order by force if one did not restore moral order" (Le Van-Mesle, 1980, 286).

The radicalism of the Revolution did not last long, as we know, but political economy was not restored as a discipline. Perhaps it was considered too centrist and insufficiently conservative in the aftermath of the revolution. By 1864, however, Victor Duruy persuaded the emperor to found a chair of political economy in the Law Faculty. He argued that Great Britain had avoided a bloody revolution in 1848 precisely because "the principles of political economy were widespread in all strata" (Weisz, 1979, 87). France was returning to centrist liberalism.

In the Germanies, the Cameralism of the eighteenth century, which emphasized the economics of public administration, gave way to the "national economy" of the early nineteenth century. *Staatskunst* (the art of the state) was replaced in Prussia by *Staatswissenschaft* (the science of the state), of "governing in relation to economic processes" (Tribe, 1988, 8). And once again, the simple advocacy of market principles was replaced by what was called in Germany *historical economics,* the last defense of a political economy that was as much political as it was economic. In effect, Germany was still holding on to a variety of political economy at a time when Great Britain, the United States, and France were finally ready to bury it in favor of (neoclassical) economics.

The big shift occurs with the change of name. *Political economy* became *economics*. The widely influential W. S. Jevons suggested this in 1879.[46] But it was Alfred Marshall who institutionalized this change when he became professor of political economy at Cambridge in 1884. He had already written a text entitled *The Principles of Economics* in 1881. And in 1885 he argued that the Statistical Society should change its name to the Society for Economic Science and Statistics. He would proceed to be a founder of the British Economics Association (later the Royal Economics Society) in 1890, which he and his followers firmly controlled (Kadish, 1982, 143–144, 152; Coats and Coats, 1970). By 1903, Marshall was able to establish Economics Tripos as an undergraduate course at the University of Cambridge.

What did Marshall institutionalize, however? One way to describe it is as a shift in the focus of economic enquiry:

> The change of name signified a break with a "classical" economics preoccupied with the capital and labour in the production of value and the distribution of national wealth, and relaunched economics as a science of exchange and price formation. In place of a theory of production and distribution centred on rent, profit and wages with their corresponding agents of production—landlords, capitalists and labourers—the new science of economics became a theory in which the allocation of scarce resources was effected by the calculations of an abstract economic agent. A new theory of value turned on the interactions of these self-interested agents, whose drive to satisfy their own wants led them in turn to satisfy the needs of others and hence create market prices. (Tribe, 2005, 116–117)

Another way to describe it might be to say that neoclassical economics ended definitively the connection of economics and history. The marginalization in Marshall's Cambridge program of the economic historian William Cunningham is notorious, and his actions seem to have led Cunningham to leave Cambridge by 1891. There were no doubt personality conflicts between the two men. Still,

---

46. In the preface to the second edition of *The Theory of Political Economy*, revised and enlarged in 1879, Jevons writes (xiv): "Among minor alterations, I may mention the substitution for the name Political Economy of the single convenient term *Economics*. I cannot help thinking that it would be well to discard, as quickly as possible, the old troublesome double-worded name of our Science. Several authors have tried to introduce totally new names, such as Plutology, Chrematistics, Catallactics, &c. But why do we need anything better than Economics?"

The issue of the name had long been a problem. In the first half of the nineteenth century, Robert Whately defended political economy against "those who saw it impugning the social arrangements of the day." He assured them that "the first half of the title of Political Economy was really a misnomer." He himself suggested the name of Catallactics, but that did not catch on. (Checkland, 1951, 56). Checkland credits Whately with being "one of the founding fathers of the concept of a neutral science of political economy."

Geoffrey Hodgson disagrees with the idea that Marshall was hostile to economic history as such. Hodgson points to Marshall's sympathetic praise and support of the German historical school. He also points to the fact that he did not side in the *Methodenstreit* with Carl Menger despite the fact that Menger, like Marshall, was a pioneer of marginal utility theory.[47]

Perhaps the correct way to interpret Marshall's organizational transformation of economics is to see it as a way to consolidate the ability of economists to influence policy making more effectively by becoming professional and abstaining from direct partisanship—in short, of being centrist liberals.[48] To guarantee that, Marshall needed to control the program of university training by creating an economic orthodoxy, the true source of his dispute with Cunningham.[49] Church then explains that the very process of professionalization led economists away from historicist leanings.[50] But at the same time, this pro-

47. Marshall seemed more sympathetic to the position of the German historical school. Marshall had himself studied in Dresden and Berlin, and was in contact there with Wilhelm Roscher. "Most specifically, in contrast to Menger, *Marshall did not reject the problem of historical specificity:* unlike Menger he saw it as a legitimate and important question for economists" (Hodgson, 2005, 334).

Reading the great debate between Cunningham and Marshall lends weight to Hodgson's analysis. Cunningham had launched an attack on Marshall (and also Thorold Rogers) in the *Economic Journal* in 1892. He entitled it "The Perversion of Economic History." His basic argument (494–495) was this: "From the point of view of economic theory neglect of patient study of actual fact seems excusable; from my point of view it is disastrous because it prevents the economist from finding out the narrow limits within which his generalisations are even approximately true."

Marshall replied in the same issue, saying (1892, 507): "Dr. Cunningham is mistaken in supposing that my book proceeds on 'the underlying assumption . . . that the same motives have been at work in all ages, and have produced similar results . . . and that the same laws hold good.' On the contrary, the chapter on The Growth of Economic Science insists that modern economists are learning from biology 'that if the subject matter of a science passes through different stages of development, the laws of one stage will seldom apply without modification to others.'" Marshall is at least nuanced on the universality of economic laws. Accused by Cunningham of accepting Ricardo's laws of rent as explanatory of the realities of medieval England, Marshall replies (p. 510): "But in fact custom is more or less plastic; and the theory of rent often gives the upper limit to the exactions which can be forced from the actual cultivator by a superior holder, who is in a strong position and is not effectively controlled by the supreme holder, the ruler of the land."

48. This is how Maloney, in his analysis (1985, 2), sees Marshall's three main objectives: "First, he wanted economists to be trained in a body of theory which—without excessive grief—he recognized would be inaccessible to laymen. Secondly, he sought, via the development of welfare economics[,] to give the economist a specialist voice in the art of policy-making. Thirdly, he wanted to enhance the scientific authority of his subject by keeping it clear of political partisanship."

49. Maloney explains (1985, 4) what happened in economics between 1880 and 1914: "[E]conomic orthodoxy, accused on all sides in the 1870s and 80s of both theoretical inadequacy and social irrelevance, resolved this position not by a successful answer to these criticisms, but by capturing a dominant position in which it could largely ignore its critics."

50. "The economists could professionalize more readily around neoclassical theory than around the doctrines of the historical, inductive school. The historical school's view that economic

fessionalization permitted the same economists to rescue economics for social reform.[51]

The emphasis on the ability to influence policy affected the practice of French economists equally, although there economics tended to be located within the Faculty of Law rather than in the Arts and Sciences faculties, as in most countries.[52]

---

generalizations were relative and that each economic problem must be approached *de novo* undermined the academic economist's claims that his superior training made his views more authoritative than those of men without that training. . . . Without the concept that the trained economist had mastered widely applicable principles and specialized techniques unknown to the general public, the economist could make little claim to authority" (Church, 1974, 2:593).

Maloney shares this view (1985, 215–216): "Economists . . . seldom struggle effectively against the world view inherent in the paradigm they choose. Economic paradigms—classical, Marxist, neoclassical, Keynesian—differ above all in their philosophical points of departure. . . . An economist is constrained both by his philosophical point of departure, and by the patterns of factual emphasis to which it leads. His attempts to round out the picture are likely to stick less firmly in readers' minds than the picture's methodological essence will. And such attempts will be enfeebled by the process of professionalization. . . . Professionalization . . . favors just that type of paradigm that takes a particularly selective view of the world."

Away from historicism, then, but not away from public policy. If one goes to the 2008 Web page of the very mainstream Faculty of Economics of the University of Cambridge, one finds the following statement concluding the "Brief History of the Faculty": "Another tradition upheld by current Faculty members is that of involvement in public policy, active on, among other bodies, the Monetary Policy Committee, the Competitive Commission, the Low Pay Commission, and the Accounting Standards Board. As the Faculty of Economics and Politics approaches its hundredth birthday, it remains committed to keeping economics useful" (www.econ.cam.ac.uk/contacts/history.html).

51. Tribe (2005, 130) explains this intention: "Jevons, Marshall, Pigou and Keynes clearly thought the Political Economy of the early nineteenth century a truly 'dismal science,' and sought to create a new science capable of transforming the world. The transition from Political Economy to Economics is therefore, in this reading, not one in which an abstract, formal 'hard' science displaces a broader, more ethical body of knowledge. The abstract, formal science created by Ricardo, McCulloch and their associates was, from the standpoint of the later nineteenth and early twentieth centuries, widely accepted to have been an unfortunate deviation. This was no basis for the construction of a positive science of social reform, and it is this understanding that drove teachers and students alike into the new science of economics. It was the new educational structure of the later nineteenth century that made it possible to elaborate a new alternative."

52. This political pressure transformed the law faculties themselves, as Karady (1976, 281) explains: "In effect, these new courses of instruction, whether economic—political economy proper, the history of economic doctrines, finance, statistics—or juridical—international law, public law, legal history, constitutional law, etc.—had in common that they met the needs less of practicing lawyers that of administrators and higher civil servants, that is governmental personnel. Their introduction represents in a sense an adaptation of the university curricula to the demand for certain kinds of competence, more specifically those linked to the new roles attributed by the reformers to legal training, henceforth called upon to furnish competent political and administrative personnel, while at the same time contributing to legitimating, via this very competence, the power which it disposed. In this sense the transformations of the law faculties cannot be explained without taking into account the ideology of

Nor was this different in Germany, where training in economics had its historicist focus that was linked to the long-dominant role of the Verein für Sozialpolitik.[53]

With this in mind, it seems that one should not think of the famous struggle in the early days of the American Economic Association as one between advocacy and expertise—the usual line of analysis—but rather as a debate of what was the most effective way to achieve appropriate reforms in public policy.

In the United States, the key figure in the late nineteenth century was Richard T. Ely. Ely was trained in Germany at Heidelberg under Karl Knies. He was very impressed by the German historical school and, when he returned, become a professor of economics at Johns Hopkins University in 1881. As early as 1882, he was urging acceptance of the German social legislation of Bismarck (Dorfman, 1955b, 24–25). He formulated a plan to create an association of economists who, as he wrote in a letter in 1884, "repudiate *laissez-faire* as a scientific doctrine" (cited in Coats, 1960, 556).

In 1885, he was one of the founders of the American Economics Association (AEA), of which he became the first secretary. In the AEA's founding statement of principles, the first point read: "We regard the state as an agency whose positive assistance is one of the indispensable conditions of human progress." Its other three points emphasized "the historical and statistical study of actual conditions"; the need to solve the social problems resulting from the conflict of labor and capital; and the insistence that, although the AEA was not partisan, it felt that that a "progressive development of economic conditions . . . must be met by a corresponding development of legislative policy" (Dorfman, 1955, 27).

Ely himself asserted twenty-five years later (1910, 60) that this statement "was a compromise in behalf of catholicity. . . . [E]ach modification represent[ed] what has been called a 'toning-down' process." The compromise did not work. In 1892, Ely ceased being secretary, and although he was later elected president of the AEA for a year, his view that the AEA should engage in relatively public advocacy was rejected in favor of a more "professional" orientation.[54] This did not mean, how-

---

the [Third] republic which was both democratic and meritocratic and which sought to reinforce the professionalization of public service."

53. "[The Verein] was intended not only to encourage scholarly and technical discussions of contemporary economic and social problems but also to exert a guiding influence upon the government and public opinion" (Ringer, 1969, 146). And since in Germany up to just before the First World War, as Oberschall underlines (1965, 139), "social scientist meant actually political economist," this orientation to influencing public policy remained central.

54. "Ely's vision of the American Economics Association as an organization of empirical economists bent on discovering solutions to immediate social problems and on generating widespread public support for those solutions did not materialize. Members of both the classical and historical schools came to reject the notion that the economist could serve as both investigator and popular educator. . . . Most economists grew to believe that the public airing of disagreement would hinder their efforts to

ever, that there was a turn away from seeking to influence public policy, precisely because the "upper and middle classes" saw this as a positive role.[55] It simply meant that the political implications—primarily those of centrist liberalism—of a professional, neutral economics became *sub rosa,* not to be avowed publicly.

2. Sociology

Sociology underwent the same process of professionalization as economics. It was, however, as a discipline somewhat less coy about its commitment to social reform. As is well known, the term *sociology* was invented by Auguste Comte, who considered the study of social relations the culminating positivist activity, the "queen of the sciences." But where can we place Comte's work in the political spectrum? For Koyré (1946, 56), Comte's ideas were those of the ultraconservative Bonald, "dressed-up, or rather disguised in modern garb." Nisbet (1952, 173) gives a similar appreciation:

> Comte himself was no scientist; but through his romantic worship of science, the social structures of family, community, language, religion were removed from the frankly theological and reactionary context in which they lay in Bonald's thought and were given the context and terminology, if not the substance, of science. . . . Comte's work was the means of translating the conservative principles into a perspective more acceptable to later generations of social scientists.

Yet we know also that Comte started his career as the secretary of Saint-Simon, who may be difficult to characterize politically but was certainly someone openly hostile to a Bonaldian view of society. Hayek (1941, 9, 11, 18) sees Comte evolving from a more left position to arrive more squarely in the political center. For Hayek, the two great intellectual forces of the nineteenth century were socialism and positivism (which he preferred to call scientism):

> Both . . . spring directly from this body of professional scientists and engineers that grew up in Paris, and more particularly from . . . the *Ecole polytechnique.* . . .

> [T]hroughout the development of French positivism this rationalist element, probably due to the influence of Descartes, continued to play an important role. . . .

---

affect public policy. How could economists expect outsiders to listen to them if they could not agree among themselves as to the conclusions of economic science?" (Church, 1974, 2:588).

55. "The application of science to government was especially attractive to the upper and middle classes of American society because it promised to reduce conflict and restore order. Unaware or unwilling to admit that social conflict could reflect fundamental value disagreements or structural inequities in the society, the more comfortable social classes attributed the conflicts besetting their society to ignorance or emotionalism that blinded the parties involved to their true interests which, when identified, would surely turn out to be mutually harmonious. The social scientific expert, of course, would help discover that truth which would harmonize the competing interests and bring them into accord with those of the society at large" (Church, 1974, 2:598).

That synthetic spirit which would not recognize sense in anything that had not been deliberately constructed . . . was a strong new element which was added to—and in the course of time even began to replace—the revolutionary ardour of the young polytechnicians.

The other major figure of French sociology in midcentury was Frédéric Le Play. His training was that of a metallurgist, a graduate of the elite École des Mines. What he drew from this education was an aversion to abstract theorizing and the belief that social science was not analogous to physics but rather to "the classificatory and eminently practical [science] of metallurgy" (Goldfrank, 1972, 134). He thus pursued an empirical, observational sociology, quite the opposite of Comte. At the same time, he was a devout Catholic, again the opposite of Comte. But he was what might be called a pastoral Catholic. From this, he derived an aversion to Saint-Simonian rationalism and individualism.

The Revolution of 1848 was a formative experience for Le Play. In a political atmosphere riven between the Party of Order and the working classes, he sought to promote "a reformist social policy" (Kalaora and Savoye, 1989, 100). He founded the Société d'Économie Sociale in 1855, which was specifically concerned with the social implications of economic development for the working classes. He established links with the British SSA and pursued an objective of social harmony, with a conservative coloring:

> Le Play, being a careful but not value-free social scientist, insisted that "social peace" could be achieved only through an understanding of "social reality." That reality . . . consisted of a hierarchy of unequal classes reproduced in the industrial division of labour. He thereby threw out the market-place as a model for social relations, and brought in the *seigneurie,* with the *grande bourgeoisie* acting as the ascendant "social authority." (Elwitt, 1988, 212)

Le Play's reformism was not that of social and economic change but of "moral reforms, reasserting the five bases of social organization: religion, family, property, work, and patronage" (Chapelle-Dulière, 1981, 745). But despite his paternalistic conservatism, Goldfrank (1972, 148) considers him "a curiously contemporary figure: the upwardly mobile conservative (liberal) technocrat hoping to solve 'scientifically' problems perpetuated by the very ruling groups he begs to serve." It is noteworthy that, in Great Britain at the end of the nineteenth century, Le Play was perceived as linked to the new liberalism of the nascent welfare state. He was seen as representing a "third alternative to the anomie of disordered capitalism and the tyrannies of socialism" (Abrams, 1968, 60)—in short, as a centrist liberal.

The other great figure of preuniversity sociology was Herbert Spencer. Spencer was by far the most widely read and esteemed sociologist in the English-speaking world in the last half of the nineteenth century. His sociology was of a totally deterministic variety. He adopted an extreme version of Darwin's "survival of the fittest." This harsh, unforgiving version of evolution asserted that whatever is, is beneficial. It followed, as Abrams argues (1968, 73), that "the greater purpose of sociology was to impress upon men the fatuity of efforts to accelerate the improvement of their condition by legislative measures."[56] Social Darwinism was, needless to say, incompatible with the image of centrist liberalism. So, despite his fame in Great Britain and the United States,[57] Spencer's meteoric presence came and went, leaving little residue in the emerging discipline of sociology.

The three birthplaces of academic professional sociology were France, Germany, and the United States. We have already discussed the ambiguities of the version of value-free sociology professed by the leading figure of the new German academic sociology, Max Weber. These ambiguities were in fact analogous to those that were part of the institutionalization of sociology in France and the United States.

In France, the key figure, both intellectually and organizationally, was Émile Durkheim. Durkheim, like Marshall, was an organizer. His academic training was in philosophy, which he found too arcane and too removed from the moral and political questions of the day. In 1887, he received an appointment in Bordeaux in philosophy. But at the instigation of Louis Liard, the director of higher education for the government, he was permitted to teach a course in social science. By 1896, he had become a full professor of social science, the first such appointment in the French university system. In 1898, he founded a scholarly journal with the name of sociology, *L'Année sociologique*. It became a major institutional meeting ground for all those, in France and elsewhere, who were oriented to empirical social science. In 1902 he was called to the Sorbonne in Paris and in 1908 became a professor of "the Sociology of Education"—a title changed by ministerial decree in 1913 to "the Science of Education and Sociology."[58]

56. Abrams continues (p. 78): Spencer "had turned the Invisible Hand into an Invisible Fist. And now he invited his contemporaries to watch quietly as it did its malignant work."

57. Hofstadter (1992, 43) tells us of Spencer's memorable visit to the United States in 1882 at the height of his popularity. In his one interview with the press, "Spencer expressed (it was a slightly jarring note) his fear that the American character was not sufficiently developed to make use of its republican institutions." But he evinced hope, from "biological truths," that "the essential mixture of the allied varieties of the Aryan race forming the population would produce 'a finer type of man than has hitherto existed.'"

58. In this way, Durkheim is usually considered the founder of sociology, as we know it today, in France. Lacroix (1981, 30–31) considers this to be "a reconstruction of the past on the basis of present-day disciplines" and therefore a "double anachronism, epistemological and biographic." He says everyone throughout the nineteenth century was using many different names and not at all consistently. "And these names reflect the uncertainty of frontiers, the confusion of objects, the quarrel about methods in a field of knowledge in full reorganization. The only constant in this tempest of ideas was the faith in science."

During this time, he was also active politically, notably during the Dreyfus affair. He was the secretary-general in Bordeaux of the Ligue pour la Défense des Droits de l'Homme, the principal Dreyfusard organization, and was a "favorite speaker at rallies in the Bordeaux area" (Clark, 1972, 161). The question here, as it is in discussing Weber, is how close the link was between Durkheim's professional activities and his political ones. And here, too, the answer is ambiguous.

Clark offers us one answer (1972, 170):

> [Durkheim] had a remarkable ability to formulate problems strategic both for socio-logical theory and pressing moral and political concerns. His prestige both with his collaborators and the general public was enhanced by the timeliness of his theoreti-cal works for definition of a secular morality, development of a theory of solidarity, and isolation of causes of social deviance. The Durkheimians also shared a common training and career pattern. They were brought together again by a series of impor-tant political experiences.

But Clark's answer is itself ambiguous. For it evades the issue of intention. If Durkheim sought to turn sociology into a genuinely positive science,[59] it is also true, as Richter argues (1960, 172), that for Durkheim

> sociology was to create a solid base for the Republic. It would indicate what reforms were needed; it would provide principles of order in politics, as well as a moral doc-trine on which the country could unite; for he believed that beneath the choppy sur-face of political and ideological differences lay a real consensus of values. This belief motivated his effort to discover what the ties are that hold together the members of a society and produce at least that minimum of order and harmony requisite to its maintenance.

There is considerable agreement that Durkheim saw himself as, and was, a firm supporter of the Third Republic. The question is where this put him on a political spectrum. Conservative members of the academy often labeled him a socialist. And there is evidence to indicate that, at a personal level, he was a fellow traveler of French socialists, if never a party member.[60]

---

59. He is taken to task quite severely for this by Wolf Lepenies (1989, 49): "Nothing characterized the scientific excess of the New Sorbonne more than its obsession with questions of method; it was the reformer's favourite catchword. . . . The most curious example of this was . . . furnished by Émile Durkheim through his *Règles de la méthode sociologique,* which was full of metaphysics; philosophers were introduced to a sociology founded on the axiom, as astonishing as it was scandalous, that the 'facts of society' were something quite different from and wholly independent of the individuals that composed it."

60. See Clark's sober assessment (1972, 171–172): "Durkheim's own relations with socialism were extremely complex and have been the subject of considerable scholarly controversy. His original thesis topic had been the relation of individualism to socialism, and although changed to the individual and society, socialism was never far below the surface of *The Division of Labor in Society;* nor was it in

On the other hand, Lewis Coser (1960, 212) makes the case for his "abiding conservatism."[61]

But most analysts place him in between the two, a proper example of centrist liberalism. Weisz (1979, 111) catches, I believe, exactly where French social science in general, and Durkheim in particular, stood:

> One should note the intimate links of the social sciences in the university with a certain republican-progressive ideology, one that was clearly anti-socialist. It is true that the case of Durkheim was more ambiguous in the degree to which certain circles considered him a socialist. But, by emphasizing how his thought was evolutionist, pragmatic, anti-utopian, and sometimes even conservative, Durkheim managed to reassure the leading university figures.

To which Logue adds (1983, 151):

> For Durkheim rejected traditional conservatism, laissez-faire liberalism, and collectivist socialism, while much of his thought was occupied with the main

---

Suicide or several other works. He planned a history of socialist thought, although he completed only the section on Saint-Simon. Jaurès came to Durkheim's home for Sunday dinner several times and he was in close contact with Lucien Herr. . . . He was known to arrive at lectures and walk out of the Sorbonne conspicuously carrying *L'Humanité,* a political act in itself. He never joined a socialist party, however, nor did he participate in partisan activities with his younger collaborators. Repelled by the emotion and lack of rigor of most socialist writers, he remained deeply concerned with many phenomena they treated. But to many less concerned with these subtleties, there was no doubt that Durkheim was a socialist." Clark further notes (182, n. 72) that "until as late as 1925, there was a combined heading of 'Socialism; Social Science' in Otto Lorenz, *Catalogue général de la librairie française,* the major bibliography of books published in France."

This flirting at the edge of the socialist movement was engaged in as well by a number of members of the Durkheimian circle—Mauss, Simiand, Bouglé, Halbwachs, Hertz—who regularly wrote for *L'Humanité* and *Revue socialiste,* "but still without making a full transition to a political career" (Karady, 1976, 294).

61. Coser defines conservatism as "an inclination to maintain the existing order of things or to re-inforce an order which seems threatened." He continues (p. 214): "The liberal or radical thinker contrasts an ideal state with a real state. Durkheim, to the contrary, substituted the distinction between the normal and the pathological for the disjunction between the ideal and the real . . . and thus introduced bias toward conservatism."

Neyer, by contrast, argues (1960, 45) that "Durkheim regarded the development toward a 'socialist' organization of society as an inevitable response to the ethics of individualism and progress, as well as a consequence of what he termed 'the emergence of the individual.' " Similarly, Richter (1960, 181) says: "The problem is not how to achieve social order by restraining or combating individualism, but rather how to complete and extend it. . . . [Durkheim's] restatement of liberalism ought to be read beside his better-known polemics against Spencer and the laissez-faire economists. His plea that all artificial obstacles to individual development be removed . . . reveals a liberal social philosophy justifying state intervention in economic life."

problem of the new liberalism: how to combine social integration with individual freedom.[62]

Overall, Durkheim's variety of centrist liberalism was perhaps a bit closer to the position formulated by the German *Katheder-Sozialisten* than to Weber's national-liberalism. But Schmoller, Weber, and Durkheim all emphasized the importance of the state as the incarnation of collective values, and in the end all three were nationalists. As Maier (1992, 134) puts it:

> Sociology from Comte to Durkheim represented, in effect, an intellectual project for encouraging an organization of civil society that might stabilize an increasingly democratic politics. And not only in France.[63]

The United States was in fact the country in which academic sociology was institutionalized the earliest. The debates and the solutions were not too different from those in France and Germany. The principal organizational figure in the history of American sociology was Albion Small. His own career illustrates well the trajectory of most of his contemporaries. Son of a Baptist minister, he studied at a seminary but was not ordained. Instead he went to Germany in 1879 to study history and *Sozialwissenschaft*. He then was appointed to Colby College in 1881 to teach history and political economy. He decided to obtain a Ph.D. at Johns

62. Logue continues (1983, 179): "Durkheim's sociology offered democratic liberalism intellectual weapons useful on several fronts at once. It provided a defense against those socialists who sought to use the argument of man's interdependence and debt to society as a justification for collectivism. It offered a defense against those conservatives who sought to promote the social value of the family over that of the individual and insisted on man's need for a guidance which transcended his rational understanding."

Giddens (1971, 513) makes the same argument: "Durkheim's sociology was rooted in an attempt to re-interpret the claims of political liberalism in the face of a twin challenge: from an anti-rationalist conservatism on the one hand, and from socialism on the other."

See also Ringer (1992, 210) on solidarism, which "obviously functioned as a progressive bourgeois alternative to revolutionary socialism. The political virtue of solidarist thinking was that it reconciled *laissez-faire* thinking with a rationalization for state action on behalf of moderate social reform. . . . Durkheim's *The Division of Social Labor* . . . may serve as an example of positivist social science sustaining solidarist principles."

63. Robert Nisbet, a self-designated conservative, asserted (1952, 167) that sociological concepts were in fact conservative in origin and consequence: "Such ideas as *status, cohesion, adjustment, function, norm, symbol* are conservative ideas not merely in the superficial sense that each has as its referent an aspect of society that is plainly concerned with the maintenance of or the *conservation* of order but in the important sense that all these words are integral parts of the intellectual history of European conservatism." Nisbet's view is specifically endorsed by Coser (1960, 213).

The problem here is to assume that concern for order is exclusively a conservative ideological objective. But the issue that separates conservatives from centrist liberals is not whether or not order is desirable but rather how order can be achieved. Centrist liberals believe that order is guaranteed only by judicious but significant reform, which involves necessarily a certain amount of economic redistribution.

Hopkins in economics and history. In 1889 he returned to Colby as its president. There he replaced the course in moral philosophy with one in sociology—one of the very first courses so entitled.

In 1892, he was called to the newly founded University of Chicago to found the first accredited department of sociology in the United States (and indeed in the world). In 1895, he founded at Chicago the *American Journal of Sociology* (*AJS*). And in 1905, he was one of the founders of the American Sociological Society. That same year, he published a basic text, *General Sociology*. His fundamental outlook is well defined by Bulmer (1984, 34–35):

> Small believed that sociology was a science, that it was changing from a discursive to an objective discipline grounded in empirical study, and that it was a cumulative discipline with a nomothetic, theoretical character. . . .
>
> At the same time, sociology was also an ethical discipline and the sociologist had a distinctive role to play in the improvement of society. His expertise and commitment enabled him to be involved in social reform without espousing the position of any class or interest group. Scientism and moralism were integrally connected.

For Oberschall, this meant that Small "literally walked a tightrope."[64] When J. W. Burgess, as dean of the Faculty of Political Science at Columbia University, recruited Franklin Giddings in 1891 to teach sociology, it was because he felt that "many special questions of penology, charity and poor relief could not be treated from the standpoint of pure political economy and many problems of social ethics could not be studied from the point of view of individual ethics" (Dorfman, 1955a, 176). Oberschall calls this the demand for courses in the "3 Ds: the defective, dependent, and delinquent classes."

All the other leading figures in the early history of American sociology also linked their sociology in varied ways to social reform. Lester Ward "replaced an older passive determinism with a positive body of social theory adaptable to the uses of reform" (Hofstadter, 1992, 68). E. A. Ross wanted the "wise sociologist" to speak to "those who administer the moral capital of society" in order that he "make himself an accomplice of all good men for the undoing of all bad men" (cited in Dorothy Ross, 1984, 163). Even Sumner, generally identified as a conser-

64. "On the one hand, in trying to enlist religious backers, he proclaimed that 'the ultimate sociology must be essentially Christian,' and that the 'principles of ultimate social science will be reiterations of essential Christianity'; on the other hand, he wrote in the programmatic statement for the *American Journal of Sociology*: 'To many possible readers the most important question will be with reference to its attitude to "Christian sociology." The answer is . . . toward Christian sociology [this journal will be] sincerely deferential, towards alleged "Christian sociologists," severely suspicious'" (Oberschall, 1972, 203).

Small, like the economist Richard Ely, was an active adherent of the Social Gospel movement, who strove "to overcome the currently assumed conflict between religion and science" (Potts, 1965, 92).

vative, was critical of "the *laissez-faire* content of [Spencer's theories, seeking to] put the case that 'progress' meant government by skilled social scientists" (Crick, 1959, 50).

As both Bulmer (1984, 39) and Oberschall (1972, 188) note, the underlying influence of liberal Protestantism, very influential in the Progressive movement of the time, permeated the work of these sociologists. Still, all of them were aware of the possible confusion of sociology and socialism. When Albion Small sought to convince President Harper of Chicago to allow him to found the *AJS*, he wrote him that a journal was "needed both to exert restraint on utopian social effort and to encourage and direct well advised attempts at social cooperation" (cited in Dibble, 1976, 301). Government in the hands of the specialists was a key element in centrist liberalism.

3. Political Science

Of the three nomothetic social science disciplines, political science was the last to emerge as an autonomous discipline. Its early period was marked by the establishment of three major institutions—Sciences Po in Paris, the Faculty of Political Science at Columbia University, and the London School of Economics (LSE) in London. The curious thing is that none of the three was originally designed to establish an autonomous discipline of political science. Indeed, they were all three intended to be pluridisciplinary, and indeed were so in practice. And yet, the three all left a lasting imprint on the discipline of political science, even though, in the twentieth century, political science went its own and separate way as an autonomous discipline, first of all in the United States, and later (particularly after 1945) throughout the world.

The three institutions were not founded simultaneously. Sciences Po was the first, established in 1871. It is harder to date the establishment of Columbia's Faculty of Political Science, since it went through many organizational versions. But the best date to use is probably 1880. LSE was the last, officially founded in 1895. Their stories are linked, but need to be told in order.

Sciences Po is the popular locution for the school, but it is not its formal name. In the semiofficial history of Sciences Po, written by Richard Descoings in 2007, we read (p. 27):

> Émile Boutmy founded the *École libre des sciences politiques* [the original name of Sciences Po] in 1871. . . . Who was Émile Boutmy? Why 1871? What should we understand by a "free school"? How should we define "political science"? That is what at Sciences Po one calls "*baliser le sujet*."[65]

---

65. "*Baliser le sujet*" is very tricky to translate. Fortunately, Descoings himself explains its meaning in another text (2008): "To accept complexity is first of all to deploy it. It is also and always to raise questions about the question, never to take the pronouncement as a postulate. To state 'from whence one speaks', to dissect the words that are used and the expressions employed, to think about what is not

Boutmy was a center-left bourgeois, a cultured political commentator (*publiciste cultivé*), a man with many connections and much influence. An entrepreneur. All this at the same time.

Why 1871? This is perhaps the place to begin. The years 1870–1871 were very traumatic ones for France. France was militarily defeated by Prussia. The empire of Napoleon III came to an end, and the Third Republic was proclaimed. The Prussian monarch, Wilhelm, somewhat flamboyantly used the Hall of Mirrors at Versailles to have himself proclaimed emperor of Germany. And, perhaps most important of all, Paris was the site of a profound social revolution, the Commune, which was finally repressed with much bloodshed.

The French world of knowledge suffered as a consequence the "German crisis of French thought" (Descoings, 2007, 32–33). Vincent says (1987, 28) that "Germany's victory was perceived as that of knowledge over ignorance." But more than that, the experience of the military defeat plus the Commune transformed French political life:

> [The combination of these two events] led to the belief that another social explosion was probable, and another (military) defeat possible. One had to borrow from Germany its formulas to use them against her. The pilgrimage to Germany became thereupon part of the educational program [*cursus*] of the French academic, and it is from German universities that Émile Boutmy borrowed the new pedagogical system that he established at the *École libre*. (Vincent, 1987, 13)

Nor could the Commune be separated from the experience of the French Revolution, still a subject of great controversy in France, and about which the centrist liberals had ambivalent feelings. Vincent suggests (1987, 13) that this, too, was on Boutmy's mind:

> In six years (1789–1794), the traditional elites were . . . swept away and replaced by others who, by and large, did not manage to rule for more than a brief time. The leaders of 1792 were all practically unknowns in 1788, which leads one to think that the "mass" has some "formidable" potentialities, dangerous but—why not?—utilizable, "recuperable," as we would say today.[66]

Boutmy's principal solution was the formation of elites. As Vincent notes (1987, 12),

> Boutmy did not hesitate to use the word [*elite*], and for him this meant endowing France with economic and political deciders recruited in the superior strata of the

---

said in the question, to evaluate the intentions of the author, in short, to take up a well-known formula of the students of Sciences-Po, 'baliser le sujet.'"

66. "The faculty of the *École libre* . . . were all preoccupied with ensuring 'progress in order,' to use the formula of Auguste Comte. They were all obsessed with the [French] Revolution. They were all convinced that the French Revolution broke out because of the failure of the political structures to adapt themselves to the enormous changes of customs and mentalities. Better to prevent than to punish" (Vincent, 1987, 211).

dominant class—including in the group a few exceptionally gifted persons coming from the "lower classes" (better to have them on your side than against you).[67]

So Boutmy used his connections to raise the money to establish a private institution. But in the first year he did not find too many students who were ready merely to study the political situation, to pursue what we might think of today as academic political science. So he quickly adjusted his strategy, adding a professional objective to the imparting of knowledge. In his report to his investors in 1872, he suggested that what was necessary was "to offer something such that the two top-rated (*haut vol*) professions that have such a great influence on the destinies of nations—diplomacy and the higher civil service—find in this institution that first-class preparation which has up to now not been available" (cited in Descoings, 2007, 40). In Vincent's metaphor, it was the shift from being an institution of knowledge to being an institution of power. "Liberal, anti-state, the *École* became a center to prepare the examinations for appointment to the *Inspection des Finances*, the *Conseil d'État*, the *Cour des Comptes*, and the *Quai d'Orsay* (the French Foreign Ministry)" (Vincent, 1987, 61).[68]

Boutmy thus created an *École libre*—that is, a private institution, one that was not subordinated to the Sorbonne but also was not clerical. It was a school of "political sciences" (note the plural). But the words *political* and *sciences* were both somewhat ambiguous. *Sciences* in French was still being used to mean knowledge

67. Boutmy laid these arguments out explicitly in a letter to his friend Ernest Vinet, published in 1871: "The new educational program is intended for those classes whose social position is assured and who have the leisure time to cultivate their mind. These classes have heretofore dominated the political scene. But their position is threatened. . . . Under pressure to submit to the rights of the more numerous, the classes who call themselves the elite can no longer maintain their political hegemony other than by invoking the rights of the most capable. Behind the collapsing wall of their prerogatives and tradition, the democratic torrent must come up against a second rampart, that of shining and useful merit, of superiority whose prestige is obvious, of capabilities of which it would be folly to deprive oneself" (*Quelques idées sur la création d'une Faculté d'enseignement supérieur*, Lettres de E. Boutmy et E. Vinet. Programme. Paris: Imp. de A. Lainé, 1871, 15–16, cited in Favre, 1981, 433).

68. Boutmy rapidly found a rationale for this shift to professional education: "Our political science, purely French or Latin, deliberately ignores modern Europe and the New World. . . .

"There are in France educational institutions for physicians, lawyers, engineers, military officers. There is none for the political person. . . . It will surely be a great and joyous revolution if France manages to produce each year two to three thousand minds furnished with political knowledge, having the social position to make themselves heard, and the arguments to get people to realize that all questions are difficult and most solutions complex. The curriculum organized for the education of the statesman would furnish the country at the same time the educated and judicious middle class that is the ballast of a democratic society. There has been up to now a middle class characterized by a conservative instinct, good manners, and riches. But this class has never held its position, it must be said, by virtue of its political enlightenment" (cited in Descoings, 2007, 34). Boutmy sought a name for this program. With some hesitation, he finally decided on *sciences camérales*, the translation of the eighteenth-century German concept of *Cameralwissenschaft* (Vincent, 1987, 84).

in general, like the German *Wissenschaften*. And *political sciences* was still a term that could mean social sciences in general. Indeed, what Boutmy actually offered was mostly what we would call today history, economics, and sociology, rather than political science more narrowly defined.[69]

John Burgess was called to Columbia University from Amherst College in 1876 with the title Professor of Political Science, History, and International Law (Hoxie, 1955, 6). The intent of the Columbia administration, as Burgess later recounted in 1893, was "to neutralize the intense professionalism of the Law School by supplying the students in private law . . . with those studies in ethics, history, and public law necessary to complete the science of jurisprudence" (cited in Bryson, 1932, 322). Burgess found the Law School "impenetrable" and turned to creating a School of Political Science instead.

In Hoxie's official history of the Faculty of Political Science, written for Columbia's bicentennial, he delineates the link to Sciences Po:

> The story of the Ecole Libre was an inspiring one for John Burgess. He, like many other students of our government, was much concerned in 1879 about the state of the United States Civil Service and was carefully following the reforms attempted by the Hayes administration. Moreover, the ideas he had gained from Sir Stafford Northcote regarding the British Civil Service had made a strong impression on him. He had noted during his visit to England in 1878 that civil service was viewed as a professional career for which one prepared much as for medicine or law. Could not a graduate school be established in this country for the training of civil servants—a school, or at least a department, not unlike the Ecole Libre des Sciences Politiques? Might it not also provide the complement to the apparently unalterable professionalism of Columbia's law curriculum? (1955, 11)

This fit in very well with a political movement of independent Republicans called the "Mugwumps"—a group drawn from the social elite and devoted to civil service reform. They were quintessential centrist liberals. They opposed the so-called Greenbackers and the labor unions, who they thought wanted to confiscate property. They also opposed the so-called Radical Republicans, who had been leaders in the struggle to ensure political rights for the liberated Negro slaves. The Mugwumps considered the Radical Republicans to be fanatics. On the other hand, the Mugwumps also inveighed against the social irresponsibility of the rich, which gave them their centrist credentials. They saw salvation in an educated elite. It followed that "enlarging social science's place in the curriculum was another part of this educational effort" (Church, 1974, 577).[70]

---

69. See the discussion of pluridisciplinarity in Descoings (2007, 39). See also the discussion of the rationale for the name that Boutmy chose for the institution in Vincent (1987, 47–48).

70. Church elaborated the view of the Mugwumps about social science further (1974, 577): "They proposed to teach the future elite—and university education was then pretty nearly restricted to the

When the trustees of Columbia gave the go-ahead for a School (later called Faculty) of Political Science, they noted that Burgess "explicitly avows it to be part of his view to train men for the service of the government; but it is hardly necessary to make this a declared object, and to do so might awaken jealousies prejudicial to its success" (cited in Hoxie, 1955, 15). The trustees may have feared the reactions of other faculty but had no doubt themselves as to the merits of the objective. In Columbia's *College Handbook of 1880,* the new School of Political Science's objectives were stated this way: "[The] prime aim [is the] development of all branches of political science. Its secondary aim is the preparation of young men for all branches of public service" (cited in Crick, 1964, 28).

Just as Émile Boutmy was the driving force to create Sciences Po and John Burgess to establish the Faculty of Political Science at Columbia, so Sydney and Beatrice Webb were the driving forces to create the LSE, whose full name is the London School of Economics and Political Science. The Webbs had long wanted such an institution when, in 1894, one Henry Hunt Hutchison died and left a bequest to the Fabian Society of twenty thousand pounds—a princely sum at the time. So, at a breakfast meeting on August 4, 1895, convened by the Webbs and attended by George Wallas and George Bernard Shaw, it was decided (over Shaw's opposition) to found the LSE.

As in the case of the other two institutions, the initial intention was to improve the training of Great Britain's political and business elite. The Webbs used the curriculum of Sciences Po as the basis of their own offerings. Indeed, although their concerns were heavily oriented toward economic issues, Ralf Dahrendorf, a later director of the LSE, explains in his centennial history of the school (1995, 196) that the phrase "and Political Science" in the title was inserted because

> the Webbs did not want to lose the allusion to the Paris École Libre des Sciences Politiques and the Faculty of Political Science at Columbia University, so that political sciences had to find a place in the name.

Furthermore, Dahrendorf notes (1995, 21) that in the beginning all classes were given in the evening as a means of pursuing its object of professional education:

> Students would not be prepared especially for any degree, but attendance would be useful for Civil Service examinations as well as those of the Institute of Bankers, the London Chamber of Commerce, and others.

Although Sciences Po continued to have as one, but not the only one, of its roles to prepare students for entry into diplomacy and the higher civil service, this

---

elite—correct principles of political and social organization, the laws governing social and political relations which had to be obeyed if the society were to function properly. Social science taught just these principles and laws through studying the development of English freedoms since Magna Carta (sometimes since village communities emerged in the German forests) and their extension and

eventually ceased to be a major role of the LSE, whereas the Faculty of Political Science at Columbia became a graduate school in the social sciences, one of whose departments was political science (called at Columbia at the time Public Law and Government).

Political science, as we knew it after about 1900, emerged first in the United States.[71] Its emergence was part of what Hughes (1958, 66–67) has called the major ideas of the 1890s, one of which was "to penetrate behind the fictions of political action . . . [to the] actual wielders of power." Crick (1959, 37–38) indicates how this idea was developed:

> The theories of a necessary progress and of a therapeutic science of society both appeared upon the scene. They were to result in a new split between political theory and political practice; a predilection to psychological explanation, and an antagonism to historical and philosophical explanation. . . . They were to furnish added conditions . . . for the emergence of a unique type of philosophy, pragmatism, and of a largely unsystematized but increasingly influential positivism.

The positivist and presentist orientation of the founders of the American Political Science Association (APSA) in 1903 represented a break both with history and economics on the one hand and with the civil-service training orientation of Burgess. As Gunnell argues (2006, 481), the principal reason to break with history and economics was not, however, method but a concern about "the relationship between social science and politics."

The founders of the APSA were interested, as were their predecessors, in achieving "an effective practical role for social science, but they were also rejecting the stance of *Kathedersozialisten*" (Gunnell, 2006, 481). They were trying to do exactly what Weber and Tönnies would try to do in 1909 in the establishment of the Deutsche Gesellschaft für Soziologie. In taking this path, the American political scientists, like the German sociologists, were approaching what Dahrendorf calls (1995, v) the Sydney Webb fault line "between wanting to know the causes of things and wanting to change things."

---

further safeguarding in the United States, how the constitution protected individual liberties, property, and the rights of minorities (in this case they meant the rights of the rich against the desires of the 'mob') and how it limited the powers of democracy; and the laws and principles of classical laissez-faire economy."

71. In seeking to explain why political science did not really emerge as a separate nomothetic discipline in Great Britain until after 1945, Dahrendorf (1995, 227) attributes it to "the enormous strength . . . of traditional political philosophy in the old universities, and notably in Oxford." But then he adds another factor: "When it comes to application, modern political science has turned out to be less effective than modern economic science." I'm not sure "less effective" is the proper adjective. I would say myself "less influential."

The way to navigate the fault line was centrist liberalism, an option Lowi suggests (1985, ix) was particularly evident in the United States, and within the United States, in political science:

> National government in the United States, emerging late and slowly, built nevertheless of liberal lines. So did the social sciences, especially political science. . . . Rejecting the Right and the Left, liberalism avoided judging the morality of conduct or of capitalism. Liberal government could be justified by concerning itself with conduct deemed harmful only in its consequences. Social science could analyze such a system and also serve such a system by concerning itself with hypotheses about conduct and its consequences or, correlatively, conduct and its causes. This helps explain why political science and the emerging national government both has such an affinity for science.

THE NON-WESTERN WORLD

The institutionalization of history and the three nomothetic disciplines—economics, sociology, and political science—in the last third of the nineteenth century and the first half of the twentieth took the form of university disciplines wherein the Western world studied itself, explained its own functioning, the better to control what was happening. I say the Western world, but in practice, as we have noted, 95 percent of the scholarship was located in just five countries—Great Britain, France, the United States, Germany, and Italy—and concerned primarily those five countries. The last 5 percent was mostly about Scandinavia, the Low Countries, Russia, Iberia, and to a very small extent Latin America.

Since we are talking of a period in which the Western world, and particularly the five countries, dominated the rest of the world—politically, economically, and culturally—this should be no surprise. Still, the rest of the world was a matter of some concern to the powerful of the world, who wished to know how best to control the "others" over whom they held sway. To control, one must understand, at least minimally. So, again, it is no surprise that academic specialties emerged to produce the desired knowledge.

The rest of the world was, however, divided into two parts politically—a division that came to be designated by often inexact terminology. Analysts sometimes spoke of colonies and semicolonies—a distinction between those zones under direct colonial rule by a "European" power and those that were still nominally independent but subject to considerable European domination. As we shall see, this mode of categorizing particular places created analytic boxes that had to be transgressed if one were to read the situation accurately. Nevertheless, we can begin by noting that a discipline called *anthropology* emerged in this period, and it dealt largely with areas that were either colonies or special zones within the metropolitan powers' home territory. A second discipline, called *Orientalism,* dealt in this period largely (but not exclusively) with the semicolonies.

These two "disciplines" were entirely separate from each other, with rare exceptions. Indeed, even in the twenty-first century, few social scientists see the two "disciplines" as even vaguely connected with each other, much less two variants on a set of common themes. Nonetheless, common themes there were. The first was that both disciplines dealt with the "rest" of the world, those that were not part of the dominant pan-European zones in the late nineteenth century. The second theme was that the peoples with whom they were dealing were not considered to be "modern"—meaning that they did not have the technology and the machinery that was thought to be constitutive of modern "progress."[72] Consequently, it was not believed that they shared the values of modernity as these values were imagined and practiced in the pan-European world. And the third common theme was the assertion that these countries/zones/peoples had no history, meaning that they had not changed, developed, progressed over historical time.

There was, however, one important difference between the peoples dealt with under one or the other label. Anthropologists dealt with populations that were relatively small, both in their numbers and in the size of the area they inhabited. These peoples, with rare exceptions, had no written documents at the time they came under colonial rule. They all spoke a single language, which was normally not shared with other neighboring peoples. Their gods also were not shared. From the perspective of their European conquerors, these were denominated "primitive" peoples, strange in every way, whose modes of living and thinking were virtually incomprehensible to the ordinary European.

Orientalists dealt with quite different kinds of peoples. They dealt with peoples or "civilizations" that were large both in their numbers and in the size of the area that they inhabited. They did have written texts, albeit ones that were difficult for Europeans to decipher. There also seemed to be a shared common language over a large area, or at least a lingua franca. Hence, the number of speakers was very large. They seemed in addition to have a single dominant religion in this large zone, a religion large enough that, in the nineteenth century, Western scholars deemed it to be a "world religion." And they clearly had a history, but one that Western scholars would deem somehow "frozen" and therefore one that had not evolved into "modernity." Upon inspection, it turned out that all these large, "frozen" civilizations were the product of large, bureaucratic empires that existed at some time in the past, what we have been terming "world-empires." It was these bureaucratic empires that gave rise to a common language or lingua franca, a common "world religion," and common cultural traditions. Many, but not all, of

72. See Michael Adas (1989), who discusses the European concept of the "the machine as civilizer" (211–236) and of "material mastery as a prerequisite of civilized life" (194–198).

these zones were still coherent enough politically and militarily to be able to resist direct colonization.

As a result of this crucial difference between the two kinds of non-European zones, two different intellectual questions formed the basis of disciplinary enquiry, and two different practical methodologies of research came to be utilized. The anthropologists sought to decipher how the peoples they studied—peoples that they began to treat almost uniformly as "tribes"—actually functioned. That is, they sought to discover the rational bases of behavior under the outer layer of what seemed to most Europeans to be irrational behavior. In this sense, the quest for the hidden rationality of behavior was not all that different from what other social scientists thought they were doing when studying "modern" peoples. It was a quest that derived from Enlightenment visions of the appropriate role of social science.

But how could they do this? Initially, there was nothing for the anthropologists to read, and they were unable even to communicate orally with such peoples, at least at the outset of their work. The solution to this problem came in the form of a practical method called *participant observation*. This method required fieldwork. The anthropologists typically went to live among a particular people for some time. They sought to locate persons they thought of as "linguists"—that is, some members of the group who had acquired, for some reason, command of a European language. These persons would become not only intermediaries between the anthropologist and their people but also interpreters (both literally of the language and intellectually of the culture).

The anthropologists would seek to learn everything about their people, whose culture was defined as a single, integrated whole that was unchanging, in order eventually to write an ethnography of this people. Once done, the anthropologists became cultural and political interpreters of their people to the European world in general and quite often to the colonial authorities in particular. This is, of course, a highly idealized picture of what occurred, but this was the standard description of the activity at the time,

The Orientalists had a quite different concern and a quite different practical methodology. Since they were dealing with what they termed a "high civilization," but one that did not seem to them modern in the sense that European civilization saw itself as modern, the most obvious and immediate issue to resolve was to explain why this "high" civilization never made the evolutionary leap that Europeans were presumed to have made into modernity. This was, of course, a highly self-congratulatory question for Europeans to pose. It presumed superiority and sought less to demonstrate its reality (for it rather was a largely unquestioned premise) than to explain its origins.

The question was how this was to be done. Since there did exist a written literature, it seemed hardly urgent to engage in the kind of fieldwork that was the pride of anthropologists. Still, this literature was written in a language quite different from the languages native to the European Orientalists. Learning the language required a long training, especially since these texts were for the most part ancient and many of them were religious texts. The needed skills were largely those of philology, and the locus of research was primarily a limited number of major libraries. To be sure, the Orientalists shared the same basic premise of social science as the anthropologists. They, too, wished to explicate the rational underpinnings of seemingly irrational behavior and philosophical argument. They, too, wished to become interpreters of their civilization to the European world in general and quite often to its political authorities in particular.

The desire of the anthropologists and the Orientalists to explicate the underlying rationality of their tribe or their civilization led them almost inevitably to be centrist liberals in their implicit ideology. They sought to ameliorate the rough edges of the relations of the powerful to the weaker, while aiding the powerful to govern their charges and/or deal with other civilizations more intelligently and more effectively.[73] They abetted reforms that served to limit conflict and above all radical subversion of the status quo of pan-European geopolitical power.

Orientalism was heir to a long tradition in the Catholic Church. Already in the Middle Ages, there were monks and other Christian scholars who were studying the languages and texts of the Muslim world and of China, as part of the effort to evangelize these zones. Such scholarship got a new (and often more secular) impulsion in the late eighteenth and especially in the nineteenth century, when European expansion began to embrace all the different parts of the Asian continent.

The study of a reified Egyptian civilization—Egyptology—began in the second half of the eighteenth century. Two political events were, however, critical to the serious development of Egyptology as an Orientalist subdiscipline. One was Napoleon's unsuccessful invasion of Egypt in 1798, and the other was the Greek war for independence in 1823. Napoleon's invasion was in the end abortive politically (see Cole, 2008). But he had had the idea to bring with him a whole group of scholars to study Egypt. One major result was a multivolume work called *La Description de l'Egypte,* a compendium of articles on the history, architecture, flora, and fauna of Egypt, plus maps and engravings.

This monumental work was perhaps less important in the creation of Egyptology than the incarnation of Greece as the fount of Western civilization—a concept

73. As Adas (1989, 203) observed, there prevailed "the assumption that Europeans were the best rulers and reformers of African and Asian societies because they represented the most progressive and advanced civilization ever known."

In 1903–1904, T. W. Rhys Davies, who was a specialist in Buddhist Pali literature, preached the importance of Oriental studies to British public policy: "And we must never forget that the conditions have now changed; and that just as we consider, in our naval estimates, foreign activity, so also we should, as practical policy, make our Intelligence Department, in Oriental matters, at least as strong as that of any two of the other Great Powers. By the present neglect by our Government of this Intelligence Department, we are running great risk" (p. 196).

so common today that it is hard to remember that this was not always a given of even Western perceptions of history. Martin Bernal, in *Black Africa,* the book in which he argued for the Afro-Asiatic roots of (Western) classical civilization, entitled volume 1 (1987) *The Fabrication of Ancient Greece, 1785–1985.*

The point he was making is the counterpoint. It was Greece, as opposed to both Rome and Egypt, that represented for the Romantic movement "models of liberty" (p. 289). An overly favorable picture of Egypt might pose a threat to "the uniqueness of Greek civilization and that of Europe as a whole" (p. 269). When the Greeks rose up against the Ottoman Empire in 1823, European Romantics led the call for solidarity, proclaiming it a "struggle between European youthful vigor and Asian and African decadence, corruption and cruelty" (p. 291).

It is not important here to analyze the scholarly controversy that Bernal's book has aroused.[74] What is undeniable is that Egyptology developed in the nineteenth century as an Orientalist subdiscipline, as a study of the other. The largely deprecatory picture of Egyptian civilization that dominated the nineteenth-century literature (and indeed that of the twentieth century) corresponded to the geopolitics and geoculture of the world-system of that period.[75]

It also seems clear that the emergence of Classics as a field of study, a discipline, in British (and then American) universities reflected the thrust of centrist liberalism in the geoculture. Classics represented on the one hand, in its emphasis on a close reading of the literature, a break from the stagnant curriculum of traditional Oxbridge education. But at the same time it also represented a rejection of the radicalism bred by the French Revolution. It was a sort of "third way."[76]

Egypt was nonetheless secondary, in the emergent discipline of Orientalism, to India. In 1818, James Mill published the first edition of *A History of British India.* In it, Mill developed the thesis of Oriental despotism as something quite different

74. Mary Lefkowitz has been the most prominent scholar seeking to refute Bernal's analysis of the Egyptian roots of ancient Greek civilization. In the collection she coedited with G. R. Rogers, entitled *Black Athena Revisited* (1996), she argues: "The evidence of Egyptian *influence* on certain aspects of Greek culture is plain and undeniable. . . . But the evidence of Egyptian *origins* for Greek culture is another thing entirely" (p. 6). She accused Bernal of Afrocentrism. Indeed, her 1997 book is entitled *Not Out of Africa: How Afrocentrism Became an Excuse to Teach Myth as History.*

In Bernal's reply to the criticisms by Lefkowitz and others (Moore, 2001, 27), he denied being an Afrocentrist. He claimed rather that he was arguing an "assimilationist (position) looking for a common origin of African and European culture." He called this a position of "intercontinental hybridity" and argued that this view was "far more threatening to the view that Greece borrowed nothing of significance from Egypt than are Afrocentric notions of fundamental continental difference and separation."

75. As Bernal (1987, 442) pointed out: "The status of Egypt fell with the rise of racism in the 1820s; that of the Phoenicians declined with the rise of racial anti-Semitism in the 1880s and collapsed with its peak between 1917 and 1939."

76. The expression is again that of Bernal (1987, 282 and 317). Bernal suggested that this was equally true of *Altertumswissenschaft* in German universities.

from European enlightened despotism, drawing quite negative portraits of both Hindus and Muslims in British India, both seen as unchanging peoples (Bannerji, 1995, 60–61). The book was highly successful, republished in ever-expanded form. It led to his appointment in a senior position in India House, of which he eventually became the director.

But, despite Mill and despite the fact that India became a British colony, it was not Great Britain that became the prime locus of the study of Indian civilization. Rather, it was Germany. Dietmar Rothermund, himself a late twentieth-century German historian of India, attributes the origin of the German romantic "quest for India" to the struggle of German poets and playwrights in the late eighteenth century "against the supremacy of French style and classical literary precedent in Germany." He notes the translation by Georg Fischer in 1791 of the Indian epic *Shakuntala,* which "created a veritable sensation in literary circles" and had a "much more enthusiastic reception than the English translation by William Jones in Great Britain" (1986, vii–viii). Indology served the German rejection of Anglo-French universalism.[77]

German Indology took a heavily linguistic form. The discovery of the links among that vast group of languages we today call the Indo-European family can be traced to the late eighteenth century. Although there had been suggestions of the existence of such linguistic links by both an English Jesuit and an Italian merchant in the sixteenth century, by a Dutch linguist in the seventeenth century, and by two French Jesuits in the eighteenth century, these suggestions got little purchase until Thomas Jones, founder of the Asiatick Society, proposed it in his presidential address in 1786. The actual term *Indo-European* was subsequently coined by Thomas Young in 1813 (Decharneux, 2000, 13).

In Germany, Indo-European was, however, labeled Indo-Germanic (Shapiro, 1981), and German research emphasized the search for an *Urspache* (an "original language"), sometimes associated with a search for an *Urheimat* (an "original homeland"). This search could take on romantic notions of linguistic purity, making of Sanskrit the oldest language and German the closest language to Sanskrit in terms of its structure (Mawet, 2000, 62). This is what Rothermund (1986, 53) considers the "conservative" version of German Indology, one "which saw in the most ancient past the manifestation of the greatest purity and perfection of language and religion," one whose object was "to penetrate the veil of later decay and corruption so as to reach the fountainhead of original revelation."

Nonetheless, the most famous of Germany's nineteenth-century Indologists, Max Muller, was also infused with the liberal optimism of evolutionary doctrines,

77. Indology was quite idiographic in its emphasis, as Rothermund observes (1986, 13): "[By 1900] all major German universities had a chair of Indology meaning Sanskrit philology in the strict sense of the term, and the professors holding these chairs tended to look askance at generalists, philosophers and others indulging in speculative theories."

and he conceived of the possibility of a religious evolution of Hinduism that would bring it closer to Christianity. He was personally close to the leaders of the Brahmo Samaj, a group that actually pursued such a process, as did comparable movements in other Asian religions in the nineteenth and early twentieth centuries (Rothermund, 1986, 54).

Of course, not all German scholars were Indologists. It was precisely in opposition to Orientalist views that Hegel laid such great emphasis on the idea that it was only in ancient Greece that mankind began *in seiner Heimat zu sein* ("to live in its homeland") (Droit, 2000, 91). As with Egypt, so with India. It was point-counterpoint of European universalism versus the frozen civilizations of the Orient, which *might* evolve, but only under Western tutelage. It was therefore no accident that German (indeed all Western) nineteenth-century scholarship concerning India and other Asian countries took no interest in the contemporary history of these countries.[78]

China is in some ways the most interesting case of the tilt that the Orientalist perception involved. The image of China as an old, wealthy, far-off civilization was one that had aroused European admiration for a long time. But somewhere in the mid- to late eighteenth century, the image was inverted: "[T]he Chinese were now condemned for what the Enlightenment had considered admirable, their stability" (Bernal, 1987, 240). China became, especially in the period after the First Opium War (1839–1842), "a civilization conventionally interpreted . . . as archetypically 'static' and 'traditional'" (Blue, 1999, 94–95).[79]

Here, too, Germany seemed to take the lead. But unlike in the case of India, German thinkers seemed unforgiving on all sides. Herder led the way, arguing that China was "the definitely dated and localized product of the Eastern Mongolians, . . . a mere petrification of an ancient way of life, . . . a hibernating marmot and . . . an embalmed Egyptian mummy" (Rose, 1951, 58).

Hegel was slightly more generous. Rose (1951, 59) summarizes Hegel's views:

> The Chinese State was an admirable patriarchy and a well-functioning bureaucracy, but it also represented an unbearable despotism. . . . Hegel could not find any free spirit, inward religiosity, deep feeling, or high ethical standards in China. In their place, the dead hand of abstract reasoning had arrested all life by its withering touch. China had no share in history. "It has always remained what it was."

Finally, Gobineau, although deeply opposed to progress and modernity, nonetheless found reasons for disdaining China, if reasons that were virtually the oppo-

78. "With the exception of Karl Marx's articles on India which he wrote for a New York newspaper from London," as noted acerbically by Rothermund (1986, 4).

79. Blue (1999, 92) notes "a broadly shared (if not unanimous) disdain [for China] in the nineteenth-century Western world as 'progress' became a watchword for defining the 'modern' identity of Europe in contrast to 'other' civilizations."

site of those of other Western thinkers. Blue (1999, 134) characterizes Gobineau's analysis in this way:

> [Mediocrity, despotism, and lack of freedom] were for him typical characteristics of "the masses" and "Revolution." China was thus a striking example of democratic despotism and "progress" as he conceived it, and of the consequences he saw flowing from these—namely, slavery, stagnation, and eventual doom.

Thus, by different particular arguments but by similar logics, Orientalism as a mode of interpreting the "high civilizations"—those latter-day descendants or continuations of historic world-empires—combined to produce an image of these zones as frozen civilizations that always remained what they were. They were, in Hegel's language, zones that could advance further only through some intervention by the European world.

The anthropologists in many ways had an easier task in demonstrating their arguments. They dealt with peoples who had no written documents and whose technology was by and large beneath the level of that of nineteenth-century Europe. As Hinsley (1981, 29) says of the study of Native Americans in the United States: "The central, nagging, political and religious dilemmas were these: Are these peoples in any sense our brothers? By what right can we claim their land as our own?"

The early history of anthropology turned around a debate over so-called polygenesis—the concept we discussed previously: that Europeans and other peoples were not part of a single species. In 1910, John Lynton Myers (1916, 69) gave a presidential address to the Anthropological Section of the British Association for the Advancement of Science. He sought to explain why polygenesis, by then a totally abandoned idea, had ever been taken seriously. He starts by noting that it was never seriously suggested before the late eighteenth century. Then something changed. That something was the emergence of a strong abolitionist movement in Great Britain:

> The slave-owning eighteenth century knew quite well that Negroes and Chinamen were no more *Homo ferus* than they were chimpanzees, and justified enslavement as Aristotle had justified it of old, on the ground that, if anything, it was to the advantage of the slave.

> But it was no accident that the generation that first doubted, on the political side, the legitimacy of white man's ownership of black man, and translated these doubts into practice and acts of Parliament, was precisely the generation which first doubted on the theoretic side, whether white men and black men were of the same blood. As long as slavery was regarded as justifiable morally, no one troubled to justify it anthropologically. But no sooner was the naturalness of slavery called into question by the Abolitionists . . . than the slave-owners raised the previous question: "Granted that I am my brother's keeper, and granted that this means I may not be his master,

yet is *this* man, this black brother, in any true sense my *brother* at all? Is he not, on the face of him, only an exceptionally domesticable animal, and of different lineage from mine?"[80]

Polygenesis was a crude racist idea. It was used, even inside Great Britain, as an argument to deny the suffrage to Celts (Rainger, 1978, 69). But by the late nineteenth century, it lost out within the community of anthropologists to an older, alternative version of the "primitive"—one linked to the basic concept of progress.[81]

John Locke (1965, 383) had said in 1690: "In the beginning all the world was America." In the mid-eighteenth century, in France and in Scotland, the concept of multiple stages of mankind's evolution was put forth as a theoretical position, notably by Jacques Turgot and Adam Smith. In their presentation, the Native Americans provided "a plausible working hypothesis about the basic characteristics of the 'first' or 'earliest' stage of socio-economic development" (Meek, 1976, 128).

This hypothesis fit in better with the Zeitgeist than did polygenesis. It also fit in better with the emergent distinction between "natural history" and "science"— part of the more general divorce we have noted between philosophy and science. Whereas previously the two terms "had meant pretty much the same thing: knowledge about the natural world" (Merrill, 1989, 12), they now signified separate enterprises, as science came to be divided into separate disciplines. As Merrill notes, now "[a] naturalist could still study all of nature . . . ; a scientist only studied part of it. . . . Natural history remained accessible to amateurs, while (science) became the province of professionals."

It is clear that anthropology, in adopting its emphasis on ethnographic delineation, was a version of natural history centered on human groups. And, of course, it remained open to amateurs for quite a while before finally becoming, in the early twentieth century, a domain reserved for professionals. In the first half of the nineteenth century, anthropology still depended on the work of travelers—sometimes scientists aboard naval expeditions, sometimes explorers sent by geographic societies, sometimes members of colonial bureaucracies, sometimes missionaries, sometimes agents engaged in philanthropic tasks.

80. It is interesting to note that Myers tells us (p. 1) that this rewritten version of his 1910 talk, which I have cited here, was the result of his residence in 1914 at the University of California, Berkeley, as the Sather Professor of Classical Literature—further evidence of the link of anthropology historically to idiographic disciplines.

81. The very advance of science helped to undo polygenesis, as Lorimer (1978, 142) pointed out: "Ultimately Darwinism solved the problem of the monogenesis-polygenesis argument simply by making them irrelevant. . . . [It] changed the concept of species, and thereby undermined the whole point of the polygenist argument. . . . Darwin had proved not only that the European was related to the Negro, but that all men were related to the ape."

The crucial transition was in the definition of what constituted the "primitive." What up to the mid-nineteenth century has been "considered a social or artistic condition of simplicity" (and therefore analyzable as a biological phenomenon) "was now redefined as a particular cultural state of existence" (Betts, 1982, 67). Once that shift was made, anthropology could become a discipline with a clear object of study.

Trouillot (1991, 40) captures the heart of it: "Anthropology did not create the savage. Rather, the savage was the raison d'être of anthropology." Two famous statements made in 1871 set the stage for this. The Italian anthropologist Cesare Lombroso said: "For the dreams of the theologians and the phantasms of the metaphysicians, [we have substituted] a few dry facts . . . but they are facts" (cited in Zagatti, 1988, 24). And that same year Edward Taylor put forward his proposition in *Primitive Culture* (1920, 410) that "the science of culture is essentially a reformer's science."

The outlines of the profession were now set. It would be holistic and descriptive, producing idiographic ethnographies based on fieldwork. It would be interpretative of the rationality of "primitive" peoples. It would stand for the better integration of such peoples into the modern world, for their benefit and for the benefit of the European authorities that ruled over them. And this it would remain until the anticolonial revolutions of the post-1945 era undid the basic geopolitical and hence geocultural framework within which anthropology carved its niche in the structures of knowledge.

TO THE TEMPLE OF FAME.

Mr. Punch (with the Greatest Respect), "AFTER YOU, MY LORD!"

Punch, *To the Temple of Fame*. This famous cartoon that appeared in *Punch* on October 23, 1858, shows Lord Brougham, a Liberal peer, in whose London home the Social Science Association was founded the year before. The cartoonist lampoons the reformist aspirations of the Liberal aristocracy and its link with the social sciences in formation. (Courtesy of Bibliothèque National de France)

6

___

The Argument Restated

.

This book is about the modern world-system in the long nineteenth century, which conventionally runs from 1789 to 1914. There are endless numbers of books that have discussed the basic characteristics of this period. There exists what we may think of as a conventional view, shared by scholars of varying ideological and/or scholarly views.

It is seen as the century of multiple revolutions—the industrial revolution, the scientific-technological revolution, the popular revolutions (and notably the French Revolution). The usual view is that the combination of all these revolutions is what created, or was labeled as, modernity. Begun in the long nineteenth century, modernity would continue into the twentieth century.

The view of this work, as expressed throughout the whole of the four volumes written up to now, is different. Take first the concept of "the industrial revolution." For most scholars, it occurred first in England or Great Britain—the most common dates are sometime between 1760 and 1840—and then was copied or emulated in a number of other countries in continental Europe and North America. We have explained at length in volume 3 why we think that this is incorrect.

We consider that what occurred in that period in England was a cyclical upward increase in the mechanization of industrial production, one that had occurred a number of times previously and would occur again a number of times later. We consider also that it was a process of the world-economy as a whole, one that accrued to the particular advantage of Great Britain because of its defeat of France in the struggle to become the new hegemonic power of the world-system.

For a long time, the dominant view of the French Revolution was the so-called social interpretation, which argued that the Revolution represented the overthrow of feudal forces by the bourgeoisie, enabling France to become a "capitalist" country. In the last forty years, this interpretation has been challenged by one in which the French Revolution was seen as an attempt to pursue a liberal, parliamentary path, one that went awry.

Once again, we have disagreed with both views. In volume 3, we explained why the French Revolution could not be thought of as a bourgeois revolution that installed "capitalism," since we considered that France had long since become part and parcel of the capitalist world-economy. Rather, we saw the French Revolution as in part a last attempt to defeat England in the struggle to become the hegemonic power, and in part an "antisystemic" (that is, anticapitalist) revolution in the history of the modern world-system, one that essentially failed.

We have argued that the modern world-system has two major cyclical processes. One is that of the Kondratieff cycles, more or less fifty to sixty years in length—cycles of expansion and stagnation in the world-economy as a whole. The second major cyclical process is a much slower one. It is of the rise and decline of hegemonic powers in the interstate system. We explained in volume 2 how the United Provinces (today's Netherlands) achieved the status of hegemonic power in the mid-seventeenth century. And we explained in volume 3 how Great Britain was able to become the hegemonic power following its defeat of France in the revolutionary-Napoleonic "world war" of 1792–1815.

Finally, we recounted in volume 3 the second great geographical expansion of the functioning boundaries of the capitalist world-economy. We explained the processes by which four zones that had been essentially outside the capitalist world-economy (Russia, the Ottoman Empire, the Indian subcontinent, and West Africa) were pulled inside and transformed—economically, politically, and socially—as a result of this inclusion.

Hence, when we arrived at telling the story of the long nineteenth century, we based it on the analyses made in the first three volumes. The modern world-system had been a capitalist world-economy since the long sixteenth century. Great Britain was the hegemonic power in the mid-nineteenth century. The effective boundaries of the modern world-system had been expanded, although they did not yet include the totality of the globe. The third and last expansion would occur in the late nineteenth and early twentieth centuries. These were stories we did not need to retell in this volume. (We explained in the preface why we were postponing the story of the third and final expansion of the modern world-system until volume 5.)

Instead, we chose to concentrate in this volume on what we thought was novel in the long nineteenth century. We label that newness the "triumph of centrist liberalism." Of course, we are not the first to note the strength of liberalism as an ideology in the nineteenth century. But our approach to this issue is somewhat different from that of other scholars. This required, among other things, reviewing the difficult terminological history of the term *liberalism* and the confusion that its ambiguous usages has made for cogent analysis of ideological reality.

To pursue this task, we needed to argue, first of all, that there was something that had not yet been achieved in the historical development of the modern world-system: the creation of what we are calling its geoculture. By a geoculture, we mean values that are very widely shared throughout the world-system, both explicitly and latently.

We have argued that, until the long nineteenth century, there had been a disjunction between the political economy of the world-system and its discursive rhetoric. In this volume, we have argued that it was the cultural impact of the French Revolution that made it imperative to overcome this disjunction by the development of the three main ideologies of the modern world-system—conservatism, liberalism, and radicalism.

We have sought to explain how it is that liberalism has always been a centrist doctrine, neither of the left nor of the right. We have argued that none of the three ideologies was in practice antistatist, although all three pretended they were. And we have tried to demonstrate the ways in which centrist liberalism "tamed" the other two ideologies, transforming them into virtual avatars of centrist liberalism. In that way, we could argue that by the end of the long nineteenth century, centrist liberalism was the prevailing doctrine of the world-system's geoculture.

We develop in detail how centrist liberalism imposed its ideology in three crucial spheres. The first was the creation of "liberal states" in the core regions of the world-system, in which Great Britain and France became the initial and leading exemplars. The second was the attempt to transform the doctrine of citizenship from being one of inclusion to being one of exclusion. We illustrated this by reference to three crucial groups that were excluded—women, the working classes (propertyless and often illiterate), and ethnic/racial "minorities." The third was the emergence of the historical social sciences as reflections of liberal ideology and modes of enabling the dominant groups to control the dominated strata.

We have put forth this analysis with as much empirical evidence as we could amass, and with whatever theoretical arguments we could assemble. The case is offered as one that better fits the totality of the world social reality than alternate modes of explaining the long nineteenth century.

Abel, Wilhelm. 1973. *Crises agraires en Europe, XIIe–XXe siècle*. Paris: Flammarion.

Abensour, Léon. 1913. *Le Féminisme sous le règne de Louis-Philippe et en 1848*. Paris: Plon-Nourrit.

———. 1923. *La Femme et le féminisme avant la révolution*. Paris: E. Leroux.

Abrams, Philip. 1968. *The Origins of British Sociology, 1834–1914*. Chicago: Univ. of Chicago Press.

Abray, Jane. 1975. "Feminism in the French Revolution." *American Historical Review* 80, no. 1 (February): 43–62.

Adas, Michael. 1989. *Machines as the Measure of Men: Science, Technology, and the Ideologies of Dominance*. Ithaca, NY: Cornell Univ. Press.

Adler, Laure. 1979. *A l'Aube du féminisme: Les premières journalistes (1830–1850)*. Paris: Payot.

Aelders, Etta Palm, d'. 1791. *Appel aux Françoises sur la régénération des mœurs et nécessité de l'influence des femmes dans un gouvernement libre*. Paris: L'Imprimerie du cercle social.

Ageron, Charles-Robert. 1963. "Jaurès et les socialistes français devant la question algérienne (de 1893 à 1914)." *Le mouvement social*, no. 42 (January–March): 3–29.

Aguet, Jean-Pierre. 1954. *Contribution à l'histoire du mouvement ouvrier français: Les grèves sous la Monarchie de Juillet (1830–1847)*. Geneva: Droz.

Agulhon, Maurice. 1970. *Une ville ouvrière au temps du socialisme utopique: Toulon de 1815 à 1851*. Paris and The Hague: Mouton.

———. 1973. *1848, ou l'apprentissage de la République, 1848–1852*. Vol. 8 of *Nouvelle histoire de la France contemporaine*. Paris: Éd. du Seuil.

———. 1979. *La République au village*. Réédition, augmentée d'une Préface. Paris: Éd. du Seuil.

———. 1998. "1848, l'année du suffrage universel." *Le Monde,* March 1–2, p. 12.

Albistur, Maïté, and Daniel Armogathe. 1977. *Histoire du féminisme français du Moyen Age à nos jours.* Paris: Éd. de Femmes.

Aldcroft, D. H. 1964. "The Entrepreneur and the British Economy, 1870–1913." *Economic History Review,* n.s., 17, no. 1 (August): 113–134.

———. 1968. "Introduction, British Industry and Foreign Competition, 1875–1914." In *The Development of British Industry and Foreign Competition, 1875–1914,* ed. D. H. Aldcroft, 11–36. London: George Allen & Unwin.

Alexander, Sally. 1984. "Women, Class, and Sexual Differences in the 1830s and 1840s: Some Reflections on the Writing of a Feminist History." *History Workshop Journal,* no. 17 (Spring): 125–149.

Allen, Ann Taylor. 1991. *Feminism and Motherhood in Germany, 1800–1914.* New Brunswick, NJ: Rutgers Univ. Press.

Allen, Judith. 1990. "Contextualising Late Nineteenth Century Feminism: Problems and Comparisons." *Journal of the Canadian Historical Association,* n.s., 1:17–36.

Allen, Robert. 1979. "International Competition in Iron and Steel, 1850–1913." *Journal of Economic History* 39, no. 4 (December): 911–937.

Amin, Samir. 1979. *Classe et nation, dans l'histoire et la crise contemporaine.* Paris: Éd. du Minuit.

———. 1989. *Eurocentrism.* New York: Monthly Review Press.

Aminzade, Ronald. 1982. "French Strike Development and Class Struggle." *Social Science History* 4, no. 1 (Winter): 57–79.

Anderson, Benedict. 1991. *Imagined Communities: Reflections on the Origin and Spread of Nationalism.* Rev. ed. London: Verso.

Andreucci, Franco. 1971. "Engels, la questione coloniale e la rivoluzione in occidente." *Studi storici* 12, no. 3 (July–September): 437–479.

———. 1979. "La Questione coloniale e l'imperialismo." In *Il marxismo dell'età della Secondo Internazionale* (vol. 2 of *Storia del Marxismo*), 865–893. Turin: Einaudi.

———. 1982. "The Diffusion of Marxism in Italy during the Late Nineteenth Century." In *Culture, Ideology, and Politics, Essays for Eric Hobsbawm,* ed. R. Samuel and G. S. Jones, 214–227. London: Routledge & Kegan Paul.

Andrews, John R. 1918. "Nationalisation (1860–1877)." In *History of Labour in the United States,* by J. R. Commons et al., 1–191. New York: Macmillan.

Angenot, Marc. 1993. *L'Utopie collectiviste: Le grand récit socialiste sous la Deuxième Internationale.* Paris: Presses Univ. de France.

Anon. 1869. "The Past and Future of Conservative Policy." *London Quarterly Review* 127, no. 254 (October): 283–295.

Anteghini, Alessandra. 1988. *Socialismo e femminismo nella Francia del XIX secolo, Jenny D'Héricourt.* Genoa: ECIG.

Applewhite, Harriet B., and Darline Gay Levy. 1984. "Women, Democracy, and Revolution in Paris, 1789–1794." In *French Women and the Age of Enlightenment,* ed. Samia I. Spencer, 64–79. Bloomington: Indiana Univ. Press.

———, eds. 1990. *Women and Politics in the Age of Democratic Revolution.* Ann Arbor: Univ. of Michigan Press.

Armstrong, Sinclair W. 1942. "The Internationalism of the Early Social Democrats of Germany." *American Historical Review* 47, no. 2 (January): 245–258.

Aron, Raymond. 1950. *La Sociologie allemande contemporaine*. 2nd ed. Paris: Presses Univ. de France.

Arrighi, Giovanni. 1994. *The Long Twentieth Century: Money, Power, and the Origins of Our Times*. London: Verso.

Ashley, Percy. 1920. *Modern Tariff History, Germany-United States-France*. 3rd ed. New York: Dutton.

Auclert, Hubertine. 1879. *Égalité sociale et politique de la femme et de l'homme: Discours prononcé au Congrès ouvrier socialiste de Marseille*. Marseille: Imp. Commerciale A. Thomas.

———. 1976. "Rapport du troisième Congrès ouvrier, Marseille, 20–31 octobre 1879." *Romantisme*, nos. 13–14, 123–129.

———. 1982. *La Citoyenne: Articles de 1881 à 1891*. Préface et commentaire d'Edith Tareb. Paris: Syros.

Aulard, Alphonse. 1911. *Napoléon Ier et le monopole universitaire*. Paris: Lib. Armand Colin.

Aydelotte, William O. 1962. "The Business Interests of the Gentry in the Parliament of 1841–47." In *The Making of Victorian England*, by G. Kitson Clark, 290–305. London: Methuen.

———. 1963. "Voting Patterns in British House of Commons in the 1840s." *Comparative Studies in Society and History* 5, no. 2 (January): 134–163.

———. 1966. "Parties and Issues in Early Victorian England." *Journal of British Studies* 5, no. 2 (May): 95–101.

———. 1967. "The Conservative and Radical Interpretation of Early Victorian Social Legislation." *Victorian Studies* 11, no. 2 (December): 225–236.

———. 1972. "The Disintegration of the Conservative Party in the 1840s: A Study in Political Attitudes." In *The Dimensions of Quantitative Research in History*, ed. W. O. Aydelotte et al., 319–346. Princeton, NJ: Princeton Univ. Press.

Babel, Antony. 1934. "Jacques Necker et les origines de l'interventionnisme." In *Mélanges d'économie politique et sociale offerts à M. Edgard Milhaud*, 25–44. Paris: Presses Univ. de France.

Bairoch, Paul. 1962. "Le Mythe de la croissance économique rapide au XIXe siècle." *La Revue de l'Institut de Sociologie* 35, no. 2, 307–331.

———. 1965. "Niveaux de développement économique de 1810 à 1910." *Annales E.S.C.* 20, no. 6 (November-December): 1091–1117.

———. 1970. "Commerce extérieur et développement économique, quelques enseignements de l'expérience libre-échangiste en France." *Revue économique* 21, no. 1 (January): 1–23.

———. 1972. "Free Trade and European Economic Development in the 19th Century." *European Economic Review* 3:211–245.

———. 1973. "European Foreign Trade in the XIXth Century, The Development of the Value and Volume of Exports (Preliminary Results)." *Journal of European Economic History* 2, no. 1, (Spring): 5–36.

———. 1974a. *Révolution industrielle et sous-développement.* 4th ed. The Hague: Mouton; Paris: E.P.H.E., VIe Section.

———. 1974b. "Geographical Structure and Trade Balance of European Foreign Trade from 1800 to 1970." *Journal of European Economic History* 3, no. 3 (Winter) : 557–608.

———. 1976a. *Commerce extérieur et développement économique de l'Europe au XIXe siècle.* Paris: Mouton.

———. 1976b. "Reply to Mr. Gunder Frank's Commentary." *Journal of European Economic History* 5, no. 2, (Fall): 473–474.

———. 1976c. "Europe's Gross National Product, 1800–1975." *Journal of European Economic History* 5, no. 2, (Fall): 273–340.

———. 1982. "International Industrialization Levels from 1750 to 1980." *Journal of European Economic History* 11, no. 2 (Fall): 269–333.

———. 1989. "European Trade Policy, 1815–1914." In *The Industrial Economies: The Development of Economic and Social Policies,* ed. P. Mathias and S. Pollard, 1–161. Cambridge Economic History of Europe 8. Cambridge: Cambridge Univ. Press.

———. 1997. *Victoires et déboires: Histoire économique et sociale du monde du XVIe siècle à nos jours.* Vol. 2, *Collection Folio/Histoire.* Paris: Gallimard.

———. 1999. *L'Agriculture des pays développés, 1800 à nos jours: Production, productivité, rendements.* Paris: Economica.

Baker, Houston A., Jr. 1987. *Modernism and the Harlem Renaissance.* Chicago: Univ. of Chicago Press.

Baker, Keith Michael. 1964. "The Early History of the Term 'Social Science.'" *Annals of Science* 20, no. 3 (September): 211–226.

———. 1988. "Souveraineté." In *Dictionnaire critique de la Révolution française,* by F. Furet and M. Ozouf, 888–902. Paris: Flammarion.

Baker, Paula. 1984. "The Domestication of Politics.." *American Historical Review* 89, no. 3, (June): 620–647.

Baldwin, Robert E. 1953. "Britain's Foreign Balance and Terms of Trade." *Explorations in Entrepreneurial History* 5, no. 4 (May 15) : 248–252.

Balibar, Étienne, and Immanuel Wallerstein. 1988. *Race, nation, classe, Identités ambigües.* Paris: La Découverte.

Ballot, Charles. 1923. *L'Introduction du machinisme dans l'industrie française.* Lille: O. Marquant.

Balzac, Honoré de. 1897. *The Country Parson* and *Albert Savaron.* Philadelphia: Gerrie Publishing.

Banks, Olive. 1981. *Faces of Feminism: A Study of Feminism as a Social Movement.* Oxford: Martin Robertson.

Bannerji, Himani. 1995. "Beyond the Ruling Category to What Actually Happens: Notes on James Mill's Historiography in *The History of British India.*" In *Knowledge, Experience, and Ruling Relations: Studies in the Social Organization of Knowledge,* ed. M. Campbell and A. Manicom, 49–64. Toronto: Univ. of Toronto Press.

Barbano, Filippo. 1985. "Sociologia e positivismo in Italia, 1850–1910: Un capitolo di sociologia storica." In *Sociologia e scienze sociale in Italia, 1861–1890: Introduzione critiche e repertorio bibliografico,* ed. F. Barbano and G. Sola, 7–73. Milan: Franco Angeli.

Barkan, Elazar. 1992. *The Retreat of Scientific Racism: Changing Concepts of Race in Britain and the United States between the World Wars.* Cambridge: Cambridge Univ. Press.

Barker-Benfield, G. J. 1989. "Mary Wollstonecraft, Eighteenth-Century Commonwealthwoman." *Journal of the History of Ideas 50*, no. 1, (January–March): 95–116.

Barnave, Antoine. 1988 [circa 1792–1793]. *De la Révolution et de la Constitution.* Grenoble: Presses Univ. de Grenoble.

Barret-Ducrocq, Françoise. 1991. *Pauvreté, charité et morale à Londres au XIXe siècle: Une sainte violence.* Paris: Presses Univ. de France.

Barret-Kriegel, Blandine. 1988. *Les historiens et la monarchie.* Vol. 3, *Les Académies et l'histoire.* Paris: Presses Univ. de France.

Barrows, Susanna. 1981. *Distorting Mirrors: Visions of the Crowd in Late Nineteenth-Century France.* New Haven, CT: Yale Univ. Press.

Barry, Kathleen. 1988. *Susan B. Anthony: A Biography of a Singular Feminist.* New York: New York Univ. Press.

Bartier, John. 1948. "1848 en Belgique." In *Le Printemps des peuples: 1848 dans le monde,* ed. F. Fejtö, 1 :355–371. Paris: Éd. du Minuit.

Barzun, Jacques. 1943. *Romanticism and the Modern Ego.* Boston: Little, Brown.

———. 1961. *Classic, Romantic, and Modern.* 2nd rev. ed. Boston: Little, Brown

Basch, Françoise. 1986. "Women's Rights and the Wrongs of Marriage in Mid-Nineteenth Century America." *History Workshop Journal,* no. 22 (Autumn): 18–40.

Baster, Albert. 1934. "The Origins of British Banking Expansion in the Near East." *Economic History Review 5,* no. 1 (October) : 76–86.

Bastid, Paul. 1953. "La Théorie juridique des Chartes." *Revue internationale d'histoire politique et constitutionelle,* n.s., 3, no. 11 (July–September): 163–175.

———. 1970. *Siéyès et sa pensée.* Nouv. éd. revue et augmentée. Paris: Hachette.

Baudis, Dieter, and Helga Nussbaum. 1978. *Wirtschaft und Staat in Deutschland von Ende des 19. Jahrhunderts bis 1918/19.* Vaduz: Topos.

Bauman, Zygmunt. 1986–1987. "The Left as the Counterculture of Modernity." *Telos,* no. 70 (Winter): 81–93.

Bayly, C. A. 1989. *Imperial Meridian: The British Empire and the World, 1780–1830.* London: Longman.

Beales, H. L. 1934. "The 'Great Depression' in Industry and Trade." *Economic History Review* 5, no. 1 (October): 65–75.

Bebel, August. 1988. *Woman in the Past, Present and Future.* London: Zwan.

Bécarud, Jean. 1953. "La Noblesse dans les Chambres (1815–1848)." *Revue internationale d'histoire politique et constitutionelle,* n.s., 3, no. 11 (July–September): 189–205.

Bédarida, François. 1965. "Le Socialisme et la nation: James Connolly et l'Irlande." *Le Mouvement social,* no. 52 (July–September): 3–31.

———. 1979. "Le Socialisme en Angleterre jusqu'en 1848." In *Des Origines à 1875,* ed. J. Droz, 257–330. Vol. 1 of *Histoire générale du socialisme.* Paris: Presses Univ. de France.

Bederman, Gail. 1995. *Manliness and Civilization: A Cultural History of Gender and Race in the United States, 1880–1917.* Chicago: Univ. of Chicago Press.

Beiser, Frederick C. 1992. *Enlightenment, Revolution, and Romanticism: The Genesis of Modern German Political Thought, 1790–1800.* Cambridge, MA: Harvard Univ. Press.

Belloni, Pier Paolo. 1979. "Lotte di classe, sindicalismo e riformismo a Torino 1898–1910." In L'età giolittiana, la guerra e il dopoguerra, ed. A. Agosti and G. M. Bravo, 43–137. Vol. 2 of Storia del movimento operaio, del socialismo e delle lotte sociale in Piemonte. Bari: De Donato.

Beloff, Max. 1974. "1848–1948, A Retrospect." In A Hundred Years of Revolution, 1848 and After, ed. G. Woodcock, 41–59. New York: Haskell House.

Benaerts, Pierre, et al. 1968. Nationalité et nationalisme, 1860–1878. Peuples et civilisations 17. Paris: Presses Univ. de France.

Bendix, Reinhard. 1964. Nation-Building and Citizenship: Studies of Our Changing Social Order. New York: Wiley.

Bénéton, Philippe. 1988. La conservatisme. Que sais-je?, 2410. Paris: Presses Univ. de France.

Bennett, George, ed. 1953. The Concept of Empire: Burke to Attlee, 1774–1947. London: Adam & Charles Black.

Bennett, Jennifer. 1982. "The Democratic Association, 1837–41: A Study in London Radicalism." In The Chartist Experience: Studies in Working-Class Radicalism and Culture, 1830–1860, ed. J. Epstein and D. Thompson, 87–119. London: Macmillan.

Benson, Donald R. 1985. "Facts and Constructs: Victorian Humanists and Scientific Theorists on Scientific Knowledge." In Victorian Science and Victorian Values: Literary Perspectives, ed. J. Paradis and T. Postlewait, 299–318. New Brunswick, NJ: Rutgers Univ. Press.

Berend, Ivan T. 1996. "Instabilità, crisi economiche, rapporto centro-periferia." In L'età contemporanea, Secolo XIX–XX, ed. P. Bairoch and E. J. Hobsbawm, 175–222. Vol. 5 of Storia d'Europa. Turin: Einaudi.

Berg, Barbara J. 1978. The Remembered Gate: Origins of American Feminism: The Woman and the City, 1800–1860. New York: Oxford Univ. Press.

Berg, Maxime. 1993. "What Difference Did Women's Work Make to the Industrial Revolution?" History Workshop Journal, no. 35 (Spring): 22–44.

Bergounioux, Alain, and Bernard Maini. 1979. La Social-démocratie ou le compromis. Paris: Presses Univ. de France.

Berlinerblau, Jacques. 1999. Heresy in the University: The Black Athena Controversy and the Responsibilities of American Intellectuals. New Brunswick, NJ: Rutgers Univ. Press.

Bernal, J. D. 1953. Science and Industry in the Nineteenth Century. London: Routledge & Kegan Paul.

Bernal, Martin. 1987. The Fabrication of Ancient Greece, 1785–1985. Vol. 1 of Black Athena: The Afroasiatic Roots of Classical Civilization. New Brunswick, NJ: Rutgers Univ. Press.

———. 1991. The Archaeological and Documentary Evidence. Vol. 2 of Black Athena: The Afroasiatic Roots of Classical Civilization. New Brunswick, NJ: Rutgers Univ. Press.

———. 2006. The Linguistic Evidence. Vol. 3 of Black Athena: The Afroasiatic Roots of Classical Civilization. New Brunswick, NJ: Rutgers Univ. Press.

Bernard, L. L., and Jessie Bernard. 1943. Origins of American Sociology: The Social Science Movement in the United States. New York: Thomas Y. Crowell.

Bernstein, Samuel. 1948. "Saint-Simon's Philosophy of History." Science and Society, 12, no. 1 (Winter): 82–96.

———. 1952. "The First International and the Great Powers." *Science and Society* 16, no. 3 (Summer): 247–272.

Berry, Christopher J. 1981. "Nations and Norms." *Review of Politics* 43, no. 1 (January): 75–87.

Bertier de Sauvigny, G. de. 1970. "Liberalism, Nationalism and Socialism: The Birth of Three Words." *Review of Politics* 32, no. 2 (April): 147–166.

Besnard, Philippe. 1979. "La Formation de l'équipe de l'Année sociologique." *Revue française de sociologie* 20, no. 1 (January–March): 7–32.

Bessel, Richard. 1990. "Workers, Politics and Power in Modern German History: Some Recent Writing on the German Labour Movement and the German Working Class in the Nineteenth and Twentieth Centuries." *Historical Journal* 33, no. 1: 211–226.

Betley, Jan Andrzej. 1960. *Belgium and Poland in International Relations, 1830–1831.* The Hague: Mouton.

Betts, Raymond F. 1982. "The French Colonial Empire and the French World-View." In *Racism and Colonialism: Essays on Ideology and Social Structure,* ed. R. Ross, 65–77. The Hague: Nijhoff, for Leiden Univ. Press.

Bezucha, Robert J. 1974. *The Lyon Uprising of 1834: Social and Political Conflict in the Early July Monarchy.* Cambridge, MA: Harvard Univ. Press.

Biagini, Eugenio F. 1991. "Popular Liberals, Gladstonian Finance and the Debate on Taxation, 1860–1874." In *Currents of Radicalism, Popular Radicalism, Organised Labour and Party Politics in Britain, 1850–1914,* ed. E. F. Biagini and A. J. Reid, 134–162. Cambridge: Cambridge Univ. Press.

Biagini, Eugenio F., and Alastair J. Reid. 1991. "Currents of Radicalism, 1800–1914." In *Currents of Radicalism: Popular Radicalism, Organised Labour and Party Politics in Britain, 1850–1914,* ed. E. F. Biagini and A. J. Reid, 1–19. Cambridge: Cambridge Univ. Press.

Bidelman, Patrick K. 1982. *Pariahs Stand Up! The Founding of the Liberal Feminist Movement in France, 1858–1889.* Westport, CT: Greenwood Press.

Bigaran, Maria Pia. 1982. "Mutamenti dell'emancipazionismo alla vigilia della grande guerra: I periodici femministi italiani del primo novecento." *Memoria, Rivista di storia delle donne,* no. 4 (June): 125–132.

Billig, Michael. 1982, 1983. "The Origins of Race Psychology." Pts. 1 and 2. *Patterns of Prejudice* 16, no. 3 (July 1982) 3–16; 17, no. 1 (January 1983): 25–31.

Billington, James H. 1980. *Fire in the Minds of Men: Origins of Revolutionary Faith.* New York: Basic Books.

Birnbaum, Pierre. 1976. "La Conception durkheimienne de l'État: L'Apoliticisme des fonctionnaires." *Revue française de sociologie* 17, no. 2 (April–June): 247–258.

Black, Eugene. 1988. *The Social Politics of Anglo-Jewry, 1880–1920.* Oxford: Blackwell.

Black, R. D. Collison. 1953. "The Classical Economists and the Irish Problem." *Oxford Economic Papers,* n.s., 5, no. 1 (March): 26–40.

———. 1960. *Economic Thought and the Irish Question, 1817–70.* Cambridge: At the University Press.

Blackbourn, David. 1977. "The *Mittelstand* in German Society and Politics, 1871–1914." *Social History,* no. 4 (January): 409–433.

———. 1984. "The Discreet Charm of the Bourgeoisie: Reappraising German History in the Nineteenth Century." In *The Peculiarities of German History: Bourgeois Society and*

Politics in Nineteenth-Century Germany, ed. D. Blackbourn and G. Eley, 157–292. New York: Oxford Univ. Press.

———. 1986. "The Politics of Demagogy in Imperial Germany." *Past and Present,* no. 113 (November): 152–184.

———. 1988. "Progress and Party: Liberalism, Catholicism and the State in Imperial Germany." *History Workshop Journal,* no. 26 (Autumn): 57–78.

Blackburn, Robin. 1988. *The Overthrow of Colonial Slavery, 1776–1848.* London: Verso.

Blanc, Louis. 1841–1844. *Révolution française: Histoire des 10 ans, 1830–1840.* 5 vols. (1, 1841; 2, 1842; 3, 1843; 4, 1844; 5, 1844). Paris: Pagnerre.

Blanc, Olivier. 1981. *Olympe de Gouges.* Paris: Syros.

Blanchard, Marcel. 1956. *Le Second Empire.* 2d rev. ed. Paris: Lib. A. Colin.

Blanning, T. C. W. 1989. "The French Revolution and the Modernization of Germany." *Central European History* 22, no. 2, 109–129.

Blocker, Jack S., Jr. 1985. "Separate Paths, Suffragists and the Women's Temperance Crusade." *Signs* 10, no. 3 (Spring): 460–476.

Bloom, Solomon F. 1941. *The World of Nations: A Study of the National Implications in the Work of Karl Marx.* New York: Columbia Univ. Press.

Blue, Gregory. 1999. "Gobineau on China, Race Theory, the 'Yellow Peril,' and the Critique of Modernity." *Journal of World History* 10, no. 1 (Spring): 93–139.

Bock, Hans Manfred. 1976. *Geschichte des linken Radikalismus in Deutschland.* Frankfurt am Main: Suhrkamp.

Böhme, Helmut. 1967. "Big-Business Pressure Groups and Bismarck's Turn to Protectionism, 1873–79." *Historical Journal* 10, no. 2, 218–236.

Bolt, Christine. 2004. *Sisterhood Questioned? Race, Class and the Internationalization in the American and British Women's Movements, c. 1880s–1970s.* London: Routledge & Kegan Paul.

Bonald, Louis de. 1988 [1802]. *Législation primitive considérée par la raison.* Paris: Éd. Jean-Michel Place.

Boon, H. N. 1936. *Rêve et réalité dans l'œuvre économique et sociale de Napoléon III.* The Hague: Martinus Nijhoff.

Bortolotti, Franca Pieroni. 1978. "Anna Kuliscioff e la questione femminile." In *Anna Kuliscioff e l'età del riformismo: Atti del Convegno di Milano, dicembre 1976,* 104–139. Rome: Mondo Operaio-Ed. Avanti!

Botrel, J.-F., and J. Le Bouil. 1973. "Sur le concept de 'clase media' dans la pensée bourgeoise en Espagne au XIXe siècle." In *La Question de la "bourgeoisie" dans le monde hispanique au XIXe siècle,* 137–151. Bibliothèque de l'École des Hautes Etudes Hispaniques, fasc. 45. Bordeaux: Éd. Bière. [Discussion, 152–160.]

Bouglé, Célestin. 1918. "Le Féminisme saint-simonien." In *Chez les prophètes socialistes,* 57–110. Paris: Félix Alcan.

Bouillon, Jacques. 1956. "Les Démocrates-socialistes aux élections de 1849." *Revue française de sciences politiques,* 6, no. 1 (January–March): 70–95.

Boulle, Pierre H. 1988. "In Defense of Slavery: Eighteenth-Century Opposition to Abolition and the Origins of Racist Ideology of France." In *History from Below: Studies in Popular Protest, and Popular Ideology,* ed. Frederick Krantz, 219–246. London: Basil Blackwell.

Bourgin, Georges. 1913. "La Législation ouvrière du Second Empire. *Revue des études napo-léoniennes,* 2e année, IV, (September): 220–236.

———. 1939. *La guerre de 1870–1871 et la Commune.* Paris: Éd. Nationales.

———. 1947. "La Crise ouvrière à Paris dans la seconde moitié de 1830." *Revue historique,* 71e année, No. CXCVIII (October–December): 203–214.

———. 1948. "La Révolution de 1848 en France." In *Le Printemps des peuples: 1848 dans le monde,* ed. F. Fejtö, 1:165–253. Paris: Éd. du Minuit.

Bourguet, Marie-Noëlle. 1976. "Race et histoire : L'Image officielle de la France en 1800." *Annales E.S.C.* 31, no. 4 (July–August): 802–823.

Bouvier, Jean. 1967. *Les Rothschild.* Paris: Le club français du livre.

Bouvier, Jean, François Furet, and Marcel Gillet. 1965. *Le Mouvement du profit en France au XIXe siècle.* Paris and The Hague: Mouton.

Bouvier, Jeanne. 1931. *Les Femmes pendant la Révolution.* Paris: Éd. Eugène Figuière.

Bowler, Peter. 1984. "E. W. MacBride's Lamarckian Eugenics and Its Implications for the Social Construction of Scientific Knowledge." *Annals of Science* 41, no. 3, 245–260.

Bowles, Robert C. 1960. "The Reaction of Charles Fourier to the French Revolution." *French Historical Studies* 1, no. 3 (Spring): 348–356.

Boxer, Marilyn. 1982. "'First Wave' Feminism in Nineteenth-Century France: Class, Family and Religion." *Women's Studies International Forum* 5, no. 6, 551–559.

Boyle, John W. 1965. "Le Développement du mouvement ouvrier irlandais de 1880 à 1907." *Mouvement social,* no. 52 (July–September): 33–53.

Bramson, Leon. 1974. *The Political Context of Sociology.* Princeton, NJ: Princeton Univ. Press.

Brass, Paul R. 1991. *Ethnicity and Nationalism: Theory and Comparison.* New Delhi: Sage Publ.

Brebner, J. Bartlett. 1930. "Joseph Howe and the Crimean War Enlistment Controversy between Great Britain and the United States." *Canadian Historical Review* 11, no. 4 (December): 300–327.

———. 1948. "Halévy, Diagnostician of Modern Britain." *Thought* 13:101–113.

Briavoinne, Natalis. 1839. *De l'Industrie en Belgique: Causes de décadence et de prospérité: La Situation actuelle.* Vol. 1. Brussels: Eugène Dubois.

Bridges, Amy. 1986. "Becoming American: The Working Classes in the United States before the Civil War." In *Working Class Formation, Nineteenth-Century Patterns in Western Europe and the United States,* ed. I. Katznelson and A. R. Zolberg, 157–196. Princeton, NJ: Princeton Univ. Press.

Briggs, Asa. 1956. "Middle-Class Consciousness in English Politics, 1780–1846." *Past and Present,* no. 9 (April): 65–74.

———. 1959. *The Age of Improvement.* London: Longmans, Green.

———. 1960. "The Language of 'Class' in Early Nineteenth-Century England." In *Essays in Labour History,* ed. A. Briggs and J. Saville, 1:43–73. London: Macmillan.

———. 1967. *William Cobbett.* London: Oxford Univ. Press.

Bristow, Edward. 1974. "Profit-Sharing, Socialism and Labour Unrest." In *Essays in Anti-Labour History,* ed. K. D. Brown, 262–289. London: Macmillan.

Brock, W. R. 1941. *Lord Liverpool and Liberal Toryism, 1820 to 1827.* Cambridge: At the University Press.

Broder, André. 1976. "Le commerce extérieur: L'échec de la conquête d'une position internationale." In *Histoire économique et sociale de la France,* ed. F. Braudel and E. Labrousse, vol. 3, *L'avènement de l'ère industrielle (1879–années 1880),* 1:305–346. Paris: Presses Univ. de France.

Bron, Jean. 1968. *Le Droit à l'existence, du début du XIXe siècle à 1884.* Vol. 1 of *Histoire du mouvement ouvrier français.* Paris: Éd. Ouvrières.

———. 1970. *La Contestation du capitalisme par les travailleurs organisés (1884–1950): Histoire du mouvement ouvrier français,* vol. 2. Paris: Éd. Ouvrières.

Brown, Kenneth D., ed. 1976. *Essays in Anti-Labour History.* London: Macmillan.

Brown, Lucy. 1958. *The Board of Trade and the Free-Trade Movement, 1830–42.* Oxford: Clarendon Press.

Bruhat, Jean. 1952. *Des origines à la révolte des canuts.* Vol. 1 of *Histoire du mouvement ouvrier français.* Paris: Éd. Sociales.

———. 1972. "Le socialisme française de 1815 à 1848." In *Des Origines à 1875,* ed. J. Droz, 331–406. Vol. 1 of *Histoire générale du socialisme..* Paris: Presses Univ. de France.

Bruhat, Jean, J. Dantry, and E. Tersen. 1960. *La Commune de 1871.* Paris: Éd. Sociales.

Brunet, Georges. 1925. *Le Mysticisme social de Saint-Simon.* Paris: Les Presses Françaises.

Brunot, Ferdinand, and Charles Bruneau. 1937. *Précis de grammaire historique de la langue française.* Rev. ed. Paris: Masson.

Bruun, Geoffrey. 1938. *Europe and the French Imperium.* New York: Harpers.

Bryson, Gladys. 1932. "The Emergence of Social Science from Moral Philosophy." *International Journal of Ethics,* 42, no. 3 (April): 302–323.

———. 1945. *Man and Society: The Scottish Inquiry of the Eighteenth Century.* Princeton, NJ: Princeton Univ. Press.

Buck, Paul. 1965. Introduction to *Social Sciences at Harvard, 1860–1920: The Inculcation of the Open Mind,* ed. P. Buck, 1–17. Cambridge, MA: Harvard Univ. Press.

Bud, Robert, and K. Gerrypenn Roberts. 1984. *Science versus Practice: Chemistry in Victorian Britain.* Manchester, UK: Manchester Univ. Press.

Buechler, Steven M. 1987. "Elizabeth Boynton Harbert and the Women's Suffrage Movement, 1870–1896." *Signs* 13, no. 1 (Autumn): 78–97.

———. 1990. *Women's Movements in the United States: Women's Suffrage, Equal Rights and Beyond.* New Brunswick, NJ: Rutgers Univ. Press.

Buer, M. C. 1921. "The Trade Depression following the Napoleonic Wars." *Economica* 1, no. 2 (May): 159–179.

Buhle, Mari Jo. 1981. *Women and American Socialism, 1870–1920.* Urbana: Univ. of Illinois Press.

Buhle, Mari Jo, and Paul Buhle, eds. 1978. *The Concise History of Women Suffrage: Selections from the Classical Work of Stanton, Anthony, Gage and Harper.* Urbana: Univ. of Illinois Press.

Bulmer, Martin. 1984. *The Chicago School of Sociology: Institutionalization, Diversity, and the Rise of Sociological Research.* Chicago: Univ. of Chicago Press.

Burdeau, Georges. 1979. *Le Libéralisme.* Paris: Éd. du Seuil.

Burgess, Keith. 1975. *The Origins of British Industrial Relations: The Nineteenth-Century Experience.* London: Croom Helm.

Burke, Edmund. 1926. *The Works of the Right Honorable Edmund Burke.* London: Oxford Univ. Press.

Burke, Peter. 1988. "Ranke als Gegenrevolutionär." In *Leopold von Ranke und die moderne Geschichtswissenschaft,* ed. W. J. Mommsen, 189–200. Stuttgart: Klett-Cotta.

Burn, Duncan L. 1928. "Canada and the Repeal of the Corn Laws." *Cambridge Historical Journal* 2, no. 3, 252–272.

———. 1961. *The Economic History of Steelmaking, 1867–1939.* 2nd ed. Cambridge: At the University Press.

Burn, W. L. 1949. "The Age of Equipoise: England, 1848–1868." *Nineteenth Century and After* 146 (July–December): 207–224.

———. 1964. *The Age of Equipoise: A Study of the Mid-Victorian Generation.* London: George Allen & Unwin.

Burnham, T. H., and G. O. Hoskins. 1943. *Iron and Steel in Britain, 1870–1930.* London: George Allen & Unwin.

Burns, Gene. 1990. "The Politics of Ideology: The Papal Struggle with Liberalism." *American Journal of Sociology* 95, no. 5 (March): 1123–1152.

Burton, Antoinette M. 1990. "The White Woman's Burden: British Feminists and the Indian Woman, 1865–1915." *Women's Studies International Forum* 13, no. 4, 295–308.

Burwick, Frederick. 1996. *The Damnation of Newton: Goethe's Color Theory and Romantic Perception.* Berlin: Walter de Gruyter.

Bury, J. P. T. 1948. "La Grande-Bretagne et la Révolution de 1848." In *Le Printemps des peuples: 1848 dans le monde,* ed. F. Fejtö, 1:401–448. Paris: Éd. du Minuit.

Bussemer, Herrad-Ulrike. 1985. *Frauenemanzipation und Bildungsbürgertum: Sozialgeschichte der Frauenbewegung in der Reichsgründungszeit.* Weinheim, Germany: Beltz Verlag.

Butterfield, Herbert. 1931. *The Whig Interpretation of History.* London: G. Bell & Sons.

Cahill, Gilbert A. 1957. "Irish Catholicism and English Toryism." *Review of Politics* 19, no. 1 (January): 62–76.

Cain, P. J. 1980. *Economic Foundations of British Overseas Expansion, 1815–1914.* London: Macmillan.

———. 1985. "J. A. Hobson: Financial Capitalism and Imperialism in Late Victorian and Edwardian Britain." *Journal of Imperial and Commonwealth History* 13, no. 3 (May): 1–27.

Cain, P. J., and A. G. Hopkins. 1987. "Gentlemanly Capitalism and British Expansion Overseas, II, New Imperialism, 1850–1945." *Economic History Review,* n.s., 40, no. 1 (February): 1–26.

Caine, Barbara. 1978. "John Stuart Mill and the English Women's Movement." *Historical Studies* 18, no. 70 (April): 52–67.

———. 1982a. "Beatrice Webb and the 'Woman Question,'" *History Workshop Journal,* no. 14 (Autumn): 23–43.

———. 1982b. "Feminism, Suffrage and the Nineteenth-Century English Women's Movement." *Women's Studies International Forum* 5, no. 6, 537–550.

————. 1992. *Victorian Feminists.* New York: Oxford Univ. Press.

Cairncross, A. K. 1949. "Internal Migration in Victorian England." *Manchester School of Economic and Social Studies* 17, no. 1, 67–87.

Calhoun, Craig. 1980. "Transition in Social Foundations for Collective Action." *Social Science History* 4, no. 4 (November): 419–456.

————. 1982. *The Question of Class Struggle: Social Foundations of Popular Radicalism during the Industrial Revolution.* Chicago: Univ. of Chicago Press.

Cameron, Rondo E. 1953. "The *Crédit Mobilier* and the Economic Development of Europe." *Journal of Political Economy* 61, no. 6 (December): 461–488.

————. 1957a. "Profit, croissance et stagnation en France au XIXe siècle." *Économie appliquée* 10, nos. 2–3 (April–September): 409–444.

————. 1957b. "French Finance and Italian Unity: The Cavourian Decade." *American Historical Review* 62, no. 3 (April): 552–569.

————. 1957c. "Le Développement économique de l'Europe du XIXe siècle, Le Rôle de la France." *Annales E.S.C.* 12, no. 2 (April–June): 243–257.

————. 1958. "Economic Growth and Stagnation in France, 1815–1914." *Journal of Modern History* 30, no. 1 (March): 1–13.

————. 1961. *France and the Economic Development of Europe, 1800–1914.* Princeton, NJ: Princeton Univ. Press.

————. 1989. *A Concise Economic History of the World: From Paleolithic Times to the Present.* New York: Oxford Univ. Press.

Cameron, Rondo E., et al. 1967. *Banking in the Early Stages of Industrialization: A Study in Comparative Economic History.* New York: Oxford Univ. Press.

Cameron, Rondo E., and Charles E. Freedeman. 1983. "French Economic Growth: A Radical Revision." *Social Science History* 7, no. 1 (Winter): 3–30.

Camparini, Aurelia. 1978a. "La Questione femminile come problema de classe." In *Anna Kulischoff e l'età del riformismo: Atti del convegno di Milano, dicembre 1976,* 318–328. Rome: Mondo Operaio-Ed. Avanti!

————. 1978b. *Questione femminile e Terza Internazionele.* Bari: De Donato.

Campbell, Stuart L. 1978. *The Second Empire Revisited: A Study in French Historiography.* New Brunswick, NJ: Rutgers Univ. Press.

Cantimori, Delio. 1948. "1848 en Italie." In *Le Printemps des peuples: 1848 dans le monde,* ed. F. Fejtö, 1:255–318. Paris: Éd. du Minuit.

Carlisle, Robert B. 1968. "Saint Simonian Radicalism: A Definition and a Direction." *French Historical Studies* 5, no. 4 (Fall): 430–445.

Carlson, Andrew R. 1972. *Anarchism in Germany.* Metuchen, NJ: Scarecrow Press.

Carnot, Sadi. 1875. Preface to *La Révolution de 1848 et ses détracteurs,* by J. S. Mill, v–xxx. Paris: Lib. Germer Baillière.

Caron, François. 1979. *An Economic History of Modern France.* New York: Columbia Univ. Press.

Carrère d'Encausse, Hélène. 1963. "La Révolution de 1905 au Turkestan." *Le Mouvement social* 45 (oct.-December): 86–92.

————. 1971. "Unité prolétarienne et diversité nationale: Lénine et la théorie de l'autodétermination." *Revue française de science politique* 21, no. 2 (April): 221–255.

Casalini, Maria. 1981. "Femminismo e socialismo in Anna Kuliscioff, 1890–1907." *Italia contemporanea* 33, no. 143 (April–June): 11–43.

Cashdollar, Charles D. 1989. *The Transformation of Theology, 1830–1890: Positivism and Protestant Thought in Britain and America.* Princeton, NJ: Princeton Univ. Press.

Catt, Carrie Chapman, and Nettie Rogers Shuler. 1923. *Woman Suffrage and Politics: The Inner Story of the Suffrage Movement.* New York: Charles Scribner's.

Cecil, Lord Hugh. 1912. *Conservatism.* London: Williams & Northgage.

Cerati, Marie. 1966. *Le Club des citoyennes républicaines révolutionnaires.* Paris: Éd. Sociales.

Césaire, Aimé. 1948. "Introduction, Victor Schoelcher et l'abolition de l'esclavage." In V. Schoelcher, *Esclavage et colonisation,* 1–28. Paris: Presses Univ. de France.

———. 1981. *Toussaint Louverture: La Révolution française et le problème colonial.* Paris: Présence Africaine.

Chafe, William. 1977. *Women and Equality: Changing Patterns in American Culture.* New York: Oxford Univ. Press.

Chafetz, Janet Saltzman, and Anthony Gary Dworkin. 1986. *Female Revolt: Women's Movements in World and Historical Perspective.* Totowa, NJ: Rowman & Allenheld.

Chandra, Bipan. 1979. *Nationalism and Colonialism in Modern India.* New Delhi: Orient Longman.

Chapelle-Dulière, Jacqueline. 1981. "Le 'Socialisme' de Frédéric Le Play (1806–1882), membre de la Commission du Luxembourg en 1848." *Revue de l'Institut de Sociologie* 4:741–769.

Charlton, Donald Geoffrey. 1959. *Positivist Thought in France during the Second Empire, 1852–1870.* Oxford: Clarendon Press.

Charvet, John. 1982. *Feminism.* London: Dent.

Chauvet, P. 1951. "Le Coup d'état vu par un ouvrier." *1848. Revue des révolutions contemporaines,* no. 189 (December): 148–152.

Checkland, S. G. 1951. "The Advent of Academic Economics in England." *Manchester School of Economic and Social Science,* n.s., 19, no. 5 (January): 43–70.

———. 1964. *The Rise of Industrial Society in England, 1815–1885.* London: Longmans.

Checkland, S. G, and E. O. A. Checkland 1974. Introduction to *The Poor Law Report of 1834,* ed. S. G. and E. O. A. Checkland, 9–59. Harmondsworth, UK: Penguin.

Chevalier, Louis. 1958. *Classes laborieuses et classes dangereuses à Paris pendant la première moitié du XIXe siècle.* Paris: Plon.

Chlepner, B.-S. 1926. *La banque en Belgique: Étude historique et économique.* Brussels: M. Lamertin.

———. 1931. "Les Débuts du crédit industriel modern." *Revue de l'Institut de Sociologie* 9, no. 2 (April–June): 293–316.

Church, R. A. 1975. *The Great Victorian Boom, 1850–1873.* London: Macmillan.

Church, Robert L. 1974. "Economists as Experts, 1870–1920." In *The University in Society,* ed. L. Stone, 2:571–609. Princeton, NJ: Princeton Univ. Press.

Clapham, J. H. 1910. "The Last Years of the Navigation Acts." Pts. 1 and 2. *English Historical Review* 25, no. 99 (July): 480–501; no. 100 (October): 687–707.

———. 1916. "The Spitalfield Acts, 1773–1824." *Economic Journal* 26, no. 104 (December): 459–471.

————. 1930. *An Economic History of Modern Britain.* Vol. 1, *The Early Railway Age, 1820–1850.* 2nd ed. Cambridge: Cambridge Univ. Press.

————. 1932. *An Economic History of Modern Britain.* Vol. 2, *Free Trade and Steel, 1820–1850.* Cambridge: Cambridge Univ. Press.

————. 1944. *The Bank of England.* Vol. 1, *1694–1797.* Cambridge: Cambridge Univ. Press.

Clark, Terry N. 1972. "Emile Durkheim and the French University: The Institutionalization of Sociology." In *The Establishment of Empirical Sociology: Studies in Continuity, Discontinuity, and Institutionalization,* ed. A. Oberschall, 152–186. New York: Harper & Row.

————. 1973. *Prophets and Patrons: The French University and the Emergence of the Social Sciences.* Cambridge, MA: Harvard Univ. Press.

Clemens, Barbel. 1988. *"Menschenrechte haben kein Geschlecht": Zum Politikverständnis der Bürgerlichen Frauenbewegung.* Pfaffenweiler, Germany: Centaurus Verlagsgesellschaft.

Clements, R. V. 1955."Trade Unions and Emigration, 1840–1880." *Population Studies* 9, no. 2 (November): 167–180.

————. "British Trade Unions and Popular Political Economy, 1850–1875." *Economic History Review,* n.s., 14, no. 1 (August): 93–104.

Coates, Willson H. 1950. "Benthamism, Laissez-faire, and Collectivism." *Journal of the History of Ideas* 11, no. 3 (June): 357–363.

Coats, A. W. 1960. "The First Two Decades of the American Economic Association." *American Economic Review* 50, no. 4 (September): 555–574.

Coats, A. W., and S. E. Coats. 1970. "The Social Composition of the Royal Economic Society and the Beginnings of the British Economics 'Profession,'1890–1915." *British Journal of Sociology* 21, no. 1 (March): 73–85.

Cobb, Richard. 1970. *The Police and the People: French Popular Protest, 1789–1820.* Oxford: Clarendon Press.

Cobban, Alfred. 1950. Introduction to *The Debate on the French Revolution,* ed. A. Cobban, 1–32. London: Nicholas Kaye.

————. 1967. "The 'Middle Class' in France, 1815–1848." *French Historical Studies* 5 (Spring): 41–52.

Cobbe, Frances Power. 1881. *The Duties of Women.* London: Williams & Norgate.

Cohen, Philip N. 1996. "Nationalism and Suffrage: Gender Struggle in Nation-Building America." *Signs* 21, no. 3 (Spring): 717–727.

Cohen, William B. 1980. *The French Encounter with Africans: White Response to Blacks, 1530–1880.* Bloomington: Indiana Univ. Press.

Cole, G. D. H. 1937. "British Trade Unionism in the Third Quarter of the Nineteenth Century." *International Review for Social History* 2:1–22.

————. 1953. *Socialist Thought: The Forerunners, 1789–1850.* Vol. 1 of *A History of Socialist Thought.* New York: St. Martin's Press.

Cole, Juan. 2008. *Napoleon's Egypt: Invading the Middle East.* New York: Palgrave-Macmillan.

Cole, Stephen. 1972. "Continuity and Institutionalization in Science: A Case Study of Failure." In *The Establishment of Empirical Sociology: Studies in Continuity, Discontinuity, and Institutionalization,* ed. A. Oberschall, 73–129. New York: Harper & Row.

Coleman, Bruce. 1973. *The Idea of the City in Nineteenth-Century Britain.* Boston: Routledge & Kegan Paul.

———. 1988. *Conservatism and the Conservative Party in Nineteenth-Century Britain.* London: Edward Arnold.

Collini, Stefan. 1978. "Sociology and Idealism in Britain, 1880–1920." *Archives européennes de sociologie* 19, no. 1, 3–50.

———. 1979. *Liberalism and Sociology: L. T. Hobhouse and Political Argument in England, 1880–1914.* Cambridge: Cambridge Univ. Press.

Collini, Stefan, Donald Winch, and John Burrow, eds. 1983. *That Noble Science of Politics.* Cambridge: Cambridge Univ. Press.

Collins, Henry. 1964. "The International and the British Labour Movement." *Society for the Study of Labour History Bulletin,* no. 9 (Autumn): 24–39.

Collins, Irene, ed. 1970. *Government and Society in France, 1814–1848.* London: Edward Arnold.

Cominos, Peter T. 1963. "Late-Victorian Sexual Respectability and the Social System." *International Review of Social History* 8:18–48, 216–250.

Commons, John R. 1918. Introduction to *History of Labour in the United States,* ed. J. R. Commons et al., 13–21. New York: Macmillan.

———. 1935. "Introduction to Volumes III & IV." In *History of Labour in the United States,* ed. J. R. Commons et al., 3:ix–xxx. New York: Macmillan.

Condliffe, J. B. 1951. *The Commerce of Nations.* London: George Allen & Unwin.

Condorcet, Jean-Antoine Nicolas de Capitat Marquis de. 1778. *Réflexions d'un citoyen catholique sur les lois de France relatives aux protestants.* N.p., n.d.

———. 1788. *Réflexions sur l'esclavage des nègres.* Rev. and corrected ed. Neuchâtel, Switzerland.

Conze, Werner, and Dieter Groh. 1966. *Die Arbeiterbewegung in der nationalen Bewegung: Die deutsche Sozialdemokratie vor, während und nach der Reichsgründung.* Stuttgart: Ernst Klett Verlag.

———. 1971. "Working-Class Movement and National Movement in Germany between 1830 and 1871." In *Mouvements nationaux et indépendance et classes populaires aux XIXe et XXe siècles en Occident et en Orient,* by Comité International des Sciences Historiques and Commission Internationale d'Histoire des Mouvement Sociaux et des Structures Sociales, ed. E. Labrousse, 1:134–174. Paris: Lib. Armand Colin.

Cookson, J. E. 1975. *Lord Liverpool's Administration: The Crucial Years, 1815–1822.* Edinburgh: Scottish Academic Press.

Coole, Diana H. 1993. *Women in Political Theory: From Ancient Mysogyny to Contemporary Feminism.* 2nd ed. Hertfordshire, UK: Harvester Wheatsheaf.

Coornaert, Emile. 1950. "La pensée ouvrière et la conscience de classe en France de 1830 à 1848." In *Studi in Onore de Gino Luzzatto,* 3:12–33. Milan: Dott. A. Giuffrè-Ed.

Copans, J., and J. Jaurin, eds. 1994. *Aux origines de l'anthropologie française: Les Mémoires de la Société des Observateurs de l'Homme en l'an VIII.* Paris: Jean Michel Place.

Coppock, D. J. 1964. "British Industrial Growth during the Great Depression (1873–96): A Pessimist's View." *Economic History Review,* n.s., 17, no. 2 (December): 389–396.

Cordillot, Michel. 1990. *La Naissance du mouvement ouvrier à Besançon: La Première Internationale, 1869–1872.* Rev. ed. Annales Littéraires de l'Université de Besançon, Cahiers D'Etudes Comtoises, no. 45. Paris: Les Belles-Lettres.

Corry, B. A. 1958. "The Theory of the Economic Effects of Government Expenditure in English Classical Economy." *Economica*, n.s., 25, no. 97 (February): 34–48.

Coser, Lewis. 1960. "Durkheim's Conservatism and Its Implications for His Sociological Theory." In *Emile Durkheim, 1858–1917,* ed. K. H. Wolff, 211–232. Columbus: Ohio State Univ. Press.

Cosslett, Tess. 1982. *The "Scientific Movement" and Victorian Literature.* New York: St. Martin's Press.

Cottereau, Alain. 1980. "Vie quotidienne et résistance ouvrière à Paris en 1870." Étude préalable to *Le Sublime,* by Denis Poulet. Paris: François Maspéro.

———. 1986. "The Distinctiveness of Working-Class Cultures in France, 1848–1900." In *Working-Class Formation: Nineteenth-Century Patters in Western Europe and the United States,* ed. I. Katznelson and A. Zolberg, 111–154. Princeton, NJ: Princeton Univ. Press.

Coudert, Alison.1989. "The Myth of the Improved Status of Protestant Women: The Case of the Witchcraze." In *The Politics of Gender in Early Modern Europe,* ed. J. R. Brink et al., 61–90. Sixteenth Century Essays & Studies 12. Kirksville, MO: Sixteenth Century Journal Publ.

Coussy, Jean. 1961. "La Politique commerciale du Second Empire et la continuité de l'évolution structurelle française." *Cahiers de l'Institut de Science Economique Appliquée,* no. 120 [série P, no. 6] (December): 1–47.

Craeybeckx, Jan. 1968. "Les débuts de la révolution industrielle en Belgique et les statistiques de la fin de l'Empire." In *Mélanges offerts à G. Jacquemyns,* 115–144. Brussels: Université Libre de Bruxelles, Ed. de l'Institut de Sociologie.

Crafts, N. F. R. 1984. "Economic Growth in France and Britain, 1830–1910: A Review of the Evidence." *Journal of Economic History* 44, no. 1 (March): 49–67.

Crick, Bernard R. 1955. "The Strange Quest for An American Conservatism." *Review of Politics* 17, no. 3 (July): 359–376.

———. 1964. *The American Science of Politics: Its Origins and Conditions.* 3rd printing. Berkeley: Univ. of California Press.

Croce, Benedetto. 1934. *History of Europe in the Nineteenth Century.* London: George Allen & Unwin.

Cronin, James E. 1983. "Politics, Class Structure, and the Enduring Weakness of British Social Democracy." *Journal of Social History* 16, no. 3 (Spring): 123–142.

Cross, Máire, and Tim Gray. 1992. *The Feminism of Flora Tristan.* Oxford: Berg.

Crouch, R. L. 1967. "Laissez-faire in Nineteenth-Century Britain: Myth or Reality?" *Manchester School of Economic and Social Studies 35,* no. 3 (September): 199–213.

Crouzet, François. 1964. "Wars, Blockade, and Economic Change in Europe, 1792–1815." *Journal of Economic History* 24, no. 4: 567–590.

———. 1967. "Agriculture et révolution industrielle: Quelques réflexions." *Cahiers d'histoire* 12, nos. 1–2, 67–85.

———. 1970. "Essai de construction d'un indice annuel de la production industrielle française au XIXe siècle." *Annales E.S.C.* 25, no. 1 (January–February): 56–99.

———. 1972a. "Encore la croissance économique française au XIXe siècle." *Revue du nord* 54, no. 214 (July–September): 271–288.

————. 1972b. "Western Europe and Great Britain: Catching Up in the First Half of the Nineteenth Century." In *Economic Development in the Long Run,* ed. A. J. Youngson, 98–125. London: George Allen & Unwin.

————. 1975. "Trade and Empire: The British Experience from the Establishment of Free Trade until the First World War." In *Great Britain and Her World, 1750–1914,* ed. B. M. Ratcliffe, 209–235. Manchester, UK: Manchester Univ. Press.

————. 1978. *L'économie de la Grande-Bretagne victorienne.* Paris: S.E.D.E.S.

————. 1985. *De la supériorité de l'Angleterre sur la France: L'économique et l'imaginaire, XVIIe-XXe siècle.* Paris: Lib. Académique Perrin.

Cruz Seoane, María. 1968. *El Primer lenguaje constitucional español (Las Cortes de Cádiz).* Madrid: Ed. Moneda y Crédito.

Cullen, L. M. 1980. "The Cultural Basis of Modern Irish Nationalism." In *The Roots of Nationalism, Studies in Northern Europe,* ed. R. Mitchison, 91–106. Edinburgh: John Donald.

Cullen, Michael J. 1975. *The Statistical Movement in Early Victorian Britain: The Foundations of Empirical Social Research.* Hassocks, Sussex, UK: Harvester Press.

Cunningham, Andrew, and Nicholas Jardine. 1990. "Introduction: The Age of Reflexion." In *Romanticism and the Sciences,* ed. A. Cunningham and N. Jardine, 1–9. Cambridge: Cambridge Univ. Press.

Cunningham, Hugh. 1981. "The Language of Patriotism, 1750–1914." *History Workshop Journal* 12 (Autumn): 8–33.

Cunningham, William. 1892. "The Perversion of Economic History." *Economic Journal* 2, no. 3 (September): 491–508.

————. 1907. *The Growth of English Industry and Commerce in Modern Times: The Mercantile System.* 4th ed. London: Cambridge Univ. Press.

————. 1908. *The Industrial Revolution; Being the Parts Entitled Parliamentary Colbertism and Laissez Faire, Reprinted from "The Growth of English Industry and Commerce in Modern Times," by W. Cunningham.* Cambridge: Cambridge Univ. Press.

Currie, R., and R. M. Hartwell. 1965. "The Making of the English Working Class?" *Economic History Review,* n.s., 18, no. 3, 633–643.

Curtin, Philip. 1990. "The Environment beyond Europe and the European Theory of Empire." *Journal of World History* 1, no. 2 (Fall): 131–150.

Daget, Serge. 1973. "Le Mot esclave, nègre, Noir et les jugements de valeur sur la traite négrière dans la littérature abolitionniste française de 1770 à 1845." *Revue française d'histoire d'Outre-Mer* LX, 4, no. 221, 511–548.

Dahrendorf, Ralf. 1987. "Max Weber and Modern Social Science." In *Max Weber and His Contemporaries,* ed. W. J. Mommsen and J. Osterhammel, 574–581. London: Unwin Hyman.

————. 1995. *LSE: A History of the London School of Economics and Political Science, 1985–1995.* Oxford: Oxford Univ. Press.

Dale, Peter Allan. 1989. *In Pursuit of a Scientific Culture: Science, Art and Society in the Victorian Age.* Madison: Univ. of Wisconsin Press.

Darvall, Frank O. 1934. *Popular Disturbance and Public Order in Regency England.* London: Oxford Univ. Press.

Daston, Lorraine. 1988. *Classical Probability in the Enlightenment.* Princeton, NJ: Princeton Univ. Press.

Daumard, Adeline. 1963. *La Bourgeoisie parisienne de 1815 à 1848.* Paris: S.E.V.P.E.N.

——. 1976. "L'Etat libéral et le libéralisme économique." In *Histoire économique et sociale de la France,* vol. 3, pt. 1 (MSP 419), ed. F. Braudel and E. Labrousse. Paris: Presses Univ. de France.

Davies, Emily. 1988. *The Higher Education of Women.* London: Hambledon.

Davis, David Brion. 1966. *The Problem of Slavery in Western Culture.* Ithaca, NY: Cornell Univ. Press.

——. 1984. *Slavery and Human Progress.* New York: Oxford Univ. Press.

Davis, Horace B. 1941. "The Theory of Union Growth." *Quarterly Journal of Economics* 55 (August): 611–637.

Davis, John A., ed. 1979. *Gramsci and Italy's Passive Revolution.* London: Croom Helm.

——. 1989. "Industrialization in Britain and Europe before 1850." In *The First Industrial Revolutions,* ed. P. Mathias and J. A. Davis, 44–68. Oxford: Basil Blackwell.

Davis, Mary. 1993. *Comrade or Brother? A History of the British Labour Movement, 1789–1951.* London: Pluto Press.

Davis, T. W. Rhys. 1903–1904. "Oriental Studies in England and Abroad." *Proceedings of the British Academy,* 183–197.

Deacon, Desley. 1985. "Political Arithmetic: The Nineteenth-Century Australian Census and the Construction of the Dependent Woman." *Signs* 11, no. 1 (Autumn): 27–47.

Deane, Phyllis, and W. A. Cole. 1967. *British Economic Growth, 1688–1959: Trends and Structures.* 2nd ed. London: Cambridge Univ. Press.

Debs, Eugene V. 1903. "The Negro in the Class Struggle." *International Socialist Review* 4, no. 5 (November): 257–260.

DeCaux, Charles. 1835. "L'Université catholique. Premier semestre. Programme des Cours, Faculté des Sciences Sociales, Cours d'économie politique." *L'Université Catholique* 1 (July): 53–54.

Decharneux, Baudouin. 2000. "Introduction philosophique: Les Indo-Européens, de l'étude aux fantasmes." In *Modèles linguistiques et idéologies, "Indo-Européen",* ed. S. Vanséveren, 13–29. Brussels: Éd. Ousia.

Degler, Carl N. 1956. "Charlotte Perkins Gilman on the Theory and Practice of Feminism." *American Quarterly* 8, no. 1 (Spring): 21–39.

DeGroat, Judith A. 1997. "The Public Nature of Women's Work: Definitions and Debates during the Revolution of 1848." *French Historical Studies* 20, no. 1 (Winter): 31–48.

Dehio, Ludwig. 1962. *The Precarious Balance: Four Centuries of the European Power Struggle.* New York: Vintage Books.

Delacampagne, Christian. 1983. *L'Invention du racisme, Antiquité et Moyen Age.* Paris: Fayard.

Delaisi, Francis. 1905. *La Force allemande.* Paris: Pages libres.

Demangeon, Albert, and Lucien Febvre. 1935. *Le Rhin: Problèmes d'histoire et d'économie.* Paris: Lib. Armand Colin.

DeMarchi, N. B. 1976. "On the Early Dangers of Being Too Political an Economist: Thorold Rogers and the 1868 Election to the Drummond Professorship." *Oxford Economic Papers*, n.s., 28, no. 3 (November): 364–380.

Démier, Francis. 1992. "Nation, marché et développement dans la France de la Restauration." *Bulletin du Centre d'Histoire de La France Contemporaine*, no. 13, 95–103.

Demoulin, Robert. 1938. *Guillaume 1er et la transformation économique des provinces belges*. Bibliothèque de la Faculté de Philosophie et Lettres de l'Université de Liège 80. Paris: Lib. E. Droz.

———. 1950. *La Révolution de 1830*. Brussels: La Renaissance du Livre.

———. 1960. "L'Influence française sur la naissance de l'Etat belge." *Revue historique*, 84e année, CCXXIII, 1 (January–March) : 13–28.

Derainne, Pierre-Jacques. 1993. "Naissance d'un protectionnisme national ouvrier au milieu du XIXe siècle." In *Prolétaires de tous les pays, unissez-vous? Les difficiles chemins de l'internationalisme, 1848–1956*, ed. S. Wolikow and M. Cordillot, 27–34. Dijon: EUD.

Desanto, Dominique. 1980. *Flora Tristan: La femme révoltée*. New ed. Paris: Hachette.

Deschamps, Henry-Thierry. 1956. *La Belgique devant la France de Juillet: L'Opinion et l'attitude françaises de 1839 à 1848*. Paris: Société d'Edition 'Les Belles Lettres.'

Descoings, Richard. 2007. *Sciences Po: De La Courneuve à Shanghai*. Paris: Presses de Sciences Po.

———. 2008. ". . . et assumer la complexité." 8 December. http://www.richard-descoings .net/2009/10/04/et-assumer-la-complexite (accessed August 18, 2010).

Dessal, M. 1949. "Les incidents franco-belges en 1848." In *Actes du Congrès historique du Centenaire de la Révolution de 1848*, 107–113. Paris: Presses Univ. de France.

Devance, Louis. 1976. "Femme, famille, travail et monde sexuelle dans l'idéologie de 1848." *Romantisme*, nos. 13–14, 79–103.

Devleeshouwer, Robert. 1970. "Le Consultât et l'Empire: Période de 'take-off' pour l'économie belge?" *Revue d'histoire moderne et contemporaine* 17:610–619.

Devreese, Daisy Eveline. 1989. "L'Association Internationales des Travailleurs, Bilan de l'historiographie et perspectives de recherché." *Cahiers d'histoire de L'IRM*, no. 37, 9–32.

Devulder, Catherine. 1987. "Histoire allemande et totalité, Leopold von Ranke, Johann Gustav Droysen, Karl Lamprecht." *Revue de synthèse*, 4th ser., 108, no. 2 (April–June): 177–197.

Dhondt, Jean. 1949. "La Belgique en 1848." In *Actes du Congrès historique du Centenaire de la Révolution de 1848*, 115–131. Paris: Presses Univ. de France.

———. 1955. "L'Industrie cotonnière gantoise à l'époque française." *Revue d'histoire moderne et contemporaine* 2 (October–December): 233–279.

———. 1969. "The Cotton Industry at Ghent during the French Régime." In *Essays in European Economic History, 1789–1914*, ed. François Crouzet et al., 15–52. London: Edward Arnold.

Dhondt, Jean, and Marinette Bruwier. 1973. "The Industrial Revolution in the Low Countries, 1700–1914." In *The Emergence of Industrial Societies*, ed. C. Cipolla, 1:329–366. The Fontana Economic History of Europe 4. London: Collins.

Dibble, Vernon. 1976. " 'Review Essay' of Herman and Julia R. Schwendinger's *Sociologists of the Chair: A Radical Analysis of the Formative Years of North American Sociology*." *History and Theory* 15, no. 3, 293–321.

Dicey, Alfred Venn. 1914 [1965]. Lectures on the Relation between Law and Public Opinion in England, during the Nineteenth Century. 2nd ed. London: Macmillan.

Dijkstra, Sandra. 1992. *Flora Tristan: Feminism in the Age of George Sand.* London: Pluto Press.

Djordjevíc, Dimitrije, and Stephen Fisher-Galati. 1981. *The Balkan Revolutionary Tradition.* New York: Columbia Univ. Press.

Dolléans, Édouard. 1947. *Histoire du mouvement ouvrier.* 2 vols. Paris: Colin.

Dominick, Raymond H. III. 1982. *Wilhelm Liebknecht and the Founding of the German Social Democratic Party.* Chapel Hill : Univ. of North Carolina Press.

Donzelot, Jacques. 1977. *La Police des familles.* Paris: Éd. du Minuit.

———. 1984. *L'Invention du social: Essai sur le déclin des passions politiques.* Paris: Fayard.

Dorfman, Joseph. 1955a. "The Department of Economics." In *A History of the Faculty of Political Science,* by R. G. Hoxie et al., 161–206. New York: Columbia Univ. Press.

———. 1955b. "The Role of the German Historical School in American Economic Growth." *American Economic Review, Papers and Proceedings,* 45, no. 2 (May): 17–28. [Discussion, 29–39.]

Dorpalen, Andrew. 1969. "The German Struggle against Napoleon: The East German View." *Journal of Modern History* 41, no. 4 (December): 485–516.

Drachkovitch, Milorad. 1953. *Les Socialismes français et allemand et le problème de la guerre, 1870–1914.* Geneva: Droz.

Drescher, Seymour. 1981. "Art Whip and Billy Roller; Or Anti-slavery and Reform Symbolism in Industrializing Britain." *Journal of Social History* 15, no. 1 (Fall): 3–24.

Dreyer, F. A. 1965. "The Whigs and the Political Crisis of 1848." *English Historical Review* 80, no. 316 (July): 514–537.

Droit, Roger-Pol. 2000. "L'Orient comme paradis ou comme enfer: Science des religions et mythes philosophiques à l'époque contemporaine." In *Sciences, mythes et religions en Europe, Royaumont, 14–15 octobre 1997,* ed. D. Lecourt, 97–103. Luxembourg: European Communities.

Droixhe, Daniel, and Klaus Keifer, eds. 1987. *Images de l'africain de l'Antiquité au XXe siècle.* Frankfurt am Main: Verlag Peter Lang.

Droz, Jacques. 1963. "L'Origine de la loi des trois classes en Prusse." In *Réaction et suffrage universel en France et en Allemagne (1848–1850),* ed. J. Droz, 1–45. Bibliothèque de la Révolution de 1848 22. Paris: Lib. Marcel Rivière.

———. 1967. *Europe between Revolutions, 1815–1848: The Fontana History of Europe.* London: Collins.

———. 1971. "Cisleithanie, Les Masses laborieuses et le problème national." In *Mouvements nationaux d'indépendance et classes populaires aux XIXe et XXe siècles en Occident et en Orient,* by Comité International des Sciences Historiques and Commission Internationale d'Histoire des Mouveent Sociaux et des Structures Sociales, ed. E. Labrousse, 1:74–92. Paris: Lib. Armand Colin.

———. 1977a. Introduction to *Des origines à 1875,* ed. J. Droz, 9–24. Vol. 1 of *Histoire Générale du Socialisme.* Paris: Presses Univ. de France.

———. 1977b. "Le Socialisme allemand du *Vormärz.*" In *Des Origines à 1875,* ed. J. Droz, 407–456. Vol. 1 of *Histoire Générale du Socialisme.* Paris: Presses Univ. de France.

Dubofsky, Melvyn. 1974. "Socialism and Syndicalism." In *Failure of a Dream? Essays in the History of American Socialism,* ed. J. Laslett and S. M. Lipset, 252–285. Garden City, NY: Anchor.

DuBois, Ellen Carol. 1978. *Feminism and Suffrage: The Emergence of an Independent Women's Movement in America, 1848–1869.* Ithaca, NY: Cornell Univ. Press.

Duchet, Michèle. 1975. *Anthropologie et histoire au siècle des Lumières.* Paris: Albin Michel.

Duffy, A. E. P. 1961. "New Unionism in Britain, 1889–1890: A Reappraisal." *Economic History Review,* n.s., 14, no. 2 (December): 306–319.

Duhet, Paule-Marie. 1971. *Les Femmes et la Révolution, 1789–1794.* Paris: Julliard.

———, ed. 1989. *1789, Cahiers de doléances des femmes et autres textes.* Nouv. éd. augm. Paris: Des Femmes.

Dunbabin, J. D. D. 1963. "The 'Revolt of the Field': The Agricultural Labourers' Movement in the 1870s." *Past and Present,* no. 26 (November): 68–97.

Dunham, Arthur Louis. 1930. *The Anglo-French Treaty of Commerce 1861 and the Progress of the Industrial Revolution in France.* Ann Arbor: Univ. of Michigan Press.

Dupuis, Charles. 1909. *Le Principe d'équilibre et le concert européen, de la Paix de Westphalie à l'Acte d'Algéciras.* Paris: Perrin.

Durkheim, Emile. 1925. "Saint-Simon, fondateur du positivisme et de la sociologie." *Revue philosophique de la France et de l'étranger,* 50e année, XCIX, nos. 5–6 (May–June): 321–341.

Duroselle, Jean-Baptiste. 1951. *Les Débuts du catholicisme social en France (1822–1870).* Paris: Presses Univ. de France.

Duverger, Maurice. 1967. *La Démocratie sans le peuple.* Paris: Éd. du Seuil.

Echard, William E. 1983. *Napoleon III and the Concert of Europe.* Baton Rouge: Louisiana State Univ. Press.

Eichtal, Eugène d'. 1903. "Carlyle et le Saint-Simonisme: Lettres à Gustave d'Eichtal." *Revue historique,* 28e année, LXXXII, 2 (July–August): 292–306.

Einaudi, Mario. 1938. "Le Prime ferrovie piemontesi ed il conte di Cavour." *Rivista di storia economica* 3:1–38.

Eisenstein, Elizabeth L. 1959. *The First Professional Revolutionist, Filippo Michele Buonarroti (1761–1837).* Cambridge, MA: Harvard Univ. Press.

Eisenstein, Zillah R. 1981. *The Radical Future of Liberal Feminism.* Boston: Northeastern Univ. Press.

Elbaum, B., and W. Lazowick. 1984. "The Decline of the British Economy: An Institutional Perspective." *Journal of Economic History* 44, no. 2 (June): 567–583.

Elesh, David. 1972. "The Manchester Statistical Society: A Case Study of Discontinuity in the History of Empirical Social Research." In *The Establishment of Empirical Sociology, Studies in Continuity, Discontinuity, and Institutionalization,* ed. A. Oberschall, 31–72. New York: Harper & Row.

Eley, Geoff. 1976." Social Imperialism in Germany: Reformist Synthesis or Reactionary Sleight of Hand?." In *Imperialismus im 20. Jahrhundert: Gedenkschrift für George W. F. Hallgarten,* ed. J. Radkau and I. Geiss, 71–86. Munich: C. H. Beck.

———. 1980. *Reshaping the German Right: Radical Nationalism and Political Change after Bismarck.* New Haven, CT: Yale Univ. Press.

———. 1984. "The British Model and the German Road: Rethinking the Course of German History Before 1914." In . *The Peculiarities of German History: Bourgeois Society and Politics in Nineteenth Century Germany*, ed. D. Blackbourn and G. Eley, 37–155. New York: Oxford Univ. Press.

———. 1996. *From Unification to Nazism: Reinterpreting the German Past*. Boston: Unwin and Hyman.

Ellis, John. 1974a. "Patterns of Political Violence during the Second Republic, 1845–51." In *Revolt to Revolution: Studies in the 19th and 20th Century European Experience*, ed. M. Elliott Bateman et al., 59–112. Manchester, UK: Manchester Univ. Press.

———. 1974b. "Revolutionary Trends in Europe, A Historical Introduction." In *Revolt to Revolution: Studies in the 19th and 20th Century European Experience*, ed. M. Elliott Bateman et al., 31–57. Manchester, UK: Manchester Univ. Press.

Elshtain, Jean Bethke. 1981. *Public Man, Private Woman: Women in Social and Political Thought*. Princeton, NJ: Princeton Univ. Press.

Elton, Godfrey Lord. 1923. *The Revolutionary Idea in France (1789–1871)*. London: Edward Arnold.

Elvin, Mark. 1986. "A Working Definition of 'Modernity'?" *Past and Present*, no. 113 (November): 209–213.

Elwitt, Sanford. 1975. *The Making of the Third Republic: Class and Politics in France, 1868–1884*. Baton Rouge: Louisiana State Univ. Press.

———. 1988. "Debate, Social Science, Social Reform and Sociology." *Past and Present*, no. 121 (November): 209–214.

Ely, Richard T. 1890. The Labor Movement in America. Rev. ed. New York: T. Y. Crowell.

———. 1910. "The American Economic Association, 1885–1909." *American Economic Association Quarterly*, 3rd ser., 11, no. 1, 47–92.

Emerit, Marcel. 1941. *Les Saint-simoniens en Algérie*. Paris: Les Belles-Lettres.

———. 1943. "Les Saint-simoniens au Maroc." *Bulletin de l'Enseignement Public du Maroc*, 30e année, no. 176 (April–June).

———, ed. 1949. *La Révolution de 1848 en Algérie*. Paris: Larose.

Emy, Hugh Vincent. 1973. *Liberals, Radicals and Social Politics, 1892–1914*. Cambridge: At the University Press.

Endres, Robert. 1948. "1848 en Autriche." In *Le Printemps des peuples: 1848 dans le monde*, ed. F. Fejtö, 2:65–122. Paris: Éd. du Minuit.

Engel, Arthur. 1974. "Emerging Concepts of the Academic Profession at Oxford: 1800–1854." In *The University in Society*, ed. L. Stone, 1:305–351. Princeton, NJ: Princeton Univ. Press.

Erickson, Charlotte. 1949. "The Encouragement of Emigration by British Trade Unions, 1850–1900." *Population Studies* 3, no. 3 (December): 248–273.

Evans, David Owen. 1951. *Social Romanticism in France, 1830–1848*. Oxford: Clarendon Press.

Evans, Eric J., ed. 1978. *Social Policy, 1830–1914: Individualism, Collectivism and the Origins of the Welfare State*. London: Routledge & Kegan Paul.

———. 1983. *The Forging of the Modern State: Early Industrial Britain, 1783–1870*. London: Longman.

Evans, Richard J. 1976. *The Feminist Movement in Germany, 1894–1933*. London and Beverly Hills: Sage Publications.

———. 1977. *The Feminists: Women's Emancipation Movements in Europe, America and Australasia, 1840–1920*. London: Croom Helm.

———. 1986. "The Concept of Feminism: Notes for Practicing Historians." In *German Women in the Eighteenth and Nineteenth Centuries: A Social and Literary History*, ed. R.-E. B. Joeres and J. M. Maynes, 247–268. Bloomington: Indiana Univ. Press.

———. 1987. *Comrades and Sisters: Feminism, Socialism, and Pacifism in Europe, 1870–1945*. Brighton, Sussex, UK: Wheatsheaf Books.

Fairlie, Susan. 1965. "The Nineteenth-Century Corn Law Reconsidered." *Economic History Review*, n.s., 18, no. 3 (December): 562–575.

———. 1969. "The Corn Laws and British Wheat Production, 1829–76." *Economic History Review*, n.s., 22, no. 1 (April): 88–116.

Faivre, Jean-Paul. 1954. *L'Expansion française dans le Pacifique, de 1800 à 1842*. Paris: Nouvelles Éd. Latines.

Fakkar, Rouchdi. 1968. *Sociologie, socialisme et internationalisme prémarxistes: Contribution à l'étude de l'influence internationale de Saint-Simon et de ses disciples. (Bilan en Europe et portée extraeuropéenne)*. Neuchâtel, Switzerland: Delachaux & Niestlé.

Farnie, D. A. 1979. *The English Cotton Industry and the World Market, 1815–1896*. Oxford: Clarendon Press.

Farr, James. 1988. "The History of Political Science." *American Journal of Political Science* 32, no. 4 (November): 1175–1195.

Faure, Alain, and Jacques Rancière. 1976. *La Parole ouvrière, textes rassemblées et présentées, 1830/1851*. Paris: UGE.

Fauré, Christine. 1991. *Democracy without Women: Feminism and the Rise of Liberal Individualism in France*. Bloomington: Indiana Univ. Press.

Favre, Pierre. 1981. "Les Sciences d'Etat entre déterminisme et libéralisme: Emile Boutmy et la création de l'Ecole libre de sciences politiques." *Revue française de sociologie* 22, no. 3 (July–September): 429–468.

Fay, C. R. 1920. *Life and Labour in the Nineteenth Century*. Cambridge: At the University Press.

———. 1926. "Price Control and the Corn Averages under the Corn Laws." *Economic Journal (Economic History)* 1, no. 1 (January): 149–154.

———. 1932. *The Corn Laws and Social England*. Cambridge: At the University Press.

Fay, Victor. 1981. Remarks in *Jaurès et la classe ouvrière*, 187–188. Collection mouvement social. Paris: Ed. Ouvrières.

Feaveryear, A. E. 1931. *The Pound Sterling: A History of English Money*. London: Oxford Univ. Press.

Fehér, Ferenc. 1987. *The Frozen Revolution: An Essay on Jacobinism*. Cambridge: Cambridge Univ. Press.

Feis, Herbert. 1930. *Europe, the World's Banker, 1870–1914*. New Haven, CT: Yale Univ. Press.

Fejtö, François. 1948a. "Introduction: L'Europe à la veille de la Révolution." In *Le Printemps des peuples: 1848 dans le monde*, ed. F. Fejtö, 1:25–125. Paris: Éd. du Minuit.

————. 1948b. "La Guerre de l'indépendance hongroise." In *Le Printemps des peuples: 1848 dans le monde*, ed. F. Fejtö, 2:123–204. Paris: Éd. du Minuit.

————. 1948c. "Conclusion." In *Le Printemps des peuples: 1848 dans le monde*, ed. F. Fejtö, 2:435–466. Paris: Éd. du Minuit.

————. 1948d. "Le Sens de la Révolution de 1848 en Hongrie et an Autriche." *Revue socialiste*, n.s., nos. 17–18 (January–February): 107–116.

————. 1949. "Paris des années 40, capitale de la Révolution." In *Actes du Congrès historique du Centenaire de la Révolution de 1848*, 357–369. Paris: Presses Univ. de France.

Feldman, Gerald D. 1986. "German Economic History." *Central European History* 19, no. 2 (June): 174–185.

Feray, E. 1881. *Du Traité de commerce de 1860 avec l'Angleterre*. Paris: Plon.

Festy, Octave. 1908. *Le Mouvement ouvrier au début de la Monarchie de Juillet (1830–1834)*. Vol. 2, part 3, of *Bibliothèque d'Histoire Moderne*. Paris: Éd. Cornély.

————. 1913. "Le Mouvement ouvrier à Paris en 1840." 3 pts. *Revue de l'Ecole Libre des Sciences Politiques* 6 (July–August): 67–79; (September–October): 226–240; (November–December): 333–361.

Fetter, Frank W. 1943. "The Early History of Political Economy in the United States." *Proceedings of the American Philosophical Society* 87, no. 1 (July): 51–60.

————. 1959. "The Politics of the Bullion Report." *Economica*, n.s., 26, no. 102 (May): 99–120.

————. 1965. *Development of British Monetary Orthodoxy, 1797–1875*. Cambridge, MA: Harvard Univ. Press.

Fitchett, W. H. 1899–1900. *How England Saved Europe: The Story of the Great War (1798–1815)*. 4 vols. London: Smith, Elder & Co.

Fitzpatrick, David. 1984. *Irish Emigration, 1801–1921*. Vol. 1 of *Studies in Irish Economic and Social History*. Dublin: Economic and Social History Society of Ireland.

Flamant, Maurice. 1988. *Histoire du libéralisme*. Que sais-je?, no. 1797bis. Paris: Presses Univ. de France.

Fletcher, Roger. 1984. *Revisionism and Empire: Socialist Imperialism in Germany, 1897–1914*. London: George Allen & Unwin.

Flexner, Eleanor. 1975. *A Century of Struggle: The Women's Rights Movement in the United States*. Rev. ed. Cambridge, MA: Belknap Press.

Flinn, M. W. 1961. "The Poor Employment Act of 1817." *Economic History Review*, n.s., 14, no. 1 (August): 82–92.

Fohlen, Claude. 1956. "Bourgeoisie française, liberté économique et intervention de l'état." *Revue économique* 7, no. 3 (May): 414–428.

————. 1961. "Sociétés anonymes et développement capitaliste sous le Second Empire." *Histoire des entreprises*, no. 6 (November): 65–77.

Folbre, Nancy. 1991. "The Unproductive Housewife: Her Evolution in Nineteenth-Century Economic Thought." *Signs* 16, no. 3 (Spring): 463–484.

Foner, Eric. 1983. *Nothing but Freedom: Emancipation and Its Legacy*. Baton Rouge: Louisiana State Univ. Press.

————. 1984. "Why Is There No Socialism in the United States?" *History Workshop Journal*, no. 17 (Spring): 57–80.

Foner, Philip S. 1977. *The Great Labor Uprising of 1877.* New York: Monad.

Fong, H. D. 1930. *Triumph of Factory System in England.* Tientsin, China: Chihli Press.

Fontvieille, Louis. 1976. "Evolution et croissance de l'Etat français de 1815 à 1969" *Économies et sociétés* 10 (September–December): 9–12 [Cahiers de l'I.S.M.E.A., Série AF, no. 13].

Fontvieille, Louis, with Anita Bringent. 1982. "Evolution et croissance de l'administration départementale française, 1815–1974." *Économies et sociétés* 16 (January–February): 1–2 [Cahiers de l'I.S.M.E.A., Séries AF, no. 14].

Foote, George A. 1951. "The Place of Science in the British Reform Movement, 1830–1850." *Isis* 42, pt. 3, no. 129 (October): 192–208.

Forbes, Geraldine H. 1982. "Caged Tigers: 'First Wave' Feminists in India." *Women's Studies International Forum* 5, no. 6, 525–536.

Forman, Michael. 1998. *Nationalism and the International Labor Movement: The Idea of Nation in Socialist Anarchist Theory.* University Park: Pennsylvania State Univ. Press.

Fossaert, Robert. 1955. "La Théorie des classes chez Guizot et Thierry." *La Pensée,* no. 59 (January–February): 59–69.

Foster, John. 1974. *Class Struggle and the Industrial Revolution: Early Industrial Capitalism in Three English Towns.* New York: St. Martin's Press.

——. 1976. "Some Comments on 'Class Struggle and the Labour Aristocracy, 1830–60." *Social History* 1, no. 3 (October): 357–366.

Foucault, Michel. 1976. *La Volonté du savoir.* Vol. 1 of *L'Histoire de la sexualité.* Paris: Gallimard.

Fox, Robert, and George Weisz, eds. 1980. *The Organization of Science and Technology in France, 1808–1914.* Cambridge: Cambridge Univ. Press.

France, Ministre de l'Agriculture du Commerce et des Travaux Publics. 1860. *Enquête, Traité de commerce avec l'Angleterre.* Paris: Imprimerie Nationale.

Frank, Andre Gunder. 1976a. "Multilateral Merchandise Trade Imbalances and Uneven Economic Development." *Journal of European Economic History* 5, no. 2 (Fall): 407–438.

——. 1976b. "Trade Balances and the Third World: A Commentary on Paul Bairoch." *Journal of European Economic History* 5, no. 2 (Fall): 469–472.

——. 1977. "Imbalance and Exploitation." *Journal of European Economic History* 6, no. 3 (Winter): 750–753.

Fraser, Derek. 1969. "The Agitation for Parliament Reform." In *Popular Movements, 1830–1850,* ed. J. T. Ward, 31–53. London: Macmillan.

Fredrickson, George M. 1971. *The Black Image in the White Mind: The Debate on Afro-American Character and Destiny, 1817–1914.* New York: Harper & Row.

Freedeman, Charles E. 1965. "Joint Stock Business Organization in France, 1807–1867." *Business History Review* 39, no. 2 (Summer): 184–204.

Frei, Annette. 1987. *Rote Patriarchen: Arbeiterbewegung und Frauenemanzipation in der Schweiz um 1900.* Zurich: Chronos.

Fridieff, Michel. 1952. L'Opinion publique française devant l'insurrection polonaise de 1830–1831." 3 pts. *Revue internationale d'histoire politique et constitutionnelle,* n.s., 2, no. 6 (April–June): 111–121; no. 7 (July–September): 205–214; no. 8 (October–December): 280–304.

Fulford, Roger. 1957. *Votes for Women: The Story of a Struggle.* London: Faber & Faber.

Fuller, Margaret. 1992. "Women in the Nineteenth Century." In *The Essential Margaret Fuller*, ed. Jeffrey Steele, 243–378. New Brunswick, NJ: Rutgers Univ. Press.

Furet, François. 1963. "Pour une définition des classes inférieures à l'époque moderne." *Annales E.S.C.* 18, no. 3 (May–June): 459–474.

———. 1988. Preface to *De la Révolution et de la constitution*, by A. Barnave, 9–29. Paris: Presses Univ. de Grenoble.

Furner, Mary O. 1975. *Advocacy and Objectivity: A Crisis in the Professionalization of American Social Science, 1865 -1905.* Lexington: Univ. Press of Kentucky for Organization of American Historians.

———. 1990. "Knowing Capitalism: Public Investigation and the Labor Question in the Long Progressive Era." In *State and Economic Knowledge: The American and British Experience*, ed. M. O. Furner and B. Supple, 241–286. Washington, DC: Woodrow Wilson International Center for Scholars; Cambridge: Cambridge Univ. Press.

Gabaccia, Donna. 1999. "The 'Yellow Peril' and the 'Chinese of Europe': Global Perspectives on Race and Labor, 1815–1930." In *Migration, Migration History, History, Old Paradigms and New Perspectives*, ed. J. L. Lucassen, 177–196. Bern: Peter Lang.

Galbraith, John S. 1961. "Myths of the 'Little England' Era." *American Historical Review* 67, no. 1 (October): 34–48.

Gallagher, John, and Ronald Robinson. 1953. "The Imperialism of Free Trade." *Economic History Review*, n.s., 6, no. 1 (August): 1–15.

Gallisot, René. 1979. "Nazione e nazionalità nei dibattiti del movimento operaio." In *Il Marxismo dell'età della Secondo Internazionale*, 785–864. Vol. 2 of *Storia del Marxismo*. Turin: Einaudi.

Garden, Maurice. 1978. "Un exemple régionale: L'industrie textile des Pays-Bas autrichiens." In *Histoire économique et social du monde*, ed. Pierre Léon, vol. 3, *Inerties et Révolutions, 1730–1840*, ed. Louis Bergeron, 20–27. Paris: Lib. Armand Colin.

Garnier, Joseph. 1852. "De l'Origine et de la filiation du mot économie politique et les divers autres noms donnés à la science économique." 2 pts. *Journal des économistes*, IIe année, XXXII, nos. 135–136 (July–August): 300–316; XXXIII, nos. 137–138 (September–October): 11–23.

Gash, Norman. 1935. "Rural Unemployment, 1815–34." *Economic History Review* 6, no. 1 (October): 90–93.

———. 1951. "Peel and the Party System, 1830–50." *Transactions of the Royal Historical Society*, 5th ser., 1:47–70.

———. 1956. "English Reform and French Revolution in the General Election of 1830." In *Essays Presented to Sir Lewis Namier*, ed. R. Pares and A. J. P. Taylor, 258–288. London: Macmillan.

———. 1965. *Reaction and Reconstruction in English Politics, 1832–1852.* Oxford: Clarendon Press.

———. 1977. "From the Origins of Sir Robert Peel." In *The Conservatives*, ed. Lord Butler, 19–108. London: George Allen & Unwin.

———. 1979. *Aristocracy and People: Britain 1815–1865.* Cambridge, MA: Harvard Univ. Press.

Gates, Henry Louis, Jr. 1988. "The Trope of the New Negro and the Reconstruction of the Image of the Black." *Representations*, no. 24 (Fall): 129–155.

Gay, Peter. 1993. *The Cultivation of Hatred*. Vol. 3 of *The Bourgeois Experience, Victoria to Freud*. New York: W. W. Norton.

Gayer, Arthur D., W. W. Rostow, and Anna Jacobson Schwartz. 1953. *The Growth and Fluctuation of the British Economy, 1790–1850*. 2 vols. Oxford: Clarendon Press.

Geanakoplos, Deno J. 1976. "The Diaspora Greeks: The Genesis of Greek National Consciousness." In *Hellenism and the First Greek War of Liberation (1821–1830): Continuity and Change*, ed. N. P. Diamandouros, 59–77. Thessalonica: Institute for Balkan Studies.

Geary, Dick. 1976. "The German Labour Movement, 1848–1918." *European Studies Review* 6, no. 3 (July): 297–330.

———. 1981. *European Labour Protest, 1848–1939*. London: Croom Helm.

Gellner, Ernest. 1983. *Nations and Nationalism*. Oxford: Blackwell.

Gemelli, Giuliana. 1987. "Communauté intellectuelle et stratégie institutionnelles: Henri Berr et la Fondation du Centre International de Synthèse." *Revue de synthèse*, 4th ser., 8, no. 2 (April–June): 225–259.

Genovese, Elizabeth Fox. 1987. "Culture and Consciousness in the Intellectual History of European Women." *Signs* 12, no. 3 (Spring): 329–347.

George, M. Dorothy. 1927. "The Combination Laws Reconsidered." *Economic Journal (Economic History)* 1, no. 2 (May): 214–228.

———. 1936. "The Combination Laws." *Economic History Review* 6, no. 2 (April): 172–178.

George, Margaret. 1976–1977. "The 'World Historical Defeat' of the *Républicaines-Révolutionnaires*." *Science and Society* 40, no. 4 (Winter): 410–437.

Gerbod, Paul. 1965. *La Condition universitaire en France au XIXe siècle*. Paris: Presses Univ. de France.

Gerhard, Ute. 1982. "A Hidden and Complex Heritage: Reflections on the History of German's Women's Movements." *Women's Studies International Forum* 5, no. 6, 561–567.

Gerschenkron, Alexander. 1943. *Bread and Democracy in Germany*. Berkeley: Univ. of California Press.

Giddens, Anthony. 1971. "Durkheim's Political Sociology." *Sociological Review*, n.s., 19, no. 4 (November): 477–519.

Gignoux, C.-J. 1923. "L'Industrialisme de Saint-Simon à Walther Rathenau." *Revue d'histoire des doctrines économiques et sociales* 11, no. 2, 200–217.

Gille, Bertrand. 1959a. *La Banque et le crédit en France de 1815 à 1848*. Paris: Presses Univ. de France.

———. 1959b. *Recherches sur la formation de la grande entreprise capitaliste (1815–1848)*. Paris: S.E.V.P.E.N.

———. 1965. *Histoire de la Maison Rothschild*. Vol. 1, *Des origines à 1848*. Geneva: Droz.

———. 1967. *Histoire de la Maison Rothschild*. Vol. 2, *1848–1870*. Geneva: Droz.

———. 1970. *La Banque en France au XIXe siècle*. Geneva: Droz.

Gillis, John R. 1970. "Political Decay and the European Revolutions, 1789–1848." *World Politics* 22, no. 3 (April): 344–370.

Gilroy, Paul. 2000. *Against Race: Imagining Political Culture beyond the Color Line*. Cambridge, MA: Belknap Press of Harvard Univ. Press.

Girard, Louis. 1952. *La Politique des travaux publics sous le Second Empire*. Paris: Lib. Armand Colin.

———. 1966. "Révolution ou conservatisme en Europe (1856): Une Polémique de la presse parisienne après la guerre de Crimée." In *Mélanges Pierre Renouvin: Etudes d'histoire des relations internationales*, 125–134. Paris: Presses Univ. de France.

———. 1977. "Caractères du Bonapartisme dans la seconde moitié du XIXe siècle." In *Le Bonapartisme, phénomène historique et mythe politique*, ed. K. Hammer and P. C. Hautmann, 22–28. Munich: Artemis Verlag.

Glaser, John F. 1958. "English Nonconformity and the Decline of Liberalism." *American Historical Review* 63, no. 2 (January): 352–363.

Glenn, Evelyn Nakano. 1992. "From Servitude to Service Work: Historical Continuities in the Racial Division of Paid Reproductive Labor." *Signs* 18, no. 1 (Autumn) : 1–43.

Godechot, Jacques. 1965. *Les Révolutions: 1770–1799*. 2nd ed. Paris: Presses Univ. de France.

———. 1971. "Nation, patrie, nationalisme et patriotisme en France au XVIIIe siècle." *Annales historiques de la Révolution française*, 43e année, no. 206 (October–December): 481–501.

Goldfrank, Walter L. 1972. "Reappraising Le Play." In T*he Establishment of Empirical Sociology: Studies in Continuity, Discontinuity and Institutionalization*, ed. A. Oberschall, 130–151. New York: Harper & Row.

Goldman, Lawrence. 1986. "The Social Science Association, 1857–86: A Context for Mid-Victorian Liberalism." *English Historical Review* 101, no. 398 (January): 95–134.

———. 1987. "A Peculiarity of the English? The Social Science Association and the Absence of Sociology in Nineteenth-Century Britain." *Past and Present*, no. 114 (February): 133–171.

———. 1998. "Exceptionalism and Internationalism: The Origins of American Social Science Reconsidered." *Journal of Historical Sociology* 11, no. 1 (March): 1–36.

———. 2002. *Science, Reform, and Politics in Victorian Britain: The Social Science Association, 1857–1886*. Cambridge: Cambridge Univ. Press.

———. 2005. "Victorian Social Science: From Singular to Plural." In *Organization of Knowledge in Victorian Britain*, ed. M. Daunton, 87–114. Oxford: Oxford Univ. Press.

Goldstein, Jan. 1982. "The Hysteria Diagnosis and the Politics of Anticlericalism in Late Nineteenth-Century France." *Journal of Modern History* 54, no. 2 (June): 209–239.

Goldstein, Leslie. 1980. "Mill, Marx, and Women's Liberation." *Journal of the History of Philosophy* 18, no. 3 (July): 319–334.

———. 1982. "Early Feminist Themes in French Utopian Socialism: The St.-Simonians and Fourier." *Journal of the History of Ideas* 43, no. 1 (January–March): 91–108.

Goliber, Sue Helder. 1982. "Marguerite Durand: A Study in French Feminism." *International Journal of Women's Studies* 5, no. 5 (November–December): 402–412.

Gonnet, Paul. 1955. "Esquisse de la crise économique en France de 1827 à 1832." *Revue d'histoire économique et sociale* 33, no. 3, 249–292.

Gooch, Brison D. 1956. "A Century of Historiography on the Origins of the Crimean War." *American Historical Review* 62, no. 1 (October): 33–58.

Goode, William J. 1960. "Encroachment, Charlatanism, and the Emerging Profession: Psychology, Sociology, and Medicine." *American Sociological Review* 25, no. 6 (December): 902–965.

Gordon, Ann D., ed. 1997. *Selected Papers of Elizabeth Cady Stanton and Susan B. Anthony.* New Brunswick, NJ: Rutgers Univ. Press.

Gordon, Barry L. 1976. *Political Economy in Parliament, 1819–1823.* London: Macmillan.

———. 1979. *Economic Doctrine and Tory Liberalism, 1824–1830.* London: Macmillan.

Gordon, H. Scott. 1973. "Alfred Marshall and the Development of Economics as a Science." In *Foundations of Scientific Methods, the Nineteenth Century,* ed. R. N. Giere and R. S. Westfall, 234–258. Bloomington: Indiana Univ. Press.

Gordon, Linda. 1991. "On 'Difference.'" *Genders,* no. 10 (Spring): 91–111.

Goriély, Benjamin. 1948a. "La Pologne en 1848." In *Le Printemps des peuples: 1848 dans le monde,* ed. F. Fejtö, 2:267–318. Paris: Éd. du Minuit.

———. 1948b. "La Russie de Nicolas 1er en 1848." In *Le Printemps des peuples: 1848 dans le monde,* ed. F. Fejtö, 2:355–393. Paris: Éd. du Minuit.

Gouges, Olympe de. N.d. *Les Droits de la Femme.* N.p.: A la Reine.

———. 1980. "The Declaration of the Rights of Woman." In *Women in Revolutionary Paris, 1789–1795, Selected Documents,* ed. D. G. Levy et al., 87–113. Urbana: Univ. of Illinois Press.

———. 1993. *Ecrits Politiques.* Paris: Côté Femmes.

Gough, Barry. 1990. "Pax Britannica, Peace, Force and World Power." *Round Table,* no. 314, 167–188.

Gourevitch, Peter Alexis. 1977. "International Trade, Domestic Coalitions, and Liberty: Comparative Responses to the Crisis of 1873–1896." *Journal of Interdisciplinary History* 8, no. 2 (Autumn) : 281–313.

Granger, Gilles-Gaston. 1989. *La Mathématique sociale du Marquis de Condorcet.* Paris: Éd. Odile Jacob.

Gray, Robert Q. 1979. "The Political Incorporation of the Working Class." *Sociology* 9, no. 1 (January): 101–104.

Greer, Donald M. 1925. *L'Angleterre, la France et la Révolution de 1848: La Troisième Ministère de Lord Palmerston au Foreign Office (1846–1851).* Paris: F. Rieder.

Grew, Raymond. 1962. "How Success Spoiled the Risorgimento." *Journal of Modern History* 34, no. 3 (September): 239–253.

Griewank, Karl. 1954. *Der Wiener Kongress und die europäische Restauration, 1814/15.* 2nd rev. ed. Leipzig: Koehler & Amelany.

Griffith, Elisabeth. 1984. *In Her Own Right: The Life of Elizabeth Cady Stanton.* New York: Oxford Univ. Press.

Groh, Dieter. 1966. "The 'Unpatriotic' Socialists and the State." *Journal of Contemporary History* 1, no. 4 (October): 151–178.

———. 1973. *Negative Integration und Revolutionärer Attentismus: Die deusche Sozialdemocratie am Vorabend der Ersten Weltkrieges.* Frankfurt am Main: Propyläen.

Gross, Leo. 1968. "The Peace of Westphalia, 1648–1948." In *International Law and Organization,* ed. R. A. Falk and W. F. Hanreider, 45–67. Philadelphia: J. B. Lippincott.

Grossman, Henryk. 1943. "The Evolutionist Revolt against Classical Economics." 2 pts. *Journal of Political Economy* 51, no. 5 (October): 381–393; no. 6 (December): 506–522.

Gruner, Wolf D. 1985. *Die Deutsche Frage: Ein Problem der Europäischer Geschichte seit 1800.* Munich: C. H. Beck.

———. 1992. "Was There a Reformed Balance of Power System or Cooperative Great Power Happening?" *American Historical Review* 97, no. 3 (June): 725–732.

Gueniffey, Patrice. 1988a. "Introduction au texte et notes." In *De la Révolution et de la Constitution,* by A. Barnave, 31–38 and notes passim. Grenoble: Presses Univ. de Grenoble.

———. 1988b. "Suffrage." In *Dictionnaire critique de la Révolution française,* by F. Furet et al., 614–624. Paris: Flammarion.

Guérard, Albert. 1943. *Napoleon III.* Cambridge, MA: Harvard Univ. Press.

Guichen, Eugène, vicomte de. 1917. *La Révolution de juillet 1830 et l'Europe.* Paris: Émile-Paul Frères.

Guilbert, Madeleine. 1966. *Les Femmes et l'organisation syndicale avant 1914.* Paris: Éd. du CNRS.

Guillaumin, Colette. 1972. *L'Idéologie raciste: Genèse et langage actuel.* Paris: Mouton.

Guiral, Pierre. 1960. "Le libéralisme en France (1815–1970): Thèmes, succès et lacunes." In *Tendances politiques dans la vie française depuis 1789,* 17–40. Colloques, Cahiers de Civilisation. Paris: Hachette.

Guizot, François. 1820a. *Du Gouvernement de la France depuis la Restauration et du ministère actuel.* Paris: Chez Ladvocat.

———. 1820b. "Avant-propos de la troisième édition." *Supplément aux deux premières éditions du "Gouvernement de la France depuis la Restauration et du Ministère actuel."* Paris: Ladvocat.

———. 1846. *Histoire de la civilisation en France depuis la chute de l'Empire romain jusqu'à la Révolution française.* Paris: Didier.

Gunnell, John G. 2006. "The Founding of the American Political Science Association: Discipline, Profession, Political Theory, and Politics." *American Political Science Review* 100, no. 4 (November): 479–486.

Guyot, Raymond. 1901–1902. "La Dernière négociation de Talleyrand: L'Indépendance de la Belgique." 2 pts. *Revue d'histoire moderne et contemporaine* 2 (1901): 573–594; 3 (1902): 237–281.

———. 1926. *La Première entente cordiale.* Paris: F. Rieder.

Haag, Henri. 1960. "La Social-démocratie allemande et la Première Guerre Mondiale." In *Histoire contemporaine.* Comité International des Sciences Historiques. XIe Congrès Internationale des Sciences Historiques, Stockholm, 21–28 Août 1960. Rapports 5:61–96. Uppsala: Almquist & Wiksell.

Hackett, Amy. 1972. "The German Women's Movement and Suffrage, 1890–1914: A Study of National Feminism." In *Modern European Social History,* ed. R. J. Bezucha, 354–386. Lexington, MA: D. C. Heath.

Halévy, Elie. 1900. *La Révolution de la doctrine de l'utilité (1789–1815).* Thèse pour le doctorat. Paris: Félix Alcan.

———. 1901a. *La Jeunesse de Bentham.* Vol. 1 of *La Formation du radicalisme philosophique.* Paris: Félix Alcan.

———. 1901b. *L'Évolution de la doctrine utilitaire de 1789 à 1815*. Vol. 2 of *La Formation du radicalisme philosophique*. Paris: Félix Alcan.

———. 1904. *La formulation du radicalisme philosophique*, vol. 3. Paris: F. Alcan.

———. 1905. *L'Angleterre et son Empire*. Paris: Pages Libres.

———. 1930. *The World Crisis, 1914–1918: An Interpretation*. Oxford: Clarendon Press.

———. 1935. "English Public Opinion and the French Revolution of the Nineteenth Century." In *Studies in Anglo-French History*, ed. A. Coville and H. Temperley, 51–60. Cambridge: At the University Press.

———. 1947. *The Age of Peel and Cobden: A History of the English People, 1841–1852*. London: Ernest Benn.

———. 1948. *Histoire de socialisme européen*. Rédigée d'après des notes de cours par un groupe d'amis et d'élèves. Paris: Gallimard.

———. 1949. *England in 1815*. 2nd rev. ed. Vol. 1 of *A History of the English People in The Nineteenth Century*. London: Ernest Benn.

———. 1950. *The Triumph of Reform (1830–1841)*. 2nd rev. ed. Vol. 3 of *A History of the English People in the Nineteenth Century*. London: Ernest Benn.

Hall, Alex. 1974. "By Other Means: The Legal Struggle against the SPD in Wilhelmine Germany, 1890–1900." *Historical Journal* 17, no. 2 (June): 365–386.

Hall, Catherine. 1992a. "Competing Masculinities: Thomas Carlyle, John Stuart Mill and the Case of the Governor Eyre." In *White, Male and Middle Class: Explorations in Feminism and History*, 255–295. New York: Routledge.

———. 1992b. "The Early Formation of Victorian Domestic Ideology." In *White, Male and Middle Class: Explorations in Feminism and History*, 75–93. New York: Routledge.

———. 1992c. "The History of the Housewife." In *White, Male and Middle Class: Explorations in Feminism and History*, 43–71. New York: Routledge.

Halpérin, Jean. 1848. "La Transformation de la Suisse, prélude aux révolutions." in *Le Printemps des peuples: 1848 dans le monde*, ed. F. Fejtö, 1:127–161. Paris: Éd. du Minuit.

Hammen, Oscar J. 1958. "1848 et le 'Spectre du Communisme.'" *Le Contrat Social* 2, no. 4 (July) : 191–200.

Hammond, J. L. 1930. "The Industrial Revolution and Discontent." *Economic History Review* 2, no. 2 (January): 218–228.

Hammond, J. L., and M. R. D. Foot. 1952. *Gladstone and Liberalism*. London: English Universities Press at Saint Paul's House.

Hangland, Kjell. 1980. "An Outline of Norwegian Cultural Nationalism in the Second Half of the Nineteenth Century." In *The Roots of Nationalism: Studies in Northern Europe*, ed. R. Mitchison, 21–29. Edinburgh: John Donald.

Hansen, Alvin H. 1921. "Cycles of Strikes." *American Economic Review* 11, no. 4 (December): 616–621.

Hansen, Erik. 1977. "Workers and Socialists: Relations between the Dutch Trade-Union Movement and Social Democracy, 1894–1914." *European Studies Review* 7, no. 2 (April): 199–225.

Haraszti, Eva H. 1978. *Chartism*. Budapest: Akadémiai Kiadó.

Hargreaves, E. L. 1930. *The National Debt*. London: Edward Arnold.

Harley, C. Knick. 1982. "British Industrialization before 1841: Evidence of Slower Growth during the Industrial Revolution." *Journal of Economic History* 42, no. 2 (June): 267–289.

Harlow, Vincent T. 1953. *British Colonial Developments, 1774–1834*. Oxford: Clarendon Press.

Harrison, Royden. 1960–1961. "The British Working Class and the General Election of 1868." 2 pts. *International Review of Social History* 5, no. 3 (1960): 424–455; 6, no. 1 (1961): 74–109.

Harsin, Paul. 1936. "La Révolution belge de 1830 et l'influence française." *Revue des sciences politiques* 53 (April–June): 266–279.

Hart, Jennifer. 1965. "Nineteenth-Century Social Reform: A Tory Interpretation of History." *Past and Present*, no. 31 (July): 39–61.

———. 1974. "Nineteenth-Century Social Reform: Tory Interpretation of History." In *Essays in Social History*, ed. M. W. Flinn and T. C. Smout, 196–217. Oxford: Clarendon Press.

Hartmann, Heidi. 1976. "Capitalism, Patriarchy, and Job Segregation by Sex." *Signs* 1, no. 3, pt. 2 (Spring): 137–169.

Hartog, François. 1988. *Le XIXe siècle et l'histoire: Le Cas Fustel de Coulanges*. Paris: Presses Univ. de France.

Hartwell, R. M. 1961. "The Rising Standard of Living in England, 1800–1850." *Economic History Review*, n.s., 13, no. 3 (April): 397–416.

———. 1963. "The Standard of Living during the Industrial Revolution: A Discussion." *Economic History Review*, n.s., 16, no. 1 (August): 135–146.

Hartz, Louis. 1948. *Economic Policy and Democratic Thought: Pennsylvania, 1774–1860*. Cambridge, MA: Harvard Univ. Press.

Haskell, Thomas L. 1977. *The Emergence of Professional Social Science: The American Social Science Association and the Nineteenth-Century Crisis of Authority*. Urbana: Univ. of Illinois Press.

———. 1984. "Professionalism *versus* Capitalism: R. H. Tawney, Emile Durkheim, and C. S. Peirce on the Disinterestedness of Professional Communities." In *The Authority of Experts*, ed. T. L. Haskell, 180–225. Bloomington: Indiana Univ. Press.

Hasquin, Hervé. 1971. *Une mutation: Le "Pays de Charleroi" aux XVIIe et XVIIIe siècles; aux origines de la Révolution industrielle en Belgique*. Brussels: Ed. de l'Université de Bruxelles.

Haupt, Georges. 1965. *Le Congrès manqué: L'Internationale à la veille de la première guerre mondiale*. Paris: François Maspéro.

———. 1972. *Socialism and the Great War: The Collapse of the Second International*. Oxford: Clarendon Press.

———. 1974. "Les Marxistes face à la question nationale: L'Histoire du problème." In *Les Marxistes et la question nationale, 1848–1914*, by G. Haupt et al., 9–61. Paris: François Maspéro.

———. 1986. *Aspects of International Socialism, 1871–1914: Essays*. Cambridge: Cambridge Univ. Press.

Haupt, Georges, and Claudie Weill. 1974. "L'Eredità de Marx ed Engels e la questione nazionale." *Studi Storici* 15, no. 2 (April–June): 270–324.

Haupt, Georges, and Madeleine Rebérioux, dirs. 1967a. *La Deuxième Internationale et l'Orient.* Paris: Éd. Cujas.

———. 1967b. "L'Internationale et le problème colonial." In *La Deuxième Internationale et l'Orient,* ed. G. Haupt and M. Rebérioux, 17–48. Paris: Éd. Cujas.

Haupt, Georges, Michael Löwy, and Claudie Weill. 1974. *Les Marxistes et la question nationale, 1848–1914.* Paris: François Maspéro.

Hause, Steven C., and Anne R. Kenney. 1981. "The Limits of Suffragist Behavior: Legalism and Militancy in France, 1876–1922." *American Historical Review* 86, no. 4 (October): 781–806.

———. 1984. *Women's Suffrage and Social Politics in the French Third Republic.* Princeton, NJ: Princeton Univ. Press.

Hauser, Henri. 1901. "L'Entrée des Etats-Unis dans la politique 'mondiale' d'après un américain." *Annales des sciences politiques* 16, 444–456.

———. 1903. *L'Enseignement des sciences sociales: Etat-actuel de cet enseignement dans les divers pays du monde.* Paris: Lib. Marescq Aîné.

———. 1905. *L'Impérialisme américain.* Paris: Pages Libres.

Hayek, Frederick A. von. 1941. "The Counter-Revolution of Science." *Economica,* n.s., 8 (February): 9–36.

———. 1952. *The Counter-Revolution of Science: Studies on the Abuse of Reason.* Glencoe, IL: Free Press.

Hazelkorn, Ellen. 1980. "Capital and the Irish Question." *Science and Society* 44, no. 3 (Fall): 326–356.

Heilbron, Johan. 1985. "Les Métamorphoses du durkheimisme, 1920–1940." *Revue française de sociologie* 26, no. 2 (March–April): 203–237.

Heinen, Jacqueline. 1978. "De la Ière à la IIIe Internationale, la question des femmes." *Critique communiste,* nos. 20/21, 109–179.

Heiniger, Ernstpeter. 1980. *Ideologie des Rassismus: Problemsicht und ethische Verurteilung in der kirchlichen Sozialverkündigung.* Immensee, Switzerland: Neue Zeitschrift für Missionswissenschaft.

Henderson, W. O. 1934. *The Lancashire Cotton Famine, 1861–1865.* Manchester, UK: Manchester Univ. Press.

———. 1950. "Prince Smith and Free Trade in Germany." *Economic History Review,* n.s., 2, no. 3, 295–302.

———. 1954. *Britain and Industrial Europe, 1750–1870.* Liverpool: At the University Press.

———. 1976. *Studies in German Colonial History.* London: Frank Cass.

Hendricks, Margo, and Patricia Parker. 1994. Introduction to *Women, "Race," and Writing in the Early Modern Period,* ed. M. Hendricks and P. Parker, 1–14. London: Routledge.

Henriques, Ursula. 1968. "How Cruel Was the Victorian Poor Law?" *Historical Journal* 11, no. 2, 365–371.

Hentschel, Volker. 1978. *Wirtschaft und Wirtschaftspolitik im Wilhelminischen Deutschland: Organisierter Kapitalismus und Intervertionsstaat?* Stuttgart: Klein-Cotta.

———. 1981. "Produktion, Wachstum und Produktivität in England, Frankreich und Deutschland von der Mitte des 19. Jahrhunderts bis zum Ersten Weltkrieg: Statitische

Grenzen und Nöte beim Internationaler wirtschaftshistorischen Vergleich." *Vierteljahr-schrift für Sozial- und Wirtschaftsgeschichte* 68, no. 4, 457–510.

Herbst, Juergen. 1965. *The German Historical School in American Scholarship.* Ithaca, NY: Cornell Univ. Press.

Hericourt, Jenny P. d'. 1860. *La Femme affranchie: Réponse à MM. Michelet, Proudhon, E. de Giradin, A. Comte et aux autres novateurs modernes.* 2 vols. Brussels: A. LaCroix, van Meenen.

Hersh, Blanche Glassman. 1978. *The Slavery of Sex: Feminist-Abolitionists in America.* Urbana: Univ. of Illinois Press.

Hertneck, Friedrich. 1927. *Die Deutschen Sozialdemokratie und die orientalische Frage in Zeitalter Bismarcks.* Berlin: Deutsche Verlaggeselltschaft für Politik und Geschichte.

Hertz, Deborah. 1988. *Jewish High Society in Old Regime Berlin.* New Haven, CT: Yale Univ. Press.

Hervé, Florence. 1983. " 'Dem Reich der Freiheit werb'ich Bürgerinnen': Die Entwicklung der deutschen Frauenbewegung, von den Anfängen bis 1889." In *Geschichte der deutschen Frauenbewegung*, ed. F. Hervé, 12–40. Cologne: Pahl-Rugenstein.

Hexter, J. H. 1936. "The Protestant Revival and the Catholic Question in England, 1778–1829." *Journal of Modern History* 8, no. 3 (September): 297–318.

Heywood, Colin. 1988. *Childhood in Nineteenth-Century France: Work, Health and Education among the "Classes Populaires."* Cambridge: Cambridge Univ. Press.

Heywood, Paul. 1990. *Marxism and the Failure of Organised Socialism in Spain, 1879–1936.* Cambridge: Cambridge Univ. Press.

Higham, John. 1979. "The Matrix of Specialization." In *The Organization of Knowledge in Modern America, 1860–1920*, ed. A. Oleson and J. Voss, 3–18. Baltimore: Johns Hopkins Univ. Press.

Higonnet, Patrick L. R., and Trevor B. Higonnet. 1967. "Class, Corruption, and Politics in the French Chamber of Deputies, 1846–1848." *French Historical Studies* 5, no. 2 (Autumn): 204–224.

Hill, Christopher. 1958. "The Norman Yoke." In *Puritanism and Revolution: Studies in Interpretation of the English Revolution of the Seventeenth Century*, 50–122. London: Secker & Warburg.

Hill, R. L. 1929. *Toryism and the People, 1832–1846.* London: Constable.

Hilton, Boyd. 1977. *Corn, Cash, Commerce: The Economic Policies of the Tory Governments, 1815–1830.* Oxford: Oxford Univ. Press.

Hilts, Victor L. 1973. "Statistics and Social Science." In *Foundations of Scientific Method: The Nineteenth Century*, ed. R. N. Giere and R. S. Westfall, 206–233. Bloomington: Indiana Univ. Press.

Himmelfarb, Gertrude. 1966. "The Politics of Democracy: The English Reform Act of 1867." *Journal of British Studies* 6, no. 1 (November): 97–138.

Hinsley, Curtis M., Jr. 1981. *Savages and Scientists: The Smithsonian Institution and the Development of American Anthropology, 1846–1910.* Washington, DC: Smithsonian Institution Press.

Hinton, James. 1983. *Labour and Socialism: A History of the British Labour Movement, 1867–1974.* Brighton, UK: Wheatsheaf Books.

Hoagland, Henry E. 1918. "Humanitarianism (1840–1860)." In *History of Labour in the United States,* by J. R. Commons et al., 1:485–623. New York: Macmillan.

Hoagwood, Terence Allen. 1996. *Politics, Philosophy and the Production of Romantic Texts.* De Kalb: Northern Illinois Univ. Press.

Hobhouse, L. T. 1911. *Liberalism.* London: Oxford Univ. Press.

Hobsbawm, Eric J. 1949. "General Labour Unions in Britain, 1889–1914." *Economic History Review,* n.s., 1, nos. 2/3, 123–142.

———. 1952. "Economic Fluctuations and Some Social Movements since 1800." *Economic History Review,* n.s., 5, no. 1, 1–25.

———. 1957. "The British Standard of Living, 1790–1850." *Economic History Review,* n.s., 10, no. 1 (August): 46–68.

———. 1962. *The Age of Revolution, 1789–1848.* London: Abacus.

———. 1963. "The Standard of Living during the Industrial Revolution: A Discussion." *Economic History Review,* n.s., 16, no. 1 (August): 119–134.

———. 1964. *Labouring Men: Studies in the History of Labour.* London: Weidenfeld & Nicolson.

———. 1974. "La Diffusione del Marxismo (1890–1905)." *Studi storici* 15, no. 2 (April–June): 241–269.

———. 1975. *The Age of Capital, 1848–1875.* London: Weidenfeld & Nicolson.

———. 1978. "Sexe, symboles, vêtements et socialisme." *Actes de la recherche en sciences sociales,* no. 23 (September): 2–18.

———. 1979. "Soziale Ungleichheit und Klassenstrukturen in England: Die Arbeiterklasse." In *Klassen in der europäischen Sozialgeschichte,* ed. Hans-Ulrich Wehler, 53–65. Göttingen: Vandenhoek & Ruprecht.

———. 1983. "Mass Producing Traditions: Europe, 1870–1914." In *The Invention of Tradition,* ed. E. J. Hobsbawm and T. Ranger, 263–307. Cambridge: Cambridge Univ. Press.

———. 1984a. "The Making of the Working Class 1870–1914." In *Worlds of Labour: Further Studies in the History of Labour,* 194–213. London: Weidenfeld & Nicolson.

———. 1984b. "The 'New Unionism' in Perspective." In *Worlds of Labour: Further Studies in the History of Labour,* 152–175. London: Weidenfeld & Nicolson.

———. 1984c. "Men and Women: Images on the Left." In *Worlds of Labour: Further Studies in the History of Labour,* 83–102. London: Weidenfeld & Nicolson.

———. 1984d. "Der *New Unionism*: Eine comparative Betrachtung." In *Auf dem Wege zur Massengewerkschaft,* ed. Wolfgang J. Mommsen and Hans-Gerhard Husung, 19–45. Stuttgart: Ernst Klett.

———. 1987. *The Age of Empire, 1875–1914.* New York: Pantheon.

———. 1988. "Working-Class Internationalism." In *Internationalism in the Labour Movement, 1830–1940,* ed. F. van Holthoon and M. van den Linden, 1:3–16. Leiden: E. J. Brill.

———. 1990. *Nations and Nationalism since 1780: Programme, Myth, Reality.* Cambridge: Cambridge Univ. Press.

Hobsbawm, Eric J., and Terence Ranger, eds. 1992. *The Invention of Tradition.* New York: Cambridge Univ. Press.

Hodgson, Geoffrey M. 2005. "Alfred Marshall versus the Historical School?" *Journal of Eonomic Studies* 32, no. 4, 331–348.

Hoffman, Ross J. S. 1933. *Great Britain and the German Trade Rivalry, 1875–1914.* Philadelphia: Univ. of Pennsylvania Press.

Hoffmann, Walther. 1949. "The Growth of Industrial Production in Great Britain: A Quantitative Study." *Economic History Review,* n.s., 2, no. 2, 162–180.

Hofstadter, Richard. 1992. *Social Darwinism in American Thought.* Boston: Beacon Press.

Hohenberg, Paul. 1972. "Change in Rural France in the Period of Industrialization, 1830–1914." *Journal of Economic History* 32, no. 1 (March): 219–240.

Holland, Bernard. 1913. *Fall of Protection, 1840–1850.* London: Edward Arnold.

Hollinger, David A. 1984. "Inquiry and Uplift: Late Nineteenth Century American Academics and the Moral Efficacy of Scientific Practice." In *The Authority of Experts: Studies in History and Theory,* ed. T. L. Haskell, 142–156. Bloomington: Indiana Univ. Press.

Hollis, Patricia. 1980. "Anti-Slavery and British Working-Class Radicalism in the Years of Reform." In *Anti-Slavery, Religion and Reform: Essays in Memory of Roger Anstey,* ed. C. Bolt and S. Drescher, 294–315. Folkestone, UK: Dawson; Hamden, CT: Archon.

Holmes, Stephen. 1984. *Benjamin Constant and the Making of Modern Liberation.* New Haven, CT: Yale Univ. Press.

Hone, J. Ann. 1982. *For the Cause of Truth: Radicalism in London, 1796–1821.* Oxford: Clarendon Press.

Honeycutt, Karen. 1979. "Socialism and Feminism in Imperial Germany." *Signs* 5, no. 1 (Autumn): 30–41.

———. 1981. "Clara Zetkin: A Socialist Approach to the Problem of Women's Oppression." In *European Women on the Left: Socialism, Feminism, and the Problems Faced by Political Women, 1880 to the Present,* ed. Jane Slaughter and Robert Kern, 29–49. Westport, CT: Greenwood Press.

hooks, bell. 1988. *Talking Back: Thinking Feminist, Thinking Black.* Toronto: Between the Lines.

Horn, Norbert, and Jürgen Kocka, eds. 1979. *Recht und Entwicklung der Grossunternehmen im 19. und früher 20. Jahrhurdert: Wirtschafts-, sozial- und rechtshistorische Untersuchungen zur Industrialisierung in Deutschland, Frankreich, England und den USA.* Göttingen: Vandenhoeck & Ruprecht.

Horsefield, J. K. 1949. "The Bankers and the Bullionists in 1819." *Journal of Political Economy* 57, no. 5 (October): 442–448.

Horvath-Peterson, Sandra. 1984. *Victor Duruy and French Education: Liberal Reform in the Second Empire.* Baton Rouge: Louisiana State Univ. Press.

Houssaye, Henri. 1901. "Allocution." In *Annales internationales d'histoire,* vol. 1, *Histoire générale et diplomatique,* 5–8. International Congress of Historical Sciences, Paris, 1900. Paris: Lib. Armand Colin.

Howkins, Alun. 1977. "Edwardian Liberalism and Industrial Unrest: A Class View of the Decline of Liberalism." *History Workshop Journal,* no. 4 (Autumn): 143–161.

Hoxie, R. Gordon. 1955. *A History of the Faculty of Political Science, Columbia University.* New York: Columbia Univ. Press.

Hroch, Miroslav. 1968. *Die Vorkämpfer der nationalen Bewegung bei den kleinen Völkern Europas.* Prague: Univ. Karlova.

Hufton, Olwen. 1971. "Women in Revolution, 1789–1796." *Past and Present,* no. 53 (November): 90–108.

Hughes, H. Stuart. 1958. *Consciousness and Society: The Reorientation of European Social Thought, 1890–1930.* New York: Knopf.

Humphreys, R. A. 1965. "British Merchants and South American Independence." *Proceedings of the British Academy* 51:151–174.

Humphries, Jane. 1977. "Class Struggle and the Persistence of the Working-Class Family." *Cambridge Journal of Economics* 1, no. 3 (September): 241–258.

Huskisson, William. 1825. "Substance of Two Speeches Delivered in the House of Commons on the 21st and 25th March, 1825 . . . ." *Edinburgh Review* 42, no. 84 (August): 271–303.

Hyman, Richard. 1984. "Massenorganisation und Basismilitanz in Großbritanien 1888–1914." In *Auf dem Wege zur Massengewerkschaft,* ed. Wolfgang J. Mommsen and Hans-Gerhard Husung, 311–331. Stuttgart: Ernst Klett.

Iggers, Georg G. 1958a. *The Cult of Authority, The Political Philosophy of the Saint-Simonians. A Chapter in the Intellectual History of Totalitarianism.* The Hague: Martinus Nijhoff.

———. 1958b. *The Doctrine of Saint-Simon, An Exposition, First Year, 1828–1829.* Trans. with notes and introduction by Georg G. Iggers. Boston: Beacon Press.

———. 1962. "The Image of Ranke in American and German Historical Thought." *History and Theory* 2, no. 1, 17–40.

———. 1970. "Le Saint-Simonisme et la pensée autoritaire." *Économies et sociétés,* 4, no. 4 (April): 673–691.

———. 1983. *The German Conception of History: The National Tradition of Historical Thought from Herder to the Present.* Rev. ed. Middleton, CT: Wesleyan Univ. Press.

Ignatiev, Noel. 1995. *How the Irish Became White.* New York: Routledge.

Iliasu, A. A. 1971. "The Cobden -Chevalier Commercial Treaty of 1860." *Historical Journal* 14, no. 1 (March): 67–98.

Imlah, Albert H. 1948. "Real Values in British Foreign Trade, 1798–1853." *Journal of Economic History* 8, no. 2 (November): 132–152.

———. 1949. "The Fall of Protection in Britain." In *Essays in History and International Relations in Honor of George Hubbard Blakeslee,* ed. Dwight Erwin Lee, 306–320. Worcester, MA: Clark Univ. Publications.

———. 1950. "The Terms of Trade of the United Kingdom, 1798–1913." *Journal of Economic History* 10, no. 2 (November): 170–194.

———. 1952. "British Balance of Payments and Export of Capital, 1816–1913." *Economic History Review,* n.s., 5, no. 2, 208–239.

———. 1958. *Economic Elements in the Pax Britannica: Studies in British Foreign Trade in the Nineteenth Century.* Cambridge, MA: Harvard Univ. Press.

Ivray, Jehan d'. 1928. *L'Aventure saint-simonienne et les femmes.* Paris: Félix Alcan.

Jacobitti, Edmund K. E. 1981. *Revolutionary Humanism and Historicism in Modern Italy.* New Haven, CT: Yale Univ. Press.

Jacquemyns, Guillaume. 1934. "Les Réactions contre l'individualisme de 1789 à 1848." *Revue de l'Université de Bruxelles* 39, no. 4 (May–July): 421–437.

Jacquey, Marie-Clotilde. 1988. *Images de Noir dans la littérature occidentale.* Vol. 1, *Du Moyen-Age à la conquête colonial.* Cultures Sud/Notre Librairie. Paris: La Documentation Française.

Janes, R. M. 1978. "On the Reception of Mary Wollstonecraft's *A Vindication of the Rights of Woman.*" *Journal of the History of Ideas* 39, no. 2 (April-June): 293–302.

Janowitz, Morris. 1972. "The Professionalization of Sociology." In *Varieties of Political Expression in Sociology,* ed. R. K. Merton, 105–135. Chicago: Univ. of Chicago Press.

Jardin, André, and André-Jean Tudesq. 1973. *Le France des notables.* 2 vols. Nouvelle histoire de la France contemporaine 6 and 7. Paris: Éd. du Seuil.

Jaurès, Jean. 1903. "La Doctrine saint-simonienne et le socialisme." *Revue socialiste* 38 (July–December): 129–149.

———. 1968. *Histoire socialiste de la Révolution française.* Paris: Éd. Sociales.

Jayawardena, Kumari. 1986. *Feminism and Nationalism in the Third World.* Rev. ed. New Delhi: Kali for Women; London: Zed.

Jelarich, Barbara. 1976. "The Balkan Nations and the Greek War of Independence." In *Hellenism and the First Continuity and Change,* ed. N. P. Diamandouros, 157–169. Thessalonica: Institute for Balkan Studies.

Jenks, Leland H. 1927. *The Migration of British Capital to 1875.* New York: Knopf.

Jennings, Louis J., ed. 1884. *The Correspondence and Diaries of the Late Right Honorable John Wilson Croker, LL.D., F.R.S.* 3 vols. London: John Murray.

Jeremy, David J. 1977. "Damming the Flood: British Government Efforts to Check Outflow of Technicians and Machinery, 1780–1843." *Business History Review* 51, no. 1 (Spring): 1–34.

Jervis, Robert. 1992. "A Political Science Perspective on the Balance of Power and the Concert." *American Historical Review* 97, no. 3 (June): 716–724.

Johnson, Christopher H. 1966. "Etienne Cabet and the Problem of Class Antagonism." *International Review of Social History* 11, no. 3, 403–443.

———. 1971. "Communism and the Working Class before Marx: The Icarian Experience." *American Historical Review* 76, no. 3 (June): 642–689.

———. 1974. *Utopian Communism in France: Cabet and the Icarians, 1839–1851.* Ithaca, NY: Cornell Univ. Press.

———. 1975. "The Revolution of 1830 in French Economic History." In *1830 in France,* ed. J. M. Merriman, 139–189. New York: Franklin Watts.

———. 1983. "Response to J. Rancière, 'Le Mythe de l'Artisan.'" *International Labor and Working Class History,* no. 24 (Fall): 21–25.

Johnson, Richard. 1970. "Educational Policy and Social Control in Early Victorian England." *Past and Present,* no. 49 (November): 96–119.

Johnston, Hugh J. M. 1972. *British Emigration Policy, 1815-30: "Shovelling Out Paupers."* Oxford: Clarendon Press.

Joll, James, ed. 1950. *Britain and Europe: Pitt to Churchill, 1793–1940.* London: Nicholas Kaye.

Jones, Charles. 1980. "'Business Imperialism' and Argentina, 1875–1900: A Theoretical Note." *Journal of Latin American Studies* 12, no. 2 (November): 437–444.

Jones, D. Caradog. 1941. "Evolution of the Social Survey in England since Booth." *American Journal of Sociology* 46, no. 6 (May): 818–825.

Jones, Gareth Stedman. 1971. *Outcast London: A Study in the Relationship between Classes in Victorian Society.* Oxford: Clarendon Press.

———. 1977. "Society and Politics at the Beginning of the World Economy." *Cambridge Journal of Economics* 1, no. 1 (March): 77–92.

———. 1983. *Languages of Class: Studies in English Working Class History, 1832–1982.* Cambridge: Cambridge Univ. Press.

———. 1984. "Some Notes on Karl Marx and the English Labour Movement." *History Workshop Journal,* no. 18 (Autumn): 124–137.

Jones, Kathleen, and Françoise Vergès. 1991. "Women of the Paris Commune." *Women's Studies International Forum* 14, no. 5, 491–503.

Jones, Robert Alan, and Robert M. Anservitz. 1975. "Saint-Simon and Saint-Simonism: A Weberian View." *American Journal of Sociology* 80, no. 5 (March): 1095–1123.

Jordan, Constance. 1990. *Renaissance Feminism: Literary Texts and Political Models.* Ithaca, NY: Cornell Univ. Press.

Jordan, Winthrop D. 1968. *White over Black: American Attitudes toward the Negro, 1550–1812.* Chapel Hill: Univ. of North Carolina Press.

Jore, Léonce. 1959. *L'Océan pacifique au temps de la Restauration et de la Monarchie de Juillet, 1815–1848.* 2 vols. Paris: Éd. Besson & Chantemerle.

Jorland, Gérard. 2000. "L'Orient et le mythe du peuple primitif." In *Sciences, mythes et religions en Europe, Royaumont, 14–15 octobre 1997,* ed. D. Lecourt, 67–90. Luxembourg: European Communities.

Judt, Tony. 1986. *Marxism and the French Left: Studies in Labour and Politics in France, 1830–1981.* Oxford: Clarendon Press.

Juglar, Clément. 1862. *Des Crises commerciales et de leur retour périodique en France, en Angleterre et aux Etats-Unis.* Paris: Guillaumin.

Julien, Charles-André. 1981. Preface to *Toussaint Louverture: La Révolution française et le problème colonial,* by Aimé Césaire, 7–19. Paris: Présence Africaine.

Kadish, Alon. 1982. *The Oxford Economists in the Late Nineteenth Century.* Oxford: Clarendon Press.

Kalaora, Bernard, and Antoine Savoye. 1989. *Les Inventeurs oubliés.* Seyssel, France: Champ Vallon.

Kaplan, Marion A. 1979. *The Jewish Feminist Movement in Germany: The Campaigns of the Jüdischer Frauenbund, 1904–1938.* Westport, CT : Greenwood Press.

Kaplan, Steven L. 1979. "Réflexions sur la police du monde du travail, 1700–1818." *Revue historique,* 103e année, CCLXI, 1, no. 529 (January–March) : 17–77.

———. 1993. *Adieu 89.* Paris: Fayard.

Karady, Victor. 1976. "Durkheim, les sciences sociales et l'Université, bilan d'un demi-échec." *Revue française de sociologie* 17, no. 2 (April-June): 267–312.

Karlsson, Gunnar. 1980. "Icelandic Nationalism and the Inspiration of History." In *The Roots of Nationalism: Studies in Northern Europe,* ed. R. Mitchison, 77–89. Edinburgh: John Donald.

Kasler, Dirk. 1984. *Die Frühe deutsche Soziologie 1909 bis 1934, und ihre Entstehungs-Milieux.* Opladen, Germany: Westdeutscher Verlag.

Katznelson, Ira. 1985. "Working-Class Formation and the State: Nineteenth-Century England in American Perspective." In *Bringing the State Back In,* ed. P. B. Evans et al., 257–284. Cambridge: Cambridge Univ. Press.

Kealey, Gregory S. 1980. *Toronto Workers Respond to Industrial Capitalism, 1867–1892.* Toronto: Univ. of Toronto Press.

Kedourie, Elie. 1985. *Nationalism.* 3rd ed. London: Hutchison.

Kehr, Eckart. 1965. "Englandhass und Weltpolitik." In *Der Primat der Innenpolitik: Gesammelte Aufsätze zur preussisch-deutschen Sozialgeschichte im 19. und 20. Jahrhunderts,* 149–175. Berlin: Walter de Gruyter.

Kelly, Gary. 1993. *Women, Writing, and Revolution, 1790–1827.* Oxford: Clarendon Press.

Kelly, Joan. 1982. "Early Feminist Theory and the *Querelle des Femmes,* 1400–1789." *Signs* 8, no. 1 (Autumn): 4–28.

———. 1984. "Did Women Have a Renaissance?." In *Women, History and Theory: The Essays of Joan Kelly,* 19–50. Chicago: Univ. of Chicago Press.

Kemp, Betty. 1962. "Reflections on the Repeal of the Corn Laws." *Victorian Studies* 5, no. 3 (March): 189–204.

Kemp, Tom. 1971. *Economic Forces in French History.* London: Dennis Dobson.

Kennedy, Marie, and Chris Tilly. 1985. "At Arm's Length: Feminism and Socialism in Europe, 1890–1920." *Radical America* 19, no. 4, 35–51.

———. 1987. "Socialism, Feminism and the Stillbirth of Socialist Feminism in Europe, 1890–1920." *Science and Society* 51, no. 1, 6–42.

Kennedy, Paul. 1987. *The Rise and Fall of the Great Powers: Economic Change and Military Conflict from 1500 to 2000.* New York: Random House.

Keylor, William R. 1975. *Academy and Community: The Foundation of the French Historical Profession.* Cambridge, MA: Harvard Univ. Press.

Keynes, John Maynard. 1926. *The End of Laissez-Faire.* London: Hogarth Press.

Kiernan, Victor. 1967. "Marx and India." In *The Socialist Register 1967,* 159–189. London: Merlin Press.

Kilmuir, Lord. 1960. "The Shaftesbury Tradition in Conservative Politics." *Journal of Law and Economics* 3 (October): 70–74.

Kindleberger, Charles P. 1951. "Group Behavior and International Trade." *Journal of Political Economy* 59, no. 1 (February): 30–46.

———. 1961a. *Economic Growth in France and Britain, 1851–1950.* Cambridge, MA: Harvard Univ. Press.

———. 1961b. "Foreign Trade and Economic Growth: Lessons from Britain and France, 1850 to 1913." *Economic History Review,* n.s., 14, no. 2 (December): 289–305.

———. 1975. "The Rise of Free Trade in Western Europe, 1820–1875." *Journal of Economic History* 35, no. 1 (March): 20–55.

———. 1984. "Financial Institutions and Economic Development: A Comparison of Great Britain and France in the Eighteenth and Nineteenth Centuries." *Explorations in Economic History* 21, no. 2 (April): 103–124.

Kintzler, Catherine. 1987. *Condorcet: L'Instruction publique et la naissance du citoyen.* Paris: Gallimard.

Kissinger, Henry A. 1973. *A World Restored.* Gloucester, MA: Peter Smith.

Kitson Clark, G. 1951a. "The Electorate and the Repeal of the Corn Laws." *Transactions of the Royal Historical Society,* 5th ser., 1:109–126.

———. 1951b. "The Repeal of the Corn Laws and the Politics of the Forties." *Economic History Review,* n.s., 4, no. 1, 1–13.

———. 1962. *The Making of Victorian England.* London: Macmillan.

———. 1967. *An Expanding Society: Britain, 1830–1900.* Cambridge: At the University Press.

Klein, Ira. 1971. "English Free Traders and Indian Tariffs, 1874–1896." *Modern Asian Studies* 5, no. 3 (July): 251–271.

———. 1980. "Prospero's Magic: Imperialism and Nationalism in Iran, 1909–1911." *Journal of Asian History* 14, no. 1, 47–71.

Kleinau, Elke. 1987. *Die Freie Frau: Soziale Utopien des frühen 19. Jahrhunderts.* Düsseldorf: Schwan.

Klejman, Laurence, and Florence Rochefort. 1989. *Légalité en marche: Le Féminisme sous la Troisième République.* Paris: Presses de la Fondation Nationale des Sciences Politiques.

Klima, Arnost. 1948. "La Révolution de 1848 en Bohême." In *Le Printemps des peuples: 1848 dans le monde,* ed. F. Fejtö, 2 :205–237. Paris: Éd. du Minuit.

Klinge, Matti. 1980. "'Let Us Be Finns': The Birth of Finland's National Culture." In *The Roots of Nationalism: Studies in Northern Europe,* ed. R. Mitchison, 67–75. Edinburgh: John Donald.

Knibiehler, Yvonne. 1976. "Les médecins et la 'nature féminine' au temps du Code Civil." *Annales E.S.C.* 31, no. 4 (July–August): 824–845.

Knibiehler, Yvonne, and Catherine Fouquet. 1983. *La femme et les médicins.* Paris: Hachette.

Knight, David. 1984. *The Age of Science: The Scientific World-View of the Nineteenth Century.* Oxford: Basil Blackwell.

———. 1990. "Romanticism and the Sciences." In *Romanticism and the Sciences,* ed. A. Cunningham and N. Jardine, 13–24. Cambridge: Cambridge Univ. Press.

Kocka, Jürgen. 1980. "The Study of Social Mobility and the Formation of the Working-Class in the Nineteenth Century." *Le mouvement social,* no. 111 (April–June): 97–117.

———. 1984. "Craft Traditions and the Labour Movement in Nineteenth-Century Germany." In *The Power of the Past: Essays for Eric Hobsbawm,* ed. Pat Thane et al., 95–117. Cambridge: Cambridge Univ. Press.

———. 1986. "Problems of Working-Class Formation in Germany: The Early Years, 1800–1875." In *Working-Class Formation: Nineteenth-Century Patterns in Western Europe and the United States,* ed. I. Katznelson and A. R. Zolberg, 279–351. Princeton, NJ: Princeton Univ. Press.

———. 1988. "German History before Hitler: The Debate about the German *Sonderweg.*" *Journal of Contemporary History* 23, no. 1 (January): 3–16.

———. 1995. "The Middle Classes in Europe." *Journal of Modern History* 67 (December): 783–806.

Kocka, Jürgen, and Heinz-Gerhard Haupt. 1996. "Vecchie e nuove classi nell'Europa del XIX secolo." In *L'Età contemporanea, Secoli XIX–XX,* ed. P. Bairoch and E. J. Hobsbawm, 675–751. Vol. 5 of *Storia d'Europa.* Turin: Einaudi.

Koerner, Konrad. 1982. "Observations on the Sources: Transmission and Meaning of 'Indo-European' and Related Terms in the Development of Linguistics." In *Papers from the 3rd International Conference on Historical Linguistics,* ed. J. P. Maher et al., 153–180. Amsterdam: John Benjamins.

Kohlstedt, Sally Gregory. 1976. *The Formation of the American Scientific Community: The American Association for the Advancement of Science, 1848–1860.* Urbana: Univ. of Illinois Press.

Kohlstedt, Sally Gregory, Michael M. Sokal, and Bruce V. Lewenstein. 1999. *The Establishment of Science in America: 150 Years of the American Association for the Advancement of Science.* New Brunswick, NJ: Rutgers Univ. Press.

Kohn, Hans. 1946. *The Idea of Nationalism.* 3d printing, with additions. New York: Macmillan.

———. 1956. *The Idea of Nationalism: A Study in Its Origins and Background.* New York: Macmillan.

———. 1965. "Nationalism and Internationalism in the Nineteenth and Twentieth Centuries." In *Grands Thèmes. Comité International des Sciences Historiques. XIIe Congrès International des Sciences Historiques, Rapports,* 1:191–240. Horn/Vienna: F. Berger & Söhne.

Kolakowski, Leszek. 1978. *Main Currents of Marxism: Its Rise, Growth, and Dissolution.* 3 vols. Oxford: Clarendon Press.

Kollontai, Alexandra. 1971. "The Social Basis of the Woman Question." In *Selected Writings of Alexandra Kollontai,* 58–73. Translated [from the Russian] with an introduction and commentaries by Alix Holt. London: Allison & Busby.

Koonz, Claudia. 1987. *Mothers in the Fatherland: Women, the Family, and Nazi Politics.* New York: St. Martin's Press.

Koyré, Alexandre. 1946. "Louis de Bonald." *Journal of the History of Ideas* 7, no. 1 (January): 56–73.

Kraditor, Aileen S. 1965. *The Ideas of the Woman Suffrage Movement, 1890–1920.* New York: Columbia Univ. Press.

———, ed. 1968. *Up from the Pedestal: Selected Writings in the History of American Feminism.* New York: Quadrangle Books.

Kraehe, Enno E. 1992. "A Bipolar Balance of Power." *American Historical Review* 97, no. 3 (June): 707–715.

Kriegel, Annie. 1979. "L' Association Internationale des Travailleurs (1864–1876)." In *Des Origines à 1875,* ed. J. Droz, 603–634. Vol. 1 of *Histoire générale du socialisme.* Paris: Univ. de France.

Kriegel, Annie, and Jean-Jacques Becker. 1964. *1914: La guerre et le mouvement ouvrier français.* Paris: Lib. Armand Colin.

Krug, Charles. 1899. *Le Féminisme et le droit civil français.* Nancy: Imp. Nancéienne.

Krüger, Dieter. 1987. "Max Weber and the 'Younger' Generation in the Verein für Sozialpolitik." In *Max Weber and His Contemporaries,* ed. W. J. Mommsen and J. Oberhammel, 71–87. London: Unwin Hyman.

Kuczynski, Jürgen. 1975. *Studien zu einer Geschichte der Gesellschaftswissenschaften.* Berlin: Akademie-Verlag.

Kuhn, Thomas. 1976. "Mathematical vs. Experimental Traditions in the Development of Physical Science." *Journal of Interdisciplinary History* 7, no. 1 (Summer): 1–31.

Kukiel, Marian. 1953. "La Révolution de 1830 et la Pologne." *Revue internationale d'histoire politique et constitutionnelle,* n.s., 3, no. 11 (July–September): 235–248.

Kulstein, David I. 1962. "The Attitude of French Workers towards the Second Empire." *French Historical Studies* 2, no. 3 (Spring): 356–375.

———. 1964. "Bonapartist Workers during the Second Empire." *International Review of Social History* 9:226–234.

———. 1969. *Napoleon III and the Working Class: A Study of Government Propaganda under the Second Empire.* N.p.: A Publication of the California State Colleges.

Kumar, Krishan. 1983. "Class and Political Action in Nineteenth-Century England: Theoretical and Comparative Perspectives." *Archives européennes de sociologie* 24, no. 1, 3–43.

Labrousse, Ernest. 1948. "Les Deux révolutions de 1848." *Revue socialiste,* n.s., nos. 17–18 (January–February): 1–6.

———. 1949a. "1848–1830–1789: Comment naissent les revolutions." In *Actes du Congrès historique du Centenaire de la Révolution de 1848,* 1–20. Paris: Presses Univ. de France.

———. 1949b. *Le mouvement ouvrier et les idées sociales en France le 1815 à la fin du XIXe siècle.* Les Cours de la Sorbonne. Paris: Centre de Documentation Universitaire.

———. 1952. *Le Mouvement ouvrier et les théories sociales en France au XIXe siècle.* Les Cours de la Sorbonne. Paris: Centre de Documentation Universitaire.

———. 1954. *Aspects de l'évolution économique et sociale de la France et du Royaume-Uni de 1815 à 1880.* 3 vols. Paris: Centre de Documentation Universitaire.

———, ed. 1956a. *Aspects de la crise et de la dépression de l'économie française au milieu du XIX siècle, 1846–1851.* Bibliothèque de la Révolution de 1848, 19. La Roche-sur-Yon: Impr. Centrale de l'Ouest.

———. 1956b. "Panoramas de la crise." In *Aspects de la crise et de la dépression de l'économie française au milieu du XIXe siècle, 1846–1851,* ed. E. Labrousse, iii–xxiv. Bibliothèque de la Révolution de 1848, vol. 19. La Roche-sur-Yon: Impr. Centrale de l'Ouest.

———. 1976. "A Livre ouvert sur les élans et les vicissitudes des croissances." In *Histoire économique et sociale de la France.* Tome 3, *L'Avènement de l'ère industrielle (1789–années 1880),* 2:859–1024. Paris: Presses Univ. de France.

Lacour, Leopold. 1900. *Les Origines du féminisme contemporaine. Trois femmes et la Révolution: Olympe de Gouges, Théoigne de Mericourt, Rose Lacombe.* Paris: Plon-Nourrit.

Lacroix, Bernard. 1981. *Durkheim et la politique.* Paris: Presses de la Fondation Nationale des Sciences Politiques.

Laidler, David. 1987. "Bullionist Controversy." In *The New Palgrave: A Dictionary of Economics,* ed. J. Eatwell et al. London: Macmillan.

Lambi, Ivo Nikolai. 1963. *Free Trade and Protection in Germany, 1868–1879.* Vierteljahrschrift für Sozial- und Wirtschaftsgeschichte, Beihefte no. 44. Weisbaden: Franz Steiner Verlag.

Landauer, Carl. 1961. "The Guesdists and the Small Farmer: Early Erosion of French Marxism." *International Review of Social History* 6, pt. 2, 212–225.

Landes, David S. 1949. "French Entrepreneurship and Industrial Growth in the Nineteenth Century." *Journal of Economic History* 9, no. 1 (May): 45–61.

———. 1956. "Vieille banque et banque nouvelle: La révolution financière du dix-neuvième siècle." *Revue d'histoire moderne et contemporaine* 3:204–222.

Landes, Joan B. 1981. "Feminism and the Internationals." *Telos,* no. 49 (Fall): 117–126.

———. 1988. *Women and the Public Sphere in the Age of the French Revolution*. Ithaca, NY: Cornell Univ. Press.

Lange, David. 1977. "London in the Year of Revolutions, 1848." In *London in the Age of Reform*, ed. J. Stevenson, 177–211. Oxford: Basil Blackwell.

Langewiesche, Dieter. 1987. "The Impact of the German Labor Movement on Workers' Culture." *Journal of Modern History* 59, no. 3 (September): 506–523.

———. 1993. "Liberalism and the Middle Classes in Europe." In *Bourgeois Society in Nineteenth-Century Europe*, ed. J. Kocka and A. Mitchell, 40–69. Oxford: Berg.

Lasch, Christopher. 1958. "The Anti-Imperialists, the Philippines, and the Inequality of Man." *Journal of Southern History* 24, no. 3 (August): 319–331.

Laslett, John H. M. 1964. "Reflections on the Failure of Socialism in the American Federation of Labor." *Mississippi Valley Historical Review* 50, no. 4 (March): 634–651.

———. 1974. "Comment [on Daniel Bell]." In *Failure of a Dream? Essays in the History of American Socialism*, ed. J. H. M. Laslett and S. M. Lipset, 112–123. Garden City, NY: Anchor/Doubleday.

Lasserre, Adrien. 1906. *La Participation collective des femmes à la Révolution: Les antécédents du féminisme*. Paris: Félix Alcan.

Lazarsfeld, Paul F. 1961. "Notes on the History of Quantification in Sociology: Trends, Sources, and Problems." *ISIS* 52, pt. 2, no. 168 (June): 277–331.

Le Bon, Gustave. 1978 [1894]. *Les Lois psychologiques de l'évolution des peuples*. Paris: Les Amis de Gustave Le Bon.

Lebrun, Pierre. 1948. *L'industrie de la laine à Verviers pendant le XVIIIe et le début du XIXe siècles: Contribution à l'étude des origines de la révolution industrielle*. Faculté de Philosophie et Lettres, fasc. 114. Liège.

———. 1961. "La rivoluzione industriale in Belgio: Strutturazione e destrutturazione delle economie regionali." *Studi storici* 2, nos. 3/4: 548–658.

Leclercq, Yves. 1991. "Les Débats d'orientation économique de la France (1815–1850)." *Cahiers de l'I.S.E.A.*, Series AF: Historie quantitative de l'économie française, no. 4 (July): 91–119.

Le Cour Grandmaison, Olivier. 1987. "La Citoyenneté à l'époque de la Constituante." *Annales historiques de la Révolution française*, nos. 269–270 (July–December): 248–265.

Lecuyer, Bernard-Pierre. 1983. "Les Statistiques démographiques et sociales et les statisticiens durant la Restauration." In *Sciences, médecines et technologies sous la Restauration*. Paris: Maison des Sciences de l'Homme.

———. 1988. Preface to *Législation primitive considérée par la raison*, by L. de Bonald, i–vi. Paris: Jean-Michel Place.

Ledru-Rollin, A.-A. 1850. *De la décadence de l'Angleterre*. 2 vols. Paris: Escudier Frères.

Lee, Dwight E., and Robert N. Beck. 1954. "The Meaning of Historicism." *American Historical Review* 59, no. 3 (April): 568–577.

Lee, Richard E., and Immanuel Wallerstein, coord. 2004. *Overcoming the Two Cultures: Science versus the Humanities in the Modern World-System*. Boulder, CO: Paradigm.

Lee, W. R., and Eve Rosenhaft, eds. 1997. *State, Social Policy and Social Change in Germany, 1880–1994*. Updated and rev. 2nd ed. Oxford: Berg.

Lefkowitz, Mary R. 1996. "Ancient History, Modern Myths." In *Black Athena Revisited,* ed. M. R. Lefkowitz and G. M. Rogers, 5–23. Chapel Hill: Univ. of North Carolina Press.

———. 1997. *Not Out of Africa: How Afrocentrism Became an Excuse to Teach Myth as History.* Rev. ed. New York: Basic Books.

Lefrane, Georges. 1930. "The French Railroads, 1823–1842." *Journal of Economic and Business History* 2, no. 2 (February): 299–331.

Lehning, Arthur. 1938. *The International Association, 1855–1859: A Contribution to the Preliminary History of the First International.* Leiden: E. J. Brill.

———. 1970. *From Buonarroti to Bakunin: Studies in International Socialism.* Leiden: E. J. Brill.

Lemoine, Robert J. 1932. "Les Étrangers et la formation du capitalisme en Belgique." *Revue d'histoire économique et sociale* 20, no. 3, 252–336.

Lentini, Orlando, ed. 1981. *La Sociologia italiana nell'età del positivismo.* Bologna: Il Mulino.

Léon, Pierre. 1960. "L'industrialisation en France en tant que facteur de croissance économique, du début du XXVIIIe siècle à nos jours." In *Première conférence internationale d'histoire économique,* 165–204. Paris and The Hague: Mouton.

Léon, Pierre, François Crouzet, and Richard Gascon, eds. 1972. *L'Industrialisation en Europe au XIXe siècle, Cartographie et typologie. Colloque International du C.N.R.S., Lyon, 7–10 Octobre, 1970.* Paris: Éd. du C.N.R.S.

Leopold, Joan. 1970. "The Aryan Theory of Race in India, 1870–1920: Nationalist and Internationalist Visions." *Indian Economic and Social History Review* 7, no. 2 (June): 271–297.

———. 1974. "British Applications of the Aryan Theory of Race to India, 1850–1870." *English Historical Review* 89, no. 352, 578–603.

Lepenies, Wolf. 1989. *Between Literature and Science: The Rise of Sociology.* Cambridge: Cambridge Univ. Press. [Originally published as *Die Drei Kulturen.*]

Lerner, Gerda. 1993. *The Creation of Feminist Consciousness: From the Middle Ages to Eighteen-seventy.* New York: Oxford Univ. Press.

Leslie, R. F. 1952. "Polish Political Divisions and the Struggle for Power at the Beginning of the Insurrection of November 1830." *Slavonic Review* 31, no. 76 (December): 113–132.

———. 1956. *Polish Politics and the Revolution of November 1830.* London: Athlone Press.

Leuilliot, Paul. 1953. "Notes et remarques sur l'histoire économique et social de la France, sous la Restauration." *Revue de synthèse,* n.s., 33 (74, sér. gén.) (July–December): 149–172.

Le Van-Mesle, Lucette. 1980. "La Promotion de l'économie politique en France au XIXe siècle, jusqu'à son introduction dans les facultés (1815–1881)." *Revue d'histoire moderne et contemporaine* 27 (April–June): 270–294.

Levasseur, Emile. 1903–1904. *Histoire des classes ouvrières et de l'industrie en France de 1789 à 1870.* 2nd ed. entièrement refondue. 3 vols. Paris: A. Rousseau.

Levy, Darline Gay, et al., eds. 1979. *Women in Revolutionary Paris, 1789–1795: Selected Documents.* Urbana: Univ. of Illinois Press.

Lévy-Leboyer, Maurice. 1964. *Les Banques européennes et l'industrialisation internationale dans la première moitié du XIXe siècle.* Paris: Presses Univ. de France.

———. 1968a. "La Croissance économique en France au XIXe siècle: Résultats préliminaires." *Annales E.S.C.* 23, no. 4 (July–August): 788–807.

———. 1968b. "Le Processus d'industrialisation: Le Cas de l'Angleterre et la France." *Revue historique,* 92e année, CCXXXIX (April–June): 281–298.

———. 1970. "L'Héritage de Simiand: Prix, profit et termes d'échange au XIXe siècle." *Revue historique,* 94e année, no. 243 (January–March): 77–120.

———. 1971. "La Décélération de l'économie française dans la seconde moitié du XIXe siècle." *Revue d'histoire économique et sociale* 49, no. 4, 485–507.

Lévy-Leboyer, Maurice, and François Bourguignon. 1985. *L'Economie française au XIXe siècle: Analyse macro-économique.* Paris: Economica.

Lewis, Gordon K. 1978. *Slavery, Imperialism, and Freedom: Studies in English Radical Thought.* New York: Monthly Review Press.

———. 1983. *Main Currents in Caribbean Thoughts: The Historical Evolution of Caribbean Society in Its Ideological Aspects, 1492–1900.* Baltimore: Johns Hopkins Univ. Press.

Lewis, Jane. 1984. *Women in England 1870–1950: Sexual Divisions and Social Change.* Brighton, UK: Wheatsheaf Books.

———, ed. 1987. *Before the Vote Was Won: Arguments for and against Women's Suffrage.* London: Routledge & Kegan Paul.

Lewis, W. A. 1957. "International Competition in Manufacturers." *American Economic Review* 47, no. 2, 578–587.

Lhomme, Jean. 1960. *La Grande bourgeoisie au pouvoir (1830–1880).* Paris: Presses Univ. de France.

Lichtheim, George. 1969. *The Origins of Socialism.* London: Weidenfeld & Nicolson.

Liddington, Jill, and Jill Norris. 1984. *One Hand Tied Behind Us: The Rise of the Women's Suffrage Movement.* Reprinted and corrected ed. London: Virago.

Lidtke, Vernon. 1980. "The Formation of the Working Class in Germany." *Central European History* 13, no. 4 (December): 393–400.

Lincoln, Andrew. 1980. "Through the Undergrowth: Capitalist Development and Social Formation in 19th Century France." In *People's History and Socialist Theory,* ed. R. Samuel, 255–267. London: Routledge & Kegan Paul.

Lindenlaub, Dieter. 1967. *Richtungskämpfe im Verein für Sozialpolitik: Vierteljahresschaft für Sozial- und Wirtschartsgeschichte.* Beiheft no. 53. Wiesbaden: Franz Steiner Verlag.

Lindholm, Marika. 1991. "Swedish Feminism, 1835–1945: A Conservative Revolution." *Journal of Historical Sociology* 4, no. 2 (June): 121–142.

Linebaugh, Peter, and Marcus Rediker. 1990. "The Many Headed Hydra: Sailors, Slaves and the Atlantic Working Class in the Eighteenth Century." *Journal of Historical Sociology* 3, no. 3 (September): 225–522.

Lipset, S. M. 1983. "Radicalism or Reformism: The Sources of Working-Class Politics." *American Political Science Review* 77, no. 1 (March): 1–18.

Lis, Catharine, and Hugo Soly. 1977. "Food Consumption in Antwerp between 1807 and 1859: A Contribution to the Standard of Living Debate." *Economic History Review,* 2nd. ser., vol. 30, no. 3: 460–486.

Lisanti, Nicola. 1979. "La Nascità del movimento operaio, 1815–1860." In *Dall'Età preindustriale alla fine dell'Ottocento,* ed. A. Agosti and G. M. Bravo, 219–267. Vol. 1 of *Storia del movimento operaio, del socialismo e delle lotte sociale in Piemonte.* Bari: De Donato.

Lissagaray, Prosper-Olivier. 1976. *Histoire de la Commune de 1871.* Paris: La Découverte.

Lladonosa, Manuel, and Joaquím Ferrer. 1977. "Nacionalisme català i reformisme social en els treballadors mercantila a Barcelona entre 1903 i 1939. El C.A.D.C.I." In *Teoría y práctica del movimiento obrero en España, 1900–1936,* ed. A. Balcells, 281–329. Valencia: Fernando Torres, Ed.

Locke, John. 1965 [1689]. *Two Treatises of Government.* New York: New American Library/ Mentor.

Logue, William. 1979. "Sociologie et politique: Le Libéralisme de Célestin Bouglé." *Revue française de sociologie* 20, no. 1 (January–March): 141–161.

———. 1983. *From Philosophy to Sociology: The Evolution of French Liberalism, 1870–1914.* De Kalb: Northern Illinois Univ. Press.

Longuet, Jean. 1913. *Le Mouvement socialiste international.* Paris: A. Quillet.

Lora, Guillermo. 1990. *A History of the Bolivian Labour Movement, 1848–1971.* Cambridge: Cambridge Univ. Press.

Lorimer, Douglas A. 1978. *Colour, Class, and the Victorians: English Attitudes to the Negro in the Mid-Nineteenth Century.* Leicester, UK: Leicester Univ. Press.

———. 1990. "Nature, Racism, and Late Victorian Science." *Canadian Journal of History* 25, no. 3 (December): 369–385.

Lorwin, Val. 1958. "Working-Class Politics and Economic Development in Western Europe." *American Historical Review* 63, no. 2 (January): 338–351.

Louis, Paul. 1905. *Le Colonialisme.* Bibliothèque Socialiste, no. 36. Paris: Société Nouvelle de Librairie et d'Edition.

Lovett, Clara M. 1982. *The Democratic Movement in Italy, 1830–1876.* Cambridge, MA: Harvard Univ. Press.

Lowi, Theodore J. 1985. Foreword to *Disenchanted Realists, Political Science and the American Crisis, 1884–1984,* by R. Seidelman, vii–xvii. Albany: State Univ. of New York Press.

Löwy, Michael. 1974. "Le Problème de l'histoire (remarques de théorie et de méthode)." In *Les Marxistes et la question nationale, 1848–1914,* by G. Haupt et al., 370–391. Paris: Maspéro.

Lukes, Steven. 1973. *Individualism.* Oxford: Basil Blackwell.

Lutfalla, Michel. 1972. "Aux Origines du libéralisme économique en France, Le 'Journal des Economistes.' Analyse du contenu de la première série, 1841–1853." *Revue d'histoire économique et social* 50, no. 4, 494–517.

Luzzatto, Gino. 1948. "Aspects sociaux de la Révolution de 1848 en Italie." *Revue socialiste,* n.s., nos. 17–18 (January–February): 80–86.

Lyon, Peyton V. 1961. "Saint-Simon and the Origins of Scientism and Historicism." *Canadian Journal of Economics and Political Science* 27, no. 1 (February): 55–63.

Lytle, Scott H. 1955. "The Second Sex (September, 1793)." *Journal of Modern History* 27, no. 1 (March): 14–26.

Lyttleton, Adrian. 1993. "The National Question in Italy." In *The National Question in Europe in Historical Context,* ed. M. Teich and R. Porter, 63–105. Cambridge: Cambridge Univ. Press.

MacCoby, S., ed. 1952. *The English Radical Tradition, 1763–1914.* London: Nicholas Kaye.

MacDonagh, Oliver. 1958. "The Nineteenth Century Revolution in Government: A Reappraisal." *Historical Journal* 1, no. 1, 52–67.

————. 1962. "The Anti-Imperialism of Free Trade." *Economic History Review*, n.s., 14, no. 3 (April): 489–501.

————. 1981. "Ambiguity in Nationalism: The Case of Ireland." *Historical Studies* 19, no. 76 (April): 337–352.

Macpherson, C. B. 1962. *The Political Theory of Possessive Individualism: Hobbes to Locke*. Oxford: Clarendon Press.

Maehl, William. 1952. "The Triumph of Nationalism in the German Socialist Party on the Eve of the First World War." *Journal of Modern History* 24, no. 1 (March): 15–41.

Magraw, Roger. 1985. *France, 1815–1914: The Bourgeois Century*. Fontana History of Modern France. London: Fontana Press/Collins.

Maier, Charles S. 1992. "Democracy since the French Revolution." In *Democracy, the Unfinished Journey: 500 B.C. to A.D. 1993*, ed. John Dunn, 125–153. Oxford: Oxford Univ. Press.

Malefakis, Edward. 1977. "Un Análisis comparativo del movimiento obrero en España e Italia." In *Teoría y práctica del movimiento obrero en España, 1900–1936*, ed. A. Balcells, 95–111. Valencia: Fernando Torres, Éd.

Maloney, John. 1985. *Marshall, Orthodoxy and the Professionalisation of Economics*. Cambridge: Cambridge Univ. Press.

Manacorda, Gaston. 1981. Remarks in *Jaurès et la classe ouvrière*, 184–186. Collection mouvement social. Paris: Ed. Ouvrières.

Mann, Michael. 1970. "The Social Cohesion of Liberal Democracy." *American Sociological Review* 35, no. 3 (June): 423–431.

Manning, D. J. 1976. *Liberalism*. London: J. M. Dent & Sons.

Manuel, Frank E. 1956. *The New World of Henri Saint-Simon*. Cambridge, MA: Harvard Univ. Press.

Marcuse, Herbert. 1974. "Marxism and Feminism." *Women's Studies* 2, no. 3, 279–288.

Marczewski, Jean. 1961. "Y a-t-il eu un 'take off'' en France?" *Cahiers de l'I.S.E.A.*, Series AD: Évolution des techniques et progrès de l'économie, no. 1 (February): 69–94.

————. 1963. "The Take-Off Hypothesis and French Experience." In *The Economics of Take-Off into Sustained Growth*, ed. W. W. Rostow, 119–138. London: Macmillan.

————. 1965. "Le Produit physique de l'économie française de 1789 à 1913 (comparison avec la Grande-Bretagne)." *Cahiers de l'I.S.E.A.*, Series AF: Historie quantitative de l'économie française, no. 4 (July): vii–cliv.

————. 1987. "Préface" to "Le Produit intérieur brut de la France de 1789 à 1982," by Jean-Claude Toutain. *Cahiers de l'I.S.M.E.A.*, Series AF: Historie quantitative de l'économie française, no. 15 (May): 3–48.

Marichal, Juan. 1955. "España y las raíces semánticas del liberalisme." *Cuadernos*, no. 11 (March–April): 53–60.

————. 1956. "The French Revolution Background in the Spanish Semantic Change of 'Liberal.'" In *American Philosophical Society Yearbook 1955*, 291–293. Philadelphia: American Philosophical Society.

Markovitch, Timohir J. 1965. "La crise de 1847–1848 dans les industries parisiennes." *Revue d'histoire économique et social* 43, no. 2, 256–260.

————.1966. "L'Industrie française de 1789 à 1964: Conclusions générales." *Cahiers de l'I.S.E.A*, Series AF: Histoire quantitative de l'économie française, no. 7 (November).

———. 1967. "Le revenu industriel et artisanal sous la Monarchie de juillet et le Second Empire." *Cahiers de l'I.S.E.A,* Series AF: Histoire quantitative de l'économie française, no. 8 (April).

Marks, Harry J. 1939. "The Sources of Reformism in the Social Democratic Party of Germany, 1890–1914." *Journal of Modern History* 11, no. 3 (September): 334–356.

Marriott, Sir J. A. R. 1918. *The Eastern Question: An Historical Study in European Diplomacy.* 2nd ed. Oxford: Clarendon Press.

Marrus, Michael R. 1972. "French Jews, the Dreyfus Affair, and the Crisis of French Society." In *Modern European Social History,* ed. R. J. Bezucha, 335–353. Lexington, MA: D. C. Heath.

Marshall, Alfred. 1892. "Reply" [to "The Perversion of Economic History"], *Economic Journal* 2, no. 3 (September): 507–519.

———. 1921. *Industry and Trade.* London: Macmillan.

Marshall, Susan E. 1986. "In Defense of Separate Spheres: Class and Status Politics in the Antisuffrage Movement." *Social Forces* 65, no. 2 (December): 327–351.

Martin, Gaston. 1948. *L'Abolition de l'esclavage (27 avril 1848). Collection du Centenaire de la Révolution De 1848.* Paris: Presses Univ. de France.

Martin, Kingsley. 1963. *The Triumph of Lord Palmerston.* Rev. ed. London: Hutchison.

Martin, Wendy. 1972. *The American Sisterhood: Writings of the Feminist Movement from Colonial Times to the Present.* New York: Harper & Row.

Marx, Karl, and Frederick Engels. 1976. "Manifesto of the Communist Party." In *Collected Works,* vol. 6, *Marx and Engels, 1845–1848,* 477–519. New York: International Publishers.

Mason, E. S. 1931. "Saint-Simonism and the Rationalisation of Industry." *Quarterly Journal of Economics* 45 (August): 640–683.

Mastellone, Salvo. 1957. *La Politica estera del Guizot (1840–1847).* Florence: La Nuova Italia.

Masure, Auguste. 1892–1893. "La Reconnaissance de la monarchie de juillet." 2 pts. *Annales de l'École Libre de Sciences Politiques* 7 (October 1892): 696–721; 8 (January 1893): 72–117.

Mathias, Eric. 1971. "The Social Democratic Working-Class Movement and the German National State Up to the End of World War I." In *Mouvements nationaux d'indépendance et classes populaires aux XIXe et XXe siècles en Occident et en Orient,* 1:175–183. Paris: Lib. Armand Colin.

Matoré, Georges. 1967. *Le Vocabulaire et la société sous Louis-Philippe.* 2nd ed. Geneva: Slatkine Reprints.

Matthew, H. C. G. 1973. *The Liberal Imperialists: The Ideas and Politics of a Post-Gladstonian Elite.* London: Oxford Univ. Press.

———. 1979. "Disraeli, Gladstone, and the Policy of Mid-Victorian Budgets." *Historical Journal* 22, no. 3 (September): 615–643.

Mawet, Francine. 2000. "Inde, réponses ou questions?" In *Modèles linguistiques et idéologies, "Indo-Européen,"* ed. S. Vanséveren, 61–84. Brussels: Éd. Ousia.

May, Arthur J. 1948. "L'Amérique et les révolutions du milieu du siècle dernier." In *Le Printemps des peuples: 1848 dans le monde,* ed. F. Fejtö, 2:395–434. Paris: Éd. du Minuit.

May, Martha. 1982. "The Historical Problem of the Family Wage: The Ford Motor Company and the Five Dollar Day." *Feminist Studies* 8, no. 2 (Summer): 399–424.

Mayer, Arno J. 1969. "Internal Courses and Purposes of War, 1870–1956: A Research Assignment." *Journal of Modern History* 41, no. 3 (September): 291–303.

———. 1981. *The Persistence of the Old Regime: Europe to the Great War*. New York: Pantheon.

McBride, Theresa M. 1976. *The Domestic Revolution: The Modernization of Household Science in England and France, 1820–1920*. London: Croom Helm.

McCalman, Iain. 1986. "Anti-slavery and Ultra Radicalism in Early Nineteenth-Century England: The Case of Robert Wedderburn." *Slavery and Abolition* 7, no. 2 (September): 99–117.

McClelland, Charles E. 1980. *State, Society, and University in Germany, 1700–1914*. Cambridge: Cambridge Univ. Press.

McCloskey, Donald N. 1971. "International Differences in Productivity? Coal and Steel in America and Britain before World War I." In *Essays on a Mature Economy: Britain after 1840*, ed. D. N. McCloskey, 285–304. London: Methuen.

———. 1980. "Magnanimous Albion: Free Trade and British National Income, 1841–1881." *Explorations in Economic History* 17, no. 3 (July): 303–320.

McCloskey, Donald N., and Kars G. Sandberg. 1971. "From Damnation Entrepreneur." *Explorations in Entrepreneurial History* 9, no. 1 (Fall): 89–108.

McCloskey, Donald N., and J. Richard Zesher. 1976. "How the Gold Standard Worked, 1880–1913." In *The Monetary Approach to the Balance of Payments*, ed. J. A. Frenkel and H. G. Johnson, 357–385. London: George Allen & Unwin.

McCord, Norman. 1958. *The Anti-Corn Law League, 1838–1846*. London: George Allen & Unwin.

McCormmach, Russell. 1974. "On Academic Scientists in Wilhelmian Germany." *Daedalus* 103, no. 3, 157–171.

McDougall, Mary Lynn. 1978. "Consciousness and Community: The Workers of Lyon, 1830–1850." *Journal of Social History* 14, no. 1 (Fall): 129–145.

McGregor, O. R. 1957. "Social Research and Social Policy in the Nineteenth Century." *British Journal of Sociology* 8, no. 2 (June): 146–157.

McGrew, William W. 1976. "The Land Issue in the Greek War of Independence." In *Hellenism and the First Greek War of Liberation (1821–1830): Continuity and Change*, ed. N. P. Diamandouros, 111–129. Thessaloniki: Institute for Balkan Studies.

McKenzie, Robert, and Allan Silver. 1968. *Angels in Marble: Working Class Conservatives in Urban England*. London: Heinemann.

McLaren, Angus. 1978a. "Abortion in France: Women and the Regulation of Family Size, 1800–1914." *French Historical Studies* 10, no. 3 (Spring): 461–485.

———. 1978b. *Birth Control in Nineteenth-Century England*. London: Croom Helm.

McMillan, James F. 1981a. "Clericals, Anticlericals and the Women's Movement in France under the Third Republic." *Historical Journal* 24, no. 2, 361–376.

———. 1981b. *Housewife or Harlot: The Place of Women in French Society, 1870–1940*. Brighton, Sussex, UK: Harvester Press.

Meek, Ronald L. 1967. "The Scottish Contribution to Marxist Sociology." In *Economics and Ideology and Other Essays*, 34–50. London: Chapman & Hall.

———. 1976. *Social Science and the Ignoble Savage*. Cambridge: Cambridge Univ. Press.

Melder, Keith. 1977. *The Beginnings of Sisterhood: The American Woman's Rights Movement, 1800–1850*. New York: Schocken Books.

Mellon, Stanley. 1958. *The Political Uses of History: A Study of Historians in the French Restoration*. Stanford, CA: Stanford Univ. Press.

Mellor, G. R. 1951. *British Imperial Trusteeship, 1783–1850*. London: Faber & Faber.

Menager, Bernard. 1981. "Forces et limites du bonapartisme populaire en milieu ouvrier sous le Second Empire." *Revue historique*, 105e année, CCLXV, 2, no. 538 (April–June): 371–388.

Merle, Marcel, ed. 1969. *L'Anticolonialisme européen de Las Casas à Marx*. Textes choisis et présentés. Collection U. Paris: Lib. Armand Colin.

Merrill, Lynn L. 1989. *The Romance of Victorian Natural History*. New York: Oxford Univ. Press.

Merriman, John M. 1975. "Radicalism and Repression: A Study of the Demobilisation of the 'Democ-Socs' during the Second French Republic." In *Revolution and Reaction: 1848 and the Second French Republic,* ed. R. Price, 210–235. London: Croom Helm.

———. 1978. *Agony of the Republic: The Depression of the Left in Revolutionary France, 1848– 1851*. New Haven, CT: Yale Univ. Press.

Meyssonier, Simone. 1989. *La Balance et l'horloge: La Genèse de la pensée libérale en France au XVIIIe siècle*. Montreuil: Éd. de la Passion.

Michaud, Stéphane, ed. 1984. *Un Fabuleux destin, Flora Tristan. Actes Du Premier Colloque International Flora Tristan, Dijon, 3 et 4 mai 1984*. Dijon: Éd. Univ. de Dijon.

Michelet, Jules. 1860. *La Femme*. 3rd ed. Paris: Hachette.

Michels, Roberto. 1908. *Il Proletariato e la borghesia nel movimento socialista italiana*. Turin: Fratelli Bocca, Ed.

Michie, Ranald. 1993. "The City of London and International Trade, 1850–1914." In *Decline and Recovery in Britain's Overseas Trade, 1873–1914,* ed. D. C. M. Platt et al., 21–63. London: Macmillan.

Middleton, Lucy, ed. 1977. *Women in the Labour Movement: The British Experience*. London: Croom Helm.

Mill, John Stuart. 1849. "The French Revolution of 1848, and Its Assailants." *Westminster Review* LI, April-July, 1–47. [Published anonymously.]

———. 1970. "The Subjection of Women." In *Essays on Sex Equality by John Stuart Mill and Harriet Taylor Mill,* ed. A. Rossi, 123–242. Chicago: Univ. of Chicago Press.

Miller, Sally M., ed. 1981. *Flawed Liberation: Socialism and Feminism*. Westport, CT: Greenwood Press.

Milward, Alan S., and S. B. Saul. 1973. *The Development of the Economics of Continental Europe, 1850–1914*. London: George Allen & Unwin.

Mink, Gwendolyn. 1986. *Old Labor and New Immigrants in American Political Development: Union, Party, and State, 1875–1920*. Ithaca, NY: Cornell Univ. Press.

———. 1990. "The Lady and the Tramp: Gender, Race, and the Origins of the American Welfare State." In *Women, the State and Welfare,* ed. L. Gordon, 92–122. Madison: Univ. of Wisconsin Press.

Minogue, K. R. 1963. *The Liberal Mind.* London: Methuen.

Mitchison, Rosalind. 1980. "Nineteenth Century Scottish Nationalism: The Cultural Background." In *The Roots of Nationalism: Studies in Northern Europe,* ed. R. Mitchison, 131–142. Edinburgh: John Donald.

Mock, Wolfgang. 1981. "The Function of 'Race' in Imperialist Ideologies: The Example of Joseph Chamberlain." In *Nationalist and Racialist Movements in Britain and Germany before 1914,* ed. P. Kennedy and A. Nicholls, 190–203. Basingstoke, UK: Macmillan.

Mokyr, Joel. 1974. "The Industrial Revolution in the Low Countries in the First Half of the Nineteenth Century." *Journal of Economic History* 34, no. 2: 365–391.

Mokyr, Joel, and John V. C. Nye. 1990. "La Grande quantification" [review of *L'Économie française au XIXe siècle,* by M. Lévy-Leboyer and F. Bourgnignon], *Journal of Economic History* 50, no. 1 (March): 172–176.

Molnár, Miklós. 1971. "Mouvements d'indépendance en Europe: Rôle de la question agraire et du niveau de culture." In *Mouvements nationaux d'indépendance et classes populaires aux XIXe et XXE siècles en Occident et en Orient,* ed. E. Labrousse, 217–227. Comité International des Sciences Historiques, Commission Internationale d'Histoire des Mouvement Sociaux et des Structures Sociales. Paris: Lib. Armand Colin.

———. 1975. *Marx, Engels et la politique internationale.* Paris: Gallimard.

Mommsen, Hans. 1979. *Arbiterbewegung und nationale Frage; ausgew. Aufsätze.* Göttingen: Vandenhoek & Ruprecht.

Mommsen, Wolfgang J., and Jürgen Osterhammel, eds. 1985. *Imperialism and After: Continuities and Discontinuities.* London: George Allen & Unwin.

Montgomery, David. 1980. "Strikes in Nineteenth-Century America." *Social Science History* 4, no. 1 (Winter): 81–104.

Mooers, Colin. 1991. *The Making of Bourgeois Europe: Absolutism, Revolution, and the Rise of Capitalism in England, France and Germany.* London: Verso.

Moore, David Chioni, ed. 2001. *Black Athena Writes Back: Martin Bernal Responds to His Critics.* Durham, NC: Duke Univ. Press.

Moore, David Cresap. 1961. "The Other Face of Reform." *Victorian Studies* 5, no. 1 (September): 7–34.

———. 1965. "The Corn Laws and High Farming." *Economic History Review,* n.s., 18, no. 3 (December): 544–561.

———. 1967. "Social Structure, Political Structure, and Public Opinion in Mid-Victorian England." In *Ideas and Institutions of Victorian Britain,* ed. Robert Robson, 20–57. London: G. Bell & Sons.

Moore, R. J. 1964. "Imperialism and 'Free Trade' Policy in India, 1853–54." *Economic History Review,* n.s., 17, no. 1 (August): 135–145.

Moorhouse, H. F. 1973. "The Political Incorporation of the British Working Class: An Interpretation." *Sociology* 7, no. 3 (September): 341–359.

———. 1975. "On the Political Incorporation of the Working Class: Reply to Gray." *Sociology* 9, no. 1 (January): 105–110.

———. 1978. "The Marxist Theory of the Labour Aristocracy." *Social History* 3, no. 1 (January): 61–82.

Moravio, Sergio. 1980. "The Enlightenment and the Sciences of Man." *History of Science* 18, pt. 4, no. 142 (December): 247–268.

Morazé, Charles. 1957. *Les Bourgeois conquérants, XIX siècle*. Paris: A. Colin.

Morgan, David. 1975. *Suffragists and Liberals: The Politics of Women Suffrage in England*. Oxford: Blackwell.

Morgan, E. Victor. 1965. *The Theory and Practice of Central Banking, 1797–1913*. London: Frank Cass.

Morley, Charles. 1952. "The European Significance of the November Uprising." *Journal of Central European Affairs* 11, no. 4 (January): 407–416.

Morrell, Jack, and Arnold Thackray. 1981. *Gentlemen of Science: Early Years of the British Association for the Advancement of Science*. Camden Fourth Series 30. Oxford: Clarendon Press.

Moses, Claire Goldberg. 1982. "Saint-Simonian Men/Saint-Simonian Women: The Transformation of Feminist Thought in 1830s' France." *Journal of Modern History* 54, no. 2 (June): 240–267.

———. 1984. *French Feminism in the Nineteenth Century*. Albany: State Univ. of New York Press.

———. 1992. "Debating the Present, Writing the Past: 'Feminism' in French History and Historiography." *Radical History Review*, no. 52 (Winter): 79–84.

Moses, John A. 1990. *Trade Union Theory from Marx to Walesa*. New York: Berg.

Moses, Wilson J. 1978. *The Golden Age of Black Nationalism, 1850–1925*. Hamden, CT: Archon.

Moss, Bernard H. 1975a. "Parisian Workers and the Origins of Republican Socialism, 1830–1833." In *1830 in France*, ed. J. M. Merriman, 203–221. New York: Franklin Watts.

———. 1975b. "Parisian Producers' Associations (1830–51): The Socialism of Skilled Workers." In *Revolution and Reaction: 1848 and the Second French Republic*, ed. R. Price, 73–86. London: Croom Helm.

———. 1976. *The Origins of the French Labor Movement, 1830–1914: The Socialism of Skilled Workers*. Berkeley: Univ. of California Press.

Mosse, George L. 1947. "The Anti-League, 1844–1846." *Economic History Review* 17, no. 2, 134–142.

———. 1985. *Nationalism and Sexuality: Respectability and Abnormal Sexuality in Modern Europe*. New York: Howard Fertig.

Mouralis, Bernard. 1987. "Le Concept du primitif: L'Europe, productrice d'une science des autres." *Notre Librairie*, no. 90 (October–December): 86–91.

Muret, Maurice. 1925. *La Crépuscule des nations blanches*. Paris: Payot.

Murphy, Marjorie. 1986. "The Aristocracy of Women's Labor in Autumn." *History Workshop Journal*, no. 22 (Autumn): 56–69.

Musson, A. E. 1959. "The Great Depression in Britain, 1873–1896: A Reappraisal." *Journal of Economic History* 19, no. 2 (June): 199–228.

———. 1963. "British Growth during the Great Depression (1873–96): Some Comments." *Economic History Review*, n.s., 15, no. 3, 529–533.

———. 1964. "British Industrial Growth, 1873–96: A Balanced View." *Economic History Review*, n.s., 17, no. 2 (December): 397–403.

———. 1972a. *British Trade Unions, 1800–1875*. London: Macmillan.

———. 1972b. "The 'Manchester School' and Exportation of Machinery." *Business History* 14, no. 1 (January): 17–50.

———. 1976. "Class Struggle and the Labour Aristocracy, 1830–60." *Social History* 1, no. 3 (October): 335–356.

Myers, John Lynton. 1916. "The Influence of Anthropology on the Course of Political Science." *University of California Publications in History* 4, no. 1 (February 29): 1–81.

Neale, R. S. 1972. *Class and Ideology in the Nineteenth Century*. London: Routledge & Kegan Paul.

Neff, Emery. 1926. *Carlyle and Mill: Mystic and Utilitarian*. New York: Columbia Univ. Press.

Neuman, R. P. 1974. "The Sexual Question and Social Democracy in Imperial Germany." *Journal of Social History*, no. 7 (Spring): 271–286.

Newbold, J. T. Walton. 1932. "The Beginnings of the World Crisis, 1873–96." *Economic Journal (Economic History)* 2, no. 7 (January): 425–441.

Newell, William H. 1973. "The Agricultural Revolution in Nineteenth Century France." *Journal of Economic History* 33, no. 4 (December): 697–731.

Newman, Edgar Leon. 1974. "The Blouse and the Frock Coat: The Alliance of the Common People of Paris with the Liberal Leadership in the Middle Class during the Last Years of the Bourbon Restoration." *Journal of Modern History* 46, no. 1 (March): 26–59.

———. 1975. "What the Crowd Wanted in the French Revolution of 1830." In *1830 in France*, ed. J. M. Merriman, 17–41. New York: Franklin Watts.

Newman, Gerald. 1987. *The Rise of English Nationalism: A Cultural History, 1740–1830*. New York: St. Martin's.

Newsinger, John. 1979. "Revolution and Catholicism in Ireland, 1848–1923." *European Studies Review* 9, no. 4 (October): 457–480.

Neyer, Joseph. 1960. "Individualism and Socialism in Durkheim." In *Emile Durkheim, 1858–1917*, ed. K. H. Wolff, 32–76. Columbus: Ohio State Univ. Press.

Nicolson, Harold. 1946. *The Congress of Vienna: A Study in Allied Unity, 1812–1822*. London: Constable and Co.

Nipperdey, Thomas. 1988. "Zum Problem der Objektivität bei Ranke." In *Leopold von Ranke und die moderne Geschichtswissenschaft*, ed. W. J. Mommsen, 215–222. Stuttgart: Klein-Cotta.

Nisbet, Robert A. 1944. "De Bonald and the Concept of the Social Group." *Journal of the History of Ideas* 5, no. 3 (June): 315–331.

———. 1952. "Conservatism and Sociology." *American Journal of Sociology* 58, no. 2 (September): 167–175.

———. 1966. *The Sociological Tradition*. New York: Basic Books.

Nolan, Mary. 1986. "Economic Crisis, State Policy, and Working-Class Formation in Germany, 1870–1900." In *Working-Class Formation: Nineteenth-Century Patterns in Western Europe and the United States*, ed. I. Katznelson and A. R. Zolberg, 352–393. Princeton, NJ: Princeton Univ. Press.

Nora, Pierre. 1988. "Nation." In *Dictionnaire critique de la Révolution française*, ed. F. Furet et al., 801–812. Paris: Flammarion.

Norrell, Robert J. 1990. "After Thirty Years of 'New' Labour History, There Is Still No Socialism in Reagan Country." *Historical Journal* 33, no. 1, 227–238.

Norton, Philip, and Arthur Aughay. 1981. *Conservatives and Conservatism*. London: Temple Smith.

Novick, Peter. 1988. *That Noble Dream: The "Objectivity" Question and the American Historical Profession*. Cambridge: Cambridge Univ. Press.

Noyes, P. H. 1966. *Organization and Revolution: German Worker Associations and the Revolutions of 1848 and 1849*. Princeton, NJ: Princeton Univ. Press.

Nye, John Vincent. 1987. "Firm Size and Economic Backwardness: A New Look at the French Industrialization Debate." *Journal of Economic History* 47, no. 3 (September): 649–669.

———. 1991. "The Myth of Free-Trade Britain and Fortress France: Tariffs and Trade in the Nineteenth Century." *Journal of Economic History* 51, no. 1 (March): 23–46.

Nye, Robert A. 1975. *The Origins of Crowd Psychology: Gustave Le Bon and the Crisis of Mass Democracy in the Third Republic*. London: Sage.

———. 1981. "Degeneration, Hygiene, and Sports in Fin-de-Siècle France." In *Proceedings of the Eighth Annual Meeting of the Western Society for French History*, ed. E. L. Newman, 404–412. Las Cruces: New Mexico State Univ. Press.

———. 1984. *Crime, Madness, and Politics in Modern France: The Medical Concept of National Decline*. Princeton, NJ: Princeton Univ. Press.

———. 1993. *Masculinity and Male Codes of Honor in Modern France*. New York: Oxford Univ. Press.

Obermann, Karl. 1965."Der Wiener Kongress, 1814/1815." *Zeitschrift für Geschichtswissenschaft* 13, no. 3, 474–492.

Oberschall, Anthony. 1965. *Empirical Social Research in Germany, 1848–1914*. Paris and The Hague: Mouton.

———. 1972. "The Institutionalization of American Sociology." In *The Establishment of Empirical Sociology: Continuities, Discontinuities, and Institutionalization*, ed. A. Oberschall, 187–251. New York: Harper & Row.

O'Boyle, Lenore. 1966. "The Middle Class in Western Europe, 1815–1848." *American Historical Review* 71, no. 3 (April): 826–845.

———. 1967. "The 'Middle Class' Reconsidered: A Reply to Professor Cobban." *French Historical Studies* 5, no. 1 (Spring): 53–56.

———. 1979. "The Classless Society: Comment on Stearns." *Comparative Studies in Society and History* 21, no. 3 (July): 397–413.

O'Brien, Patrick. 1986. "Do We Have a Typology for the Study of European Industrialization in the XIXth Century?" *Journal of European Economic History* 15, no. 2 (Fall): 291–333.

O'Brien, Patrick, and Çağlar Keyder. 1978. *Economic Growth in Britain and France, 1780–1914: Two Paths to the Twentieth Century*. London: George Allen & Unwin.

O'Brien, Patrick, and Geoffrey Allen Pigman. 1992. "Free Trade, British Hegemony and the International Economic Order in the Nineteenth Century." *Review of International Studies* 18:89–113.

Offen, Karen. 1983. "The Second Sex and the Baccalauréat in Republican France, 1880–1924." *French Historical Studies* 13, no. 2 (Fall): 252–286.

———. 1984. "Depopulation, Nationalism, and Feminism in *Fin-de-Siècle* France." *American Historical Review* 89, no. 3 (June): 648–676.

———. 1986. "Ernest Legouve and the Doctrine of 'Equality in Difference' for Women: A Case Study of Male Feminism in Nineteenth-Century French Thought." *Journal of Modern History* 58, no. 2, 452–484.

———. 1987a. "Feminism, Antifeminism, and National Family Politics in Early Third Republic France." In *Connecting Spheres: Women in the Western World, 1500 to the Present,* ed. M. J. Boxer and J. H. Quataert, 177–186. New York: Oxford Univ. Press.

———. 1987b. "Sur l'origine des mots 'féminisme' et 'féministe.'" *Revue d'histoire moderne et contemporaine,* 34 (July–September): 492–446.

———. 1988. "Defining Feminism: A Comparative Historical Approach." *Signs* 14, no. 1 (Autumn): 119–157.

O'Gorman, F. 1967. *The Whig Party and the French Revolution.* London: Macmillan.

Olcott, Teresa. 1976. "Dead Centre: The Women's Trade Union Movement in London: 1874–1914." *London Journal* 2, no. 1 (May): 33–50.

O'Neill, William L. 1969. *The Woman Movement: Feminism in the United States and England.* London: George Allen & Unwin.

———. 1971. *Everyone Was Brave: A History of Feminism in America.* With a new Afterword by the author. New York: Quadrangle.

Ortega López, Margarita. 1988. "'La Defensa de las mujeres' en la sociedad del Antiguo Régimen: Las Aportaciones del pensamiento ilustrado." In *El Feminismo en España: Dos siglos de historia,* ed. P. Folguer, 3–28. Madrid: Ed. de la Fundación Pablo Iglesias.

Ortner, Sherry B. 1974. "Is Female to Male as Nature Is to Culture?." In *Woman, Culture, and Society,* ed. M. Z. Rosaldo and L. Lamphere, 67–87. Stanford, CA: Stanford Univ. Press.

Ottaviano, Chiara. 1982. "Antonio Labriola e il problema dell'espansione coloniale." *Annali della Fondazione Luigi Einaudi* 16:305–328.

Paish, George. 1909. "Great Britain's Capital Investment in Other Lands." *Journal of the Royal Statistical Society* 72, no. 3 (September 30): 465–480 (with discussion, 481–495).

———. 1911. "Great Britain's Capital Investment in Individual Colonial and Foreign Countries, Pt. 2." *Journal of the Royal Statistical Society* 74 (January): 167–187 (with discussion, 187–200).

Palencia-Roth, Michael. 2008. "The Presidential Addresses of Sir William Jones: The Asiatic Society of Bengal and the ISCSC." *Diogenes* 55, no. 2, 103–115.

Palmade, Guy P. 1961. *Capitalisme et capitalistes français au XIXe siècle.* Paris: Lib. A. Colin.

Pancaldi, Giuliano. 1994. "The Technology of Nature: Marx's Thoughts on Darwin." In *The Natural Sciences and the Social Sciences: Some Critical and Historical Perspectives,* ed. I. B. Cohen, 257–274. Boston Studies in the Philosophy of Science 150. Dordrecht, Netherlands: Kluwer Academic Publishers.

Pankhurst, Richard K. P. 1957. *The Saint-Simonians: Mill and Carlyle.* London: Lalibela Books, Sidgwick & Jackson.

Pannekoek, A. 1912. "Révolution mondiale." *Le Socialisme,* no. 214, 6e année, no. 21 (January): 4.

Paquot, Thierry. 1980. *Les faiseurs des nuages: Essai sur la genèse des marxismes français, 1880–1914*. Paris: Le Sycomore.

Parker, C. J. W. 1981. "The Failure of Liberal Racialism: The Racial Ideas of C. A. Freeman." *Historical Journal* 24, no. 4 (December): 825–846.

Parris, Henry. 1960. "The Nineteenth-Century Revolution in Government: A Reappraisal Reappraised." *Historical Journal* 3, no. 1, 17–37.

Paxton, Nancy L. 1991. *George Eliot and Herbert Spencer: Feminism, Evolutionism and the Reconstruction of Gender*. Princeton, NJ: Princeton Univ. Press.

Payne, Howard C. 1956. "Preparation of a Coup d'Etat: Administrative Centralization and Police Powers in France, 1849–1851." In *Studies in Modern European History in Honor of Franklin Charles Palm*, ed. F. J. Cox et al., 175–202. New York: Bookman Associates.

Payne, Peter L. 1967. "The Emergence of the Large-Scale Company in Great Britain, 1870–1914." *Economic History Review*, n.s., 20, no. 3 (December): 519–542.

———. 1968. "Iron and Steel Manufactures." In *The Development of British Industry and Foreign Competition, 1875–1914*, ed. D. H. Aldcroft, 71–99. London: George Allen & Unwin.

Pelling, Henry, ed. 1954. *The Challenge of Socialism*. London: Adam & Charles Black.

———. 1968. "The Working Class and the Origins of the Welfare State." In *Popular Politics and Society in Late Victorian Britain*, 1–18. London: St. Martin's Press.

———. 1976. *A History of British Trade Unionism*. London: Macmillan.

Perkin, Harold. 1969. *The Origins of Modern English Society, 1780–1880*. London: Routledge & Kegan Paul.

———. 1977. "Individualism versus Collectivism in Nineteenth Century Britain: A False Antithesis." *Journal of British Studies* 17, no. 1 (Fall): 105–118.

Perkins, Dexter. 1927. *The Monroe Doctrine, 1823–1826*. Cambridge, MA: Harvard Univ. Press.

Perlman, Selig. 1918. "Upheaval and Reorganization (since 1876)." In *History of Labor in the United States*, by J. R. Commons, et al., 193–537. New York: Macmillan.

———. 1922. *A History of Trade Unionism in the United States*. New York: Macmillan.

Perlman, Selig, and Philip Taft. 1935. *Labor Movements*. Vol. 4 of *History of Labor in the United States, 1896–1932*. New York: Macmillan.

Perrot, Jean-Claude, and Stuart J. Woolf. 1984. *State and Social Statistics in France*. Chur, Switzerland: Harwood Academic Publishers.

Perrot, Michelle. 1967. "Les Guesdistes: Controverses sur l'introduction du marxisme en France." *Annales E.S.C.* 22, no. 3 (May–June): 701–710.

———. 1974. *Les ouvriers en grève: France, 1871–1890*. 2 vols. Paris: Mouton.

———. 1976. "L'Éloge de la ménagère dans le discours des ouvriers français au XIXe siècle." *Romantisme*, nos. 13–14, 105–121.

———. 1986. "On the Formation of the French Working-Class." In *Working-Class Formation: Nineteenth-Century Patterns in Western Europe and the United States*, ed. I. Katznelson and A. R. Zolberg, 71–110. Princeton, NJ: Princeton Univ. Press.

———. 1988. "Naissance du féminisme." In *Le Féminisme et ses enjeux: Vingt-sept femmes parlent*, 29–60. Paris: FEN–Edilig.

Phillips, G. A. 1971. "The Triple Industrial Alliance in 1914." *Economic History Review*, 2nd ser., 24, no. 1 (February): 55–67.

Picavet, François. 1891. *Les idéologues*. Paris: Félix Alcan.

Pieroni Bortolotti, Franca. 1963. *Alle origini del movimento femminile in Italia, 1848–1892*. Rome: Einaudi.

———. 1974. *Socialismo e questione femminile in Italia, 1892–1922*. Milan: G. Mazzotta.

Pierrard, Pierre. 1984. *L'Eglise et les ouvriers en France, (1890–1940)*. Paris: Hachette.

Pinchbeck, Ivy. 1930. *Women Workers and the Industrial Revolution, 1750–1850*. London: George Routledge & Sons.

Pinkney, David H. 1958. *Napoleon III and the Rebuilding of Paris*. Princeton, NJ: Princeton Univ. Press.

———. 1963. "Laissez-Faire or Intervention? Labor Policy of the First Months of the July Monarchy." *French Historical Studies* 3, no. 1 (Spring): 123–128.

———. 1964a. "The Crowd in the French Revolution of 1830." *American Historical Review* 70, no. 1 (October): 1–17.

———. 1964b. "The Myth of the French Revolution of 1830." In *A Festschrift for Frederick B. Artz*, ed. D. H. Pinkney and T. Rapp, 52–71. Durham, NC: Duke Univ. Press.

———. 1972. *The French Revolution of 1830*. Princeton, NJ: Princeton Univ. Press.

Plamenatz, John. 1952. *The Revolutionary Movement in France, 1815–1870*. London: Longman, Green.

Platt, D. C. M. 1968a. "The Imperialism of Free Trade: Some Reservations." *Economic History Review*, 2nd ser., 21 (August): 296–306.

———. 1968b. *Finance, Trade, and Politics: British Foreign Policy, 1815–1914*. Oxford: Clarendon Press.

———. 1973. "Further Objections to an 'Imperialism of Free Trade,' 1830–1860." *Economic History Review*, 2nd ser., 26, no. 1 (February): 77–91.

———. 1993a. "Introduction: Britain's Decline." In *Decline and Recovery in Britain's Overseas Trade, 1873–1914*, ed. D. C. M. Platt et al., 1–12. London: Macmillan.

———. 1993b. "Particular Points of Strength in Britain's Overseas Trade." In *Decline and Recovery in Britain's Overseas Trade, 1873–1914*, ed. D. C. M. Platt et al., 65–76. London: Macmillan.

———. 1993c. "Trade Competition in the Regions of Recent Settlement." In *Decline and Recovery in Britain's Overseas Trade, 1873–1914*, ed. D. C. M. Platt et al., 91–138. London: Macmillan.

Plechanow, Georg. 1902–1903. "Über die Anfänge der Lehre vom Klassenkampf." *Die Neue Zeit* 21, no. 1: 275–286, 292–305.

Pleck, Elizabeth. 1983. "Feminist Responses to 'Crimes against Women,' 1868–1896." *Signs* 8, no. 3 (Spring): 451–470.

Plessen, Marie-Louise. 1975. *Die Wirksamkeit des Vereins für Sozialpolitik von 1872–1890: Studien zum Katheder- und Staatssozialismus*. Berlin: Duncker & Humboldt.

Plessis, Alain. 1973. *De la Fête impériale au mur des fédérés, 1852–1871*. Paris: Éd. du Seuil.

———. 1987. "Le 'Retard français,' la faute de la banque? Banques locales, succursales de la Banque de France et financement de l'économie sous le second Empire." In *Le capitalisme français, 19e-20e siècle: Blocages et dynamismes d'une croissance,* ed. P. Fridenson and A. Straus, 199–210. Paris: Fayard.

Poggi, Stefano, and Maurizio Bossi, eds. 1994. *Romanticism in Science: Science in Europe, 1790–1840.* Boston Studies in the Philosophy of Science 152. Dordrecht, Netherlands: Kluwer Academic Publ.

Pohl, Hans. 1989. *Aufbruch der Weltwirtschaft: Geschichte der Weltwirtschaft von der Mitte des 19. Jahrhunderts bis zum Ersten Weltkrieg.* Stuttgart: Franz Steiner Verlag.

Polanyi, Karl. 1957. *The Great Transformation: The Political and Economic Origins of Our Time.* Boston: Beacon Press.

Poliakov, Léon. 1974. *The Aryan Myth: A History of Racist and Nationalist Ideas in Europe.* London: Sussex Univ. Press.

———. 1982. "Racism from the Enlightenment to the Age of Imperialism." In *Racism and Colonialism: Essays on Ideology and Social Structure,* ed. Robert Ross, 55–64. The Hague: Martinus Nijhoff.

Poliakov, Léon, Christian Delacampagne, and Patrick Girard. 1976. *Le racisme: Collection Point de Départ.* Paris: Éd. Seghers.

Pollard, Sidney. 1963. "Factory Discipline in the Industrial Revolution." *Economic History Review,* 2nd ser., 16, no. 2 (December): 254–271.

———. 1964. "The Factory Village in the Industrial Revolution." *English Historical Review* 79, no. 312 (July): 513–531.

———. 1973. "Industrialization and the European Economy." *Economic History Review,* n.s. 26, no. 4: 636–648.

———. 1977. "Merchandise Trade and Exploitation." *Journal of European Economic History* 6, no. 3 (Winter): 745–749.

———. 1983. "England, Der unrevolutionäire Pionier." In *Europäische Arbeiterbewegungen im 19. Jahrhurderts, Deutschland, Österreich, England und Frankreich im Vergleich,* ed. J. Kocka, 21–38. Göttingen: Vandenhoeck & Ruprecht.

———1984. "Wirschaftliche Hintergründe des *New Unionism.*" In *Auf dem Wege zur Massengewerkschaft,* ed. Wolfgang J. Mommsen and Hans-Gerhard Husung, 46–75. Stuttgart: Ernst Klett.

Ponteil, Félix. 1968. *L'Eveil des nationalités et le mouvement libéral (1815–1848).* Nouv. éd. mise à jour. Peuples et Civilisations 15. Paris: Presses Univ. de France.

Poovey, Mary. 1988. *Uneven Developments: The Ideological Work of Gender in Mid-Victorian England.* Chicago: Univ. of Chicago Press.

Poper, Barbara Corrado. 1987. "The Influence of Rousseau's Ideology of Domesticity." In *Connecting Spheres: Women in the Western World, 1500 to the Present,* ed. M. J. Boxer and J. H. Quataert, 136–145. New York: Oxford Univ. Press.

Portal, Magda. 1983. *Flora Tristán, precursora.* Lima: La Equidad.

Postel-Vinay, Gilles, and Jean-Marc Robin. 1992. "Eating, Working, and Saving in an Unstable World: Consumers in Nineteenth-Century France." *Economic History Review,* n.s. 45, no. 3 (August): 494–513.

Postgate, Raymond. 1974. "The Principles of 1848." In *A Hundred Years of Revolution, 1848 and After,* ed. G. Woodcock, 93–119. New York: Haskell House.

Potter, J. 1955. "The British Timber Duties, 1815–60." *Economica,* n.s., 22 (May): 122–136.

Potts, David B. 1965. "Social Ethics at Harvard, 1881–1931: A Study in Academic Activism." In *Social Sciences at Harvard, 1860–1920: From Inculcation to the Open Mind*, ed. Paul Buck, 91–128. Cambridge, MA: Harvard Univ. Press.

Pouthas, Charles H. 1962. "La réorganisation du Ministère de l'Intérieur et la reconstitution de l'administration préfectorale par Guizot en 1830." *Revue d'histoire moderne et contemporaine* 9 (October–December): 241–263.

Pouthas, Charles H., et al. 1983. *Démocratie, réaction, capitalisme, 1848–1860*. Peuples et Civilisations 16. Paris: Presses Univ. de France.

Prewitt, Kenneth. 2004. "Political Science and Its Audiences." *Political Science and Politics* 37, no. 4 (October): 781–784.

Preyer, Robert O. 1985. "The Romantic Tide Reaches Trinity." In *Victorian Science and Victorian Values: Literary Perspectives*, ed. J. Paradis and T. Postlewait, 39–68. New Brunswick, NJ: Rutgers Univ. Press.

Price, Richard. 1990. "Britain." In *The Formation of Labour Movements, 1870–1914: An International Perspective*, ed. M. van der Linden and J. Rojahn, 3–24. Leiden: E. J. Brill.

Price, Roger. 1972. *The French Second Republic: A Social History*. London: B. T. Batsford.

———. 1975a. *The Economic Modernization of France*. London: Croom Helm.

———. 1975b. Introduction to *Revolution and Reaction: 1848 and the Second French Republic*, ed. R. Price, 1–72. London: Croom Helm.

Prinz, Michael. 1989. "Wandel durch Beharrung: Sozialdemokratie und 'Neue Mittelschichten' in historischer Perspektive." *Archiv für Sozialgeschichte* 24:35–73.

Procacci, Giuliano. 1972. *La lotta di classe in Italia agli inizii del secolo XX*. Rome: Ed. Riuniti.

Proctor, Robert N. 1991. *Value-Free Science? Purity and Power in Modern Knowledge*. Cambridge, MA: Harvard Univ. Press.

Prothero, I. J. 1969. "Chartism in London." *Past and Present*, no. 44 (August): 76–105.

———. 1971. "London Chartism and the Trades." *Economic History Review*, 2nd ser., 24, no. 2 (May): 202–219.

———. 1979. *Artisans and Politics in Early Nineteenth-Century London: John Gast and His Times*. Folkestone, Kent, UK: William Dawson & Son.

Proudhon, Pierre-Joseph. 1912. *Les Femmelins: Les grandes figures romantiques*. Paris: Nouvelle Librairie Nationale.

Przeworski, Adam. 1980. "Social Democracy as a Historical Phenomenon." *New Left Review*, no. 122 (July–August): 27–58.

Przeworski, Adam, and Michael Wallerstein. 1982. "The Structure of Class Conflict in Democratic Capitalist Societies." *American Political Science Review* 76, no. 2 (June): 215–238.

Puccini, Sandra. 1976. "Condizione della donne e questione femminile (1892–1922)." *Problemi del Socialismo* 17, no. 4 (October–December): 9–23.

Puech, Jules-L. 1925. *La Vie et l'œuvre de Flora Tristan*. Paris: Marcel Rivière.

Pugh, Evelyn L. 1982. "Florence Nightingale and J. S. Mill Debate Women's Rights." *Journal of British Studies* 21, no. 2 (Spring): 118–138.

Puryear, Vernon John. 1931. *England, Russia, and the Straits Question, 1844–1856*. Berkeley: Univ. of California Press.

Quataert, Jean H. 1979. *Reluctant Feminists in German Social Democracy, 1885–1917*. Princeton, NJ: Princeton Univ. Press.

Quero Molares, J. 1948. "L'Espagne en 1848." In *Le Printemps des peuples: 1848 dans le monde,* ed. F. Fejtö, 1:319–354. Paris: Éd. du Minuit.

Rabaut, Jean. 1983. "1900, tournant du feminisme français." *Bulletin de la société d'histoire modern,* 82e année, sér. 14, no. 17, 5–16. [Supplement to *Revue d'histoire moderne et contemporaine,* no. 1, 1983.]

Racz, Elizabeth. 1952. "The Women's Rights Movement in the French Revolution." *Science and Society* 16, no. 2 (Spring): 151–174.

Ragionieri, Ernesto. 1961. *Socialdemocrazia tedesca e socialisti italiani, 1875–1895.* Milan: Feltrinelli.

Rainger, Ronald. 1978. "Race, Politics and Science: The Anthropological Society of London in the 1860's." *Victorian Studies* 22, no. 1 (Autumn): 51–70.

Ralle, M. 1973. "La notion de 'bourgeoisie' dans l'idéologie de la Première Internationale en Espagne." *La Question de la 'bourgeoisie' dans le monde hispanique au XIXe siècle,* 119–131. Bibliothèque de l'Ecole des Hautes Etudes Hispaniques 45. Bordeaux: Éd. Bière. [Discussion, 131–135.]

Rancière, Jacques. 1981. *La nuit des prolétaires: Archives du rêve ouvrier.* Paris: Fayard.

———. 1983. "The Myth of the Artisan: Critical Reflections on a Category of Social History." *International Labor and Working Class History,* no. 24 (Fall): 1–16.

———. 1984. "A Reply." *International Labor and Working Class History,* no. 25 (Spring): 42–46.

Ravera, Camilla. 1978. *Breve storia del movimento femminile in Italia.* Rome: Ed. Riuniti.

Read, Donald. 1958. *Peterloo: The " Massacre" and Its Background.* Manchester, UK: Manchester University Press.

Reardon, Bernard. 1976. *Liberalism and Tradition: Aspects of Catholic Thought in Nineteenth-Century France.* Cambridge: Cambridge Univ. Press.

Rebérioux, Madeleine. 1978a. Preface to *Les femmes et le socialisme,* by C. Sowerwine, xi–xxiii. Paris: Presses de la FNSP.

———. 1978b. "La questione femminile nei dibatti della II Internazionale." In *Anna Kuliscioff e l'età del riformismo: Atti del Convegno di Milano, dicembre 1974,* 140–154. Rome: Mondo Operaio—Ed. Avanti!

———. 1989. Preface to *1789: Cahiers de doléances des femmes et autres textes,* ed. Paule Duhet, i-xii. Nouv. éd. augm. Paris: Des Femmes.

Rebérioux, Madeleine, Christiane Dufrancantel, and Béatrice Slema. 1976. "Hubertine Auclert et la question des femmes à 'l'immortel congrès' (1879)." *Romantisme,* nos. 13–14, 123–152.

Rebérioux, Madeline, and Georges Haupt. 1963. "L'attitude de l'Internationale." *Le Mouvement social,* no. 45 (October–December): 7–37.

Reddy, William M. 1979. "Skeins, Scales, Discounts, Steam, and Other Objects of Crowd Justice in Early French Textile Mills." *Comparative Studies in Society and History* 21, no. 2 (April): 204–213.

———. 1984. *The Rise of Market Culture: The Textile Trade and French Society, 1750–1900.* Cambridge: Cambridge Univ. Press.

Redford, Arthur. 1956. *Manchester Merchants and Foreign Trade.* Vol.2, *1850–1939.* Manchester, UK: Manchester Univ. Press.

————. 1968. *Labour Migration in England, 1800–50.* 2nd ed., rev. W. H. Chaloner. New York: A. M. Kelley.

Reichand, Richard W. 1953. "The German Working Class and the Russian Revolution of 1905." *Journal of Central European Affairs* 13, no. 2 (July): 136–153.

Reid, Alastair. 1978. "Politics and Economics in the Formation of the British Working Class: A Response to H. F. Moorhouse." *Social History* 3, no. 3 (October): 347–361.

————. 1983. "Intelligent Artisans and Aristocrats of Labour: The Essays of Thomas Wright." In T*he Working Class in Modern British History: Essays in Honor of Henry Pilling,* ed. J. M. Winter, 171–186. London: Cambridge Univ. Press.

————. 1991. "Old Unionism Reconsidered: The Radicalism of Robert Knight, 1870–1900." In *Currents of Radicalism: Popular Radicalism, Organised Labour and Party Politics in Britain, 1850–1914,* ed. E. F. Biagini and A. J. Reid, 214–243. Cambridge: Cambridge Univ. Press.

Rémond, René. 1982. *Les Droites en France.* Paris: Aubier Montaigne.

Rendall, Jane. 1985. *The Origins of Modern Feminism: Women in Britain, France and the United States, 1780–1860.* London: Macmillan.

Renouvier, Charles. 1868. "De la philosophie du XIXe siècle en France." *L'Année philosophique—Première Année (1867).* Paris: Lib. Geemer Baillière.

Renouvin, Pierre. 1949. "L'idée d'Etats-Unis d'Europe pendant la crise de 1848." In *Actes du Congrès historique du Centenaire de la Révolution de 1848,* 31–45. Paris: Presses Univ. de France.

————. 1954. *Le XIXe siècle.* Vol. 1, *De 1815 à 1871: L'Europe des nationalités et l'éveil de nouveaux mondes.* Histoire des Relations Internationales 5. Paris: Lib. Hachette.

Rerup, Lorenz. 1980. "The Development of Nationalism in Denmark." In *The Roots of Nationalism: Studies in Northern Europe,* ed. R. Mitchison, 47–59. Edinburgh: John Donald.

Reynolds, James A. 1954. *The Catholic Emancipation Crisis in Ireland, 1823–1829.* New Haven, CT: Yale Univ. Press.

Rhys Davies, T. W. 1903–1904. "Oriental Studies in England and Abroad." *Proceedings of the British Academy, 1903–1904,* 183–197.

Richard, Gaston. 1914. *La Question sociale et le mouvement philosophique au XIXe siècle.* Paris: Lib. Armand Colin.

Richter, Melvin. 1960. "Durkheim's Politics and Poitical Theory." In *Emile Durkheim, 1858–1917,* ed. K. H. Wolff, 170–210. Columbus: Ohio State Univ. Press.

————. 1964. *The Politics of Conscience: T. H. Green and His Age.* Cambridge, MA: Harvard Univ. Press.

Ringer, Fritz. K. 1969. *The Decline of the German Mandarins: The German Academic Community, 1890–1933.* Cambridge, MA: Harvard Univ. Press.

————. 1979. *Education and Society in Modern Europe.* Bloomington: Indiana Univ. Press.

————. 1992. *Fields of Knowledge: French Academic Culture in Comparative Perspective, 1890–1920.* Cambridge: Cambridge Univ. Press.

Rist, Charles. 1897. "La Durée du travail dans l'industrie française de 1820 à 1870." *Revue d'économie politique* 11, no. 4 (May): 371–393.

Rist, Marcel. 1956. "Une Expérience française de libération des échanges au dix-neuvième siècle, le traité de 1860." *Revue d'économie politique,* 66e année (November–December): 908–961.

Roberts, David. 1958. "Tory Paternalism and Social Reform in Early Victorian England." *American Historical Review* 63, no. 2 (January): 323–337.

———. 1959. "Jeremy Bentham and the Victorian Administrative State." *Victorian Studies* 2, no. 3 (March): 193–210.

———. 1963. "How Cruel Was the Victorian Poor Law?" *Historical Journal* 6, no. 1, 97–107.

Roberts, J. M. 1978. *The French Revolution.* Oxford: Oxford Univ. Press.

Robertson, William Spence. 1939. *France and Latin American Independence.* Baltimore: Johns Hopkins Univ. Press.

Robinson, Ronald E. 1991. "Introduction: Railway Imperialism." In *Railway Imperialism,* ed. C. B. Davis Jr. and K. E. Wilburn, 1–6. New York: Greenwood.

Rodgers, Brian. 1952. "The Social Science Association, 1857–1886." *Manchester School of Economic and Social Studies* 20, no. 3 (September): 283–310.

Roehl, Richard. 1976. "French Industrialization: A Reconsideration." *Explorations in Economic History* 13, no. 3 (July): 233–281.

Rogers, J. D. 1963. "Laissez-faire in England." *Palgrave's Dictionary of Political Economy,* 2:535–537. Reprint of rev. ed.. New York: Augustus M. Kelley.

Roller, Michel. 1948. "Les Roumaines en 1848." In *Le printemps des peuples: 1848 dans le monde,* ed. F. Fejtö, 2:239–266. Paris: Éd. du Minuit.

Romalis, Coleman, and Shelly Romalis. 1983. "Sexism, Racism and Technological Change: Two Cases of Minority Protest." *International Journal of Women's Studies* 6, no. 3 (May/June): 270–287.

Rosanvallon, Pierre. 1985. *Le moment Guizot.* Paris: Gallimard.

Rosdolsky, Roman. 1964. "Engels und das Problem der 'geschichtlosen' Völker (Die Nationalitätenfrage in der Revolution 1848–1849 im Lichte der 'Neuen Rheinischen Zeitung')." *Archiv für Sozialgeschichte* 4:87–282.

Rose, Ernst. 1951. "China as a Symbol of Reaction in Germany, 1830–1880." *Comparative Literature* 2, no. 1 (Winter): 57–76.

Rose, Michael E. 1974. *The Relief of Poverty, 1834–1914.* London: Macmillan.

Rose, R. B. 1984. "The 'Red Scare' of the 1790's: The French Revolution and the 'Agrarian Law,'" *Past and Present,* no. 103 (May): 113–130.

Rose, Sonia O. 1986. "Gender and Work: Sex, Class, and Industrial Capitalism." *History Workshop Journal,* no. 21 (Spring): 113–131.

Rosen, Andrew. 1974. *Rise Up Women! The Militant Campaign of the Women's Social and Political Union, 1903–1914.* London: Routledge & Kegan Paul.

Rosenberg, Charles E. 1976. *No Other Gods: On Science and American Social Thought.* Baltimore: Johns Hopkins Univ. Press.

Rosenberg, Hans. 1943. "Political and Social Consequences of the Great Depression of 1873–1896 in Central Europe." *Economic History Review* 13, nos. 1 and 2, 58–73.

Ross, Dorothy. 1979. "The Development of the Social Sciences." In *The Organization of Knowledge in Modern America, 1860–1940,* ed. A. Olesen and J. Voss, 107–138. Baltimore: Johns Hopkins Univ. Press.

———. 1984. "American Social Science and the Idea of Progress." In *The Authority of Experts, Studies in History and Theory,* ed. T. L. Haskell, 157–175. Bloomington: Indiana Univ. Press.

———. 1991. *The Origins of American Social Science.* Cambridge: Cambridge Univ. Press.

Ross, Sydney. 1962. "Scientist: The Story of a Word." *Annals of Science* 18, no. 2 (June): 65–85.

Rosselli, John. 1980. "The Self-Image of Effeteness: Physical Education and Nationalism in Nineteenth-Century Bengal." *Past and Present,* no. 86 (February): 121–148.

Rossi, Alice S., ed. 1970. *Essays on Sex Equality [by] John Stuart Mill and Harriet Taylor Mill.* Chicago: Univ. of Chicago Press.

———. 1973. *The Feminist Papers, from Adams to de Beauvoir.* New York: Columbia Univ. Press.

Rostow, W. W. 1938. "Investment and the Great Depression." *Economic History Review* 8, no. 2 (May): 136–158.

———. 1939. "Investment and Real Wages, 1877–86." *Economic History Review* 9, no. 1 (November): 144–159.

———. 1942. "Adjustments and Maladjustments after the Napoleonic Wars." *American Economic Review* 32, no. , part 2, suppl., *Papers and Proceedings of the Fifty-fourth Annual Meeting of the American Economic Association* (March): 13–23.

———. 1948. *British Economy of the Nineteenth Century.* New York: Oxford Univ. Press, 1948.

———. 1971. *The Stages of Economic Growth.* 2nd ed. Cambridge: At the University Press.

Roth, Guenther. 1963. *The Social Democrats in Imperial Germany: A Study in Working-Class Isolation and National Integration.* Totowa, NJ: Bedminster Press.

Rothermund, Dietmar. 1986. *The German Intellectual Quest for India.* New Delhi: Manohar.

Rougerie, Jacques. 1964. *Procès des Communards, présenté par Jacques Rougerie. Collection 'Archives.'* Paris: Juilliard.

———. 1965. "Sur l'histoire de la Première Internationale." *Le Mouvement social,* no. 51 (April–June): 23–45.

———. 1968. "Remarques sur l'histoire des salaires à Paris au XIXe siècle." *Le Mouvement social,* no. 63 (April–June): 71–108.

———. 1972. "1871, jalons sur une histoire de la Commune de Paris: Livraison spéciale préparée sous la direction de Jacques Rougerie avec la collaboration de Tristan Haan, Georges Haupt et Miklós Molnár." *International Review of Social History* 17, pts. 1 and 2, i–ix, 1–624.

Rousseaux, Paul. 1938. *Les Mouvements de force de l'économie anglaise, 1800–1913.* Brussels: L'Edition Universelle; Paris: De Brouwer & Cie.

Rover, Constance. 1967. *Women's Suffrage and Party Politics in Britain, 1866–1914.* London: Routledge & Kegan Paul.

Rowbotham, Sheila. 1974. *Women, Resistance and Revolution: A History of Women and Revolution in the Modern World.* New York: Pantheon.

———. 1977. *Hidden from History: 300 Years of Women's Oppression and the Fight Against It.* 3rd ed. London: Pluto Press.

Rowe, D. J. 1967. "The London Working Men's Association and 'The Peoples' Charter.'" *Past and Present,* no. 36 (April): 73–86.

Royle, Edward. 1986. *Chartism.* 2d ed. London: Longman.

Rubel, Maximilien. 1960. *Karl Marx devant le bonapartisme.* Paris and The Hague: Mouton.

Rubin, Gayle. 1975. "The Traffic in Women." In *Toward an Anthropology of Women,* ed. R. R. Reiter, 157–210. New York: Monthly Review Press.

Rudé, Fernand. 1940. "La première expédition de Savoie (février 1831)." *Revue historique,* CLXXXVIII–CLXXXIX, 65e année (July–December): 413–443.

———. 1969. *L'Insurrection lyonnaise de novembre 1831: Le mouvement ouvrier à Lyon de 1827–1832.* 2nd ed. Paris: Éd. Anthropos.

Rudé, George. 1967. "English Rural and Urban Disturbances on the Eve of the First Reform Bill, 1830–1831." *Past and Present,* no. 37 (July): 87–102.

———. 1969. "Why Was There No Revolution in England in 1830 or 1848?" In *Studien über die Revolution,* ed. M. Kossok, 231–244. Berlin: Akademie-Verlag.

Rueschmayer, Dietrich, and Roman Van Rossen. 1996. "The Verein für Sozialpolitik and the Fabian Society: A Study in the Sociology of Policy-Relevant Knowledge." In *States, Social Knowledge, and the Origins of Modern Social Policies,* ed. D. Rueschmayer and T. Skocpol, 117–162. Princeton, NJ: Princeton Univ. Press.

Ruggiero, Guido de. 1959. *The History of European Liberalism.* Boston: Beacon Press.

Rule, John. 1988. "The Formative Years of British Trade-Unionism: An Overview." In *British Trade-Unionism, 1750–1850,* ed. John Rule, 1–28. London: Longman.

Ruwet, Joseph. 1967. *Avant les révolutions: Le XVIIIe siècle.* Brussels: Fondation Charles Plisnier.

Ryan, Barbara. 1992. *Feminism and the Women's Movement: Dynamics of Change in Social Movement, Ideology and Activism.* New York: Routledge.

Sagnac, Philippe. 1901–1902. "Les Juifs et Napoléon (1806–1808)." *Revue d'histoire moderne et contemporaine* 2:595–604.

Said, Edward W. 1978. *Orientalism.* New York: Pantheon Books.

———. 1985. "Orientalism Reconsidered." ." *Race and Class 27,* no. 2 (Autumn): 1–15.

Sakellariou, Michel. 1948. "L'Hellénisme et 1848." In *Le printemps des peuples: 1848 dans le monde,* ed. F. Fejtö, 2:319–354. Paris: Éd. du Minuit.

Salvadori, Massimo. 1977. *The Liberal Heresy: Origins and Historical Development.* London: Macmillan.

Samuel, Raphael. 1977. "Workshop of the World: Steam Power and Hand Technology in Mid-Victorian Britain." *History Workshop,* no. 3 (Spring): 6–72.

Santarelli, Enzo. 1964. *La Revisione del marxismo in Italia.* Milan: Feltrinelli.

Sartorius von Waltershausen, A. 1931. *Die Enstehung der Weltwirtschaft: Geschichte des zwischenstaatlichen Wirtschaftslebens von letzten Viertel des achtzehnten Jahrhundests bis 1914.* Jena: Gustav Fischer.

Saul, S. B. 1960. "The American Impact on British Industry, 1895–1914." *Business History* 3, no. 1 (December): 19–38.

———. 1971. "Some Thoughts on the Papers and Discussion on the Performance of the Late Victorian Economy." In *Essays on a Mature Economy, Britain after 1840,* ed. D. N. McCloskey, 393–397. London: Methuen.

Saville, John. 1990. *1848: The British State and the Chartist Movement.* Cambridge: Cambridge Univ. Press.

Sayers, R. S. 1932. "The Question of the Standard in the Eighteenth-Fifties." *Economic History* 2, no. 7 (January): 575–601.

Schapiro, J. Salwyn. 1934. *Condorcet and the Rise of Liberalism*. New York: Harcourt, Brace & Co.

———. 1939. "Utilitarianism and the Foundations of English Liberalism." *Journal of Social Philosophy* 4, no. 2 (January): 121–137.

———. 1949. *Liberalism and the Challenge of Fascism: Social Forces in England and France (1815–1870)*. New York: McGraw-Hill.

Schefer, Christian. 1907. *Les Traditions et les idées nouvelles, la réorganisation administrative, la reprise de l'expansion (1815–1830)*. Vol. 1 of *La France moderne et le problème colonial*. Paris: Félix Alcan.

———. 1928. *L'Algérie et l'évolution de la colonisation française*. Paris: Lib. Anc. Honoré Champion.

———. 1939. *Les Origines de l'expédition du Mexique (1858–1862): La Grande Pensée de Napoléon III*. Paris: Marcel Rivière .

Schenk, H. G. 1947. *The Aftermath of the Napoleonic Wars: The Concert of Europe—An Experiment*. New York: Oxford Univ. Press.

Schlesinger, Arthur M., Jr. 1962. *The Vital Center: The Politics of Freedom*. Boston: Houghton Mifflin.

Schlote, Werner. 1952. *British Overseas Trade from 1700 to the 1930s*. Oxford: Basil Blackwell.

Schmoller, Gustav von. 1920. "Zur 25jährigen Feier des Vereins für Sozialpolitik." In *Zwanzig Jahre Deutscher Politik (1897–1917), Aufsätze und Vortrage*, 23–34. Munich: Duncker & Humblot.

Schnerb, Robert. 1936. "Napoleon III and the Second French Empire." *Journal of Modern History* 8, no. 3 (September): 338–355.

———. 1963. *Libre échange et protectionnisme*. Que sais-je?, no. 1032. Paris: Presses Univ. de France.

———. 1968. *Le XIXe siècle: L'Apogée de l'expansion européenne*. Histoire Générale des Civilisations. Paris: Presses Univ. de France.

Schnetzler, Barbara V. 1971. *Die frühe amerikanische Frauenbewegung und ihre Kontakte mit Europa (1836–1869)*. Bern: Peter Lang.

Schoelcher, Victor. 1948. *Esclavage et colonisation*. Paris: Presses Univ. de France.

Schorske, Carl E. 1955. *German Social Democracy, 1905–1917: The Development of the Great Schism*. Cambridge, MA: Harvard Univ. Press.

Schöttler, Peter. 1985. *Naissance des Bourses de travail, un appareil idéologique d'état à la fin du XIXe siècle*. Paris: Presses Univ. de France.

Schroeder, Paul W. 1989. "The Nineteenth Century System: Balance of Power or Political Equilibrium?" *Review of International Studies* 15:135–153.

———. 1992a. "Did the Vienna Settlement Rest on a Balance of Power?" *American Historical Review* 97, no. 2 (April): 683–706.

———. 1992b. "A Mild Rejoinder." *American Historical Review* 97, no. 3 (June): 733–735.

Schuman, Frederick L. 1958. *International Politics: The Western State System and the World Community*. 6th ed. New York: McGraw-Hill.

Schumpeter, Joseph. 1964. *Business Cycles*. 1st abr. ed. Philadelphia: McGraw-Hill.

Schuyler, Robert L. 1921. "The Climax of Anti-Imperialism in England." *Political Science Quarterly* 36, no. 4 (December): 537–560.

———. 1922. "The Rise of Anti-Imperialism in England." *Political Science Quarterly* 37, no. 3 (September): 440–471.

———. 1945. *The Fall of the Old Colonial System: A Study in British Free Trade, 1770–1870.* London: Oxford Univ. Press.

Schwab, Raymond. 1950. *La Renaissance orientale.* Paris: Payot.

Schwartz, Anna Jacobson. 1987. *Money in Historical Perspective.* Chicago: Univ. of Chicago Press.

Schweber, S. S. 1985. "Scientists as Intellectuals: The Early Victorians." In *Victorian Science and Victorian Values: Literary Perspectives,* ed. J. Paradis and T. Postlewait, 1–37. New Brunswick, NJ: Rutgers Univ. Press.

Schwendinger, Herman, and Julia R. Schwendinger. 1974. *Sociologists of the Chair: A Radical Analysis of the Formative Years of North American Sociology (1883–1922).* New York: Basic Books.

Scott, James C. 1998. *Seeing Like a State: How Certain Schemes to Improve the Human Condition Have Failed.* New Haven, CT: Yale Univ. Press.

Scott, Joan Wallach. 1974. *The Glassworkers of Carmaux: French Craftsmen and Political Action in a Nineteenth-Century City.* Cambridge, MA: Harvard Univ. Press.

———. 1981. "French Feminists and the Rights of 'Man': Olympe de Gouge's Declarations." *History Workshop Journal,* no. 28 (Autumn): 1–21.

———. 1988. "A Statistical Representation of Work: Le Statistique de l'Industrie à Paris, 1847–1848." In *Gender and the Politics of History,* 113–138. New York: Columbia Univ. Press.

Sée, Henri. 1921. *Esquisse d'une histoire du régime agraire en Europe aux XVIIIe et XIXe siècles.* Paris: M. Giard.

———. 1923. "Esquisse de l'évolution industrielle de la France de 1815 à 1848: Les progrès du machinisme et de la concentration." *Revue d'histoire économique et social* 11, no. 4, 473–497.

———. 1924. "Quelques aperçus sur la condition de la classe ouvrière et sur le mouvement ouvrier en France de 1815 à 1848." *Revue d'histoire économique et social* 12, no. 4, 493–521.

———. 1927. *La vie économique de la France sous la monarchie censitaire (1815–1848).* Paris: F. Alcan.

———. 1951. *Histoire économique de la France.* 2nd ed. 2 vols. Paris: A. Colin.

Seecombe, Wally. 1986. "Patriarchy Stabilized: The Construction of the Male Breadwinner Wage Norm in Nineteenth-Century Britain." *Social History* 11, no. 1 (January): 53–76.

Semidei, Manuela. 1966. "De l'Empire à la décolonisation à travers les manuels salaires français." *Revue française de science politique* 16, no. 1 (February): 56–86.

Semmel, Bernard. 1970. *The Rise of Free Trade Imperialism.* Cambridge: At the University Press.

Sergent, Bernard. 1982. "Penser—et mal penser—les Indo-Européens (Note critique)." *Annales E.S.C.* 27, no. 4 (July–August): 669–681.

Seton-Watson, Hugh. 1977. *Nations and States: An Enquiry into the Origins of Nations and the Politics of Nationalism.* London: Methuen.

Seton-Watson, R. W. 1937. *Britain in Europe, 1789 to 1914.* Cambridge: At the University Press.

Sewell, William H., Jr. 1974. "Social Change and the Rise of Working Class Politics in Nineteenth-Century Marseille." *Past and Present,* no. 65, 75–109.

———. 1979. "Property, Labor, and the Emergence of Socialism in France, 1789–1848." In *Consciousness and Class Experience in Nineteenth-Century Europe,* ed. J. Merriman, 45–63. New York: Holmes & Meier.

———. 1983. "Response to J. Rancière, 'The Myth of the Artisan,'" *International Labor and Working-Class History,* no. 24 (Fall): 17–20.

———. 1985. "Ideologies and Social Revolutions: Reflections on the French Case." *Journal of Modern History* 57, no. 1 (March): 57–85.

———. 1986. "Artisans, Factory Workers, and the Formation of the French Working Class, 1789–1848." In *Working-Class Formation: Nineteenth Century Patterns in Western Europe and the United States,* ed. I. Katznelson and A. R. Zolberg, 45–70. Princeton, NJ: Princeton Univ. Press.

———. 1988. "Le citoyen/la citoyenne: Activity, Passivity, and the Revolutionary Concept of Citizenship." In *The Political Culture of the French Revolution: The French Revolution and the Creation of Modern Political Culture,* ed. C. Lucas, 2:105–123. Oxford: Pergamon Press.

———. 1990. "Collective Violence and Collective Loyalties in France: Why the French Revolution Made a Difference." *Politics and Society,* 68, no. 4 (December): 527–552.

Shapiro, Fred R. 1981. "On the Origin of the Term 'Indo-Germanic,'" *Historiographia Linguistica* 8, no. 1, 165–170.

Shefter, Martin. 1986. "Trade Unions and Political Machines: The Organization and Disorganization of the American Working Class in the Late Nineteenth Century." In *Working Class Formation: Nineteenth-Century Patterns in Western Europe and North America,* ed. I. Katznelson and A. R. Zolberg, 197–278. Princeton, NJ: Princeton Univ. Press.

Sherman, Dennis. 1974. "The Meaning of Economic Liberalism in Mid-Nineteenth-Century France." *History of Political Economy* 6, no. 2 (Summer): 171–199.

Shine, Hill. 1941. *Carlyle and the Saint-Simonians: The Concept of Historical Periodicity.* Baltimore: Johns Hopkins Univ. Press.

Sievers, Sharon. 1983. *Flowers in Salt: The Beginnings of Feminist Consciousness in Modern Japan.* Stanford, CA: Stanford Univ. Press.

Siéyès, Emmanuel-Joseph. 1789. "Préliminaire de la Constitution, lu les 20 et 21 juillet 1789, au Comité de Constitution." In *Recueil des pièces authentiques approuvés par l'Assemblée Nationale de France,* 178–200. Geneva: 1e éd.

———. 1985. *Ecrits politiques.* Paris: Éd. des Archives contemporaines.

Silbering, Norman J. 1923. "Financial and Monetary Policy of Britain during the Napoleonic Wars." *Quarterly Journal of Economics* 38 (November): 214–233.

Silva, Pietro. 1917. *La Monarchia di luglio e l'Italia.* Turin: Fratelli Bocca Ed.

Silver, Allan. 1967. "The Demand for Order in Civil Society: A Review of Some Theories in the History of Urban Crime, Police and Riots." In *The Police,* ed. D. J. Bordua, 1–24. New York: Wiley.

Simon, André. 1946. "Les Origines religieuses de l'indépendance belge." *Chantiers* 11, no 2 (15 November): 1–28.

———. 1949. *L'Eglise catholique et les débuts de la Belgique indépendante.* Wetteren, Belgium: Éd. Scaldis.

———. 1959. "Lamennais en Belgique." *Revue belge de philologie et d'histoire* 37:408–417.

———. 1991. "Théoriciens français du racisme au 19e siècle." *Gavroche,* no. 55 (January–February): 21–25.

Simon, Walter M. 1956. "History for Utopia: Saint-Simon and the Idea of Progress." *Journal of the History of Ideas* 17, no. 3 (June): 311–331.

Simoni, Pierre. 1980. "Science anthropologique et racisme à l'époque de l'expansion coloniale: Le cas du Grand Dictionnaire Universel du XIXe siècle de Pierre Labrousse." *Historical Papers (Ottawa)* 15, no. 1, 167–184.

Singelmann, Joachim, and Peter Singelmann. 1986. "Lorenz von Stein and the Paradigmatic Function of Social Theory in the Nineteenth Century." *British Journal of Sociology* 37, no. 3 (September): 431–452.

Sked, Alan, ed. 1979. *Europe's Balance of Power, 1815–1848.* London: Macmillan.

Skinner, Andrew S. 1965. "Economics and History: The Scottish Enlightenment." *Scottish Journal of Political Economy* 12 (February): 1–22.

Skocpol, Theda. 1985. "Cultural Idioms and Political Ideologies in the Revolutionary Reconstruction of State Power: A Rejoinder to Sewell." *Journal of Modern History* 57, no. 1 (March): 86–96.

Slaughter, Jane, and Robert Kern. 1981. *European Women on the Left: Socialism, Feminism, and the Problems Faced by Political Women, 1880 to the Present.* Westport, CT: Greenwood Press.

Slicher van Bath, B. H. 1963. *The Agrarian History of Western Europe, A.D. 500–1850.* New York: St. Martin's.

Smelser, Neil J. 1991. *Social Paralysis and Social Change.* Berkeley: Univ. of California Press.

Smith, Carol H. 1995. "Race-Class-Gender Ideology in Guatemala: Modern and Anti-Modern Forms." *Comparative Studies in Society and History* 37, no. 4 (October): 723–749.

Smith, Paul. 1967. *Disraelian Conservatism and Social Reform.* London: Routledge & Kegan Paul.

———. 1989. "Liberation as Authority and Discipline." *Historical Journal* 32, no. 2 (September): 723–737.

Snyder, Carl. 1934. "Measures of the Growth of British Industry." *Economica,* n.s., 1 (November): 421–435.

Soboul, Albert. 1948. "La Question paysanne en 1848." 3 pts. *La Pensée,* no. 18, 55–66; no. 19, 25–37; no. 20, 48–56.

———. 1962. "A propos des réflexions de Georges Rudé sur la sans-culotterie." *Crítica storica* 1, no. 4 (July 31): 391–398.

Soffer, Benson. 1960. "A Theory of Trade Union Development: The Role of the 'Autonomous' Workman." *Labor History* 1, no. 2 (Spring): 141–163.

Soffer, Reba N. 1982. "Why Do Disciplines Fail? The Strange Case of British Sociology." *English Historical Review* 97, no. 385 (October): 767–802.

Solle, Zdenek. 1969. "Die tschechische Sozialdemokratie zwischen Nationalismus und Internationalismus." *Archiv für Sozialgeschichte* 9:181–266.

Soloway, Richard A. 1990. *Demography and Degeneration: Eugenics and the Declining Birthrate in Twentieth-Century Britain.* Chapel Hill: Univ. of North Carolina Press.

Somit, Albert, and Joseph Tanenhaus. 1982. *The Development of American Political Science: From Burgess to Behavioralism.* New York: Irvington Publ.

Sonenscher, Michael. 1989. "Editorial, 1789–1989." *History Workshop Journal,* no. 28 (Autumn): v–vi.

Soreau, Edmond. 1931. "Le loi Le Chapelier." *Annales historiques de la Révolution française,* 8e année, no. 46 (July–August): 287–314.

Sorenson, Lloyd R. 1952. "Some Classical Economists, Laissez Faire, and the Factory Acts." *Journal of Economic History* 12, no. 3 (Summer): 247–262.

Southgate, Donald G. 1965. *The Passing of the Whigs, 1832–1886.* London: Macmillan.

——. 1977. "From Disraeli to Law." In *The Conservatives,* ed. Lord Butler, 109–270. London: George Allen & Unwin.

Sowerwine, Charles. 1976. "The Organisation of French Socialist Women, 1880–1914: A European Perspective for Women's Movements." *Historical Reflections* 3, no. 2 (Winter): 3–24.

——. 1978. *Les Femmes et le socialisme: Un siècle d'histoire.* Paris: Presses de la Fondation Nationale des Sciences Politiques.

——. 1982. *Sisters or Citizens? Women and Socialism in France since 1876.* Cambridge: Cambridge Univ. Press.

——. 1983. "Workers and Women in France before 1914: The Debate over the Courian Affair." *Journal of Modern History* 55, no. 3 (September): 411–441.

Spain, Jonathon. 1991. "Trade Unionists, Gladstonianian Liberals and the Labour Law Reforms of 1875." In *Currents of Radicalism: Popular Radicalism, Organised Labour and Party Politics in Britain, 1850–1914,* ed. E. F. Biagini and A. J. Reid, 109–133. Cambridge: Cambridge Univ. Press.

Spengler, Oswald. 1926. *The Decline of the West: Form and Actuality.* New York: A. A. Knopf.

Spitzer, Alan B. 1962. "The Good Napoleon III." *French Historical Studies* 2, no. 3 (Spring): 308–329.

Stanton, Elizabeth Cady, Susan B. Anthony, and Matilda Joslyn Gage, eds. 1881. *History of Woman Suffrage.* 6 vols. Rochester, NY: Charles Mann.

Stark, W. 1943. "Saint-Simon as a Realist." *Journal of Economic History* 3, no. 1 (May): 42–55.

——. 1945. "The Realism of Saint-Simon's Spiritual Program." *Journal of Economic History* 5, no. 1 (May): 24–42.

Starzinger, Vincent. 1965. *Middlingness: "Juste Milieu" Political Theory in France and England, 1815–48.* Charlottesville: Univ. Press of Virginia.

Stearns, Peter N. 1965. "Patterns of Industrial Strike Activity during the July Monarchy." *American Historical Review* 70, no. 2 (January): 371–394.

——. 1974. *1848: The Revolutionary Tide in Europe.* New York: W. W. Norton.

——. 1979a. "The Middle Class: Toward a Precise Definition." *Comparative Studies in Society and History* 29, no. 3 (July): 377–396.

——. 1979b. "Reply." *Comparative Studies in Society and History* 29, no. 3 (July): 414–415.

Stengers, Jean. 1950–1951. "Sentiment national, sentiment orangiste et sentiment français à l'aube de notre indépendance." 2 pts. *Revue belge de philologie et d'histoire* 28:993–1029 (pt. 1); 29:61–92 (pt. 2).

Stepan, Nancy. 1982. *The Idea of Race in Science: Great Britain, 1800–1960.* Hamden, CT: Archon Books.

Stern, Fritz. 1971. *The Failure of Illiberalism: Essays on the Political Culture of Modern Germany.* New York: Knopf.

Stern, Leo, and Rudolf Sauerzapf. 1954. Introduction to *Die Auswirkungen der ersten russischen Revolution von 1905–1907 auf Deutschland,* ed. L. Stern, xi-lxxvi. Berlin: Rütten & Loening.

Stevenson, John. 1977. "The Queen Caroline Affair." In *London in the Age of Reform,* ed. J. Stevenson, 117–148. Oxford: Basil Blackwell.

———. 1979. *Popular Disturbances in England, 1700–1870.* London: Longman.

Stewart, Robert. 1971. *The Politics of Protection: Lord Derby and the Protectionist Party, 1841–1852.* Cambridge: At the University Press.

Stieg, Margaret F. 1986. *The Origin and Development of Scholarly Historical Periodicals.* Tuscaloosa: Univ. of Alabama Press.

Stigler, George J. 1965. "The Politics of Political Economists." In *Essays in the History of Economics,* 51–65. Chicago: Univ. of Chicago Press.

Stites, Richard. 1957. "The Russian Revolution and Women." In *Connecting Spheres: Women in the Western World, 1500 to the Present,* ed. M. Boxer and J. Quataert, 246–255. New York: Oxford Univ. Press.

———. 1978. *The Women's Liberation Movement in Russia: Feminism, Nihilism, and Bolshevism, 1860–1930.* Princeton, NJ: Princeton Univ. Press.

Stocking, George W., Jr. 1971. "What's in a Name? The Origins of the Royal Anthropological Institute." *Man,* n.s., 6, no. 3 (September): 369–390.

Stoddard, Lothrop. 1920. *The Rising Tide of Color against White World-Supremacy.* New York: Charles Scribner's Sons.

Stokes, Eric. 1959. *The English Utilitarians and India.* Oxford: Clarendon Press.

———. 1980. "Bureaucracy and Ideology: Britain and India in the Nineteenth Century." *Transactions of the Royal Historical Society,* 5th ser., 30:131–156.

Stolcke, Verena. 1981. "Women's Labours: The Naturalisation of Social Inequality and Women's Subordination." In *Of Marriage and the Market: Women's Subordination Internationally and Its Lessons,* ed. K. Young et al., 159–177. London: CSE Books.

Storr, Marthe Severn. 1932. *Mary Wollstonecraft et le mouvement féministe dans la littérature anglaise.* Paris: Presses Univ. de France.

Strandmann, Hartmut Pogge von. 1969. "Domestic Origins of Germany's Colonial Expansion under Bismarck." *Past and Present,* no. 42 (February): 140–159.

Strumingher, Laura S. 1984. "The Legacy of Flora Tristan." *International Journal of Women's Studies* 7, no. 2 (May/June): 232–247.

Stuart, Robert. 1992. *Marxism at Work: Ideology, Class and French Socialism during the Third Republic.* Cambridge: Cambridge Univ. Press.

Stürmer, Michael. 1977. "Krise, Konflikt, Entscheidung, die Sache nach dem neuen Cäser als europäische Verfassungsproblem." In *Le Bonapartisme, phénomène historique et mythe politique,* ed. K. Hammer and P.C. Hartmann, 102–118. Munich: Artemis Verlag.

Suel, Marc. 1953. "L'Adresse et sa discussion de 1814 à 1830." *Revue internationale d'histoire politique et constitutionnelle,* n.s., 3, no. 11 (July–September): 176–188.

Sugihara, Kaoru. 1986. "Patterns of Asia's Integration into the World Economy, 1880–1913." In *The Emergence of a World Economy, 1500–1914: Papers of the IX. International Congress of Economic History*, by W. Fischer et al., 2:709–746. Wiesbaden: Franz Steiner.

Super, R. H. 1977. "The Humanist at Bay: The Arnold-Huxley Debate." In *Nature and the Victorian Imagination*, ed. U. C. Knoepflmacher and G. B. Tennyson, 231–245. Berkeley: Univ. of California Press.

Swingewood, Alan. 1970. "Origins of Sociology: The Case of the Scottish Enlightenment." *British Journal of Sociology* 21, no. 2 (June): 164–180.

Sydie, Rosalind A. 1991. "From Liberal to Radical: The Work and Life of Mary Wollstonecraft." *Atlantis* 17, no. 1 (Fall–Winter): 36–51.

Sykes, Robert. 1988. "Trade Unionism and Class Consciousness: The 'Revolutionary' Period of General Unionism, 1829–1834." In *British Trade-Unionism, 1750–1850*, ed. J. Rule, 178–199. London: Longmans.

Sztejnberg, Maxime. 1963. "La Fondation du Parti Ouvrier Belge et le ralliement de la classe ouvrière à l'action politique." *International Review of Social History* 8, pt. 2, 198–215.

Talmon, J. H. 1952. *The Origins of Totalitarian Democracy*. London: Secker & Warburg.

Taricone, Fiorenza. 1992. "Cronologia per una storia sociale femminile, dall'Unità al fascismo." *Il Politico*, no. 162 (April–June): 341–364.

Tarlé, Eugène. 1929. "L'insurrection ouvrière de Lyon." 3 pts. *Revue marxiste*, no. 2 (March): 132–153; no. 3 (April): 265–294; no. 4 (May): 412–428.

Taylor, Arthur J. 1960. "Progress and Poverty in Britain, 1780–1850: A Reappraisal." *History* 45, no. 153 (February): 16–31.

———. 1972. *Laissez-Faire and State Intervention in Nineteenth-Century Britain*. London: Macmillan.

Taylor, Barbara. 1983. *Eve and the New Jerusalem: Socialism and Feminism in the Nineteenth Century*. New York: Pantheon.

———. 1992. "Mary Wollstonecraft and the Wild Wish of Early Feminism." *History Workshop Journal*, no. 33 (Spring): 197–219.

Taylor, Edward B. 1920. *Primitive Culture*. New York: J. P. Putnam.

Taylor, Keith. 1982. *The Political Ideas of the Utopian Socialists*. London: Frank Cass.

Temperley, Harold. 1925a. *The Foreign Policy of Canning, 1822–1827*. London: G. Bell & Sons.

———. 1925b. "French Designs on Spanish America in 1820–5." *English Historical Review* 40, no. 158 (January): 34–53.

Terlinden, Charles. 1922. "La Politique économique de Guillaume 1er, roi des Pays-Bas en Belgique (1814–1830)." *Revue historique*, 47e année, CXXXIX (January–April): 1–40.

Therbom, Göran. 1974. *Science, Class, and Society: On the Formation of Sociology and Historical Materialism*. Göteborg: Tryck Revo Press.

Théret, Bruno. 1989. "Régimes économiques de l'ordre politique." Doctorat d'Etat en Science Economique, Université Paris-I Panthéon-Sorbonne. 2 vols.

———. 1991. "Le Système fiscal français libéral du XIXe siècle, bureaucratie ou capitalisme?" *Etudes et documents* 3:137–224.

Theriot, Nancy M. 1993. "Women's Voices in Nineteenth-Century Medical Discourse: A Step toward Deconstructing Science." *Signs* 19, no. 1 (Autumn): 1–31.

Thibert, Marguerite. 1926. *Le Féminisme dans le socialisme français de 1830 à 1850.* Paris: Marcel Giard.

Tholfsen, Trygve R. 1961. "The Transition to Democracy in Victorian England." *International Review of Social History* 6, pt. 2, 226–248.

———. 1976. *Working Class Radicalism in Mid-Victorian England.* London: Croom Helm.

Thomas, Edith. 1948. *Les Femmes en 1848: Collection du Centenaire de la Révolution de 1848.* Paris: Presses Univ. de France.

Thomis, Malcolm I. 1970. *The Luddites: Machine-Breaking in Regency England.* Newton Abbot, Devon, UK: David & Charles.

Thomis, Malcolm I., and Peter Holt. 1977. *Threats of Revolution in Britain, 1789–1848.* London: Macmillan.

Thompson, Dorothy. 1976. "Women and Nineteenth-Century Radical Politics." In *The Rights and Wrongs of Women,* ed. J. Mitchell and A. Oakley, 112–138. Baltimore: Penguin.

———. 1984. *The Chartists: Popular Politics in the Industrial Revolution.* London: Temple Smith.

Thompson, E. P. 1997. *The Romantics: England in a Revolutionary Age.* New York: New Press.

Thompson, F. M. L. 1963. *English Landed Society in the Nineteenth Century.* London: Routledge & Kegan Paul.

Thompson, Victoria, 1996. "Creating Boundaries: Homosexuality and the Changing Social Order in France, 1830–1870." In *Feminism and History,* ed. Joan Wallach Scott, 398–428. Oxford: Oxford Univ. Press.

Thompson, William. 1983. *Appeal of One Half of the Human Race, Women, against the Pretensions of the Other Half, Men, to Retain them in Political, and Hence in Civil and Domestic Slavery.* London: Virago.

Thönnessen, Werner. 1973. *The Emancipation of Women: The Rise and Decline of the Women's Movement in German Social Democracy, 1863–1933.* London: Pluto Press.

Thysser, A. Pontoppidon. 1980. "The Rise of Nationalism in the Danish Monarchy 1800–1864, with Special Reference to Its Socio-Economic and Cultural Aspects." In *The Roots of Nationalism: Studies in Northern Europe,* ed. R. Mitchison, 31–45. Edinburgh: John Donald.

Tickner, Lisa. 1987. *The Spectacle of Women: Imagery of the Suffrage Campaign, 1907–1914.* London: Chatto & Windus.

Tilly, Charles. 1964. "Reflections on the Revolutions of Paris: An Essay on Recent Historical Writing." *Social Problems* 12, no. 1 (Summer): 99–121.

———. 1972. "How Protest Modernized in France, 1845–1855." In *The Dimensions of Quantitative Research in History,* ed. W. O. Aydelotte et al., 192–255. Princeton, NJ: Princeton Univ. Press.

———. 1986. *The Contentious French: Four Centuries of Popular Struggle.* Cambridge, MA: Belknap Press of Harvard Univ. Press.

Tilly, Charles, Louise Tilly, and Richard Tilly. 1975. *The Rebellious Century, 1830–1930.* Cambridge, MA: Harvard Univ. Press.

Tilly, Charles, and Lynn Lees. 1974."Le Peuple de juin 1848." *Annales, E.S.C.* 29, no. 5 (September–October): 1061–1091.

Tilly, Richard H. 1990. *Vom Zollverein zum Industriestaat: Die wirtschaftlichsoziale Entwicklung Deutschlands, 1834 bis 1914*. Munich: Deutscher Taschenbuch Verlag.

Tissot, Louis. 1948. "Les Événements de 1848 dans les pays du Nord." In *Le Printemps des peuples: 1848 dans le monde*, ed. F. Fejtö, 1:373–400. Paris: Éd. du Minuit.

Tixerant, Jules. 1908. *Le Féminisme à l'époque de 1848, dans l'ordre politique et dans l'ordre économique*. Paris: V. Giard & E. Brière.

Todorov, Tzvetan. 1989. *The Deflection of the Enlightenment*. Stanford, CA: Stanford Humanities Center.

Tomaszewski, Jerzy. 1993. "The National Question in Poland in the Twentieth Century." In *The National Question in Europe in Historical Context*, ed. M. Teich and R. Porter, 293–316. Cambridge: Cambridge Univ. Press.

Tønnesson, Kåre D. 1978. *La Défaite des sans-culottes: Mouvement populaire et réaction bourgeoise en l'an III*. Oslo: Presses Univ. d'Oslo.

Torstendahl, Rolf. 1993. "The Transformation of Professional Education in the Nineteenth Century." In *The European and American University since 1800: Historical and Sociological Essays*, ed. S. Rothblatt and B. Wittrock, 109–141. Cambridge: Cambridge Univ. Press.

Toutain, Jean-Claude. 1987. "Le Produit intérieur brut de la France de 1789 à 1982." *Économies et sociétés. Cahiers de l'I.S.M.E.A.*, ser. AF 15, 21, no. 5 (May).

Treble, J. H. 1973. "O'Connor, O'Connell and the Attitudes of Irish Immigrants towards Chartism in the North of England, 1838–48." In *The Victorians and Social Protest: A Symposium*, ed. J. Butt and I. F. Clarke, 33–70. Newton Abbot, Devon, UK: David & Charles; Hamden, CT: Archon Books.

Tribe, Keith. 1988. *Governing Economy: The Reformation of German Economic Discourse, 1750–1840*. Cambridge: Cambridge Univ. Press.

———. 2005. "Political Economy and the Science of Economics in Victorian Britain." In *Organization of Knowledge in Victorian Britain*, ed. M. Daunton, 115–137. Oxford: Oxford Univ. Press.

Tristan, Flora. 1846. *L'Emancipation de la femme ou le testament de la paria*. Ouvrage posthume, complété d'après ses notes et publié par A. Constant Éd. Paris.

———. 1983. *The Workers' Union*. Urbana: Univ. of Illinois Press.

Trouillot, Michel-Rolph. 1991. "Anthropology and the Savage Slot: The Poetics and Politics of Otherness." In *Recapturing Anthropology: Working in the Present*, ed. T. G. Fox, 17–44. Santa Fe, NM: School of American Research Press.

———. 1995. *Silencing the Past: Power and the Production of History*. Boston: Beacon Press.

Tudesq, André-Jean. 1964. *Les Grands notables en France (1840–1849): Etude historique d'une psychologie sociale*. 2 vols. Paris: Presses Univ. de France.

Tuñon de Lara, Manuel. 1972. *El Movimento obrero en la historia de España*. Madrid: Taurus.

Turin, Yvonne. 1989. *Femmes et religieuses au XIXe siècle: Le Féminisme "en religion."* Paris: Éd. Nouvelle Cité.

Turner, R. Steven. 1974. "University Reformers and Professional Scholarship in Germany, 1760–1806." In *The University in Society*, ed. L. Stone, 2:495–531. Princeton, NJ: Princeton Univ. Press.

——. 1980. "The Prussian Universities and the Concept of Research." *Internationales Archiv für Sozialgeschichte der deutschen Literatur* 5:68–93.

Twellmann, Margrit. 1972. *Die deutsche Frauenbewegung: Ihre Anfange und erste Entwicklung.* Vol. 2, *Quellen 1843–1889.* Marburger Abhandlungen zur Politischen Wissenschaft, vol. 17, no. 1–2. Meisenheim-am-Glan, Germany: Verlag Anton Hain.

Valensi, Lucette. 1977. "Nègre/Negro : Recherches dans les dictionnaires français et anglais du XVIIIème au XIXème siècles." In *L'Idée de race dans la pensée politique française contemporaine,* ed. P. Guiral and E. Temine, 157–170. Paris: Éd. du CNRS.

——. 1993. *The Birth of the Despot: Venice and Sublime Porte.* Ithaca, NY: Cornell Univ. Press.

van der Linden, Marcel. 1988. "The Rise and Fall of the First International: An Interpretation." In *Internationalism in the Labour Movement, 1830–1940,* ed. F. Holthoon and M. van der Linden, 323–335. Leiden: E. J. Brill.

——. 1989. "Pourquoi le déclin de la Première Internationale était-il inéluctable?" *Cahiers d'histoire de L'I.R.M.,* no. 37, 125–131.

van Kalken, Frans. 1930. "La révolution de 1830, fut-elle prolétarienne?." *Le Flambeau* 13, nos. 1–2 (January): 45–54.

Veblen, Thorstein. 1964a [1918]. *The Higher Learning in America.* New York: Augustus Kelley.

——. 1964b [1915]. *Imperial Germany and the Industrial Revolution.* New York: Augustus Kelley.

Vellacott, Jo. 1987. "Feminist Consciousness and the First World War." *History Workshop Journal,* no. 23 (Spring): 81–101.

——. 1987. "Lecteurs forts et secteurs faibles dans l'économie française des années 1860: Une simulation économétrique." In *Le capitalisme français, 19e–20e siècle: Blocages et dynamismes d'une croissance,* ed. P. Fridenson and A. Straus, 151–173. Paris: Fayard.

Verley, Patrick. 1989. *L'Industrialisation, 1830–1914: Nouvelle histoire économique de la France contemporaine.* Vol. 2. Paris: La Découverte.

Vermeil, Edmond. 1948a. "Pourquoi la tentative de 1848 a-t-elle échoué en Allemagne?" *Revue socialiste,* n.s., nos. 17–18 (January–February): 99–106.

——. 1948b. "Un Paradoxe historique: La Révolution de 1848 en Allemagne." In *Le Printemps des peuples: 1848 dans le monde,* ed. F. Fejtö, 2:9–63. Paris: Éd. du Minuit.

Veysey, Lawrence R. 1965. *The Emergence of the American University.* Chicago: Univ. of Chicago Press.

——. 1979. "The Plural Organized World of the Humanities." In *The Organization of Knowledge in Modern America, 1860–1920,* ed. A. Oleson and J. Voss, 51–106. Baltimore: Johns Hopkins Univ. Press.

Vidal, César. 1931. *Louis-Philippe, Metternich et la crise italienne de 1831–1832.* Paris: E. de Boccard.

Vigier, Philippe. 1977. "Le Bonapartisme et le monde rural." In *Le Bonapartisme, phénomène historique et mythe politique,* ed. K. Hammer and P. C. Hartmann, 11–21. Munich: Artemis Verlag.

Villieurs, Marc de Baron. 1910. *Histoire des clubs de femmes et des Régions d'Auragones, 1793–1848–1871.* Paris: Plon.

Vincent, Gérard. 1987. *Sciences Po: Histoire d'une réussite.* Paris: Éd. Olivier Orban.

Vincent, J. R. 1981. "The Parliamentary Dimension of the Crimean War." *Transactions of the Royal Historical Society,* 5th ser., 31:37–49.

Viner, Jacob. 1927. "Adam Smith and Laissez Faire." *Journal of Political Economy* 35, no. 2 (April): 198–232.

———. 1949. "Bentham and J. S. Mill: The Utilitarian Background." *American Economic Review* 39, no. 2 (March): 360–382.

———. 1960. "The Intellectual History of Laissez Faire." *Journal of Law and Economics* 3 (October): 45–69.

Vogel, Lise. 1983. *Marxism and the Oppression of Women: Toward a Unitary Theory.* New Brunswick, NJ: Rutgers Univ. Press.

von Laue, Theodore H. 1953. "The High Cost and the Gamble of the Witte System: A Chapter in the Industrialization of Russia." *Journal of Economic History* 13, no. 4 (Fall): 425–448.

———. 1961. "Russian Peasants in the Factory, 1892–1904." *Journal of Economic History* 21, no. 1 (March): 61–80.

———. 1964. "Russian Labor between Field and Factory, 1892–1903." *California Slavic Studies* 3:33–65.

Vovelle, Michel. 1993. *La Découverte de la politique: Géopolitique de la Révolution française.* Paris: La Découverte.

Waelti-Walters, Jennifer. 1990. *Feminist Novelists of the Belle Epoque: Love as a Lifestyle.* Bloomington: Indiana Univ. Press.

Wagner, Donald O. 1931–1932. "British Economists and the Empire." 2 pts. *Political Science Quarterly* 46, no. 2 (June 1931): 248–276; 47, no. 1 (March 1932): 57–74.

Walker, Kenneth O. 1941. "The Classical Economists and the Factory Act." *Journal of Economic History* 1, no. 2 (November): 168–177.

Walker-Smith, Derek. 1933. *The Protectionist Case, 1840–1846.* Oxford: Basil Blackwell.

Walkowitz, Judith R. 1982. "Male Vice and Feminist Virtue: Feminism and the Politics of Prostitution in Nineteenth Century Britain." *History Workshop Journal,* no. 13 (Spring): 79–90.

Wallerstein, Immanuel. 1989. *The Modern World-System.* Vol. 3, *The Second Era of Great Expansion of the Capitalist World-Economy, 1730–1840s.* San Diego: Academic Press.

———. 1995. "Three Ideologies or One? The Pseudo-Battle of Modernity." In *After Liberalism,* 72–92. New York: New Press.

Wallerstein, Immanuel, et al. 1996. *Open the Social Sciences: Report of the Gulbenkian Commission on the Restructuring of the Social Sciences.* Stanford, CA: Stanford Univ. Press.

Walmsley, Robert. 1969. *Peterloo: The Case Reopened.* Manchester, UK: Manchester Univ. Press.

Ward, J. T. 1962. *The Factory Movement, 1830–1855.* London: Macmillan.

———. 1973. *Chartism.* London: B. T. Batsford.

Ward-Perkins, C. N. 1950. "The Commercial Crisis of 1847." *Oxford Economic Papers,* n.s., 2, no. 1 (January): 75–94.

Ware, Vron. 1992. *Beyond the Pale: White Women, Racism, and History.* London: Verso.

Washington, Joseph R., Jr., ed. 1984. *Jews in Black Perspectives: A Dialogue*. Rutherford, NJ: Fairleigh Dickinson Univ. Press.

Watson, George. 1973. *The English Ideology: Studies in the Language of Victorian Politics*. London: Allan Lane.

Webster, C. K. 1925. *The Foreign Policy of Castlereagh, 1815–1822: Britain and the European Alliance*. London: G. Bell & Sons.

———. 1931. *The Foreign Policy of Castlereagh, 1812–1815: Britain and the Reconstruction of Europe*. London: G. Bell & Sons.

Wehler, Hans-Ulrich. 1970. "Bismarck's Imperialism, 1862–1890." *Past and Present*, no. 48 (August): 119–155.

———. 1971. *Sozialdemokratie und Nationalstaat: Nationalitätenfrage in Deutschland, 1840–1914*. 2nd ed., rev. Göttingen: Vandenhoeck & Ruprecht.

———. 1985. *The German Empire, 1871–1918*. Leamington Spa, UK: Berg.

Weigall, David. 1987. *Britain and the World, 1815–1986*. New York: Oxford Univ. Press.

Weil, Cdt. Maurice-Henri. 1919. *Metternich et l'Entente Cordiale, une dépêche inédite, les manœuvres et les inquiétudes du Chancelier*. Paris: Auguste Picard.

———. 1921. *Guizot et l'Entente Cordiale*. Paris: Félix Alcan.

Weill, Georges. 1913. "Les Saint-Simoniens sous Napoléon III." *Revue des études napoléoniennes*, 2e année, III (May): 391–406.

———. 1924. *Histoire du mouvement social en France (1852–1924)*. 3rd ed, rev. Paris: F. Alcan.

———. 1930. *L'Eveil des nationalités et le mouvement libéral (1815–1848)*. Paris: Lib. Felix Alcan.

Weindling, Paul. 1989. "The 'Sonderweg' of German Eugenics: Nationalism and Scientific Internationalism." *British Journal for the History of Science* 22, pt. 3, no. 74 (September): 321–333.

Weingart, Pater. 1989. "German Eugenics between Science and Politics." In *Science in Germany, The Intersection of Institutional Intellectual Issues*, ed. K. M. Olesko, 260–282. *Osiris*, 2nd ser., 6.

Weisz, George. 1979. "L'Idéologie républicaine et les sciences sociales: Les durkheimiens et la chaire d'historie d'économie sociale à la Sorbonne." *Revue française de sociologie* 20, no. 1 (January–March): 83–112.

Wengenroth, Ulrich. 1994. *Enterprise and Technology: The German and British Steel Industries, 1865–1895*. Cambridge: Cambridge Univ. Press.

Werner, Karl Ferdinand. 1977. Preface to *Le Bonapartisme, phénomène historique et mythe politique*, ed. K. Hammer and P. C. Hartmann, ix–xii. Munich: Artemis Verlag.

White, R. J. 1950. Introduction to *The Conservative Tradition*, ed. R. J. White, 1–24. London: Nicholas Kaye.

———. 1973 [1957]. *Waterloo to Peterloo*. New York: Russell & Russell.

Willard, Claude. 1965. *Le Mouvement socialiste en France (1893–1905): Les Guesdistes*. Paris: Éd. Sociales.

———. 1971. *Le Socialisme de la Renaissance à nos jours*. Paris: Presses Univ. de France.

———. 1978. *Socialisme et communisme français*. Rev. ed. Paris: Lib. Armand Colin.

Williams, Glarmor. 1980. "Wales: The Cultural Bases of Nineteenth and Twentieth Century Nationalism." In *The Roots of Nationalism: Studies in Northern Europe,* ed. R. Mitchison, 119–129. Edinburgh: John Donald.

Williams, Gwyn A. 1982. "Druids and Democrats: Organic Intellectuals and the First Welsh Radicalism." In *Culture, Ideology, and Politics: Essays for Eric Hobsbawm,* ed. R. Samuel and G. S. Jones, 246–276. London: Routledge & Kegan Paul.

Williams, Judith Blow. 1972. *British Commercial Policy and Trade Expansion, 1750–1850.* Oxford: Clarendon Press.

Williams, Raymond. 1983. *Culture and Society, 1780–1950.* With new preface. New York: Columbia Univ. Press.

Williamson, Jeffrey G. 1962. "The Long Swing: Comparisons and Interactions between British and American Balance of Payments, 1820–1913." *Journal of Economic History* 22, no. 1 (March): 21–46.

Willson, A. Leslie. 1964. *A Mythical Image: The Ideal of India in German Romanticism.* Durham, NC: Duke Univ. Press.

Wilson, Charles. 1965. "Economy and Society in Late Victorian Britain." *Economic History Review,* n.s., 18, no. 1 (August): 183–198.

Winterarl, Barry D., and Stanley N. Katz. 1987. "Foundations and Ruling Class Elites." *Daedalus,* no. 1 (Winter): 1–39.

Winch, Donald. 1963. "Classical Economics and the Case for Colonization." *Economica,* n.s., 43rd year, vol. 30, no. 120 (November): 387–399.

———. 1965. *Classical Political Economy and Colonies.* London: G. Bell & Sons.

———. 1990. "Economic Knowledge and Government in Britain: Some Historical and Comparative Reflections." In *State and Economic Knowledge: The American and British Experience,* ed. M. O. Furner and B. Supple, 40–47. Washington, DC: Woodrow Wilson International Center for Scholars; Cambridge: Cambridge Univ. Press.

Wittrock, Björn. 1993. "The Modern University: The Three Transformations." In *The European and American University since 1800: Historical and Sociological Essays,* ed. S. Rothblatt and B. Wittrock, 303–362. Cambridge: Cambridge Univ. Press.

Wolff, Richard J. 1986. "Christian Democracy and Christian Unionism in Italy, 1890–1926." *Italian Quarterly* 27, no. 103 (Winter): 49–57.

Wood, George H. 1909. "Real Wages and the Standard of Comfort Since 1850." *Journal of the Royal Statistical Society* 72, pt. 1 (March 31): 91–103.

Woolf, Stuart. 1989. "French Civilization and Ethnicity in the Napoleonic Empire." *Past and Present,* no. 124 (August): 96–120.

———. 1991. *Napoleon's Integration of Europe.* London: Routledge, Chapman & Hill.

———. 1992. "The Construction of a European World-View in the Revolutionary-Napoleonic Years." *Past and Present,* no. 137 (November): 72–101.

Wright, Gordon. 1938. "The Origins of Napoleon III's Free Trade." *Economic History Review* 9, no. 1 (November): 64–67.

Wright, H. R. C. 1955. *Free Trade and Protection in the Netherlands, 1816–30.* Cambridge: At the University Press.

Wright, Vincent. 1975. "The Coup d'Etat of December 1851: Repression and the Limits to Repression." In *Revolution and Reaction: 1848 and the Second French Republic,* ed. R. Price, 303–333. London: Croom Helm.

Wurms, Renabe. 1983. "Kein einig Volk von Schwestern: Frauenbewegung 1890–1914." In *Geschichte der deutschen Frauenbewegung,* ed. F. Hervé, 41–83. Cologne: Pahl-Rugenstein.

Yaari, Aryeh. 1978. *Le Défi national.* Vol. 1, *Les Théories marxistes sur la question nationale à l'épreuve de l'histoire.* Paris: Éd. Anthropos.

———. 1979. *Le Défi national.* Vol. 2, *Les Révolutions éclatées.* Paris: Éd. Anthropos.

Yeo, Eileen. 1981. "Christianity in Chartist Struggle, 1838–1842." *Past and Present,* no. 91 (May): 109–139.

———. 1982. "Some Practices and Problems of Chartist Democracy." In *The Chartist Experience: Studies in Working-Class Radicalism and Culture, 1830–1860,* ed. J. Epstein and D. Thompson, 345–380. London: Macmillan.

Yeo, Richard R. 1993. *Defining Science: William Whewell, Natural Knowledge and Public Debate in Early Victorian Britain.* Cambridge: Cambridge Univ. Press.

Yeo, Stephen. 1977. "A New Life: The Religion of Socialism in Britain, 1883–1896." *History Workshop,* no. 4 (Autumn): 5–56.

Zagatti, Paola. 1988. "Colonialismo e razzismo: Immagini dell'Africa nella pubblicistica postunitaria." *Italia contemporanea,* no. 170 (March): 21–37.

Zak, L. A. 1971. "Die Grossmächte und die deutschen Staaten am Ende der napoleonischen Kriege." *Zeitschrift für Geschichtswissenschaft* 19, no. 11, 1536–1547.

Zeldin, Theodore. 1958. *The Political System of Napoleon III.* London: Macmillan.

———. 1959. "English Ideals in French Politics during the Nineteenth Century." *Historical Journal* 2, no. 1, 40–58.

———. 1967. "Higher Education in France, 1848–1940." *Journal of Contemporary History* 2, no. 3 (July): 53–80.

———. 1979. *France, 1848–1945.* Vol. 1, *Politics and Anger.* Oxford: Clarendon Press.

Zévaès, Alexandre. 1953. "La Fermentation sociale sous la Restauration et sous la Monarchie de Juillet." *Revue internationale d'histoire politique et constitutionnelle,* n.s., 3, no. 11 (July-September): 206–234.

Ziolkoski, Theodore. 1990. *German Romanticism and Its Institutions.* Princeton, NJ: Princeton Univ. Press.

Zolberg, Aristide R. 1972. "Moments of Madness." *Politics and Society* 2, no. 2 (Winter): 183–207.

———. 1999. "The Great Wall against China: Responses to the First Immigration Crisis, 1885–1925." In *Migration, Migration History, History: Old Paradigms and New Perspectives,* ed. J. L. Lucassen, 291–315. Bern: Peter Lang.

Zubrzycki, J. 1953. "Emigration from Poland in the Nineteenth and Twentieth Centuries." *Population Studies* 6, no. 3 (March): 248–272.

Zylberberg-Hocquard, Marie-Hélène. 1978. *Féminisme et syndicalisme en France.* Paris: Anthropos.

INDEX

I have adapted some conventions to organize this index. Regions within countries or within continents; names of monarchs and presidents; and events, groups, or laws that refer only to a particular country are listed as subcategories under the larger entities. However, overseas colonies and cities are listed separately, as are individual personalities other than monarchs or presidents. Furthermore, generalized categories that may be used to discuss phenomena in multiple entries are given their own entry, and multinational phenomena, such as treaties or wars, are listed separately under their most common names.

Abd-el-Kader, 86
Abel, Wilhelm, 63
Abensour, Léon, 193
Aberdeen, 4th Earl of (George Hamilton-
    Gordon), 82, 127
Abrams, Philip, 225, 252–53
Abray, Jane, 150, 152, 193
Absolutism, xiv, 7, 12, 16, 24, 62, 80, 85, 111
Abyssinia, 127
Adams, Herbert Baxter, 233
Adas, Michael, 265, 267
Adler, Laure, 193, 196
Adrianople, Treaty of, 62
Africa, 86
    Guinea Coast, 121
    Scramble for, xvi, 16, 121, 131
    West Africa, xv, 15, 128, 276
Ageron, Charles-Robert, 215
Aguet, Jean-Pierre, 81
Agulhon, Maurice, 16, 108, 141
Aix-la-Chapelle, 55

Albistur, Maïté, 191, 194
Albert, Prince, 225
Alexander, Sally, 185
Algeria, 61, 85–86, 127
Aliens, 82, 126, 144–45, 154, 171, 195, 209
Allen, Ann Taylor, 196, 201
Amar, André, 150–51
American Economics Association (AEA), 250
American Federation of Labor, 183
American Journal of Sociology, 257
American Political Science Association (APSA),
    263
American Social Science Association (ASSA),
    228–29
American Women's Suffrage Association
    (AWSA), 206
America (the Americas), 31, 58, 99
    Caribbean, 130
    Central, 130
    Latin, 30, 43, 54–55, 58, 68, 111, 121, 264
    North, 54, 70, 98, 162, 275

America (the Americas) *(continued)*
  South, 30, 54–55
  Spanish, 54, 56
  See also United States
Aminzade, Ronald, 164
Amsterdam, 112
Ancien régime, 11, 27, 42, 60, 64, 79, 112, 131,
    149–50, 152, 155, 164, 196
Anderson, Benedict, 184, 211
Andreucci, Franco, 180
Andrews, John R., 181–82, 190
Anglo-Chinese Wars, 120
Anglo-French Treaty of Commerce (Chevalier-
    Cobden Treaty, 1860), 105, 116,
    122–23, 125
Anglo-Saxons, 128, 215
Anglo-Turkish Commercial Convention (1838),
    121
Année sociologique, L', 253
Anteghini, Alessandra, 195
Anthropology, 213–14, 222, 264–73
Antiracism. *See* Racism
Anti-Semitism, 58, 210, 268
Anti-statism. *See* Statism
Antisystemic movements, xvi, 147, 159, 161, 229,
    276
Antwerp, 65, 67, 70
Applewhite, Harriet B., 150, 152
Apponyi, Comte Antoine, 63, 87
Aquinas, St. Thomas, 221
Archaeology, 238
Argentina, Republic of La Plata, 54
Aristocracy, 15, 22, 26, 40, 45, 47, 53, 61, 71–72,
    78–79, 83, 87, 91, 93, 97–98, 104, 144,
    149, 151–52, 162, 168, 210–11, 229,
    232, 274
Arnold, Matthew, 225
Aron, Raymond, 234–35
Arrighi, Giovanni, v
Artisans. *See under* Classes
Aryan, 214, 253
Ashley, Lord Anthony, 100
Ashley, William James, 179
Asia, 31, 128
  East, xvi, 16
  Far East, 121
  South, 214
Association Internationale pour le Progrès des
    Sciences Sociales, 219
Atheism, 119
Atlantic Monthly, 208

Auclert, Hubertine, 190, 195, 199–200
Australia, 126, 203
  Queensland, 121
Austria, 39, 42, 63–64, 87, 95, 114, 119, 131, 159, 191
  Austrian Netherlands, 63, 66
  Bohemia, 94
  Joseph II, Emperor, 64
  Suffrage, 191
Aydelotte, William O., 97, 115

Bagehot, Walter, 103, 133
Bairoch, Paul, 31–32, 118, 122–24
Baker, Keith Michael, 143, 222
Baker, Robert, 97
Bakunin, Mikhail, 171
Balance of power, 15, 21, 39, 44, 95–96
Balibar, Étienne, 210
Balkans. *See under* Europe
Ballanche, Pierre-Simon, 23
Banks, Olive, 151, 192, 207
Bannerji, Himani, 269
Banque de Belgique, 109
Banque de France, 110
Barings Bank, 108
Barkan, Elazar, 213
Barre, Raymond, 106
Bartier, John, 88
Barzun, Jacques, 56–57, 131, 140
Basch, Françoise, 203
Baster, Albert, 129
Bastid, Paul, 3
Basutoland, 121
Bayly, C. A., 27, 53, 126
Bebel, August, 177–78, 189
Bédarida, François, 165, 184
Bederman, Gail, 215–16
Beecher, Henry Ward, 206
Belgium, 17, 29–30, 37, 62–71, 73, 75, 84–85,
    87–88, 102, 105, 109, 114, 119, 122, 149,
    157, 173, 264
  Austrian Netherlands, 63, 66
  Flanders, 65
  Leopold I, 69, 88, 109, 149
  Liège, 64, 66
  Malines, School of, 67
  Suffrage, 191
  Wallonia, 65–67
Belloni, Pier Paolo, 180
Beloff, Max, 22–23, 89
Bendix, Reinhard, 170, 174
Bénéton, Philippe, 2, 12, 48, 60, 139, 239

Benson, Donald R., 225
Bentham, Jeremy, 6, 8–10, 15, 17, 100–101, 114–15, 132, 137
Benthamism, 15, 53, 114–15. *See also under* Great Britain
Berg, Barbara J., 204, 207
Berg, Maxime, 185
Berlin, 88, 193, 230, 248
Bernal, Martin, 57–58, 268, 270
Bernard, Jessie, 227
Bernard, L. L., 227
Bernstein, Edouard, 177–78, 180, 184
Bertier de Sauvigny, G. de, 2
Bessemer, Sir Henry, 104
Betley, Jan Andrzej, 65–69
Betts, Raymond F., 273
Bezucha, Robert J., 80–82
Biagini, Eugenio F., 102, 168
Bidelman, Patrick K., 195, 199
Bigaran, Maria Pia, 203
Billington, James H., 1–2, 23–24, 47, 56, 136, 146–49
Binary categories. *See* Civilization vs. barbarism
Birmingham, 45
Bismarck, Otto van, 36, 93, 131, 135, 174, 177–78, 231, 250
Blackburn, Robin, 27, 119–20, 154
Black Sea, 99, 129
Blacks, 153–54. *See also* United States
Blanc, Louis, 48, 61, 72, 85–86
Blanchard, Marcel, 93, 107
Blandford, Marquis of, 72
Blanqui, Louis Auguste, 17, 57
Blocker, Jack S., Jr, 202
Blondel, Léon, 86
Blue, Gregory, xii, 270
Bonald, Louis de, 12–13, 18, 23, 47–48, 160, 212, 223, 251
Boon, H. N., 108
Bortolotti, Franca Pieroni, 191
Botrel, J.-F., 166
Bougainville, Louis de, 127
Bouglé, Célestin, 193, 255
Bouillon, Jacques, 90
Boulle, Pierre H., 212
Bourgeoisie, xviii, 2, 8, 14, 23, 57, 59–61, 66, 75, 77–79, 90–94, 107–8, 123, 126, 146, 152–53, 155, 158, 162–64, 166–68, 170, 174, 177–78, 184, 189, 191, 196, 199–201, 211, 215–17, 219, 230, 252, 256, 259, 276

Bourgin, Georges, 59–60, 90–91, 107, 116–17
Bourguet, Marie-Noëlle, 21
Bourguignon, François, 37
Boutmy, Émile, 258–62
Bouvier, Jean, 36
Bouvier, Jeanne, 112
Bowler, Peter, 236
Boyle, John W., 41, 167
Brassists, the, 190
Brebner, J. Bartlett, 9, 17, 77, 100–101, 113, 129
Briavoinne, Natalis, 63–64, 105
Bridges, Amy, 162, 169, 178, 185
Briggs, Asa, 44–45, 51, 74–75, 83, 100, 103, 128, 133, 162
Bright, John, 74, 88, 126
British Association for the Advancement of Science, 225, 271
Brock, W. R., 43–46, 51
Broder, André, 124
Broglie, Duc de, 84
Bron, Jean, 181
Brook, Timothy, xiii
Broughan, Lord Henry, 97, 274
Brown(e), Commodore William, 54
Browning, Elizabeth Barrett, 128
Bruhat, Jean, 59, 81–82, 158
Bruneau, Charles, 2, 220
Brunet, Georges, 78
Brunot, Ferdinand, 2, 220
Brupbacker, Fritz, 189
Brussels, 66, 88, 110, 229
Bruun, Geoffrey, 18
Bruwier, Marinette, 64–65
Bryson, Gladys, 261
Bucharest, 171
Buechler, Steven M., 206, 229
Buenos Aires, 54
Buer, M. C., 28
Buhle, Mari Jo, 209
Bull, George, 100
Bulmer, Martin, 257–58
Bulwer, Lord Henry, 95
Buonarroti, Filippo, 60, 69
Burdeau, Georges, 112
Burgess, John W., 257, 261–63
Burgess, Keith, 175
Burke, Edmund, 2, 5, 12, 25, 87, 139
Burke, Peter, 238–39
Burma, Lower, 121
Burn, Duncan L., 11
Burn, W. L., 113, 115, 125, 131

Burton, Antoinette M., 207
Bury, J. P. T., 87–88, 95
Byron, Lord (George Gordon Byron), 54

Cabet, Étienne, 86–87
Cahill, Gilbert A., 114
Cain, P. J., 34, 119
Caine, Barbara, 197, 201
Cairncross, A. K., 113
Calhoun, Craig, 161, 164
California, University of, 272
Cambridge University, 221, 247, 249
Cameralism, 246
Cameron, Rondo E., 30–31, 34, 37, 106, 108–11,
    122–23
Campbell, Stuart L., 91, 93
Canada, 71, 98, 125, 129, 180
    British Columbia, 121
    Liberal Party, 180
    Newfoundland, 71
    Quebec, 70
    Victoria, 88
Canadian Pacific Railway, 128
Canning, George, 54–56, 60, 68, 130
Cantimori, Delio, 17, 94–95
Canuts. See under France
Capacity. See under Suffrage
Carlisle, Robert B., 107
Carlson, Andrew R., 177
Carlyle, Thomas, 18, 57, 125, 223, 225
Carrère d'Encausse, Hélène, 149
Casalini, Maria, 199
Cashdollar, Charles D., 224
Castlereagh, Viscount Robert Stewart, 2, 39–42,
    54–55
Catholicism, 4, 12–13, 18, 47, 50, 60–67, 70–72, 74,
    85, 114, 132, 139, 152, 157–58, 169, 182,
    190, 197–98, 202, 217, 221, 241–42,
    246, 252, 267
Catholic University (Paris), 246
Catt, Carrie Chapman, 206, 208
Cavaignac, Gen. Louis-Eugène, 90–91
Cecil, Lord Hugh, 4, 15–16, 18
Cerati, Marie, 152
Césaire, Aimé, 90, 153–54, 183
Ceylon, 126
Chabrol, Comte Christophe, 59
Chadwick, Edwin, 137
Chafetz, Janet Saltzman, 200
Chapelle-Dulière, Jacqueline, 250
Charte d'Amiens, 181

Chateaubriand, François-René de, 2, 23, 47, 57,
    80
Chaumette, Pierre-Gaspard, 152
Checkland, E. O. A., 114
Checkland, S. G., 31, 114, 220, 247
Cheney, Edna B., 208
Chevalier, Louis, 161
Chevalier, Michel, 112
Chicago, University of, 257
Chile, 54
China, vii, 30, 57, 120, 123, 127, 130, 203, 267,
    270–71
Chlepner, B.-S., 66, 70, 108–9
Church, R. A., 104, 251
Church, Robert L., 247–49, 261
Citizens, active-passive distinction, 145–47, 160,
    164, 182, 188, 193, 197, 200, 205, 211,
    225
Civilization vs. barbarism, 80, 84, 126, 146–47,
    156, 158, 197, 216–17
Clapham, J. H., 40, 45, 50, 52, 102–5, 113, 119, 131
Clark, G. Kitson. See Kitson Clark, G.
Clark, John Bates, 233
Clark, Terry N., 254–55
Class conflict, 77–141, 155, 171, 225
Classes
    Dangerous, 90, 132, 135–37, 140–41, 181–82,
        212, 243, 259
    Dominant strata, 79, 146, 153, 157, 166, 170, 172,
        204, 260, 277
    Middle (see Bourgeoisie)
    Working
        Artisans, 60, 80–81, 84, 90, 103, 113, 158,
            162–64, 167, 169
        Workers, xviii, 25, 32–33, 37, 57, 59–60,
            63–64, 66, 70, 79–83, 85–86, 89–90,
            94, 114, 116–17, 133–36, 149, 154–55,
            158, 161–72, 174–77, 180–90, 209, 212,
            215
    Mutual aid societies, 80
Classics, 212, 226, 268
Clemens, Barbel, 197
Coates, Willson H., 114
Coats, Alfred William, 247, 290
Coats, S. E., 247
Cobb, Richard, 155
Cobban, Alfred, 167
Cobden, Richard, 88, 98, 103, 119–20, 122, 126
Cochran, Thomas, 10th Earl of Dundonald, 54
Cochin, 130
Cohen, William B., 207, 211, 214, 216

Colbert, Jean-Baptiste, 65, 115
Colbertism, 112
Colby College, 256
Cole, G. D. H., 13, 32, 51, 78, 107, 126–27, 159–60, 175
Cole, Juan, 267
Cole, Stephen, 229
Coleman, Bruce, 45, 103, 105
Collège de France, 221
Collins, Henry, 183
Collins, Irene, 79
Colman, H., 37
Cologne, 230
Colonial scramble. *See under* Africa
Coloureds, 149
Columbia University, 257–58, 261–62, 265
Commons, John R., 181, 183
Communism, 76, 84, 87–88, 93–94, 161, 163, 183, 195
Competence, as criterion for decision-making, 228, 232, 243, 249
Comte, Auguste, 23, 69, 78, 232, 251–52, 256, 259
Concert of Europe. *See* Vienna, Congress of/ Treaty of
Condliffe, J. B., 28, 31, 43, 123, 125–26
Condorcet, Jean–Antoine Nicolas de Capitat, Marquis de, 149, 221, 226, 241
Confédération Générale du Travail (CGT), 181
Conservatism, 2–6, 11–18, 23–25, 27, 43–44, 47, 49, 51, 58, 60–61, 66, 72, 74–75, 78, 86, 88, 92–93, 97, 99, 107, 111–13, 115–19, 129, 131–36, 138–41, 160–61, 170, 174–76, 191, 201–3, 207, 209, 219, 229, 237, 239–40, 242–43, 246, 251–52, 254–56, 260, 269
    Enlightened, 43, 71, 92, 95, 112, 131, 161, 170
Constant, Benjamin, 2, 6, 23–24
Constantine, Grand Duke, 63, 68
Constantinople, 55, 73
Continental Blockade, 64, 96, 118, 122
Conze, Werner, 158, 169
Coornaert, Emile, 78
Coser, Lewis, 255–56
Cottereau, Alain, 179
Couriau, Emma, 190–91
Cousin, Victor, 212
Coussy, Jean, 105, 124
Cracow, 87
Crafts, N. F. R., 38
Cranborne, Lord, 3rd Marquess of Salisbury, 133
Crédit Foncier, 110

Crédit Mobilier, 109–11
Crick, Bernard R., 4, 58, 262–63
Crimean War, 104, 128–31, 183, 229
Croats, 159, 239
Croce, Benedetto, 61, 80
Croker (Crocker), John Wilson, 2, 97
Crouch, R. L., 138
Crouzet, François, 30, 38, 64, 122
Cruz Seoane, María, 2, 148
Cuba, 130–31
Cullen Michael J., 227–28
Cunningham, Andrew, 222
Cunningham, William, 31, 118, 247–48
Czechs, 99, 239

Dahrendorf, Ralf, 234–35, 262–63
Dale, Peter Allan, 225, 232
Darvall, Frank O., 21, 32, 51, 137
Daumard, Adeline, 59–60, 78–80, 86, 112, 117
Davies, Emily, 267
Davis, Mary, 214
Deacon, Desley, 203
Deane, Phyllis, 32
Debs, Eugene V., 207, 216
Decharneux, Baudouin, 269
Decolonization, xiii, xv, 32, 54, 70
D'Eglantine, Fabre, 150
DeGroat, Judith Ann, 185
Deindustrialization. *See* Industrialization
Delacampagne, Christian, 209, 212
Delacroix, Eugène, 186
Delaive, Victor, xviii
De Lamartine, Alphonse, 127
De Maistre, Joseph, 2, 47–48, 78, 162
Demangeon, Albert, 24, 64
Démier, Francis, 122
De Morgan, Augustus, 222
Demoulin, Robert, 30, 65–68
Denmark, 97
De Pisan, Christine, 152
Derainne, Pierre-Jacques, 165
Derby, Lord (Frederick Stanley, 16th Earl of Derby), 133–34
Deroin, Jeanne, 193–94
Descoings, Richard, 258–60
Despotism, 14–15, 23, 49, 54, 67, 97, 120, 126, 251, 268–71
    Enlightened, 15, 269. *See also under* Conservatism
Deutsche Gesellschaft für Soziologie, 263
Devance, Louis, 195

Devleeshouwer, Robert, 64
Dhondt, Jean, 64–65, 87
Dibble, Vernon, 258
Dicey, Albert Venn, 9
Dijkstra, Sandra, 194
Disraeli, Benjamin, 99, 120–21, 130–31, 133–34, 138, 140, 174–75
Divine right of kings. *See* Absolutism
Djordjevíc, Dimitrije, 159
Dohn, Hedwig, 196
Dolléans, Edouard, 60, 81, 165, 168
Donzelot, Jacques, 24, 116, 201
Dorfman, Joseph, 230, 250, 257
Douglass, Frederick, 206
Drescher, Seymour, 119
Droit, Roger-Pol, 163, 226
Droit de cité, 79, 83, 166. *See also* Suffrage
Droz, Jacques, 158–59
Dubofsky, Melvyn, 180
DuBois, Ellen Carol, 199, 206
Duffy, A. E. P., 176
Dunham, Arthur Louis, 123–24
Dupont de Nemours, Pierre Samuel, 154
Dupuis, Charles, 41
Durkheim, Emile, 253–56
Duruy, Victor, 246
Dutch East Indies, 65–66, 126
Duverger, Maurice, 93–117
Dworkin, Anthony Gary, 200

Economics, 15–16, 51–53, 88, 100–101, 113, 119, 126, 159, 228, 230, 244–45, 248–52, 255, 257
Economist, the, 104
Eden Treaty (1786), 118
Egypt, 57–58, 111, 218, 267–68, 270
Eisenstein, Elizabeth L., 60, 69
Eisenstein, Zillah R., 200
Elesh, David, 227
Ellis, John, 89–90, 161
Elton, Godfrey Lord, 24, 47, 60
Elvin, Mark, 60
Elwitt, Sanford, 136, 252
Ely, Richard T., 182, 250, 257
Emerit, Marcel, 127
Endres, Robert, 94
Enfantin, Barthélemy Prosper, 107
Engel, Arthur, 224
Engels, Friedrich, 14, 188, 239
England. *See* Great Britain
Enlightenment, 5, 138, 148, 162, 202, 204, 211, 214, 239, 241, 260, 266, 270

Entente cordiale, 22, 70, 84–87, 121, 127–28
Equality, 7, 23, 47, 64, 107, 114, 116, 138, 143–48, 153, 155, 163, 165, 186, 188, 190, 197, 199, 201, 211, 213, 215, 217, 221
Erfurt, 178
Eugenics, 235–37
Eupen, 64
Europe, xii-xiii, 2, 21, 24, 27, 29–31, 39, 41–42, 44, 46, 49, 54–58, 60, 62–63, 65–66, 69, 72, 82, 84–85, 87–89, 92–96, 102–3, 110, 112, 115, 117–25, 129, 131, 134, 136, 141, 146–47, 156–57, 159, 165, 171, 173–75, 184, 192, 195, 198, 209–14, 220–21, 237, 240, 256, 260, 264–73
    Central, 106, 141, 161, 209
    Concert of (*see* Vienna, Congress of)
    Continental, 28, 30–31, 39, 110, 114, 131, 170, 174, 195
    Eastern, 42, 69–70, 98, 141
    Latin, 114
    Northern (Scandinavia), 94, 264
    Northwestern, 95, 99
    Revolutions of 1848, 8, 56, 86–89, 91–92, 95–96, 114, 118, 126, 141, 157–62, 168, 189, 194–98, 206, 240, 246 (*see also under* France)
    Southern, 94
    Western, 33, 69, 90, 98, 100
Evans, David Owen, 188, 200, 208
Evans, Eric J., 9, 21–22, 25–26, 33–34, 43, 55, 69, 72, 83, 98, 100–101, 114, 118
Evans, Richard J., 189, 191, 199–202, 206, 209

Fabvrier, Col., 59
Fairlie, Susan, 33, 97, 99
Faivre, Jean-Paul, 127–28
Family wage, 186–88
Faraday, Michael, 235
Farnie, D. A., 120–21, 125, 130
Fauriel, Claude, 59
Favre, Pierre, 260
Fay, C. R., 20, 26, 32, 83, 101
Fay, Victor, 81, 177
Febvre, Lucien, 24, 64
Fédération Française des Travailleurs du Livre (FFTL), 187, 191
Fejtö, François, 89, 94, 96, 103, 159
Feminist and suffragist movements. *See* Women
Ferguson, Adam, 244
Ferrero, Gugliemo, 199
Ferry, Jules, 242
Festy, Octave, 80

Fetter, Frank W., 50, 103, 244
Fichte, Johann Gottlieb, 240
First World War. *See* World War I
Fisher-Gelati, Stephen, 159
Fitzgerald, Vesey, 71
Flahant, Comte de, 87
Flexner, Eleanor, 207
Flinn, M. W., 52
Fohlen, Claude, 123
Folbre, Nancy, 203
Foner, Eric, 84, 180
Fontvieille, Louis, 115
Forbes, Geraldine H., 199
Foreigners. *See* Aliens
Forman, Michael, 171–72
Fossaert, Robert, 78
Foster, John, 162, 183
Foucault, Michel, 202
Fould, Achille, 123
Fourier, François Marie Charles, 59
France, passim.
    Amis des Noirs, 154
    Assignats, 154
    Avignon, 148
    Bibliothèque Nationale, 195
    Bicentennial (1989), 2, 49
    Bonapartism, 47, 91–93, 106–7, 116, 117, 135, 157
    Bourbons, 41, 55, 85, 93
    Cahiers de doléance, 148–49
    Canuts, 76, 81, 165, 146
    Catholic League, 67
    Champ de Mars massacre (1791), 180
    Charles X, 3, 8, 47, 55, 59–62, 72, 85, 127, 162–63
    Charter of 1814, 3, 46–47, 49, 60, 79
    Collapse, political (1870), 111
    Committee of Public Safety, 150
    Commune of Paris, 135–36, 165, 171–72, 179, 189, 225, 241–42, 259
    Comtat Venaisson, 148
    Constitution of 1875, 117
    Council of Five Hundred, 152
    Declaration of Rights of Women and the Citizen, 152
    Dreyfus affair, 254
    Elba, Napoleon's return from (Hundred Days), 39, 46–47 (*see also* Waterloo)
    Enragés, 150
    Estates-General, 149–50
    Fifth Republic, 115
    Fourmies killings (1891), 180
    French Revolution, xv–xvi, 1–4, 13, 16, 21–23, 28, 50, 56–57, 60, 79, 82, 91–92, 105,

115–16, 143–64, 197, 199, 204, 210–11, 213, 217, 219–21, 225–26, 235, 240, 245, 259, 268, 275–77
    Convention, 149–55, 153–55
    National Assembly, 149, 153–55
    Idéologues, 245
    Jacobins, 115, 150–52, 155
    July Monarchy, 8, 10, 12, 22–23, 32, 60, 79, 82, 85–86, 89, 91, 94, 106, 108, 110, 115, 127, 145, 157, 166, 195, 241
    July Revolution *(Trois glorieuses)* (1830), 40, 47, 60–62, 66, 70, 72, 77, 79–81, 84–85, 139, 163, 186, 210, 241
    La Marseillaise, 61
    Legitimists, 12, 16, 47–50, 60–61, 66–67, 71–72, 75, 157, 163
    Loi Le Chapelier, 80, 82, 155
    Louis XI, 7
    Louis XV, 90
    Louis XVI, 8, 220
    Louis XVIII, 3, 41, 46–48, 55, 60, 62, 71, 85, 249 (*see also* Restoration)
    Louis Napoleon (Napoleon III), 36, 89–93, 106–8, 110, 112, 114, 116–17, 123–24, 129–36, 170, 258–59
    Louis-Philippe, 3, 61–62, 67–68, 72, 87–90, 94–95, 105, 110, 127, 149, 157 (*see also* July Monarchy)
    Maximum, the, 155
    Méline tariff, 124
    Millerand, Pres. Alexandre, 180
    Napoleon Bonaparte, 48, 64, 116, 122
    Orleans, House of, 87, 93
    Orleanist monarchy (*see* July Monarchy)
    Party of Movement, 156
    Party of Order, 91, 108, 136, 156, 252
    Philip the Fair, 150
    Prince Napoleon, 117
    Race gauloise vs. *race franque,* 210
    Republicans, 10, 16, 82, 91–93, 95, 117, 134–36, 163, 206
    Restoration, 3, 5, 12, 46–50, 60, 71, 80, 105, 122, 162, 245
    Revolution of 1848, 10, 16, 59, 75, 88–90, 93–94, 105, 107, 109–10, 112–13, 252
    Social revolution, xviii, 89–90, 92, 135–36, 157–62, 168, 246
    Revolutionary-Napoleonic period, 1, 23–25, 29, 58, 105, 276
    Royalists, 47–49, 92, 117, 135–36, 155, 169
    Saint-Simonians, 16–18, 27, 78, 91, 106–8, 127, 135, 179, 193–94

France *(continued)*
    Second Empire, 90–91, 93, 105–8, 110, 115–17,
        127, 131, 134–36, 158, 169, 174
    Second Republic, 116
    Slavery, abolition of, 90, 181
    Society of Republican-Revolutionary Women,
        150
    Suffrage, 7, 24, 48, 86, 89–90, 92–93, 116, 131,
        133–34, 190
    Suffrage censitaire, 31, 86, 107
    Terror, the, 8, 24, 91, 152, 189
    Third Republic, 115, 136, 189, 197, 241, 250, 254,
        259
    Tuppenny riot *(émeute de deux sous),* 81
    Ultras *(see* Legitimists)
    Vendée, 67
    Volontaires du Rhône, 62
    White Terror, 47
Franco-German War (1870–1871), 134–35
Fraser, Derek, 73
Free trade. *See* Laissez-faire
Freedeman, Charles E., 37
Freemasons, 198
Frei, Annette, 189
Fulford, Roger, 191–92, 204
Furet, François, 49
Furner, Mary O., 233

Galbraith, John S., 125
Gallagher, John, 121
Gallars, M., 41
Gambia, 128
Garibaldi, Giuseppe, 183–84
Garnier-Pagès, Louis-Antoine, 78
Gash, Norman, 4, 14, 42–43, 71–72, 74, 79, 83,
        87–88, 101, 129–30, 138–39, 166
Gay, Peter, 219, 224, 231
Gayer, Arthur D., 30–32
Geary, Dick, 161, 163, 169, 171–72, 178
Geisteswissenschaften, 238
Geoculture, xiii, xv, 2, 19, 58, 96, 100, 131, 196, 217,
        219, 268, 277
Geopolitics. *See* Interstate system
George, M. Dorothy, 25
George, Margaret, 76–77, 150–52
Germany (Germanies), xvi, 21, 27, 31, 41, 53–54,
        58, 65, 70–73, 85, 87, 92–94, 97, 102,
        105–6, 119, 131, 135–39, 141, 157–58,
        160, 163, 167, 169, 171–74, 177–79,
        184–85, 188–90, 195, 197, 199–203,
        207–10, 212, 214, 217, 229–30, 234,

        237, 240–43, 246, 248, 250, 253, 256,
        259–64, 268–70
    Bavaria, 64, 119, 188
    Frankfurt Assembly, 189
    Katheder-Sozialisten, 230–31, 256, 263
    Nazis, 214, 237
    Palatinate, 64
    Prussia, 39, 42, 64, 65, 68, 104, 119, 135, 138,
        188, 240, 246, 259
    Suffrage, 174, 177, 191, 200, 207
    Wilhelm I, Kaiser, 179
    Vaterlandlos, 181
    Zollverein, 119
Ghent, 64–65
Giddens, Anthony, 256
Giddings, Franklin, 257
Gille, Bertrand, 34, 106, 108, 110
Gilman, Charlotte Perkins, 207
Gilroy, Paul, 211, 214
Girard, Louis, 93, 110, 131, 135–36
Gladstone, William Ewart, 35, 74, 125, 183
Glasgow University, 244
Gobineau, Joseph Arthur, Comte de, 211, 213,
        270
Godechot, Jacques, 147–48
Godkin, Edwin, 229
Gold Coast, 121
Goldfrank, Walter L., 252
Goldman, Lawrence, 133, 227–29, 231, 237, 243
Gold standard, 51, 96, 103, 109
Gompers, Samuel, 183
Gonnet, Paul, 59, 79
Gordon, Ann D., 206
Gordon, H. Scott, 245
Goriély, Benjamin, 95
Gottesdienst, 239
Gouges, Olympe de, 152
Gough, Barry, 125
Graham, Sir James, 88
Great Britain, passim.
    Abolitionist movement, 27, 119–20, 183, 192,
        197, 205–8, 271
    Act of Union (1800), 70
    Anglicans *(see* Church of England)
    Anti-Combination Acts, 25, 80, 113, 137, 162
    Bank of England, 50, 103
    Bank Charter Act (1844), 103, 109
    Benthamites *(see* Utilitarians)
    Board of Trade, 35, 71, 119, 227
    Catholic Dissenters Relief Bill (1791), 70
    Catholic Emancipation, 70–72, 132

Great Britain (continued)
  Chartism, 21, 73, 75, 83–84, 87–88, 114, 128,
      137–38, 165–68, 175, 192–93, 200
  Christian socialism, 125, 140
  Church of England, 58, 70, 126, 130
  Colonial Preference, 71, 118
  Contagious Diseases Act, 201
  Corn Laws (and Repeal of), 33, 35, 44–45, 71,
      75, 83, 87–88, 95–100, 102, 109, 113,
      119–21, 125, 132, 139–40, 200
  Conservatives (see Tories)
  East India Company, 95–96, 126
  "Entrepôt of the world," 101
  Fabianism, 57, 115, 261
  Factory Acts, 15, 113, 137, 142
  Fair Trading League, 105
  Financial crisis of 1816, 111
  Fleet Street, 128
  Food and Drug Acts, 114
  Gordon Riots, 44, 70
  Great Victorian Boom, 101, 104
  Home Counties, 126
  House of Commons, 43, 72, 134, 158
  Ireland, 35, 70–72, 74, 84, 88, 95, 128, 141, 165,
      184, 215
    Catholic Association, 71, 165
    Easter Rebellion, 184
    Potato famine, 88
    Ulster, 35
  Irish Coercion Bill, 83
  Irish workers in England, 84
  John Bull, 126
  Labo(u)r Party, 99, 174, 176, 191
  Lancashire, 120–21, 130
  Liberals (see Whigs)
  Little Englandism, 125, 130
  Luddites, 26, 44
  Manchester School, 8, 29, 101, 130, 134, 230
  Masters and Servants Bill (1844), 83
  Methodists, 27, 73
  Municipalities Act, 83
  Navigation Acts, 53, 71, 99, 125
  Noncomformism, 52, 125
  Norman Yoke, 210
  Pax Britannica, 43, 125, 129
  Pentrich Rising, 44
  Peterloo Massacre, 25–26, 45–46, 51
  Police Acts, 114
  Poor Laws, 26, 52–53
    New Poor Laws, 83–84, 100, 114, 163
  Pre-Raphaelitism, 125

  Presbyterians, 126
  Public Health Acts, 114
  Reform Act (1867), 99, 132–34, 140
  Reform Bill (1832), 75, 82–84, 100, 109, 113, 132,
      136, 163, 204–5
  Reform League, 133
  Repeal of the Sliding Scale (1846), 99
  Royal Society, 221
  Scotland, x, 24, 27, 51, 74, 172, 241, 244–45
    Lowlands, 126
  Speenhamland, 113
  Stuarts, 41
  Suffrage, 2, 9, 131–34, 136, 145, 165, 174, 191–92,
      195, 200, 207, 272
  Tamworth Manifesto, 17, 96
  Ten Hours' Bill, 83–84, 100, 113, 163
  Tories, 4, 14, 18, 22, 26, 40–41, 43–44, 46, 51,
      56, 59, 66, 70–72, 84, 88, 95–97, 99,
      113, 115, 129–34, 138–42, 165
    National Toryism, 140
    Peelism, 97, 140
    Tory Evangelicals, 100
    Tory interpretation of history, 44
    Tory Reaction, 114, 22, 43–44
    Tory workers, 134, 140
  Utilitarians, 8–9, 17, 23, 44, 63, 75, 100, 114, 132
  Victoria, Queen, 95, 115
  Whig interpretation of history, 240–41
  Whigs, 2, 14, 25–26, 31, 44, 46, 51, 70–74, 83,
      88, 97–100, 120, 125, 133–35, 138–40,
      163, 175–76, 228–29, 274
  White settler colonies/White Dominions, 125,
      173
  "Workshop of the world," 31, 120
  Young Englandism, 125
  See also under Hegemony
Great Depression, 111, 115
Greece, 24, 43, 55–58, 62, 94, 141, 267–70
Greeley, Horace, 206
Greer, Donald M., 87
Grégoire, Abbé Henri Jean-Baptiste, 153–54
Grey, Lord, 69–70, 73–74
Griffith, Elisabeth, 206
Grimm, Jacob, 214, 240
Groh, Dieter, 158, 169, 174, 179, 181
Gross, Leo, 41
Grossman, Henryk, 226, 245
Gruner, Wolf D., 39
Gueniffey, Patrice, 145
Guérard, Albert, 108
Guesdists, 179–80, 184–85, 189–90

Guichen, Eugène, Vicomte de, 61–63, 67–68, 85
Guilbert, Madeleine, 185–88, 190
Guillaumin, Colette, 210, 213, 236–37
Guizot, François, 6–9, 48–49, 59, 68, 77–79, 85–87, 91, 108, 116, 127, 136, 210, 212, 241
Gunnell, John G., 235, 263
Guyot, Raymond, 61, 68, 84–85

Hackett, Amy, 195
Hainault, 64
Halbwachs, Maurice, 255
Halévy, Elie, 2, 9, 14–17, 21, 27, 38–39, 43–44, 51–52, 72–74, 83–84, 87–88, 101, 114, 138, 158, 160
Halifax, 129
Hall, Alex, 179
Hall, Catherine, 196
Halpérin, Jean, 87
Hamburg, 65
Hamilton, Sir William, 224
Hammen, Oscar J., 87
Hammond, J. L., 112
Hansen, Erik, 176, 180
Hardy, Gathorne, 133
Harley, C. Knick, 32
Harper, William Rainey, 258
Harsin, Paul, 66
Hart, Jennifer, 44, 115
Hartmann, Heidi, 185
Haskell, Thomas L., 229, 232, 237
Hasquin, Hervé, 63
Hasselman, Wilhelm, 177
Haupt, Georges, 171, 176–77, 184
Hause, Steven C., 150, 189, 200
Hauser, Henri, 223, 225, 241
Haussmann, Georges-Eugène, 110
Haute banque, 110–11
Hayek, Frederick A. von, 18, 78, 219, 244, 251
Hegel, Georg Wilhelm Friedrich, 240, 270–71
Hegelians, Young, 78
Hegemony, 104
    American, xii, xvi
    British, xii, xv–xvi, 21, 30, 33, 39, 41, 43, 54, 84, 103, 118, 129, 135
    Dutch, xii, xiv
Heiniger, Ernstpeter, 236
Henderson, W. O., 35, 70
Hendricks, Margo, 210
Herberg, Will, 180
Herbst, Juergen, 238

Herr, Lucien, 255
Hersh, Blanche Glassman, 205–6
Hertz, Deborah, 193
Hertz, Robert, 225
Hervé, Florence, 186, 199
Herz, Henriette, 193
Hexter, J. H., 70
Heywood, Colin, 52, 100, 180
Higham, John, 232
Hill, Christopher, 210
Hill, R. L., 51–52, 137, 140
Hilton, Boyd, 45
Himmelfarb, Gertrude, 132
Hinsley, Curtis M. Jr., 233, 272
Hinton, James, 133, 169, 174–75, 183, 185–86, 191
Historicism, 238, 240–41, 249
Historische Zeitung, 242
History, as science or humanism, 222, 224–25, 228, 235, 237–44, 247–49, 261, 263–65, 267–68, 272
Hoagland, Henry E., 169
Hobhouse, L. T., 16
Hobsbawm, Eric J., 8, 17, 29–30, 37–39, 51, 56–57, 77, 79, 89–90, 102, 113, 155, 161, 167, 171, 174–78, 186, 212, 240–42
Hodgson, Geoffrey M., 248
Hoffmann, Walther, 32
Hofstadter, Richard, 236–37, 251, 257
Hogg, Quintin, 4
Hohenberg, Paul, 37
Holland. See Netherlands
Holland, Bernard, 44, 71, 121
Hollis, Patricia, 183
Holt, Peter, 25–26, 46, 71, 73
Holy Alliance, 20, 40, 42–44, 48–49, 55–56, 58, 60–62, 65, 67, 75, 108, 117, 131
Holyoake, George Jacob, 128
Holy Roman Empire, 64
Honeycutt, Karen, 189
Hong Kong, Kowloon, 121
Hope, House of, 112
Horton, Wilmot, 52
Hoxie, R. Gordon, 261–62
Hufton, Olwen, 151
Hughes, H. Stuart, 263
Humanité, L', 255
Humbolt, Alexander von, 240
Hungary, 95, 128, 157, 159–60, 184
Huskisson, William, 53, 101
Hutchison, Henry Hunt, 262

Hutton, R. H. 121
Huxley, Julian, 213
Hyndman, Henry Mayers, 184

Ideologies, xvi, 1–19, 23–25, 27, 31, 36, 43, 77, 91,
        112, 114–15, 119, 123, 125–26, 138–41,
        144, 147, 155–60, 162–64, 169, 178,
        193, 196–97, 201, 204, 210, 213, 215,
        217, 219–21, 227, 234–35, 237, 245, 249,
        252, 255–56, 267, 275–77
Iggers, Georg G., 48, 72, 78, 140
Ignatiev, Noel, 215
Imlah, Albert H., 30–31, 34–36, 49, 54, 104, 104,
        124, 129
India, xv, 30, 53, 58, 111, 121, 126–27, 268–70
    Berar, 114
    India Office, 127
    Oudh, 121
    Punjab, 121
    Sepoy Mutiny, 125, 127
Indian Ocean, 127
Indo-European languages, 269–70
Industrial revolution, xiii, xv–xvi, 8, 38, 69, 85,
        101, 105, 275
Industrialization, xii, 36, 104, 120, 164, 167, 171,
        173–74, 188, 196, 227
    "Take-off," 36, 64
Industrial Workers of the World (IWW), 183
Inequality. See Equality
Institut d'Études Politiques (IEP). See Sciences
        Po
International Workingmans' Association
        (IWMA) (1st International), 117, 170,
        172, 176, 182, 186, 188
Interstate system, 22, 39, 68, 95, 111, 117, 176, 203
Ireland. See Great Britain
Irving, Washington, 126
Italy (Italies), 7, 17, 41, 47, 54, 58, 61–62, 81, 82,
        85, 105, 116, 124, 126, 128, 141,
        146–48, 157, 159, 175, 180, 187, 191–92,
        195, 198, 202, 210, 219, 240, 264, 269,
        273
    Carbonari, 62
    Naples, 46, 95
    Northern and Central, 94
    Piedmont, 68, 82, 123
    Risorgimento, 180
    Savoy, 63, 82
    Sicily, 95
    Southern, 24
    Suffrage, 191–92

Jacob, William, 227
Jacobinism, 2, 18, 77, 112. See also under France
Jacquemyns, Guillaume, 86
Jacqueries, 94
Japan, 123, 189, 203, 212
Jardin, André, 22, 85
Jardine, Nicholas, 222
Jaurès, Jean, 155, 215, 255
Java, 126
Jayawardena, Kumari, 208
Jenks, Leland H., 43, 50, 88, 111, 119, 127
Jennings, Louis J., 97
Jeremy, David J., 35
Jervis, Robert, 39
Jevons, William Stanley, 113, 247, 249
Jews, 198, 210
Johns Hopkins University, 250, 256–57
Johnson, Christopher H., 29, 61, 87
Johnson, Richard, 138
Johnston, Hugh J. M., 52
Jones, Gareth Stedman, 83, 162–63, 166–68, 173,
        184
Jones, Thomas, 269
Jones, William, 269
Jordan, Winthrop D., 213
Jore, Léonce, 127–28
Judt, Tony, 165, 185
Juárez, Benito, 131

Kadish, Alon, 247
Kalaora, Bernard, 252
Kaplan, Steven L., 2, 49, 155
Karady, Victor, 249, 255
Katznelson, Ira, 114
Kautsky, Karl, 177–78, 198
Kealey, Gregory S., 181
Kelly, Joan, 252
Kemp, Betty, 98
Kemp, Tom, 108, 116
Kennedy, Marie, 192
Keyder, Çaglar, 31, 36–37
Keylor, William R., 242
Keynes, John Maynard, 115, 219, 249
Kilmuir, Lord (David Maxwell Fyfe, 1st Earl of
        Kilmuir), 140
Kindleberger, Charles P., 34, 115, 119
Kingsley, Charles, 140
Kissinger, Henry A., 5, 40, 42
Kitson Clark, G., 44, 74, 88, 97, 99, 102, 114
Kleinau, Elke, 185
Klejman, Laurence, 192, 199, 203

Klima, Arnost, 94
Knibiehler, Yvonne, 152
Knies, Karl, 250
Knight, David, 225, 227
Knights of Labor, 181
Kocka, Jürgen, 158, 163–64, 167, 169
Kolakowski, Leszek, 17
Kollontai, Alexandra, 191
Kondratieff cycles, 96, 102, 104, 118, 276
Koyré, Alexandre, 48, 251
Kraditor, Aileen, 206–8
Kraehe, Enno E., 39
Krefeld, 64
Kriegel, Annie, 170–71
Kruger, Dieter, 230
Krupskaya, Nadezhda, 191
Kuliscioff, Anna, 191
Kulstein, David I., 116–17
Kumar, Krishan, 168

Labriola, Antonio, 186
Labrousse, Ernest, 5–9, 77, 86, 90, 101, 141, 158,
    162, 171
Lacroix, Bernard, 253
Lafayette, Marquis de, 62–63, 68
Lagos, 121
Laidler, David, 50
Laissez-aller, 101
Laissez-faire, 8–11, 15, 31, 34–36, 53, 83, 85, 88, 98,
    100–103, 105, 109, 112, 114–26, 130,
    137, 229–30, 250, 255–56, 258, 263
Lamennais, Hugues Félicité Robert de, 23, 66–67,
    90
Landes, David S., 34, 108
Landes, Joan B., 149–52, 155, 196
Lanjuinais, Jean-Denis, 151
La Plata. *See* Argentina
Lasch, Christopher, 215
Lassalle, Ferdinand, 186
La Vallet(t)e, Duchess of, 54
Le Bon, Gustave, 24
Lebrun, Pierre, 63–65
Lechard (engraver), 76
Leclerc, Jean-Théophile, 152
Lecuyer, Bernard-Pierre, 48
Ledru-Rollin, Alexandre Auguste, 91, 95–96
Lee, Richard L., 223
Leeds, 45
Lefkowitz, Mary R., 268
Legouvé, Ernest, 197
Lehning, Arthur, 158
Lenin, Vladimir Ilyich, 184, 191

Léon, Pierre, 115
Lepenies, Wolf, 220, 223, 254
Leslie, R. F., 63, 96
Le Van-Mesle, Lucette, 245–46
Levant, 121
Levasseur, Emile, 81–82, 85
Levy, Darline Gay, 150–52
Lévy-Leboyer, Maurice, 28–31, 36–37, 110, 122
Lewis, Gordon K., 213
Lewis, Jane, 187–88, 201
Lhomme, Jean, 79
Liard, Louis, 250
Lichtheim, George, 68, 159, 163
Liebknecht, Karl, 177
Liège. *See under* Belgium
Limburg, 71
Linders, Else, 208
Linnaeus, Carl (Carl von Linné), 235
Lipset, Seymour Martin, 180
Lis, Catharine, 65
Lisbon, 59
List, Friedrich, 103, 105
Liverpool, Lord (Robert Jenkinson), 44, 52, 79
Lloyd George, David, 74
Locke, John, 162, 272
Lombroso, Cesare, 198–99, 273
London, 10, 25, 41–42, 68, 74, 83, 95, 108, 117, 120,
    127, 161, 177, 184, 208, 222, 258, 262,
    270, 274
    Hyde Park, 133
London, University of, 222
Longuet, Jean, 177–78
Lorenz, Otto, 255
Lorimer, Douglas A., 236, 272
Lovett, Clara M., 147
Lowi, Theodore J., 264
Lucerne, 87
Luddism, 66, 161. *See also under* Great Britain
Luxemburg, 71, 189
Luzzatto, Gino, 94
Lyon, 59, 65, 76, 80–82, 136, 162, 165, 246

Macauley, Thomas Babington, 83, 100
MacBride, Ernest, 236
MacDonagh, Oliver, 44, 115, 216
MacGregor, Brig. Gen. Gregor, 54
Maehl, William, 179
Magraw, Roger, 107
Maistre. *See* De Maistre
Maloney, John, 237, 248–49
Malthus, Thomas, 9, 52, 201
Manacorda, Gaston, 176

Managerial revolution, 107

Manchester, 26, 334, 335, 45, 65, 125, 130, 200. *See also under* Great Britain

Manchester Statistical Association, 227

Manning, D. J., 2, 5, 7, 16, 219, 240

Manuel, Frank E., 18, 78, 212, 222

Marat, Jean-Paul, 154

Marczewski, Jean, 32, 36, 105

Marichal, Juan, 2, 6, 49

Maries, Marcel, 255

Market(s), 10, 14–15, 26, 29–31, 34–35, 38, 43, 45, 53, 65–66, 92, 96, 102, 104–5, 108, 110–11, 113, 120, 122, 130, 137, 143, 149, 165, 184, 196, 201, 203, 241, 244–45, 247, 252

Markovitch, Timohir J., 30, 33–34, 36, 81, 86, 106

Marks, Harry J., 179

Marquesas Islands, 127

Marrast, Armand, 90

Marshall, Alfred, 15, 101, 113, 144, 251, 247–49

Martineau, Harriet, 193

Marx, Karl, 14, 57, 77, 87, 107, 133, 155, 162, 171, 176, 178, 188, 216, 241, 244, 270

Marxism, 17, 19, 78, 161, 167, 171–73, 176–80, 184, 199, 230, 241, 249

Mason, E. S., 17

Masure, Auguste, 61–62

Mathias, Eric, 178

Mawet, Francine, 269

Mazzini, Giuseppe, 82, 94, 159

McClelland, Charles E., 24, 239

McCloskey, Donald N., 124

McCord, Norman, 96, 98–99

McCulloch, J. R., 52, 113, 240

McGregor, O. R., 229

McKenzie, Robert, 133

McLaren, Angus, 201

McMillan, James F., 190, 194, 198

Meek, Ronald L., 244, 272

Mellon, Stanley, 48–49, 67

Mellor, G. R., 96

Mendel, Gregor, 236

Menger, Carl, 248

Merrill, Lynn L., 271

Merriman, John M., 91

Mestro (Director of Colonies), 90

Methodenstreit, 248

Metternich, Prince Klemens Wenzel von, 50, 20, 39–40, 42, 46, 55, 69, 87–88, 108, 117, 160

Mexico, 131, 183, 185
    Archduke Maximilien, King of, 131
    Zuloaga, Pres. Félix María, 131

Mexico City, 131

Meyssonier, Simone, 17

Michelet, Jules, 152, 198, 211

Migration, 34–35, 38, 52–54, 59, 64, 81, 113, 165, 181–83, 186, 207–9, 217

Miguel, Dom, 69

Mill, James, 145, 268, 269

Mill, John Stuart, 17, 52–53, 73, 89, 100, 105, 126, 126, 192, 212, 232

Millar, John, 244

Milward, Alan S., 64, 70

Mink, Gwendolyn, 204

Minogue, K. R., 5

Mock, Wolfgang, 213

Moerenhaut (French consul in Tahiti), 128

Mokyr, Joel, 64, 102, 124

Moltke, Helmuth Bernhard Graf von, 130

Moluccas, the, 127

Mommsen, Wolfgang J., 163

Monod, Gabriel, 241

Montesquieu, Baron de (Charles-Louis Secondat), 12, 210

Montgomery, David, 181

Montlosier, Comte François Dominique de Reynaud de, 210

Monzoni, Anna, 192

Moore, David Chioni, 268

Moore, David Cresap, 71, 97–98, 134

Moore, R. J., 127

Moorhouse, H. F., 170, 174

Moravian Brethren, 27

Morley, Charles, 68

Morley, John, 212

Morocco, 184

Mortgage banks, 110

Moses, Claire Goldberg, 158, 193–94, 200

Moses, John A., 176

Moses, Wilson J., 208

Moss, Bernard H., 80, 163–64, 169, 179

Mosse, George L., 97, 99, 202, 216

Murad Bey, 218

Musson, A. E., 34, 118, 168

Myers, John Lynton, 271–72

Naples. *See under* Italy

Napoleon Bonaparte. *See under* France

Narváez, Gen, Ramon María, 1st Duke of Valencia, 95

Nation, xvi, 23–24, 26–27, 39–40, 47, 49, 53, 56–58, 61, 66–68, 71, 74, 79, 82, 84–87, 89–95, 103, 106, 108, 110, 115–18, 124–26, 129–30, 135, 137–38, 140–41, 143, 145, 147–50, 153–54, 156–61, 164–65, 171–74, 176–84, 187, 190–91, 197–99, 201, 205–6, 210–17, 229, 233, 237, 239–44, 246–47, 256, 260, 264

National American Women's Suffrage Association (NAWSA), 206

National Association for the Promotion of Social Science. *See* Social Science Association (SSA)

National Federation of Women's Clubs, 208

National Women's Suffrage Association (NWSA), 206

Nationalism. *See* Nation

Nationalist and National Liberation Movements. *See* Nation

Neale, R. S. 126

Negroes, 125, 207, 271. *See also* United States

Nesselrode, Count, 68

Netherlands, 64–68, 71, 85, 97, 112, 120, 122, 126, 148, 180, 269

  Orange, House of, 67–68

  William, King, 65–67, 109

Newbold, J. T. Walton, 111

New Caledonia, 127–28

New Hebrides, 127

Newman, Edgar Leon, 61, 81

Newman, Gerald, 25

Newman, John Henry, 225

Newmarch, William, 113

New Zealand, 121, 127

Niboyet, Eugénie, 194

Nice, 124

Nicolson, Harold, 40–41

Niebuhr, Berthold, 240

Nipperdey, Thomas, 238

Nisbet, Robert A., 13, 18, 251, 268

Nolan, Mary, 178

Nora, Pierre, 148

Novick, Peter, 235, 239

Nye, John Vincent (V. C.), 34–36, 107, 124

Nye, Robert A., 196, 203, 211

Oastler, Richard, 100, 140

O'Boyle, Lenore, 167

O'Brien, Bronterre, 162

O'Brien, Patrick, 30, 36–37, 122

O'Connell, Daniel, 71, 165, 215

O'Connor, Feargus, 84

O'Neill, William L., 192, 195, 206, 209

Oberschall, Anthony, 230, 250, 257–58

Oceania, 54, 126–28

Offen, Karen, 188, 194, 197–98

Olcott, Teresa, 187

Orientalism, 218, 264–73

  Egyptology, 262–68

  Indology, 268–70

Orientals, 181, 214, 217

Orleans, Duke of, 60, 73

Ortega López, Margarita, 196

Ottoman Empire, xv, 42, 55, 110, 121, 128–29, 268, 276

Owenism, 52, 193

Oxford University, 224

Pacific Ocean. *See* Oceania

Paine, Tom, 161

Palmade, Guy P., 91, 106

Palmerston, Viscount Henry John Temple, 84, 87–89, 95, 120, 129–30, 134

Panama Canal, 107

Pankhurst, Emmeline, ii

Pankhurst, Richard K. P., ii

Paris, 41, 54, 60–63, 66, 68, 79, 81–82, 86–90, 93, 106, 108, 110, 135–36, 150, 153, 155, 165, 168, 171, 185, 190, 194, 218, 225, 241–42, 251, 253, 258–60, 262

Parker, C. J. W., 210, 237

Parris, Henry, 9, 115

Participant observation, 266

Parti Ouvrier Français (POF), 179

Paulet, Lord George, 127

Paxton, Nancy L., 198

Peasants, 31, 45, 53, 81, 89, 93, 97–98, 101–3, 106–8

Peel, Sir Robert, 14, 17, 52, 71, 75, 79, 84, 87–88, 97–98, 101–3, 107, 109, 113, 119, 138–40

Pelling, Henry, 162, 171, 175

Péreire brothers, 108–9, 135

Péreire, Émile, 110, 112

Péreire, Isaac, 107

Perkin, Harold, 9

Perkins, Dexter, 54

Perlman, Selig, 182

Pernambuco, 59

Perrot, Michelle, 172, 180, 190, 194, 196, 200, 212

Peters, Louise-Otto, 199

Peyerinhoff, Henri de, 112

Phillips, Wendell, 205–6
Phoenicians, 269
Physiocracy, 245
Pieroni Bortolotti, Franca, 191
Pierrard, Pierre, 157
Pigman, Geoffrey Allen, 122
Pinchbeck, Ivy, 188
Pinkney, David H., 61
Pitcairn Islands, 125
Pitt, William, the Younger, 25, 50
Place, Francis, 73, 109
Plamenatz, John, 10, 77, 82, 91–92, 117, 134–36,
    163
Platt, D. C. M., 120–21
Plechanow (Plekhanov), Georgi, 78
Plessen, Marie-Louise, 230–31
Plessis, Alain, 105, 107, 110
Poland, 47, 58, 60, 62–63, 68–69, 71, 90, 94–97,
    123, 126, 128, 141, 149, 183, 239–40
    Posen, 126
Polanyi, Karl, 10, 43, 96, 113, 118, 128
Poliakov, Léon, 209–10, 213–14
Polignac, Prince Jules de, 61, 85
Political Economy. See Economics
Political Science, 237, 243, 245, 257–64
Politics, popular participation in, x, 25–26
Pollard, Sidney, 69–70, 175
Ponteil, Félix, 24, 59, 65, 67, 70
Poovey, Mary, 197
Popelinière, Lancelot Voisin de la, 238
Portal, Magda, 194
Portugal, 17, 24, 43, 54, 69, 210, 264
Postgate, Raymond, 57
Potts, David B., 257
Pouthas, Charles H., 79, 106, 110, 116
Prebisch, Raúl, xiii
Prewitt, Kenneth, 232, 234
Price, Roger, 61, 89, 92
Pritchard, George, 127–28
Procacci, Giuliano, 180
Proctor, Robert N., 222, 234
Protestants, 16, 27, 52, 65–67, 70–71, 180, 198,
    209–10, 258
Prothero, I. J., 45, 83
Proudhon, Pierre-Joseph, 194, 198
Puech, Jules-L, 194

Quadruple Alliance, 41
Quataert, Jean H., 186, 188–89
Quellenkritik, 238–39
Querelle des femmes, 152

Quero Molares, J., 94–95
Quintuple Alliance, 41

Rabaut, Jean, 189
Racism, 58, 153, 172, 181–83, 204–17, 235–37, 268,
    271, 277
Racz, Elizabeth, 151
Ragionieri, Ernesto, 177, 179
Raimbach, Abraham, x
Ralle, Michel, 166
Ranger, Terence, 240
Ranke, Leopold von, 238–40
Ravenna, 54
Ravera, Camilla, 191
Read, Donald, 26, 45, 51
Rebérioux, Madeleine, 149, 184, 190, 194, 196
Redford, Arthur, 125
Reformism, 4, 6, 17, 50, 67, 107, 112, 114, 120, 139–
    40, 171, 173, 177–80, 190, 200, 226–27,
    233, 243, 252, 274
Rémond, René, 6, 47
Renan, Ernest, 224
Rendall, Jane, 199, 210
Renner, Karl, 184
Rennes, 186
Renouvin, Pierre, 42–43, 56, 58, 63, 67, 85, 240
Revue historique, 241
Reynolds, James A., 71
Rhys Davis, T. W., 267
Ricardo, David, 43, 51–52, 113, 115, 248–49
Richelieu, Armand Jean du Plessis, Cardinal-
    Duc, 115
Richter, Melvin, 254–55
Ringer, Fritz K., 230, 239, 250, 256
Rist, Marcel, 125
Roberts, David, 4, 8–9, 44, 87, 100, 115, 124, 156
Robertson, William, 244
Robertson, William Spence, 55
Robespierre, Maximilien de, 8, 148, 151–52,
    154–55
Robinson, Ronald E., 121
Rodgers, Brian, 228
Roehl, Richard, 37
Rogers, Guy Maclean, 268
Rogers, J. D., 101
Rogers, Thorold, 248
Rogier, Charles, 88
Romania, 98, 159, 239
Romanticism, 54, 56–58, 66–67, 91, 139–41, 149,
    213, 215, 239, 251, 268–69
Romorino, Gen. Girolano, 82

Rosanvallon, Pierre, 2, 7–8, 23, 49, 59, 138–39, 144–45, 224
Roscher, Wilhelm, 248
Rosdolsky, Roman, 239
Rose, Ernst, 170
Rose, Michael E., 100
Rosenberg, Charles E., 236
Ross, Dorothy, 222–23, 257
Ross, Edward Alsworth, 257
Rossi, Alice, 192, 195
Rostow, W. W., 28–31, 36, 64, 104
Roth, Guenther, 174, 177, 178–79
Rothermund, Dietmar, 269–70
Rothschilds, the, 43, 108, 110
Rougerie, Jacques, 135–36
Rousseau, Jean-Jacques, 7–8, 12, 32–33, 148, 160
Rouzade, Léonie, 190
Rover, Constance, 200–204
Rowbotham, Sheila, 188, 196, 208
Rowe, D. J., 83
Royal Statistical Society, 187
Royer-Collard, Pierre-Paul, 23
Royle, Edward, 166
Rubin, Gayle, 198
Rudé, Fernand, 59, 62–63, 80, 162
Rudé, George, 73, 163
Rueschmayer, Dietrich, 231, 235
Ruffin, Josephine St. Pierre, 208
Ruggiero, Guido de, 10, 42, 48–49, 115, 239–41
Ruskin, John, 121
Russia, xv, 21, 39, 41, 55, 62, 64, 68–69, 73, 98, 119, 125, 128–29, 173, 177, 191, 199, 207, 229, 264, 276
    Cadet League, 68
    Decembrists, 63
    Nicholas, Tsar, 149
    Suffrage, 199, 297, 229
Russell, Lord John, 1st Earl Russell, 130, 218
Ruthenians, 239
Ruwet, Joseph, 64
Ryan, Barbara, 205

Sadler, Michael Thomas, 100
Saint-Gaudens, Auguste, 142
Saint-Simon, Comte Claude Henri de Rouvroy, 16, 23, 76–79, 107, 127, 166, 212, 251, 252, 255
Sakellariou, Michel, 94
Samoa, 127
Samuel, Raphael, 32
Sapieha, Prince Léon, 69

Saul, S. B., 64, 70
Saumoneau, Louise, 189
Saville, John, 158–59
Savoye, Antoine, 252
Scandinavia. See under Europe
Schapiro, J. Salwyn, 6, 21, 132, 141
Schefer, Christian, 62, 85, 127, 130–31
Scheldt, the, 65
Schenk, H. G., 40–42, 55
Schlegel, Friedrich von, 214
Schlesinger, Arthur M., Jr., 6
Schleswig-Holstein, 130
Schlote, Werner, 31, 105
Schmoller, Gustav von, 230–31, 256
Schoelcher, Victor, 90
Schopper, Carl, 161
Schorske, Carl E., 171, 177–78
Schöttler, Peter, 179, 181
Schroeder, Paul W., 39–40
Schuyler, Robert L., 53, 88, 118–19, 129, 134
Schwab, Raymond, 214
Schwartz, Anna Jacobson, 30–32, 50
Schweber, S. S., 222
Science, natural, 7, 9, 15, 50, 53, 57, 77–78, 91, 97, 105, 114, 119, 138, 141, 190, 196–98, 201–3, 213–14, 217, 220, 222–27, 233–34, 236, 271–72, 275
Sciences Po, 258–59, 261–63
Scientists. See Science, natural
Scott, Joan Wallach, 152, 155, 158, 168
Scott, Walter, 57
Second International, 176–77, 184
Second World War. See World War II
Section Française de l'Internationale Ouvrière (SFIO), 176
Sée, Henri, 30, 32, 80–81, 86, 106, 117
Semites. See Anti-Semitism
Semmel, Bernard, 120–21
Seneca Falls Convention (1848), 195, 206
Senior, Nassau William, 100–101, 113
Serbs, 159, 239
Seton-Watson, Hugh, 69, 129–30
Seton-Watson, R. W., 42, 54, 58, 129–30
Sewell, William H., Jr., 161, 163–64, 169
Shaftesbury, Lord (Anthony Ashley Cooper, 3rd Earl of), 100, 140
Shapiro, Fred R., 6, 269
Shaw, Robert Gould, 142
Shefter, Martin, 181–82
Sierra Leone, 121
Sievers, Sharon, 187, 203

Siéyès, Emmanuel-Joseph, 145, 147, 160
Silva, Pietro, 69
Silver, Allan, 133
Simiand, François, 255
Simon, André, 66–67
Simon, Jules, 198
Simon, Walter M., 16, 210
Skinner, Andrew S., 241
Slave trade, Atlantic, 27
Sleiden, John, 238
Slicher van Bath, B. H., 63
Slovaks, 230
Slovenes, 239
Small, Albion, 256–57
Smith, Adam, 7, 100, 115, 126, 161, 344, 272
Smith, Gerrit, 203
Smith, Paul, 134, 140
Snow, Charles Percy, 221
Soboul, Albert, 155
Social Darwinism, 199, 253
Social Gospel movement, 257
Socialism, 10–19, 77–78, 80, 85–93, 102, 106–7,
        114–15, 125–26, 135–36, 140–41, 152,
        158–65, 168–81, 184, 188–95, 198–200,
        203, 214–16, 231, 234, 251–58
Social Science, xvi, 36, 157, 167, 170, 187, 203,
        219–73, 276–77
    Professionalization and Value Neutrality,
        231–37
Social Science Association (SSA), 228–29, 231,
        252
Société des Droits de l'Homme, 163
Société d'Économie Sociale, 252
Société Générale, 109
Sociology, 234, 241, 251–58, 261, 263–64
Soffer, Benson, 18
Solomon Islands, 127
Soly, Hugo, 65
Soreau, Edmond, 154
Sorenson, Lloyd R., 101
South Africa, 54, 183
    Griqualand, 121
    Natal, 121
    Transvaal, 121
Southgate, Donald G., 71, 74–75, 114, 133
Sovereignty, popular (of the people), xvi, 1–2, 5,
        7, 11–13, 21–27, 111, 116, 143–44, 148,
        150, 156, 220
Sowerwine, Charles, 189–92
Spain, 2, 17, 24, 42–43, 46, 53–56, 69, 94–95, 121,
        130–31, 148, 164, 166, 180, 210, 264

Carlists, 69
Cortés, 2, 95, 148
Ferdinand, 2
Spencer, Herbert, 18, 198, 213, 231, 252–53, 255,
        258
Staël, Mme. de (Anne-Louise Germaine
        Necker), 23, 193
Stanton, Elizabeth Cady, 191, 205–6, 208
Stark, Werner, 78
Starzinger, Vincent, 79
Statism, 9–10, 13–16, 22, 27, 113, 137, 139–40
Stearns, Peter N., 80, 167
Stengers, Jean, 66–68
Stepan, Nancy, 214
Stern, Leo, 178
Stevenson, John, 44, 70
Stieg, Margaret F., 242
Stites, Richard, 191, 199, 207
St.-Malo, 127
Stocking, George W., Jr., 99
Stoddard, Lothrop, 212
Stone, Lucy, 206
Stuart, Robert, 179–80
Stuart, Sir Charles, 41
Stürmer, Michael, 91
Suel, Marc, 46, 60
Suez Canal, 107
Suffrage, 15, 75, 132, 137–38, 174, 199, 200–201, 209
    Capacity as basis for suffrage, 7, 138, 145, 191,
        233
    See also under Austria; Belgium; France; Ger-
        many; Great Britain; Italy; Russia;
        United States
Sumner, Charles, 206, 257
Super, R. H., 224
Switzerland, 17, 37, 87, 95, 122, 176, 189, 229
    Sonderbund, 87
Sykes, Robert, 165
Sztejnberg, Maxime, 181

Tahiti, 127–28
"Take-off." See under Industrialization
Talabot, Leon, 122
Talleyrand, Charles Maurice de, 41, 61–62, 68,
        84, 136
Tampico, 131
Tarlé, Eugène, 61
Taylor, Arthur J., 44, 101
Taylor, Barbara, 145, 193
Taylor, Edward B., 273
Taylor, W. Cooke, 50

Temperley, Harold, 42, 55–56

Tenant farmers. *See* Peasants

Terlinden, Charles, 66

Thatcher, Margaret, 140

Théret, Bruno, 115, 117

Theriot, Nancy M., 201

Thibert, Marguerite, 193–95

Thiers, Adolphe, 60, 80, 91, 136

Thomas, Edith, 90

Thomis, Malcolm I., 25–26, 46, 71, 73

Thompson, Dorothy, 192

Thompson, E. P., 44, 156

Thompson, F. M. L., 33, 99

Thompson, Victoria, 195

Thönnessen, Werner, 185

Tilly, Charles, 81, 89, 161

Tilly, Chris, 192

Tissot, Louis, 94

Titian (Tiziano Vecelli), 121

Tixerant, Jules, 194–95

Todorov, Tzvetan, 213

Tønnesson, Kåre D., 155

Tönnies, Ferdinand, 263

Tooke, Thomas, 113

Torstendahl, Rolf, 232

Toussaint L'Ouverture, 154

Train, George Francis, 206

Treaty of 1831 (Netherlands-Belgium), 109

Treaty of Nanking (China-Great Britain), 127

Tribe, Keith, 246–47, 249

Tristan, Flora, 165, 185, 194

Troppau, Congress of, 46

Trouillot, Michel-Rolph, 242, 273

Tuamolu, 127

Tudesq, André-Jean, 2, 12, 16, 22, 79, 85–86, 94

Tuñon de Lara, José Manuel, 165

Turati, Filippo, 180, 191, 199

Turgeon, Charles Marie Joseph, 194

Turgot, Jacques, 272

Turin, Yvonne, 197–98

Turkey. *See* Ottoman Empire

Turner, R. Steven, 222, 224

Two Cultures, 220–26

Ukrainians, 239

United Kingdom. *See* Great Britain

United Provinces. *See* Netherlands

United States, xiii, xvi-xvii, 14, 22, 28–30, 32–33, 35, 53–54, 98–99, 104, 111, 118, 125, 128–31, 141, 162, 167, 169, 173–74, 179–83, 191, 195, 199–201, 204, 206–9, 213, 215–16, 221, 227–29, 231–33, 236, 243–44, 246, 250, 253, 256–58, 261, 263–64, 268, 271, 275

Buchanan, Pres. James, 131

California, 88

Chinese Exclusion Act (1880), 162

Civil Rights Act (1962), 206

Civil War, 111, 118, 129, 131, 142, 182, 205, 228

Declaration of Independence, 22

Democratic Party, 122, 128, 180, 206

Hawaii, 127–28

Lincoln, Pres. Abraham, 205

Monroe, Pres. James, 68

Monroe Doctrine, 54, 128

Mugwumps (*see* Republican Party)

Point Four, 107

Republican Party, 204–5, 261

Slavery and Jim Crow, 215

Suffrage, 174, 195, 200, 205–7, 209

Texas, 87

Thirteenth, Fourteenth, and Fifteenth Amendments, 205–6

Truman, Pres. Harry S., 107

Wilson, Pres. Woodrow, 183

See also under America; Hegemony

Unkiau-Skelessi, Treaty of, 85

Urquhart, David, 128

Vallette, Aline, 185

Van der Linden, Marcel, 179, 178

Van Kalken, Frans, 66

Van Kol, Henri, 184

Van Rossen, Roman, 231, 235

Varnhagen, Rachel, 193

Vatican, the, 66

Gregory XVI, 67

Mirari vos, 67

Pius IX, 87

Vellacott, Jo, 203

Venezuela, 54

Venice, 64–65, 112

Vénil, (Jeanne-)Désirée, 193

Veracruz, 131

Verein für Sozialpolitik, 230–31, 234–35, 250

Verley, Patrick, 107

Vermeil, Edmond, 94

Versailles, 136, 149–50, 259

Verviers, 64

Veysey, Lawrence R., 233

Vidal, César, 40

Vienna, 88

Vienna, Congress of/Treaty of (Concert of Europe), 39–41, 49
Vigier, Philippe, 106
Villemain, Abel-François, 212
Villermé, Louis-René, 81
Vincent, Gérard, 259–61
Viner, Ernest, 260
Viner, Jacob, 9, 100
Voltaire, François Marie Arouet, 148, 213
Von Courland, Dorothea, 193
Vovelle, Michel, 23

Wagner, Donald O., 126
Wakefield, E. G., 53
Waldeck-Rousseau, Pierre, 180
Walker, Kenneth O., 101
Walker-Smith, Derek, 119
Walkowitz, Judith R., 201
Wallerstein, Immanuel, 2, 36, 40, 80, 113, 118–22, 153, 155, 188, 210
Wallis, 128
Walras, Léon, 244
Waterloo, 22, 39, 45–46, 54, 65
Ward, J. T., 52, 73, 83, 101, 166
Ward, Lester, 257
Ware, Vron, 207–8, 215
Warsaw, 90
Washington, Booker T. (Mr. & Mrs.), 208
Washington, DC, 121
Watson, George, 1, 13, 115
Webb, Sydney and Beatrice, 262–63
Weber, Max, 228, 234–35, 253–54, 256, 263
Webster, C. K., 40, 46
Webster, Daniel, 128
Wells, Ida B., 215
Weil, Cdt. Maurice-Henri, 87

Weill, Georges, 50, 56–57, 69, 84, 87, 107
Weingart, Pater, 237
Weisz, George, 242–46, 255
Wellington, Duke of, 41, 52, 61–62, 70–75, 84, 109, 140
Werner, Karl Ferdinand, 116
West Indies, 96
Whateley, Robert, 247
White, R. J., 1, 4, 12, 45–46
White settlers, 58, 126, 153–54, 173
Wilkie, David, x
Willard, Claude, 179–80, 184
Willard, Frances, 208, 215
Wilson, Sir Robert, 54
Winch, Donald, 53
Wittrock, Björn, 227, 233
Wolff, Richard J., 50, 117, 148, 156, 211
Women, iv, 145, 149–52, 184–204, 206, 208, 216
    Politics of breach vs. politics of assault, 200
    Temperance movements, 202
Woolf, Stuart, 50, 117, 148, 156, 211
Wollstonecraft, Mary, 193
World religions, 268
World War I, 103, 105, 123, 128, 131, 173, 177, 183, 201, 209, 219, 250
World War II, 123
Wright, H. R. C., 64–66
Wright, Vincent, 91

Yeo, Eileen, 166
Yeo, Richard R., 222, 225

Zeldin, Theodore, 47, 91, 93, 97, 117, 138
Ziolkoski, Theodore, 123
Zurich, 165, 177
Zylberberg-Hocquard, Marie-Hélène, 72

TEXT
10/12.5 Minion Pro

DISPLAY
Minion Pro

COMPOSITOR
Toppan Best-set Premedia Limited